KT-222-873

A MODERN ILLUSTRATED MILITARY HISTORY

SEA POWER

A MODERN ILLUSTRATED MILITARY HISTORY

SEA POWER

Phoebus

This edition © 1979 Phoebus Publishing
Company/BPC Publishing Limited
52 Poland Street, London W1A 2JX

Material previously published in *Battleships 1856–1919*
© 1977 Phoebus Publishing Co/BPC Publishing Ltd;
Battleships 1919–1977 © 1977 Phoebus Publishing Co/
BPC Publishing Ltd; *The First Submarines* © 1974
Phoebus Publishing Co/BPC Publishing Ltd; *Submarines
since 1919* ©1974 Phoebus Publishing Co/BPC Publishing
Ltd; *Naval Aircraft 1914–1939* © 1977 Phoebus Publishing
Co/BPC Publishing Ltd and *Naval Aircraft 1939–1945*
© 1975 Phoebus Publishing Co/BPC Publishing Ltd

All rights reserved. No part of this publication may
be reproduced, stored in a retrieval system or
transmitted in any form or by any means, electronic,
mechanical, photocopying, recording or otherwise,
without the prior permission of the copyright owner

Made and printed in Great Britain by
Redwood Burn Limited

ISBN 0 7026 0046 6

JOHN BATCHELOR, after leaving the RAF, served his
'apprenticeship' in the technical publications departments
of several British aircraft firms, and went on to contribute
on a freelance basis to many technical magazines. Since
then, his work for Purnell's *Histories of the World Wars*,
and subsequently the Purnell's *World War Specials*, has
confirmed him as being one of the most outstanding artists
in his field.

ANTONY PRESTON was born in England and educated
in South Africa where he studied at the University of
Witwatersrand. He worked for some time at the National
Maritime Museum, Greenwich, primarily on Admiralty
records. He is Naval Editor of *Defence* and has written
numerous articles and reviews on warship design and
aspects of nineteenth- and twentieth-century naval history
for various specialised journals and periodicals. Among his
books are *Send a Gunboat* (with John Major), *V & W
Destroyers*, *Battleships of World War I*, *Submarine: A
History of the Underwater Fighting Vessel*, *Navies of the
Second World War*, *Battleships 1856–1977*, *Destroyers*,
U-Boats and the translation from the German of *Ships of
the Japanese Navy* (with J D Brown). His latest book is
Aircraft Carriers.

LOUIS S. CASEY is curator of Aircraft, Department of
Aeronautics, National Air and Space Museum, Smithsonian Institution, Washington DC. A pilot in the USAAF
during the Second World War, he subsequently became
Assistant to the Director of Civil Aviation in Bermuda, and
is a qualified FAA instructor in several aspects of aircraft
and aviation. A regular contributor to aviation journals
both in the US and elsewhere, he is one of the leading
authorities in his field. His special interest is the Curtiss
Aircraft Company, of which he is engaged in writing the
definitive history.

Imperial War Museum

INTRODUCTION

This book tells the story of Sea Power from the early battle-ships and submarines to the naval aircraft and carriers which provided the basis for the long-range sea battles of the Second World War. It is illustrated throughout by John Batchelor, with many expert full colour and black and white cutaway drawings which show off the machines to perfection.

The first section of the book describes the rise and fall of the battleship from the ironclad *La Gloire*, laid down in 1858, to the *New Jersey*, which saw action during the Vietnam War.

The second section deals with the concept of underwater travel, from the first recorded design for an underwater vessel which appeared as early as 1578. It goes on to describe how, with the invention of the torpedo and the battery-powered electric motor, the submarine became a lethal weapon, and how during the First World War it really came into its own. The section continues with the development of submarines between the Wars and their vital role in all the major theatres of war during the Second World War, and concludes with a survey of postwar development culminating in the almost limitless power of ICBM-armed nuclear submarines of today.

The final section details the evolution of the naval aircraft from frail and primitive observation biplanes to the deadly instruments of power at sea which played such a great part in the Allied victories in the Pacific during the Second World War.

HMS Resolution, *the Royal Navy's first ballistic missile submarine, was commissioned in 1967 and was followed by three other members of the class*

CONTENTS

The Iowa *Class battleship USS* New Jersey *in 1954. She was recommissioned in 1968 for service off Vietnam, thus becoming the world's last operational battleship*

Imperial War Museum

Bekan

HMS Camperdown, *commissioned in 1889 at the high water-mark of the Victorian navy*

THE EARLY BATTLESHIPS
Antony Preston

In 1914 the ultimate deterrent was the battleship. In the fifty years since the first ironclads, the combination of steel armour plate and the hitting power of the big gun had produced the most powerful weapon the world had ever seen.

This first chapter details the development of the battleship from sailing ships armed with muzzle-loading guns, through the fascinating nineteenth-century period of tactical and design experimentation to the First World War itself and the high-tide of the battlefleets' power. Antony Preston's expert and highly readable text charts the rise of the steel leviathans from the Crimea to Tsushima. Then Britain's revolutionary *Dreadnought* stoked up the naval race, left unresolved in the fog of Jutland in 1916 but culminating in the surrender of the High Seas Fleet at Scapa Flow.

CONTENTS

Musée de la Marine

Jean Bart, one of the French navy's first dread-noughts, kicks up spray on a high-speed run. The combination of superimposed heavy fore turrets and a short foredeck resulted in a great deal of water being shipped in rough seas

The Battle of Navarino Bay, October 20, 1827. In the last major fleet action fought by wooden sailing ships, the Turkish fleet was destroyed by the combined British, French and Russian fleets

THE FIRST IRONCLADS

The battleship epitomizes naval warfare in a way that no other warship can. Many people associate the passing of the battleship with the decline of navies, and yet it had a short life. The first 'ironclad,' the *Gloire*, was begun only in 1858, just over a century ago, while the *New Jersey*, the last battleship to see action, was decommissioned in 1968. When Drake and Howard fought the Spanish Armada in 1588 'ship-of-the-line' was a term unknown to them, and the 'great gun' had not yet come to dominate warfare at sea. Although the requirements of eighteenth-century warfare were to foster the growth of warships, the battleship as we know it had no reason to exist until such time as guns threatened to destroy the traditional ship-of-the-line. Until that day dawned the seas were ruled by majestic two- and three-deckers, armed with tiers of smooth-bore guns on the broadside. It was these ships which fought the great sea battles of the Napoleonic Wars, culminating in Trafalgar, and the outstanding example of the type, the 100-gun ship HMS *Victory*, can be seen today at Portsmouth.

The first step in the evolution of the modern battleship came in 1822, when a French artillery colonel, Henri Paixhans, published his ideas about using shell-guns at sea. The French Navy had only just sustained a shattering defeat at the hands of the Royal Navy, the British having captured or destroyed enough French ships to make up a fair-sized navy in its own right. Both sides had relied almost solely on the cast-iron smooth-bore ship-gun, firing a solid iron shot. At any distance the stout wooden walls of a two- or three-decked man-o'-war sufficed to keep out cannon-balls, and it was only at short distances that guns could act as 'ship-smashers'. France had only the remnants of her once-large navy, and Paixhans knew that there could be no question of building enough big ships to equal or overtake the Royal Navy.

What he wanted was a devastating weapon which could give France an advantage in quality, and he was sure that he had the answer in the shell-gun. With hollow explosive shells instead of solid shot, Paixhans argued, a small warship could inflict tremendous destruction on the largest wooden warships; if France were to build a large number of these small (and therefore cheap) warships she could nullify the British three-to-one preponderance in ships by making them all obsolete.

Many writers are under the impression that Paixhans invented the shell-gun. This is not true, as the shell had been a naval weapon since the seventeenth century in the form of the mortar-bomb. What Paixhans did was to adapt the principle of the fuzed delayed-action projectile on the 'long' ship gun. The great value of a hollow cast-iron sphere filled with gunpowder was that it could so easily set fire to a wooden ship if it burst inside the hull. Nothing was feared as much as a fire aboard a wooden ship, with its tarred cordage and its enormous quantity of combustible material, and even the threat of fire was enough to make the captain of a three-decker wary of taking on a ship capable of setting him alight. Sailors remembered with a shudder that Admiral Brueys' flagship *l'Orient* had been lost with all hands during the Battle of the Nile because she had had an 'infernal machine' aboard, or so it was believed.

Unlike many visionaries Paixhans had an attentive audience, for the French Navy wanted to erase the stain of the recent catastrophe. In 1824 the first *canon-obusier* was adopted by the Navy, and tests against target hulks showed that in most cases the explosion of shells caused a fire. If all had gone as planned the French would have immediately become the world's leading navy. But of course Paixhans, like so many theorists, had assumed that the opposition would be hypnotised by the awesome destructive power of his shell-gun. The

Napoléon was one of the first examples of the screw-propelled ship-of-the-line. Although fully rigged, she was designed from the start for steam propulsion

Musée de la Marine

The iron-hulled floating battery HMS Terror *on the slip at Palmer's shipyard, Yarrow in 1856, too late for the Crimea. The period of British supremacy in iron shipbuilding was beginning*

Royal Navy met the French challenge by designing its own shell-guns, with the result that French warships were now just as vulnerable to damage. By the end of the 1840s it was normal for a three-decker to have a mixed battery of about 40% shell-guns and 60% firing solid shot. Apart from the understandable temptation to retain a proven weapon for as long as possible, the solid-shot gun fired further and more accurately; the hollow shell was difficult to cast with perfect balance, and the fuze made for erratic flight.

In addition to the shell-gun, another invention had a profound effect on the traditional wooden ship-of-the-line. The Royal Navy first tried to put a steam engine in a small sloop in 1814, but without success. Undeterred by this the Admiralty sanctioned the building of six paddle vessels in 1821 – a remarkably far-sighted step. But there was no doubt that the paddle-wheel was not the right method of propulsion for ships relying on massed broadside guns. Apart from reducing the area on the broadside which could carry guns, the paddle-wheel was highly vulnerable to damage. Not until the screw-propeller was perfected in the early 1840s did the Admiralty feel confident enough to embark on building a steam-powered battle fleet. But once the screw-propelled HMS *Ajax* went to sea in the autumn of 1846 the pace of conversion was only limited by the cost. By 1854 both France and Great Britain had either converted ships under construction or had designed new steam-powered wooden ships with propellers, and other navies were following their example. The outstanding examples of this type were the British *Agamemnon* and the French *Napoléon*, both fast for their day and well armed, but still curious hybrids. Some observers feared that a naval action was likely to last minutes rather than hours, with both sides consumed by fire and blast as the explosive shells tore through the wooden hulls.

Shell-Guns in Action

Actually the record of shell-guns in action proved rather disappointing. Their first recorded use was at the Battle of Yucatan, fought in April 1843 between the fledgling Texan Navy and a Mexican squadron. As if this does not sound unlikely enough, two weeks later at the Battle of Campeche two Texan sailing brigs defeated the same squadron, including an English-built iron steamer, the *Guadelupe*. It was the first action involving an iron ship and the only

known case of sailing ships defeating steamers. In both actions the heavier Mexican shells inflicted casualties but failed to destroy the Texan ships. In November 1853 the 'massacre' of Sinope occurred, in which six Russian ships-of-the-line took some hours to sink ten Turkish frigates and smaller warships. Naval and public opinion, anxious both for a war against Russia and for a scare about a new horror weapon, harped on the fact that the Turkish ships caught fire and blew up, without mentioning that at Navarino in 1827 a Turkish squadron, similarly trapped without hope of escape, had also been destroyed by fire.

By itself Sinope did not cause the introduction of armour protection, but it acted as a tremendous spur to progress. As early as 1835 the French had tried to produce iron plate which was proof against shells, and the Royal Navy in the early 1840s carried out trials with an iron-hulled steamer, the *Ruby*. The quality of iron at this period was not sufficiently good to allow it to be used as armour; under the shock of impact it shattered into flying shards which were as deadly as the fragments of the original shell. Like the French, the British concluded that they could not recommend the use of iron in warships, and, although this is derided as a triumph of prejudice over scientific advance, their admirals were

The wooden-hulled battery Devastation, *ironclad veteran of the bombardment of Kinbourn Kosa*

right. But the science of metallurgy was making giant strides, notably in England, and in only ten years many of the drawbacks were eliminated. As a result, when the call came in 1854 for a sure method of protection against shellfire, iron was found to be satisfactory. The reason for this was partly that wrought iron now had greater tensility and partly because it was used in such a way as to absorb the stresses set up by the impact of a shell.

The lesson of Sinope was followed by the unsatisfactory performance of the Anglo-French ships against the Russian fortifications at Sevastopol in 1855. The Allies found that they could avoid serious damage from the red-hot and explosive shells fired by the forts, but only at a price of staying so far out that their own fire against the batteries was ineffective. What was needed was a means of taking ships in close, and it was this rather than any exaggerated fear of the Russian Fleet which inspired the French *Directeur de Matériel* to draw up plans for a 'floating battery.'

Floating Packing-cases

The first proposals were to pack the hollow sides of a ship with iron solid shot, but after consultation with their British allies the French constructors decided that 100-mm wrought-iron plates were far more suitable. The result was that in the autumn of 1854 the first five floating batteries were laid down in France. Their names were *Congreve* (to flatter their English allies), *Devastation*, *Foudroyante*, *Lavé* and *Tonnante*. The Royal Navy ordered a further five of almost identical design: the *Aetna*, *Glatton*, *Meteor*, *Thunder* and *Trusty*; they were unwieldy craft like floating packing-cases, with bluff bows and sterns, feeble machinery to drive them at no more than 4 knots, and three masts with barque-rig to assist the engines. Their massive timber hulls had a strake of wrought iron 110 mm (4.3 in) thick at its maximum, sloping to half that thickness at its upper edge, but it covered the length of the hull. The French batteries had a length of 53 m (174 ft) over all, a beam of 13.14 m (43 ft) and drew 2.88 m ($9\frac{1}{2}$ ft) of water. The single gun deck carried sixteen 50-pdr guns, and two 18-pdr carronades.

The French quintet commissioned in the summer of 1855, nearly a year after they had been laid down, and their English sisters were ready in April (minus the *Aetna*, which caught fire on the stocks, launched herself and had to be written off as a total loss). But the French were less dilatory in getting their batteries out to the Black Sea, with the result that the *Devastation*, *Lavé* and *Tonnante* arrived in time for the big attack on Kinbourn Kosa, a complex of five forts guarding the approaches to the mouths of the Dnieper and Bug rivers, near Odessa.

On the morning of 17 October, 1855 these 'formidable engines of war' came into action at a range of 900-1200 yds. Despite being hit by red-hot shot and shell from the Russian guns their armour proved invincible, although 28 casualties were caused by shot and splinters going through the gun-embrasures and the overhead hatch. What was more to the point, Kinbourn surrendered after an hour-and-a-half, a dramatic reversal of the normal supremacy of forts over ships. The British batteries arrived too late, despite the fact that the French ships had travelled nearly as far, from Brest, Rochefort and Lorient on the Atlantic coast.

'THE BLACK SNAKES OF THE CHANNEL'

Despite their instant fame the floating batteries were not battleships. Their lack of speed and manoeuvrability meant that they could never control the seas in the way that other warships could. But they had proved the principle of using armour to keep out shells, and the next step was to build a seagoing armoured ship. The French, fired with enthusiasm for the new idea which they had developed, started work immediately. In this they were aided by the fact that they possessed in Dupuy de Lôme one of the finest naval architects of the century. As the new *Directeur de Matériel* for the French Navy, de Lôme had the backing of the *Conseil des Travaux* and the Emperor Napoléon III. De Lôme had already proposed an ironclad 12 years before, and had achieved fame as the designer of the fast steam-powered two-decker *Napoléon* in

Gloire, with her steam power and iron plating, made the rival navy across the Channel suddenly seem obsolete. The ironclad race was on and the all-iron hulled battleship was only a few years away

1850. Early in 1857 all work on conventional wooden ships-of-the-line stopped, and by March 1858 the French were ready to start work on four ironclad warships.

The four ships were the prototype *La Gloire*, her sisters *Invincible* and *Normandie*, and a slightly larger vessel, *La Couronne*. The most famous of these was the *Napoléon*, and built of timber in the conventional manner, but protected by iron plating. This plating varied from 4,7 in on the waterline to 4.3 in thickness at gun-deck level, and was calculated to keep out the new Model 1855 16-cm (6.5-in) shell, which

was fired from a rifled muzzle-loading gun known also as a 50-pdr. Although even her admirers could not call her a beautiful ship, as she was squat and plain in appearance, the *Gloire* was a sound, workmanlike design which gave the French Navy a head start, and she rightly deserves her place as the first true battleship.

Across the Channel, the Royal Navy was still wallowing in the wave of unpopularity which washed over both services as a result of the revelations of muddle and incompetence during the Crimean War. The news of the laying down of four French ironclads in March 1858 caused a 'naval scare' in Parliament. As ever, Press and Parliament did little to assist the Admiralty in coming to a sensible decision. At one stage the French ships were described as 'huge polished steel frigates,' and at another they

Musée de la Marine

Gloire

The world's first fully seagoing armour-clad ship, Gloire was timber-built with iron plating and is regarded as the first true battleship. The building of Gloire and her sisters provoked a response from the Royal Navy

Displacement: 5617 tons *Length:* 80.4 m
Armament: 36×160-mm *Armour:* 120-mm waterline, 110-m battery *Max speed:* 12.5 knots

Gloire: Inboard Section

Note the relatively small space devoted to engines but the very large uptake required to provide draught for the inefficient rectangular boilers. The hull was mainly of wood with iron stiffening to compensate for the weight of armour

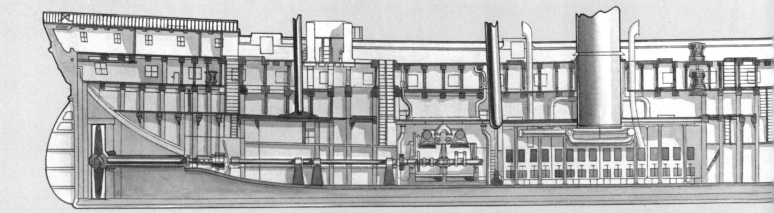

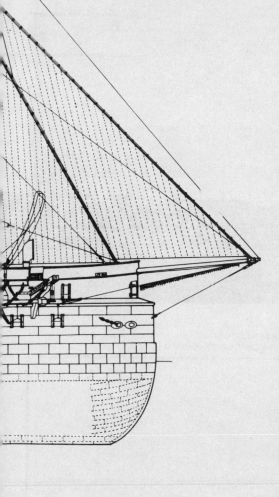

Solférino
A French armour-clad ship similar to the *Magenta*, and developed from the *Gloire* design, *Solférino* had its armament arranged on the broadside on two levels
Displacement: 7000 tons *Length:* 92 m
Armament: 16×50-pdr, 34×30-pdr *Armour:* 100/120-mm *Max speed:* 12 knots

were credited with gunpower they could never have possessed. Yet a Parliamentary Committee recommended nothing more than an accelerated programme to convert the remaining wooden three-deckers to steam!

These were enormous ships, twice the tonnage of HMS *Victory*, armed with 131 8-in and 68-pdr shell-guns capable of firing at a range of 1200 yards. But they were expensive anachronisms, even before the building of ironclads, for the greater range and accuracy of guns meant that there was no longer any need for the massive concentration of fire from three decks. There was strong pressure from naval tacticians for the building of two-deckers or even single-decked frigates, which were smaller, handier and required smaller crews. The Americans had shown the way in 1854 when they laid down five big frigates, which included the *Roanoke* and *Merrimack* (of which more later), and the British had built six big frigates in 1856-58 as a reply. These ships relied on speed and long-range gunfire in place of armour, and they showed that a single-decked warship could carry sufficient armament to make her a threat to a capital ship.

The nervousness in England engendered by the building of ironclads in France was not allayed by the strong reaction in France to the Orsini conspiracy, an attempt on Napoléon III's life which had been plotted by exiles in England. French newspapers talked wildly of invasion to 'hunt down the assassins.' A visit by Queen Victoria and Prince Albert to Cherbourg in August 1858 simply underlined the fact that the French were feverishly expanding their navy, and the Admiralty plucked up courage to demand the immediate construction of ironclads to match the French programme.

The British were fortunate in one respect; when and if they decided to turn to iron for warship-building they had far better resources than the French. Not only had their shipbuilders more experience in building iron ships, but their iron foundries could produce far greater quantities of armour. In fact the British had built four floating batteries with iron hulls at the end of the Crimean War, and in William Scott Russell they had the leading designer of iron ships; all they needed was the will to act.

When that will finally manifested itself the results were dramatic. Throughout the summer of 1858 tests were carried out against the old ship-of-the-line *Alfred*, fitted out as a target with sample plates, and the floating batteries *Erebus* (iron-hulled) and *Meteor* (wooden-hulled). The Admiralty called for designs for ironclads from no fewer than 12 private firms as well as their own designers, some indication of the resources that could be called upon. In November 1858 the estimates for the following year included the sum of £252,000 for the building of two armoured frigates.

The first was laid down on the River Thames on 25 May, 1859 and launched as the *Warrior* on 29 December, 1869, shortly after the *Gloire* had successfully completed her trials; her sister *Black Prince* was launched on the Clyde in February 1861. HMS *Warrior* joined the Fleet in October 1861 and the *Black Prince* just 11 months later. They were the world's first iron-hull seagoing ironclads, as the French *Couronne*, although laid down in March 1858 with the *Gloire*, was not launched until March 1861.

The British choice of an all-iron hull resulted in two important advantages: watertight bulkheads could be provided to close the ends of the battery, and the gunports could be positioned further apart. This last was important, for having gunports close together as in the *Gloire* weakened the armour and increased the risk of several guns being disabled by a hit. Like the *Gloire*, the *Warrior* and *Black Prince* were frigates, ie with a single gun-deck, and their long, low profile resulted in the nickname 'the black snakes of the Channel'. Certainly their arrival in the Channel Fleet in 1861-62 led to a distinct improvement in Anglo-French relations.

Iron Ship-building
The *Black Prince* and *Warrior* were the *only* warships which ever merited the title 'invincible', even if they deserved it for little more than six months. When new they could outrun the *Gloire* (14.3 knots against 12.8) and stand up to any shell-guns afloat; the worst that could have happened would have been to run aground and be slowly pounded to pieces by a squadron of floating batteries.

What the French press had not borne in mind was the fact that France did not have anything like the industrial potential to sustain a massive programme of iron ship-building. The *Couronne*, far more successful than the original *Gloire* design by virtue of her iron hull, was followed by only two more by 1866, during which time the Royal Navy had completed an additional nine. Admittedly some of the British ironclads had timber hulls, in order to make use of the enormous supplies of seasoned timber which had been stored in the Royal Dockyards

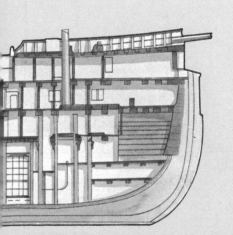

HMS Minotaur's *full-length armour and broadside batteries made the ship long and unwieldy. The brief reign of the broadside ironclad ship was drawing to a close, inevitably dictating the frenzied period of experimentation in the 1870s to devise means of concentrating fire from barbettes and turrets*

Gloire and Warrior in Comparison

	Warrior	Gloire
Displacement:	9000 tons	5617 tons
Length:	367·5 ft	252 ft
Weight of armour:	1200 tons	820 tons
Armament:	26 × 68-pdrs (8-in) ML smooth-bore 10 × 110-pdrs (7-in) BL rifled 4 × 70-pdrs (4·7-in) BL rifled	26 × 50-pdrs (16-cm) BL rifled
Machinery:	Single-screw horizontal direct-acting trunk engines, 1200 hp	Single-screw horizontal 2-cylinder reciprocating engines, 900 hp
Max speed:	14 knots	12 knots

since before the Crimean War, but it gradually dawned on the British that their shipbuilding industry's speed and facility was a safe enough insurance against the French threat. In any case, France's need to spend money on her large conscript army for continental defence meant that the momentum of the naval programme was soon lost.

But both countries had changed the course of ship design permanently. The term 'frigate' was obviously no longer adequate as an expression of fighting worth, and the ironclad was the cause of the abandonment of the old rating system of warship classification. It was absurd to pretend that a 1st Rate wooden 131-gun ship-of-the-line was superior to the 6th Rates Gloire and Warrior, and the distinctions were soon abandoned in favour of the term ironclad, and then line-of-battle ship, subsequently shortened to battleship.

The supremacy of the Gloire and Warrior did not last long. Within months a series of much larger broadside ironclads were under construction for the Royal Navy, such as the 380-ft Achilles and the 400-ft Minotaur. The length of these monsters and the lofty rig needed to move them under sail made it evident that the type could not develop much further. The answer was the turret, a revolving mounting capable of carrying one or two guns. A ship fitted with one or more turrets could bring guns to bear on a number of bearings, and this would do away with the need for a lengthy broadside of guns. The enormous armoured sides of the original ironclads demanded a great weight of iron, but a turret-ship could have a much shorter hull.

HMS Warrior
Britain's first seagoing armoured warship, Warrior (commissioned in 1861) was designed for the maximum possible speed and the French practice of using an extensive armoured belt was therefore not adopted
Displacement: 8600 tons *Length:* 380 ft
Armament: 10 × 110-pdr, 4 × 70-pdr, 26 × 68-pdr,
Armour: 4½-in amidships *Max speed:* 14 knots

HMS Warrior: Section
Made of iron throughout, with teak backing to the wrought-iron armour, Warrior's hull form with its one gun-deck was derived from the conventional large frigate. Warrior's hull still survives at Pembroke Dock, Wales, as an oil pontoon

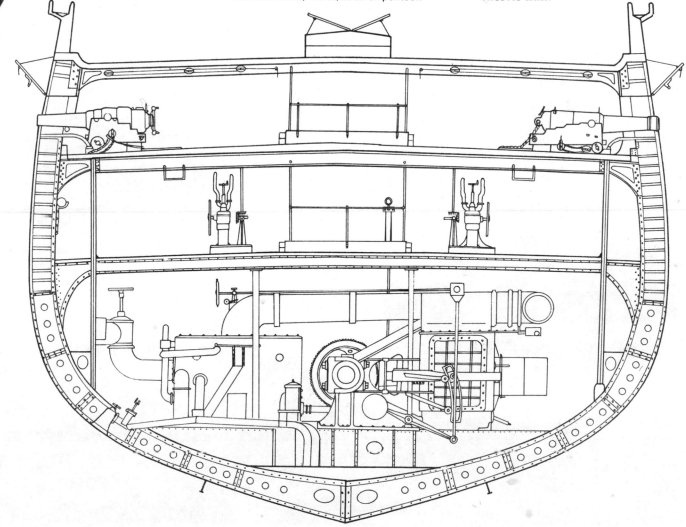

BROADSIDES AND BARBETTES

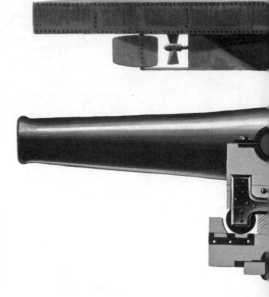

Federal sailors relax on the deck of Monitor *after her one action against the CSS* Virginia *– note the dent*

The turret or cupola mounting had been put forward in 1854 by the Swedish engineer John Ericsson and an English naval officer, Captain Henry Cowper Coles. Both men appear to have stumbled on the idea at the same time, an occurrence which is more common than people might think, but we do know that Coles designed an armoured raft after his experience with a wooden gun-raft in the Crimean War. By 1859 his ideas had

matured to the point where he could file patents, and in 1861 the first turret was mounted in the floating battery *Trusty* for trials. Although hit 33 times by heavy shells the turret was still in working order, and the Navy began to take Coles seriously.

The outbreak of the American Civil War in 1861 caught the United States Navy in a very poor state, with only 42 warships, none of them armoured. The Confederate

States Army's successes on land merely worsened the problem by over-running the main naval dockyard at Norfolk, Virginia, on 20 April, 1861. Among the debris was the brand-new wooden steam frigate USS *Merrimack*, which had been burned and scuttled to avoid capture. The waterlogged hulk was raised and found to be in good condition below the waterline, and so in June work started on rebuilding her as an armoured

CSS *Virginia*
An ironclad floating battery, with 68-pdr shell-guns contained in a sloping iron casemate. The *Virginia* was based on the wooden hull of the frigate USS *Merrimack,* captured when the South overran the Norfolk naval dockyard, with the addition of armour cladding built up from railway lines. The North responded by building the *Monitor* as a counter, and the two ships fought one inconclusive battle against each other
Displacement: 4500 tons *Length:* 275 ft
Armament: 6 × 9-in, 2 × 7-in, 2 × 6-in *Armour:* rails bolted in groups of three *Max speed:* 9 knots

A Dahlgren cannon points through the sloping casemate protecting the side of the CSS Virginia

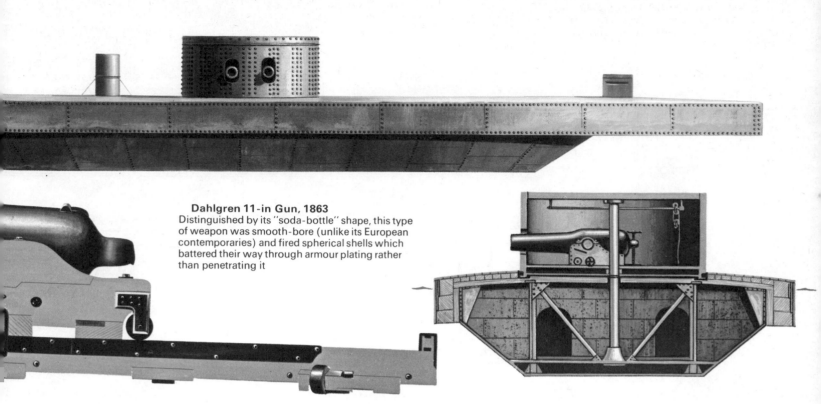

Dahlgren 11-in Gun, 1863
Distinguished by its "soda-bottle" shape, this type of weapon was smooth-bore (unlike its European contemporaries) and fired spherical shells which battered their way through armour plating rather than penetrating it

ship. Explosive shells from forts were as big a menace to ships as they had been in the Crimean War, and it was hoped that the new CSS *Virginia* would be able to withstand the Federal batteries and drive off the blockading warships.

The warship which resulted bore a likeness to the British and French floating batteries, apart from lacking masts and yards; she had a sloped iron casemate containing 68-pdr shell-guns and an iron ram. She was not a battleship, and her machinery was never reliable enough to allow her to venture far afield. Nor could the ingenuity of the South match the industrial might of the North. Knowledge of the new ironclad quickly reached Washington and in August 1861 Congress authorized the construction of iron armoured ships to match her.

Although other designs were started, the main effort was concentrated on a design put forward by John Ericsson, which alone promised to carry enough armour and armament to deal with the *Virginia*. The ship which resulted was the *Monitor*, a 172-ft armoured raft surmounted by a single turret carrying two 11-in smooth-bores.

Armoured Box
Speed of building was the essence of the *Monitor*'s design, and everything was subordinated to that end. The main feature was the raft-like top to the hull, an armoured box which was laid on top of the hull and overhung it all around. This served three purposes. First, it improved stability to provide a good gun-platform; secondly, the overhang provided good protection against

USS *Monitor*
An armoured raft carrying a single two-gun turret, *Monitor* was the North's response to the Confederate *Virginia*. The armoured box enclosing the hull improved stability, protected against ramming and deflected incoming shells. *Monitor* gave her name to a type of ironclad generally used as floating artillery
Displacement: 987 tons *Length:* 172 ft
Armament: 2 × 11-in *Armour:* 3¼-in waterline, 8-in turret, 1-in deck *Max speed:* 9 knots

ramming; and thirdly, the flat trajectory of the shells fired against the deck would tend to make them bounce off, leaving the turret as the main target. The deck was covered with 1-in iron plate but the turret had 8-in plates made up of 1-in laminated layers. British armour was rolled in mills as solid 4-in plates, but American foundries could only roll 1-in plates.

Despite the problems associated with her highly novel design, the little *Monitor* was launched just under four months after the signing of the contract, and she was commissioned on 25 February, 1862. She was just in time, for the *Virginia* (perversely known to history under her original name *Merrimack*) appeared on 8 March in Hampton Roads and destroyed the wooden frigates *Congress* and *Cumberland*. That night the little turret ship joined the Federal squadron and prepared for battle the next day.

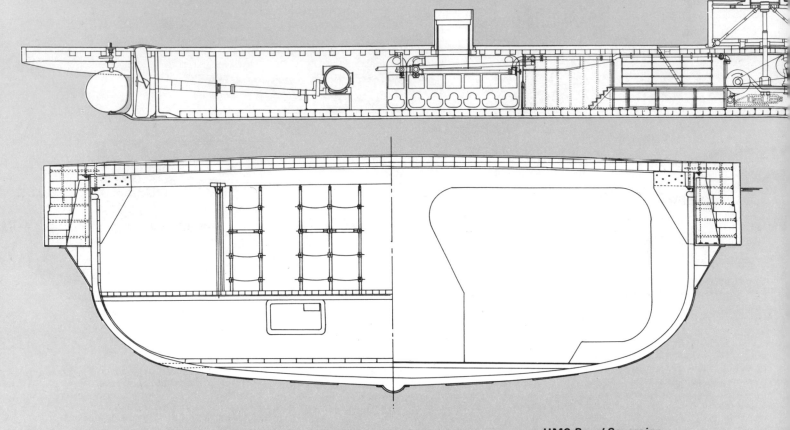

USS*Tecumseh*
One of the third group of monitors, incorporating many of the improvements which could not be used earlier because of a rapid building programme. Armament comprised 15-in smooth-bore guns

HMS *Royal Sovereign*
A wooden ship of the line, *Royal Sovereign* was converted to a turret-ship during building and has been described as the ugliest battleship ever built, with three masts and a huge funnel. She was completed in 1864
  Displacement: 5080 tons *Armament:*
5×10.5-in in four turrets

USS Tecumseh *sinking at the Battle of Mobile Bay*

The confident Confederates in the *Merrimack* were surprised to see what they called a 'cheesebox on a raft', but they soon discovered that their shells could make no impression.

Unfortunately the *Monitor*'s guns made no impression either, for her captain had strict orders to use only single charges (15 lb) as his guns had not been proof-fired. Had the *Merrimack* fired solid shot and the *Monitor* fired 30-lb charges the world's first ironclad fight might have had some interesting results, but as it was the 'Battle of Hampton Roads' was a draw. Some idea of the state of naval gunnery in 1862 can be gained from the fact that the *Merrimack* fired a broadside every 15 minutes and the

Monitor replied with two shells every 7 minutes. Firing continued for about $3\frac{1}{2}$ hours, with frequent attempts at ramming. Finally the contestants drew apart, never to meet again.

Although the battle had a profound impact on public opinion it had little effect on the design of battleships. In March 1862, some days *before* the Battle of Hampton Roads, the British Controller of the Admiralty announced plans for building two turret ships. One was to be built of iron and the other was to be converted from the incomplete hull of a three-decker wooden ship-of-the-line, to see if money could be saved by conversion of the now useless 1st and 2nd Rates. The first was the *Prince*

Albert and the second was the *Royal Sovereign*. Neither ship bore any resemblance to the *Monitor*, being seagoing vessels with four turrets and side armour. Both ships were quickly overshadowed by later developments, but they are outstanding as they enshrine basic features which did not reappear until 1903: multiple centre-

line turrets and a virtual absence of masts and yards. They were in fact the true ancestors of the twentieth-century battleships, rather than the original broadside type exemplified by the *Warrior* and *Gloire*.

As the Civil War progressed more 'monitors' were built, and so a new type of armoured ship came into being. But there were no more encounters like Hampton Roads, although the *Manhattan* helped to finish off the *Tennessee*, another Southern ironclad similar to the *Merrimack*. For a time the Northern press talked of taking on the Royal Navy, for feeling was running high over British sympathy for the Southern cause, but the miserable seakeeping of the monitors precluded them from fighting in the Atlantic, or indeed anywhere other than sheltered waters. In the words of a modern authority, they were nothing more than 'river-going rafts,' and their influence on proper battleship design must not be over-emphasized.

Another battle was soon to take place, one which was much more important in the development of battleships for it involved two ocean-going fleets. This was the Battle of Lissa fought on 20 July, 1866 between the Austrians and the Italians. On paper the Italian fleet was impressive, with brand-new ironclads bought at a high price from

England, France and the United States. The *Re d'Italia* and *Re di Portogallo* were 300-ft steam frigates, protected by 4.7-in armour belts and armed with a mixture of 100-pdr (6.3-in) Armstrong guns, 150-pdrs (7.8-in) and 300-pdrs (10-in). A further five ironclad frigates were backed up by the new English-built 'turret-ram' *Affondatore*, which had only just joined the fleet. She carried two single 10-in guns in Coles turrets at the extremities of the ship, and in addition to these she was 'armed' with a huge projecting spur underwater. During the American Civil War several ships had been sunk by ramming, one of the few ways of letting water into an ironclad hull if you lacked armour-piercing guns, and this revival from the days of galleys seemed likely to be useful.

Armour-piercing guns were just what the Austrian fleet lacked. The barque-rigged *Ferdinand Max* and *Hapsburg* resembled the *Gloire*, but their designed armament of rifled Krupp 21-cm guns had not been delivered (Austria was at war with Prussia as well as Italy) and so they mounted 48-pdr smooth-bore shell-guns. The smaller ironclad frigates had some rifled guns, but the Austrian Rear-Admiral Wilhelm Tegetthoff mustered only 74 rifled guns in all against

HMS Agincourt *of 1871, although fully rigged, was an intermediate design with a central battery. The development of turret ships for the Royal Navy had been checked by the loss of HMS* Captain *in 1870*

National Maritime Museum

23

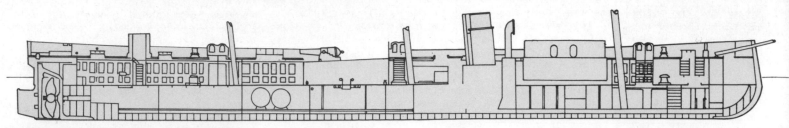

the 200 modern weapons of his opponent, Count Carlo Pellion di Persano. As a further disadvantage a large part of the Austrian fleet was composed of unarmoured wooden ships, the sort which could be destroyed in minutes. The largest of these was the screw two-decker *Kaiser*, armed with 90 30-pdr smooth-bores and two 24-pdr rifled guns.

Tegetthoff was not dismayed by these odds, and chose to remedy his material deficiences with leadership and imagination. He knew that the Italian Navy was a new creation, like the incomplete Italian state itself; it lacked training and confidence. Knowing that his guns were outranged he decided to come to close quarters – at short range some of his shells might have a chance of penetrating the Italian armour. He also chose to engage end-on, as Nelson had done at Trafalgar, to allow his ships to break into the Italian line, but as his fleet was so weak in gunpower he ordered it to sink by ramming. Like Nelson, Tegetthoff was prepared to accept the risk of damage during the initial phase, confident that superior training and morale would enable his men to survive long enough.

Clumsy Ironclads

With such determination on one side and lack of it on the other it is hardly surprising that Lissa was an overwhelming victory for the Austrians. It was a scrappy melée, reminiscent of the sea fights of the seventeenth century, and it proved singularly difficult for the clumsy ironclads to aim themselves with enough precision. For some time both sides charged about, colliding with one another or missing by a few feet; the *Affondatore* failed to ram the *Kaiser* but wrecked her upperworks with 300-pdr shells at point-blank range. The *Kaiser* then tried to ram the *Re di Portogallo* but lost her foremast figurehead and bowsprit and was set on fire.

Then came the unlucky moment in all battles. The *Re d'Italia* was hit in the rudder by a shell and became unmanoeuvrable; while her crew fought desperately to effect repairs she was spotted through the billowing clouds of powder smoke by Tegetthoff

Rolf Krake
Built by Robert Napier for the Danes, this small double-turreted coast-defence ship engaged the Prussian batteries, besieging the Düppel fortress in 1864

in the *Ferdinand Max*. Inexorably the Austrian ship bore down at 11½ knots and her ram bow tore into the *Re d'Italia* full amidships, tearing an enormous hole below her waterline. As the *Ferdinand Max* backed off the stricken ship listed slowly to starboard, righted herself as the water poured in, and then rolled quickly over to port and disappeared. The corvette *Palestro* made a gallant attempt to divert the Austrian flagship from the *Re d'Italia* but she took a shell in the wardroom which set her ablaze, and she later blew up. The Italian fleet withdrew to lick its wounds, leaving the Austrians in possession of the Adriatic.

Lissa was in its way as indecisive and insignificant as Hampton Roads, but it had a disproportionate effect on ideas and tactics. For the next 30 years all navies were obsessed with ramming, and ships were even built for the sole purpose of ramming. Yet the weapon had proved singularly ineffective against moving ships. The lessons that were *not* learned from Lissa were the important ones: the slow rate of fire, the dense powder-smoke and the relative clumsiness of big ships made it very difficult to hit anything, either with rams or shells. Another point that was overlooked was the superior training and morale of Tegetthoff's fleet. Yet for many years naval designers continued to equip battleships with monster guns which promised the mythical 'knockout blow', and apparently ignored the problem of achieving that hit.

Another effect of the Civil War actions and Lissa was an increased pace of development of guns and armour. Within five years of the building of the first ironclads armour thickness had increased from 4 inches to 6 inches, but in the same period gunmakers produced guns which pierced 9½ inches. This reinforced the arguments about doing away with a broadside armament and its full-

length armoured belt, to allow thicker armour to be fitted over a shorter length. The British designer Edward Reed (later Sir Edward Reed KCB) pioneered the 'box-battery' or 'central battery' ship, in which the guns were mounted in the central part of the hull, with the guns firing through two ports on either broadside and alternative angled ports to give some measure of fore-and-aft fire. Reed's prototype, the sloop *Research*, was only 195 ft long and displaced a mere 1743 tons, but was armoured with 4½-in plates similar to the *Warrior's*; her armament of four 100-pdr (7-in) guns was rated as equal to her original designed armament of 17 68-pdrs.

Oval Bore

Gun-design was in a state of flux in the early 1860s, making the naval architect's task even more difficult. Just before the Crimean War the British had introduced the rifled muzzle-loading Lancaster gun, which used an oval bore to impart a twist to the shell. The French followed in 1855 with their *système la Hitte*, using shells with zinc studs to fit three shallow spiral grooves. This was also known as 'shunt' rifling, for the shell was rammed into the gun base-first, when fired it 'shunted' into shallower grooves which gripped the studs. However crude this sounds, it imparted more accuracy to the shell than the old smooth-bore muzzle-loaders, but it still failed to solve the problem of 'windage', the gap between the shell and the bore of the gun which had to to be left to allow loading from the muzzle.

Naval guns had originally been breechloaders, as far back as the sixteenth century, but muzzle-loading guns replaced them entirely, because a gun cast in one piece could eliminate virtually all weaknesses. But the need for more powerful charges and the novel forms of rifling adopted in the 1850s imposed new stresses which were too much for the old cast-iron guns, and they developed a distressing habit of bursting. The British gun-manufacturer William Armstrong started to experiment with strengthening barrels by shrinking hoops of iron around them, and found that these guns

10-in Armstrong Rifled Muzzle-loader
This gun, mounted on a wrought-iron carriage, fired a shell fitted with gun-metal studs which shunted into the shallow-groove rifling of the barrel

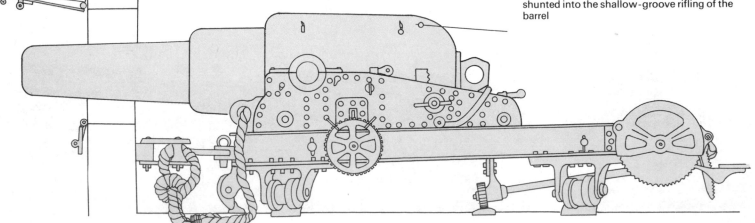

Musée de la Marine

French gun-makers developed the interrupted screw, with part of the threads cut away so that the block could be screwed home with only one-third of a turn. This 270-mm weapon, mounted in the bow of the Redoutable, *was a Model 1881 built in 1884 and weighed 28,240 kg*

could withstand much greater pressures. From there he moved on to the problem of windage, and decided to adopt a 'wedge' system of breech-loading similar to the sliding block tried in Prussia by Krupp.

The French had come to much the same conclusions, but chose a different system, with a hinged threaded block. The time taken to screw the threads home made loading too slow, and so the French soon improved the system by cutting away every sixth part of the threads, making an 'interrupted screw' which needed only a sixth-turn to lock it in place. The Prussians clung to their sliding block, but Armstrong switched to another system, with a vent-piece dropped into a slot cut into the rear

part of the gun and a hollow screw plug. This system had features of both the Prussian and the French systems but lacked the virtues of either, but nevertheless the Royal Navy adopted it in 1859.

The Royal Navy took only four years to find out about the Armstrong gun's vices. In 1863 a squadron in action in Japan reported 28 accidents in 365 rounds and the larger types of Armstrong were thereafter abandoned. But the Armstrong principle of strengthening the barrel by shrinking hoops survived this fiasco, and it was used with a modified version of the French system.

Meanwhile the Americans had taken a different direction entirely. Under the aegis of Admiral Dahlgren a series of large-calibre

smooth-bores was developed, culminating in a 15-in monster used in the monitors. These 'soda bottle' guns were intended to batter a way through armour by firing a heavy low-velocity spherical shell, whereas European guns were now using elongated conical shells which could punch through a solid plate.

Guns grew very rapidly now that they could be made to take bigger charges. The smooth-bore jumped from the previous maximum of 10 inches at the time of the Crimean War to a monster 13-in 600-pdr developed by Armstrong, while the new rifled muzzle-loaders and breech-loaders grew from 6.3-in to 12.5-in calibre. Weights went up in proportion, from the 4-ton 110-pdr to the

Armstrong 110-pdr Gun
The British gun-manufacturer William Armstrong developed a method of strengthening barrels by shrinking iron hoops on to them. This 7-in 110-pdr of 1860 weighed just over four tons, and as bigger charges became practicable the size of Armstrong weapons grew rapidly to 600-pdrs weighing 22 tons

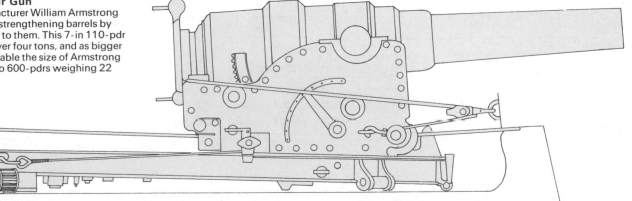

Océan *(1868) introduced guns mounted on barbette,* ie in circular armoured towers inside which the guns themselves revolved. Reduction in weight allowed *such guns to be mounted higher and the high-freeboard battleship made its reappearance*

Musée de la Marine

22-ton 600-pdr Armstrong guns. New mountings had to be designed to cope with this problem. For many years small warships had used a 'central pivot' mounting in which the gun was mounted on a slide instead of the traditional 'truck' mounting on four wooden wheels. This idea was developed into wooden and later wrought-iron slide mountings, with plate compressor systems for checking the recoil.

In France designers showed little sympathy for the turret, preferring the 'barbette' mounting. Taking its name from land fortifications, the barbette was a circular iron or steel tower, inside which the guns were carried on turntables. The main advantage was that it allowed the guns to be carried fairly high above the waterline, whereas the great weight of the turret limited the height at which it could be mounted if ship dimensions were not to grow inordinately. The *Ocean*, *Marengo* and *Suffren* of 1868 had four 14-ton guns in a high central battery of four barbettes.

The 1870s were the 'Dark Ages' not only for the Royal Navy but for others. The much-feared French Navy of the previous decade had been very slow to complete its ambitious programmes, and furthermore did little to justify its existence against the considerably inferior Prussian Navy during the Franco-Prussian War in 1870. In that year the Royal Navy's pride in its new ships suffered a tragic blow, when the new turret ship *Captain* turned turtle during a gale in the

Bay of Biscay. What made the matter worse was that she took with her Captain Coles, the man who had invented the turret, and in addition had designed the ship. Ever since the ordering of the *Prince Albert* and *Royal Sovereign* and the vindication of that decision at Hampton Roads, Coles had pestered the Admiralty to build a seagoing turret ship. Nobody but the Americans believed in the seagoing properties of monitors, and it was necessary for a blue-water-navy to have ships which could cross the Atlantic.

Naval Architect

In 1866 the Admiralty ordered the world's first seagoing turret ship, the *Monarch*, but Coles was not satisfied with her. Making adroit use of support in the Press and in Parliament he orchestrated a campaign to be allowed to design his own ship, and finally the Admiralty bowed to the inevitable, however preposterous it sounds to modern ears. But Coles was a sick man, and furthermore he had a grossly inflated idea of his capabilities as a ship designer. What he and many officers did not realise was that the introduction of armour and steam machinery had totally altered the funda-

Brazil
Another solution to the weight problem was the box-battery concentrating guns and armour in a central armoured citadel. The ironclad corvette *Brazil* was built in France in the late 1860s

mentals of naval architecture; the days when a sea-officer had as good an idea of how to build a ship as most shipwrights were gone for ever. Needless to say, the dispute over the *Monarch* had alienated the Chief Constructor, Reed, who refused to have anything to do with the design of the *Captain*. Coles was anxious to have a ship with maximum endurance and so he insisted on the maximum scale of masting, three tripod masts and about 26,000 sq ft of canvas.

The *Captain* went to sea in January 1870, and was an immediate success, although she was overweight and drawing about $2\frac{1}{2}$ ft more than her designed draught. She joined the Channel Squadron and on the night of 6 September in a full gale the *Captain* heeled over on her beam ends and then sank with the loss of 473 officers and men. Reed would not have been human if he had not drawn some satisfaction from the way in which the Admiralty and Parliament turned to him for an explanation, having previously allowed the unqualified Coles to impugn his ability. The court martial found that the ship was capsized by the 'pressure of sail assisted by the heave of the sea', something which should not have been possible in a fully stable ship. At the time the chief cause of instability was seen as excess weight which had been incorporated as a result of Admiralty inspectors not being allowed to weigh materials in the yard, but modern opinion is that the ship's unusual hurricane deck helped to act as a wind-trap.

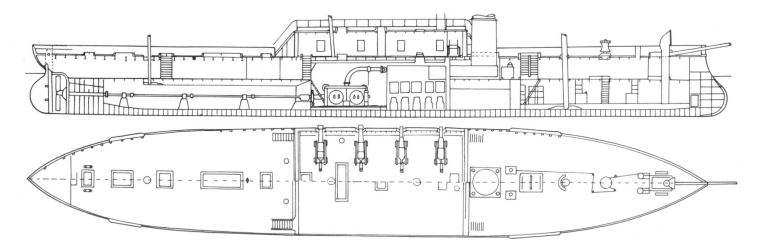

The First True Battleships
CAPITAL SHIPS

Fortunately the disaster had no effect on future battleships, apart from ensuring that no more fully rigged, low-freeboard ships were built. In the next class low-freeboard and turrets were retained but masts and yards were discarded. In their place was sufficient coal to allow them to steam nearly 5000 miles. The two ships, called *Devastation* and *Thunderer*, entered service under a cloud of pessimism and foreboding, and when the *Devastation* was commissioned an anonymous notice was fixed to the gangway, reading macabrely 'Letters for the *Captain* may be posted here.' In fact she proved remarkably steady, and amply justified her designer's faith in her. 'Steady as the old *Thunderer*' became a byword and they served for over 30 years.

Throughout the 1870s a variety of unusual ships were built, and it seemed as if the purity and simplicity of the *Devastation* design were unappreciated. The French continued to favour barbettes for ocean-going ships, and the French *Admiral Duperré* of 1879 had two single barbettes forward, side by side, and two aft on the centreline. Italy had recovered from Lissa, and in 1876 she launched the *Duilio*, the most provocative design of the decade.

Monster Guns
The talented designer Benedetto Brin was ordered to build a ship armed with four 38-ton 12.5-in guns with the thickest armour and the highest speed possible. Unfortunately the British firm of Armstrongs egged

the Italians on to upgun the ships with 50-ton 15-in guns, and then again with 100-ton 17.7-in, and the luckless Brin was forced to 'adjust' the design accordingly. The armour had to be increased in case any competitor introduced similar monster guns, and eventually he settled on a heavily armoured citadel less than a third of the length of the ship.

The hulls of the *Duilio* and her sister *Dandolo* would never have withstood the stress of firing the 100-tonners for any length of time (only one gun could fire at a time, to avoid structural damage), and the slow rate of fire made it unlikely that they would hit anything. Furthermore, Brin's theory of an underwater 'raft body', on which the ship would float if the unarmoured two-thirds of

Redoutable in a French channel port, forming part of the Défense Mobile, the reserve fleet. She was a turreted development of the high-freeboard barbette ship developed from the Océan. 'Lozenge' disposition of main armament remained a feature of French battleship design until the end of the century

Musée de la Marine

the ship were flooded, was over-optimistic. In action progressive flooding would have caused the ship to founder, even if the watertight compartments had all remained watertight, which was rarely the case.

However, the *Duilio* and *Dandolo's* drawbacks were ignored, and a wave of panic ensued. The Chief Constructor of the Royal Navy, Nathaniel Barnaby, was ordered to reply with something similar, and in 1874 the keel of the *Inflexible* was laid. This remarkable ship epitomizes the transitional stage of battleship design in the 1870s, with a preposterous brig rig, twin turrets *en*

echelon amidships, and a squat hull only four times as long as it was wide. She had not only the heaviest armour ever mounted in a battleship, 24-in compound (steel and iron), but the largest muzzle-loading guns ever used by the RN, four 80-ton 16-in. She would have carried 100-ton guns just like the *Duilios* but the Navy was only allowed to buy guns from the Government Arsenal at Woolwich, and Woolwich could only produce a 16-in gun.

The *Inflexible's* guns were also transitional. Experience had shown that the new slow-burning gunpowders being deve-

Redoutable

In 1872, after the land war with Germany, France began battleship construction again in the form of *Redoutable*—the first armoured ship with steel frames. The bow did not contain a ram, despite its appearance, but was cut away to avoid damage from the bow-mounted chaser gun
Displacement: 9200 tons *Armament:* 4 × 108-mm *Armour:* 350-mm belt, 240-mm battery

loped were not suited to short-barrelled guns, as part of the powder remained unburnt when the shell left the gun. Increasing the length of barrel solved the problem, but of course it increased the difficulties of muzzle-loading. The Royal Navy was not alone among the front-rank navies in clinging to the muzzle-loader, but the *Inflexible's* problems convinced even the doubters. To cope with the extra length of barrel the loading gear was put *outside* the turret and beneath the deck. The barrels were depressed until the muzzles were below a glacis or ramp, underneath which rammers pushed the charges and the shells up the bore.

Like the *Duilio*, the *Inflexible* relied on a raft body, with a buoyant unarmoured superstructure carried above the raft, on

HMS Devastation, *the first ocean-going battleship without sails. The weight formerly devoted to masts and full-rig could now be used for increased coal capacity to give far greater endurance. As such HMS* Devastation *was the progenitor of the modern battleship and as important as the* Dreadnought

Dandalo, with four turret-mounted 17-in guns, caused panic in rival navies in the mid-1870s

National Maritime Museum

Museo Storico Navale

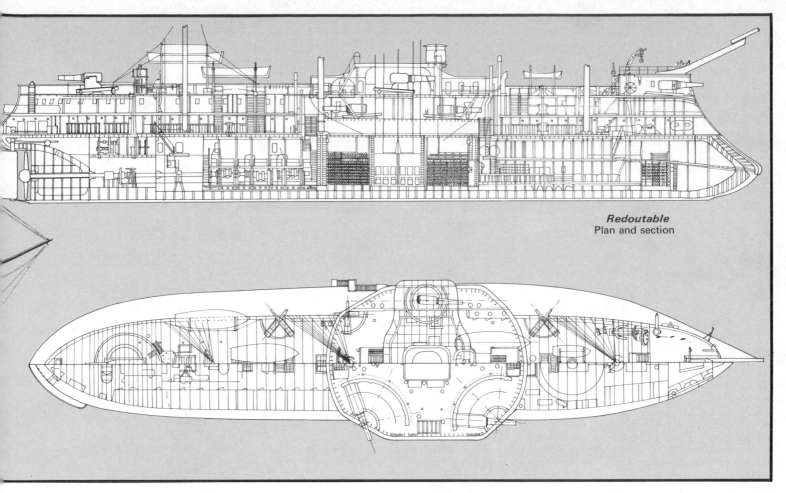

Redoutable
Plan and section

which the turrets were mounted. She was the first ship illuminated throughout by electric light, and also the first with anti-rolling tanks. But she was without doubt the most ungainly ship yet built for the Royal Navy, and the British would have done well to have ignored the *Duilio* for the freak that she was.

As the *Inflexible* was largely experimental she was full of complicated new machinery, and in addition her layout was far more involved than in any previous battleship. Her first captain was John Fisher, later to erupt in volcanic fashion as Sir John Fisher, the man who refashioned the Royal Navy. The new captain was dismayed to find that his ship's company were losing themselves in the 'iron labyrinth', and so he designed a series of colour-symbols for marking bulkheads, passage-ways and deck-levels. But all this zeal passed for nothing until Fisher, having worked his men up to fighting efficiency, then turned them to drilling aloft. And only when the most modern steam-powered battleship in the world could shift a topsail quicker than her squadron-mates was she judged to be efficient.

The *Inflexible* was commissioned in 1881, and a year later she fired her guns in anger at the Bombardment of Alexandria, when the Mediterranean Fleet opened fire on the Egyptian forts in protest against a rebellion and massacre of Europeans. She fired 88 of her enormous shells and was hit by a 10-in shell, which did less damage than the concussion of her own guns. The glamour of her big guns and heavy protection soon wore off, and although she was followed by smaller editions she marked the end of the era of bizarre designs. Enormous technological changes were on the way, and the emergence of the true battleship was close.

The Italians however could not resist one last attempt at out-doing the rest of the world. In 1876, the year in which the *Inflexible* was launched, they began the *Italia* and *Lepanto* as much improved *Duilios*. They were armed with 103-ton 17-in breech-loaders, but in place of the armoured citadel Benedetto Brin gave them a heavily armoured redoubt around the guns and a raft body running the length of the ship below the waterline. For their time they represented a rare example of maximum offence and defence in one hull, among the masterpieces of warship design.

Unfortunately a new development promised to discredit many of the ships of the 1870s and early 1880s. This was the quick-firing gun of 3- to 6-in calibre, which could deliver a large number of high-explosive shells against the large unarmoured parts of the hulls of such ships as the *Inflexible* and *Italia*, destroying the cellular com-

HMS Inflexible *was an overhasty reply to the Italian* Duilio, *adopting the same configuration, and carrying the largest muzzle-loading rifled guns ever mounted in the Royal Navy*

Duilio, *as potent as her sister but again weakly armoured and only suitable for the Mediterranean*

Museo Storico Navale

National Maritime Museum

partmentation which gave them additional buoyancy. Although the quick-firer shells would not sink a battleship by themselves they could cause fires and widespread destruction, sufficient to disable the largest battleships. It was like the shell-scare after Sinope, with some ludicrous claims about small cruisers vanquishing mighty battleships, but there was no doubt that a ship like the *Italia*, firing one shell every four or five minutes from her 17-in guns, might well be unable to prevent a fast and manoeuvrable ship from coming within range to smother her with 6-in shells. The quick-firer was simply a gun with an improved breech-mechanism, which automatically readied the firing mechanism as the breech was closed, thereby speeding up the rate of fire considerably, but it revolutionized tactics and ship-design.

Not only light guns were being improved. The British had dropped the breech-loader for good reasons in 1863 – not least because of inferior construction of the Armstrong gun. Although the French and German systems of breech-loading were retained they were by no means perfect, and accidents occurred through weaknesses at the breech. But in 1875 the Prussians produced at Meppen the so-called 'mantle-ring', a mantle or jacket shrunk over the breech end. This strengthened the body of the gun, and allowed much lighter construction for a given charge. The Royal Navy was not slow to hear of the progress at Meppen, particularly as there was a strong body of opinion within the Service in favour of a return to breech-loading. A bad explosion in one of the *Thunderer*'s turrets in January 1879 also helped to shake faith in the reliability of muzzle-loaders.

The *Thunderer* explosion not only illustrates how a gun could be double-loaded, but also gives some clue to what it was like to fire the great guns of a Victorian battleship. Both guns were being fired simultaneously, and apparently one 'hung fire'. But as the men in the turrets often put their fingers in their ears (no ear-plugs were issued until well after the First World War) and even shut their eyes just before the guns fired, they then immediately operated the run-in levers without noticing that one gun

HMS Benbow, *last of the 'Admirals' and in fact an individual design. Weight considerations allowed only two of the 16.25-in guns to be mounted, one in each main turret. The midships battery carried ten 6-in guns*

had not recoiled as far as the other. The 38-ton guns were run inside the turret and then depressed for loading, but this time one gun was loaded twice, and the indicator on the rammer simply jammed without being noticed by the loading number. Understandably the gun burst on being fired, wrecking the turret and killing two officers, nine ratings and wounding a further 30.

The French continued to build battleships with high freeboard and barbette-mounted heavy guns into the early 1880s, and it was in reply to the last of these, the *Formidable* and *Courbet* classes, that the British built what was to prove their best design since the *Devastation*. This was the handsome *Collingwood* class, the first fruits of the genius of William White, the naval architect who was to dominate warship design for 20 years.

The layout of the *Devastation* was revived, a return to simplicity and balance, but this time the guns were in French-style barbettes. The reason for this was to allow the guns to be carried at 22 ft above the waterline, as White had to restrict freeboard to save weight. There was a tacit understanding between the Admiralty and Parliament that displacement should not exceed 10,000 tons, despite the fact that this was only 10% more than the *Warrior*'s tonnage 20 years before. To stay within this unofficial limit White had no choice but to go for a short and heavy waterline armour belt, closed by a transverse bulkhead and protected additionally by coal bunkers. The ends were left completely unarmoured, and could be penetrated even by machine-gun bullets, but, although speed and stability might be diminished, this could not be avoided even if another 1000 tons of armour were added to protect the ends. So White plumped for an 'all or nothing' scheme some 30 years before it became widely accepted as the only method of armouring.

The armament of the *Collingwood* also reflected the revolution in naval architecture. In place of the giant muzzle-loaders familiar for so long she carried four 12-in breech-loaders, widely separated at either end of the superstructure. On each side of the superstructure at upper deck level there were three 6-in guns, with good arcs of fire before and abaft the beam. She was also an extremely handsome ship, in total contrast to the angular freaks which had been

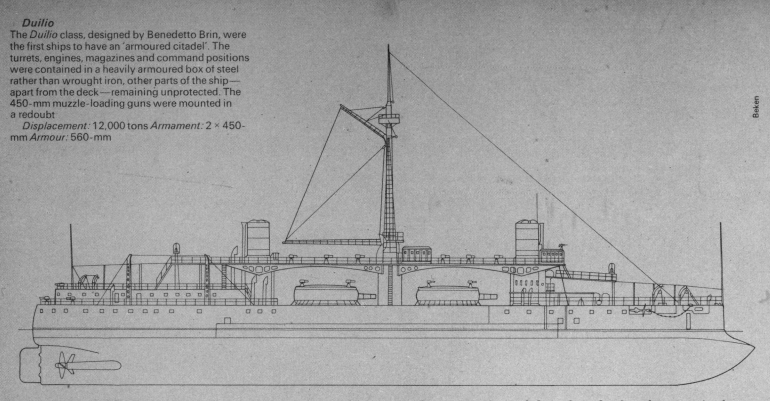

Duilio
The *Duilio* class, designed by Benedetto Brin, were the first ships to have an 'armoured citadel'. The turrets, engines, magazines and command positions were contained in a heavily armoured box of steel rather than wrought iron, other parts of the ship—apart from the deck—remaining unprotected. The 450-mm muzzle-loading guns were mounted in a redoubt
  Displacement: 12,000 tons *Armament:* 2 × 450-mm *Armour:* 560-mm

common for many years. Her two tall funnels and single mast stamped her as a creation of William White, and began what was later regarded as a typically British 'look' for battleships.

Sir Edward Reed had resigned from the post of Chief Surveyor after the loss of HMS *Captain* in 1870, and from his position as a Member of Parliament he ceaselessly attacked all official Admiralty designs. The *Collingwood* gave him what he saw as a chance to undermine confidence in the current administration, and to allow him to return to take charge. But this time Reed went too far, and his rancour was instrumental in persuading the Japanese and Spanish navies not to order new battleships from British yards. Although there were doubts about the *Collingwood*'s 'soft ends' it gradually dawned on her critics that Reed's fulminations were not based on precise knowledge of the design. Some idea of the value of soft ends was gained some years later, at the Battle of the Yalu River in 1894, when the Chinese turret ships *Chen Yuen* and *Ting Yuen* were hit nearly 200 times each without sinking, and certainly without their soft ends being blown to pieces, as the *Collingwood*'s critics claimed would happen.

The French were not idle in the face of this challenge, and in 1880 they laid down the *Hoche*, *Magenta*, *Marceau* and *Neptune*,

HMS Collingwood, *William White's brilliant design of 1887. A development of the* Devastation, *she was the forerunner of the 'Admiral' class*

impressive ships armed with four guns: two in barbettes fore and aft, and two in barbettes on either side amidships, or 'lozenge' fashion. The French Navy had been expanding for some years, having built 22 battleships since 1874, as against 13 British, and although the French programme was not to continue after 1881 the Admiralty felt bound to reply to maintain the relative strength. The choice was far from easy, for not only were there a number of tempting freakish designs like the *Inflexible* and *Italia* to recommend themselves, but to complicate matters the RN was in the middle of its change-over from muzzle-loading guns to breech-loaders. Four types of large-calibre guns had been adopted in 1881, ranging from the 29-ton 10-in to the 110-ton 16.25-in.

The five ships built were improved versions of the *Collingwood*, and they became known as the 'Admiral' class: *Anson, Camperdown, Howe, Rodney* and *Benbow*. But in place of the 12-in guns four were armed with a new 30-cal 13.5-in gun weighing 30 tons, giving them a more massive look that the prototype. But the ship which caught the public eye was the fifth vessel, the *Benbow*, for she was armed with two of the 16.25-in monsters. Despite the fact that they could only fire a round every four or five minutes, and that the barrel-life was only 75 rounds, the public thought very highly of her. The 'Admirals' were much admired professionally too, and the Italian Navy built the *Sardegna* class along similar lines.

HMS *Victoria*
Designed for use in the Mediterranean, *Victoria* and her sister *Sanspareil* carried a main armament of only two guns but mounted weapons of eight calibres in all. *Victoria* was lost following a collision with the *Camperdown* during an exercise

Displacement: 10,470 tons *Length:* 340 ft
Armament: 2×16.25-in, 1×9.2-in, 12×6-in, 12×6-pdr, 12×3-pdr, 8×mg *Armour:* 16/18-in belt, 18-in turret, 3-in deck *Max speed:* 17.5 knots

Sanspareil class

Name	Completed	Fate
Sanspareil	1889	
Victoria	1891	Sunk in collision 1893

It might be thought that the successful 'Admirals' might have been followed by a series of improved vessels, but this was not so. Instead a new series of freaks appeared. Obsessed by the 'lozenge' disposition of guns in French ships, the British opted for end-on fire, despite the fact that the *Hoche* class could only fire their forward guns over a 180° arc and their midship guns over 90°, because of the blast damage to their superstructure. It is an unchanging rule of naval architecture that foreign designers must be credited with special exemptions from the problems one's own team find intractable. The results of this particular aberration were the two turret ships *Sans Pareil* and *Victoria*, armed with two 16.25-in guns in a turret forward and a single 10-in on the after superstructure. They looked like giant slippers, with low freeboard forward, two funnels side-by-side and massive superstructure aft.

The voices of those who lent their support to this awkward-looking pair were remarkably silent when the *Victoria* sank after a collision with the *Camperdown* off Tripoli in the Levant. On 22 June, 1893 the Mediterranean Fleet, eight battleships and five cruisers under Vice-Admiral Sir George Tryon, was entering Tripoli Bay in two columns, with the Port Division headed by Rear-Admiral Markham in HMS *Camperdown* and the Starboard Division led by the flagship, HMS *Victoria*. One point must be made clear: Sir George Tryon was an unorthodox tactician, and was regarded as one of the Navy's ablest flag-officers. The two columns were steaming 6 cables (1200 yards) apart, and as the two leading battleships had turning circles of about 3½ cables (700 yards) Admiral Markham was not the only officer to be puzzled by a signal from Tryon ordering each division to turn inwards 180° 'preserving the order of the Fleet'. The normal distance for such a manoeuvre would be eight cables (1600 yards), but when Markham indicated that he did not understand the signal (by leaving the answering signal pendants 'at the dip') Tryon asked the *Camperdown* what she was waiting for.

As the two leading ships began their ponderous turns inward it became more and more clear to Markham that his ship was going to strike the *Victoria* on her starboard side. Tryon's flag-captain had already ordered the *Victoria*'s port propeller to be reversed to tighten her turning circle, but nothing could slow down the *Camperdown*; a 10,000-ton ship travelling at eight knots has no brakes, and even reversing both engines had little effect. With a terrible grinding of steel the *Camperdown*'s ram bow struck the *Victoria* on her starboard bow, penetrating about 9 ft, some 12 ft below the waterline. But this was not all, for the impact swung the *Victoria* nearly 70 ft to port and so the *Camperdown*'s ram enlarged the hole to an enormous gash over 100 sq ft in area.

Both ships had gone to 'collision stations' about a minute before the impact, but closing watertight doors and hatches took all of three minutes, and in addition many of the smaller drainage valves were either inaccessible or clogged with dirt and rust. Water flooded in as the *Victoria* headed slowly for shallow water in an attempt to beach herself, but 12 minutes after the collision she suddenly lurched to starboard and capsized. Only half of the 700 men on board were saved, partly because of the devotion of the ship's company who did not desert their posts until ordered to save themselves, and partly because the old-fashioned sailor rarely learned to swim. The *Camperdown* was also holed, and it was feared that she would sink too, but she was saved by the quick action of her carpenter, who built a wooden cofferdam across the main deck. In neither ship could basic design be blamed; the same lessons had to be relearned in 1914, that small openings and minor leakages will make nonsense of any

HMS Nile, *and her sister the* Trafalgar, *were updated versions of the* Devastation, *launched in 1886. The Financial Secretary to the Admiralty predicted that they would be the last battleships, made obsolete by the mine and torpedo*

The Italian Sardegna *class copied the best features of the British 'Admirals' but had splinter-proof shields over the two barbettes*

theoretically watertight system. Still, there was profound alarm at the rapid sinking of a modern battleship, and even more disquiet at the spectacle of two admirals colliding in broad daylight while attempting an apparently simple manoeuvre.

The discussion of Tryon's intentions continued long after the Royal Navy had quietly made several improvements to the drainage of its battleships and had studied the problems of rapid flooding. All hinged on the distance between the columns, for Tryon had either made a mistake or had been misunderstood. The likeliest explanation lies in the fact that the manoeuvre was unorthodox, and did not even appear in the signal book. Quarter-circle turns were made constantly, whereas half-circle turns (the ones ordered by Tryon) were very rare. It is possible that Tryon automatically allowed a safe distance (a minimum of four cables or 800 yards) for a quarter-circle turn, forgetting that he needed twice that distance for the turn he was making. Admiral Mark Kerr claimed that Tryon had made a similar mistake during the 1890 Manoeuvres, and that his attention had been drawn to it in time. If so, we must assume that this was a blind spot in Tryon's considerable tactical skill, and Admiral Kerr's anonymous informant went on to say that Tryon had admitted as much on the bridge of the *Victoria* as she went down.

Premature Obituary

The next ships to be built for the RN were far from ideal, as they were little more than up-to-date versions of the *Devastation*, but were nevertheless a considerable improvement over such flights from sanity as the *Victoria*. The *Nile* and *Trafalgar* at least had thick armour, a citadel which reached a maximum thickness of 20 inches of compound armour, because the Admiralty was allowed to increase displacement to nearly 12,000 tons. But the design was overshadowed by a new fear, the possibility of the torpedo boat making the battleship redundant. In the first of many premature obituaries for the battleship the financial secretary to the Admiralty said of the *Nile* and *Trafalgar* in 1886, 'these large ironclads will probably be the last of this type that will ever be built in this or any other country'.

Although the automobile or 'fish' torpedo dated back to 1868, when Robert Whitehead brought his device to England, little had been achieved in the way of making it a dominant weapon at sea. The British had shown more interest than anyone else, and had built large numbers of torpedo boats. Naturally the French were not going to be left behind and so they followed the British lead in ordering large numbers. In the only torpedo action of the 1870s, the fight between the British unarmoured ships *Amethyst* and *Shah* and an ex-Peruvian 'pirate' ship, the *Huascar* out-ran the *Shah's* torpedo at a speed of about 9½ knots!

French enthusiasm for the torpedo was remarkably similar to the excitement caused first by the Paixhans shell and then by the introduction of armour. Here was another 'David' weapon which would offset the uncomfortable and inescapable fact that Great Britain could build 'Goliath' battleships faster. In 1874 the French Admiral Aube pointed out that Britain's seaborne trade was still her most vulnerable asset, and that a blockading fleet of battleships was no more an effective way of preventing

individual commerce-raiding ships from slipping out of French harbours than Nelson's three-deckers. Aube and his disciples, soon dubbed the New School or *Jeune Ecole*, went further in saying that France ought to devote more of her maritime resources to commerce destruction and much less to trying to equal the Royal Navy in battleships and cruisers.

None of this was particularly novel, but the Whitehead torpedo lent a great deal of point to these theories, for it could be launched by small, fast craft. Unlike the big gun, which needed a stable and well designed platform to function properly, the torpedo needed only a tube or launching cradle to eject it into the water, and the weight saved could be devoted to machinery for high speed. The limited range of the torpedo was not important; guns were slow-firing and inaccurate at long range, and so were unlikely to register annihilating hits on small, highly mobile targets.

The introduction of the quick-firing gun demolished much of the basis for the theories of the *Jeune Ecole*, for it was not likely that alert gunners would allow a torpedo boat to approach to within 400 yards of a battleship. And there were other defences, notably the anti-torpedo net, which could be extended on booms around a ship at anchor. But this restricted movement and although heavier nets allowed the ship to use them at low speeds, they were hardly ever used outside harbour. Machine guns were developed for use against torpedo boats, a .65-in Gatling which was later replaced by the more effective 1-in Nordenfelt, and searchlights were introduced to provide illumination at night. The *Jeune Ecole* arguments paid little attention to the improvements in ships' gunnery, for the quick-firing gun was regarded as a menace equal to that of the battleship. But the torpedo continued to inhibit designers and tacticians, and by the end of the 1880s all modern battleships were armed with numbers of light guns, searchlights and torpedo nets.

So far the story has been almost exclusively about British and French innovations; this is not surprising, for other navies had not shown the same inclination to experiment. The US Navy had suffered a relapse after the end of the Civil War, and no new construction in any category was sanctioned after 1874. The last big monitors had been laid up, as if somehow their inflated reputations would suffice as a deterrent. Monitors had caught the attention of the Swedes, one suspects partly because of Ericsson's Swedish origins, and they built four. France bought the double-turretted *Onondaga* from the US Navy after the Civil War and Chile bought two of the *Canonicus* class. Russia invested in no fewer than 14 Ericsson-type monitors, and for some years they were the only Russian armoured ships.

Although the British clearly regarded the seagoing ironclad as the only proper answer to the monitor they showed some interest in the type as a coast-defence ship, and were active in building them for other navies. Thus the *Rolf Krake* (1863) was built for Denmark, the *Huascar* for Peru and the *Buffel* and *Tijer* for the Netherlands. The navies of Argentina and Brazil also featured monitors, such as the French-built *Javary*. The US Navy was, however, unique in clinging to the idea of the big monitor long after every other major power had aban-

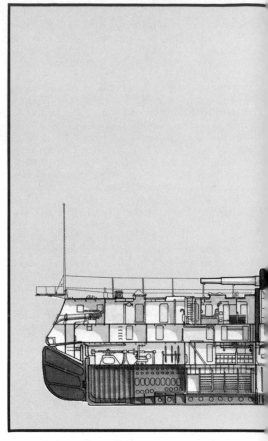

USS *Indiana*
The three battleships in this class were similar to the later *Royal Sovereigns* but had paired turrets, giving a low freeboard. Neither seakeeping ability nor top speed was impressive
Displacement: 10,200 tons *Armament:* 4×13-in, 8×8-in, 4×6-in *Max speed:* 16 knots

Indiana class

Name	Completed	Fate
Indiana	Nov 1895	Scrapped 1924
Massachusetts	Jun 1896	Sunk as target 1920
Oregon	1896	Scrapped 1956

doned the type as a front-line battle unit. The circumstances were unusual in that Congress would not allow new construction. In 1874, in a desperate attempt to provide some sort of shipbuilding programme, the US Navy resorted to the old eighteenth-century trick of a 'great repair'. An unsuspecting legislature voted money for the 'repair' of five Civil War monitors whose hulls had been attacked by dry rot.

The five ships, *Puritan*, *Amphitrite*, *Monadnock*, *Terror* and *Miantonomoh*, bore no resemblance to the original ships, apart from their low freeboard; they had breech-loaders and other refinements, and might more correctly be described as coast-defence battleships. The ships took 17 to 22 years to build, partly because it was necessary to allocate money in driblets to avoid alerting suspicious Congress watchdogs. To make matters worse the Navy's insistence on the right to build the monitors resulted in over-enthusiastic support from senior officers and the few navy-minded politicians. A further five were authorized between 1887 and 1898, and by a happy coincidence they turned out to be ideal submarine tenders because of their low freeboard. But seagoing ships they were not, as witness the conditions aboard the *Amphitrite*, which recorded a temperature of 205° in her boiler-room. During one Atlantic 'cruise' in 1895 so many of her stokers were prostrated by

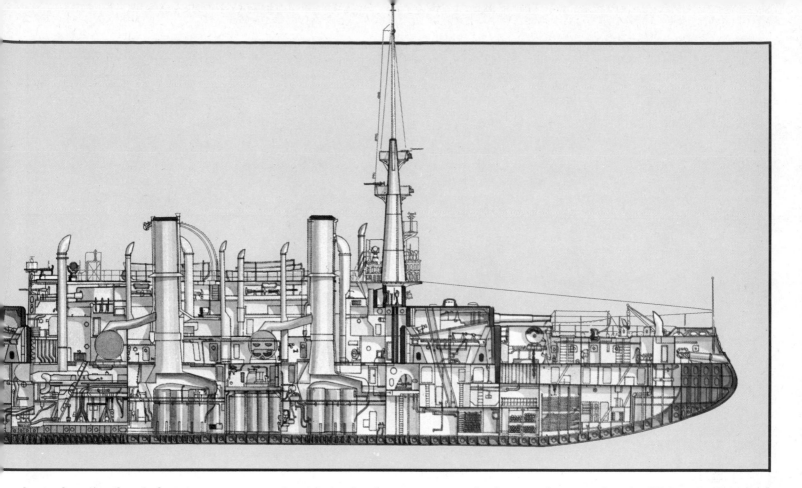

heat exhaustion that she lost steam pressure and had to anchor until the temperature had cooled.

From this nadir the US Navy could only make slow progress. For a start the domestic steel industry's capacity had to be built up. Battleships could only be built if the right industrial base existed, and so the first two ships ordered in 1886 were the 2nd Class battleship *Texas* and the armoured cruiser *Maine* (re-rated as a 2nd Class battleship during construction). Neither ship struck terror into her foes, for they were turret ships of small, obsolescent design, with turrets amidships. The *Maine*'s only memorable achievement was to be blown up in Havana in February 1898, thus providing the US Government with the excuse it wanted to go to war with Spain. With noteworthy zeal for truth and justice the US Government refused to allow an international committee of ordnance experts to examine the hull for proof of sabotage, but modern opinion inclines to the view that the *Maine* suffered an internal explosion from deteriorating powder rather than an external detonation caused by a time-bomb or mine.

Despite the slow start America soon discovered the extent of her industrial resources. In 1890 Congress authorized the building of three seagoing battleships. The designation 'seagoing' was insisted upon to stress that the ships were for coast defence, for Congress had no intention of allowing ambitious naval officers to agitate for bigger and better ships than the European navies. Despite this the *Indiana*, *Massachusetts* and *Oregon* compared favourably in gunpower and protection, with four 13-in guns, a heavy secondary battery of eight 8-in guns and an armour belt 18-in thick. The value of the four twin 8-in turrets at the corners of the superstructure was not as great as it looked on paper. Blast interference from them made the 13-in turrets unusable, as the sight-setters in

the sighting hoods were concussed when the 8-in guns fired overhead.

There was a much more serious fault in the design of the 13-in turrets: the positioning of the carriages of the guns too far forward. This had been done to avoid having too large a gunport, but its effect was to make the turret unbalanced. When the guns were trained on the beam the ship listed several degrees and submerged the armour belt. On one occasion the *Indiana*'s turrets broke loose from their stops and it took the efforts of 100 men to bring them

under control again. With so much armour and armament on a limited displacement there was no room for coal, and the normal load of 400 tons (theoretically a maximum of 1800 tons could be carried) would be good for about 700 miles' steaming at full speed (probably not more than 2000 miles at economical speed). A fourth ship, the *Iowa*, was ordered in 1892 to a similar design, but she was armed with four 12-in guns to allow for greater freeboard, as the 12-ft freeboard of the *Indianas* had proved inadequate.

USS Texas, *launched in 1892, was heavily influenced by both French and German ideas emphasising gunpower at the expense of speed. Poor sea-keeping and range reflected US emphasis on coast defence*

To maintain a high freeboard, French battleship designs of the late 1880s (above Masséna) adopted an exaggerated tumblehome, the maximum waterline width sloping to a narrower upper-deck. The snout bow was not a ram but a device to avoid excessive blast damage from the foremost turret

Beken

République

The two vessels in this class, along with those of the *Vérité* class, formed the backbone of the French battle fleet for many years. They continued the practice of mounting the secondary armament in turrets

Displacement: 14,865 tons full load *Length:* 135 m *Armament:* 4 × 305-mm, 18 × 165-mm, 13 × 65-mm, 10 × 47-mm, 5 × 450-mm torpedo tubes *Armour:* 180/280-mm belt, 320-mm main turrets, 60-mm main deck *Max speed:* 18 knots

République class

Name	Completed	Fate
République	1906	Scrapped 1921
Patrie	1906	Scrapped 1927

The French Navy's actual building rate contrasted dramatically with its predictions. The four ships which inspired the British to build the 'Admirals' were laid down in 1880-81 but not completed until 1890-92, whereas the British ships were commissioned two to three years sooner. The new *Directeur de Matériel*, Emile Bertin, produced a series of designs which marked him as a worthy successor to Dupuy de Lôme, but the slow pace of construction made them look somewhat dated by the time they appeared. In other respects, too, the French Navy seemed curiously reluctant to embrace progress. Having pioneered the

barbette system they dropped it in favour of the turret, but kept turrets years after every other navy had dropped them. The obsession with the 'lozenge' disposition of guns meant that French battleships had to pay a heavy penalty.

Like the Chinese, the French believed that opponents should be frightened before the battle, and their ships had a 'fierce-face' appearance, with massive funnels and built-up masts. The hulls were given very high freeboard, which was of course a good feature as it allowed a high command for the guns, but this resulted in unacceptable topweight, which had to be reduced by

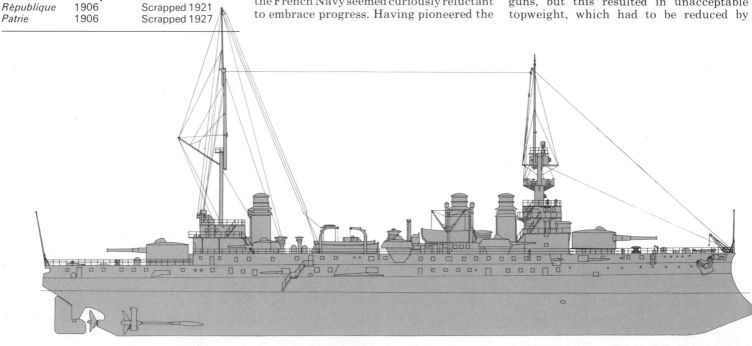

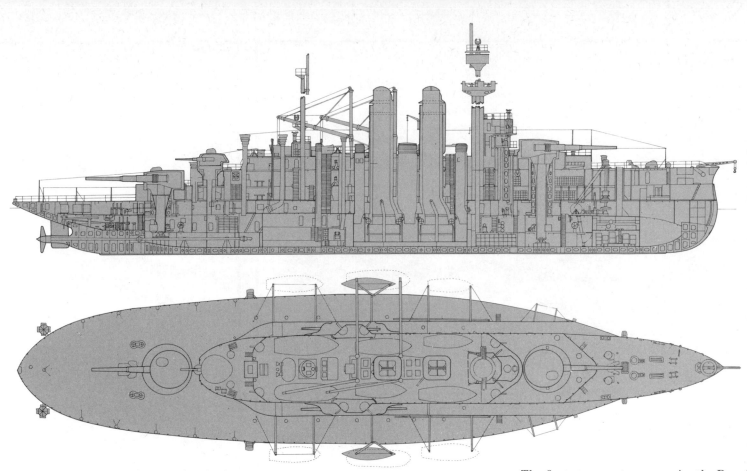

'tumblehome', the archaic term for sloping the sides to make the upper deck beam narrower than the waterline width. Again, this was quite logical, but it had to be exaggerated to allow the beam guns to fire end-on, at best a theoretical advantage. Armour was limited to a very narrow waterline belt running the length of the ship, a waterline deck and virtually nothing else apart from armour on the turrets. The worst feature of this system was that the ship lost stability at any moderate angle of heel; with only 4-in armour starting about $1\frac{1}{2}$ ft above the load waterline, the sides could be perforated and water would enter the ship above the armoured deck during a roll of only 9°.

At the end of the 1880s the British position was not nearly as bad as the critics had assumed. In 1886 the French Chamber of Deputies learned that only ten seagoing battleships were ready for sea. Only one of six ships laid down between 1878 and 1881 was near to completion, and one, the *Neptune*, was only 38% complete after five

Henri IV

Although intended only for coast defence *Henri IV* was guardship at Bizerta at the outbreak of the First World War and was later sent to the Dardanelles

Displacement: 8,800 tons *Length:* 108 m
Armament: 2 × 275-mm, 7 × 140-mm, 12 × 45-mm, 2 × mg, 2 × 355-mm or 450-mm torpedo tubes
Armour: 180/280-mm belt, 300-mm turrets, 76-mm deck *Max speed:* 17·2 knots

Name	Completed	Fate
Henri IV	1902	Scrapped 1921

years on the stocks. In contrast the Royal Navy had got rid of all but two of the old wooden-hulled ironclads and had virtually written off the old *Warrior*-type broadside ironclads. But there were a number of new technical developments in ship design, and it was felt in Parliament and in the Navy that the time had come for an overhaul of the system. What was needed was not a vast increase in the nominal strength of the Fleet but more efficient building.

The first step was to reorganize the Royal Dockyards, and this task was given to Sir William White, the gifted naval architect who had left the Navy in 1882 to work for a private firm. In 1885 he returned, and transformed the Dockyards from being grossly inefficient into the cheapest and fastest building yards in the world. Much was made of the building of HMS *Dreadnought* in just over a year, but the same dockyard built HMS *Majestic* in only 22 months. And these were the same yards which in 1884 had been officially considered to be capable only of repair work. White's reforms were made possible because of a virtual moratorium on battleship-building; until the reforms were completed only small cruisers and gunboats were ordered.

On the material side the old ironclad *Resistance* was used as a target to test various types of armouring and shells. Even torpedoes were fired at the ship, and from these experiments White and the newly formed Royal Corps of Naval Constructors were able to prepare revolutionary new de-

Charlemagne running trials without armament, emphasising the theoretical advantages of 'fierce-face' appearance with heavily built-up masts and superstructure, long a preoccupation of French warship design

St Louis, a sister of Charlemagne, seen in the later overall grey paint scheme. The shape of the ship and the pronounced tumblehome is much more recognisable, emphasising the camouflage properties of the peacetime scheme

USS Massachusetts, *the second unit of the* Indiana *class. Low freeboard prevented the use of the main battery in a seaway*

Marius Bar

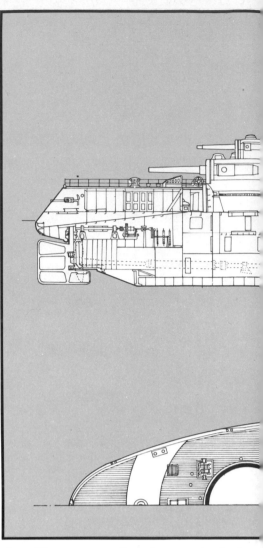

HMS Repulse *(seen in 1904) of the* Royal Sovereign *class broke new ground in combining the barbette system with high freeboard to produce a more effective sea-going battleship*

Imperial War Museum

The design of SMS Baden, *launched in 1884, reflected the continuing emphasis put on the embryonic German Navy as a coast-defence force*

Imperial War Museum

signs. The scare over French expansion had loosened the purse-strings, and so, when White proposed larger battleships than ever before, for the first time there was no political opposition.

In July 1886 the Conservatives under Lord Salisbury were returned to power, and Lord George Hamilton returned as First Lord of the Admiralty with hardly a break in policy, since the Liberal Government was only in power for six months. The public suddenly became very Navy-minded, having taken the Navy for granted since the Crimean War, and a powerful Press campaign helped the politicians to make up their minds. In March 1889 the Government introduced the Naval Defence Act, a special programme to modernize and strengthen the Fleet:

    8—1st Class battleships
    2—2nd Class battleships
    9—1st Class cruisers
   29—2nd Class cruisers
    4—3rd Class cruisers
  18—torpedo gunboats

These 70 ships were to cost £21.5 million, a staggering sum by the standards of the day, and construction was to be spread over five years.

Having achieved such a remarkable degree of political support William White responded by producing ships of exceptional military qualities. His 1st Class battleships, the *Royal Sovereign* class, were remarkable ships. With the 10,000-ton limit behind him he was able to take the best feature of his 'Admiral' class, the barbette-mounted gun armament, and combine it with proper freeboard. Not only was spray interference thus

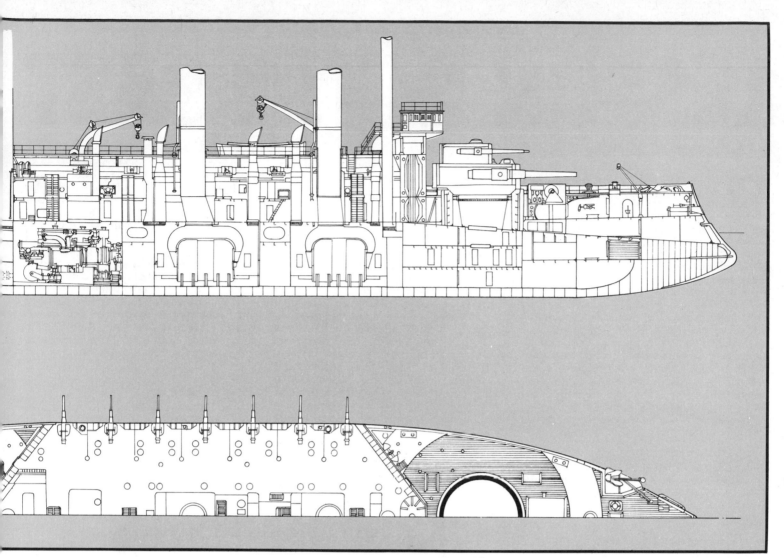

reduced, but the sea speed was increased. Tumblehome was used to avoid excessive topweight. The main armament was the same as in the 'Admirals', four 13.5-in, but the 6-in guns were mounted in two casemates or enclosed armoured boxes at maindeck level on each side, and three ordinary shielded mountings a deck higher. These secondary guns were quick-firers, and were the equivalent of about double the number of the older slow-firing breech-loaders.

The *Royal Sovereigns* were an outstanding success, and what is more they struck a new note in being handsome ships, with funnels side by side and a symmetrical silhouette. The odd man out was the eighth ship, the *Hood*. The First Sea Lord, Sir Arthur Hood, was adamant in his belief in the turret, despite all White's arguments about its great weight. In deference to the First Sea Lord's prejudices the last unit of the class was given two twin 13.5-in turrets, and if she did nothing else she clinched the argument for good. Because of the weight she had to have low freeboard and so was always slower than the other seven ships. Also, when they were rearmed with additional 6-in casemates in 1902–04 the *Hood* was found to have insufficient stability to allow the alteration. She only redeemed herself by her valuable service in testing the first anti-torpedo 'bulges' in 1913, and was sunk as a blockship at Portland in 1914, where she can be seen to this day.

White was not content with one masterpiece. There was one serious disadvantage in the *Royal Sovereign* design; the main armament was unprotected from shells bursting overhead, as the guns were mounted in barbettes. In 1893, with the Naval Defence Act building programme still under way, the Admiralty was pressing for a continuation of the drive for supremacy. Seven more battleships were authorized, and White took the chance to make several technical improvements, such as the provision of 'hoods' for the barbettes, adopting a lighter but more powerful 12-in gun and putting all the 6-in guns in casemates. The result was not only the ultimate nineteenth-century battleship design but also an even better looking ship than the *Royal Sovereign*, with a compact, balanced profile and two funnels set close together, side by side. The US Navy paid the most sincere compliment of all by building the *Alabama* class along almost identical lines.

After making such a strenuous effort the British settled down to build more battleships along very similar lines. With the completion of the last *Majestic* the Royal Navy had 16 new battleships of basically similar design, which could manoeuvre together and therefore be handled as one homogeneous force. To preserve this homogeneity the Royal Navy made few demands for detailed changes in succeeding classes for nearly ten years, and so a total of nearly 40 ships were built in quick succession. The speed with which British shipyards could turn out battleships is demonstrated by the fact that the *Majestic* was built by Portsmouth Dockyard in less than 22 months, a record which was only equalled by the *Dreadnought*'s 14 months from the same yard. But the *Dreadnought*'s record was achieved by using gun turrets earmarked for two other ships, whereas all nine

USS Kearsage
The battleships in this class employed the two-storey turret arrangement in an attempt to save weight so that the ships could operate more easily off the Mexican coast. The disadvantages outweighed the benefits, however
Displacement: 11,540 tons *Length:* 368 ft
Armament: 4×13-in, 4×8-in, 18×5-in, 2×3-in AA (from 1918), 4×6-pdr, 1×18-in torpedo tube
Armour: 9¼/16¼-in belt, 15/17-in turrets *Max speed:* 16 knots

Majestics were built on time.

From this point the French Navy went into relative decline. The *Jeune École* stressed the importance of numbers, and wanted to replace battleships with torpedo boats and submarines. But manoeuvres showed that however useful small torpedo boats and submarines might be in defence, they were not yet good enough to fight on the oceans. And even if French cruisers could harry British shipping around the world there was still the risk of the French coast being attacked by the British battle fleet, and so the battleship was still needed. But the latest French battleships were hardly a match for ships like the *Royal Sovereign*s and the *Majestic*s. They carried less than 700 tons of coal, as against the 2000 tons specified for the *Majestic*, and carried their guns in single turrets. Although French designers favoured high freeboard they also liked complex superstructures, which raised the centre of gravity. Great expanses of their sides were unarmoured, and this factor combined with the exaggerated tumblehome made them potentially unstable if the hull was holed.

The Battle of Tsushima
LESSON IN THE EAST

The German Navy was still at this stage a coastal defence force committed to do no more than protect the Baltic shores. Not until the late 1890s did Admiral Tirpitz get permission to increase the size of new battleships. But once that decision was made, and given the authority of long-term policy in the form of Navy Laws modelled on the Naval Defence Act, the German Navy rose swiftly in power and reputation.

Paradoxically the French Navy, which reached a peak of new efficiency at the end of the 1890s, was suddenly turned into a political football. An ardent political supporter of the *Jeune Ecole*, M. Pelletan, became Minister of Marine and proceeded to cripple the battle fleet by such dubious methods as reducing coal allowance to restrict manoeuvres. Pelletan's reign was comparatively brief, but it achieved more lasting harm than anything since the Battle of Trafalgar. When he was finally replaced France's declining industrial strength was not up to the effort needed to modernize her battle fleet. Nor was the political will present, for the *Entente* with Great Britain removed much of the exaggerated fear of a naval war in the Channel or the Mediterranean which had previously sustained the expansion of the navy.

Technical Advance
One of the problems facing naval architects at the turn of the century was the lack of practical experience. With no battle of any consequence later than Lissa and such a hectic pace of technical advance, particularly in the years from 1885 to 1900, there was little to guide the theorists apart from target practice against old ships. The Sino-Japanese war of 1896 did little to help, as it was an affair of fast, modern cruisers against slow, obsolescent coast-defence battleships. As at Lissa, the dash of the Japanese gave them an easy victory over the tactically inept Chinese at the Battle of the Yalu River, but the result was interpreted by everybody to prove their chosen views. To the British the 'hail of fire' from medium- and light-calibre guns had been the clincher, whereas the French claimed that cruisers could now fight any battleship!

The Japanese provided the next object lesson, when they fought the Russians at Tsushima in 1904, but again the disparity between the two sides baffled and misled the naval theorists. The naval side of the Russo-Japanese War in general, and Tsushima in particular, was a trial of strength between ships and tactics of British and French origin. Many of the modern Russian ships were built according to French ideas, for

A Japanese battleship, one of two lost to Russian mines in May 1904, is seen about to meet its end (from a contemporary French print)

The Russian battleship Petropavlovsk, *flagship of Admiral Makarov, explodes after being lured into a Japanese minefield (also depicted in a French print)*

Le Petit Journal Illustré

The 12,000-ton Petropavlovsk *was completed in 1894 and blew up outside Port Arthur ten years later after hitting a Japanese mine*

The Retvizan *was fitted with a 250-ft long steel belt to protect her against torpedoes, but was damaged by just such a weapon while at anchor*

Asahi *and her sister,* Shikishima, *breached the 15,000-ton barrier. Each carried five torpedo tubes, used to good effect against the Russian fleet*

Russian shipyards relied heavily on French investment, whereas the Japanese were ordering their ships from Britain, in most cases following the latest British innovations in weapons and equipment. Ironically the Japanese equipment was hardly exposed to severe testing, whereas the Russian ships were tested in every conceivable way. The Russian ships and the French ideas they represented failed lamentably, whereas British ideas were largely vindicated.

The most unusual feature about the Battle of Tsushima was the enormous range at which the Japanese opened fire, 7000 yards. The fact that they hit nothing, and

continued to hit nothing until they had closed the range to something more reasonable, was lost on the observers who reported on the battle. The British learned most; being the mentors of the Japanese they were allowed to examine the Russian ships salvaged at Port Arthur and those surrendered after Tsushima. Other countries had all sent observers, and opinion was unanimous that all future naval actions would be fought at long range.

This immediately created a new set of problems. Nobody had yet designed a battleship to fight at a range of more than about 4000 yards, which was little more than the extreme range of the guns at Trafalgar. This

was not, as has been claimed, because it never occurred to anyone to fire a gun at a greater range. For many years guns had been capable of much greater ranges, but the powders available produced irregular rates of burning, and at extreme range this resulted in a wide scatter of shots. Only after the introduction of large-grain, slow-burning powders in the 1890s was it possible to 'calibrate' a gun to land shots repeatedly on the same spot at ranges of more than 3000-4000 yards. And even when this became possible there was a delay before ships' gun-mountings could be given higher elevation. At 7000 yards or more the only thing visible was a plume of smoke from the target and the enormous 100-ft high splashes made by one's own shells. To complicate matters the slow rate of fire of a large gun like a 12-in (one shell every two-and-a-half minutes) meant that the target had time to move away (the 'rate of change') and might well be missed by the next salvo of shells. Even when a crude rangefinder was provided, this time-lag between salvoes was inescapable.

Even before Tsushima, gunnery experts were studying the problem, Cpt Percy

Potemkin
Having been taken over by her crew in 1905, *Potemkin* was renamed *Panteleimon*, served in the Black Sea during the First World War, resumed her original name and then became the *Boretz Za Svobodu* before being broken up in 1922—24

Displacement: 12,600 tons full load *Length:* 113 m *Armament:* 4×305-mm, 16×152-mm, 14×76-mm, 6×47-mm, 5×450-mm torpedo tubes *Armour:* 152/230-mm belt, 250-mm turrets, 63/75-mm decks *Max speed:* 16 knots

Fuji, along with sister-ship Yashima, *was built to counter the Chinese Navy's pair of German-constructed battleships. The 1892 Sino-Japanese war was over by the time they were completed, however, and Fuji's first action was against the Russians in 1904. She sank the Russian battleship* Borodino *at Tsushima*

Scott in the Royal Navy and Captain William Sims in the United States Navy. But the Japanese experience proved that battleships would have to fight at a greater range than before. Sims and his British and Japanese contemporaries knew that the one way to improve shooting at long range was to fire larger numbers of shells, dividing them into two salvoes to provide a smaller gap between firing. The Americans had for many years insisted on a heavy secondary battery of 8-in guns in their battleships, the Germans had 6.7-in guns and the Italians had also produced ships with 8-in batteries.

The British finally followed the trend in the *King Edward VII* class of 1901, the last battleships of the William White era. These handsome ships had four single 9.2-in guns at the corners of the superstructure, with 6-in guns in a battery a deck lower, and in theory both 9.2-in and 12-in shells could penetrate the heaviest armour afloat at 7000 yards. The Japanese copied the *King Edward VII* class in the *Kashima* and *Katori*, giving them 10-in guns instead of 9.2-in, but neither ship was ready in time for the war. The British quickly followed with the *Lord Nelson* and *Agamemnon*, armed with a secondary battery of ten 9.2-in guns in a mixture of twin and single turrets on the beam, and again the Japanese ordered something similar, with four 12-in and 12 10-in guns.

The race to produce a bigger secondary battery might have gone on unchecked had a practical objection not suddenly raised its head. At 7000 yards or more shell-splashes from 8-in, 9.2-in or 10-in shells looked very like 12-in shell-splashes. This meant that the gun layers could not distinguish the fall of shot of individual guns, and so could not correct their aim. The only way to minimize this difficulty was to arm ships with a uniform armament of a single calibre, devoting the weight saved on smaller guns to a larger number of 12-in guns. The logic of this was inescapable, and the Americans took the plunge first in 1903 when they designed the *Michigan* and *South Carolina* with four 12-in turrets, two forward and two aft. Even more significant was the fact that the intermediate guns were replaced entirely by 3-in guns, suitable only for

defence against torpedo boats. The Japanese came to the same conclusion during the war against Russia, and drew up plans for two ships armed with 12 12-in guns. The British might have been left standing by these developments, but they turned the tables by using their vastly superior shipbuilding resources. In secret they produced a design for a new, fast ship with five twin 12-in gun turrets to outmatch anything afloat.

12-in Gun Turret, 1899
The British battleships *Albion* and *Glory* introduced a new type of hydraulic turret mounting 12-in guns. They had all-round loading, speeding up the rate of fire. With only minor refinements this design of turret was retained until 1945

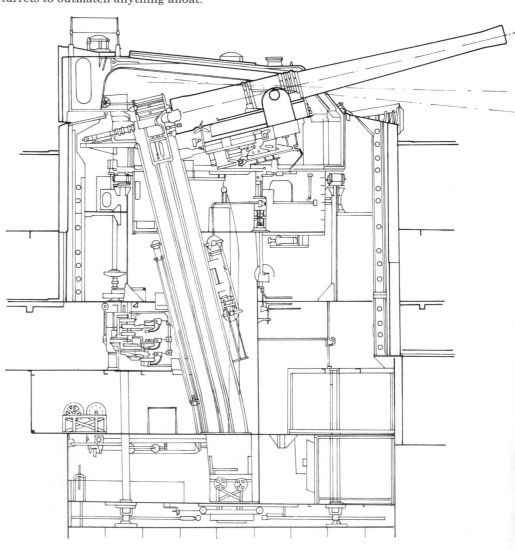

DREADNOUGHT

The new First Sea Lord, Sir John Fisher, immediately grasped the potential of the design, to be called HMS *Dreadnought*, but his motives for doing so were different from the intentions of her designers. Fisher had very little grasp of such matters as long-range gunnery, and his main concern was to modernize and enlarge the Royal Navy to meet what he saw as the threat from the rapidly expanding German Fleet. To achieve this overhaul of *matériel* Fisher knew that he had to make great economies in some directions, for the British taxpayer was in no mood to sanction vast expenditure on the Navy.

What attracted Fisher about the *Dreadnought*'s design was simply economy. Her four-shaft Parsons steam turbines, the first to be installed in a major warship, were cheaper to run and easier to maintain. They also dispensed with secondary and tertiary batteries, thereby saving the problem of maintaining the armament. The fact that the gunnery branch also valued the arrangement of heavy guns for long-range gunnery does not appear to have entered into

Fisher's head, and he valued her simply on the basis that 30 *Dreadnoughts* could be run at the same annual cost of 29 of the preceding *Lord Nelson* Class.

Fisher's demonic energy was harnessed to the building of this monster, for he wanted to astound the world and give Britain a lead over her rivals: the French, Russians, Germans and Americans. The major delay would be caused by the lack of gun turrets, which took at least 2½ years to assemble. Fisher immediately sanctioned the diversion of the four turrets already earmarked for the *Lord Nelson* and *Agamemnon*, and by such shortcuts Portsmouth Dockyard was able to beat its own record set up when the *Majestic* was built in 22 months. On 2 October, 1905 the keel was laid, and with much material already stockpiled it was only four months later, on 10 February, 1906, that she slid down the launching way. To the consternation of Britain's rivals HMS *Dreadnought*'s completion was announced on 3 October, 1906, 366 days after her keel-laying. In fact this was a typical piece of Fisher bombast; the ship

moved for the first time on that day, but was in no sense complete for another two months. Nevertheless, the building of the *Dreadnought* in only 14 months is a record which has never been beaten.

The *Dreadnought* gave her name to a whole generation of battleships, and today the term is still used loosely to describe any big battleship. She was a complete break with previous ships in every way, with her starkly simple superstructure, massive tripod mast between two funnels, and hull devoid of small guns. But even more remarkable was the vindication of the decision to engine her with Parsons turbines. Not only was she three knots faster than her contemporaries, but her turbines gave virtually no trouble. Gone were the days when the engine-room of a battleship was a 'cross between an inferno and a snipe-marsh', with massive pistons and connecting rods and a shroud of leaking steam. There was little or no mercantile experience to guide the Royal Navy's Engineer-in-Chief in this audacious experiment, for the first large turbine-driven passenger liner was not

National Maritime Museum

Although the advent of the Dreadnought *rendered the vast predominance of the Royal Navy's battleship strength obsolete at a stroke, British shipyards were in a commanding position to compete in the new naval race. The next three battleships were virtually repeats of* Dreadnought. *The Hercules class (below) were, however, the first to break away from the original disposition of turrets, with the midships armament staggered to give a big-gun broadside*

HMS Invincible, *prototype of the battle-cruiser idea. The combination of speed and heavy armament was bought at the expense of armour, and in action the battle-cruiser concept was to prove very vulnerable*

Imperial War Museum

completed until 1907, and any one of a number of minor faults could have condemned the *Dreadnought* to failure. Another point in her favour was that she achieved her massive increase in speed without any sacrifice of armour; her 11-in belt of armour was equal to that of any of her contemporaries.

The drawback to the *Dreadnought* was her cost, but Fisher solved this problem by reducing the enormous number of old ships of all sizes which had swollen the Navy List, partly because of the reassuring effect that numbers had on Parliament and the press when the time came to prepare returns of numerical strength. Fisher condemned hundreds of ships to be scrapped, on the grounds that they were 'too weak to fight and too slow to run away', but he also tried to get rid of cruisers, because he convinced himself that the future lay with the destroyer, the submarine and the fast battleship. Undoubtedly there were too many obsolescent small warships around the world, and Fisher's reorganization of the Reserve Fleet produced a smaller, cheaper and much more effective battle fleet, but it was not long before the Navy found itself desperately short of minor warships, and had to reprieve some of Fisher's victims. But Fisher reinforced the public's tendency

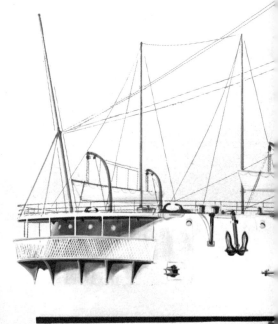

to see naval strength as a matter of numbers only, a fault which was dutifully copied by the politicians and the press. Henceforth all naval issues tended to boil down to numbers of 'dreadnoughts', with the older ships dismissed as useless.

Fisher disliked cruisers, as we have seen, and just after the *Dreadnought* was laid down he ordered a '*Dreadnought* armoured cruiser' to render the existing large cruiser obsolete. This was a ship of approximately the same tonnage as the *Dreadnought* but designed to steam at $25\frac{1}{2}$ knots, with thinner armour and only four twin 12-in turrets to allow the horsepower to be doubled. Known later as the 'battleship cruiser' and then the battle-cruiser, the new *Invincible* proved even more successful than the *Dreadnought*. Her purpose was to hunt down armoured cruisers on the trade routes and to replace them as scouting units for the main battle fleet. The idea was that they could shoulder aside the cruisers which tried to bar their way, and as they were armed with 12-in guns they could only be safely chased away by battleships. Like other creations of the fertile Fisher brain the idea had not been worked out to its logical conclusion. The battle-cruiser idea was quite reasonable so long as the enemy fleet did not possess its own battle-cruisers.

HMS Dreadnought, *the ship which gave her name to a whole new kind of warship*

Imperial War Museum

At the high tide of the Royal Navy's world-wide command of the seas, Admiral Sir John Fisher portrayed in the sea-cabin on board HMS Renown, in 1899. Already the Germans were stirring, beginning to challenge British supremacy at sea

P A Vicary

Brazil's second battleship, São Paulo, *on trials in 1910. Unlike* Dreadnought, *she had superimposed end turrets*

São Paulo

This ship and her sister, closely resembling the *Dreadnought* but more heavily armed, ensured Brazilian naval supremacy over neighbouring Chile and Argentina

Displacement: 21,200 tons full load *Length:* 530 ft *Armament:* 12 × 12-in, 22 × 4·7-in, 8 × 3-pdr *Armour:* 4/9-in belt, 8/12-in turrets, 2¼-in deck *Max speed:* 21 knots

Minas Geraes class

Name	Completed	Fate
Minas Geraes	Jan 1910	Scrapped 1954
São Paulo	Jul 1910	Sank in North Atlantic 1951

Beken

Petty Officer's cap badge, Imperial German Navy

C Campbell

BIRTH OF THE HIGH SEAS FLEET

If Fisher hoped to frighten the Germans out of naval rivalry he was badly mistaken. The advent of the *Dreadnought* and particularly the rapidity of her building did take the German Navy by surprise, and all battleship construction was suspended to give the *Marineamt* a chance to work out its reply. The Kiel Canal would have to be deepened and locks widened if similar ships were to be built, and this vast programme was immediately sanctioned; the German Navy relied on the canal to move squadrons from the Baltic to the North Sea, and regarded it in much the same way as the American Navy does the Panama Canal. The *Nassau* class was not started until the summer of 1907, by which time six improved *Dreadnoughts* had been started in England. The *Nassaus* were inferior to the *Dreadnought* in many ways; they did not have turbines for the simple reason that the only firm capable of making turbines was building a set for the first German battle-cruiser, and although they had a cumbersome arrangement of six twin 11-in guns they could only fire four of them on the beam, giving them less gunpower than the British ship. However, in one respect the *Nassaus*

Imperial War Museum

Admiral von Tirpitz, force behind the German Navy

were better: their armour was better distributed and their underwater protection against torpedoes was superior.

The German prototype battle-cruiser *Von der Tann* was a worthy opponent of the *Invincible*, with eight 11-in guns, slightly less speed but heavier armour. As soon as she appeared the rationale of the battle-cruiser idea disappeared, but Fisher was not easily persuaded that his toys had been superseded, and three more were ordered, two to be paid for by Australia and New Zealand. Now the dreadnought race was on between Germany and Great Britain, and each year more ships were laid down. Whenever the diplomats of both countries tried to negotiate a reduction of the tempo they were answered by arguments about national survival. Germany feared British 'encirclement', but above all the Navy Laws were an obstacle to any political understanding. Tirpitz had asked for long-term legislation to prevent any future government from cancelling or trimming his programmes, but this had a disastrous political side-effect; any suggestion from the Wilhelmstrasse about reductions of naval armaments was rejected on the

SMS Von der Tann, *the German reply to the British* Invincible *class battle-cruisers. Fisher's bluff had been called and the German ships had lighter armament, devoting the weight saved to a heavier scheme of protection. At Jutland the British battle-cruisers proved fatally vulnerable*

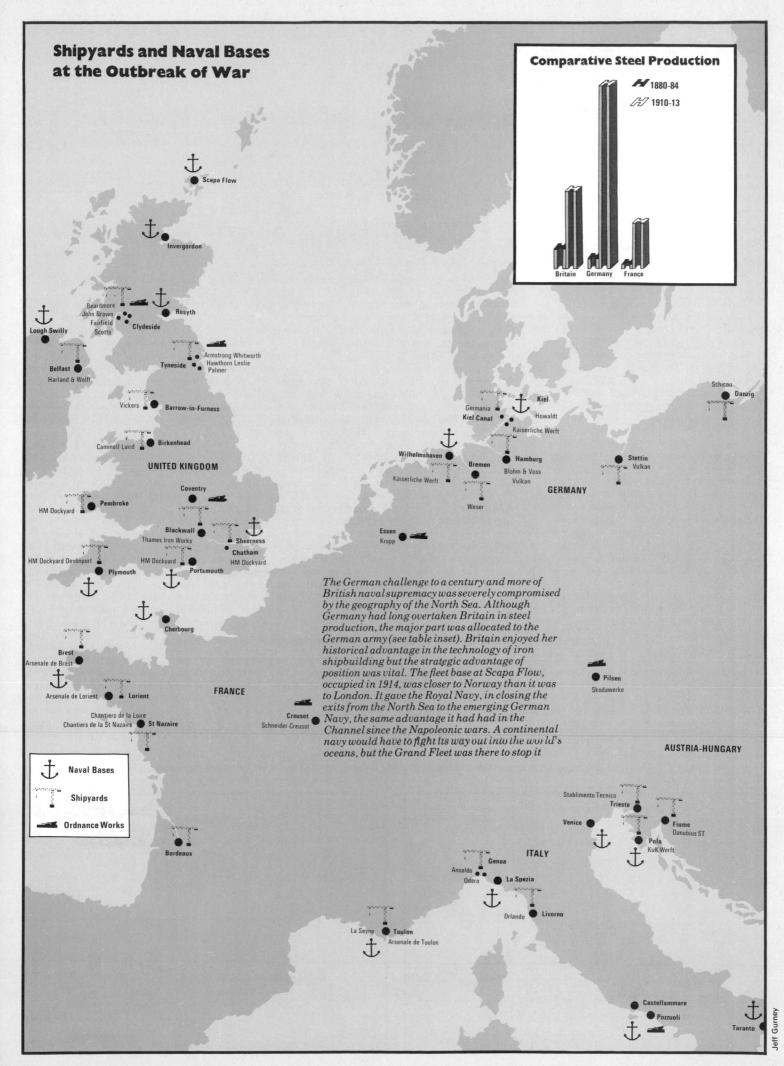

Shipyards and Naval Bases at the Outbreak of War

Comparative Steel Production

1880-84
1910-13

Britain Germany France

Scapa Flow

Invergordon

Rosyth

Beardmore
John Brown
Fairfield
Scotts
Clydeside

Lough Swilly

Belfast
Harland & Wolff

Tyneside
Armstrong Whitworth
Hawthorn Leslie
Palmer

Vickers
Barrow-in-Furness

Cammell Laird Birkenhead

UNITED KINGDOM

Coventry

Pembroke
HM Dockyard

Blackwall
Thames Iron Works

Sheerness

Chatham
HM Dockyard

HM Dockyard Devonport

HM Dockyard
Portsmouth

Plymouth

Cherbourg

Brest
Arsenale de Brest

Arsenale de Lorient Lorient

Chantiers de la Loire
Chantiers de la St Nazaire St Nazaire

FRANCE

Bordeaux

La Seyne Toulon
Arsenale de Toulon

Creusot
Schneider-Creusot

Essen
Krupp

Kiel
Germania
Howaldt
Kiel Canal
Kaiserliche Werft

Wilhelmshaven
Kaiserliche Werft

Bremen
Hamburg
Blohm & Voss
Vulkan

Weser

GERMANY

Schichau
Danzig

Stettin
Vulkan

Pilsen
Skodawerke

AUSTRIA-HUNGARY

Stablimento Tecnico
Trieste
Venice
Fiume
Danubius ST
Pola
KuK Werft

ITALY

Ansaldo
Genoa
Odero
La Spezia

Orlando Livorno

Castellammare
Pozzuoli

Taranto

The German challenge to a century and more of
British naval supremacy was severely compromised
by the geography of the North Sea. Although
Germany had long overtaken Britain in steel
production, the major part was allocated to the
German army (see table inset). Britain enjoyed her
historical advantage in the technology of iron
shipbuilding but the strategic advantage of
position was vital. The fleet base at Scapa Flow,
occupied in 1914, was closer to Norway than it was
to London. It gave the Royal Navy, in closing the
exits from the North Sea to the emerging German
Navy, the same advantage it had had in the
Channel since the Napoleonic wars. A continental
navy would have to fight its way out into the world's
oceans, but the Grand Fleet was there to stop it

Legend
⚓ Naval Bases

⊥ Shipyards

Ordnance Works

Jeff Gurney

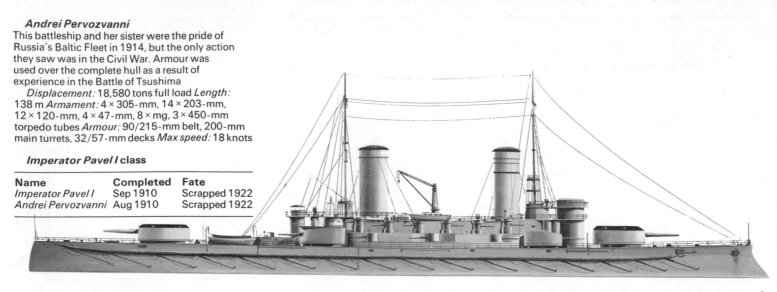

Andrei Pervozvanni
This battleship and her sister were the pride of Russia's Baltic Fleet in 1914, but the only action they saw was in the Civil War. Armour was used over the complete hull as a result of experience in the Battle of Tsushima
Displacement: 18,580 tons full load *Length:* 138 m *Armament:* 4 × 305-mm, 14 × 203-mm, 12 × 120-mm, 4 × 47-mm, 8 × mg, 3 × 450-mm torpedo tubes *Armour:* 90/215-mm belt, 200-mm main turrets, 32/57-mm decks *Max speed:* 18 knots

Imperator Pavel I class

Name	Completed	Fate
Imperator Pavel I	Sep 1910	Scrapped 1922
Andrei Pervozvanni	Aug 1910	Scrapped 1922

grounds that the size and building programme of the navy was fixed by law, and could not therefore be set aside. From 1906 the British had a Liberal Government dedicated to retrenchment on defence to release money for social reform, and the climate was ripe for some sort of Anglo-German understanding, but again and again the diplomats and politicians failed to reach a compromise. The world was going through an extraordinary upsurge of violent nationalism, and the German and British newspapers echoed jingoistic demands for stronger armaments. Dreadnought battleships were the visible embodiment of sea power, and as they also provided employment in shipyards there was an understandable reluctance to make the first cut.

The turning point came in 1908, when Tirpitz used a loophole in the Navy Law to increase the strength of the German Fleet. The original law had allowed for the building of eight *Grosse Kreuzer*, the original armoured cruisers now made redundant by the battle-cruiser, and Tirpitz simply referred to his future battle-cruisers as 'large cruisers' and added them to the programme. The battle-cruiser, although she was still known as a dreadnought armoured cruiser, was widely regarded as the equivalent of a battleship, and Tirpitz had in effect added eight battleships to the future strength of his fleet. The British saw this as chicanery, and even the Liberal Government had to bow to pressure for an expansion of the

British building programme. Thereafter until August 1914 there was no pretence that each navy was building for its own requirements, and the British adopted a policy of 'two keels to one', doubling whatever figure the Germans announced.

Across the Atlantic the Americans were also expanding their fleet, but without the same frantic haste as the British and Germans. The French and Russians dropped out of the race, largely because of the enormous expense involved, and did not start to build dreadnoughts until 1911. Economic reality caught up with the Japanese when the post-war boom collapsed, and their dreadnought-building was slowed down. The Americans had considerable trouble with turbines, and took the remarkable step of reverting to reciprocating machinery for a while in order to force the machinery suppliers to accept General Board specifications. In 1911 the battleships *Nevada* and *Oklahoma* were designed to radically new principles, making them the most revolutionary since the *Dreadnought*.

Zone of Immunity

Unfettered by the need to match a rival programme, the Americans sat down to work out theoretically the best way to protect battleships against long-range gunfire. They discarded the medium armour used in contemporaries against lighter shells, and concentrated on keeping out large shells at 10,000 yards or more. This

led them to the discovery of the 'zone of immunity', ranges between which heavy shell cannot penetrate either side armour or deck armour. As the range increases the shells tend to plunge more and so the number of hits on deck armour tends to rise. What had been learned at Tsushima was that light armour tended to burst shells, with the result that splinters did nearly as much damage; on the other hand, unarmoured structures were unlikely to trigger off the relatively insensitive fuze of an armour-piercing shell, and so shells would pass through without bursting. From this the US Navy formulated the 'all or nothing' theory of armouring, that armour should be put on the deck or on the side, at maximum thickness or not at all.

The ship which resulted had some of the classic simplicity of the *Dreadnought* or even the old *Devastation*, with her single massive funnel, minimal superstructure and lofty 'cage' masts, all in a balanced profile. With twin and triple 14-in turrets forward and aft and 13½-in armour, the *Nevada* class were the most powerful warships in the world when designed, and had they appeared sooner they might have had the reputation that they deserve. Part of their success was due to the adoption of oil fuel, which saved a great deal of weight, and part was due to the reduction of weight by concentrating ten guns in only four turrets.

As British and German dreadnoughts appeared each year it became clear that

The Austro-Hungarian battleship Radetzky *and her two sisters were completed in 1910–11. They had a heavy secondary battery, typical of the later intermediate dreadnoughts*

Had the USS Michigan *(below) and her sister the* South Carolina *been completed earlier they would have beaten* Dreadnought *into service as the first all big-gun ships*

Kriegsarchiv Vienna

Imperial War Museum

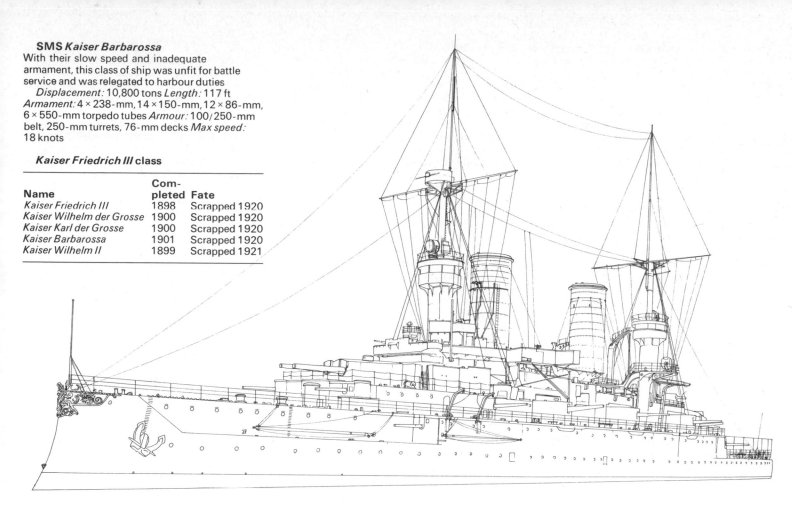

SMS Kaiser Barbarossa
With their slow speed and inadequate
armament, this class of ship was unfit for battle
service and was relegated to harbour duties
   Displacement: 10,800 tons *Length:* 117 ft
Armament: 4 × 238-mm, 14 × 150-mm, 12 × 86-mm,
6 × 550-mm torpedo tubes *Armour:* 100/250-mm
belt, 250-mm turrets, 76-mm decks *Max speed:*
18 knots

Kaiser Friedrich III class

Name	Com-pleted	Fate
Kaiser Friedrich III	1898	Scrapped 1920
Kaiser Wilhelm der Grosse	1900	Scrapped 1920
Kaiser Karl der Grosse	1900	Scrapped 1920
Kaiser Barbarossa	1901	Scrapped 1920
Kaiser Wilhelm II	1899	Scrapped 1921

British and German designers were pursuing different objectives. The Germans
emphasized protection, preferring to retain
the 11-in gun for as long as possible to
save weight for armour, whereas British
designers emphasized gunpower at the
expense of armour. Thus the 12-in gun gave
way in 1910 to the 13.5-in gun in HMS *Orion*,
whereas the Germans only reluctantly
adopted a 12-in gun in the *Helgoland* class
in 1909. This divergence was much criticised
by British observers, and has been blamed
on Fisher's unhappy influence over design,
but looked at dispassionately it can be seen
as the logical outcome of British strategic
aims. The British wanted a quick decisive
victory over the German Fleet if war should
come, a clear-cut victory along the lines of
Tsushima or even Trafalgar, whereas the
Germans, whatever their propagandists
might boast, intended to survive by avoiding
just that sort of battle. Their strategy was
to use torpedo craft, submarines and mines
to whittle down the British margin of
superiority, and use the surface fleet only
to cut off and destroy isolated portions of
the British fleet. Therefore the British had
to emphasize speed and gunpower, to bring
the enemy to battle and to sink him, while
the Germans had to concentrate on defensive characteristics if they were to survive
the heavier shells likely to be fired at their

SMS Ostfriesland
The *Helgoland* class battleships adopted the 12-in
gun, at a time when their British adversaries were
introducing the 13·5-in. They were better protected
and less cramped than their predecessors but,
despite having reciprocating machinery, took
nearly three years to build
   Displacement: 24,300 tons full load *Length:*
166 m *Armament:* 12 × 305-mm, 14 × 150-mm,
14 × 86-mm, 6 × 500-mm torpedo tubes *Armour:*
100/300-mm belt, 280-mm turrets, 75-mm decks
Max speed: 20 knots

Helgoland class

Name	Completed	Fate
Ostfriesland	Aug 1911	Sunk in bombing demonstration 1921
Thüringen	Jul 1911	Scrapped 1923
Helgoland	Aug 1911	Scrapped 1924
Oldenburg	May 1912	Scrapped

ships. For this reason a straight comparison between British and German designs is not easy, and a mere comparison of dimensions and armour thicknesses is misleading. Other factors are also important; for example, German battleships tended to cost more and used less standard equipment.

When Fisher left the Admiralty in 1911 he took many of his obscurantist opinions about ship design with him, and British battleships improved noticeably in consequence. In 1912 work started on a class which more than wiped out the disparity between British and German designs. This was the famous *Queen Elizabeth* class, which were the first British battleships to adopt all-oil fuel, for the same reason as the American *Nevadas*. But there was more to the *Queen Elizabeths*. Alarmed by news about the Americans and the Japanese arming new ships with 14-in guns, the Admiralty decided to give itself a comfortable margin for some years by making a big jump from the fairly new 13.5-in gun to a 15-in 42-calibre weapon. What sounds like a small increase in shell diameter resulted in a very large increase in shell weight: whereas the 12-in shell weighed 850 lb, the 13.5-in weighed 1400 lb and the 15-in jumped to 1920 lb. Another virtue of the new gun was its low muzzle velocity. The British were the first to appreciate that too much muzzle velocity was actually detrimental to long-range gunnery; although the shell travelled further it 'wobbled' more in flight. The 13.5-in shell had been increased from 1250 lb to 1400 lb and was greatly improved as a result, and this characteristic was built into the 15-in as well. Another reason for the phenomenal accuracy of the 15-in was

the phenomenal accuracy of the 15-in was that improved manufacture of steel produced bigger forgings, which gave greater rigidity to the barrel. To make everybody even happier lower muzzle velocities produced less wear on the barrel-liner.

Fast Division

The greatly increased power of the 15-in gun made another innovation possible. Tacticians were hankering after a breakaway from rigid line-of-battle tactics, and the idea of a 'Fast Division' of battleships was mooted. This was in complete contrast to the battle-cruiser concept, and called for ships with a four-knot advantage over existing ships, but with full armour protection. The fundamental weakness of the battle-cruiser, as the more perceptive observers could see, was that it really dared not spend too long in action against a battleship. There were those who might be called the 'whizz-kids' of naval tactics, like Fisher and some of the less cautious admirals, who convinced themselves that speed was protection in itself and that battle-cruisers could be used as fast battleships. But the fact that the Fast Division was proposed as early as 1911 shows that someone in the Admiralty had spotted the flaws in their

France
The last ship in the *Courbet* class, which were the first French Dreadnoughts. The long building time, three years, resulted in the ships being outclassed by the time they entered service
Displacement: 25,850 tons full load *Length:* 165 m *Armament:* 12 × 305-mm, 22 × 138-mm, 4 × 47-mm, 4 × 450-mm torpedo tubes *Armour:* 270-mm, 230-mm turrets, 70-mm main deck *Max speed:* 21 knots

Courbet class

Name	Completed	Fate
Jean Bart	Jun 1913	Scrapped 1945
Courbet	Sep 1913	Used as breakwater, Normandy, June 1944
Paris	Aug 1914	Scrapped 1956
France	Jul 1914	Sank in Quiberon Bay, 1922

argument. The introduction of the 15-in gun made a true fast battleship feasible for the first time, for by dropping the fifth turret room could be found for double the horsepower. As in the *Nevada* design the use of oil fuel meant that the weight formerly taken up by coal could be devoted to armour, and space could be saved on stokers' messdecks, etc. Also the greater thermal efficiency of oil meant that the higher horsepower could be achieved economically.

To change the whole of the British Battle Fleet from coal to oil was, in Churchill's words, 'to take arms against a sea of troubles'. Coal of the highest quality was available in the British Isles, whereas oil had to be imported from far-off countries. But in the tactical field there could be no doubt of the advantages: ships could refuel in a quarter of the time and so be ready for action faster, and full speed could be maintained for a longer time. Tactical considerations triumphed and the Admiralty immediately bought a large shareholding in Iranian oilfields to ensure a plentiful supply of crude oil. There were many critics of the change to oil, but the main objection, that coal provided a defence against torpedoes, was invalid, since the equivalent weight of coal could be easily spared for armour which would do more good.

The 15-in was ordered in great secrecy as the '14-in Experimental' in 1912, and at first there were grave doubts about the wisdom of ordering a whole class of ships before their armament had been proved. Should the new ships not be armed with 13.5-in guns in case the 15-in was a failure? The Admiralty Board and the Director of Naval Ordnance were assured by the manufacturers, Armstrong, Whitworth of Elswick, Newcastle-on-Tyne, that they had such faith in the new gun and its mounting that they would guarantee that it would meet its specification. To insure against accidents and to reassure the Admiralty one gun was to be advanced and put through a series of tests, but in due course Armstrongs' confidence was completely justified. The *Queen Elizabeth* was ready just after the outbreak of war in August 1914, and a total of nine other 15-in-gunned ships were under construction or completing at the same time.

When war broke out between Germany and her allies and Great Britain, Russia and France the line-up showed how rapidly the major nations had been building battleships.

SMS Goeben

Moltke and her sister, *Goeben,* were enlarged versions of the *Von der Tann.* The layout of the armament was not ideal, but both vessels served with distinction throughout the First World War
Displacement: 25,000 tons full load *Length:* 186 m *Armament:* 10 × 280-mm, 12 × 150-mm, 12 × 86-mm, 4 × 500-mm torpedo tubes *Armour:* 100/280-mm belt, 250-mm turrets, 65-mm decks
Max speed: 25½ knots

Moltke class

Name	Completed	Fate
Moltke	Sep 1911	Scrapped 1927-29
Goeben	Jul 1912	Scrapped 1972 (sold to Turkey 1914)

SMS *Prinzregent Luitpold*

The *Kaiser*-class vessels were the first German battleships with turbine propulsion, and this made mounting of the heavy armament simpler. All five of the main turrets could fire to either side
Displacement: 26,500 tons *Length:* 172.4 m *Armament:* 10×305-mm, 14×150-mm, 8×88-mm, 2-4×88-mm AA, 5×500-mm torpedo tubes *Armour:* up to 350-mm side, 300-mm main turrets, 60/100-mm deck
Max speed: 21 knots

Kaiser class

Name	Completed	Fate
Kaiser	Aug 1912	Scrapped 1929–30
Friedrich der Grosse	Oct 1912	Scrapped 1937
Kaiserin	May 1913	Scrapped 1936
Prinzregent Luitpold	Aug 1913	Scrapped 1931–33
König Albert	Jul 1913	Scrapped 1935–36

The battleship had changed beyond recognition since the turn of the century. Average displacement had jumped from 15,000 tons to 28,000 tons, and speed from 18 knots to 28. As we have seen, gunpower was not overwhelming, with armaments of eight to twelve guns, and gunnery practices at 10,000 yards were normal. Both British and Germans regarded this as the range at which future battles would be fought; attempts at firing at greater ranges produced such poor results that the idea of ultra-long-range gunnery was dismissed as a mere waste of ammunition. The British, under the direction of Percy Scott, introduced a new system known as director-firing for controlling fire at long range. This meant in essence that a single master-sight mounted as high up in the ship as possible (usually on a masthead platform) calculated the range and bearing, and from there the guns were fired electrically. In 1912 HMS *Thunderer* was fitted with the first director, and beat the previous top gunnery ship of the Home Fleet. The Germans preferred the 'follow-the-pointer' system, in which individual gunlayers still fired their guns according to range and bearing information shown on a pointer in the turret, relayed from a master-sight abaft the forebridge.

Although the German fire-control system was generally inferior to the British it was greatly superior in one important respect. In place of the 9-ft incidence-type range-finder used in British dreadnoughts, German ships were given 20-ft or 27-ft Zeiss stereoscopic range-finders. The British range-finders were capable of producing reliable ranges at 10,000 yards or under, but they took time to find longer ranges, whereas the longer-base Zeiss instruments picked up all ranges quickly. The British became aware of the limitations of their range-finders but only the new *Queen Elizabeth* class had a better 15-ft model suitable for longer ranges. On the other hand the British range-finders performed well under stress, whereas the Zeiss range-finders were hard to operate when the range-taker was put off by such distractions as damage to his own ship, gun-blast, etc, and so British shooting tended to get better in battle, while German shooting started well but fell in action.

The German dreadnought SMS Friedrich der Grosse *entering Copenhagen in 1913. Completed in 1912, she was commissioned immediately as the flagship of the High Seas Fleet which she remained until March 1917. The guard of honour is presenting arms on the quarterdeck, sailors raise their caps in salute, and the fore and after bridges are lined with saluting officers*

Battleships and Battlecruisers in Service: 1914

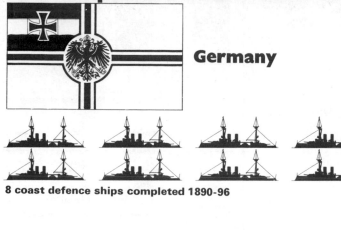

Germany

Great Britain

8 coast defence ships completed 1890-96

23 pre-dreadnoughts completed 1893-1908*

30 pre-dreadnoughts completed 1895-1904*
10 'intermediate dreadnoughts' completed 1902-08

4 dreadnoughts armed with 11-in guns, completed 1909-10
11 dreadnoughts armed with 12-in guns, completed 1911-14†

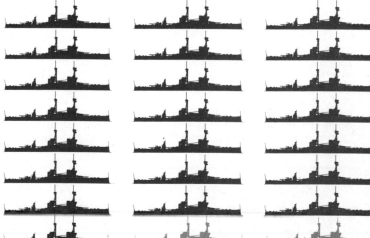

10 dreadnoughts armed with 12-in guns, completed 1906-11
12 dreadnoughts armed with 13·5-in guns, completed 1912-14

4 battlecruisers armed with 11-in guns, completed 1910-13

*Two ships sold to Turkey 1911
†Two more ships nearing completion, and the
 battlecruiser SMS *Derfflinger* (12-in guns)

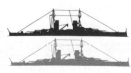

Completed

Under Construction

6 battlecruisers armed with 12-in guns, completed 1908-12
3 battlecruisers armed with 13·5-in guns, completed 1912-13†

*HMS *Montagu* lost 1906, two bought from Chile 1904
†A fourth ship, HMS *Tiger* was nearly complete. Additional ships were HMS
 Queen Elizabeth (15-in guns) nearly complete and two Turkish dreadnoughts
 which were seized after the declaration of war: HMS *Erin* (13·5-in guns) and
 HMS *Agincourt* (12-in guns)

Jeff Gurney

53

THE BATTLESHIPS' GREAT WAR

By a stroke of luck the entire Royal Navy in home waters had been mobilized in July 1914 for a giant fleet manoeuvre to test the mobilization plans. Thus when the news from Sarajevo set Europe on the road to war the Admiralty was able to delay the demobilization and ensure that the Fleet was at its war station before the ultimatum to Germany expired at midnight on 4 August. The dominant fear had been of a surprise attack by German torpedo craft, but in fact the German High Seas Fleet had not planned such an operation and indeed was not fully mobilized for some weeks. The British fleet, now known as the Grand Fleet in honour of the name given to the fleet gathered to fight the Spanish Armada in 1588, steamed in majestic lines out of Spithead and simply vanished from sight. Its chosen base was top secret: the desolate anchorage of Scapa Flow in the Orkney Islands. From here the Fleet was well placed to block the exit routes from the North Sea to the Atlantic, for Scapa Flow is nearer to Norway than to London. The old battleships were stationed in the Channel in case the High Seas Fleet should try to attack the shipping carrying troops to France.

The Germans, too, mustered their battleships at Kiel and Wilhelmshaven. Like the British, they expected action within hours, but apart from skirmishes between light forces the North Sea remained quiet. It was the battle-cruisers which saw action, first at the Battle of the Heligoland Bight on 28 August, when the British sent three battle-cruisers into the Bight to rescue their light forces from defeat. The risks were higher, but the gamble paid off and three German cruisers were sunk by the guns of HMS *Lion* and her sisters. What the Germans had banked on was a close blockade

The Iron Duke *arrives at Scapa Flow on the outbreak of war. This desolate anchorage in the Orkneys had been designated as fleet base some years before but had been kept secret*

by the Grand Fleet, with dreadnoughts lying off German ports to enforce the blockade, just as the British Fleet had done against the French a hundred years before. But the British had dropped all ideas of a close blockade by 1913 and were content to guard the exits to the North Sea and leave the business of day-to-day contesting of the North Sea and Channel waters to light cruisers and destroyers.

In the Mediterranean the French Fleet was following a similar policy of penning the Austro-Hungarian battle fleet in the Adriatic, but there had been one bad miscalculation. The British allowed the only German capital ship on an overseas station, the battle-cruiser *Goeben*, to escape from them. She offered herself for internment in Turkey, which promptly 'purchased' the ship and her entire crew, and joined the Central Alliance. The result was that the British and French could no longer hope to use the Dardanelles to get supplies to their Russian allies in the Black Sea without first forcing the Straits. It was a triumph of German diplomacy which was to cause untold suffering before long.

Battle-cruisers showed their qualities again in December. When the news came through in November 1914 that a squadron of German cruisers had annihilated a British cruiser squadron off Coronel on the coast of Chile, Lord Fisher sent two battle-cruisers to the South Atlantic to avenge them. The *Invincible* and *Inflexible* arrived at the Falkland Islands just 24 hours before the German cruisers under Admiral Spee arrived to capture the coaling station. This was the battle the *Invincibles* had been designed to fight, and they did it magnificently, running down their quarry in a long stern-chase and sinking them with relative impunity at a range of about 12,500 yards. Only one small German cruiser escaped the slaughter, to be hunted down later, and the battle-cruisers' victory was no less welcome because it wiped out the bitter memory of the disaster at Coronel and cleared the oceans of the last German commerce raiders.

The German battle-cruisers under Admiral Hipper were used in a series of raids on the east coast of England, firing shells at what were believed to be fortified towns, such as Scarborough. The purpose was to distract the Grand Fleet from its watch, and to lure a small part of it into battle on favourable terms. There were several near-misses, and on one occasion the High Seas Fleet nearly ran into a single squadron of four battleships, but the only practical result of the raids was that public alarm forced the Admiralty to move the battle-cruiser force south from Scapa Flow

to Rosyth, on the Firth of Forth. From here they were better placed to intercept raids, although poorly placed to stop a break-out into the Atlantic. The new disposition paid off on 24 January, 1915 when Admiral Beatty, with five battle-cruisers under his command, met the German First Scouting Group under Admiral Hipper, comprising three battle-cruisers and a large cruiser.

The Battle of the Dogger Bank was disappointing for the British, for, although they had the advantage of numbers, speed and gunpower over the Germans, and although they managed to sink the slow armoured cruiser *Blücher*, a series of signalling errors allowed Hipper to escape virtually unscathed. The battle showed

NPC

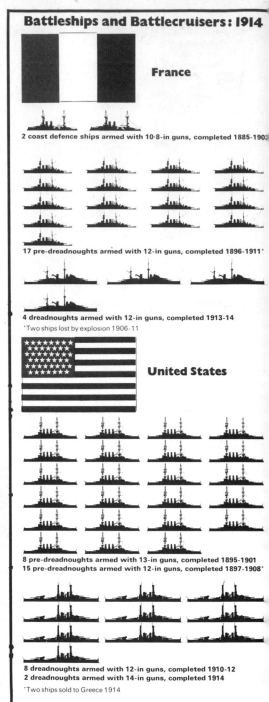

Battleships and Battlecruisers: 1914

France

2 coast defence ships armed with 10·8-in guns, completed 1885-1902

17 pre-dreadnoughts armed with 12-in guns, completed 1896-1911*

4 dreadnoughts armed with 12-in guns, completed 1913-14

*Two ships lost by explosion 1906-11

United States

8 pre-dreadnoughts armed with 13-in guns, completed 1895-1901
15 pre-dreadnoughts armed with 12-in guns, completed 1897-1908*

8 dreadnoughts armed with 12-in guns, completed 1910-12
2 dreadnoughts armed with 14-in guns, completed 1914

*Two ships sold to Greece 1914

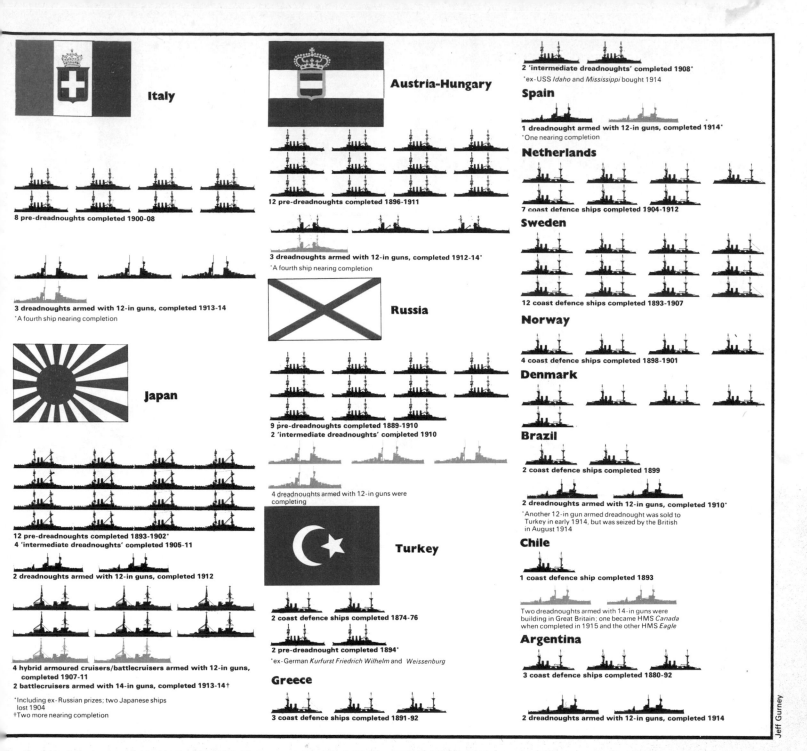

Italy

8 pre-dreadnoughts completed 1900-08

3 dreadnoughts armed with 12-in guns, completed 1913-14
*A fourth ship nearing completion

Japan

12 pre-dreadnoughts completed 1893-1902*
4 'intermediate dreadnoughts' completed 1905-11

2 dreadnoughts armed with 12-in guns, completed 1912

4 hybrid armoured cruisers/battlecruisers armed with 12-in guns, completed 1907-11
2 battlecruisers armed with 14-in guns, completed 1913-14†

*Including ex-Russian prizes; two Japanese ships lost 1904
†Two more nearing completion

Austria-Hungary

12 pre-dreadnoughts completed 1896-1911

3 dreadnoughts armed with 12-in guns, completed 1912-14*
*A fourth ship nearing completion

Russia

9 pre-dreadnoughts completed 1889-1910
2 'intermediate dreadnoughts' completed 1910

4 dreadnoughts armed with 12-in guns were completing

Turkey

2 coast defence ships completed 1874-76

2 pre-dreadnought completed 1894*
*ex-German Kurfurst Friedrich Wilhelm and Weissenburg

Greece

3 coast defence ships completed 1891-92

2 'intermediate dreadnoughts' completed 1908*
*ex-USS Idaho and Mississippi bought 1914

Spain

1 dreadnought armed with 12-in guns, completed 1914*
*One nearing completion

Netherlands

7 coast defence ships completed 1904-1912

Sweden

12 coast defence ships completed 1893-1907

Norway

4 coast defence ships completed 1898-1901

Denmark

Brazil

2 coast defence ships completed 1899

2 dreadnoughts armed with 12-in guns, completed 1910*
*Another 12-in gun armed dreadnought was sold to Turkey in early 1914, but was seized by the British in August 1914

Chile

1 coast defence ship completed 1893

Two dreadnoughts armed with 14-in guns were building in Great Britain; one became HMS *Canada* when completed in 1915 and the other HMS *Eagle*

Argentina

3 coast defence ships completed 1880-92

2 dreadnoughts armed with 12-in guns, completed 1914

Jeff Gurney

German fire-control at its best, with the British flagship HMS *Lion* hit by two shells from the *Derfflinger* and crippled by flooding; by comparison the British shooting was patchy, the *Tiger* not scoring a single hit. But British shells caused a disastrous fire in the after turrets of the *Seydlitz*, and burning killed nearly 200 men. Then a series of imprecise signals from Beatty was misinterpreted, and the remaining British battle-cruisers turned away from the fleeing Germans and concentrated on the slowest ship, the *Blücher*. By the time the mistake was sorted out (Beatty had been forced to shift his flag to a destroyer in a frantic attempt to catch up with his squadron) Hipper's ships were too far away to be caught. The *Blücher* fought doggedly but could not hope to survive the rain of hits, and capsized.

For the Germans the Dogger Bank had some disquieting lessons. The fire which burnt out the after turrets of the *Seydlitz* showed that too many cordite charges had been stored in the turrets for safety, but it did prove that German cordite was extremely stable. The British, whose cordite was less stable due to a relatively minor fault in the manufacturing process, knew nothing of the near-escape of the *Seydlitz*, and remained happily unaware of the fact that their own cordite might flash off instead of merely burning, as it was meant to do.

The Grand Fleet led by HMS Iron Duke *on manoeuvres just before the outbreak of war*

Imperial War Museum

JUTLAND

Kaiser *class battleship fires her full broadside armament of eight 12-in guns*

The appointment of *Vizeadmiral* Scheer to the command of the High Seas Fleet in February 1916 brought a new offensive spirit to German fleet operations. For the next sortie he planned to use Hipper's battle-cruisers boldly to lure part of the Grand Fleet into a trap. He first sent out U-Boats to mine the routes likely to be followed by the British battle squadrons coming out of Scapa Flow and Rosyth, and then on 30 May took the entire High Seas Fleet to sea from the Jade River. Only one flaw marred the plan. Since 1914 the Admiralty had been reading a large number of German naval messages, and it was correctly deduced in London that the High Seas Fleet was putting to sea. The British followed Scheer's plan in essence, sending the battle-cruisers out from Rosyth separately to scout off the Skagerrak, where they would eventually be joined by the Grand Fleet coming south from Scapa Flow. Purely by chance the C-in-C Grand Fleet, Admiral Sir John Jellicoe, had chosen the

area in which Hipper's battle-cruisers would be operating, and the long-awaited main fleet action was imminent. Beatty's battle-cruisers by chance included four of the fast *Queen Elizabeth* class battleships, as three 12-in gunned battle-cruisers had been detached to Scapa Flow to practise their gunnery.

Even though fate had put the two rival battle-cruiser groups in the same area they

still met by chance on 31 May, when both sides' light forces turned to investigate a Danish steamer. The big ships sighted one another at a range of 14 miles (over 24,000 yards) and eagerly closed the range, each admiral confident that he was leading his opponent into a trap. The Germans had only five battle-cruisers, the British six, so Beatty did not hesitate to pursue them to the south, leaving the four battleships to

HMS *Agincourt*
Designed to meet a Brazilian requirement, sold to Turkey before completion and finally taken over by the Royal Navy, *Agincourt* was very heavily armed but generally under-armoured
Displacement: 30,250 tons full load *Length:* 632 ft *Armament:* 14 × 12-in, 20 × 6-in, 10 × 3-in, 2 × 3-in AA, 3 × 21-in torpedo tubes *Armour:* 4/9-in belt, 8/12-in turrets, 1/2½-in decks
Max speed: 22 knots

Name	Completed	Fate
Agincourt	Aug 1914	Sold for breaking 1922

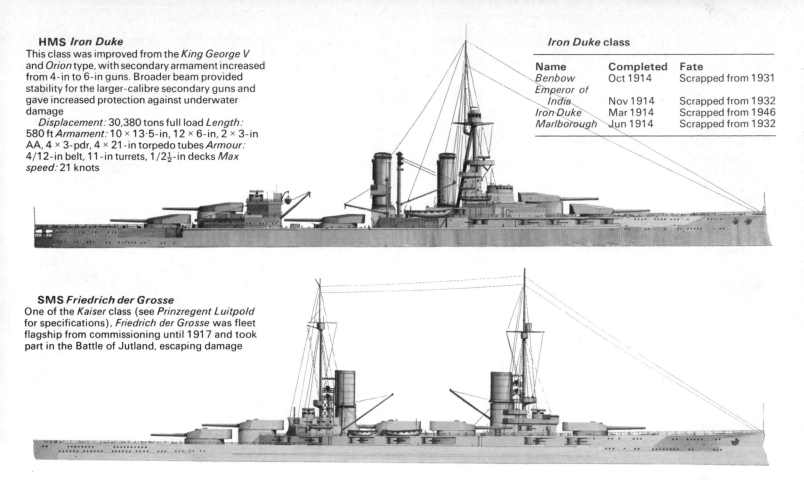

HMS Iron Duke
This class was improved from the *King George V* and *Orion* type, with secondary armament increased from 4-in to 6-in guns. Broader beam provided stability for the larger-calibre secondary guns and gave increased protection against underwater damage
Displacement: 30,380 tons full load *Length:* 580 ft *Armament:* 10 × 13·5-in, 12 × 6-in, 2 × 3-in AA, 4 × 3-pdr, 4 × 21-in torpedo tubes *Armour:* 4/12-in belt, 11-in turrets, 1/2½-in decks *Max speed:* 21 knots

Iron Duke class

Name	Completed	Fate
Benbow	Oct 1914	Scrapped from 1931
Emperor of India	Nov 1914	Scrapped from 1932
Iron Duke	Mar 1914	Scrapped from 1946
Marlborough	Jun 1914	Scrapped from 1932

SMS Friedrich der Grosse
One of the *Kaiser* class (see *Prinzregent Luitpold* for specifications), *Friedrich der Grosse* was fleet flagship from commissioning until 1917 and took part in the Battle of Jutland, escaping damage

catch up. The *Queen Elizabeth*s with their distinctive silhouettes had been stationed some miles astern so as not to tempt Hipper to avoid action, and above all it was essential to bring the Germans to action. It was already early afternoon, and, although the weather was calm, visibility was hazy; there was a distinct possibility that the Grand Fleet might not arrive in time to clinch the matter.

Both admirals reacted instinctively, Beatty swinging east to put his squadrons between Hipper and the German bases and Hipper turning south-east to draw the British towards the High Seas Fleet, now only 50 miles away. The *Lion* was in the lead, followed by the *Princess Royal, Queen Mary, Tiger, New Zealand* and *Indefatigable*, while Hipper was also leading his line in the *Lützow*, followed by the *Derfflinger, Seydlitz, Moltke* and *Von der Tann*.

At 1546 the duel began, fire gongs rang and ships shuddered as their guns belched flame and cordite smoke. The advantage lay with Hipper, for he had the sun behind him to illuminate the British, and his own ships were hard to see against the mist haze; to make matters worse, in a few minutes rolling clouds of coal smoke and cordite fumes reduced visibility even further. There was little Beatty could do about the light, but an error by his signals staff (reminiscent of the mix-up at the Dogger Bank) caused two of his ships to fire at the same German ship, and as a result the *Princess Royal* and *Lion* fired at the same ship and HMS *Indefatigable*, the last in the line and the weakest battle-cruiser, was left shooting

against the *von der Tann*. The German shooting was good, particularly the *Moltke*'s, and she soon scored two hits on the *Tiger*. Then the *Derfflinger* found the range of the *Princess Royal* and the *Lützow* began to score hits on the *Lion* and a hit on 'Q' turret amidships knocked out both guns. But the *Queen Mary* was hitting back with full broadsides, fired with 'fabulous rapidity' according to a German observer, and a range which came down to 14,000 yards.

At the rear of the line the *Von der Tann* registered three 11-in shell hits on the *Indefatigable* right aft. The stricken ship hauled out of line with smoke billowing from her stern, but before she could give any indication of the extent of her damage another shell hit near her forward 12-in gun turret and another hit the turret itself. For some seconds she seemed unhurt but then she blew up violently in a cloud of brown cordite smoke and sheets of orange flame. As debris hurtled into the air the hull turned over and sank, leaving only a handful of survivors out of her complement of nearly 1000 men. The time was 1603 and it had taken Hipper only twenty minutes to reduce the odds against him. But worse was to follow; at 1625 the *Derfflinger* shifted fire from the *Lion* to her sister *Queen Mary*, lying third in the line, and straddled her. Once again a vivid red flame shot up from

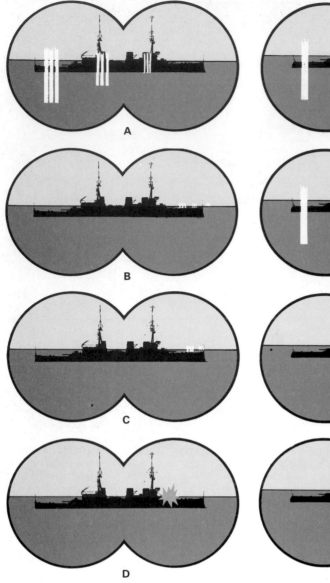

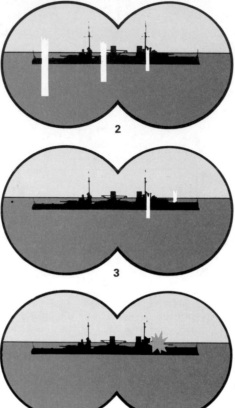

Gunnery Fire Control: German System
- A: Main armament ladder, short
- B: Main armament ladder, over
- C: Down ladder, range found
- D: Main armament, rapid fire

Gunnery Fire Control: British System
- 1: Ranging shot, short
- 2: Ranging shots, approaching target
- 3: Ranging shots, straddle
- 4: Main armament, rapid fire

At the battle of Jutland the opponents used two different systems of fire-control. At ranges of 10,000 yards or more, as at Jutland, the only means of correcting the fire of heavy guns was by spotting the 200-ft shell splashes. The speed at which accurate full armament fire could be brought to bear on a target was crucial to the outcome of the battle, and in their system the Germans had an advantage. The German ladder system fired at maximum rate, increasing range by fixed distances or ladders. The British system relied on one or two guns actually estimating the range, trying to get a bracket, then going into rapid fire. Although the bracket system appeared to be more reliable, in practice the ladder system for finding the range was more successful and was adopted by the British after 1916

Opponents at Jutland: Admiral Sir John Jellicoe, Commander-in-Chief of the Royal Navy's Grand Fleet (left), and Vizeadmiral Reinhard Scheer, his German counterpart

the forepart of the British ship, followed immediately by a tremendous explosion. The ship astern, HMS *Tiger*, had to alter course to dodge the clouds of debris, and horrified watchers testified later that the ship had 'opened out like a puffball'. The *New Zealand* reported seeing the stern sticking out of the water with men scrambling out of the after gun turret, but only nine officers and men out of 1285 survived. Beatty was now in trouble, with only four ships left to face five apparently undamaged Germans, but help was on its way. The slower battleships of the 5th Battle Squadron, the *Barham*, *Valiant*, *Warspite* and *Malaya*, were catching up by cutting corners wherever they could, and with their 15-in guns and vastly superior fire-control they were able to open fire at the astounding range of 19,000 yards. Within six minutes the *Barham* was hitting the *Von der Tann* and the *Valiant* was taking on the *Moltke*. At this range the Germans could not reply, and all they could do was to alter course slightly in an attempt to throw off the British range-takers. To gain time and to

National Maritime Museum

further harass the Germans Beatty ordered his destroyers to attack with torpedoes, and this forced Hipper to turn away. The *Seydlitz* was hit by a 21-in torpedo which tore a hole 13 ft × 39 ft in her side up forward, but despite heavy flooding which cut her speed the German battle-cruiser kept her station in the line.

Suddenly the 2nd Light Cruiser Squadron signalled to Beatty that battleships had been sighted, and two minutes later the High Seas Fleet was visible at a distance of 12 miles. Now it was Beatty who turned about, pretending to avoid action to tempt the German Fleet to follow him into the arms of the Grand Fleet. The British battle-cruisers made their 16° turn without difficulty, but once again sloppy signalling on the bridge of the *Lion* left the 5th Battle Squadron to its own devices. By the time its commander, Rear-Admiral Evan-Thomas, realized that the rest of the British force

was retreating in the opposite direction, his ships were nearly within range of the High Seas Fleet. The next few minutes were crowded and hectic as the four British battleships were exposed to the firepower of what seemed to them like the whole German Fleet. Battleships took time to turn, and the four *Queen Elizabeth*s were exposed to concentrated fire as they slowly hauled around. The *Barham* and *Malaya* were hit and suffered casualties, but all four continued to fire and scored hits on the *Grosser Kurfürst* and *Markgraf* as well as the battle-cruisers.

The Grand Fleet had been pushing southwards at maximum speed since 1555, and the Commander-in-Chief, Admiral Jellicoe, detached three *Invincible* class battle-cruisers under Rear-Admiral Hood to reinforce Beatty. These three ships arrived on the scene just as Beatty's ships had stopped their 'run to the north' to re-engage Hipper

Queen Elizabeth-class battleships practise their shooting. The Royal Navy's accuracy tended to improve as an action progressed, but the long-base Zeiss rangefinders in German ships were difficult to use accurately in battle, so the High Seas Fleet's gunnery started well but deteriorated. Inset: HMS Queen Elizabeth takes aboard cordite in containers and a one-ton 15-in shell. Magazine design was to prove crucial in battle

in an effort to stop him from sighting and reporting the Grand Fleet. This movement to the east across Hipper's bows began at 1726 and this time the advantage of the light lay with the British. Beatty manoeuvred his ships across the van of the battle-cruiser line, forcing it to turn away. The *Lützow* was hit badly, the *Derfflinger* began to take in water from bow damage, the *Seydlitz* was ablaze and the *Von der Tann* had all her 11-in guns out of action. In desperation Hipper ordered his destroyers to attack the British battle line, but just as the German light forces began to deploy at 1735 Hood's three battle-cruisers erupted on the scene and chased them away.

HMS *Inflexible*

The controversial *Invincible* class battle-cruisers combined the heavy guns of a battleship with the speed of a cruiser. They inevitably came off second-best when used as dreadnoughts
Displacement: 17,250 tons *Length:* 530 ft
Armament: 8 × 12-in, 16 × 4-in, 3 × 4-in AA, 1 × 3-in, 7 × mg, 5 × 18-in torpedo tubes *Armour:* 6-in belt, 7-in turrets, 10-in conning tower, $2\frac{1}{2}$/1-in decks *Max speed:* 25 knots

Invincible class

Name	Completed	Fate
Indomitable	Jun 1908	Sold 1922
Inflexible	Oct 1908	Sold 1922
Invincible	Mar 1908	Blew up at Jutland

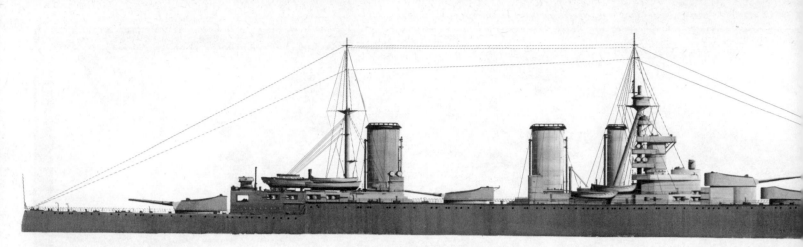

HMS *Lion*

This class of battle-cruiser was fast, powerful and heavily armed, but the main turrets were arranged in an inefficient way and the armour was inadequate. Other drawbacks necessitated extensive modifications

Displacement: 29,680 tons full load *Length:* 660 ft *Armament:* 8×13.5-in, 16×4-in, 1×4-in AA, 4×3-pdr, 2×21-in torpedo tubes *Armour:* 4/9-in belt, 4/9-in turrets, 1/2½-in decks *Max speed:* 27 knots

Lion class

Name	Completed	Fate
Lion	May 1912	Scrapped 1924
Princess Royal	Nov 1912	Scrapped 1926
Queen Mary	Sep 1915	Blew up at Jutland

To Jellicoe in the Fleet Flagship HMS *Iron Duke* the tactical situation must have been baffling. Visibility was dropping as the early spring twilight closed in, and he had only a series of estimates of the last known position, bearing and speed of the High Seas Fleet. He could see only seven miles from the flag-deck of the *Iron Duke*, which was much less than maximum gun-range, and it was essential that his fleet should be properly deployed in line, with all guns pointing in the right direction, ready to open fire as soon as a target presented itself. Anything less than that would forfeit the tactical advantage to the Germans and would expose the Grand Fleet to the risk of serious damage before it could reply. But Jellicoe was the ablest ship-handler and tactician in the Royal Navy, and possibly the best in the world. He studied the plot for no more than ten seconds, then ordered a deployment from the box-shaped cruising formation into a single line nine miles long, using the port column as the head of the line. This had the effect of simultaneously putting the Grand Fleet between the High Seas Fleet and its bases, avoiding complex

SMS *Seydlitz*

Developed from the *Moltke* class, with a raised forecastle to improve seakeeping and a longer, narrower hull to give a higher speed. She was hit more times at Jutland than any other German ship which survived the battle yet was able to return safely to the Jade River

Displacement: 25,150 tons full load *Length:* 200·6 m *Armament:* 10 × 280-mm, 12 × 150-mm, 12 × 88-mm, 2 × 88-mm AA, 4 × 500-mm torpedo tubes *Armour:* 100/300-mm side, 250-mm main turrets, 30/80-mm deck *Max speed:* 26½ knots

Seydlitz class

Name	Completed	Fate
Seydlitz	May 1913	Scrapped from 1928

wheeling and 'marking time', and putting the most modern and powerful battleships into action first. Few tacticians faced by an able opponent have had the good fortune to achieve such perfection, and although controversy raged over the deployment for years after Jutland, no serious historian today questions that Jellicoe achieved all that an admiral could ask:

The British battle-cruisers now effected the junction with the main fleet for which they had worked so hard, and indeed for which they had been built. But one more tragedy was to darken their achievement. Admiral Hood's flagship, the battle-cruiser

HMS Lion, *Beatty's flagship, making full speed during the battle. Shortly afterwards she was nearly blown up by a hit on 'Q' turret*

Invincible, was hit at 9000 yards, caught by a sudden improvement in visibility which left her clearly outlined against the setting sun – it was an opportunity which the *Derfflinger* and *König's* gunlayers could not waste. A salvo fell on the *Invincible's* midships turrets, and within seconds she collapsed in a huge cloud of smoke and coal dust. Because the battle was taking place over the shallow Jutland Bank off the coast of Denmark the two halves of the 567-ft ship rested on the bottom, standing up 'like gravestones to her 1026 dead'. Ironically, the officers and men of the Grand Fleet assumed that she was the remains of a German ship sunk, and cheers rang out as each battleship swept past at 20 knots.

The third phase of Jutland now began, a series of gun actions between the two fleets. Admiral Scheer suddenly found his 'T' crossed by the fully deployed British line, the one thing that he and his predecessors had tried to avoid since the war began. From eight points of the compass a line of battleships, whose extremities vanished into the mist, poured shells into his van. The *Lützow* was completely disabled and the other battle-cruisers suffered heavily. Scheer was in a trap, and he had only one way out – a complete 180° turn by each ship, the so-called 'battle turnaway' which had been assiduously practised. This achieved its aim and contact was lost as the German battleships headed on a reciprocal course under cover of a smokescreen laid by destroyers.

Jellicoe swung the Grand Fleet round to the south-east at 1844 and again to the south at 1856 to keep himself between Scheer and his escape route. At 1908 the High Seas Fleet blundered into the Grand Fleet a second time while trying to feel its way around the flank. Once again Scheer's 'T' was crossed, and the British battle fleet opened fire from one end to the other at ranges of 9000 to 12,000 yards. But this time the German position was worse, with the British closer and their own line bent. Scheer was desperate, and threw his destroyers into an attack. To his battle-cruisers he said, 'Charge the enemy. Ram. Ships denoted are to attack without regard to consequences'. This 'death ride' of the battle-cruisers was led by the *Derfflinger*, which soon had two turrets destroyed by exploding ammunition, and lost her fire-control. The *Lützow* was burning fiercely, and her fighting days were over, but Hipper's 1st Scouting Group saved the day for his Commander-in-Chief. Amid the encircling gloom and the pall of smoke from gunfire, burning ships and funnels, the British could not see the second battle turnaway; although they did not know it, they had

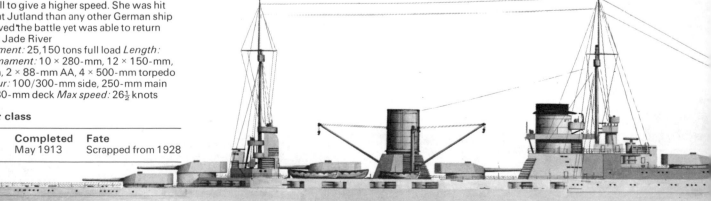

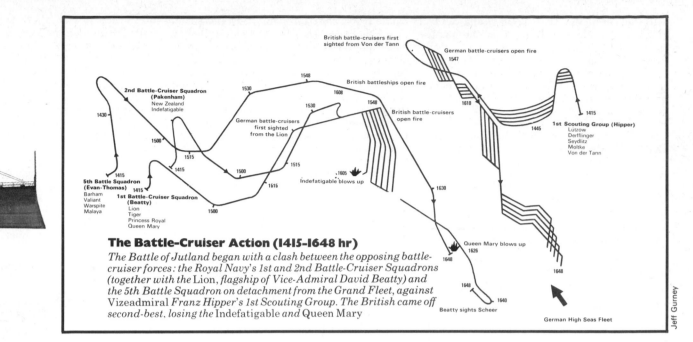

The Battle-Cruiser Action (1415-1648 hr)

The Battle of Jutland began with a clash between the opposing battle-cruiser forces: the Royal Navy's 1st and 2nd Battle-Cruiser Squadrons (together with the Lion, *flagship of Vice-Admiral David Beatty) and the 5th Battle Squadron on detachment from the Grand Fleet, against Vizeadmiral* Franz Hipper's *1st Scouting Group. The British came off second-best, losing the* Indefatigable *and* Queen Mary

seen the last of Germany's High Seas Fleet.

The only damage suffered by the Grand Fleet during this phase were two shell hits on the *Colossus* and a torpedo hit on the *Marlborough*, but neither ship was put out of action. Although the rival battle-cruisers exchanged a few more shots, the firing finally died away and by 2035 the fleet action was over. In the night action which followed British capital ships played no part, but German battleships engaged cruisers and destroyers when they forced their way through the British light forces stationed to the rear of the Grand Fleet. Jellicoe did not want to risk a night action, with all its fearful possibilities of mistaken identity and collision, but Scheer dared not wait for daylight and so he had to fight his way through at night. Also, his ships were equipped for night-fighting, so that he could take a calculated risk. This paid off handsomely, and Scheer got back to harbour safely, but minus the pre-dreadnought battleship *Pommern* which blew up with the loss of all hands when hit by a British destroyer's torpedo, and the *Lützow*, which had to be sunk by her destroyers when she could no longer steam.

The figures make it clear that, in terms of ships sunk, Jutland was more or less a

Vice-Admiral Sir David Beatty, commander of the Royal Navy's battle-cruisers at Jutland

drawn battle. In tactical terms there was no doubt that the Germans had sunk more valuable ships – three capital ships and three armoured cruisers as against one capital ship and one obsolescent battleship. But victories are not decided simply by numbers. The British were clearly in possession of the battlefield on the morning of 1 June, whereas the Germans were thankfully negotiating the swept channels outside Wilhelshaven, and it could even be claimed that they lost another battle-cruiser, since the *Seydlitz* came to rest on the bottom of the North Sea *outside* her home port, and had to be salvaged. There is no doubt that the *Seydlitz* and the *Derfflinger* could not have faced a long voyage across the North Sea, whereas the entire Grand Fleet arrived safely in its harbours, docked its lame ducks, coaled and was ready for sea within 24 hours. But in a broader sense, Jutland, if not a defeat for the British, was a strategic stalemate. Millions of pounds had been lavished on the dreadnought battle fleet in the hope that it would provide a quick, decisive victory over Germany, but when the moment came nothing had happened and the slaughter in the trenches was still going on.

The inquisition began immediately after

Seydlitz was the most heavily damaged German warship to survive Jutland. Thanks to her captain's careful nursing she escaped the fate of the Lützow but still sank outside Wilhelmshaven, having shipped 2000 tons of water and being completely burnt out

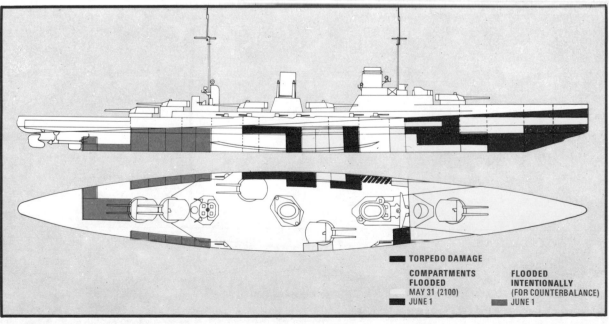

TORPEDO DAMAGE

COMPARTMENTS FLOODED
☐ MAY 31 (2100)
■ JUNE 1

FLOODED INTENTIONALLY (FOR COUNTERBALANCE)
JUNE 1

Jutland. Jellicoe, true to his character, refused to issue a statement on the battle until all his crippled ships had been accounted for, so an anxious Admiralty caved in to pressure from the press and, incredibly, published the German communiqué. Naturally this made little of the fearful pounding taken by the High Seas Fleet and Scheer's two turns away from Jellicoe, and made much of the loss of three British battle-cruisers and three armoured cruisers. From this moment on British opinion divided into two camps, pro-Beatty and pro-Jellicoe, with a third lobby claiming that both admirals had been let down by inferior material.

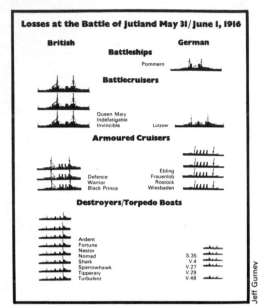

Losses at the Battle of Jutland May 31/June 1, 1916

British		German
Battleships		
		Pommern
Battlecruisers		
Queen Mary		
Indefatigable		
Invincible		Lützow
Armoured Cruisers		
		Ebling
Defence		Frauenlob
Warrior		Rostock
Black Prince		Wiesbaden
Destroyers/Torpedo Boats		
Ardent		
Fortune		
Nestor		
Nomad		S.35
Shark		V.4
Sparrowhawk		V.27
Tipperary		V.29
Turbulent		V.48

Jeff Gurney

SMS König *seen running trials just before the war*

Bundesarchiv

The truth, as so often happens, lies somewhere between the two extremes. Beatty had handled his battle-cruisers well; although this staffwork left a lot to be desired he had been acutely aware that time was essential, and he had delivered Scheer into Jellicoe's grasp. Jellicoe, on the other hand, had produced a masterly deployment with very little information to hand, and had positioned his fleet so well that twice he had achieved tactical perfection in crossing Scheer's 'T'. On the German side, Hipper had also handled his battle-cruisers well and had followed a difficult set of orders dutifully and had made much more out of the situation than anyone had dared hope. Of Scheer's tactics the less said the better. It has been claimed by a recent English commentator that British tactics were inferior to German in not having a 'battle turnaway', but 200 years of British naval history had demonstrated that naval victories were not to be won by a 180° turn in the face of the enemy. If the Royal Navy did not practise such a manoeuvre it was because they felt that it did little to bring a reluctant enemy to battle.

Many years later an earnest student asked Scheer what grand strategic design he had been pursuing at the time of his second encounter with the Grand Fleet; with more candour than regard for reputation Scheer replied, 'I don't know. As the virgin said when told she was pregnant, "It just happened".'

On the *matériel* side Jutland raised far more puzzling questions. Why had three modern British ships been blown up, but no German ships? The loss of the *Invincible* and *Indefatigable* could be explained away

by the fact that they had only a 6-in armour belt, but the *Queen Mary* was protected by 9-in armour, and evidence from her two sisters showed that only two shells had penetrated British armour of that thickness. Disturbing reports also filtered through from neutral sources that British shells had failed to burst, and it was clear that something had gone wrong.

With only a handful of survivors from all three battle-cruisers there was little direct evidence as to the cause of the losses. But the *Lion* had suffered a nearly disastrous fire in 'Q' turret during the early stages of the action. According to Beatty's flag captain the shell hit the front plate at its joint with the roof plate, blowing half the roof into the air and bursting over the guns. The

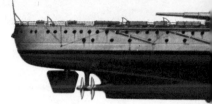

blast of the shell killed or wounded every man in the turret and severed the hydraulic pipes. Several cordite cartridges caught fire, and the left-hand gun tilted upwards from the weight of the breech-mechanism, causing the cordite charges in the breech to fall into the fire already burning below. But the unfortunate and disturbing fact about this fire was that although the ship's fire parties ran hoses into the turret and doused the fire, half an hour later the still-smouldering charges burst into flame, and ignited eight more charges jammed in the hoist. A tongue of flame leapt down the ammunition hoist, killing the 70 men of the magazine and shell-room crews, but fortunately the Royal Marine officer in charge of the turret, Major Marvey RMLI, had earlier given the order to flood 'Q' magazine, and so the ship did not blow up.

Examination of the *Lion* showed that her cordite charges were extremely unstable, whereas it had hitherto been assumed that they would merely burn rather than flash off if ignited. The Germans, on the other hand, had no such trouble. Their charges were encased in metal covers as against silk bags, but the matter went deeper than that. British cordite manufacturers still used a

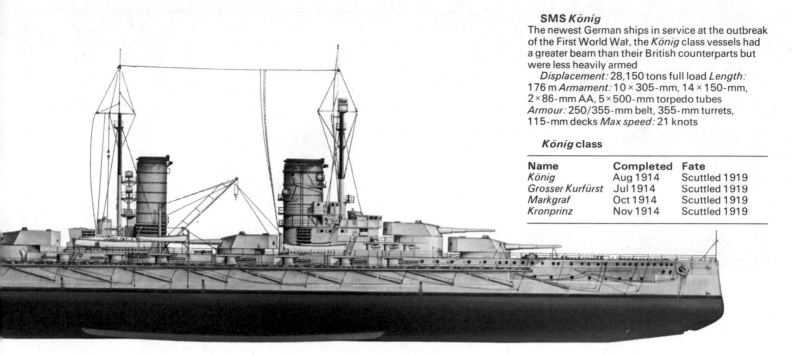

SMS *König*
The newest German ships in service at the outbreak of the First World War, the *König* class vessels had a greater beam than their British counterparts but were less heavily armed
Displacement: 28,150 tons full load *Length:* 176 m *Armament:* 10 × 305-mm, 14 × 150-mm, 2 × 86-mm AA, 5 × 500-mm torpedo tubes *Armour:* 250/355-mm belt, 355-mm turrets, 115-mm decks *Max speed:* 21 knots

König class

Name	Completed	Fate
König	Aug 1914	Scuttled 1919
Grosser Kurfürst	Jul 1914	Scuttled 1919
Markgraf	Oct 1914	Scuttled 1919
Kronprinz	Nov 1914	Scuttled 1919

vaseline-based solvent to stabilize the propellant, whereas the Germans had moved on to solventless cordite. Tests showed that the so-called stabilizer actually reduced the stability of cordite, making it all the more likely to flash off. No German ship using solventless propellant blew up in the First World War, whereas the three navies using British-pattern cordite – British, Japanese and Italian – all suffered from magazine explosions:

British – *Bulwark* (1914), *Vanguard* (1917)
Italian – *Benedetto Brin* (1915), *Leonardo da Vinci* (1916)
Japanese – *Tsukuba* (1917), *Kawachi* (1918)

The British were worried by reports that many of their armour-piercing shells had failed to detonate properly. On investigation this was found to be true, and to its chagrin the Royal Navy realized that many German ships had reached harbour safely when they should have been sunk. Again, the problem was one of quality control rather than design. The nose-caps of the armour-piercing shell were too brittle and the Lyddite burster was too sensitive, so that when a shell hit armour it broke up or detonated prematurely. British ships scored a number of hits on German ships at Jutland, and had the shells detonated properly, *after* the intended delay to allow them to pass through the armour, they would have

SMS *Grosser Kurfürst*
One of the *König* class (see that ship for specifications), *Grosser Kurfürst* had an eventful war which included action at Jutland, being torpedoed, colliding with the *Kronprinz* and hitting a mine

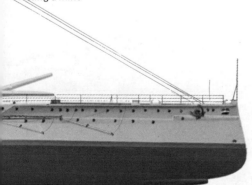

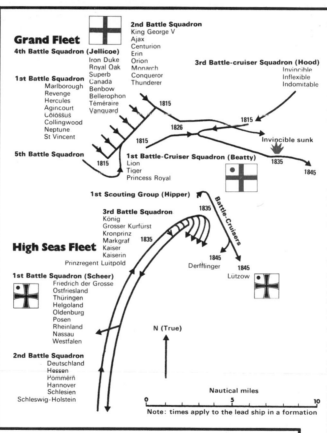

Grand Fleet

4th Battle Squadron (Jellicoe)
Iron Duke
Royal Oak
Superb
Canada
Benbow
Bellerophon
Téméraire
Vanguard

1st Battle Squadron
Marlborough
Revenge
Hercules
Agincourt
Colossus
Collingwood
Neptune
St Vincent

2nd Battle Squadron
King George V
Ajax
Centurion
Erin
Orion
Monarch
Conqueror
Thunderer

3rd Battle-cruiser Squadron (Hood)
Invincible
Inflexible
Indomitable

5th Battle Squadron

1st Battle-Cruiser Squadron (Beatty)
Lion
Tiger
Princess Royal

1st Scouting Group (Hipper)

High Seas Fleet

3rd Battle Squadron
König
Grosser Kurfürst
Kronprinz
Markgraf
Kaiser
Kaiserin
Prinzregent Luitpold

1st Battle Squadron (Scheer)
Friedrich der Grosse
Ostfriesland
Thüringen
Helgoland
Oldenburg
Posen
Rheinland
Nassau
Westfalen

2nd Battle Squadron
Deutschland
Hessen
Pommern
Hannover
Schlesien
Schleswig-Holstein

Invincible sunk
Derfflinger
Lützow

Battle-Cruisers

N (True)

Nautical miles
0   5   10

Note: times apply to the lead ship in a formation

The Fleets Collide : 1

The long-awaited first clash between the Royal Navy's Grand Fleet and the German High Seas Fleet followed on the heels of the initial battle-cruiser action. Admiral Jellicoe in the *Iron Duke* ordered the 1st, 2nd and 4th Battle Squadrons to deploy from their cruising formation of six columns into a single line nine miles long, with the 5th Battle Squadron rejoining them.

This enabled Jellicoe's force to cross the 'T' of Vice-Admiral Scheer's 1st, 2nd and 3rd Battle Squadrons, which were steaming in line ahead. Scheer, in the *Friedrich der Grosse*, had little choice but to order a battle turnaway to starboard, turning each ship through 180° and reversing its order in the line.

Meanwhile Beatty's 1st Battle-Cruiser Squadron, minus the sunken *Queen Mary*, was joined by the 3rd Battle-Cruiser Squadron under Hood. This force steamed parallel with the battleship line, between those ships and the enemy. It was to suffer another setback, however; at 1835, after being pounded by the *König* and *Derfflinger*, the *Invincible* exploded.

But Hipper's 1st Scouting Group did not escape unscathed. The *Lützow* was disabled and her sisters were damaged, although the High Seas Fleet was intact.

Just over half an hour later the fleets clashed again. Scheer, finding his 'T' crossed for a second time, ordered his battle-cruisers to attack the enemy while his battleships carried out their second battle turnaway. A smoke screen laid by the accompanying torpedo-boats added to the gloom, and the High Seas Fleet yet again emerged intact.

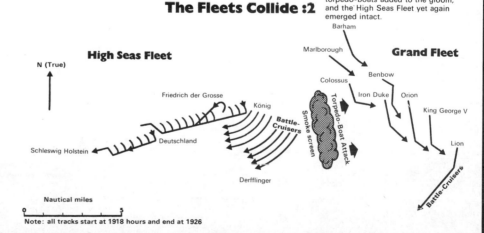

The Fleets Collide : 2

High Seas Fleet

N (True)

Friedrich der Grosse
König
Deutschland
Schleswig Holstein
Derfflinger

Battle-Cruisers

Smoke screen

Torpedo-Boat Attack

Grand Fleet

Barham
Marlborough
Benbow
Colossus
Iron Duke
Orion
King George V
Lion

Battle-Cruisers

Nautical miles
0   5

Note: all tracks start at 1918 hours and end at 1926

Jeff Gurney

63

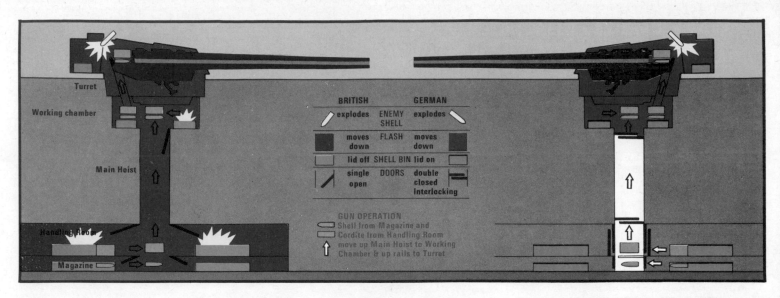

Diagrammatic explanation of the way in which British battle-cruisers blew up at Jutland. The German practice of encasing cordite in brass saved them from fatal magazine explosions

caused more serious damage. This is not to suggest that all German ships escaped without serious damage, as several battle-cruisers were badly damaged, and the common or high-explosive shell used by British ships was extremely destructive. However, the stable nature of German cordite meant that cordite fires were less of a hazard.

The British took energetic steps to remedy the faults in their ships; the armour-piercing shell was completely redesigned with a TNT burster, and all ships of the Grand Fleet were given extra deck armour around the turrets and new flash-tight scuttles in the ammunition supply system. But the opportunity to settle the outcome of the war had been lost. There was to be no second chance, as the two fleets were not to meet again, apart from a brief sortie by the High Seas Fleet in 1917, which was cancelled as soon as reconnoitring Zeppe-lins revealed that the Grand Fleet was heading southwards. In November 1917 a small battle-cruiser force tried to push into the Heligoland Bight, but after a brief skirmish with German outposts the fear of minefields proved too much and the British withdrew. Life for the two fleets became monotonous as the battleships swung at their anchors. In the end it was the High Seas Fleet's morale which cracked; the British had a much less hospitable base at Scapa but they were at least able to keep themselves busy by going to sea.

Adversaries in the Adriatic
The Naval Race between Britain and Germany was duplicated in the Mediterranean before the war as Austria-Hungary and Italy built up their fleets

Duilio
Similar to the ships of the *Cavour* class, but having greater power and with secondary armament upgraded in order to keep pace with foreign battleships. The secondary armament was exposed to spray interference
Displacement: 24,730 tons full load *Length:* 176 m *Armament:* 13 × 305-mm, 16 × 152-mm, 13 × 76-mm, 6 × 76-mm AA, 3 × 450-mm torpedo tubes *Armour:* 250-mm belt, 240-mm turrets, 40-mm deck *Max speed:* 21 knots.

Andrea Doria class

Name	Completed	Fate
Andrea Doria	Mar 1916	Scrapped 1958
Duilio	May 1915	Scrapped 1958

Viribus Unitis

Construction of this class of Austro-Hungarian battleships was prompted by the building of similar vessels in Italy. *Viribus Unitis* herself was fleet flagship from 1914 to 1918

Displacement: 22,500 tons *Length:* 161 m *Armament:* 12×305-mm, 12×150-mm, 18× 70-mm, 2×75-mm AA (from 1918), 4×533-mm torpedo tubes *Armour:* 150/280-mm side, 305-mm main turrets, 48-mm deck *Max speed:* 20 knots

Viribus Unitis class

Name	Completed	Fate
Viribus Unitis	Oct 1912	Mined 1918
Tegetthoff	Jul 1913	Scrapped 1924–25
Prinz Eugen	Jul 1914	Sunk as target 1922
Szent Istvan	Nov 1915	Torpedoed 1918

Giulio Cesare

Intended to match Austria's *Viribus Unitis* class, the three battleships of the *Conte di Cavour* class were fast and heavily armed but never met their adversaries

Displacement: 24,300 tons full load *Length:* 169 m *Armament:* 13 × 305-mm, 18 × 120-mm, 13 × 76-mm, 3 × 450-mm torpedo tubes *Armour:* 250-mm belt, 250-mm turrets, 40-mm decks *Max speed:* 22½ knots

Conte di Cavour class

Name	Completed	Fate
Conte di Cavour	Apr 1915	Torpedoed at Taranto 1940, broken up 1947-52
Giulio Cesare	May 1914	Transferred to Russia 1948, mined ? in Black Sea 1955
Leonardo da Vinci	May 1914	Blew up 1916

Giulio Cesare *at Taranto after the armistice, one of six Italian dreadnoughts. Unfortunately British pattern cordite was responsible for the loss of her sister, the* Leonardo da Vinci

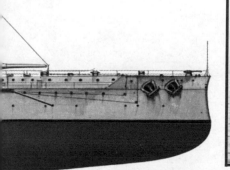

Imperial War Museum

THE OLD SHIPS FIGHT BACK

Paradoxically the pre-dreadnoughts, which had been written off by all the naval pundits as useless, had a much more exciting war. The old battleship *Canopus* was sent to South America in a vain attempt to reinforce Admiral Cradock against von Spee's squadron, but she did manage to put herself on the mud at the Falkland Islands to act as a fixed battery in defence. When the German armies reached the Belgian coast late in 1914 their right flank was vulnerable to bombardment from the sea, and so the Royal Navy mustered a scratch force of elderly ships to harass them. The *Venerable* was used for a time, and then someone remembered that the old *Revenge*, which had been struck off the Navy List in 1911, had not yet been scrapped. Her 13.5-in guns had already been relined to convert them to 12-in calibre when she was serving as a gunnery training ship, and as she also had a relatively modern outfit of fire-control she was eminently suited to the job. All that remained to be done was to fit her with the first primitive anti-torpedo 'bulges' and a few anti-Zeppelin guns on high-angle mountings, and she was ready. Apart from having to take the name *Redoubtable* in February 1915 to release her name for a new *Royal Sovereign* class battleship, she led an uneventful life. To

The old battleship HMS Revenge *bombards the coast of German-occupied Belgium, listing to increase the range of her guns*

increase the range of her guns she was often heeled over, but eventually she was replaced by specially built monitors in October 1915.

Only two British dreadnought battleships were sunk during the entire war, the *Vanguard* by ammunition explosion and the *Audacious* by a mine off Northern Ireland. The pre-dreadnoughts, on the other hand, soon showed that they were more vulnerable. In November 1914 HMS *Bulwark* blew up while loading ammunition at Sheerness, and in January 1915 the *Formidable* was torpedoed in the English Channel.

To the Dardanelles

When the Allies decided to attack the Dardanelles they sent all the old battleships they could spare, and it was even hoped that some could act as 'mine-bumpers' to clear the minefields. Seventeen pre-dreadnoughts were mustered for the attack on the Narrows

on 18 March, 1915, backed up by a British battle-cruiser and the brand-new *Queen Elizabeth*. It was fondly hoped that the new battleship would be able to calibrate her 15-in guns against the Turkish forts, but it should have been realized earlier that ships had very little effect against forts. On 3 November, 1914, the battle-cruisers *Indefatigable* and *Indomitable* and the French battleships *Verité* and *Suffren* had fired at Seddulbahir (Sedd-el-Bahr) and Kum Kale forts; despite a lucky hit in a magazine, neither fort was destroyed. Vice-Admiral Carden, the British admiral commanding in the Aegean, asked for 12 battleships, two battle-cruisers and smaller warships such as cruisers, destroyers and minesweepers. In view of what happened later it is worth noting that he also forecast a heavy expenditure of 12-in shells. What he was finally given was:

Allied Battleships at the Dardanelles

1 modern battleship (*Queen Elizabeth*, 15-in guns).
1 battle-cruiser (*Inflexible*, 12-in guns).
2 modern pre-dreadnoughts (*Lord Nelson, Agamemnon*, 12-in and 9.2-in guns).
10 old pre-dreadnoughts (*Ocean, Albion, Vengeance, Majestic, Prince George, Canopus, Irresistible, Cornwallis, Swiftsure* and *Triumph*, 12-in and 10-in guns).
4 French pre-dreadnoughts (*Suffren, Charlemagne, St Louis* and *Gaulois*, 12-in and 10.8-in guns).

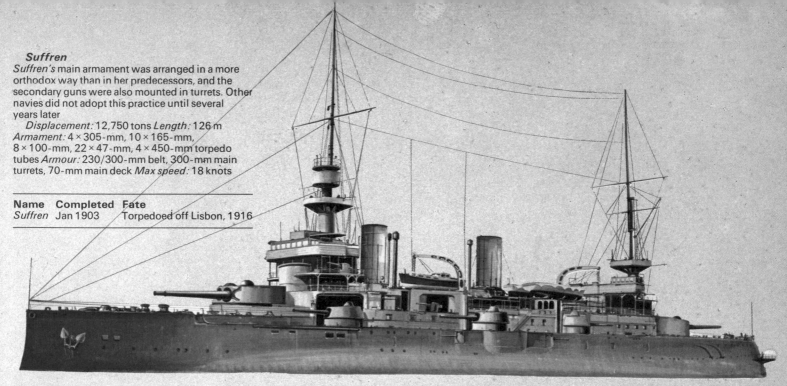

Suffren

Suffren's main armament was arranged in a more orthodox way than in her predecessors, and the secondary guns were also mounted in turrets. Other navies did not adopt this practice until several years later

Displacement: 12,750 tons *Length:* 126 m
Armament: 4 × 305-mm, 10 × 165-mm, 8 × 100-mm, 22 × 47-mm, 4 × 450-mm torpedo tubes *Armour:* 230/300-mm belt, 300-mm main turrets, 70-mm main deck *Max speed:* 18 knots

Name	Completed	Fate
Suffren	Jan 1903	Torpedoed off Lisbon, 1916

Ten of these battleships went into action on 19 February, 1915, against the outer forts. The *Cornwallis* opened fire at about 12,000 yards and the others joined in at about 8000 yards, but it was soon obvious that the ships would not be able to hit anything until they anchored. What had not been foreseen was that ships' gunners would have great difficulty in spotting fall of shot on a flat, featureless landscape. Each gun position ashore needed a direct hit to disable it, and nothing short of a direct hit on a magazine could knock out a fort. To make matters worse the ships fired 139 12-in shells from 42 guns, an average of only 3.3 rounds per gun over a period of nearly eight hours.

A further bombardment the next day was cancelled because of bad weather, but on 25 February the battleships went in again in much the same formation as before. This time the ships did better because other battleships had been stationed on the flanks to spot the fall of shot (known in naval parlance as 'flank marking'). The *Queen Elizabeth* did much better this time, taking only 18 rounds to find the range and disable both the modern 9.4-in guns at Cape Helles. Even the older ships did well, the *Irresistible*, for example, knocking out the guns at Orkanie with 35 rounds. As the afternoon wore on the ships moved in closer to be able

HMS *Prince Rupert*

Old battleships drew too much water for shore bombardment and were vulnerable, so they were replaced by specially built monitors. The *Prince Rupert* and her sisters used 12-in guns and turrets removed from four old *Majestic* class battleships

to use their 6-in and 5.5-in secondary guns to silence all the forts and allow mine-sweepers to clear the dense minefields. Landing parties were able to demolish 50 guns with little loss from the demoralized Turkish troops.

The inner forts proved much harder to deal with. The Straits widen out above Seddulbahir, and so the gun batteries were too far away for accurate firing. There was no short-wave radio, and even the seaplanes present were too primitive to be of much use. Three more bombardments between 2 and 8 March achieved little, although the *Queen Elizabeth* again showed off by firing *over* the Gallipoli Peninsula at the Nagara forts on the European side. The methods indicate the crudity of long-range gunnery; the *Queen Elizabeth* used three pre-dreadnoughts as flank-markers, seaplanes and a cairn on a hilltop as an aiming mark, but it still took four hours at 14,000 yards. Once again the expenditure of ammunition was laughable, 33 rounds of 'common' (high-explosive) shell, one round per gun per hour.

Next day the *Queen Elizabeth* was involved in a dangerous and unique action. While she was firing at Fort Chemenlik on the Asiatic side of the Straits, the Turks brought up the old pre-dreadnought *Hairredin Barbarossa* (formerly the German *Kurfürst Friedrich*

Wilhelm built in 1894) in an attempt to interfere with her fire. The old battleship had one advantage in that her old 11-in (28-cm) guns had 25° elevation, and she was able to drop three shells near her giant adversary. The *Queen Elizabeth* at first assumed that the shells came from a mobile field-howitzer battery, and she moved out about a thousand yards, pausing only to demolish the German ship's spotting position on shore. But the Germans were not finished yet, and as soon as the spotting party was established in a new position the *Hairredin Barbarossa* found the range again in three rounds, this time hitting the *Queen Elizabeth* three times on her armour below the waterline. No battleship of that era was designed to withstand plunging fire, and the old Turkish battleship might well have crippled or even sunk the pride of the Royal Navy if she had scored a hit on the deck.

Although the *Queen Elizabeth* was not damaged in this bizarre action she was too valuable to be risked in this sort of work, and in any case the Admiralty was reluctant to ship too many 15-in shells out to the Dardanelles until stocks had been built up at home. Sending her out had been foolhardy and one of the 13.5-in-gunned *Orion* class would have been more useful, and now the Admiralty insisted that she be recalled as soon as Carden could get the major assault on the Narrows over, to force his way past the minefields. The problem was quite simple now: the mines prevented the ships from dealing effectively with the guns, and the guns prevented the minesweepers from sweeping the mines. To finish once and for all the Allies planned a massive sweep with all 18 battleships. Although Carden had a nervous breakdown his second-in-command, Vice-Admiral de Robeck, was able to take over with virtually no delay, and the attack was launched on 18 March, 1915.

The day began in brilliant sunshine and de Robeck's fleet looked magnificent as it advanced up the Narrows. First to open fire was the *Queen Elizabeth* followed by the other three ships, and by 1130 the whole of Line 'A' was in action, with the Turkish artillery firing back. All the ships were hit but not seriously. Things seemed to be going well, and de Robeck ordered the French Admiral Guepratte to bring up Line 'B'. Guepratte responded with great verve, taking his ships between the first line as if carrying out a drill manoeuvre, and soon both lines were firing at the forts. The Turkish guns were beginning to score more

hits now; the *Inflexible*'s bridge was set on fire, the *Gaulois* was holed below the line, and the *Agamemnon* was hit 12 times within half an hour. But even pre-dreadnoughts were built to take this sort of punishment, and casualties remained low, fewer than 40 killed and wounded. The Turkish gunners were beginning to run low in ammunition and fire slackened; de Robeck judged that the time had come to bring up his reserve line of ships to take the pressure off the elderly French battleships in Line 'B' which had been taking a fair amount of punishment.

Just after 1400 hours the *Suffren* began a wide turn to starboard into Erenkoy Bay, at the start of her turn towards Kum Kale and the open sea. Her three consorts followed her in a huge arc, but then, suddenly, the second ship *Bouvet* lurched as a huge explosion stopped her in a cloud of steam and smoke. In a matter of seconds she capsized and sank, taking nearly 600 men down with her. The unfortunate ship had already been hit by several heavy projectiles, and as she was turning under fire it was assumed that she had been hit in the magazine by a lucky shell. The bombardment continued, but two hours later the *Inflexible*, also manoeuvring in Erenkoy Bay, struck a mine and began to take in water fast. This time the cause was clearly understood, and three minutes later the *Irresistible* also reported that she had been mined. Admiral de Robeck had little choice but to cancel the bombardment until the extent of the danger was known.

The most obvious explanation was that the Turks had released drifting mines above the Narrows, but de Robeck feared that torpedoes might have been fired from fixed tubes ashore. Nobody suspected Erenkoy Bar, for the area had been swept repeatedly. In fact the sweepers had found three mines earlier but had not suspected that they formed part of a larger line, and the Allies had placed too much faith in the ability of seaplanes to spot mines. What they had missed was possibly the most effective minefield in the history of naval warfare.

On the night of 8 March a small Turkish minelayer, the *Nousret* under the command of Lieutenant-Colonel Geehl, had slipped down through the Narrows to lay 20 mines

to lay a trap. His gamble was more successful than he could have imagined, for a third battleship was to be claimed by the small minefield. The *Ocean* chose to ignore a request from Commodore Keyes to take the stricken *Irresistible* in tow (her captain would not take orders from a mere temporary commodore), and she steamed backwards and forwards at maximum speed, firing her 12-in guns at nothing in particular. This comic sideshow was brought to an end by one of the *Nousret*'s mines, and the *Ocean* drifted off up the Straits turning helpless circles. Neither she nor the *Irresistible* were seen again. Keyes made an eerie trip after dark to try to find the two battleships, with everything dark and silent, and only the searchlights probing the darkness.

The losses were made good, for both the French and British had plenty of obsolescent battleships, but the catastrophe unnerved the leaders of the expedition and their masters at home. The irony of it all was that those old battleships had been sent out as expendable units, but as soon as three were sunk the admirals began to talk about unbearable losses. Only the *Queen Elizabeth* and the *Inflexible* could be regarded as strategically important ships, and they should not have been there anyway. The alternative was the bloody attempt to take the Gallipoli Peninsula by means of amphibious landings, and when thinking of the colossal casualties incurred by British, French and ANZAC troops in trying to gain a foothold on that barren spur it is hard to avoid the thought that more attention to the problems of shore bombardment and a few more pre-dreadnought battleships sunk by mines would have been a cheaper price to pay. And if the Allies had been able to get reinforcements and supplies to Russia through the Black Sea, might the Revolu-

Charlemagne, *another 'expendable' old battleship sent to the Dardanelles*

Marius Bar

in Erenkoy Bay. Geehl was a mine-warfare expert and had seen how the battleships used the bay for turning, and so he decided

tion of 1917 have been postponed? Unlikely, for there is no evidence that the British and French would have known what to do if their battleships had arrived off Istanbul.

Many of the battleships stayed on at Mudros, for they were needed to provide covering fire for the landings. This they did very well, and the hard-pressed troops were encouraged by the sight of battleships

HMS Queen Elizabeth

The *Queen Elizabeth* class introduced the use of oil as the sole fuel, thereby allowing a greater weight of armour and higher speed. It also greatly speeded up refuelling and improved morale by removing the dirty chore of shovelling coal

Displacement: 33,000 tons full load *Length:* 600 ft *Armament:* 8 × 15-in, 16 × 6-in, 2 × 3-in AA, 4 × 3-pdr, 4 × 21-in torpedo tubes *Armour:* 6/13-in belt, 11/13-in turrets, 1/3-in decks *Max speed:* 24 knots

Queen Elizabeth class

Name	Completed	Fate
Barham	Oct 1915	Torpedoed off Sollum 1941
Malaya	Feb 1916	Sold 1948
Queen Elizabeth	Jan 1915	Sold 1948
Valiant	Feb 1916	Sold 1948
Warspite	Mar 1915	Scrapped from 1947

pouring shells into the Turkish trenches. Under these circumstances the old battleships could fire much more accurately, for the troops ashore could spot and report the fall of shot, so that corrections could be made. But this happy state of affairs did not last. On the night of 13 May a Turkish torpedo boat crept down the Straits and torpedoed the *Goliath*, which was lying off the beaches. Then, on May 25, 1915, the German submarine *U-21* arrived after a long voyage from Germany via Austria, and torpedoed the *Triumph* off Gaba Tepe. Two days later *U-21* returned to find the old *Majestic*, once the pride of the Channel Fleet and newly appointed as a flagship, anchored with her torpedo nets out. In a desperate attempt to protect the battleship

she had been surrounded by a screen of colliers and transports, but Otto Hersing waited until a gap opened for a moment between two ships, and fired a single torpedo. The net-cutter did its work, the torpedo went straight through the nets, and within seven minutes the old ship capsized in only 50 ft of water.

The loss of three battleships off the beaches meant that it was no longer possible to give heavy fire-support and the battleships were withdrawn. The French ships went to Corfu and four British pre-dreadnoughts were sent to Taranto to strengthen the already-strong Italian Navy in its task of coping with the Austro-Hungarian Fleet in the Adriatic. The old ships saw a lot of activity in the Mediterranean but very little action, apart from bombardments carried out by Italian ships in northern Italy from 1916 onwards. The most curious career of all the old ships is that of the little French coast-defence ship *Requin*. Laid down in 1879,

completed in 1885 and modernized, she had been stricken from the effective list in 1908 and was not listed in any 1914 reference book. But, like many other French warships, she was still used for training and in August 1914 was stationed at Bizerta as local guardship. From there she went to the Suez Canal in December 1914 to help repel the Turkish attack on Egypt, and she took part in a massive bombardment of Gaza in November 1917.

Odd uses were also found for the old *Majestic* class. Early in 1915 the *Hannibal*, *Magnificent*, *Mars* and *Victorious* were disarmed to provide 12-in gun turrets for a new class of eight 'monitors'. These were shallow-draught ships designed to bombard the coast of Belgium, now under what promised to be long-term occupation by the right flank of the German Army. They bore little resemblance to the monitors of the 1860s, but they had the shallow draught and single gun turret so characteristic of Ericsson's creations. The four disarmed battleships were then used as troop transports and sent out to the Dardanelles. The *Jupiter* was sent to Archangel in North Russia at the end of 1914 to clear a path through the ice, and she created a record by being the first ship ever to dock in that port as early as February. Like the *Caesar*, she had an active career and did not return to the United Kingdom until 1918, the oldest British battleships still in commission.

Several ships were altered in various ways, usually to improve their fire-control, but the *London* was unique. In January 1918 she emerged from a year-long conversion to a large minelayer. Her 12-in guns were removed and a continuous mine deck was installed at main deck level. Most other navies made use of their old ships for patrol work and shore bombardment, but the German Navy paid off many of its old coast-defence ships and pre-dreadnoughts in 1915-16. The Germans lacked the manpower to keep too many useless ships in commission, and as they were virtually confined to the Baltic and North Sea they had no need for ships on distant stations.

This busy life led by the older battleships took its toll in casualties from mines and submarine torpedoes. In contrast the dreadnoughts led such sheltered lives that comparatively few were lost. The nature of the conflict in the North Sea meant that virtually all British and German dreadnoughts were committed to watching each other, apart from the few British ships despatched to the Falklands and the Dardanelles and the German ships involved against the Russians in 1916-17. The significant exception to this was the battle-cruiser *Goeben*, the only German capital ship on a foreign station at the outbreak of war. She escaped from British battle-cruisers just before the expiry of the Anglo-French ultimatum and reached Turkey, where she was first interned and then purchased. Renamed the *Yavuz Sultan Selim* she embroiled Turkey in the war by attacking the Russians at Sevastopol. She was in action with the Russian Black Sea Fleet more than once, fired on the *Queen Elizabeth* in April 1915, was mined and bombed. On January 20, 1918, she and a light cruiser sallied out of the Dardanelles and sank two British monitors off Imbros. Despite being mined twice and running aground immediately afterwards and being bombed by British aircraft, she was towed off by the old battleship *Torgud Res* (sister of the *Hairredin Barbarossa* mentioned earlier) and was finally scrapped in 1971 after 60 years of service.

FROM JUTLAND TO SCAPA FLOW

SMS *Baden*
Designed to counter the firepower of the Royal Navy's *Queen Elizabeth* class, the German ships were slower and intended to fight only in the comparatively sheltered conditions of the North Sea
Displacement: 28,000 tons *Length:* 170 m
Amament: 8×380-mm, 16×150-mm, 8×88-mm, 5×600-mm torpedo tubes *Max speed:* 22¼ knots

Bayern class

Name	Completed	Fate
Baden	Oct 1916	Sunk as target 1921
Bayern	Mar 1916	Scrapped 1935

USS New Mexico
The first major warship to use electric transmission, *New Mexico* was armed with a new type of 14-in gun and was unusual for the period in having a clipper bow. Power was provided by geared turbines

The leading navies virtually stopped building any new capital ships at the outbreak of the war, although ships under construction were nearly all accelerated. The Germans were badly hit by the Army's overriding claims to heavy guns and steel, and the third ship of the *Derfflinger* class, the *Hindenburg*, was not completed until mid-1917. Only two of the four *Bayern* class were completed by mid-1916; the *Bayern* was still working up in the Baltic at the time of the Battle of Jutland, when her 15-in guns might have been useful. Seven battle-cruisers laid down in 1915-1916 were never completed.

The British completed five of their eight *Royal Sovereign* class ships in 1916-17; the remaining three were replaced by two battle-cruisers, *Renown* and *Repulse*, but unfortunately the design of this pair was approved by Lord Fisher, who had returned in triumph as First Sea Lord late in 1914. Although armed with 15-in guns and capable of 32 knots they had no more armour than the old *Invincible* class of 1908. When *Repulse* arrived at Scapa Flow in August 1916 a horrified Admiral Jellicoe sent her straight back into dock to have some extra magazine protection added. Three other Fisher-inspired freaks are worth

Displacement: 32,000 tons *Length:* 624 ft
Armament: 12 × 14-in, 14 × 5-in, 4 × 3-in, 2 × 21-in torpedo tubes *Armour:* 14-in belt, 9/18-in turrets *Max speed:* 21 knots

New Mexico class

Name	Completed	Fate
New Mexico	May 1918	Scrapped from 1947
Mississippi	Dec 1917	Scrapped from 1956
Idaho	Mar 1919	Scrapped from 1947

HMS Glorious
Widely regarded as grotesque failures, the *Courageous* and *Glorious* later found fame after their conversion to aircraft carriers. In their original form they mounted extremely heavy armament on a light cruiser hull with very little armour protection
Displacement: 22,700 tons full load *Length:* 735 ft *Armament:* 8 × 15-in, 18 × 4-in, 2 × 3-in AA, 2 × 21-in torpedo tubes *Armour:* 2/3-in belt, 9-in turrets, 3/4/1-in decks *Max speed:* 31 knots

Courageous class

Name	Completed	Fate
Courageous	Jan 1917	Torpedoed 1939
Glorious	Jan 1917	Sunk 1940

SMS Hindenburg, *sister of the* Derfflinger. *They were possibly the best capital ships of the First World War, with a very battleworthy combination of gunpower, armour and speed*

Imperial War Museum

mentioning: the 15-in-gunned 'large cruisers' *Glorious* and *Courageous* and their 18-in gunned half-sister *Furious*. With only 3-in armour they embodied the Fisher ideals of speed and gunpower without armour pushed beyond the bounds of logic, and by no stretch of the imagination could they be rated as capital ships. On the only occasion the *Glorious* and *Courageous* were in action, off Heligoland in November 1917, they suffered more damage from German light cruisers than they were able to inflict themselves.

The British had not intended to build any more capital ships, on the basis that the war would be over by Christmas. The Cabinet had only given approval to build the *Repulse* and *Renown* on the strength of the battle-cruisers' showing at the Battle of the Falklands, but in 1915 news leaked out that the Germans were building 15-in-gunned battle-cruisers, and so a new super-*Queen Elizabeth* design was prepared. This was the *Hood* class, drastically re-cast after Jutland from 36,300-ton battle-cruisers with 9-in armour belts to 41,200-ton fast battle-ships with 12-in belts. In other respects they were merely enlarged *Queen Elizabeth*s with another five or six knots' speed. Work did not start until just before Jutland, and when news of the slow progress in German shipyards filtered through three were slowed

down in 1917, leaving only the *Hood* to be launched in August 1918. For those who are superstitious it might have seemed unwise to have the ship christened by Lady Hood, the widow of the admiral who lost his life so tragically in HMS *Invincible* at Jutland.

Battleship design improved little during the war, apart from the British invention of anti-torpedo 'bulges', which were fitted to new ships in 1916-17. But equipment and particularly fire-control improved radically. Ships were fitted with more searchlights to improve night-fighting, range-clocks to concentrate fire, enlarged bridges to improve efficiency and accommodation for personnel, etc. Torpedo nets disappeared completely, the Germans being the last to discard them after Jutland. The biggest single change was the British introduction of aircraft platforms in 1917 to allow fighters and reconnaissance biplanes to be flown off at sea. The fighters were needed to curb the German Navy's Zeppelins, which repeatedly gave away the position of British warships, and by the end of the war the Grand Fleet had a large number of its battleships and battle-cruisers equipped with two aircraft apiece.

When the Armistice came on 11 November, 1918, it brought to an end the era of battleship supremacy. In little more than 20 years

it had grown enormously in fighting power and size, and had come to dominate the naval scene in a remarkable way, but its days were numbered. The enormous fleets which had been existing in 1914 solely to do battle with one another had been severely restricted throughout the war by the threat of mines and torpedoes, and far more had been lost to these methods than to the guns of other battleships. In November 1918 the Royal Navy had 60 battleships on the Effective List, but 18 of those were pre-dreadnoughts and 14 were 12-in-gunned dreadnoughts, most of them with thin armour, leaving only 28 ships armed with 13.5-in, 14-in or 15-in guns. There would be further battleships, much bigger and better armed, but never again would the battleship dominate the oceans and be the sole arbiter of sea power.

Symbolically, the battle fleet which had started the race towards war, the German High Seas Fleet, surrendered to the British off the Firth of Forth ten days after the Armistice. Fourteen dreadnought battle-ships and battle-cruisers steamed across to surrender, and passed between long lines of British, American and French warships before proceeding to Scapa Flow. There they rotted until 21 June, 1919, when the entire fleet was scuttled.

Battleship Losses 1914-18

Audacious (GB) – mined off Northern Ireland 27 October 1914
Bulwark (GB) – blew up at Sheerness 26 November 1914
Mussddieh (Turkey) – torpedoed in Dardanelles by Br. submarine 13 December 1914
Formidable (GB) – torpedoed by U-Boat in Channel 1 January 1915
Bouvet (FR) – mined at Dardanelles 18 March 1915
Irresistible (GB) – mined at Dardanelles 18 March 1915
Ocean (GB) – mined at Dardanelles 18 March 1915
Goliath (GB) – torpedoed by Turkish TB at Dardanelles 13 May 1915
Triumph (GB) – torpedoed by U-Boat at Dardanelles 25 May 1915
Majestic (GB) – torpedoed by U-Boat at Dardanelles 27 May 1915
Hairredin Barbarossa (Turkey) – torpedoed by Br. submarine 8 August 1915
Benedetto Brin (It) – blew up at Brindisi 28 September 1915
King Edward VII (GB) – mined off Cape Wrath 6 January 1916
Russell (GB) – mined off Malta 27 April 1916
Invincible (GB) – blew up at Battle of Jutland 31 May 1916
Indefatigable (GB) – blew up at Battle of Jutland 31 May 1916
Queen Mary (GB) – blew up at Battle of Jutland 31 May 1916
Pommern (Ger) – torpedoed at Battle of Jutland 1 June 1916
Lutzow (Ger) – scuttled after heavy damage at Jutland 1 June 1916
Leonardo da Vinci (It) – blew up at Taranto 2 August 1916
Impertritsa Maria (Russ) – blew up at Sevastopol 20 October 1916
Suffren (Fr) – torpedoed by U-Boat in Mediterranean 26 November 1916
Regina Margherita (It) – mined off Valona 11 December 1916
Gaulois (Fr) – torpedoed by U-Boat in Mediterranean 27 December 1916
Peresviet (Russ) – mined off Port Said 5 January 1917
Cornwallis (GB) – torpedoed by U-Boat in Mediterranean 9 January 1917
Tsukuba (Jap) – blew up at Yokosuka 14 January 1917
Danton (Fr) – torpedoed by U-Boat in Mediterranean 19 March 1917
Vanguard (GB) – blew up at Scapa Flow 9 July 1917
Slava (Russ) – wrecked by gunfire and scuttled in Moon Sound, Eastern Baltic 17 October 1917
Wien (A-H) – torpedoed by Italian MTB at Trieste 10 December 1917
Szent Istvan (A-H) – torpedoed by Italian MTB off Premuda 10 June 1918
Svobodnaya Rossia (Russ) – scuttled off Novorossiisk 18 June 1918
Viribus Unitis (A-H) – sunk by Italian limpet mine at Pola 10 October 1918
Britannia (GB) – torpedoed off Cape Trafalgar by U-Boat 9 November 1918

Bundesarchiv

SMS Bayern *seen at the surrender of the High Sea Fleet. At last the enemy, last seen through the smoke of Jutland, was there in close-up. After 1916 the morale of the German fleet had been steadily eroded as key personnel were drafted to U-boats and destroyers. At Scapa, isolation, dirt and acute shortage of food contributed to a further drastic fall in morale. Main picture – the end, June 21, 1919 and* SMS Bayern *heads for the bottom of the Flow*

Imperial War Museum

BATTLESHIPS SINCE 1919
Antony Preston

The scuttling of the High Seas Fleet at Scapa Flow and the triumphant lines of British and American battleships that steamed past in review seemed to mark the high point of the battleship's power at sea. The great Battle of Jutland, however, had failed to win the war in an afternoon and new challengers, the submarine and aircraft, were waiting in the wings.

Before the Second World War the battleship had to adapt to the constrictions of disarmament treaties and the new threats to its supremacy, but the rebirth of the German Navy and the Japanese challenge in the Pacific rekindled faith in the power of the big gun. The Second World War tested that faith and from Taranto to the destruction of the greatest battleship of all time, the *Yamato*, it was found to be misplaced.

Meanwhile some of the most fascinating ships ever built had been tested in action and this book is a brilliant evocation of the greatest ships that fought at sea from the strange products of the Washington Treaty to the reborn *New Jersey* firing 16-in broadsides off the coast of Vietnam.

CONTENTS

John Batchelor

The Yamato, *pride of the Imperial Japanese Navy. She was the greatest and the last of the battleships to be sunk in action.*

The Treaty for the Limitation of Naval Armament
'CUT DOWN BY WASHINGTON'

The brand-new battle-cruiser HMS Hood *belches smoke as she ploughs through a heavy sea off the Isle of Arran while running her acceptance trials in 1920*

National Maritime Museum

When the First World War ended, the major navies seemed about to plunge into another battleship arms race like the one which had occurred between Great Britain and Germany from 1904 onwards. But this time there was a difference. The surrender and the scuttling of the High Seas Fleet at Scapa Flow in 1919 eliminated the second most powerful navy in the world. This left the Royal Navy still in an apparently unchallengeable position, followed by Japan and the United States, with France and Italy trailing some way behind.

These figures are misleading, for the British were in a much worse position than the Americans and Japanese, with all their existing battle-cruisers badly underarmoured and a third of their total strength armed with 12-in guns. By comparison the Americans had authorised in 1916 the construction of ten battleships and six battle-cruisers armed with 16-in guns, and in 1918 the Japanese had followed suit with eight battleships and battle-cruisers similarly armed. The Americans had made no secret of the fact that they wanted to overtake the British as the leading naval power in the world. Their main rival was Japan, for the United States wished to expand its trade in the Pacific, but some Big-Navy interests in Washington felt inclined to take on the British as well if they refused to accept with good grace. The entry of the United States

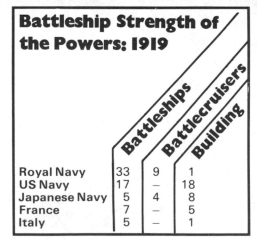

Battleship Strength of the Powers: 1919	Battleships	Battlecruisers	Building
Royal Navy	33	9	1
US Navy	17	—	18
Japanese Navy	5	4	8
France	7	—	5
Italy	5	—	1

into the war in 1917 hamstrung the battleship programme, for steel and manpower were switched to building the destroyers and merchant shipping needed by the Allies. Only one of the 16 ships authorised by Congress was laid down in 1917; the others had to wait until 1919, and the last two were not actually started until mid-1921. The Japanese did slightly better, with two battleships begun in 1917 and 1918, but—like the Americans—they could not start the others until two or three years after the war. To match the American programme the Japanese drew up their so-called '8-8

Programme', eight battleships and eight battle-cruisers, all to be started by the beginning of 1927 at the latest.

It was not only the increase in gun-calibre to 16-in which made these ships remarkable. Displacement jumped from the 32,000-ton mark in the Japanese *Nagato* class and the American *Colorado* class to 40,000-43,000 tons in the *Amagi* and *South Dakota* classes. The Americans favoured a relatively modest speed of 23 knots for their biggest battleships, but the Japanese *Nagato* and *Tosa* classes were intended to be 26½-knotters. Against this the British had only the *Queen Elizabeth*s, with 15-in guns and a speed of 24½ knots, and one survivor of the four *Hood* class, 41,000 tons and eight 15-in guns. The British, alone out of all the Allied navies, had first-hand knowledge of what happened to battleships when they were torpedoed, hit by shells or mined. Not only had their ships been much more exposed to action damage, but there had also been a chance throughout 1919 to study the design of German capital ships. German ships had suffered a certain amount of battle damage but not as much, and of course the extinction of the High Seas Fleet was followed by the dispersal of that talented group of constructors who had designed the battleships and battle-cruisers which fought at Jutland.

Armed with this knowledge and with the results of detailed tests against target ships, the British had good reason to be uneasy about their position. The Director of Naval Construction did not regard the new battle-cruiser *Hood* as a particularly suitable design, and had even suggested that the ship should be scrapped on the stocks to make way for something better. After a series of exhaustive tests against the German battleship *Baden* (the only large ship not to be successfully scuttled at Scapa Flow) and firing trials against the disarmed *Superb*, the British drew up a series of designs to outclass both the Japanese and American ships. Known as the 'G.3' design, the first class consisted of four 48,000-ton battle-cruisers armed with nine 16-in guns and capable of 32 knots. They were to be followed by 43,500-ton battleships armed with nine 18-in guns, formidable weapons capable of firing a 3200-lb shell nearly 30,000 yards.

Bulge Protection

The 'G.3's were among the most powerful capital ships ever laid down, and were certainly the most advanced ships of their day. The armour arrangement was an extension of the 'all-or-nothing'. scheme pioneered in the *Nevada* of 1911, but the side armour was sloped inboard to increase its resistance to plunging shells, and the 'bulge' protection against torpedoes was incorporated into the hull to prevent a reduction of speed. The ships were 856 ft long overall, and to avoid spreading the belt armour over too great an area the triple 16-in turrets were concentrated forward, two before the extensive bridge structure and the third between the bridge and the funnels. The massive tower bridge was another bold step dictated by war experience. The windy platforms in older ships had provided little shelter for signalmen and bridge personnel, and it was decided to accept the risk of a large target in order to provide dry, comfortable accommodation for the key personnel who controlled the ship in action. This policy was amply vindicated in the Second World War, but no other navy followed the British lead.

The US Navy now found that it had a tiger by the tail. The 1916 programme was way behind schedule; the Japanese had responded with ships as powerful; and now, to make matters worse, the British had woken up and produced designs which would eclipse their own. The British shipyards had shown their staggering proficiency by building the *Renown* and *Repulse* (a completely novel design) in 18 months, and nobody in Washington doubted that the British would have their ships in service before the American giants.

The new arms race was also preoccupying the State Department in Washington. Rivalry with Japan was becoming more acute, with both the USA and Japan facing the

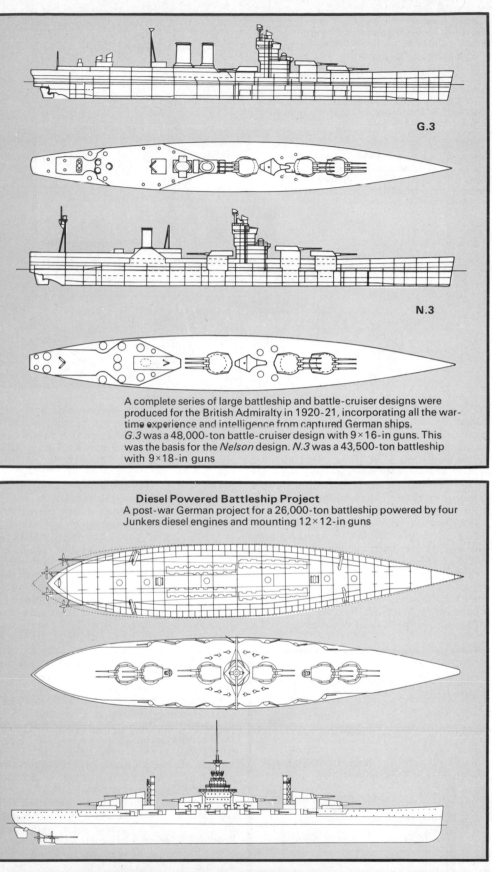

G.3

N.3

A complete series of large battleship and battle-cruiser designs were produced for the British Admiralty in 1920-21, incorporating all the war-time experience and intelligence from captured German ships. *G.3* was a 48,000-ton battle-cruiser design with 9 × 16-in guns. This was the basis for the *Nelson* design. *N.3* was a 43,500-ton battleship with 9 × 18-in guns

Diesel Powered Battleship Project
A post-war German project for a 26,000-ton battleship powered by four Junkers diesel engines and mounting 12 × 12-in guns

After 1919 the battle-cruiser Repulse *could be distinguished from her sister* Renown *by the strake of 9-in armour amidships. In 1936 she had a further partial modernisation giving her an aircraft hangar and catapult*

National Maritime Museum

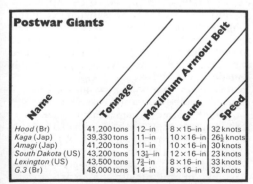

Postwar Giants

Name	Tonnage	Maximum Armour Belt	Guns	Speed
Hood (Br)	41,200 tons	12–in	8 × 15–in	32 knots
Kaga (Jap)	39,330 tons	11–in	10 × 16–in	26½ knots
Amagi (Jap)	41,200 tons	11–in	10 × 16–in	30 knots
South Dakota (US)	43,200 tons	13½–in	12 × 16–in	23 knots
Lexington (US)	43,500 tons	7⅞–in	8 × 16–in	33 knots
G.3 (Br)	48,000 tons	14–in	9 × 16–in	32 knots

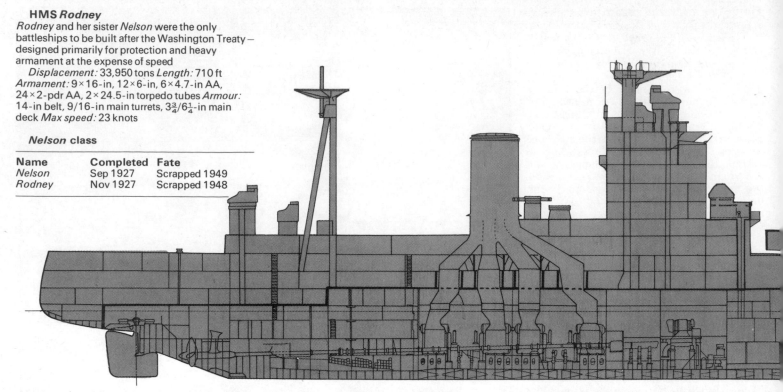

HMS Rodney
Rodney and her sister *Nelson* were the only battleships to be built after the Washington Treaty – designed primarily for protection and heavy armament at the expense of speed
Displacement: 33,950 tons *Length:* 710 ft
Armament: 9×16-in, 12×6-in, 6×4.7-in AA, 24×2-pdr AA, 2×24.5-in torpedo tubes *Armour:* 14-in belt, 9/16-in main turrets, 3¾/6¼-in main deck *Max speed:* 23 knots

Nelson class

Name	Completed	Fate
Nelson	Sep 1927	Scrapped 1949
Rodney	Nov 1927	Scrapped 1948

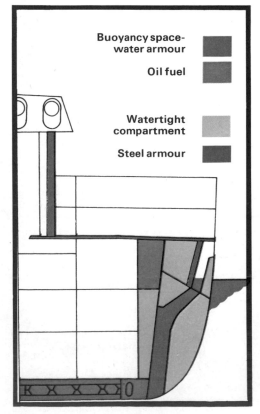

Buoyancy space-water armour

Oil fuel

Watertight compartment

Steel armour

problems of the post-war recession. Their respective economies had been greatly expanded to cope with war-production for the other Allies, and now these markets had virtually disappeared. Japan had clashed with the United States in 1915 over an attempt to coerce China, and when the US Navy began preparations to fortify its base at Cavita in the Philippines towards the end of the First World War the Japanese made it clear through diplomatic channels that they would regard any such move as a *casus belli*. The Japanese felt, with some justification, that they had not spent millions of yen and many thousands of soldiers' lives to expel the Russians from Manchuria only to have another American Port Arthur.

The Big-Navy party in Washington had a simple answer to all these problems: scrap the 1916 programme entirely and replace it with bigger and better ships that would cow the British and the Japanese. But at this point Congress intervened to bring the whole discussion back to reality. There was no hope of getting the money to finish the existing programme, for the US taxpayer was not interested in financing a huge navy two or three years after the end of a costly 'war to end wars', to say nothing of widening the Panama Canal to take the 'Mark II' version battleships. Also, the British were linked to the Japanese by treaty, and the State Department was not wholly convinced by some of the admirals' arguments about fighting both the British and the Japanese simultaneously. The only sane solution was to bring the whole mad scheme to an end by negotiation, just as the British had done with the French in 1904 and the Japanese in 1902, to free themselves to concentrate on matching Germany.

In response to an invitation from President Harding, delegates from the USA, Great Britain, Japan, France and Italy met in Washington on 21 November, 1921 for a conference on naval arms limitation. It was an historic occasion, the first time that the principal naval powers had met to discuss ways of fixing the numbers of warships by treaty, and of fixing the characteristics of the ships themselves. The President began the proceedings by proposing a 'battleship holiday', a ten-year ban on the construction of capital ships; he went on to propose the scrapping of 845,000 tons of American battleship tonnage, 583,000 tons of British construction and 449,000 tons of Japanese construction. In this sense the Americans won the political side of the conference. They had more ships under construction than anyone else, and by offering to scrap them all they laid the onus of wrecking the possibility of peace, parsimony and international disarmament on the shoulders of the British and the other foreign delegations.

In the technical sense, however, it was the British who 'won' the conference. The Japanese and American delegates fought tooth-and-nail to retain ships which had been designed without benefit of combat experience; the British fought for the right to build two ships in which they could incorporate all the lessons of the late war. Furthermore the British delegation at Washington had far superior technical briefing to the others; all technical points raised in the committees were referred back to the DNC and other technical departments for discussion. To cite one example, when the US Navy proposed limiting battleships to a tonnage of 32,500 tons the British immediately insisted on 35,000 tons on the DNC's advice. Design work on a smaller edition of the *G.3* to meet the probable size-limit which would be fixed was going on throughout the conference, so that the delegates could be constantly briefed on points that must not be conceded. The best example of this was the choice of Standard Tonnage. The displacement tonnage of warships had for the previous 60 years been listed as 'normal' or sometimes 'Navy List' for the tonnage of the ship as built, without complement, but with ammunition and the normal allowance of fuel and boiler feedwater. 'Full load' tonnage was the figure for the maximum fuel, reserve feedwater and ammunition and the ship's company.

The British delegation made a stand on the matter of defining tonnage, and insisted that a new tonnage definition should be drawn up, including men, ammunition and stores but not fuel and reserve feedwater. At the time this was put forward as necessary because British ships had to be capable of steaming greater distances in defence of the Empire; it was felt that if fuel and reserve feedwater were included in the tonnage, British ships would have to have thinner armour. The real reason was that the British had designed 'water protection' or liquid-loaded layers for the new battleships, a method of admitting fuel or seawater into a 'sandwich' compartment inside the anti-torpedo protection, with the aim of damping the effect of a torpedo hit. If fuel and feedwater could be left out of the tonnage total it would be much easier to conceal the existence of this novel type of protection,

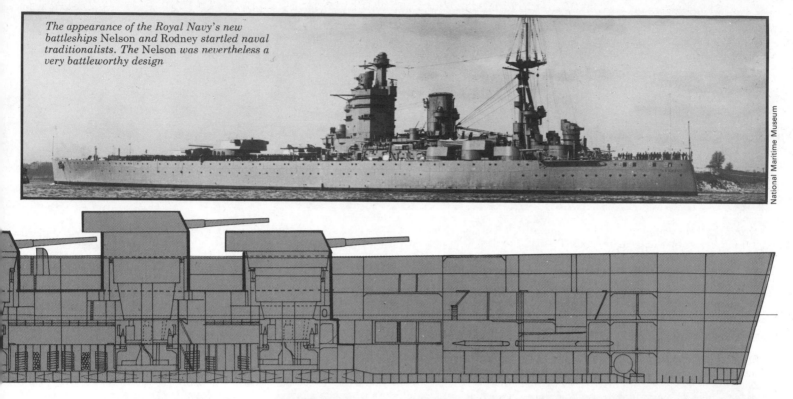

The appearance of the Royal Navy's new battleships Nelson *and* Rodney *startled naval traditionalists. The* Nelson *was nevertheless a very battleworthy design*

National Maritime Museum

and in fact the British managed to hide it from the outside world for 40 years.

The delegates finally settled on a standard displacement of 35,000 tons and a maximum gun calibre of 16-in, but the bitterest wrangling was reserved for the discussion on total strength. Eventually it was agreed that the British should be allowed 22 capital ships (580,450 tons), to be reduced to 18 by 1927; the Americans 18 (500,650 tons); but the Japanese, the French and Italians 10 each. This was accepted by the Japanese with ill grace as a 'Rolls-Rolls-Ford' arrangement, but like all the other delegations present they knew that their government was not prepared to pay for a new fleet. On 6 February, 1922 the Washington Treaty, more properly known as the Treaty for the Limitation of Armament, was signed. The British could build two new 35,000-ton ships armed with 16-in guns, the US Navy could complete one of its 16-in gunned ships and the Japanese could complete both theirs. The French and Italians were in such financial difficulties that they had given up all ideas of completing their wartime construction.

Although the British negotiators had good reason to be satisfied with themselves, the DNC and his team still faced tremendous technical problems. The *G.3* design had been a 32-knot ship protected by 14-in armour on the side of 5½-in decks. Many features had to be sacrificed or modified to reduce this 48,000-ton design to 35,000 tons. The options were limited: the 16-in guns had to be retained and so either armour or speed must be reduced. With no hesitation the latter course was followed, and the installed power was slashed from 160,000 to 45,000 shaft horsepower. This meant a speed of only 23 knots, but even so it was two knots faster than the *Colorado* and only two knots less than the Japanese *Nagato*. To further reduce the hull length the third triple 16-in gun turret was moved forward to a position just behind the two foremost turrets, and the 6-in secondary guns were similarly bunched together aft. These changes saved 15,000 tons and 150 ft in length, but produced a most unusual profile,

With the Colorado *class the US Navy adopted 16-in guns for the first time, following the Japanese lead. Both navies were, however, following the layout of the British* Queen Elizabeth *design of 1915*

US Navy

particularly as the designers retained the massive 'tower' bridge which had been a feature of the original design.

HMS *Nelson* was completed on the Tyne in June 1927, and her sister *Rodney* followed her into service from her Birkenhead builders two months later. The decision to build two new battleships had not been received with unanimous approval, for a strong lobby in navalist circles wanted smaller battleships, and an even more vociferous air-power lobby wanted the battleship to be replaced by bomber aircraft. The outlandish appearance of the ships did not help, and as the critics knew nothing of the hidden factors in their design, particularly the 2000 tons of water protection not included in their declared tonnage under

the treaty, the battleships were compared unfavourably with foreign designs. They were known as the 'Cherry Tree' class, cut down by Washington, but the unkindest cut of all was the sailors' nickname for them— 'Nelsol' and 'Rodnol'—in memory of a group of fleet oilers whose names ended in 'ol'; this was a reference to the position of the funnel so far aft.

6-in round uptakes

14-in belt

15-in round 16-in gun trunks

6-in round 6-in gun trunks

16-in armour round directors

16-in round control position

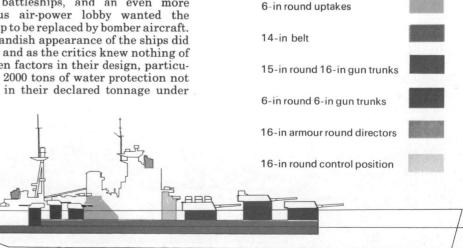

The Royal Sovereigns *were slower and smaller than the* Queen Elizabeths *but with some modernisation they gave extensive service in the Second World War*

National Maritime Museum

Ironically, in stopping the development of the battleship the Washington Treaty was responsible for advancing another type of warship, one which would eventually outstrip the battleship in destructive power, complexity and cost. Aircraft carriers had been developed during the First World War, but until 1922 the ships built or converted had all been relatively small. The large hulls made redundant by the treaty in 1922 all offered tempting opportunities to try out schemes for large aircraft carriers, but without the cost of building them from scratch. The US Navy took the incomplete battle-cruisers *Lexington* and *Saratoga* in hand and the Japanese announced that they would convert the similar-sized *Akagi* and *Amagi*. The British had already converted one of Fisher's freak 'large light cruisers', HMS *Furious*, from a paper tiger with two 18-in guns into a fleet carrier, and chose to disarm and convert her half-sisters *Glorious* and *Courageous* along similar lines. The Japanese had almost started work on their two battle-cruisers when the great earthquake of 1 September, 1923 wrecked the building slip at Yokosuka Dockyard. The hull of the *Amagi* was so badly distorted by the shock that it was decided to dismantle her, but the two *Kaga*-class battleship hulls were still in existence, and they were only 60 ft shorter. The hull of the *Kaga* was therefore reprieved and her conversion on similar lines to *Akagi* was started soon afterwards.

The 'battleship holiday' did not mean the end of work on battleships. For one thing the appearance of the 16-in gun made all the big navies conscious of the weak protection of their older battleships, and for another the lessons of the late war indicated many improvements that could be made. The British started immediately after the Armistice by re-armouring the thin-skinned *Repulse* with 9-in armour, an essential improvement which her sister did not get until 1926. In 1924 the first of the *Queen Elizabeth* class was taken in hand for improvements, including the addition of 'bulges' to the hull, strengthening anti-aircraft armament and trunking the funnels together to reduce the tendency to smoke out the bridgework. The single-funnelled *Royal Sovereigns* had no need of such drastic treatment, but some were given a funnel cap to reduce the smoke interference.

Maximum Fighting Value

With so many coal-fired ships the US and Japanese navies felt bound to devote money to reboilering their older ships and converting them to oil-burning. But the Japanese went even further. Still nursing a grievance over what they saw as a conspiracy beteen the Americans and their stooges the British to relegate Japan to second-class status, they planned a careful programme of reconstruction to extract the maximum fighting value out of their ships. Even if no new battleships could be built for ten years, each

Japanese battleship would exploit the reconstruction clauses of the treaty to the full. It was during this period that the complex 'pagoda' foremasts began to appear in Japanese ships. In reality these were only a cluster of platforms added to the original tripod masting in most cases, although the *Nagato*s went one better by having a pentapod mast.

In 1927 the Royal Navy received its two new battleships, the *Nelson* and *Rodney*, but had to say goodbye to the three *King George V* class and the *Thunderer* to reduce the numbers to 20, the same as the United States. The following year the Italians paid off the old *Dante Alighieri*, reducing their total of battleships to four, the four pre-dreadnoughts of the *Regina Elena* class having been disposed of between 1923 and 1927. The French retained their four old ships of the *Danton* class, for all their antique design, although after 1927 they were used only for training.

The French and Italian navies suffered even more than those of the major naval powers. Their ships were generally older and less powerful than the British, American and Japanese counterparts; the Italian vessels lacked heavy guns and the French ships were poorly protected. To compensate for this, special clauses in the treaty allowed France to start building a new capital ship in 1927 and another in 1929, while the Italians were permitted to build 70,000 tons of new construction. Neither the French nor the Italians took advantage of these clauses, although design work started in both countries. The French examined the idea of a

HMS *Malaya*
One of the *Queen Elizabeth* class extensively modernised between the wars. She was re-engined, the twin funnels were trunked into one, AA armament was increased and a central aircraft hangar with athwartship catapult was installed
Displacement: 31,000 tons *Length:* 600 ft
Armament: 8×15-in, 12×6-in, 8×4-in AA, 16×2-pdr AA

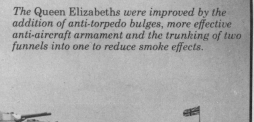

The Queen Elizabeths *were improved by the addition of anti-torpedo bulges, more effective anti-aircraft armament and the trunking of two funnels into one to reduce smoke effects.*

National Maritime Museum

croiseur de combat, or battle-cruiser, capable of handling heavy cruisers and scouting for the Fleet—which sounds dangerously like the original *Invincible*. The Italians even went so far as to divide their 70,000 tons into three parts, and considered building three 23,000-tonners; the idea was dropped when it was pointed out that these vessels would be inferior even to the existing ships.

Two navies have not been mentioned so far, the German and the Russian. For the moment the Russian Navy, or Red Fleet as it had been christened, was wallowing in the chaos that followed the Revolution and the Civil War. Those ships that survived the vicissitudes of 1917–22 were in appalling condition, and Lenin wisely decided after the Civil War that Russia's industrial position was too weak to support a large fleet. All the pre-dreadnoughts were scrapped, and one of the four surviving dreadnoughts, the *Poltava*, was 'cannibalised' for spares. Only the *Petropavlovsk* (renamed *Marat*) and *Oktyabskaya Revolutsia* (ex-*Gangut*) were back in working order by 1925–26. Although the might of the High Seas Fleet had been obliterated in the depths of Scapa Flow, the Treaty of Versailles allowed Germany to retain eight old pre-dreadnoughts as coast-defence ships. Replacement of these was allowed, but only on a ship-for-ship basis, subject to a limit of 10,000 tons and guns of 11-in calibre. In 1926 the oldest ship, the *Zähringen*, was converted to a radio-controlled target. The *Preussen* and *Elsass* followed in 1931–32, and replacements were ordered in 1930. The Versailles Treaty was not concerned with naval limitations as such, but the framers of the Washington Treaty had laboured hard to separate the categories of battleship, coast-defence ship and cruiser. They reckoned without the tenacity and skill of German designers, however, who quite deliberately strove to build a ship which could fit into the 10,000-ton limit and yet act as a commerce raider on the high seas. And furthermore, by giving the ship the 11-in guns permitted under the Versailles Treaty, they made her much more than a match for all the big, expensive heavy cruisers permitted by the Washington Treaty.

Fleet Reductions After Washington

Existing Ships to be Retained	Existing Ships to be Scrapped	New Ships to be Completed	New Ships to be Scrapped
Great Britain			
Hood	Indomitable	Nelson	Invincible*
Renown	Inflexible	Rodney	Inflexible*
Repulse	Bellerophon		Indomitable
Royal Sovereign	Superb/Temeraire		Indefatigable*
Royal Oak	Collingwood		
Revenge	St Vincent		
Ramilles	New Zealand		
Resolution	Australia (RAN)		
Queen Elizabeth	Neptune		
Warspite	Orion		
Barham	Colossus		
Malaya	Hercules		
Valiant	Monarch		
Tiger	Conqueror		
Iron Duke	Lion		
Marlborough	Princess Royal		
Emperor of India	Courageous		
Benbow	Glorious		
King George V***			
Ajax***			
Centurion***			
Thunderer****			

*These names were unofficially allocated to the G.3 class
**To be converted to aircraft carriers
***To be scrapped in 1927 on completion of *Nelson* and *Rodney*
****Used for training, to be scrapped on completion of *Nelson* and *Rodney*

Existing Ships to be Retained	Existing Ships to be Scrapped	New Ships to be Completed	New Ships to be Scrapped
United States			
Florida	South Carolina	Colorado	Washington
Utah	Michigan	Maryland	South Dakota
Wyoming	Delaware	West Virginia	Indiana
Arkansas	North Dakota		Montana
New York			North Carolina
Texas			Iowa
Nevada			Massachusetts
Oklahoma			Lexington*
Pennsylvania			Constellation
Arizona			Saratoga*
New Mexico			Ranger
Mississippi			Constitution
Idaho			United States
Tennessee			
California			

*To be converted to aircraft carriers

Existing Ships to be Retained	Existing Ships to be Scrapped	New Ships to be Completed	New Ships to be Scrapped
Japan			
Kongo	Ibuki	Mutsu	Kaga
Kirishima	Kurama		Tosa
Hiei	Aki		Akagi*
Haruna	Satsuma		Amagi*
Fuso	Settsu		Atago
Yamashiro			Takao
Hyuga			
Ise			
Nagato			

Italy

Napoli
Regina Elena
Roma
Vittorio Emmanuele
Dante Alighieri
Conte di Cavour
Giulio Cesare
Leonardo da Vinci*
Andrea Doria
Duilio

*Blown up at Taranto in 1916 and salvaged in 1919, but plans to reconstruct her were subsequently cancelled and she was scrapped in 1923

Existing Ships to be Retained	Existing Ships to be Scrapped		New Ships to be Scrapped
France			
Diderot	République*		Béarn**
Condorcet	Patrie***		Normandie
Vergniaud	Democratie		Languedoc
Jean Bart	Justice		Flandre
Courbet	Vérité		Gascogne
Paris			
France			
Bretagne			
Provence			
Lorraine			

*Disarmed and used as training ship
**To be converted to aircraft carrier
***Hulked as training ship at Toulon

New Construction Programmes
THE SECOND NAVAL RACE

It was small wonder that the appearance of the *Deutschland* in April 1933 created a sensation, or that she was hailed with hysterical delight by the German public, now beginning to fret under the humiliating restrictions of the 1919 treaty. The outside world dubbed her a 'pocket battleship', but to the German Navy she was simply called a *Panzerschiff*, or armoured ship—the best translation of which was armoured cruiser. Despite the exaggerated reports of her capabilities she was not a battleship, but a high-endurance cruiser with ultra-heavy armament and only moderate speed and no better protection than most contemporary cruisers. Two novelties gave the clue to her success: the extensive use of welding to save weight, and the use of diesel motors to give high endurance. Unfortunately, she was not a 10,000-ton ship as defined by the Washington Treaty, and if her admirers had known that her standard displacement was actually 11,700 tons (17 per cent outside the limit) they might not have waxed so enthusiastic. Although contemporary reports had credited her with the staggering range of 19,000 miles at cruising speed, the actual service endurance was about 10,000 miles and the Germans admitted later that the diesel machinery had been something of a disappointment. Two similar half-sisters, the *Admiral Scheer* and *Admiral Graf Spee*, followed in 1934 and 1936.

The *Panzerschiffe* must be regarded as more of a political gesture than a significant contribution to the history of capital-ship design. The experience of the Second World War was to expose the myths about them, and in 1940 the *Kriegsmarine* admitted as much by re-rating the surviving pair as heavy cruisers. They were effective commerce raiders but heavily over-armed for the

The Reichsmarine's *coast-defence battleship* Schlesien *was modernised twice within the terms of the Versailles Treaty. The old ships' age was the excuse for building the pocket battleships*

Deutschland—*first of the pocket battleships—seen on completion in 1933. She was hailed in a frenzy of patriotic fervour as a symbol of the rebirth of German naval power*

job, and suffered from having the prestige value of a capital unit. They were five knots slower than the cruisers they were intended to elude, and their cumbersome arrangement of two triple 11-in gun mountings put them at a disadvantage in fighting faster and more manoeuvrable cruisers.

The appearance of the *Deutschland* caused a great disturbance in the carefully regulated balance of battleship strength. The French were immediately worried at the prospect of a German commerce raider cutting communications between France and North Africa, the routes by which troop reinforcements would be ferried in time of war, and if the French took fright the

Italians would inevitably respond to keep the balance. To complicate matters the Big Powers were again signing treaties, this time the London Naval Agreement of 1930, whereby Great Britain, America and Japan agreed to extend the 'battleship holiday' to the end of 1936 and to keep the limitations in force. France refused to ratify the treaty on the grounds that she needed new ships to counter the *Deutschland*, and Italy

Admiral Graf Spee

This pocket battleship saw action, in common with her sisters, during the Spanish Civil War and then carried out commerce raids in the South Atlantic until being intercepted by the British cruisers *Ajax*, *Achilles* and *Exeter*

Displacement: 16,200 tons maximum
Length: 186 m *Armament:* 6×280-mm,
8×150-mm, 6×105-mm, 8.37-mm, 8×20-mm
(from Oct 1939) *Armour:* 60/80-mm side,
140-mm main turrets *Max speed:* 28.5 knots

Deutschland class

Name	Completed	Fate
Lützow (ex-*Deutschland*)	Apr 1933	Blown up by crew May 1945
Admiral Scheer	Nov 1934	Capsized after bombing Apr 1945
Admiral Graf Spee	Jan 1936	Scuttled Dec 1939

predictably did likewise. For her the addition of even one new French capital ship would widen the gap between France's six ships and her own ageing quartet. It must never be forgotten just how important battleships still were as symbols of national prestige, and both France and Italy felt that they had been slighted at Washington, so that there was a degree of malicious pleasure in their refusal to ratify the London agreement. Another factor was the Italians' need to maintain employment in their shipyards as part of Mussolini's policy of using military expenditure to subsidise the economy.

The French decided to build two battle-cruisers of approximately 25,000 tons and armed with 13-in guns. The reason for this was that the British had been advocating a reduction in displacement and size of guns, as part of the constant search for mutual reduction of naval armaments in Europe. The Americans had been very cool about these proposals, and of course the Japanese had no intention of making a unilateral gesture of peace, but the French Navy cast its plans on the assumption that these proposals might become fact.

The ships which resulted were remarkable. Although they were lightly armoured, with a belt varying from 9¾-in to 5¾-in at its lower edge, a great deal of weight was saved by grouping the eight 13-in (330-mm) guns in two quadruple turrets forward, as in the *Nelson* class. But unlike the slow and rather ugly *Nelson*, the *Dunkerque* was an elegant ship with a long, flared forecastle and a balanced silhouette. She was also very fast, reaching 30½ knots on an 8-hr trial. Her sister *Strasbourg* was completed four years later (1936) and reached 31 knots. The 13-in/52 cal gun fired three 1258-lb shells per minute to a distance of 45,800 yards, and had a muzzle velocity of 2803 ft/sec.

The appearance of the *Dunkerque* made the Italians think again, and in 1930 they started work on a new series of 35,000-ton designs to be armed with 15-in or 16-in guns. The British convened another round of fruitless negotiations in Rome in 1931 in an attempt to head off a Franco-Italian arms race, but all that could be agreed was that both nations would be invited to a major conference to be held in London at the end

of 1935. From then until the outbreak of the Second World War the naval treaties became less and less effective in controlling the rate of battleship building. Had the Germans not built their ingenious 'pocket battleships' the new arms race might have been delayed, but it should not be forgotten that the Washington Treaty—despite its limitations—did work remarkably well for a decade.

It was appropriate that the Italians should take the lead in designing the first of a new series of fast battleships. Their battleships had always been capable of a good turn of speed, even in the 1880s, and when they started design work on 35,000-ton designs in 1930 they plumped for a speed of 30 knots. The designers soon discarded the idea of

The impressive lines of the Graf Spee *seen from above as she surges through the water*

having 16-in guns, which would have to be designed from scratch. The Armstrong gun foundry at Pozzuoli was capable of producing the 15-in already designed in England in the First World War for the defunct *Francesco Caracciolo* class, and Ansaldo's factory at Genoa was able to produce a new and more powerful design which fired an 885 kg shell a distance of 42,800 metres at 36° elevation.

The Inspector of Naval Engineering, General Umberto Pugliese, was in charge of the project and designed a totally new scheme of underwater protection. This involved a cylindrical section running longitudinally down the length of the anti-torpedo 'bulge'. In theory a cylindrical

Reduction of Fleets: 1931-6

Retained	Scrapped
Great Britain	
Nelson	Iron Duke*
Rodney	Benbow
Hood	Emperor of India
Renown	Marlborough
Repulse	Tiger
Royal Sovereign	
Royal Oak	
Ramillies	
Resolution	
Revenge	
Queen Elizabeth	
Warspite	
Valiant	
Barham	
Malaya	
United States	
Colorado	Florida
Maryland	Utah*
West Virginia	Wyoming*
Tennessee	
California	
New Mexico	
Mississippi	
Idaho	
Pennsylvania	
Arizona	
Nevada	
Oklahoma	
New York	
Texas	
Arkansas	
Japan	
Mutsu	Hiei*
Nagato	
Hyuga	
Ise	
Fuso	
Yamashiro	
Kongo	
Haruna	
Kirishima	
France	
Dunkerque**	Jean Bart*
Strasbourg**	Condorcet*
Bretagne	Diderot
Provence	Voltaire
Lorraine	Vergniaud*
Courbet	
Paris	
Italy	
Littorio**	
Vittorio Veneto**	
Andrea Doria	
Caio Duilio	
Conte di Cavour	
Guilio Cesare	

*Retained demilitarised

**New Construction

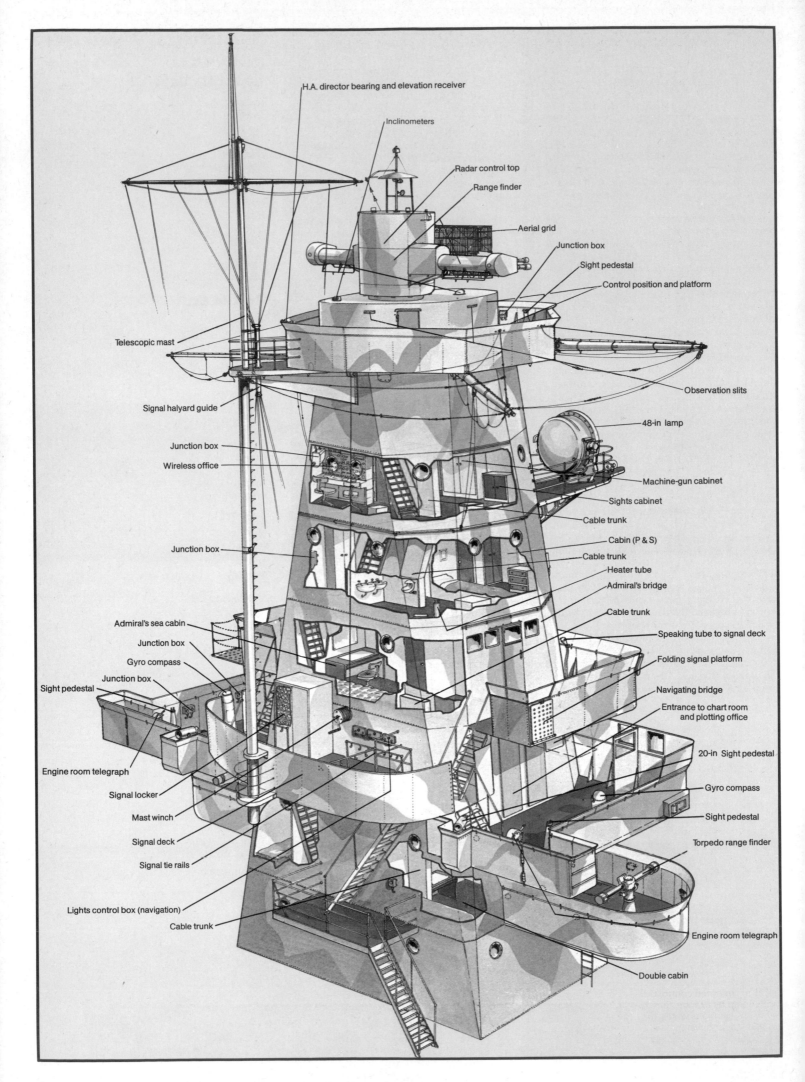

H.A. director bearing and elevation receiver

Inclinometers

Radar control top

Range finder

Aerial grid

Junction box

Sight pedestal

Control position and platform

Telescopic mast

Observation slits

Signal halyard guide

48-in lamp

Junction box

Wireless office

Machine-gun cabinet

Sights cabinet

Cable trunk

Cabin (P & S)

Junction box

Cable trunk

Heater tube

Admiral's bridge

Cable trunk

Admiral's sea cabin

Junction box

Speaking tube to signal deck

Gyro compass

Folding signal platform

Junction box

Navigating bridge

Sight pedestal

Entrance to chart room
and plotting office

20-in Sight pedestal

Engine room telegraph

Gyro compass

Signal locker

Sight pedestal

Mast winch

Torpedo range finder

Signal deck

Signal tie rails

Lights control box (navigation)

Engine room telegraph

Cable trunk

Double cabin

The elegant French battle-cruiser Dunkerque was built in reply to the German pocket battleships to counter a potential threat to France's sea-route to North Africa

Marius Bar

Strasbourg
Designed in response to Germany's construction of the *Deutschland* class of 'pocket battleships,' *Dunkerque* and her sister were fast and fairly heavily armed but had only light armour
Displacement: 35,500 tons full load
Length: 214.5 m *Armament:* 8×330-mm, 16×130-mm, 8×37-mm AA, 32×13.2-mm AA
Armour: 141/241-mm belt, 330-mm main turrets, 130/140-mm main deck *Max speed:* 29½ knots

Dunkerque class

Name	Launched	Fate
Dunkerque	Dec 1932	Scuttled at Toulon 1942
Strasbourg	Dec 1936	Scuttled at Toulon 1942, raised, bombed 1944, raised and scrapped

structure offered maximum resistance to the crushing effect of a torpedo hit and it was hoped that most of the effect would be expended in driving fragments of plating inwards. Another feature was the Ferrati 'triple hull', basically an additional floor to the double bottom to minimise the shock effect of mines. The belt armour was nearly 14 in (350 mm) thick, while the deck thickness reached a maximum of 8 in (207 mm).

Steaming Power
The most impressive aspect of the new ships was their machinery. Four Belluzzo geared turbines delivered 130,000 shaft horsepower for a projected speed of 30 knots less than the French battle-cruisers, but considerably more than any battleships with comparable protection, apart from the British battle-cruiser *Hood*. In practice the four ships of the *Littorio* class reached an average speed of more than 31 knots on trials despite displacing over 41,000 tons in normal conditions. The trials, however, gave a misleading impression of the ships' steaming powers and in practice their sea speed (ie effective maximum at sea) was only 28 knots, making them equal to such ships as the British *King George V* class. Being designed for the Mediterranean, they had less endurance than British or American ships, but even so they carried 3700 tons of oil fuel, the same amount as the *King George V*. The eight Yarrow boilers were

not very economical, however, and endurance at full speed was a miserable 1770 nautical miles.

The first two ships were laid down on 28 October, 1934: the future *Littorio* at Cantieri Ansaldo, Sestri Ponente (Genoa), and the *Vittorio Veneto* at Cantieri Navali Riuniti dell'Adriatico, Trieste. The name-ship of the class (littorio=lictor, the bearer of the fasces in ancient Rome) was launched

Dunkerque
Control tower and superstructure of the *Dunkerque* in close-up. *Dunkerque* differed from her sister *Strasbourg* in design of the control tower, superstructure and the position of the forward range-finder

Admiral Graf Spee
Left: The armoured control tower of the *Graf Spee* surmounted by a range-finder and primitive radar aerial. The Germans were a long way behind in seaborne radar development on the outbreak of war, but they were the first to use gunnery radar in action

The shallow waters of the baltic and the numerous islands forced the Scandinavian navies to retain small coast-defence battleships long after they had disappeared from other leading navies. The Swedish Drottning Victoria *(seen below in 1921) resembled a small pre-dreadnought*

Comparative Armour Protection Systems

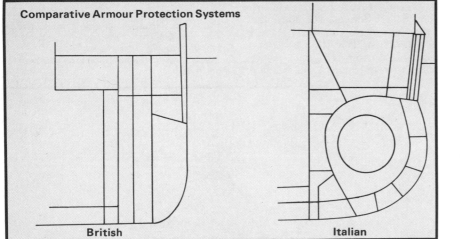

British   **Italian**

The sandwich system of armouring battleships was typical of practise in Royal Navy and US Navy vessels, using void spaces and oil bunkers to maximise resistance to projectiles and blast damage. The Italian Pugliese system of cylindrical armour did not perform well in action.

Andrea Doria

The two ships in this class were designed in 1911 as half-sisters of the *Conte di Cavour* vessels, but they did not see action until the Second World War. By then they had been extensively modernised, but they remained under-armoured

Displacement: 25,200 tons *Length:* 186.9 m
Armament (after conversion): 10×320-mm, 12×135-mm, 10×90-mm, 19×37-mm, 16×20-mm *Armour:* 130/250-mm belt, 240-mm main turrets, up to 44-mm main deck
Max speed: 27 knots

Duilio class

Name	Completed	Fate
Duilio	May 1915	Scrapped 1958
Andrea Doria	Mar 1916	Scrapped 1958

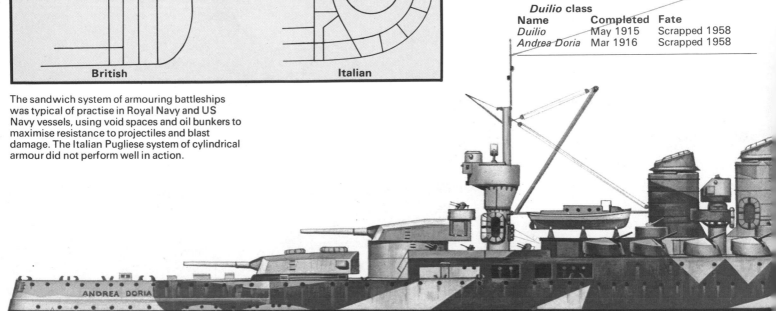

By the mid-1930s the Baltic navies were also being forced to modernise. The Swedish *Sverige* was given trunked funnels and increased anti-aircraft armament

two more battleships of the *Littorio* class. The *Impero* was started in May 1938 and the *Roma* followed in September. The possession of a squadron of four modern, fast and hard-hitting ships, backed up by the four older ships reconstructed to modern standards, was calculated by Mussolini to give him supremacy over the British in the Mediterranean and make it truly *Mare Nostrum*.

The reconstruction of the old Italian ships was one of the most remarkable feats of naval architecture, rivalling even the Japanese reconstructions in its ingenuity. The midships 12-in turret was removed and replaced by a modern two-shaft steam plant developing more than double the original power. The hull was lengthened and rebuilt to incorporate the Pugliese system of underwater protection, and the superstructure was entirely rebuilt to resemble that of the *Littorio* class. But sadly all this was achieved without increasing the protection. If the Italian constructors had been content with 24 knots to match the British *Queen Elizabeth* class, instead of aiming for 27 knots, they might have had weight to spare for better deck and side armour. The guns were relined to 12.6-in/44 cal (320-mm) to give higher velocity and range; at 27° elevation the 525-kg shell could reach a maximum of 28,600 metres.

With four modern capital ships projected it was not surprising that other countries were beginning to show signs of alarm. But it was Germany, still officially shackled by the Versailles Treaty, which made the next move. The 1933 programme included a fourth *Panzerschiff*, but after Adolf Hitler came to power in that year the German Government insisted on its 'right' to build a reply to the French *Dunkerque*—in other words a reply to the reply to the *Deutschland*. The democracies dithered and so tacitly conceded that they could do nothing to stop the Germans from building a 26,000-ton battle-cruiser armed with 11-in guns.

on 22 August, 1937, but she was preceded by nearly a month by her sister. It is interesting to speculate on what the delegates at the London Naval Conference in 1935 would have made of the proposals to build smaller battleships if they had known that Italy was building ships not only with 15-in guns but which exceeded the existing limit by the considerable margin of 6,000 tons. The Italians were to protest afterwards that they had to allow the tonnage to 'grow' during construction because they found that they could not meet the specified limits, but to the naval architect such excuses make little sense. A major project from a designer as skilled as Umberto Pugliese does not col-

lect 18 per cent more than its designed weight in *standard* condition (all warships tend to increase their full-load tonnage, both during building and in service), and there must have been official connivance at the decision to violate the treaty limits.

As the international situation worsened, for reasons not unconnected with the territorial ambitions of Benito Mussolini, France replied to the two *Littorio*s with her own 35,000-tonners. By now Italy was heavily involved in supporting General Franco in the Spanish Civil War, and as she was already angered by international criticism of her war against Abyssinia in 1936 she decided to double her stakes by laying down

Andrea Doria was transformed in the 1930s from the characteristic appearance of a First World War dreadnought to the sleek design illustrated below. The extent of the reconstruction is apparent in this drawing of the 1914 configuration

The bluff bow of the Gneisenau proved inadequate for sea-keeping. In 1939 she was rebuilt with a lengthened and raked 'Atlantic' bow

Drüppel

Professional observers shrewdly suspected that the new ship, the *Scharnhorst*, would be much bigger. Indeed, when she was completed in 1938 she displaced 32,000 tons, an 'error' of 23 per cent which, if genuine, should have resulted in the dismissal of the designer. The choice of the 11-in gun was odd, in view of the *Dunkerque*'s 13-in guns and the Italian 12.6-in and 15-in weapons, but in fact German heavy industry was not able to cope with Hitler's sudden expansion of military production. The 11-in triple turrets had been ordered for the next three *Panzerschiffe*, and it was decided to save time by using the six turrets for two nine-gunned battle-cruisers. The design allowed for eventual replacement by three twin 15-in mountings but nothing was done about it until much later.

The Versailles Treaty was now a dead letter. The *Kriegsmarine* (formerly the *Reichsmarine*) did not reveal the laying down of the *Gneisenau*, a sister ship for the *Scharnhorst*, under the 1934 programme. In the early part of the following year Hitler denounced the treaty, however, and presented a shocked world with a *fait accompli*: a new and powerful navy already well advanced. The 1935 programme added a battleship, eventually to be named

Scharnhorst

The two vessels in this class, orginally designated armour-clad ships, gradually grew as design work progressed and heavier armament than originally intended was installed. They were intended partially as replacements for two older battleships

Displacement: 32,000 tons *Length:* 226 m
Armament: 9×280-mm, 12×150-mm, 14×105-mm, 16×37-mm, up to 24×20-mm, 6×533-mm torpedo tubes (from 1941)
Armour: up to 350-mm side, 360-mm main turrets, 50-mm deck *Max speed:* 31.5 knots

Scharnhorst class

Name	Completed	Fate
Scharnhorst	Jan 1939	Sunk in Battle of North Cape, Dec 1943
Gneisenau	May 1938	Scuttled at Götenhafen Mar 1945

Bismarck, armed with eight 15-in guns; her sister *Tirpitz* was ordered in 1936.

The British Rearmament Programme
As early as 1934 the British Government realised that a war with either Germany or Japan—and possibly both—was likely by 1941, with Italy thrown in to lengthen the odds. What disturbed the Admiralty was the fact that the Royal Navy was considerably under-strength for such a struggle. Although nominally still the largest in the world, the RN had a large proportion of elderly capital ships, the majority of which would be unfit to fight their opposite numbers. It must be remembered that the aircraft carrier had not yet developed its full potential, and no major navy dared think of countering battleships with anything but its own battle fleet.

The leading naval powers were anxious to continue the limitations enshrined in the treaties, but not at the cost of their fighting efficiency. The London Naval Treaty was due to expire in December 1936, and a new conference was due to be convened to discuss how to continue the limitations on the world's fleets. With a view to rectifying what they saw as a serious weakness in the Royal Navy's strength, the Admiralty advised the Cabinet in May 1934 that the new naval treaty must allow Great Britain to build new battleships. The Admiralty was particularly anxious that they must be laid down as soon as the existing treaty expired, even if the new agreement reduced the permitted displacement and armament.

Design studies for new capital ships had begun in the spring of 1933 to allow the British delegates to have clear objectives at the 1935 conference, just as they had at Washington. Armour protection was given top priority, as it was recognised that even if the conference agreed to reduce gun calibre the new ships would have to face opponents with 15-in and 16-in guns for some years. Air attacks with bombs of up to 2000 lb weight were to be taken into account. Speed was to be no more than 23

knots, the same as foreign battleships and the *Nelson* class. The decisive battle range was held to be 12,000–16,000 yards; it was felt that although high speed (30 knots) would permit action at greater distances, experience showed that destruction of an enemy battleship would only take place at the shorter ranges.

The question of speed vexed the designers of what had now been labelled the '1937 Capital Ships'. The 1935 conference led to the Three-Power Treaty among Great Britain, the USA and France. But the French, with a nervous eye on Italy, would not renounce their right to build 35,000-ton ships with 15-in guns. The battle-cruisers *Dunkerque* and *Strasbourg* were also fast, as were the German replies to them, the *Scharnhorst* and *Gneisenau*. Gun calibre was also the subject of violent changes of policy. At the conference in 1935 the British

Above:
Scharnhorst *fires a salvo from one of her three triple 280-mm turrets*

Drüppel

Construction of the Scharnhorst effectively torpedoed the Versailles Treaty

were still pressing for a reduction to 12-in guns for battleships, although the Americans wanted to retain the 16-in, while the French and Italians had secretly already committed themselves to 15-in guns for their new ships. But the British remained optimistic about a reduction to 14-in calibre, and won the Americans round. As naval guns and their massive mountings take a long time to design and even longer to build, the guns had to be ordered before the end of 1935 if the first two battleships were to be ready in 1940.

The result was that in October 1935, two months before the convening of the London Naval Conference, the Board of Admiralty recommended that the new capital ships should be 35,000-ton, 28-knot ships armed with twelve 14-in guns. The United States insisted on a clause to allow 16-in guns to be reinstated if the Japanese refused to accept the treaty terms by April 1937. In the event this happened, and so Great Britain ended up as the only country to build 14-in-gunned battleships. This was at the core of most of the criticism levelled at these ships, although experience during the Second World War was to indicate that the theoretically greater range and hitting power of 15-in and 16-in shells made little difference in action. But in 1935 the British designers

felt that to compensate for the lighter shell they should increase the number of guns from eight or nine to 12 in three quadruple mountings, a solution adopted by the Americans as well in their 14-in design.

As work on the new ships progressed several radically novel features were incorporated. A new 5.25-in surface/anti-aircraft gun mounting was adopted for the battleships in place of the planned 4.5-in gun; this was the first example of a dual-purpose armament. The thick horizontal armour against plunging shells and bombs was raised from the middle deck to the main deck to improve stability if the ship was damaged and to reduce the volume of structure vulnerable to semi-armour-piercing (SAP) bombs. The original requirement for six aircraft had been altered, but now provision was to be made for two aircraft hangars in the superstructure, the first time this had been done in any battleships. The underwater protection system which had proved such an important feature of the *Nelson* class was retained in a much improved form.

In February 1936 a provisional programme was drawn up for the two ships. It is quoted below to give some idea of the time-scale for building battleships, and the actual completion dates are given for comparison:

	Provisional date	Actual date
1 Order for the gun mountings	Apr 1936	Apr 1936
2 Order for two ships	Sep 1936	Jul 1936
3 Laying down of ships	Feb 1937	Jan 1937
4 Launch	Jan 1939	Feb and May 1939
5 1st turret installed	Mar 1939	Feb 1940
6 2nd turret installed	May 1939	Apr 1940
7 3rd turret installed	Dec 1939	May 1940
8 Completion of ships	Jul 1940	Dec 1940, Mar 1941

It can be seen clearly from this table that the main source of delay was the armament. The guns themselves presented no problems, unlike the turrets. Three quadruple

turrets had been stipulated to achieve the maximum weight of broadside, although for a time the designers toyed with the idea of nine 14-in guns in three triple mountings. Finally it was decided to alter the number of guns to ten by substituting a twin mounting for one of the quads to save weight. As time was so short this sudden change can only be described as capricious. With hindsight it is clear that nine 14-in would have been nearly as good as twelve, for the simple reason that a triple turret was roomier and easier to work than a quadruple one. But either arrangement was preferable to incurring further delay while a new twin 14-in turret was designed. In any case the design of the new turrets proved more complex than the Director of Naval Construction had envisaged, and the quadruple turrets were eleven months late because of a shortage of draughtsmen.

The first two ships were the *King George V*, ordered from Vickers-Armstrongs, Barrow, and the *Prince of Wales* from Cammell Laird, Birkenhead. The Board of Admiralty wanted to go to a 16-in-gunned design to match the ships which it believed the Japanese were building, but to save further delay the next three battleships authorised under the 1937 programme were repeats of the *King George V*. Despite all the delays it was still hoped to have the first ship at sea in September 1940 and the others in 1941, and *King George V* began her trials in October 1940. During the crisis at the time of Dunkirk, work on the last two—*Anson* and *Howe*—was stopped, but only for a few months; they joined the Fleet in 1942.

US Battleships

Like the British, the Americans had their '1937 Battleships', and it is interesting to see that they came to much the same conclusions: that 27–28 knots was all that was needed to provide tactical flexibility without sacrificing armour. They also chose three quadruple 14-in mountings and a dual-purpose secondary armament for dealing with surface and air attack. All other contemporary designs still retained the cumbersome arrangement of low-angle guns for

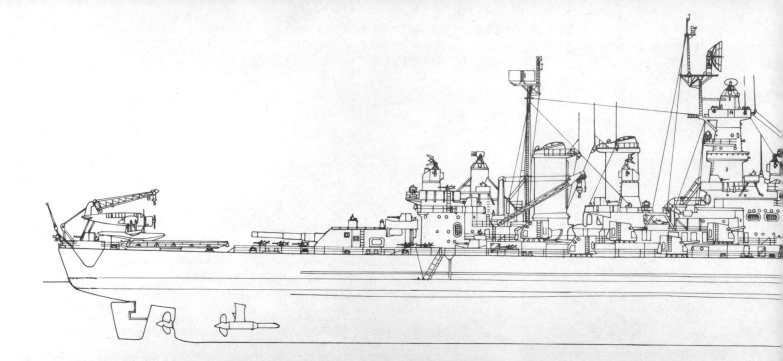

fending off destroyers and a separate lighter-calibre armament against aircraft. But, as we have seen, the Americans reserved the right to drop 14-in guns and revert to 16-in if the Japanese refused to sign the 1936 naval treaty. Nobody knows what the reaction of the British and Americans would have been if they had known just how far the Japanese had decided to depart from the spirit of the treaties, but by the time it was learned that the Japanese might be building 18-in-gunned ships it was too late to change the design of the British ships. The Americans were prepared to wait a little longer, and so the two ships of the *North Carolina* class were altered during construction from twelve 14-in guns to nine 16-in.

The *North Carolina* class had 12-in inclined armour belts with external 'bulges', a relatively light scale of protection. This was the result of being designed to fight 14-in-gunned ships, but it makes an interesting comparison with the British *King George V*, which had equally heavy deck armour but much thicker side armour. This fault was rectified in the next class, the four *South Dakotas* projected for the 1939 programme. These ships were possibly the best of the battleships designed within the restrictions of the international treaties,

and certainly the most ingenious balance of offensive and defensive qualities. The first criterion was to increase protection while keeping the displacement the same, and so it was necessary to make drastic savings in weight. The waterline length was reduced to save structural weight, but as the stubbier hull needed more horsepower than the *North Carolinas* to reach the same speed it was necessary to redesign the steam plant, and in any case the short hull meant smaller engine rooms. But once the intricate problems of squeezing 130,000-shp turbines and boilers into less space than the *North Carolina* needed for 121,000 shp, there were many compensating factors. The shorter hull reduced the areas vulnerable to damage by 7 per cent, and the compact superstructure made for good anti-aircraft defence. The armour was only slightly thicker, but it was inclined at 19° in a different way to that in the previous class, with the belt mounted internally as in the British and Japanese designs of 1920–21. The disadvantages were the risk of increased listing as a result of damage to the thin outer plating, and the loss or contamination of large quantities of oil fuel, but the overriding need was to provide protection against 16-in shells and so the risks were accepted. Like the

British ships, the *South Dakotas* concentrated deck armour in a single 5-in deck, a far more effective defence against bombs than the *North Carolinas* total of three decks.

Production time for the new US battleships was similar to the British ships, and the *North Carolina* was built in roughly the same time as the *King George V*. Both ships were commissioned in the spring of 1941. The *South Dakotas* were laid down between July 1939 and January 1940; three were ready by the spring of 1942 but the last, the *Alabama*, was not commissioned until August 1942. The two classes looked very different, the *North Carolinas* being elegant ships with two slim funnels whereas the *South Dakotas* were squat and purposeful, with a single funnel faired into the superstructure. Both classes retained the old feature of a separate bridge and conning tower, unlike the British *Nelson* and *King George V*, which incorporated both into the tower bridge. This was a weak point, for it split the command organisation in action and the slender pyramidal tower tended to suffer much more from vibration than the solid 'Queen Anne's Mansions' introduced in the *Nelson* class. These features of battleship design were of vital importance.

US Navy

USS *North Carolina*

The two vessels in this class were laid down in response to the construction of the Royal Navy's *King George V* class and similar Japanese ships. Weight-saving construction methods were used, but speed was sacrificed for the sake of firepower
Displacement: 46,770 tons full load
Length: 729 ft *Armament:* 9×16-in, 16×1.1-in AA *Armour:* $6\frac{5}{8}$/12-in belt, 7/16-in main turrets, $3\frac{5}{8}$/$4\frac{5}{8}$-in main deck *Max speed:* 28 knots

North Carolina class

Name	Completed	Fate
North Carolina	Apr 1941	Moored in Cape Fear river as memorial
Washington	May 1941	Scrapped 1961

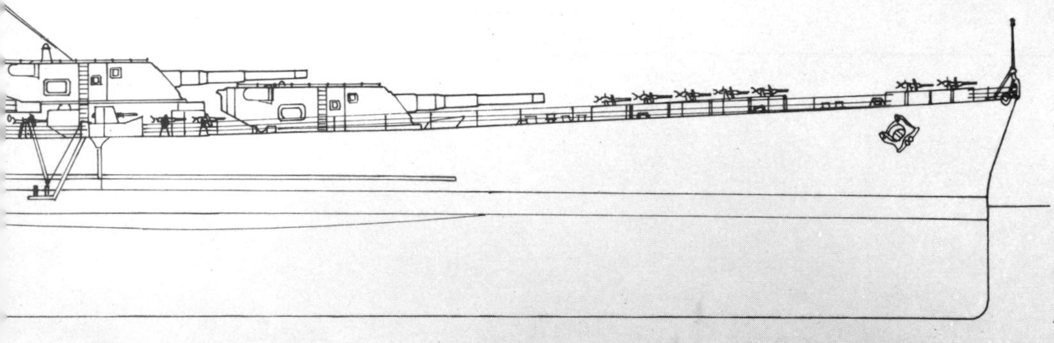

While the disarmament treaties remained effective, warship designers were set almost impossible tasks in accommodating more powerful guns, higher speed and increased anti-aircraft armaments. The South Dakota *class were the last battleships built under these conditions and were a very ingenious solution to the problem*

Challenge in the Pacific
RISING SUN

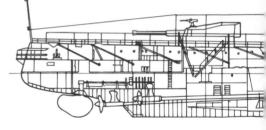

The old Japanese battleships were largely inferior to their Western contemporaries and so required a much greater degree of modernisation. The Hyuga *(seen above at Tsingtao in 1938) was re-engined and totally reconstructed to improve her fighting capacity*

US Navy

From 1934 onwards the Imperial Japanese Navy grew more and more ambitious. Under strong political pressure from the Army to support grandiose schemes for conquest in the Far East, the Navy Staff drew up plans for rebuilding the older capital ships and building new ships which could defeat the British and Americans in battle. But at every turn the designers were hampered by the treaties' limits on tonnage and numbers. Eventually the grave decision was taken to renounce the treaties, and Japan gave the statutory two years' warning of her intention not to renew the 1930 treaty when it expired in 1936. It was this announcement which led the Americans to drop their plans for 14-in-gunned ships, but Japan did agree to keep to the spirit of the 1936 treaty, although reserving the right to build ships of up to 45,000 tons. This was agreed to in June 1938 in a protocol signed by Great Britain, the United States and France.

The first step in rebuilding the Fleet was to reconstruct the four *Kongo*-class battle-cruisers, which had been completed in 1913–15 and partially modernised. Between 1933 and 1940 first the *Haruna* and then her sisters, including the officially 'demilitar-ised' *Hiei*, were rebuilt as 'fast battleships'. The ships were lengthened by 25 ft, extra deck armour was added and elevation of the 14-in guns was increased to 30° to increase their range. The machinery was completely replaced, so that horsepower went up from 64,000 to 136,000, raising speed from just under 26 to 30½ knots. When the British saw the rebuilt *Kongos* (which they had designed originally) they reflected ruefully that they could have done the same with the battle-cruiser *Tiger*, which had been prematurely scrapped in 1933 to comply with the Washington Treaty. The *Kongos* were no better

Kongo (above) in her three-funnelled configuration before the first rebuilding 1929-31. The second conversion in 1936 brought her up to modern standards. She is seen below as in 1944 equipped with a Nakajima 'Rufe' floatplane

protected against other battleships than the Italian *Cavour* and *Doria* classes, but they were ideal escorts for the new fast carriers being built.

The *Fuso* class, the similar *Hyuga* class and the two *Nagatos* were also reconstructed to bring them into line with modern requirements. In all six ships this involved massive 'bulge' protection, heavy anti-aircraft armament, new deck armour and huge 'pagoda' foremasts. But these measures only brought the Japanese battle fleet up to the standard of the latest British and American ships in quality, not in numbers. Japan's aggressions in China made her many enemies, particularly the United States, which joined the League of Nations in condemning Japan for invading Manchuria. And when Russia, in a new mood of conciliation, restored diplomatic relations with China and the United States, Japanese extremists saw this as evidence that Japan was hemmed in by hostile nations just as Germany had been 30 years before.

Japanese shipbuilding could not hope to outbuild either Great Britain or the United States and so the Naval General Staff planned for ships of the maximum fighting power in conjunction with a massive fleet of submarines to wear down the strength of the opposing fleets. In fact the Japanese strategy was only an up-dated version of Togo's Tsushima campaign—to lure the enemy fleet into Japanese waters and there finish it off in one decisive battle. The attrition was to be accomplished mainly by torpedo attacks from destroyers and submarines attacking enemy supply lines in the Pacific, but there was still the question of how to ensure that the final fleet action would go in Japan's favour. To achieve this the Naval General Staff decided that they wanted the most powerful battleships that could be built, whatever the treaties said.

The Road to Pearl Harbor

Once the decision had been taken to defy the treaties the necessary justification was created—provided that Japan signified her intention to withdraw from the international agreements, there was nothing to stop her from planning and building ships which would not be completed until after the expiry date! And with that dubious logic the Imperial Japanese Navy took the first positive step down the road to Pearl Harbor. The next step was to ask the Bureau of Naval Construction to determine what size of ship was needed. It was recognised that the US Navy had a priceless asset in being able to move its battleships from the Atlantic to the Pacific through the Panama Canal, and so the Japanese Staff demanded a battleship of such size and power that the only possible American rival would be too big to pass through the canal. This was an echo of the *Dreadnought* era, when the Germans had been forced to widen the Kiel Canal to allow them to compete in the naval race in the North Sea.

To meet this condition the new battleships would have to displace at least 63,000 tons, have a speed of 23 knots and be armed with ten 16-in guns. But the Naval General Staff wanted 18-in guns to achieve the other requirements of superior range and hitting power. Now it became clear what a monster had been hatched, for it was not possible merely to scale up, say, the *Nagato* design to produce an 18-in-gunned battleship. As the British had found in 1917, the increase in calibre caused many headaches; shell weight jumped from about 2200 to 3200 lbs, and a triple turret would weigh more than 2500 tons. Blast effects went up from about 50 lbs/sq inch from one of the *Nagato*'s twin 16-in turrets to nearly 100 lbs/sq inch from three 18-in guns at a point 50 ft from the muzzles. It should be remembered that a muzzle blast of $\frac{1}{4}$ lb/sq in could damage boats nearby and as little as 15 lbs/sq in was capable of rendering a man unconscious. The new battleship would have to have all secondary and light guns enclosed in blast-proof shields, and weather-deck fittings would have to be reduced to a minimum.

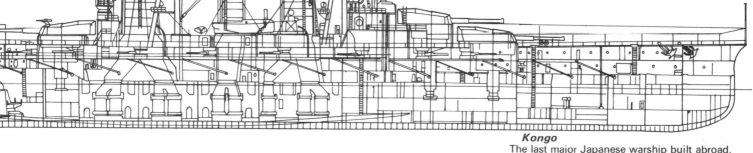

Kongo

The last major Japanese warship built abroad, *Kongo* was constructed in Britain and inspired the Royal Navy's *Tiger*-class battle-cruisers. The ship was modernised twice between 1929 and 1937

Displacement: 27,500 tons *Length:* 214 m *Armament:* 8×356-mm, 16 (later 14)×152-mm 16×76-mm, 12×127-mm (from 1944), 118 (max)×25-mm *Armour:* 76/203-mm belt, 229-mm turrets *Max speed:* 27.5 knots

Kongo class

Name	Completed	Fate
Kongo	Aug 1913	Sunk by US submarine *Sealion* 1944
Hiei	Aug 1914	Sunk by US aircraft 1942
Haruna	Apr 1915	Sunk by US aircraft 1945
Kirishima	Apr 1915	Sunk by US battleships 1942

The go-ahead for the new design was given in October 1934, with a request from the Staff to the Bureau of Naval Construction for a 30-knot ship armed with nine 18-in guns and protected by the thickest armour possible. By March 1935 a design had been produced for a 69,500-ton monster 294 metres (965 ft) long and having a beam of 135 ft; with 200,000-hp steam turbines she would have had a speed of 31 knots. With great reluctance the Staff accepted that this design was too big, and a lower speed was requested to allow better protection and more endurance. To improve endurance and to save weight steam was abandoned in favour of high-speed diesels, presumably because of favourable reports about the Germans' success with the 'pocket-battleships'. The Japanese were very proud of a new 10,000-bhp two-cycle double-acting diesel which had been used in a series of submarine tenders, and it was hoped that this unit would propel the new battleships,

in conjunction with steam on the inner shafts for top speed.

In two years the Bureau produced 23 designs, but in July 1936 a sudden setback threw the project into the melting pot again. The high-speed diesel was found to have a major design fault, and had to be abandoned. In the battleship design the diesel room was covered by 7¾-in armour, and it would have been impossible to replace the engines if they gave any trouble, so there was nothing to be done but redesign the machinery. Finally four-shaft steam turbines as in the original 1935 design were chosen, but reduced to 150,000 shp making 27 knots.

Protected Vitals

Nothing has been said so far about armouring, but, as might be expected, the Japanese had not gone to the trouble of driving a coach and horses through the naval treaties to build a poorly protected ship, and the new class would outstrip all

Nagato and her sister Mutsu *underwent a total reconstruction between the wars, which involved widening of the hull and rebuilding of the superstructure to accommodate a heavy anti-aircraft battery*

others in the scale and thickness of armour. The vitals were protected by 16.1-in Vickers face-hardened armour capable of stopping an 18-in shell at 22,000 yards, and the 7¾-in deck armour could keep out an 18-in shell at 33,000 yards. This deck armour could also stop a 2200-lb bomb dropped from 15,000 ft and even the extremities of the ship were plated with light armour capable of keeping out small bombs. The funnel was armoured, not by conventional coaming armour, but by a huge 15-in plate inside the uptakes, with 7-in-diameter perforations to allow the smoke to pass through; the coaming of the funnel was protected by 2-in plating. Even the bottom plating was armoured with two 3-in plates under the magazines to protect

Mutsu

Japan was able to forge ahead with battleship design while the European powers were locked in combat, and some of the lessons of Jutland were incorporated in their design. *Mutsu* and her sister were fast, heavily armed and were considered extremely successful

Displacement: 34,100 tons full load *Length:* 215 m *Armament:* 8×406-mm, 18×140-mm (from 1936), 8×127-mm (from 1933, 20×25 -mm (from 1936), 4×533-mm torpedo tubes *Armour:* 100/300-mm belt, 356-mm turrets, up to 75-mm decks *Max speed:* 26.7 knots

Nagato class

Name	Completed	Fate
Nagato	Nov 1920	Sunk during A-bomb test 1946
Mutsu	Oct 1921	Blew up 1943

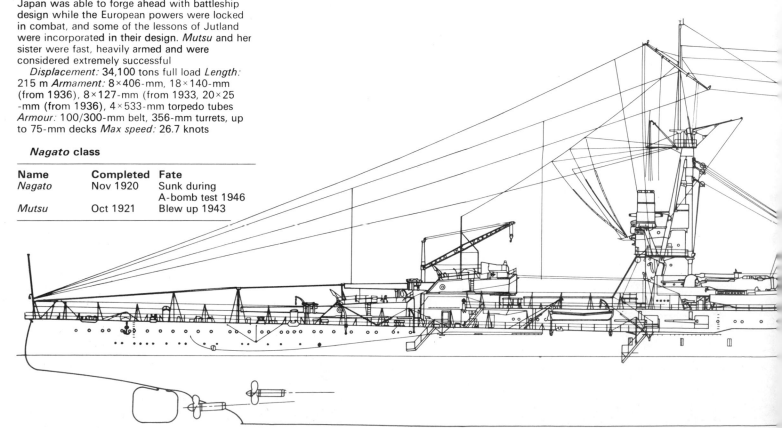

US Navy

them from mine or torpedo explosions. Even though the ship was 860 ft long the armour absorbed 34.4 per cent of the displacement.

The 18-in guns were actually 46-cm (18.1-in) 45 cal weapons which weighed 157 tons each and had a muzzle velocity of 2559 ft/sec. At 45° elevation they could fire a 3220-lb shell a maximum of 45,000 yards. The triple turrets were the most massive ever built, with 24.8-in faces, 9-in sides, 6.7-in backs and 9.8-in roof plates. The rate of fire was one round per gun every 90 sec, and the whole moving structure weighed 2730 tons.

Although the Japanese constructors were not limited by considerations of size and cost there were nevertheless restraints imposed by practicability. For example, the draught had to be restricted to allow the ships to enter Japanese harbours, a factor which contributed to the great beam. To try to save weight the lower side armour formed part of the longitudinal strength of the ship, and welding was used wherever possible.

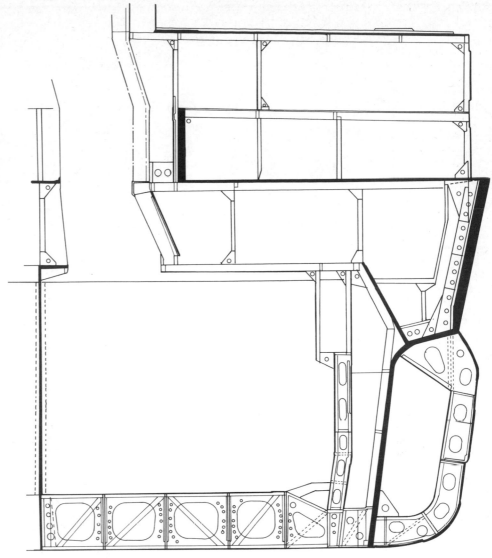

***Amagi:* Armour Diagram**
Midship section of the cancelled battle-cruiser *Amagi,* showing the inward slope of the armour designed to increase the angle of impact of shells and hence increase resistance to penetration

Unfortunately the Japanese shipbuilding industry had severe problems with welding, partly through lack of proper rods. The structure of the new battleships was much heavier than that of contemporary British and American ships, with all the important parts of the hull riveted for safety. When tests showed that armour plates had less resistance at their edges the Japanese spent $10 million on new steel mills to make large armour plates. The 16.1-in plates for the side armour were 19.36 ft × 11.81 ft and weighed 68½ tons. The great thickness of these plates forced the Japanese to use a new process for hardening the surface, one which proved to be more effective and

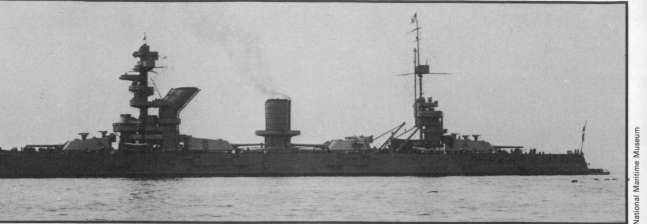

The first public outing of the Soviet Navy was in 1936 when the Marat appeared at the Coronation Naval Review. A quaint reconstruction failed to conceal the original 1915 outline of the Petropavlovsk

quicker than the traditional method of cementing.

The first of the super-battleships was given the name *Yamato* when her keel was laid in November 1937, while her sister *Musashi* was laid down in March 1938. Work started in 1940 on two more ships of slightly modified design, but a fifth unit and two more of even larger type with six 50.8-cm (20-in) guns were never started. Kure Dockyard, the builder chosen for the *Yamato*, had to deepen its building dock by 3 ft and strengthen the gantry crane to allow for the weight of the bigger armour plates. A special transport, the *Kashino*, had to be built to carry the 18-in guns and part of the mountings from the Kamegakubi Ordnance Works to the four yards selected. A special new dock was built at Yokosuka for the *Shinano*, but Mitsubishi built the *Musashi* at Nagasaki on a conventional slipway. Never before had any Japanese shipyard launched a hull weighing more than 30,000 tons, although the British had recently launched the *Queen Mary* at a weight of 37,387 tons. Because of the need to delay any announcement about these ships as long as possible there was total secrecy. At Kure the *Yamato* was hidden from prying eyes by a roof built at the landward end of the berth, while the *Musashi*'s hull was covered by a gigantic camouflage net weighing 408 tons and made out of 1370 miles of sisal rope.

The appearance of the *Yamato* and *Musashi* was unusual, with a long undulating flush deckline and a massive funnel raked well aft to take smoke clear of the tall tower mast. Two catapults at the stern could launch six floatplanes, but to avoid blast damage these aircraft had to be kept in a large hangar a deck below the boat stowage. A large lift hoisted both aircraft and boats to the deck, where a crane put the aircraft on positioning trolleys.

Russia

Despite the efforts made to revive the Red Fleet, the Soviet Union found that its industrial potential was not sufficient to produce the guns and heavy armour needed for new battleships. But to Stalin this was merely a temporary problem. Between 1935 and 1938 Italy and the United States were approached for designs of ships and asked to supply guns

The old battleship Sebastopol was renamed Parishkaya Kommuna in 1928 but in 1942, as part of Stalin's drive to rekindle the spirit of Russian patriotism, she reverted to her old Tsarist name

Sovietski Soyuz

Construction of two battleships in this class was begun, the name-ship being laid down in 1938. Work proceeded slowly, but by the time of the German invasion in 1941 the first vessel was almost ready for launching. In November of that year construction was abandoned, however, and the hull was scrapped after the war

Displacement: up to 60,000 tons *Length:* 262 m *Armament:* 9×406-mm, 12×130-mm or 12×150-mm, 12×76-mm or 8×100-mm *Max speed:* nearly 30 knots

and armour. In 1939 the Germans were also asked to supply plans of the new *Bismarck* class as well as guns, but on Hitler's orders the negotiations were spun out to avoid giving away any secrets. In 1938 two very large battleships were laid down, one at Leningrad and the other at Nikolaiev in the Black Sea. Neither was launched, and naturally nothing of any value has ever been released by the Russian authorities, but in August 1941 German forces captured the dockyard at Nikolaiev and so we have a fairly good idea of how big the ship would have been. What was gradually realised was that if the Second World War had not broken out the Russian Navy would have had two battleships nearly as big as the *Yamato* class. On a displacement of 59,000 tons they would have been a little shorter but with similar beam. The armour was lighter and nine 16-in guns would have been carried at a speed of 30 knots. During the war Stalin assured his allies that the two ships would have been stationed in the Pacific, but it is clear that the Russians were on the brink of a massive expansion to challenge both British and German seapower in the West.

Germany

In 1937–38 the German Navy drew up plans for a naval war against Great Britain and France, at about the same time as the British were putting their own naval programme in hand. Lists were drawn up of the ships needed for a successful sea war against British trade as follows:

German Z-Plan

6 battleships to be ready by 1944
8 heavy cruisers, 4 by 1943 plus 4 by 1948
4 aircraft carriers, 2 by 1941 plus 2 by 1947
223 submarines, 128 by 1943 plus 95 by 1947

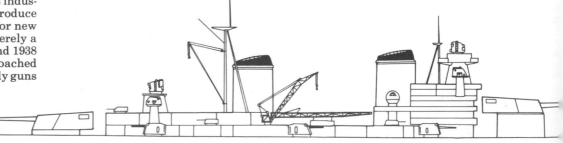

The plan was modified several times, and subsequently some of the heavy cruisers were replaced by a trio of battle-cruisers. The battleships were 56,000-ton diesel-driven ships to be armed with eight 16-in guns, and the battle-cruisers would have been 15-in-gunned versions of the *Scharnhorst* class.

The 'Z' Plan showed little sense of reality, for the German Naval Staff seems to have ignored what effect it might have on British naval programmes. The magic date of 1944 was chosen because Adolf Hitler claimed to guarantee that war between Britain and Germany could not break out before then, and it had nothing to do with the capacity of German shipyards. In fact the British had already started to lay down more ships than the Germans in every category except submarines (a type for which they had less need), and the news of the 'Z' Plan only helped to strengthen the British determination to use their superior shipbuilding resources to outbuild the *Kriegsmarine*. An improved *King George V* design with 16-in guns, known as the *Lion* class, was started in 1939 and the modernisation of the older ships was accelerated. The results can be seen below:

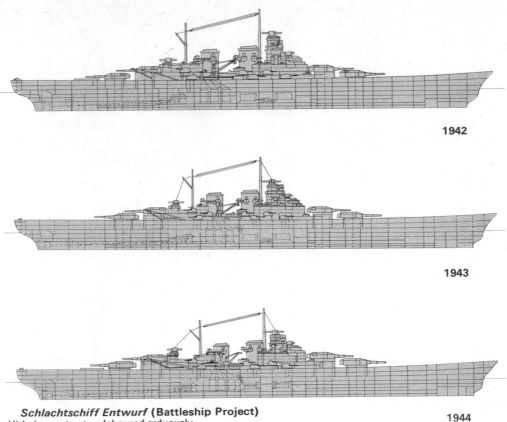

1942

1943

***Schlachtschiff Entwurf* (Battleship Project)**
Hitler's constructors laboured arduously throughout the war to avoid the Eastern Front by producing ever more colossal designs. The steel alone would have equalled a years Tiger tank production

1944

The Second Naval Race

	Begun	Completed
British		
King George V	1937	1940
Prince of Wales	1937	1941
Duke of York	1937	1941
Anson	1937	1942
Howe	1937	1942
German		
Bismarck	1936	1940
Tirpitz	1936	1941
'H'	1939	—*
'J'	1939	—*

*Stopped in October 1939 and scrapped on slipway in 1940

During the same period the British also modernised the *Queen Elizabeth*, *Valiant* and *Renown* to a degree which made them virtually new ships. The four *Lions* were fine ships, but the slow progress of German shipbuilding made them superfluous, and their cancellation in 1940 released much-needed steel and manpower for better purposes. The only way in which the 'Z' Plan could have worked would have been for the British to build no more ships whatsoever between 1937 and 1941, an eventuality so remote as to be absurd, and Hitler's naval expansion plans must be pigeon-holed alongside Stalin's megalomaniac plans for the *Sovietski Soyuz* class.

Right: *A navy band crashes out* Deutschland über Alles *as Hitler attends the launching of the* Tirpitz *in 1937. In 1941 the German surface fleet was still a threat to the Royal Navy, but by 1943 the remaining big ships would be completely overshadowed by the submarine offensive*

THE SECOND TEST

When war broke out in September 1939 none of the new generation ships was in commission, unless one counts the French *Dunkerques* and the German *Scharnhorsts*. The British had a total of 13 ships in commission, with the *Queen Elizabeth* and *Valiant* still completing reconstruction, whereas the Germans had only two battlecruisers and four new ships under construction. The French and Italians were more evenly matched, with two new ships each due to commission from mid-1940 and another pair apiece which could be ready by 1942–43. The Japanese had nearly completed their programme of reconstructing their battleships, but the *Yamato* and *Musashi* would not be ready until 1941–42. The Americans expected to have six 16-in-gunned ships in commission in the same time and were about to lay down the first two of a class of six 45,000-tonners.

The first battleship casualty of the war was the old British *Royal Oak*, which was torpedoed by a U-Boat in the supposedly safe anchorage at Scapa Flow. Under K/Lt Gunther Prien *U.47* was sent to force her way through the defences of Kirk Sound, which had not been overhauled since 1918. Prien's daring paid off, and he found himself inside the Flow on the night of 13–14 October, 1939. The first salvo of three torpedoes (one tube was faulty) had no effect, either because the single torpedo which hit struck an anchor cable, or more likely because it only detonated partially. Nearly threequarters of an hour later Prien had reloaded his forward torpedo tubes and returned to the attack. This time his three torpedoes ran true and the magnetic pistols detonated the warheads underneath the *Royal Oak*'s keel. The old ship, which had been at Jutland 23 years before, blew up and sank with the loss of 833 officers and men.

The *Royal Oak* was not a modern ship, and would have been scrapped in another

Battleship Strength of the Powers: 1939

Great Britain

Nelson
Rodney
Hood
Renown
Repulse
Royal Sovereign
Royal Oak
Revenge
Ramillies
Resolution
Queen Elizabeth
Valiant
Warspite
Barham
Malaya

United States

Colorado
Maryland
West Virginia
Tennessee
California
New Mexico
Mississippi
Idaho
Pennsylvania
Arizona
Nevada
Oklahoma
New York
Texas
Arkansas

Germany

Scharnhorst
Gneisenau

Japan

Nagato
Mutsu
Hyuga
Ise
Fuso
Yamashiro
Haruna
Kirishima
Kongo
Hiei

Note: Only units operational in September 1939 are indicated

France

Dunkerque
Strasbourg
Bretagne
Provence
Lorraine
Courbet
Paris
Ocean

Italy

Andrea Doria
Duilio
Conte di Cavour
Guilio Cesare

Russia

Marat
Oktyabrskaya Revolutsia
Parizhskaya Kommuna

Chile

Almirante Latorre

Argentina

Moreno
Rivadavia

Brazil

Sao Paulo
Minas Geraes

Turkey

Yavuz

The twisted hulk of the Graf Spee blazes in Montevideo harbour after demolition charges had ripped through her hull

three years if war had not broken out, but the brilliant attack by *U.47* shook the Home Fleet. As in 1914 the battle fleet had to desert its main base for bases in the west of Scotland until Scapa Flow could be made safe once more, and for a few crucial months the Home Fleet had to leave the exit to the North Sea unguarded. Furthermore the extemporised bases like Loch Ewe were even less secure than Scapa Flow; the Home Fleet flagship *Nelson* was badly damaged by a magnetic mine laid by a U-Boat in the entrance to Loch Ewe and the *Barham* was torpedoed by *U.30*. The defences were not fully strengthened until early in 1940, but no further casualties resulted.

Another casualty of the early months of the war was the myth of the 'pocket-battleship'. In December 1939 the *Admiral Graf Spee* was caught off the River Plate by three British cruisers, the *Exeter*, *Ajax* and *Achilles*. The *Panzerschiff* had left Germany before the outbreak of war with her sister *Deutschland* to evade the British patrols, and they had been cruising in the Atlantic spreading confusion by sinking random merchantmen and adopting disguises. No fewer than eight hunting groups, including the battle-cruisers HMS *Renown* and the French *Dunkerque* and *Strasbourg*, hunted them from Halifax, Nova Scotia, down to Pernambuco. The *Deutschland* sank only two ships before being recalled but the *Admiral Graf Spee*, under her skilled and humane captain Hans Langsdorff, sank nine ships totalling 50,000 tons. One of the ruses adopted by Langsdorff was to paint a dummy tripod on his control tower and rig a dummy triple 11-in turret. He was reported on more than one occasion as a French battleship, which tells a lot about the average merchant navy officer's skill at warship recognition.

When the *Graf Spee* met the three British cruisers off Montevideo early on the morning of 13 December, 1939 she soon showed her shortcomings. She had radar, but the rapid changes of bearing of her three adversaries made it impossible for the two triple 11-in turrets to register long enough to score hits. Eventually by concentrating on the 8-in-gunned *Excter* the German ship was able to damage her severely, but she was unable to finish her off because the *Ajax* and *Achilles* behaved like picadors drawing off the bull from a wounded matador. The *Graf Spee* was not fast enough to out-manoeuvre the cruisers and eventually, with relatively light damage, she was forced to make for neutral Uruguayan waters, from which she eventually emerged to scuttle herself. The vaunted 'pocket-battleship' had turned out to be too slow to out-distance cruisers and not well enough protected to ignore their shells.

'Salmon and Gluckstein'

The Norwegian Campaign of April 1940 saw no great fleet action, but capital ships on both sides played their part from the beginning. The British moved first, wanting to lay mines in Norwegian territorial waters to stop the flagrant violation of neutrality by German iron ore ships, and their mine-laying forces ran into German naval forces covering an invasion of Norway intended to pre-empt a British occupation. The *Renown* and four destroyers narrowly missed the heavy cruiser *Admiral Hipper* on 6 April but one of her escorts, HMS *Glowworm*, was sunk in a gallant but hopeless action after becoming detached two days later. On 9 April the Germans started to land troops at Narvik, Trondheim and other Norwegian ports, and on the same day the *Renown* and nine destroyers ran into the *Scharnhorst* and *Gneisenau* about 50 miles off Vestfjord. The British ship was keeping a sharp look-out and spotted the German battle-cruisers at 3.37 am in bad weather, amid intermittent snow squalls. The *Renown* closed the range to about nine miles, and her opening salvo about 30 minutes later came as an unpleasant surprise. 'Salmon and Gluckstein' (as they were known in Britain after a chain of teashops) turned to fight, but it was the *Renown's* 15-in guns which scored the first hit ten minutes later, putting the *Gneisenau's* forward fire-control out of action. Hitler's orders were explicit; no German capital ships were to expose themselves to the risk of loss, and so there was little choice for Admiral Lütjens but to break off. But the *Renown* pursued the Germans and hit the *Gneisenau* twice more, crippling one of her forward turrets. She herself was hit by two 11-in shells, one of which clipped the top of her funnel, but she suffered no damage. The rising sea prevented her from catching her quarry, despite working up to 29 knots.

On 10 April a British destroyer flotilla fought the First Battle of Narvik in an attempt to dislodge the German destroyer force which had landed troops to seize the vital iron-ore port. But in spite of sinking two destroyers the British lost two of their own and had left the Germans in possession of Narvik, and so the Admiralty ordered the Commander-in-Chief of the Home Fleet to finish off the remaining destroyers. This time Admiral Whitworth was given permission to take the *Warspite* up Ofotfjord to reinforce the nine destroyers, a gamble which could have resulted in the battle-ship's grounding or being torpedoed. This was the same *Warspite* which had been at 'Windy Corner' at Jutland, after two reconstructions, and far from being damaged she was about to start her glorious Second World War career. The destroyers hurried up the fjord with the *Warspite* bringing up the rear. Her Swordfish floatplane was catapulted off to reconnoitre, and soon sighted and sank a U-Boat in the small Herjangs-fjord. The booming of 15-in guns warned the German destroyers of the approach of the British force, but there was little they could do to avoid their fate. By the end of the day all eight German destroyers had been sunk, at a cost of two British destroyers damaged. Narvik was left in German hands for lack of troops to occupy the port, but a large part of the German Navy's entire destroyer force had been wiped out.

Off Norway the Home Fleet learned for the first time just how effective dive-bombing could be. The *Rodney* was hit by a heavy bomb and, although she was not seriously damaged, losses of smaller ships showed that anti-aircraft gunnery alone could not ward off bombers. The multiple pom-pom was found to be useful in breaking up massed attacks but fire-control was still at too crude a state of development to enable aircraft to be shot down except by a random hit. Another weapon was introduced in 1940, a multiple rocket-projector

The pre-dreadnought Schleswig-Holstein, *which had bombarded the Polish coastline in 1939, is seen here at Götenhafen (Gdynia) in 1940. The old ships in Hitler's navy survived until the end of the war*

known as the UP (Unrotated Projectile) mounting. This fired a salvo of rockets, which released parachutes and trailing wires in the hope of entangling an aircraft propeller. Its main disadvantages was that if it was fired too soon the aircraft could dodge the row of parachutes, and it was almost impossible with the predictors of 1940 to plant a salvo in the right place.

The *Scharnhorst* and *Gneisenau* had their moment of glory at the end of the Norwegian Campaign, during the evacuation by the British and French. On the afternoon of 9 June they met the aircraft carrier HMS *Glorious* and two destroyers. The carrier had just evacuated the last shore-based RAF Hurricanes and Gladiators from Norway, and although she had a few Swordfish torpedo-bombers still left on board she does not appear to have been able to fly any off. Thus she was defenceless when the German ships opened fire at 28,000 yards, and it was left to the destroyers *Acasta* and *Ardent* to make a desperate attack. The fight was hopelessly one-sided, but the *Acasta* managed to hit the *Scharnhorst* with a single torpedo abreast of the after turret.

The *Gneisenau* did not escape either, for on 20 June she was also badly damaged by a torpedo from a British submarine. Both battle-cruisers were out of action for a considerable time, and their absence from the scene had a considerable bearing on the German Navy's reluctance to support Hitler's plans for invading the British Isles after Dunkirk. The Norwegian Campaign was full of disappointments and mistakes on the British side but it also cost the Germans losses in ships that they could ill afford.

Right: The world had forgotten the two ex-US pre-dreadnoughts passed to the Greek Navy in 1914 until Stukas found and sank the Kilkis *(ex-Mississippi) in Salamis harbour, 1941*

HMS Warspite
A battleship which saw extensive service in two wars, *Warspite* was the most heavily engaged warship at the Battle of Jutland. She served throughout the Second World War, from Norway, through the Mediterranean to the Indian Ocean and back to Europe to support the D-Day and Walcheren landings
Displacement: 31,000 tons full load
Length: 600 ft *Armament:* 8×15-in, 8×6-in, 8×4-in AA, 16×2-pdr AA

The French Eclipse

The fall of France in June 1940 did not mean the immediate collapse of the French Navy. The old battleships *Courbet* and *Paris* escaped to England and the incomplete *Jean Bart* and *Richelieu* reached North Africa after incredible exertions. The *Dunkerque, Strasbourg, Bretagne* and *Provence* were at Mers-el-Kebir near Oran when the Armistice was signed, while the *Lorraine* was at Alexandria. The Italians had finally moved against France in her most desperate hour, and to the British it seemed unarguable that whatever sincere intentions the French Navy might give about their ships not falling into German hands, they were not in a good position to offer such guarantees. Neither Hitler nor Mussolini had a good track record as far as guarantees went, and furthermore both the *Regia Navale* and the *Kriegsmarine* needed ships badly. Means and motive existed, and only opportunity was needed for the deed to be done. On 3 July Admiral Somerville was ordered to use his new Force 'H' to back up a British 'offer' to the French, one which they could not refuse. The ultimatum offered five choices to the French:

1 Put to sea and join forces against Germany.
2 Sail with reduced crews to a British port for internment.
3 Sail with reduced crews to a French West Indian port to be laid up in a demilitarised condition.
4 Scuttle the ships within six hours.
5 Demilitarise the ships where they lay, within six hours.

Admiral Gensoul was in a difficult position. The first two conditions contradicted the conditions of the Armistice, and the third condition could also be construed that way. The fourth condition was insulting to a proud navy, and the fifth was physically impossible to fulfil in the time allowed. Probably Gensoul and Somerville were not the right people to handle such a delicate matter; Somerville seems to have been needlessly brusque, while Gensoul inexplicably reported to the French C-in-C Admiral Darlan that he had been simply ordered to sink his ships in six hours or surrender them. Not unexpectedly Darlan, who had devoted his career to building up the French Navy, instructed Gensoul to resist, and so the stage was set for the unhappiest action of the war, with the British and French fighting one another only weeks after both navies had heroically evacuated their soldiers from Dunkirk.

All that day (3 July) Force 'H', which included the battle-cruiser *Hood*, the battleships *Resolution* and *Valiant* and the carrier *Ark Royal*, patrolled to seaward of Mers-el-

Kebir. At 1730 a final signal was sent to Admiral Gensoul by Somerville, warning him that if no answer was received his ships would be fired upon. At 1754 the British ships began to fire into the crowded anchorage, and soon the 15-in salvoes were causing havoc. The French ships tried to return the fire, and obtained two straddles on the *Hood*, but the British had the range and had no difficulty in silencing their fire. The *Bretagne* blew up and the *Provence* and *Dunkerque* were seriously damaged. At 1809 the attackers shifted fire to the coastal batteries, and three minutes later the 'melancholy action' was over. The only important unit to escape the carnage was the

Strasbourg, which managed to work clear of the crowded anchorage under cover of the huge pall of smoke from burning ships. The *Hood* gave chase but her 28 knots was insufficient to catch the Frenchman, and when two French aircraft attacked her with torpedoes she turned back. To give some idea of the pace of the action, the *Hood* fired 56 15-in shells and 120 4-in in only 18 minutes, or 14 salvoes.

The *Richelieu* had reached Dakar in Senegal, but that did not put her beyond the reach of the British. On 8 July she was attacked with great daring by a motor boat, which attempted unsuccessfully to drop depth charges under her stern to wreck the

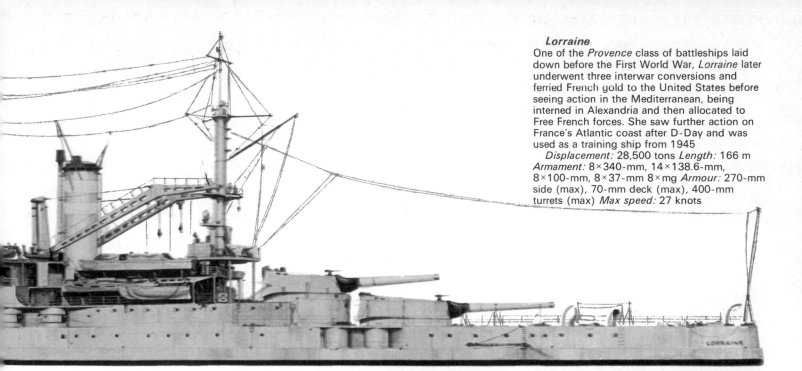

Lorraine

One of the *Provence* class of battleships laid down before the First World War, *Lorraine* later underwent three interwar conversions and ferried French gold to the United States before seeing action in the Mediterranean, being interned in Alexandria and then allocated to Free French forces. She saw further action on France's Atlantic coast after D-Day and was used as a training ship from 1945
  Displacement: 28,500 tons *Length:* 166 m *Armament:* 8×340-mm, 14×138.6-mm, 8×100-mm, 8×37-mm 8×mg *Armour:* 270-mm side (max), 70-mm deck (max), 400-mm turrets (max) *Max speed:* 27 knots

rudder and propellers. Shortly afterwards a torpedo-bomber from HMS *Hermes* scored a hit with a torpedo right aft, but the *Richelieu* remained capable of putting to sea. When the British and the Free French attempted to take Dakar in September (Operation 'Menace') her 15-in guns were a major factor in driving off the attackers. The British battleships *Barham* and *Resolution* failed to silence her or the shore batteries, and when a French submarine put a torpedo into the *Resolution* British enthusiasm for Operation 'Menace' waned noticeably. Fortunately the *Resolution*'s 'bulge' took the main force of the explosion and she was not out of action for long.

Jean Bart

Larger and better protected than the ships of the *Dunkerque* class, which they resembled, *Jean Bart* and her sister *Richelieu* sailed to African ports while still incomplete when France was invaded
  Displacement: 47,500 tons full load *Length:* 248 m *Armament:* 8×380-mm, 9×152-mm, 12×100-mm, 16×37-mm AA, 8×13.2-mm AA *Armour:* 327-mm belt, 430-mm main turrets, 170-mm main deck *Max speed:* 30 knots

Richelieu class

Name	Launched	Fate
Richelieu	Jan 1939	Scrapped 1968
Jean Bart	Mar 1940	Scrapped 1969

ECP Armées

The French battleship Provence *trains her 13·4-in turrets to starboard before opening fire on the British Force H at Mers-el-Kebir. In the background the* Strasbourg *slips her moorings—one of the few ships to escape the holocaust*

ACTION IN THE MEDITERRANEAN

The entry of Italy into the war meant that the British now had to send battleships back to the Mediterranean urgently if they were to maintain their hold on the vital Suez Canal. There were no fast battleships to spare, for the first two of the *King George V* class were earmarked for the Home Fleet to 'mark' the *Scharnhorst* and *Gneisenau* and the *Bismarck* when she appeared. The *Warspite* was sent to the Mediterranean as the flagship of Admiral Sir Andrew Cunningham, shortly to make his name as the most brilliant fighting admiral since Nelson. In May 1940 Cunningham was also given the old *Royal Sovereign* and *Malaya*, and shortly afterwards the aircraft carrier *Eagle* and the *Ramillies* came through the Suez Canal from the Far East. For all too short a period the Mediterranean Fleet was also strengthened by the modernised French battleship *Lorraine*, but she and her squadron-mates were interned at Alexandria in July when France surrendered. At first the British thought that they would have to abandon Malta, their priceless base in the central Mediterranean, but with Cunningham in command there was no need for such a concession.

On 9 July Cunningham met the Italian Fleet off the coast of Calabria; each squadron was covering the passage of a convoy at the time. After the *Eagle*'s torpedo-bombers failed to score hits the battleships came within range, and the *Warspite*'s 15-in guns scored a hit on the *Giulio Cesare* at the great range of 24,600 yards. An orange-coloured flash shot up from the Italian flagship, followed by a pillar of smoke. Admiral Campioni's flagship was not slowed down by the damage but the single shell had made a shambles out of the topsides gun positions, and the whole force turned away under cover of a smokescreen. The *Malaya* was unable to get within range and *Royal Sovereign* had been left behind, which meant that the *Warspite* had been unsupported. To complete the Italian discomfiture in what they called the Battle of Point Stilo (Punta di Stilo), the retreating squadron was bombed by Italian aircraft.

The next brush with the Italian Fleet, the Battle of Cape Spartivento on 25 November, 1940, was less satisfactory. This time the new battleship *Vittorio Veneto* was Admiral Campiano's flagship, with the repaired *Giulio Cesare*, and they faced the *Ramillies* from the Mediterranean Squadron and the *Renown* from Somerville's Force 'H'. Again, the slower *Ramillies* could not get within

range and it was only the *Renown* which was able to fire a few salvoes at extreme range. Campioni over-estimated the strength of the British squadron and broke off the action before any damage could be inflicted on either side.

Taranto

Cunningham was sent another modernised battleship, the *Warspite*'s sister *Valiant*, at the end of August 1940, but the arrival of a modern aircraft carrier, HMS *Illustrious*, was even more important. The next blow against the Italians was to be a deadly one which could have affected the outcome of the entire war and marked a turning point in naval history.

The attack on Taranto was carried out on the night of 11–12 November by the new armoured carrier *Illustrious*, using 21 Swordfish biplane bombers. For the price of a few bombs and eleven 18-in torpedoes these slow aircraft sank the battleship *Conte di Cavour* outright and damaged the new *Littorio* and the *Caio Duilio*. The shallowness of the harbour at Taranto meant that the two damaged ships would eventually return to service, but at a crucial moment three out of the six battleships of the Italian Navy were out of action, and the British could pass reinforcements through the central Mediterranean with impunity. For the first time in history a battle fleet had been crippled in harbour without a shot being fired by the opposing side's fleet. Strangely enough, a similar attack had been planned by the British for 1919, using Sopwith Cuckoos to drop torpedoes against the German Fleet. The lesson of Taranto

was not lost on the Japanese, who studied the plan very carefully when preparing their own air strike against Pearl Harbor a year later.

The *Conte di Cavour* never sailed again. She was refloated and towed to Trieste, but was still incomplete at the time of Italy's surrender. The Germans captured the ship in September 1943 but Allied bombs sank her in February 1945. The other two ships were refloated and put back into service in 1941, but the blow to the Italians' confidence was a heavy one. Like the Germans, they could build fine ships, but the High Command was reluctant to accept any risk. The Italians could easily have sacrificed two of their ships without being outnumbered by the British, and if in so doing they had cut British communications between Gibraltar, Malta and Alexandria the strategic consequences could have been overwhelming—the Germans would have reached the Middle East oil that they needed so desperately and the Mediterranean would indeed have become an Italian lake. But the advantages of boldness were obscured by anxiety about losses, and Italian fleet commanders were never given any encouragement to show a bold front to their opponents.

The next time the Italian Fleet met the British was in March 1941, when the Mediterranean Fleet was covering the ill-fated expedition to Greece. Under prodding from the German Naval Liaison Staff in Rome the Italians were persuaded that only HMS *Valiant* was ready for action, and that the time was propitious for another sortie by the 15-in-gunned *Vittorio Veneto*, accompanied by a force of heavy cruisers. But

Giulio Cesare

By 1942 the two surviving battleships of the *Conte di Cavour* class were very different in appearance from their First World War outline. Speed, armament and protection were increased, modernisation having been spurred partly by construction of the French *Dunkerque,* and *Giulio Cesare* survived the Second World War only to mysteriously sink in the Black Sea in 1955 while serving with the Russian Navy

Displacement: 29,100 tons *Length:* 186.4 m *Armament:* 10×320-mm, 12×120-mm, 8×100-mm, 16×37-mm, 12×20-mm *Armour:* 250-mm max side, 100-mm max decks, 280-mm max turrets *Max speed:* 28 knots

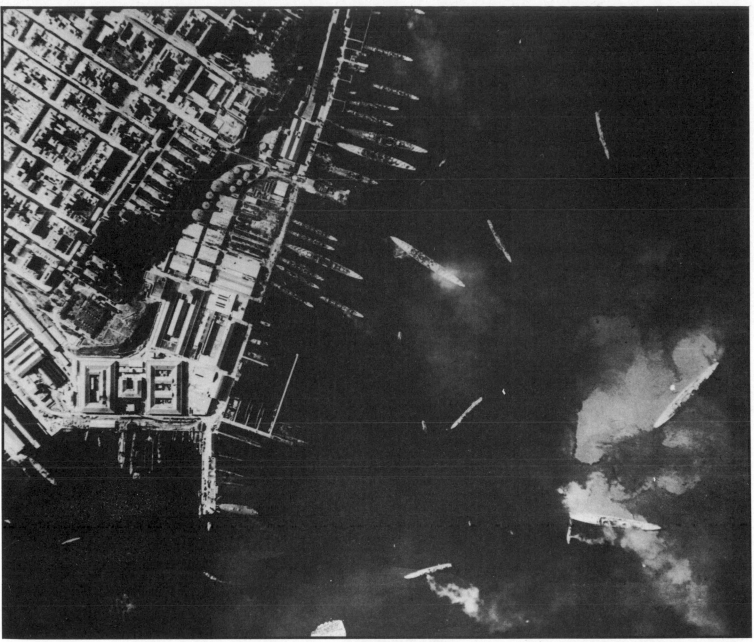

Reconaissance pilot's view of the agony of the Italian Fleet at Taranto. Battleships are surrounded by tell-tale oil slicks, and some already have their bows beneath the water. The major surface threat to Allied control of the Mediterranean had been removed at a stroke, and the aircraft had supplanted the big gun as the arbiter of power at sea

there were three British battleships at sea: the *Warspite, Barham* and *Valiant*, all veterans of Jutland but modernised to varying degrees. With the invaluable carrier *Formidable* in company Cunningham was ready to take a few chances to bring the Italians to battle, and this time his wish was granted.

The *Vittorio Veneto* was hit by a torpedo from one of the *Formidable's* bombers on the morning of 28 March, at about 11 am, and as soon as the report was received on board the flagship Cunningham tried to cut her off. As the Italian ship was not badly damaged and was about 80 miles away there was no chance of catching her that day, but the British still pressed on. The *Vittorio Veneto* bore a charmed life, for she was hit

again near the stern but managed to maintain a fair speed, varying between 12 and 15 knots. At dusk the pursuers were still there, about 65 miles astern, and Cunningham made up his mind to accept the risk of night action. It was a far cry from Jutland, when action had been declined because of the risks; this time, even though only a few ships had radar, Cunningham knew that his ships were fully exercised in night fighting.

On the Italian side there was no such confidence, for their ships had not been equipped with such items as flashless cordite to avoid dazzling the gun crews. The *Vittorio Veneto* was now clear and heading for home, but one of her escorting cruisers, the *Pola*, had been hit by a torpedo and the Commander-in-Chief sent her sisters *Fiume* and *Zara*

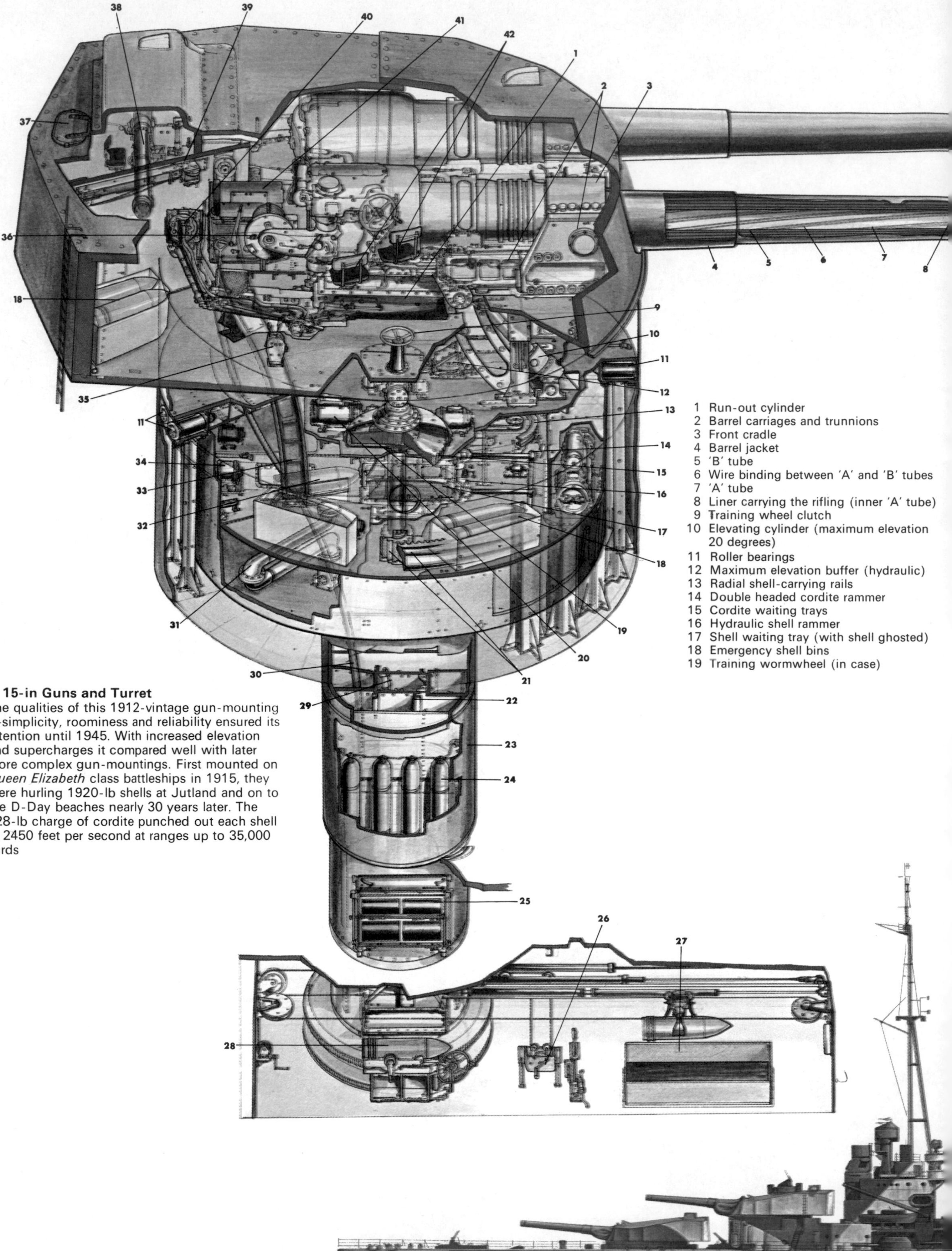

1 Run-out cylinder
2 Barrel carriages and trunnions
3 Front cradle
4 Barrel jacket
5 'B' tube
6 Wire binding between 'A' and 'B' tubes
7 'A' tube
8 Liner carrying the rifling (inner 'A' tube)
9 Training wheel clutch
10 Elevating cylinder (maximum elevation 20 degrees)
11 Roller bearings
12 Maximum elevation buffer (hydraulic)
13 Radial shell-carrying rails
14 Double headed cordite rammer
15 Cordite waiting trays
16 Hydraulic shell rammer
17 Shell waiting tray (with shell ghosted)
18 Emergency shell bins
19 Training wormwheel (in case)

15-in Guns and Turret

The qualities of this 1912-vintage gun-mounting
—simplicity, roominess and reliability ensured its
retention until 1945. With increased elevation
and supercharges it compared well with later
more complex gun-mountings. First mounted on
Queen Elizabeth class battleships in 1915, they
were hurling 1920-lb shells at Jutland and on to
the D-Day beaches nearly 30 years later. The
428-lb charge of cordite punched out each shell
at 2450 feet per second at ranges up to 35,000
yards

20 Turret training engine
21 Turret training rack and pinion gears
22 Ammunition hoist cage rails
23 Turret trunk
24 Breech air blast cylinders (four each side)
25 Cordite hopper (when empty ammunition hoist cage returns, flash proof doors open, and cordite drops onto carriers inside turret trunk)
26 Hand lifting winch
27 Shell bin
28 Shell bogie (in this position it collects shell from overhead rail. Should turret be turned to either side, the bogie is hand wound to position opposite flash proof doors)
29 Auxiliary shell supply hoist tube
30 Auxiliary cordite supply rail (used if normal supply fails)
31 Walking pipes with radial joints (allow systems to function properly while the turret is turning)
32 Emergency supply shell waiting tray (from this point shell is lifted with block and tackle up to the guns)
33 Gun loading cage rails (shape of these allows the cage to line up with breech no matter where the turret is trained)
34 Local fire control dynamo
35 Interlocking gear for gun loading cage and telegraph gear
36 Hydraulically operated breech mechanism (in open position)
37 Turret entrance through armour
38 Range finder
39 Radial crane for lifting shells from bin to emergency folding breech tray in front of open breech
40 Rammer engine and gun loading arm
41 Gun loading cage with cordite in two top sections and shell in bottom chamber (cage lines up with gun at any elevation)
42 Breech operator's and loader's seats

back to look for her. These two ships were suddenly confronted by the terrifying sight of three battleships which had been tracking them steadily on radar. Cunningham himself describes the scene:

'In the dead silence, a silence that could almost be felt, one heard only the voices of the gun control personnel putting the guns on to the new target. One heard the orders repeated in the director tower behind and above the bridge. Looking forward, one saw the turrets swing and steady when the 15-in guns pointed at the enemy cruisers. Never in the whole of my life have I experienced a more thrilling moment than when I heard a calm voice from the director tower: "Director-layer sees the target"; sure sign that the guns were ready and that his finger was itching on the trigger. The enemy was at a range of no more than 3800 yards—point blank.

'It must have been the Fleet Gunnery Officer ... who gave the signal order to open fire. One heard the "ting-ting-ting" of the firing gongs. Then came the great orange flash and the violent shudder as the six big guns bearing were fired simultaneously. At the very same moment the destroyer Greyhound ... switched her searchlight on to one of the enemy cruisers, showing her up momentarily as a silvery-blue shape in the darkness. Our searchlights shone out with the first salvo, and provided illumination for what was a ghastly sight. Full in the beam I saw our six great projectiles flying through the air. Five out of the six hit a few feet below the level of the cruiser's upper deck and burst with flashes of brilliant flame. The Italians were quite unprepared. Their guns were trained fore and aft. They were hopelessly shattered before they could put up any resistance.'

Partial Success

The *Valiant* and *Barham* dealt similarly with the other cruisers, and in a matter of a few minutes both were glowing torches. The Italian destroyers made a gallant attempt to torpedo the British squadron but they were driven off. The destroyers found the damaged *Pola* and torpedoed her, and as dawn was approaching Cunningham wisely decided to head for home. This Battle of Cape Matapan, otherwise known to the Italians as the Battle of Gaudo Island, was in Cunningham's eyes only a partial success as he had wanted to trap the *Vittorio Veneto*, but its strategic value was to be demonstrated very soon. In May the Mediterranean Fleet had to evacuate troops from Crete under constant German air attack. The *Warspite* was hit and badly damaged by a large bomb, and several smaller ships were sunk. If the Italian Fleet needed to put to sea now was the time, but it did not. The memory of Matapan was too recent.

The Italians did eventually get their

revenge for Matapan, but still they failed to reap the proper benefit. On the night of 18–19 December, 1941 the submarine *Scire* launched three 'human torpedoes', really small self-propelled craft driven by two operators wearing underwater breathing apparatus and sitting astride the body of the craft. At about 4 am sentries found two frogmen clinging to the anchor cable of HMS *Valiant*, and a few minutes later charges detonated under her and the flagship *Queen Elizabeth*. The *Valiant* was seriously damaged, but could steam, whereas the *Queen Elizabeth* was much worse, with a hole about 40 feet square under her forward boiler rooms. Both ships were quite unfit for action, and, had the Italians but known it, they had virtually sunk the last two British battleships in the Mediterranean. But the harbour at Alexandria is shallow and both ships settled on the mud, revealing very little to the snooping aircraft which flew over next day. After strenuous efforts both battleships were eventually refloated; the *Valiant* went to Durban in April 1942 for a three-month repair but the *Queen Elizabeth* needed nine months in an American yard, and did not rejoin the Fleet until June 1943.

The other battleship in the Mediterranean had been the *Barham*, but on 24 November she had been exercising with the rest of the Mediterranean Fleet off the coast of Egypt when *U.331* penetrated the screen without being detected. Three torpedoes hit the old ship, she rolled over to port and after about four minutes lay on her beam ends and blew up. She and the *Malaya* had never received the full modernisation given to the other *Queen Elizabeth*s and her loss was probably caused by her inferior underwater protection. The Board of Inquiry concluded that 4-in ammunition stored in what had once been the port underwater torpedo-tube compartment might have caught fire and set off the 15-in magazines. In the modernised ships such spaces had been given protection and converted to other uses, but in the unmodernised ships the compartments were outside the main citadel and were often used for storing the vast quantities of anti-aircraft ammunition which were needed. It is significant that four out of the five British capital ships sunk in the war were old ships which had not had their underwater and magazine protection overhauled. It is also interesting to note that the *Barham* was the only Allied battleship to be sunk at sea by a U-Boat.

HMS *Queen Elizabeth*
Queen Elizabeth, seen here in 1941, was substantially modernised a second time before the war. The superstructure was completely replaced, anti-aircraft armament was increased and a hangar and catapult were provided. Weight saved on new machinery was used to increase protection
Displacement: 36,000 tons *Length:* 639 ft *Atmament:* 8×15-in, 20×4.5-in, 32×40-mm up to 52×20-mm, 16×mg *Armour:* 13-in max side, 3-in max deck, 11-in max turrets
Max speed: 24.5 knots

Bismarck: Breakout and Destruction

It is opportune now to return to the Atlantic, for the German Navy was ready by April 1941 to send its newest and most powerful battleship to sea. On 21 May the *Bismarck* sailed from her Norwegian fjord with the 8-in gunned cruiser *Prinz Eugen*, and as the Home Fleet had been alerted it was not long before two cruisers patrolling in the Denmark Strait made contact. In the early hours of 24 May the battle-cruiser HMS *Hood* and the new battleship *Prince of Wales* moved from Iceland to intercept the German squadron. Vice-Admiral Holland in the *Hood* hoped to come into action on the most advantageous bearing, but during the night he had made an alteration of course, and as a result found that his ships would have to engage on a fine bearing which masked their after guns and so reduced the weight of fire. The *Prince of Wales* had been completed only two weeks before and was suffering teething troubles in her 14-in gun mountings, so a reduction of 40 per cent in her firepower added to her already severe problems.

The British ships turned in line ahead to close the range as fast as possible, for Admiral Holland knew that his flagship was vulnerable to 15-in shellfire down to about 18,000 yards. Vulnerability in this sense refers to the 'immunity zone' conferred by the side and deck armour, and it is interesting to compare this with *Prince of Wales'* immunity zone, which extended down to 13,000 yards. Below 18,000 yards the trajectory of shells flattened and the thinness of

Hood's deck armour would matter less and less, while her 12-in side armour was only .6-in less than that of the *Bismarck*. Another problem for Holland was that *Hood's* speed was now only about $28\frac{1}{2}$ knots, the same as that of the *Prince of Wales*; although the *Bismarck's* sea speed was only 29 knots she was credited with 31, and he must have felt that he could be out-manoeuvred by the German ships.

Massive Explosion

Many commentators claim that *Hood* made a mistake in identifying the leading ship as the *Bismarck* instead of the *Prinz Eugen* but German survivors reported that *Hood* was firing at *Bismarck* very well and found the range in three salvoes. The next salvo might well have been a hit, but *Prinz Eugen* had already scored a hit on *Hood's* boat deck which started a fire. The range was now down to just over 18,000 yards, and the *Hood* ordered a turn to port to bring full broadsides to bear, but just as she started her turn she was hit by one or possibly two shells from the *Bismarck*. Suddenly the *Hood* vanished in a sheet of flame and a massive explosion engulfed her. When the smoke cleared her shattered hull could be seen disappearing below the water.

To the onlookers in the *Prince of Wales*, as much as to the Germans, the explosion was horrifying, but there was no time to think of reasons. The *Prince of Wales*, with one forward 14-in gun defective and the after turret

jammed by a shell which had fallen out of the hoist, now faced the *Bismarck* and *Prinz Eugen* alone. She was hit seven times in quick succession by three 8-in and four 15-in shells. Six caused little damage but one hit was deadly; it passed through the bridge without exploding but shattered the binnacle on its way out. Fragments of metal scythed across the compass platform, killing or wounding everyone except Captain Leach. But the *Prince of Wales* was not put out of action, and although her gunnery radar set was not working she was able to get the range from her Type 281 air-warning set and obtained several straddles on the *Bismarck*. Two 14-in shells penetrated the German ship's hull and started a leak in a fuel bunker, but it was clearly foolhardy to allow a new ship to face two apparently undamaged German ships, and the rear-admiral commanding the cruisers, now the

HMS *Hood*

The battle-cruiser *Hood* was the only one of her class to be completed, the other three being suspended in 1917 when Germany stopped work on the *Mackensen* class. The loss of three battle-cruisers at Jutland resulted in additional armour being incorporated in the *Hood's* design, adding 5000 tons to the displacement and reducing top speed by 2 knots. The explosion which destroyed the ship in her action against the *Bismarck* and *Prinz Eugen* is thought to have resulted from anti-aircraft shells or rockets being ignited by a fire following a shell hit, rather than by the main armour being penetrated

Displacement: 41,200 tons *Length:* 860 ft
Armament: 8×15-in, 14×4-in, 24×2-pdr (3×8), 20×mg, 5×UP batteries, 4×21-in TT *Armour:* 12-in belt, 3-in deck (max), 15-in turrets (max)
Max speed: $28\frac{1}{2}$ knots

senior officer present, ordered Leach to break off action.

It will never be known just what caused the *Hood* to blow up, and two boards of inquiry were unable to do more than make educated guesses. There were hardly any witnesses; the three survivors could not provide any clue, and the majority of people on board the *Prince of Wales* were either watching the German ships or fully engaged elsewhere. Several interesting points did come to light, however. First, the *Hood* was carrying a large amount of rocket ammunition for her anti-aircraft 'UP' (Unrotated Projectile) rocket mountings, stowed in light steel lockers under the boat deck, which was the site of the fire caused by the 8-in shell from *Prinz Eugen*. Second, four out of the seven shells which hit the *Prince of Wales* did not explode, and the remaining three only detonated partially. Third, the after magazines in the *Hood* had been surrounded by additional 4-in anti-aircraft stowage outside the armoured barbettes. If

Right: The breakout and destruction of the *Bismarck*. Once she had fought her way out into the Atlantic and given the Royal Navy a bloody nose by sinking the *Hood*, the convoys were easy prey. Through a mixture of luck, the long arm of airpower, and finally the gunpower of superior surface forces, the *Bismarck* was sunk only a few hundred miles from the safety of Brest

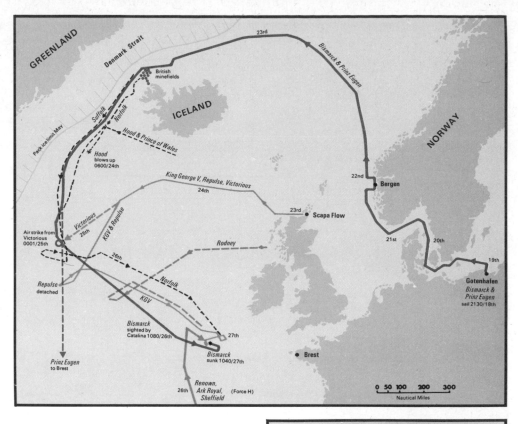

May 20, 1941 and the Bismarck *prepares in the Baltic for her final sortie against the Atlantic convoys. The aircraft recognition bands were painted out at Bergen*

Bismarck

The *Bismarck* was the *Kriegsmarine*'s first modern battleship, built under the terms of the Anglo-German Naval Agreement. Basically an enlarged version of the 1915 *Baden*, she displayed many old-fashioned features—particularly separate high-angle and low-angle batteries and a lack of vertical sandwich protection against underwater damage. In fact her most important asset was her massive beam

Displacement: 41,000 tons *Length:* 245 m *Armament:* 8×380-mm, 12×150-mm, 16× 105-mm, 16×37-mm, 12×20-mm *Armour:* 320-mm side (max), 120-mm deck (max), 360-mm turrets (max) *Max speed:* 29 knots

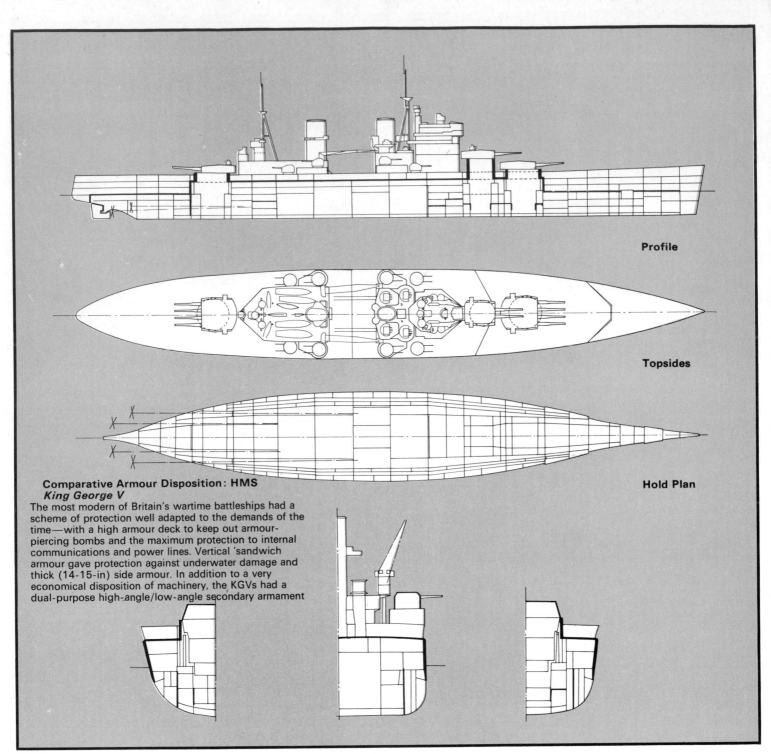

Profile

Topsides

Hold Plan

Comparative Armour Disposition: HMS *King George V*

The most modern of Britain's wartime battleships had a scheme of protection well adapted to the demands of the time—with a high armour deck to keep out armour-piercing bombs and the maximum protection to internal communications and power lines. Vertical 'sandwich' armour gave protection against underwater damage and thick (14-15-in) side armour. In addition to a very economical disposition of machinery, the KGVs had a dual-purpose high-angle/low-angle secondary armament

Left: HMS Anson, *launched in 1942, fourth of the* King George V *class*

the fire amidships did not detonate the above-water torpedo tubes, and there is no direct evidence of this, and if the *Bismarck's* shells were defective, as we know they were, then the most tenable conclusion is that the *Hood* was sunk by a fire which somehow spread to the 4-in ammunition below and thence to the after 15-in magazines. Stemming from this, the probability is that *Hood* was sunk by a fire caused by an 8-in shell, and not by a 15-in shell penetrating her side or deck armour.

The *Bismarck* and *Prinz Eugen* now succeeded in shaking off the shadowing cruisers, and during the confusion the cruiser broke away and proceeded independently to Brest. Admiral Lütjens decided that his flagship had lost too much fuel from the two shell hits, and decided to make for St Nazaire, where there was a dock large enough to take her. Late on the night of 24

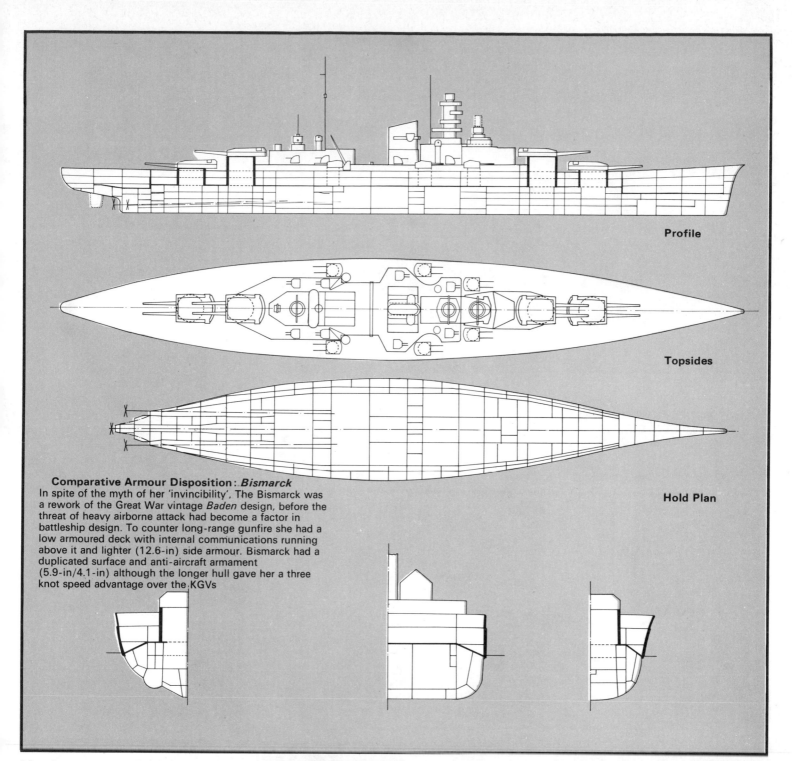

Profile

Topsides

Hold Plan

Comparative Armour Disposition: *Bismarck*
In spite of the myth of her 'invincibility', The Bismarck was a rework of the Great War vintage *Baden* design, before the threat of heavy airborne attack had become a factor in battleship design. To counter long-range gunfire she had a low armoured deck with internal communications running above it and lighter (12.6-in) side armour. Bismarck had a duplicated surface and anti-aircraft armament (5.9-in/4.1-in) although the longer hull gave her a three knot speed advantage over the KGVs

May she was attacked by Swordfish torpedo-bombers from the aircraft carrier *Victorious,* and although one torpedo hit the 18-in weapon did not carry a warhead big enough to make much impression on the thickest part of a battleship's armour belt.

Throughout the next day the British hunted the *Bismarck* with ships and aircraft in the most massive co-ordinated search of the war. Not until 26 May did a Catalina flying boat spot the *Bismarck*, but she was so far away from any ships strong enough to bring her to battle that it seemed as if she might reach safety after all. In a 'French port she could be repaired and then sail again, and this time she would be closer to the Atlantic shipping routes. It was essential to slow her down, and the carrier *Ark Royal* coming up from Gibraltar with the battle-cruiser *Renown* was ordered to fly off a strike. The first was unsuccessful, as the

Right: Bismarck, *greatest of her time, or a rework of an outdated design?*

Drüppel

111

Pulling through a 38-cm gun aboard the Tirpitz *after firing practise*

10.5-cm High-Angle Anti-Aircraft Gun
Main AA armament on *Bismarck* and *Tirpitz*.
A triaxial stabilising system ensured that the
gun and crew were on a level platform whatever
the sea conditions and angle of the ship.
Illustration bottom right shows the gun at
maximum angle of roll

The 10·5-cm high-angle anti-aircraft guns of the Tirpitz

*The 10·5-cm and 3·7-cm anti-aircraft armament
aboard German capital ships was supplemented
by 2-cm automatics in single and quadruple
mountings*

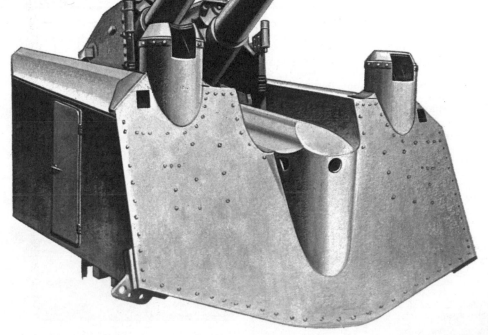

Swordfish attacked the cruiser *Sheffield* by mistake in the murky weather, but the second strike was successful. One 18-in torpedo spent itself on the armour belt as before, but the second wrecked the *Bismarck*'s steering gear and jammed her rudders.

The giant battleship was doomed; although she survived torpedo attacks from destroyers during the night she was steering erratically and trailing oil fuel. Next morning the Home Fleet flagship *King George V* and the *Rodney* hove into view, and the *Bismarck* prepared to fight her last battle. The two British battleships selected their own courses, the *Rodney* choosing to engage end-on while the flagship attacked on the broadside. All three ships opened fire at about 8.47 am, but the *Bismarck*'s firing was soon erratic; the nearest she came to scoring a hit was a straddle on the *Rodney,* and within half an hour her guns were silent and she had sustained heavy damage. By now she was so low in the water

and the range was so short that the shells were passing straight over the armoured deck. To try to get a plunging hit the *King George V* opened the range to 14,000 yards, leaving the *Rodney* to reduce the superstructure to a shambles from a range of 4000 yards. At 10.15 the C-in-C Home Fleet, Admiral Tovey, ordered his ships to cease fire and the cruiser *Dorsetshire* fired two torpedoes into the *Bismarck*'s starboard side and another one into the port side. At 10.36 she rolled over and sank, leaving a few score of dazed survivors in the water.

Myth of Invincibility

Surprisingly the last fight of the *Bismarck* has become a subject for myth and misunderstanding, with claims made to the effect that she was 'unsinkable', that she was scuttled without her armour being perforated, or even that the British could have towed her into port. Myths also surround the subject of her design; she is credited with the heaviest protection in the

world, with a 'secret formula' nickel-steel armour twice as resistant as any previous steels, etc, etc. True, she was a powerful ship but her design basically was old-fashioned. The haste with which Hitler had expanded the *Kriegsmarine* had prevented a full evaluation of designs and many of the brilliant ship designers had left the service after 1918. With nothing like the action experience of the British and the lengthy tests on target ships carried out by them, the Americans and the Japanese, there was little choice but to update the *Baden* design of 1915, just as the *Mackensen* of 1916 had served as the model for the *Scharnhorst*. Of course the machinery was more modern and far more powerful, but the essential details of armouring were more First World War than Second in conception.

Among the principal features which stamp the *Bismarck* design as elderly are the triple gun-battery, main 15-in, secondary 15-cm (5.9-in) and anti-aircraft 10.5-cm, and the relatively low level at which the main armoured deck was positioned. As we have already seen, the US Navy and the Royal Navy had independently reached the conclusion that bombs were a bigger danger than long-range gunfire, and had sited the armoured deck as high as possible. Nor was there any 'sandwich' protection against torpedoes; instead the *Bismarck* relied on

her massive 118-ft beam to provide a deep space between the ship's side and the anti-torpedo bulkhead. This gave great initial stability and resistance to underwater damage, but eventually resulted in an accelerated tendency to capsize, especially as the freeboard was quite low. Despite a flagrant evasion of the international treaty limits, involving a jump from 35,000 tons declared standard tonnage to an actual displacement of 41,700 tons, and the installation of high-pressure steam machinery delivering 138,000 horsepower, the *Bismarck* had a sea speed of only 29 knots, a fraction of a knot more than that of the smaller *South Dakota* and *King George V* classes. The belt armour was 12.6-in thick, making her equal to the *South Dakota* but inferior to the *King George V* and other classes.

These comparisons are quoted not to belittle the *Bismarck* but to debunk the myths which have grown up around her. She and the *Tirpitz* were powerful ships but they were by no means the ultimate design that many people think they were. This contrast between the facts and popular belief probably stems from the loss of HMS *Hood*. The British were downcast by the loss of a ship that had been imbued with strength she did not possess, and the Germans were correspondingly elated by the feat and justifiably proud of their battleship's last stand. Be that as it may, since 1941 there has been a flood of ill-informed and half-baked speculation about the loss of the *Bismarck*. One ludicrous report claimed that a diver had gone down to examine the hull of the *Bismarck* and had found 'no holes in the hull'. Apart from the fact that the diver could claim a world record for diving off the Continental shelf, a team of expert divers took three months to examine the hull of the *Prince of Wales* and were still unable to find the radar aerials; on such a large hull a bottom search in deep water would be impossible.

The Channel Dash

The elimination of the *Bismarck* led the German naval command to reconsider the wisdom of leaving the *Scharnhorst* and *Gneisenau* at Brest. The two battle-cruisers had cruised in the Atlantic from January to March 1941—Operation *Berlin*—during which they sank or captured 22 ships. After steaming a total of 17,800 miles they docked at Brest on 23 March, but soon the RAF began to bomb their berths. Despite an ever-increasing weight of bombs dropped, neither ship was seriously damaged, apart from a torpedo hit on the *Gneisenau* on 6 April, 1941 and bomb damage to *Scharnhorst* on 24 July. But it was only a matter of time before a lucky hit caused serious damage, and if the ships were not to be allowed to make another foray into the Atlantic better use could be made of them elsewhere. On 1 January, 1942 Naval Group Command West brought up the subject of what to do with the two battle-cruisers and the cruiser *Prinz Eugen,* and 12 days later Hitler announced his plan for a breakout through the English Channel.

The naval staff was aghast, for on the face of it three large ships had no chance of slipping through the narrow Straits of Dover without being sunk by air attack, surface torpedo attack or coastal guns. But Hitler once again showed that his imagination and skill at divining his opponent's weaknesses could out match conventional wisdom; he banked on the British convincing themselves that a daylight run could never happen. And so it turned out. The RAF failed to spot the German ships until they were off Le Havre at 10.42 am on the morning of 12 February, and even then no co-ordinated attack could be mounted. Piecemeal attacks by motor torpedo boats and aircraft were beaten off with ease, for the *Luftwaffe* had for once co-operated with the *Kriegsmarine* totally, and had provided a massive fighter 'umbrella' for Operation *Cerberus*. The coastal guns at Dover were not allowed to open fire until the German ships were almost out of range, for fear that they might hit their own MTBs' Although a small force of destroyers got within 4,000 yards their torpedoes were dodged, and an incredulous Admiral Ciliax slowly realised that the Führer's intuition had been right. Apart from mine damage to both ships late in the day, the most audacious, not to say insolent, excursion of the war had been achieved without loss.

The British were furious, and heads rolled as Churchill investigated what *The Times* chose to call the greatest humiliation inflicted on the Royal Navy since the Dutch burned the fleet at Chatham in 1667. But it was a hollow victory, for the three German ships were far less dangerous in Germany than they had been at Brest. Operation *Cerberus* was in fact a strategic withdrawal, that time-honoured euphemism for a retreat, and the high command was hard-put to work out what to do with the battle-cruisers now that they were safe in German waters. Both ships went to Kiel for repairs, and *Scharnhorst* rejoined the Fleet in August 1942. But *Gneisenau* was not so lucky. On the night of 26-27 February she was set on fire by a bomb during an air raid on Kiel, and an explosion of oil fumes wrecked the entire forepart of the ship, from the bow as far back as 'A' turret.

The ship was towed to Götenhafen

Above: *The* Scharnhorst *arms at Brest in preparation for Operation* Cerberus. *Her Arado Ar 196 is on the dockside*

(Gdynia) in April, and a long-cherished plan to re-arm the class with 15-in guns was revived. The barbettes had been designed to take the weight of the twin 38-cm turret, but the opportunity was also taken to improve seaworthiness by lengthening the bow. The wreckage of the forecastle was cut off in 1943, but by this time the Third Reich was desperately short of steel and labour. The work ground to a halt in 1944, and eventu-

ally she was no more than an inert hulk. On 27 March, 1945 she was scuttled in the entrance to the harbour of Götenhafen to deny the port to the Russians. The Poles took four years to salvage the wreck, and the work was not completed until September 1951.

The Destruction of the Scharnhorst and Tirpitz

After the sinking of the *Bismarck* the German naval command fell back on its older and safer doctrine of the 'fleet in being'. When the Allies stopped their convoys to North Russia in the summer of 1943 this was largely due to the presence of the *Scharnhorst* and *Tirpitz* in northern Norway. Despite Hitler's rage over the bungled action in the Barents Sea in December 1942, when the failure of the 'pocket battleship' *Lützow* (formerly the *Deutschland*) and the heavy cruiser *Admiral Hipper* to deal with a convoy escorted only by destroyers led to the resignation of Admiral Raeder as Commander-in-Chief.

Raeder had resigned largely because Hitler had threatened to pay off the large warships, using their steel to make tanks and their guns for coastal defence. His successor, Admiral Dönitz, was well known for his advocacy of U-Boat warfare, but even he recognised the value of the few remaining large ships in tying down large numbers of British ships and preventing supplies from reaching Russia. Not only did Dönitz win a reprieve for the surface fleet, but he even initiated a request to Hitler early in 1943 for permission to use the big ships offensively once more. Dönitz and his admirals Schniewind (Flag Officer Group North) and Kummetz (Flag Officer Northern Task Force) were determined that the commanders would have freedom to engage, without inhibiting orders of the sort that had resulted in so many abortive operations in the past.

The subject acquired new urgency in November 1943, when two convoys slipped through to Russia without loss. This was despite doubts expressed by Kummetz, who pointed out that *Tirpitz* would not complete her repairs until March, and the undeniable fact that in an action during the long Arctic winter the much superior British radar would put his ships at a disadvantage. Kummetz then went on long leave, and command of the Northern Group was handed over to Admiral 'Achmed' Bey, who commanded the destroyers. Bey seems to have been under the impression that action would be limited to a destroyer raid on a convoy but on 29 December he was told that it might be expedient to use the *Scharnhorst* as well. On 19 December Dönitz informed Hitler that the battle-cruiser would attack the next Allied convoy if the circumstances were favourable.

Dunking Dönitz

The circumstances were not very favourable, had Dönitz known, and now that the 'Ultra' story has been revealed, of how much of the highest level German intelligence was known to the Allies, we can wonder how much knowledge the C-in-C Home Fleet, Admiral Fraser, was acting upon when he took his flagship, the battleship *Duke of York*, the cruiser *Jamaica* and four destroyers as distant cover for an outward convoy (JW.55B) and an inward convoy (FA.55A) between Loch Ewe and the Kola Inlet. The *Scharnhorst* sailed from Altenfjord at 7 pm on Christmas Day, accompanied by five destroyers. Recon-

naissance had detected convoy JW.55B but not the one heading for home, and Admiral Bey did not know that Admiral Fraser had already transferred some of his destroyers to JW.55B's escort, bringing it up to 14 destroyers to oppose the *Scharnhorst*. The weather and visibility were worsening, and Bey was forced to ask permission to send his destroyers back as they could not keep up with his flagship. Despite the risk of operating a capital ship without escort he was told to press on alone if he felt justified. All the time the *Duke of York* and the *Jamaica* were pounding through the heavy seas at a steady 17 knots, closing on the *Scharnhorst*.

The bad weather grounded the *Luftwaffe*'s reconnaissance aircraft, and although U-boats provided good estimates of the convoy's escort they failed to spot the other convoy or the Home Fleet. Mindful of the way in which his forces were scattered, Admiral Fraser took care to inform them of his own position and established the whereabouts of all ships; even the risk of breaking wireless silence was preferable to any misunderstanding about the tactical dispositions. By contrast the *Scharnhorst* lost contact with her destroyers at about 7.30 am on 26 December, thanks to a mix-up in signals, and they were not able to rejoin the flagship.

It was 8.40 am when Admiral Burnett, commanding the cruisers covering the convoy, learned that the *Belfast* had picked up the *Scharnhorst* on her radar screen, only 30 miles away. The *Duke of York* was still nearly 200 miles distant, and the three

HMS *Duke of York*
Construction of the *King George V* class was spurred by the laying down of new battleships in France, Germany and Italy. The ships were more heavily armoured than those of the *Nelson* class
  Displacement: 44,790 tons max *Length:* 745 ft
Armament: 10×14-in, 16×5.25-in, 48×2-pdr AA
Armour: 15-in belt, 9/16-in main turrets,
1/6-in deck *Max speed:* 29 knots

King George V class

Name	Completed	Fate
King George V	Dec 1940	Scrapped 1958
Prince of Wales	Mar 1941	Sunk by Japanese aircraft 1941
Duke of York	Nov 1941	Scrapped 1958
Anson	Jun 1942	Scrapped 1957
Howe	Aug 1942	Scrapped 1958

cruisers would have to hold off the *Scharnhorst* for a long time. At 9.24 the *Scharnhorst* was suddenly illuminated by starshell from the *Belfast* and two minutes later an 8-in shell from HMS *Norfolk* burst on her foretop, destroying the forward radar fire-control director. With one of her 'eyes' blinded the *Scharnhorst* was in a bad position, but she was able to turn to the south and outstrip the cruisers, which could not maintain top speed in such bad weather. The cruisers therefore rejoined the convoy, putting themselves between the *Scharnhorst* and her quarry. There were terrible fears aboard the Home Fleet flagship that contact might have been lost for good, but Admiral Burnett in the *Belfast* was confident that the *Scharnhorst* would be back, and he was proved right when his flagship regained radar contact at about mid-day.

Just after 12.21 the *Scharnhorst* opened fire on the cruisers, and as the range was down to 11,000 yards she hit both *Sheffield* and *Norfolk*; the latter had an 8-in turret and all but one of her radar sets put out of action. Once again the *Scharnhorst* turned away, but this time she unwittingly steamed directly towards the *Duke of York,* with the result that the British battleship picked her up on radar at 4.17 pm.

The range rapidly came down to 12,000 yards as the *Duke of York* manoeuvred to bring her full broadside to bear on her luckless target. At 4.50 pm the dreaded starshell burst in the darkness overhead, followed by 14-in and 6-in salvoes from the *Duke of York* and *Jamaica*. Admiral Bey was taken completely by surprise by this attack from an unexpected bearing, and it was some minutes before the German guns could reply. The range quickly opened as the *Scharnhorst* tried to break away, but the *Duke of York* hung on her heels. By 5.40 the cruisers had fallen back and the two big ships fought their duel alone at range varying from 17,000 to 20,000 yards. The *Scharnhorst*'s gunnery settled down, but the only two hits she scored against the *Duke of York* went through the legs of her tripod masts and failed to explode. The British shooting was excellent, and at one stage the *Scharnhorst* was reduced to making small alterations to port to throw off the enemy fire-control, just as Hipper's battle-cruisers had done against the 5th Battle Squadron at Jutland many years before. But this time radar plotting was able to pick up these variations, and the *Duke of York*'s gunnery was good enough to be able to fire the 14-in to hit the target by aiming at her next likely position.

Glow Through the Smoke

At least one of the 14-in shells had damaged one of the *Scharnhorst*'s propeller shafts, but this did not slow her down sufficiently, and Admiral Fraser's fear was still that she would escape. After the gun action was broken off, just as Bey signalled 'We shall fight to the last shell', the four destroyers were ordered to attack with torpedoes. While two drew fire on the port side the other pair crept up to within 3000 yards on the starboard side before they were seen. The *Scorpion* hit her with at least one torpedo, and in the confusion that followed the *Savage* and *Saumarez* hit with another three. At 7 pm the *Duke of York* again opened fire, this time at only 10,400 yards, and the cruisers joined in. In half an hour the *Scharnhorst* was crawling at 5 knots, with shells bursting everywhere and fires

The topography of her fjord lair rather than any inherent invincibility of the ship protected the Tirpitz *from air attack. The* Tirpitz *never took part in any major surface action and was finally sunk by 'Tallboy' 12,000-lb bombs delivered by Lancaster bombers*

glowing through the clouds of smoke. The *Jamaica* closed in to finish her with torpedoes, and reported that she could see only a dull glow through the smoke.

No-one saw the *Scharnhorst* go down, but she must have sunk at about 7.45. Only 36 survivors were found in the icy water, out of nearly 2000 men. She had been sacrificed in an operation which had been badly planned, and with her went the last credible threat to the Arctic convoys for the time being. Once again it had been proved that only a capital ship could do the job, for at that distance from land and in such weather conditions air attacks could not have been made.

The last capital ship left to the *Kriegsmarine* was the *Tirpitz,* the sister of the *Bismarck*. Since late 1941 she had led a life of masterly inactivity. She was sent to Norway to threaten the Russian convoys, and in 1942 the threat of her going to sea was enough to cause the Admiralty to order convoy PQ.17 to scatter. In April 1943 the Royal Navy started to plan an attack on her Norwegian anchorage, using midget submarines to penetrate the net defences in Altenfjord. In this sense the X-Craft, as they were known, were the modern equivalent of the fireship, sent in to reach a ship which would not come out to fight. In this the midgets were successful, and on the night of 20-21 September, 1943 the *Tirpitz* was badly damaged by a ½-ton charge which exploded under her keel. All three sets of turbines were seriously damaged, putting the ship out of action for at least seven months.

The *Tirpitz* has acquired a formidable reputation for the way she stood up to attacks, but the reason she survived so many is because the anchorage she used afforded a superb natural defence against air attack. It was all but impossible to aim a bomb or torpedo at her when she nestled under the side of the fjord, and the story of the many attacks on her is really the story of attempts to overcome the geographical problems. On the occasion that a bomb did hit her, it went right through most of her decks but failed to explode. Once she was surprised at sea by Fleet Air Arm torpedo-bombers, and was very lucky to dodge the

torpedoes. Finally in August 1944, with the Allied Joint Planning Staff increasingly irritated at the way in which she was tying down ships urgently needed for the Pacific, it was decided to use Lancaster bombers and 12,000-lb 'Tallboy' bombs. On 15 September, 1944, 28 Lancasters flying from a Russian airfield scored a hit and two near misses.

The damage caused was too serious to be repaired so far north, and as the Germans were in any case thinking of abandoning Altenfjord they decided to move her to Tromsö, where she could act as a floating battery to defend against the invasion which Hitler was sure would be launched against Norway. Now she was 200 miles nearer to British air bases than before, and after a false start on 18 October, when low cloud obscured the anchorage, 32 Lancasters attacked on 12 November. This time all went well; the *Luftwaffe* failed to put any fighters up and in clear weather, without any distractions, the RAF bomb-aimers were able to hit the *Tirpitz* three times. She heeled over 30° to port, her after magazine exploded, and then she turned turtle. Some thousand men were trapped inside the hull, but a few trapped in an air pocket were heard, and a hole was cut in the bottom plating to allow them to escape.

In all 16 air attacks were made on the *Tirpitz,* 7 by the RAF and 9 by the Fleet Air Arm. For many years the wreck of the *Tirpitz* lay in Tromsö Fjord oozing oil, but she yielded a useful bonus to the Norwegian people who had been her unwilling hosts for three years, in the form of hundreds of electrical generators salvaged and put to good use ashore.

BATTLESHIPS IN SHADOW

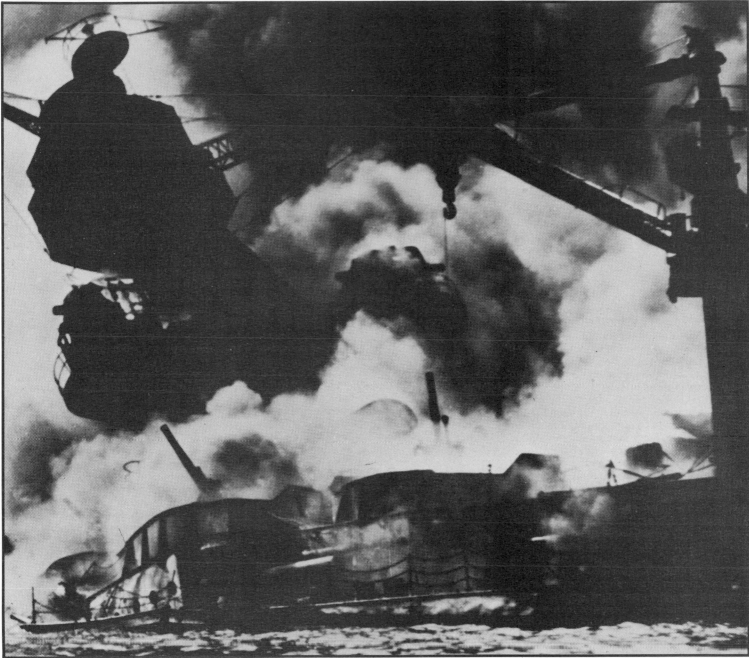

American battleships blaze at Pearl Harbor, struck by the massive Japanese carrier-launched attack. Since Taranto the message had been clear. The mighty battleship as king-pin of surface fleets was now overshadowed by air power

Across the other side of the world the Japanese had set in train events which rocked the world, and incidentally finished the reputation of the battleship. Profiting by the lessons of the British attack on Taranto, the Japanese planned an air strike against the United States' Pacific Fleet in its base at Pearl Harbor on Oahu in the Hawaiian Islands. They were acutely aware that the Americans outnumbered them, and it was hoped, just as at Port Arthur in 1904, to start the war with a knockout blow. Commercial rivalry between the United States and Japan had been growing for years, but above all the Japanese needed the strategic raw materials of Malaya and the East Indies—oil, rubber and minerals—to maintain their economic growth. It needed only the military ardour of young middle-rank officers who believed themselves invincible to turn these economic

imperatives into a bold and imaginative war plan.

On 26 November, 1941 a large fleet of six aircraft carriers, two battleships and three cruisers put to sea for a secret rendezvous; they were actually heading by a roundabout route for Pearl Harbor, and avoided shipping routes. The deception was a complete success and the attack position 275 miles north of Pearl Harbor was reached on the night of 6-7 December. At 7 am the first wave took off, and an hour later the first bombs shattered the Sunday tranquility of the great naval base.

In just under two hours two waves of aircraft wrought havoc with the unprepared Pacific Fleet. Despite having radar warning and despite a destroyer reporting a midget submarine outside the harbour, nothing was done to sound the alarm. By midday the battleships *Arizona* and *Okla-*

homa had been destroyed, and the *California, Maryland, Pennsylvania, Tennessee* and *West Virginia* all seriously damaged. Burning furiously, the *Nevada* had nearly sunk in the entrance to the harbour, but had managed to beach herself before blocking the channel. Casualties were heavy in men and aircraft, but above all the Americans' pride was hurt. They could draw some comfort from the knowledge that all four of their own aircraft carriers had been away at sea and so had escaped the holocaust, and that the ships' gunfire had punished the second wave of Japanese aircraft severely. But the fact remained that the US Pacific Fleet had been neutralised, and nothing stood between the Japanese Fleet and conquest of the Pacific.

The British had rashly sent the *Prince of Wales* and the old battle-cruiser *Repulse* to Singapore in the vague hope that their

117

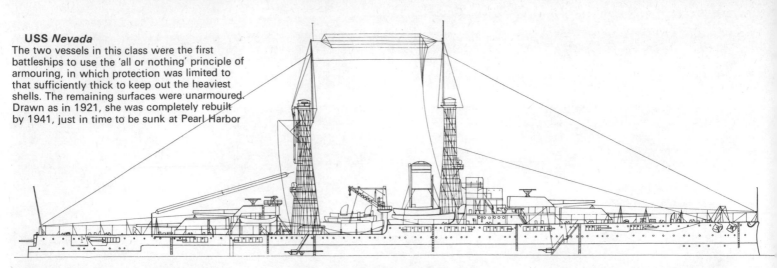

USS *Nevada*

The two vessels in this class were the first battleships to use the 'all or nothing' principle of armouring, in which protection was limited to that sufficiently thick to keep out the heaviest shells. The remaining surfaces were unarmoured. Drawn as in 1921, she was completely rebuilt by 1941, just in time to be sunk at Pearl Harbor

Displacement: 34,000 tons full load *Length:* 583 ft *Armament:* 10×14-in, 12×5-in, 8×5-in AA *Armour:* 8/14-in belt, 5/18-in main turrets, 4-in main deck *Max speed:* 20.5 knots

Nevada class

Name	Completed	Fate
Nevada	Mar 1916	Sunk as target 1948
Oklahoma	May 1916	Sank under tow 1947

presence would overawe the Japanese. With the destruction of the US Fleet these two capital ships now found themselves in a hopeless position, close to powerful land-based air squadrons in Thailand and lacking anything but the most rudimentary air cover from the obsolescent fighters of the RAF. On 8 December, six days after the two ships had arrived, Admiral Sir Tom Phillips took them to sea to carry out a 'search and destroy' mission against a reported Japanese landing at Singora and Kota Bharu. Next day the force was sighted by aircraft, and although it altered course during the night it was relocated next morning. Just after 1100 high-level bombing attacks started, and then torpedo attacks. The *Repulse* was slightly damaged by a bomb but the *Prince of Wales* was hit aft by a torpedo, which wrecked her steering.

The *Prince of Wales* was in a bad way. The torpedo hit warped the port outer shaft, and as the turbine was not stopped the bent shaft churned up the structure, opening out the bulkheads and allowing about 2500 tons of water to flood the machinery compartments. The ship listed about 11½°, and when

HMS *Repulse*

Repulse was another victim of that precocious child, the aircraft, and only three days after Pearl Harbor she succumbed to Japanese bombers while steaming off Malaya in the company of *Prince of Wales*. The birds let loose at Taranto were finally coming home to roost

Displacement: 32,000 tons *Length:* 740 ft *Armament:* 6×15-in, 9×4-in, 8×4-in AA, 24×40-mm, 8×21-in torpedo tubes *Armour:* 6-in max side, 3½-in max decks, 11-in max turrets, *Max speed:* 29 knots

the shock effect of near-misses knocked out the electrical generators the anti-aircraft gun turrets were unable to train. A second wave of aircraft scored no hits on either *Prince of Wales* or *Repulse* but the third wave hit *Prince of Wales* with four torpedoes on the starboard side. The great ship heeled over further to port but was still able to steam and made off slowly to the north. She was hit by another bomb at 12.44 but continued until 13.20, when she lurched suddenly and capsized. Two destroyers rescued 1285 officers and men but 327 officers and men including Admiral Phillips and Captain Leach were lost with their ship.

Striking Force

The *Repulse* had skilfully dodged both bombing and a torpedo attack and had even tried to help the flagship, but she was struck by a torpedo from a third wave, just after the *Prince of Wales* was hit, at 12.23 pm. Her steering was hit, and now she was at the mercy of the bombers. Three more hits finished her and Captain Tennant ordered his crew to abandon ship. The old battle-cruiser hung at an angle of 60–70° to port for several minutes and then rolled over and sank at 12.33. Again destroyers were able to save 796 out of a total company of 1309 officers and men.

If Pearl Harbor was a blow to the supremacy of the battleship, this disaster marked the end. The Japanese 22nd Air Flotilla, a striking force of some 30 bombers and 50 torpedo-bombers, had taken less than an hour-and-a-half to sink two capital ships, at a cost of only eight aircraft. True, the *Repulse* had an obsolescent anti-aircraft battery, but the *Prince of Wales* had not only the most modern anti-aircraft gunnery system with radar control but also a modern scheme of protection. Until December 1941 people fondly hoped that the battleship could hold its own against aircraft at sea; thereafter it remained a valuable but vulnerable asset which had to be given the right

protection. The loss of the two ships could nevertheless have been avoided. Had some degree of air cover been provided the Japanese pilots would not have been able to execute such perfectly co-ordinated attacks, and a properly organised standing air patrol such as became standard in the Mediterranean and Pacific would have given virtual immunity to anything but a chance hit.

The Battle of the Coral Sea was fought in May 1942 without any capital ships, and at Midway only a month later a force of American carriers forced the Japanese Commander-in-Chief to turn back, despite the fact that he had under him no fewer than seven battleships, including the giant *Yamato*. It was inevitable, if hard to grasp, that three thin-skinned carriers could deter ships armed with the heaviest guns afloat, but from that moment the Japanese too regarded the battleship as no longer relevant. All the existing construction programmes were thrown out, and a new plan for more carriers was drawn up; its most grandiose element was the conversion of the third *Yamato*-class battleship, the *Shinano*, to a 62,000-ton carrier. An even more extreme move was to convert the *Hyuga* and *Ise* to hybrid 'battleship-carriers'. Work began on *Ise* at Kure in March 1943 and she was ready seven months later; her sister started her conversion in July 1943 and was ready in only four months. The two aftermost 14-in gun turrets were removed and replaced by a large flight deck and hangar which extended from the mainmast to the stern. The aircraft were intended to be 22 floatplane bombers, launched from two catapults which effectively masked the fire of the midships turrets, but by the autumn of 1943 there were neither aircraft nor pilots available.

Battleships were still destined to fight their own kind for the time being, however. On the night of 11–12 November, 1942, during the US amphibious landings on Guadalcanal in the Solomon Islands, a Japanese force including the fast battleships *Kirishima* and *Hiei* tried to shell the newly captured airstrip at Henderson Field. In a fierce night action at relatively short range the *Hiei* was detected on radar and then savagely mauled by gunfire from a force of five cruisers and eight destroyers. She was badly damaged by 8-in shells from the *Portland* and *San Francisco* and possibly a torpedo from one of the destroyers, made a half-circle turn and then lurched northwards along the east side of Savo Island.

The *Kirishima* withdrew with only a single hit from an 8-in shell—relying totally on radar, the Americans could only aim at the largest radar echo—and joined up with another bombarding force next day. The *Hiei* was hunted down when daylight came, and aircraft from the carrier *Enterprise* found her. Throughout the day she twisted and turned in frantic efforts to dodge the bombs and torpedoes. Eventually, after 300 of her crew had died in the fires and explosions, she was abandoned the following evening. When destroyers had taken off the survivors she was torpedoed and sunk.

The new American battleships *South Dakota* and *Washington* arrived too late to join in this first part of the battle, but they were in position the following evening when a fresh bombardment force was reported making for Henderson Field. At 2316 the two ships opened fire on the Japanese cruiser *Sendai* at a range of 16,000 yards, but suddenly the tables were turned. The Japanese ships, trained to concert-pitch in night fighting, opened a furious fire with guns and torpedoes. Within minutes all four US destroyers were disabled without

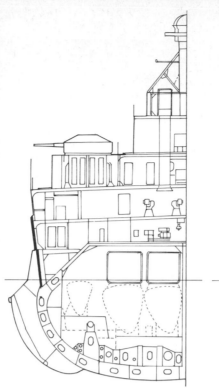
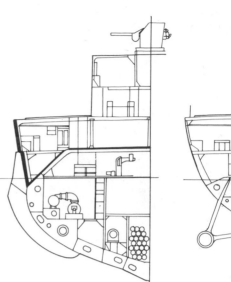

HMS *Repulse*:Sections
Repulse was partially modernised to enable her to fight a modern war on something approaching equal terms. Sectional views show added AA armament—high angle 4-in mountings and 2-pdr pom-poms

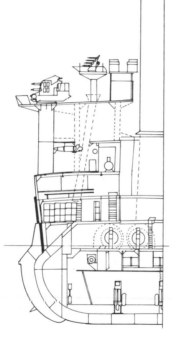
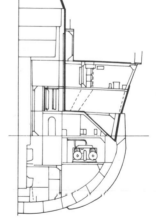

USS South Dakota *somewhere in the North Atlantic. The 'Sodak' and the* Alabama *were attached to the British Home Fleet escorting convoys to North Russia in 1942*

having fired a single torpedo. As for the *South Dakota*, her performance was less than brilliant; about 17 minutes after the start of the action the concussion from a 5-in twin gun mounting caused a short-circuit in the secondary fire-control system, and by a series of errors this 'blew' the entire electrical system for the ship. For three endless minutes the ship was in darkness without power for any of the guns, gyros or fire-control. She made a turn to avoid the burning destroyers, but then the surface-warning radar blacked out. To add to the confusion gun blast set fire to the two floatplanes on their catapults aft, but by a lucky stroke the next salvo's blast blew the aircraft overboard and put out the fires. But the battleship was now off course and blundered towards the Japanese, unable to get a 'fix' on the *Washington*. She was silhouetted by the glare from the burning destroyers and at a range of 5800 yards was illuminated by Japanese searchlights. The *Kirishima* and the cruisers *Atago* and *Takao* opened fire immediately, and although the American ship aimed at the searchlights and was successful in putting them out she was hit by a deluge of 8-in shells. Fortunately the *Washington* had kept her searchlights switched off and was free to concentrate her fire on the *Kirishima*, and so the *South Dakota* was only hit by one 14-in shell. She had 38 killed and 60 wounded, and was hit 27 times in 22 minutes; structural damage was mostly superficial but she had only one radar set still functioning, had many small fires burning, and had lost most of her fire-control and internal communications. She was clearly in no fit state for further fighting and withdrew just after midnight.

The *Washington* took advantage of the *South Dakota*'s plight to approach the Japanese unobserved, and from about 8400 yards opened a devastating fire on the *Kirishima*. Nine 16-in and about 40 5-in shells hit the *Kirishima*, her steering gear was wrecked and her upperworks were soon ablaze. Like the *Hiei*, she was eventually abandoned, and at about 0320 next morning friendly destroyers torpedoed the wreck after taking off the remnants of her crew. In only seven minutes the *Washington* had fired 75 16-in shells and 522 5-in, and had saved the day, but the Battle of Guadalcanal had shown up grave weaknesses in the American night-fighting organisation. As at Jutland 26 years earlier, one side had lavished a lot of attention to the subject of night action while the other had not, and if the US Navy had not had radar the battle could have gone against it and the Marines might have been forced to abandon Guadalcanal.

Two years later another battleship action took place in the Pacific, but this time the older American battleships were involved. Like the old Japanese ships, the battleships sunk at Pearl Harbor had been rebuilt. The *West Virginia*, *California* and *Tennessee* had been completely transformed, while the *Pennsylvania* and *Maryland* had also been repaired and given modern equipment. The first three boasted the new Mark 8 fire-control radar, which gave precise ranges as far as 44,000 yards and could pick up surface echoes out to 60,000 yards. Although these old ships were not intended to face the latest Japanese ships they were more than a match for their First World War contemporaries of the *Fuso* and *Ise* classes.

By October 1944 the tide of war had turned against the Japanese. Fast carrier task forces, composed of the new carriers and their battleship escorts, hit at the perimeter of island bases seized by the Japanese in the early days of 1942, while submarines preyed on the shipping which fed and supplied their garrisons. All this time the grand battle of annihilation, for which the Japanese had originally planned their giant battleships, remained elusive. The American invasion of the Marianas finally forced the Japanese to make a decisive move, for at last their leaders began to admit that they might soon face defeat. The Commander-in-Chief of the

USS *Iowa*
The fastest battleships ever built, the *Iowa* class were 10,000 tons heavier and 200 ft longer than the preceding *South Dakota* class. They were widely used in the Pacific for shore bombardment and anti-aircraft escorts
Displacement: 57,450 tons full load
Length: 887 ft *Armament:* 9×16-in, 20×5-in, 60×40-mm AA, 60×20-mm AA *Armour:* 12¼-in belt, 17½-in turrets, 4¾-in main deck *Max speed:* 33 knots

Iowa class

Name	Launched	Fate
Iowa	Aug 1942	Decommissioned 1958
New Jersey	Dec 1942	Decommissioned 1969
Missouri	Dec 1942	Decommissioned 1955
Wisconsin	Dec 1943	Decommissioned 1958

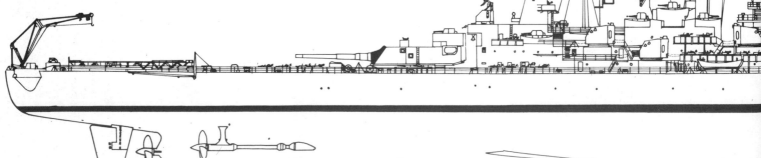

US Navy

Combined Fleet, Admiral Toyoda, and his staff had little difficulty in predicting that the next American move would be against the Philippines. The *Sho-1* or Victory Plan was to make use of the entire surface fleet in a final gambler's throw to draw the American Fleet into a battle. It was recognised that there were now too few trained

Top: USS Iowa *off Pearl Harbor in the early 1950s*

aircrew to provide adequate carrier strike forces, and so the surface forces were to be used as a bludgeon to smash their way through to the invasion beach-head, at which point the Americans would have to commit their main fleet to save the landing.

The Japanese Fleet was divided into four sections:

1 The Main Body under Vice-Admiral Ozawa, comprising the carriers *Zuikaku, Chitose, Chiyoda* and *Zuiho* and the battleship-carriers *Hyuga* and *Ise*, these last two without aircraft as we have already seen, and three cruisers and eight destroyers.
2 Force 'A' under Vice-Admiral Kurita, comprising the battleships *Yamato, Musashi, Nagato, Haruna* and *Kongo*, 12 cruisers and 15 destroyers.
3 Force 'C', divided into a Van Squadron

under Vice-Admiral Nishimura, the battleships *Fuso* and *Yamashiro*, a heavy cruiser and destroyers.
4 The Rear Squadron under Vice-Admiral Shima, with only three heavy cruisers and destroyers.

To the Americans these forces were known only by their locations: the Main Body was labelled the 'Northern Force', Force 'A' the 'Centre Force' and Force 'C' as the 'Southern Force'.

Admiral Ozawa's Force 'A' was the decoy force to lure Admiral William Halsey's Fast Carrier Task Force, comprising the cream of the US Pacific Fleet, away from the invasion fleet. The Main Body would unite with Force 'C' to sink, burn and destroy the invasion fleet, and then deal with any forces which tried to stop them. As soon as the Americans began to land in

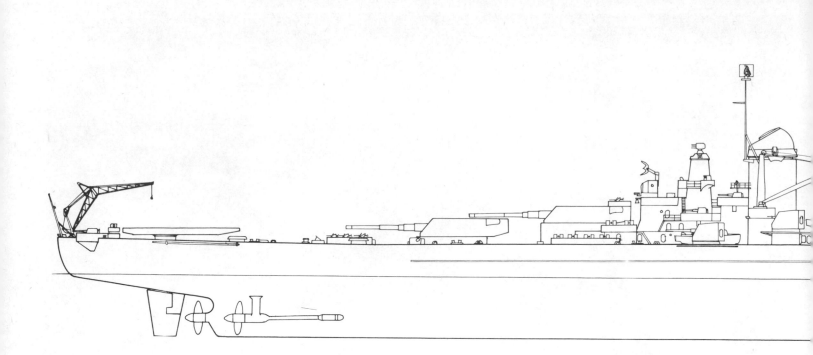

Leyte Gulf on 17 October the units of the *Sho* Plan knew the parts that they had to play: Force 'A' steamed southwards from Japan, the Main Body sailed from Borneo heading for the San Bernardino Strait and Leyte Gulf, and Force 'C' headed for Leyte Gulf via the Surigao Strait between Leyte and Mindanao.

Against this the Americans could muster the most powerful fleet ever seen. Halsey had organised Task Force 38 under Vice-Admiral Mitscher into four powerful Task Groups:

TG.38.1 carriers *Wasp, Hornet, Monterey* and *Cowpens*, four heavy cruisers and 15 destroyers.

TG.38.2 carriers *Intrepid, Hancock, Bunker Hill* and *Independence*, fast battleships *Iowa* and *New Jersey* (flagship), three light cruisers and 16 destroyers.

TG.38.3 carriers *Essex, Lexington, Princeton* and *Langley*, battleships *Massachusetts* and *Indiana* and four light cruisers and 12 destroyers.

TG.38.4 carriers *Franklin, Enterprise, San Jacinto* and *Belleau Wood*, battleships *Washington* and *Alabama*, two cruisers and 16 destroyers.

In addition there was the Landing Support Group of six older battleships, the *Mississippi, Maryland, West Virginia, Tennessee, California* and *Pennsylvania*, but as they were intended purely for shore bom-bardment the shellrooms were largely stocked with high explosive (HE) rather than armour-piercing (AP) or semi-armour-piercing (SAP) shells.

Usually American submarines provided outstanding reports of Japanese movements, but this time things went wrong and Admiral Ozawa's departure from the Inland Sea went unreported. The decoy force was thus not functioning as a decoy yet, whereas Kurita's Main Body was seen passing through the Palawan Passage three days later, and part of Admiral Shima's group was also seen. It was assumed that both forces were heading for Surigao Strait and three of the Task Groups were stationed to the east of the Philippines, 125 miles from one another.

Death of a Giant

On 24 October Admiral Halsey ordered air searches in every sector except the vital north and north-east, and so Ozawa's presence was still unsuspected. Halsey decided to concentrate his three task groups and ordered the fourth, TG.38.1, back from its position much further east. Although Ozawa's aircraft attacked the carrier *Princeton* a search could not be made for his ships until late in the day, by which time he was too far away. In the meantime strikes had been launched against Admiral Kurita's Main Body by carrier aircraft, and the 64,000-ton *Musashi* was under constant attack from 1015 to 1500. The bombs mostly bounced off her massive decks and even a torpedo hit did not slow her down, but finally a third wave hit her with three torpedoes. These opened up the bow, slowing her down to 22 knots, and further attacks reduced this to 12 knots, making a total of seven bombs and nine torpedoes. More than a hundred aircraft suddenly arrived and in the confusion the *Musashi* took another 11 torpedoes; soon she was sinking by the bows and capable of only 6 knots, as progressive flooding began to beat the frantic countermeasures. At 1700 the captain ordered his crew to abandon ship, and at 1735 she suddenly lurched to port and rolled over, taking with her 1039 officers and

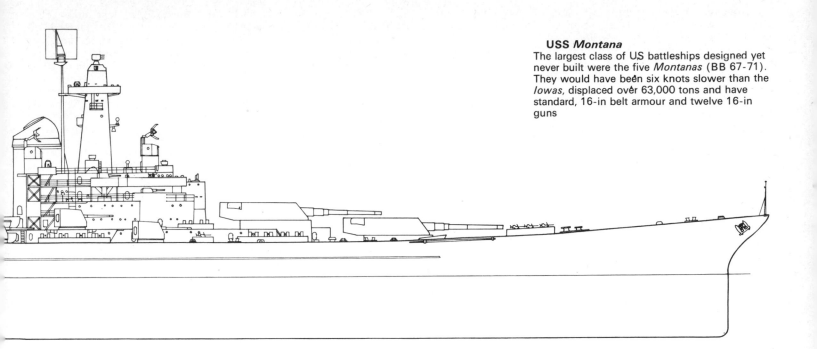

USS *Montana*
The largest class of US battleships designed yet
never built were the five *Montanas* (BB 67-71).
They would have been six knots slower than the
Iowas, displaced over 63,000 tons and have
standard, 16-in belt armour and twelve 16-in
guns

men out of her complement of 2400. She had
withstood more punishment than any previous battleship but even her massive protection could not cope with 20 torpedoes, 17
bombs and at least 15 near misses, most of
them within a space of three to four hours.

Apart from damage to the cruiser *Myoko*,
Kurita's force had otherwise escaped further
loss during these attacks, but he still insisted on maintaining his withdrawal to
avoid further attacks until he had con-
firmation that Halsey had been successfully
decoyed by Ozawa. Halsey obliged by decid-
ing that the 'Centre Force' was so badly

mauled that it no longer constituted a threat
to the invasion fleet. He compounded this
misplaced optimism by declaring Ozawa's
force to be the main Japanese fleet and
ordered all his ships in pursuit. Toyoda's
plan had worked perfectly.

What now occurred was poor staffwork,
but it turned an error into a major blunder
which nearly cost the Americans the battle.
At 1512 on 24 October Halsey had signalled
his intention of forming a new task force of
battleships and carriers off the San Bernardino Strait to stop Kurita's Main Body.
Although only an intention it was taken by
Kinkaid's 7th Fleet to mean that the force
had actually been formed, whereas the exit
was not guarded by any ships at all. To the
south, off Surigao Strait there were at least
the six old battleships under Rear-Admiral
Jesse B. Oldendorf and, as we have seen,
they had been alerted to the Japanese Force
'C' heading for the area. When Kurita reversed course and headed for Leyte Gulf
once more, however, there were no units
heavier than escort carriers and destroyers
to stop him from slaughtering the invasion
transports.

At mid-day Oldendorf was warned to prepare for a night action, and he disposed his
forces as best he could. Using destroyers and
radar-equipped PT-Boats (motor torpedo
boats) as an advance guard, he had his battleships steam across the 12-mile wide strait,
with the two cruiser divisions extending

the patrol line to the north of the
destroyers and PT-Boats. The first sighting
of Nishimura's Van Squadron was made at
about 1030 that night, but the first attacks
by PT-Boats had no effect. Nishimura
ploughed on, with four destroyers leading
the line, followed by his flagship *Yamashiro*,
the *Fuso* and the *Mogami* at one-kilometre
intervals. Even when US destroyers attacked at 0300, from a range of 8000-9000
yards, and hit three destroyers and the two
battleships he did not waver, and continued
to steam majestically towards the unseen
line of American battleships.

Eventually at 0349 the *Fuso* blew up,
breaking in two parts which drifted southwards, but the flagship seemed indestruct-
ible. She took another two torpedo hits at
about 0411 but was not stopped. When she
was within 22,000 yards the *California*,

USS *Alabama*
Battleships of the *South Dakota* class were
shorter than their *North Carolina* predecessors, to
give better protection both above and below the
waterline. This resulted in the layout of the
secondary armament being altered
 Displacement: 44,375 tons full load
Length: 680 ft *Armament:* 9×16-in, 20×5-in,
56×40-mm AA, 40×20-mm AA *Armour:* 12¼-in
belt, 18-in turrets, 5-in main deck *Max speed:*
28 knots

South Dakota class

Name	Launched	Fate
South Dakota	Jun 1941	Scrapped 1962
Indiana	Nov 1941	Scrapped 1964
Massachusetts	Sep 1941	State memorial
Alabama	Feb 1942	State memorial

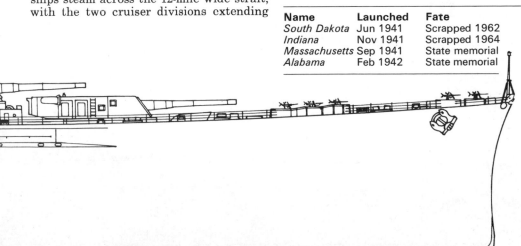

Tennessee and *West Virginia* poured in devastating broadsides of 14-in and 16-in shells, followed by the *Maryland* and *Mississippi* (fleet flagship). The *Yamashiro* could not withstand such a lethal concentration of fire and was soon blazing from end to end. She wheeled southwards with the *Mogami*, but at 0419 she suddenly capsized, taking the admiral and most of her crew with her. As the last battleship to be sunk in a straight fight with her own kind she had faced 3100 6-in and 8-in shells and 285 14-in and 16-in shells. The *Mississippi*'s last salvo, a full broadside of 12 guns, was, in the words of Samuel E. Morison, the 'funeral salute to a finished era of naval warfare'.

Just about the time that Nishimura was being wiped out by Oldendorf someone finally thought to check which ships were guarding the San Bernardino Strait, but even so a proper answer was not obtained from Halsey's staff until 0645 on the morning of 25 October. Ten minutes later the escort carriers off Samar learned the facts for themselves, when the *Yamato*'s 18-in shells began to fall around them—the Japanese were only 17 miles away. These small carriers were almost defenceless because their aircraft, like Oldendorf's battleships, had been armed for bombing shore targets and had only light bombs. But the destroyers sacrificed themselves in an heroic attempt to save the carriers and, although three of them were sunk, only the carrier *Gambier Bay* was lost. Sprague's forces were at the end of their tether, and his pilots were reduced to making dummy passes at the Japanese ships because they had no bombs left, but suddenly Kurita's ships vanished as quickly as they had appeared.

HMS *Nelson*
Being the Royal Navy's most modern capital ships in 1936, the *Nelson* and *Rodney* were never reconstructed. By 1945 their close-range armament had been vastly increased. She is seen here with a mixture of 2-pdr pom-poms, US-supplied quad 40-mm Bofors, 20-mm Oerlikon guns as well as numerous radar sets. (see *Rodney* for specifications)

USS *Tennessee*
These battleships were originally based on the *New Mexico* class but were extensively modified during their lives, especially after having been damaged at Pearl Harbor
Displacement: 35,190 tons full load
Length: 624 ft 6 in *Armament:* 12×4-in, 12×5-in 8×5-in AA *Armour:* 8/14-in belt, 5/18-in main turrets, 3½-in main deck *Max speed:* 21 knots

Tennessee class

Name	Completed	Fate
Tennessee	Jun 1920	Scrapped 1959
California	Oct 1921	Scrapped 1959

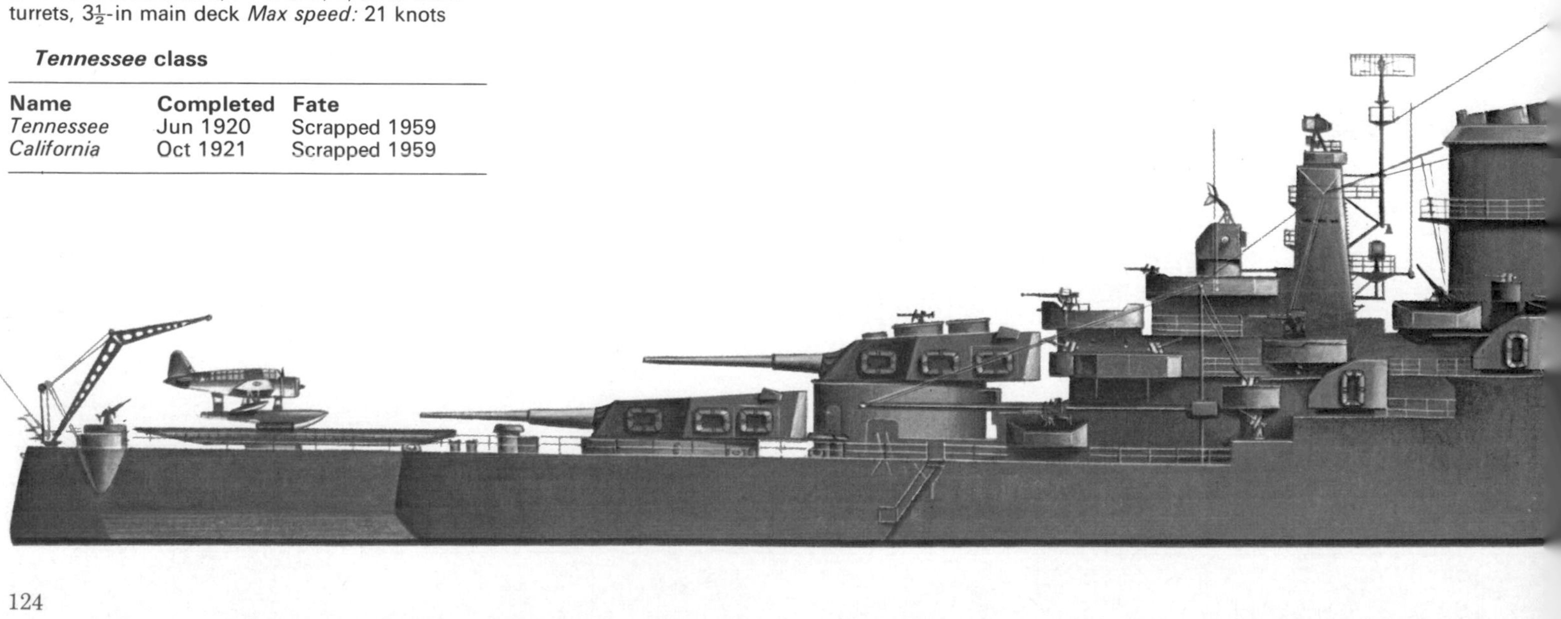

HMS Nelson *finished her wartime career of continuous service with the East Indies Fleet in 1945. She is seen here entering the harbour of Trincomalee in Ceylon with all her wartime modifications and final combat paint scheme*

The old US battleships, some of them rebuilt after Pearl Harbor, proved their worth until the end. Here an Idaho class battleship bombards the coast of Okinawa in 1945

In all probability the prolonged strain of air attacks and the lack of reliable intelligence cause Kurita to change his plans so suddenly. He knew now that Nishimura's forces had been annihilated and he had used a lot of fuel, but whatever his reasons he now threw away the last chance to affect the outcome of the war. After wasting time in manoeuvres of no consequence he withdrew at noon and headed for home, leaving Ozawa to Halsey. That gallant admiral now suffered the full wrath of the American carrier strikes, and quickly lost three carriers. But it was a paltry substitute for the general action with the main fleet, which would have earned Halsey laurels comparable to Nelson's or Togo's and his (Halsey's) wrath could not mask the fact that his intemperate handling of the battle had nearly lost it.

The Japanese were now finished as a naval power, but characteristically they used the *Yamato* in one final gesture of futile defiance. When the Americans landed on Okinawa Vice-Admiral Ito was given enough fuel for a one-way trip (not that there was enough left for the return voyage, even if it had been contemplated) and orders to hurl his 863-ft flagship at the anchorage. After blasting his way through he was then to beach the *Yamato* and use her 18-in guns to shell the US troops on shore. But the mad scheme had no hope of succeeding.

The *Yamato* was superior in gunpower and armour to any other battleship afloat, but without air cover these assets were useless. The mission's course was plotted within fifty miles of the coast of Kyushu, with its many airfields, but the Japanese C-in-C made no order for air cover to protect the 'Special Sea Attack Force'. The *Yamato's* massive anti-aircraft firepower was compromised by low cloud cover. If she was found by US aircraft the greatest battleship of all time would face a terrible test.

On April 6, 1945 she slipped out of the Inland Sea by the Bungo Strait accompanied by a screen of six destroyers. Soon after dawn the next day the *Yamato* was sighted by the first American air patrols. Zigzagging his ship to avoid submarines and to throw off the hunting carrier air-groups, Admiral Ito received reports at noon of two big aircraft formations heading northwards on interception course. Already the ship's own radar had detected the danger and at 1232 hours formations of some 150 aircraft broke cloud cover and were sighted at about thirteen miles. Immediately the Japanese fleet increased speed to 24 knots, but already US fighters were coming in fast and low using cloud as low as several hundred feet for cover, smothering the *Yamato's* anti-aircraft batteries with bombs and machine-gun fire. Following the fighters, TBF torpedo bombers came in at wave height as the Japanese fleet formation broke up, each ship having to take evasive action.

Nine minutes after the first attack the *Yamato* was struck by two bombs near the aft secondary gun turret, and a few minutes later a torpedo struck the port bow. The American pilots were concentrating on the stricken battleship's port beam and at 1300 hours two more torpedoes struck home, severing the ship's communications. Half an hour later a third wave of about 150 aircraft appeared and the attacking torpedo aircraft scored three hits on the port beam, which gave the *Yamato* a list beyond the capacity of her counter-flooding arrangements. The starboard engine and boiler rooms were flooded and the great ship's speed fell to a limping seven knots. Now circling, with her rudder jammed, the Japanese ship soaked up bombs and machine-gun fire while her own gunners' aim was thrown off by the ship's ever increasing list to port.

At 1417 hours the tenth torpedo struck, dealing the ship a decisive blow. Admiral Ito transferred to a destroyer and Captain Ariga ordered his men to abandon ship while he was lashed to the *Yamato's* binnacle. Six minutes later the *Yamato's* own exploding ammunition ripped the ship apart. She sank within seconds, taking more than 3000 men with her.

Yamato *running full speed trials, 1942*

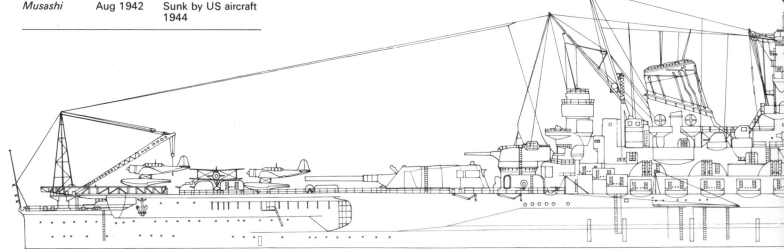

Yamato

Designed to outrange the guns of any opponent, the mighty *Yamato* class battleships were rendered obsolescent from the outset by the rise rise of the aircraft carrier. A third vessel was completed as a carrier, and a fourth was scrapped ehile incomplete

Displacement: 72,800 tons full load *Length:* 263 m *Armament:* 9×460-mm, 12×155-mm, 12 (later 24) ×127-mm AA, 24 (later 147) ×25-mm AA, 4×12.7-mm AA *Armour:* 400-mm belt, 500/650-mm turrets, 200-mm decks
Max speed: 27½ knots

Yamato class

Yamato	Dec 1941	Sunk by US aircraft 1945
Musashi	Aug 1942	Sunk by US aircraft 1944

Musashi *down at the bows and sinking after a massive air attack during the Battle for Leyte Gulf, October 24, 1944. It took hits from 20 torpedoes and 17 bombs to sink her*

Fukui

Above: Yamato *fitting out at Kure Naval Yard, 1941. Each 18-in gun weighed over 150 tons and could hurl a 3220-lb shell 45,000 yards*

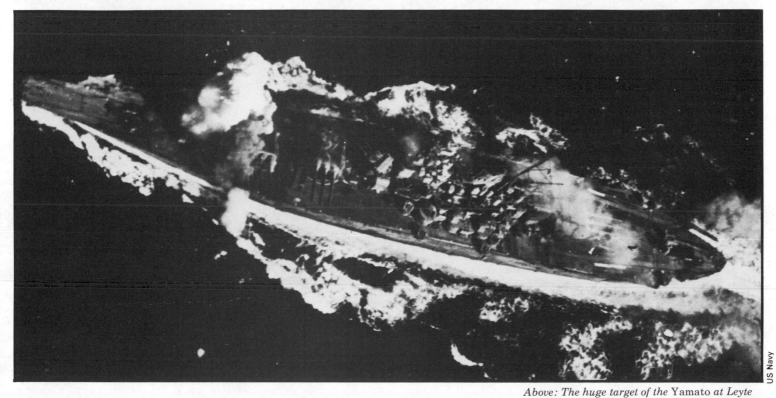

US Navy

Above: The huge target of the Yamato *at Leyte Gulf, as seen by an American pilot. The* Yamato *survived this battle but her sister was lost. The Japanese tried to build warships that could outfight anything else afloat, but without air cover the fate of the super-battleships was sealed*

The superstructure of the Yamato bristling with 5-in and 25-mm anti-aircraft guns. The Japanese provided blast-proof mountings for the 5-in guns to protect the crew from the phenomenal blast of the 18-in guns which could tear the flesh from the unprotected arm of an exposed gunner. The weight of US air attacks forced them to add 25-mm guns regardless of the risk

John Batchelor

THE GIANTS SLIP AWAY

When the Second World War ended in August 1945 the battleship's reign formally ended, although she still had the prestige she had always enjoyed—sufficient to ensure that the Japanese surrender was signed on the quarterdeck of USS *Missouri*, with HMS *Duke of York* nearby as flagship of the British Pacific Fleet. But nearly all were destined, if not for the scrapheap, then at least premature retirement. The Royal Navy at last completed the *Vanguard* in 1946, having spent most of 1944 and 1945 arguing about her anti-aircraft armament. She was a fine ship in every way, even though her 15-in guns had first gone to sea in the battle-cruisers *Courageous* and *Glorious* in 1917. This meant that they had once been fired in anger, in November 1917, despite what her critics said. All the older battleships were scrapped except those of the Americans (who retained their modernised veterans in order to placate Congress), the Russians and the Italians. Under the peace treaty the Italians were allowed to keep the *Andrea Doria* and *Caio Duilio* for training, while the Soviet Union was given the *Giulio Cesare* as reparation for war losses at the hands of Italian submarines in the Black Sea. Sadly the two elegant *Littorios* had to be scrapped, for no better reason than to stop the Russians from demanding one of them. France did better than might be expected, for the *Richelieu* had been over-hauled and modernised in the USA in 1944, and it proved feasible to complete the *Jean Bart* in 1949.

A few battleships were kept in service as flagships and for training, but the majority went into the 'mothball fleet'. But the Korean War provided a good excuse to get the rest of the *Iowa* class back into service.

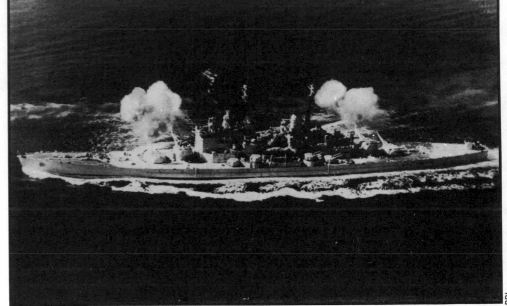

A rare aerial view of the Vanguard *firing a 15-in broadside during gunnery practice*

They performed sterling service in shore bombardment, but when they went back into reserve it was widely assumed that the next move would be to the breakers. Numerous schemes were proposed for using battleships in the 1950s. The obvious one was to replace the big guns with guided missiles, and indeed for many years the Western Press believed that the Russians had completed their big *Sovietski Soyuz* class as missile ships, until the Russians finally admitted that it had been a ponderous leg-pull. Another was to use them as giant oilers and replenishment ships, and indeed during the big NATO exercise 'Mariner' in 1953 the *Iowa* and *Wisconsin* had successfully refuelled all the destroyers in their task force. The incomplete *Kentucky* was suggested as a subject for conversion to a missile ship, but this fell through—like all the other schemes—on grounds of cost. Not only would such a job have been costly, but the running costs would have been exorbitant, for ship and missile systems.

HMS *Vanguard*

The biggest warship ever built in Britain, and the Royal Navy's last battleship, *Vanguard* was originally intended to reinforce the Singapore station and to make use of the 15-in guns in storage since 1925. She never saw action, and expressed her disapproval by running aground on the way to the breakers
    Displacement: 51,420 tons max *Length:* 248 ft 4 in overall *Armament:* 8×15-in, 16×5.2-in, 22×40-mm (final fit) *Armour:* 330/356-mm side, 330-mm main turrets *Max speed:* 29.5 knots

Vanguard class

Name	Completed	Fate
Vanguard	Apr 1946	Scrapped 1960

The USS Missouri fires a 16-in salvo at targets on the coast of Korea, 1951. A full broadside from her nine 16-in guns weighed over twelve tons

US Navy

By the 1960s the last battleships were the four *Iowa* class, all in reserve and regarded as stately white elephants. But the Vietnam war was being fought, and one of its clear lessons was that air bombardment did not have enough precision or continuity. An increasingly vociferous lobby, particularly from the US Marine Corps, demanded the re-activation of a battleship to provide cheap and effective fire support. Guided weapons were far too expensive, and air strikes too hard to organize, whereas a battleship could lie off the coast and even resume fire if the initial bombardment had not been fully effective. Eventually the 'big-gun' lobby won the day, and in mid-1967 the *New Jersey* was selected as being in the best condition. The sum of $21 million was spent, mostly on remodelling her upper control tower to take up-to-date communications and electronic-countermeasures gear, but this was offset by saving about 1000 men from her previous complement by eliminating light guns.

The recommissioning of the *New Jersey* on 6 April, 1968 caused many a battleship-lover's heart to flutter, and in one sense the whole idea was almost a gesture of contempt: only the US Navy could dare or even afford to have a battleship fighting in a war of guided weapons and supersonic aircraft. During her tour of duty on the 'gun line' in 1968-69 she served for 120 days, and at one time spent 47 days at sea. She fired 5688 rounds of 16-in shells and more than 15,000 5-in shells; by comparison, in two deployments during the Korean War she had fired only a thousand more 16-in, while in the Second World War she fired 771 rounds.

The *New Jersey*'s comeback did not last long, for she was decommissioned once

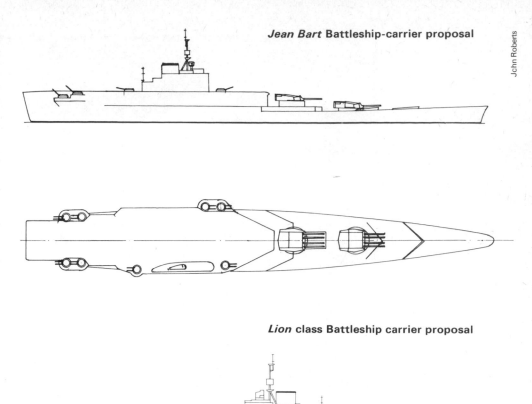

Jean Bart Battleship-carrier proposal

John Roberts

Lion class Battleship carrier proposal

Battleship-Carriers

The last attempt to save the battleship dinosaur from extinction was to mate it with the aircraft carrier. The British produced two designs for hybrid battleship-carriers using the hull of the incomplete French *Jean Bart*, and a second based on the never-built *Lion* class with six 16-in guns. Only the Japanese carried this idea into practice with the *Hyuga* and *Ise* with a flight-deck aft to operate 22 floatplane bombers. The aircraft were never allocated to the ships and both vessels fought at Leyte Gulf as even less effective battleships

Left: A broadside fired at night from the USS New Jersey, *the last operational battleship; is a spectacular reminder of the power of the big gun*

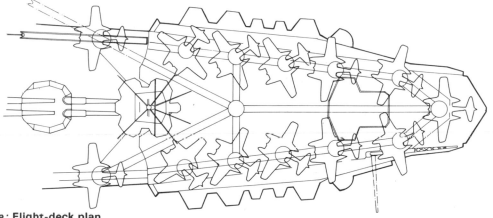

Ise: Flight-deck plan

Ise: Profile

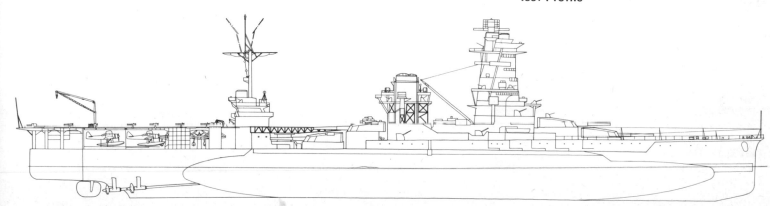

Bede Museum Jarrow

more on 17 December, 1969. The reason was an apparent shortage of 16-in barrel-liners, without which her guns would soon become worn and inaccurate. Ironically, as she was on her way home to decommission a whole field full of gun-liners was discovered in Washington, apparently missed from the inventory some time since 1945. But in a large bureaucracy decisions cannot be reversed easily; the 70 officers and 1556 enlisted men had already been allocated to other ships, and it was not possible to rescind the decision.

Apart from the *Missouri,* which is earmarked for preservation in memory of her role as the platform for the Japanese surrender in 1945, the *Iowa*s will probably not see out the decade. But other battleships

Long gone to breaker's yards or rusting hulks, sunk where they fought in two world wars, all that remains of the mighty battleships are a few museum ships' preserved armaments and fittings, and the plans, drawings and photographs which lets research continue. Above is an invitation to the launch of HMS Resolution *in Jarrow, 1892*

have been preserved—the *Texas, North Carolina, Alabama* and *Massachusetts*—to give future generations some idea of the complexity and majesty of the type. No British battleship has been preserved, although attempts were made to save first the *Warspite* in 1946 and then the *Vanguard* in 1961 as memorials, one because of her unique war record and the other because she was the last. Strangely enough, the first

British ironclad, HMS *Warrior,* is still afloat, having outlasted a whole century of later ships. She acts as a floating jetty at a fuel terminal, and could still be saved to bridge the gap between HMS *Victory* and the American battleships. Togo's flagship at Tusushima, the *Mikasa,* survives at Yokosuka. She was nearly destroyed during an air raid during the Second World War, but was later restored to her former glory and is now the only example of a pre-dreadnought battleship.

The battleship was in its day the most complex mobile structure in existence, and it pushed technology to its limits. But it was also a product of the societies which sponsored it, and was a reflection of all the factors which made up those societies.

Battleships 1950-77

Argentina
Moreno	Scrapped in Italy 1957
Rivadavia	– do –

Brazil
Minas Geraes	Sold 1953 and scrapped in Italy 1954
Sao Paulo	Sold 1951 but lost in Atlantic in tow November 1951

Chile
Almirante Latorre	Scrapped in Japan 1959

France
Richelieu	Scrapped in Italy 1968
Jean Bart	Scrapped in Japan 1969

Italy
Caio Duilio	Scrapped 1958
Andrea Doria	– do –

Great Britain
King George V	Scrapped 1958
Duke of York	– do –
Howe	– do –
Anson	Scrapped 1957
Vanguard	Scrapped 1960

Soviet Union
Oktyabrskaya Revolutsia	Scrapped 1956
Sevastopol	Scrapped about 1957
Petropavlovsk	Salved and scrapped about 1950
Novorossiisk	Sunk by mine (?) in Sevastopol 1956

Turkey
Yavuz	Scrapped 1972

United States
Mississippi	Gunnery trials ship from 1947, and scrapped 1956
Tennessee	Scrapped 1959
California	– do –
Colorado	– do –
Maryland	– do –
West Virginia	Scrapped 1961
North Carolina	State memorial 1961
Washington	Scrapped 1961
South Dakota	Scrapped 1962
Indiana	Scrapped 1964
Massachusetts	State memorial 1965
Alabama	State memorial 1964
Iowa	Still in existence (1977)
New Jersey	– do –
Missouri	– do –
Wisconsin	– do –

Last of the dreadnoughts. The Turkish battle-cruiser Yavuz (ex-Goeben) *guarded Istanbul as a museum ship for many years with only a Petty Officer and his cat as crew—until she was tragically scrapped in 1972*

Imperial War Museum

THE FIRST SUBMARINES
Antony Preston

The idea of underwater travel has always fascinated men, as much as that of flight, and the first recorded design for an underwater vessel occurs in 1578. But it was only after centuries of experiments that the submarine became a practical and a lethal weapon, with the invention of the torpedo and the development of the battery-powered electric motor in the latter part of the 19th century.

In this book we trace the history of the submarine from its earliest beginnings, the man-powered craft with primitive armament which were often more dangerous for their crews than for their targets. Of course, it was during the First World War that the submarine came into its own. Here we follow the development of the submarine up to 1919, when it had almost succeeded in defeating the entire naval might of the British Empire.

CONTENTS

THE BIRTH OF THE SUBMARINE

It was war which provided the main stimulus for the first submarine-inventors. But while the military potential of an underwater craft was obvious, all the flair and bravery of the early designers and their crews were unable to overcome the problems posed. Nevertheless, many of their designs applied surprisingly sound principles, and some were to prove many years ahead of their time

Two of Man's most illogical ambitions are to be able to fly like a bird and to be able to live underwater like a fish. He has no natural aptitude for either, but these two ideas have held Man's imagination for thousands of years. Now, human ingenuity has achieved what Nature clearly did not intend; flight has progressed to space travel and nuclear propulsion has given us the 'true submarine', almost independent of the atmosphere.

Like the aircraft, the submarine owes its startling achievements to the needs of war. However pacific the sentiments of inventors the chief purpose of submarines has been destructive. German U-Boats twice came close to a victory which would have altered the course of history, while a Polaris submarine can unleash missiles with more destructive power than all the bombs dropped in the Second World War.

The first recorded instance of a submarine, as opposed to apparatus for diving and working underwater, comes as late as 1578, when the Englishman William Bourne wrote in *Inventions and Devices* about his 'submersible boat'. Unlike later submarines, Bourne's boat actually was shaped like a boat, but its bilges were fitted with leather ballast tanks which admitted seawater through holes below the waterline. The boat would then sink, but buoyancy could be restored by screw presses which squeezed the leather tanks and forced the water out again. While below the surface, the operator could draw air through a hollow mast, but later experience with hand-operated submarines suggests that the exertions would have soon exhausted him. There was a further practical drawback to Bourne's device; it had no means of propulsion, and so we must conclude that Bourne was merely anxious to prove that a boat *could* be made to submerge.

Scarcely 40 years later a Dutch emigré, Cornelius van Drebbel, took Bourne's idea a stage further by devising an oar-propelled submersible. Van Drebbel, however, relied on his rowers to force the boat partially below the surface — in nautical parlance, it was only running awash, and since he had no means of altering the displacement it would have been impossible to actually propel under water. However, Drebbel had a flair for publicity which Bourne lacked, for when

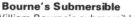

Bourne's Submersible
William Bourne's submersible boat of 1578 was never built, but this cross-section shows that it was a practicable idea. The horizontal screw presses admitted sufficient water to submerge the boat, and the hollow mast permitted the rower to breathe

he built two boats of different sizes and tested them on the Thames, he attracted great interest. He is reputed to have induced that intrepid monarch James I to travel in his boat, but when we read that it travelled from Westminster to Greenwich and was rowed at a depth of twelve or fifteen feet for several hours we can see the hand of some Jacobean public relations expert at work.

Ahead of their time

What is most interesting about both these early experimenters is that they were some 250 years ahead of their time; Bourne's principle of varying the displacement to obtain submergence is essential to the design of modern submarines, while some of the Confederate submersibles used in the American Civil War revived Van Drebbel's idea of forcing themselves below the surface by oar-power. No detailed description of Van Drebbel's submarine has survived, apart from the fact that it was wooden, and covered with greased leather.

Not until 1653 is there any indication that a submarine could be used to destroy ships, when a Frenchman, de Son, built a boat at Rotterdam which 'doeth undertake in one day to destroy a hondered Ships'. Its other qualities were no less modest, for it was to have the speed of a bird and 'no fire, nor Storme, nor Bullets can hinder her, unless it please God'.

M. de Son is immortalised as the inventor of the first mechanically powered submarine, for his craft was propelled by an internal paddle-wheel, but as it was driven by clockwork it is hardly surprising that it was too weak to move. Which was a pity, for this 72-ft craft embodied sound principles, and because of her size could

British warships, and he applied his inventive mind to the problem. The first priority was strength, and the hull was made in the form of two tortoise shells, hence the name *Turtle*; this naturally strong structure was stiffened by a baulk of timber which also served as a seat for the operator. His head came level with a cylindrical brass top, which was fitted with an access hatch and illuminated by glass windows.

The *Turtle* was a most advanced machine which could travel awash, and then ballast down for the final attack. While travelling awash, air was provided for the operator through two brass pipes in the hatch cover, fitted with a simple stop valve like a swimmer's snorkel-tube. A foot-operated valve admitted water when submerging, and there were two hand-pumps to expel water ballast for surfacing. The boat was propelled horizontally and vertically by separate propellers; the horizontal propeller was operated by hand or foot-crank, but the vertical one was only hand-cranked.

In the past, submarine-designers had avoided the most important problem, namely how to sink a ship, but Bushnell was a thorough man. He devised a detachable explosive charge which could be left beneath the hull of a ship by means of

a line attached to a screw driven into its keel. In essence this is very close to the method used in the Second World War by 'human torpedoes', and to complete the modern touch about everything done by Bushnell, he also provided a compass and depth-gauge for navigation.

Ideally, the next step should have been a successful attack on the British Fleet, but here the submarine story met another problem — a minor one, but enough to relegate the submarine to a mere nautical curiosity again. The first experiments in Long Island Sound were promising, but to avoid premature discovery the *Turtle* was removed to the Hudson River. Bushnell's brother had been operating her in these tests, and when he fell ill, possibly from the effects of carbon dioxide poisoning, General Parsons was asked to provide three 'volunteers' from the Army.

Exceptional bravery

Whatever inducements were offered to the trio, one of them, Sergeant Ezra Lee, must have been an exceptionally brave man. On the night of 6 September 1776 he climbed into the *Turtle* and was towed down river to attack the British blockading squadron anchored off Plateau Island. When within a few miles of New York harbour, the two rowing boats slipped their tow and left the tide to carry her downstream. The tide was too strong,

hold enough air to keep a man alive for three hours. The lack of any suitable power unit was to hold back the development of submarines throughout the 17th and 18th centuries, although progress was made with diving bells as Man continued in his battle to find a way of surviving underwater. For this reason the next successful step in submarine development reverted to human motive power when, in 1776, the American David Bushnell produced his one-man *Turtle*.

After the outbreak of the American War of Independence, British warships had blockaded the Atlantic coast and, as a young patriot, Bushnell was keenly aware of the need for the colonies to break the British stranglehold. With no large navy to match the Royal Navy, Bushnell reasoned that an underwater boat might cause sufficient damage to drive away the

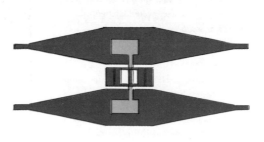

De Son's Submersible
De Son's submersible catamaran of 1653 was 72 ft long, and was the first mechanically propelled design. Unfortunately, the clockwork engine was not strong enough to move the hull, so she never had a chance to live up to any of her inventor's extravagant claims

and swept the little submarine past the anchorage, so Lee had to work for some two hours, cranking the *Turtle* back into a position where he could reach the 64-gun *Eagle*, flagship of Lord Howe, which was lying off Governor's Island.

He manoeuvred carefully under the massive hull, and proceeded to work the screw for attaching the explosive charge, but to his dismay he found that the screw could not penetrate. English warships were now being coppered and sheathed against shipworm, and this was thought to be the reason, though Bushnell felt that Lee had probably encountered iron bracing near the keel. After trying two other places on the bottom Lee realised that daylight was too near for him to continue, and so he gave up.

Fortunately, the tide was now in his favour, and he made good progress. A guard-boat gave chase, and Lee was able to discourage it and gain speed by jettisoning the 150-lb charge, but not before he set the clockwork fuse; the fact that the charge exploded indicates that Lord Howe's flagship might have been sunk or disabled with only a little more luck.

Although further attacks are said to have been made with the *Turtle*, and a copy may have been built for an attack on HMS *Ramillies* in the War of 1812, Bushnell's contribution to the submarine story was over. His fellow-countryman, Robert Fulton, claimed to have worked out his own ideas quite separately, and although he seems to have discussed them with Bushnell, he was certainly the first of the pacifist submarine-inventors, for unlike Bushnell, he wanted to perfect a machine to destroy *all* warships. He felt that the inevitable growth of the United States Navy would contaminate her spirit of republicanism and destroy its power for good.

Like other ardent republicans he regarded the French Revolution as the apotheosis of democracy, and he emigrated to France in 1797 to be able to put his inventive genius at the service of the Directory. After working on a number of engineering projects with some success, Fulton wrote to the Directory in December 1797 to offer them a 'mechanical engine' for the destruction of the Royal Navy, which was then blockading the coast of France with conspicuous effectiveness. Fulton offered to manufacture at his own expense a submarine to be called the *Nautilus*, on condition that the French Government

Extracts from David Bushnell's letter to Thomas Jefferson, 1787.

General Principles and Construction of a Sub-marine Vessel, communicated by D. Bushnell of Connecticut, the inventor, in a letter of October, 1787, to Thomas Jefferson then Minister Plenipotentiary of the United States at Paris.

The external shape of the sub-marine vessel bore some resemblance to two upper tortoise shells of equal size, joined together; the place of entrance into the vessel being represented by the opening made by the swell of the shells, at the head of the animal. The inside was capable of containing the operator, and air, sufficient to support him thirty minutes without receiving fresh air. At the bottom opposite to the entrance was fixed a quantity of lead for ballast. At one edge which was directly before the operator, who sat upright, was an oar for rowing forward or backward. At the other edge, was a rudder for steering. An aperture, at the bottom, with its valve, was designed to admit water, for the purpose of descending; and two brass forcing-pumps served to eject the water within, when necessary for ascending. At the top, there was likewise an oar, for ascending or descending, or continuing at any particular depth – A water-gauge or barometer, determined the depth of descent, a compass directed the course, and a ventilator within, supplied the vessel with fresh air, when on the surface.

When the operator would descend, he placed his foot upon the top of a brass valve, depressing it, by which he opened a large aperture in the bottom of the vessel, through which the water entered at his pleasure; when he had admitted a sufficient quantity, he descended very gradually; if he admitted too much, he ejected as much as was necessary to obtain an equilibrium, by the two brass forcing pumps, which were placed at each hand. Whenever the vessel leaked, or he would ascend to the surface, he also made use of these forcing pumps. When the skilful operator had obtained an equilibrium, he could row upward, or downward, or continue at any particular depth, with an oar, placed near the top of the vessel, forming upon the principle of the screw, the axis of the oar entering the vessel; by turning the oar one way he raised the vessel, by turning it the other way he depressed it.

Description of a magazine and its appendages, designed to be conveyed by the sub-marine vessel to the bottom of a ship.

In the forepart of the brim of the crown of the sub-marine vessel, was a socket, and an iron tube, passing through the socket; the tube stood upright, and could slide up and down in the socket, six inches: at the top of the tube, was a wood-screw (A) fixed by means of a rod, which passed through the tube, and screwed the wood-screw fast upon the top of the tube; by pushing the wood-screw up against the bottom of a ship, and turning it at the same time, it would enter the planks; driving would also answer the same purpose; when the wood-screw was firmly fixed, it would be cast off by unscrewing the rod, which fastened it upon the top of the tube.

Behind the sub-marine vessel, was a place, above the rudder, for carrying a large powder magazine, this was made of two pieces of oak timber, large enough when hollowed out to contain one hundred and fifty pounds of powder, with the apparatus used in firing it, and was secured in its place by a screw, turned by the operator. A strong piece of rope extended from the magazine to the wood-screw (A) above mentioned, and was fastened to both. When the wood-screw was fixed, and to be cast off from its tube, the magazine was to be cast off likewise by unscrewing it, leaving it hanging to the wood-screw; it was lighter than the water, that it might rise up against the object, to which the wood-screw and itself were fastened.

Experiments made to prove the nature and use of a sub-marine vessel.

The first experiment I made, was with about two ounces of gun powder, which I exploded 4 feet under water, to prove to some of the first personages in Connecticut, that powder would take fire under water.

The second experiment was made with two pounds of powder, enclosed in a wooden bottle, and fixed under a hogshead, with a two inch oak plank between the hogshead and the powder; the hogshead was loaded with stones as deep as it could swim; a wooden pipe descending through the lower head of the hogshead, and through the plank, into the powder contained in the bottle, was primed with powder. A match put to the priming, exploded the powder, which produced a very great effect, rending the plank into pieces; demolishing the hogshead; and casting the stones and the ruins of the hogshead, with a body of water, many feet into the air, to the astonishment of the spectators. This experiment was likewise made for the satisfaction of the gentlemen above mentioned.

I afterwards made many experiments of a similar nature, some of them with large quantities of powder; they all produced very violent explosions, much more than sufficient for any purpose I had in view.

KEY

1 Ventilation pipes with simple self-sealing valves to prevent water entering boat

2 One vent pipe stayed shut as shown so that foul air could escape through top of dome

3 Skylights in glass dome

4 Port holes on either side and in front of dome. These could be opened to admit air during surface running

5 Brass hinge allowed brass dome to tip sideways to admit crew. This could be screwed down from inside or out

6 Screw for attaching 'bomb' to underside of target ship. After screw was firmly attached to bottom planks, the boat was submerged even further to release screw, rope and bomb

7 Ascent and descent propeller which could effectively raise or lower boat in negative buoyancy state

8 Bomb. Made from two pieces of oak hollowed to take 150 lb of black powder. Inside an 'apparatus (most probably clockwork) was made to run up to twelve hours, when it would release a sear allowing a flintlock to fire and explode the main charge. When released, the bomb, which was lighter than the water it displaced, would float up against the target to give better performance

9 Bomb release screw

10 Depth gauge. A glass tube, its open end at the bottom, allowed outside water pressure to float a phosphorus-covered cork up and down according to depth. The light of the phosphorus allowed the operator to see the position of the cork and measure his depth against a graduated line on the glass

11 Propeller. Could move forward or astern

12 Propeller operating crank. A removable handle could be used for hand operation

13 Foot pedals for operating propeller cranks

14 Major transverse beam and operator's seat

15 Compass

16 Two brass forcing pumps for pumping out leaks and ballast water

17 Forcing pump operating handles

18 Rudder bar: down for port and up for starboard

19 Rudder bar crank

20 Rudder

21 Ventilation pump, to force fresh air in and foul air out at 2

22 Completely sealed down, the operator had enough air for about 30 minutes. This valve ensured that no water was admitted

23 Ballast reel

24 Tackle for lifting emergency ballast

25 Below deck, 200 lb of lead ballast could be released on 50 ft of line in an emergency, and recovered if and when the operator was able to continue his mission

26 Ballast water inlet valve operated by right foot. Perforated cover prevented weeds etc. entering and blocking pumps or valve

27 Although not mentioned, it is fairly certain that the operator would carry some means of 'repelling boarders' in the event of being forced to surface

would pay 4,000 francs per gun for every British warship carrying more than forty guns, and 2,000 francs per gun for smaller ships. (At this rate he would have been richer by 400,000 francs if he had sunk HMS *Victory* – in modern terms at least four million pounds.) He also stipulated, among other things, that his weapon would not be used against his own countrymen unless they used it first against France.

The impoverished Directory cut the amount of money and, on the advice of

Bushnell's *Turtle*
This illustration is John Batchelor's analysis of information supplied by Dr P Lundeberg and Howard P Hoffman from the Museum of History and Technology, Smithsonian Institution, Washington D.C. It is based on a letter from David Bushnell, the designer, to Thomas Jefferson, US Plenipotentiary in Paris, 1778

the Minister of Marine, refused to grant commissions to any future crew-members of the *Nautilus*, thus ensuring that the English could hang them as pirates. After further haggling, the disappointed inventor took his designs to Holland only to be rejected. Three years later, however, when Napoleon Bonaparte had replaced the Directory with the title of First Consul of the French Republic, Fulton was given a more friendly reception. A grant of 10,000 francs was made to allow him to build the *Nautilus*, and she was completed in Paris in about five months.

The *Nautilus* was far bigger than the *Turtle* and was closer to the modern submarine in having a conning tower, diving planes, flooding valves and space for three men. The hull was built of copper and strengthened with iron frames, and although its designed diving depth was only 25 ft this was more than enough. Without periscopes, the only way to navigate such a craft was by taking frequent sights at the surface, and for this purpose the *Nautilus* had a hemispherical conning tower fitted with lookout scuttles of thick glass.

As Bushnell's experience had shown, a submarine was useless without an efficient ship-killing weapon, and in this respect Fulton was no more successful. The *Nautilus* had a heavy hollow spike projecting through the top of her conning tower, and this was intended to be driven into the bottom of the target ship. The submarine then drew free, and pulled in a line which was towing a buoyant explosive charge; a percussion lock would fire the charge as soon as it struck the target. As before, the main motive power came from a hand-operated screw, but there was also a kite-like sail which could be used to make 2 – 3 knots and take the strain off the operator in favourable conditions.

In the spring of 1800 some startled Frenchmen saw Fulton take his boat down to 25 ft in the muddy waters of the Seine, and while the trials indicated that the lack of motive power was still the most limiting factor, he was encouraged to continue. Although Fulton was not

Fulton's *Nautilus*
Robert Fulton's *Nautilus* was built in 1800 to help the French Navy to break the British naval blockade. The sail was to reduce the strain on her three-man crew, and the explosive charge can be seen on the end of its trailing line. Although this submarine proved workable, it lacked a suitable weapon for sinking ships, and never had a chance to prove itself

allowed to use the dockyard at Brest for his experiments, the officers were instructed to give him any assistance needed. In September 1800 he claimed to have attacked two English brigs off the Normandy coast, but said that in each case the vessels had weighed anchor before he could approach them. It was also reported that the *Nautilus* had managed to remain submerged for an hour at a depth of about 20 ft, and some sources claim that the addition of a compressed air reservoir made a five-hour dive possible, though the French archives suggest that an air-tube had been fitted by Fulton to extend the endurance.

Too convincing
In August 1801 an old shallop was successfully blown up in a demonstration by the *Nautilus*, but when it was suggested that she should attack an English warship lying off Brest it was clear that the forces of orthodoxy were, if anything, too well convinced. The officers at Brest, particularly Admirals Villaret de Joyeuse and Latouche-Treville, made no secret of their dislike of Fulton's infernal machine, and as Bonaparte was trying to negotiate the Peace of Amiens with the British he was anxious not to encourage such anti-British activities.

When a final rejection came in February 1804, Fulton was so disheartened that he was able to compromise with his conscience, and went to London to present his idea to the British. One explanation of this startling abandonment

of Fulton's well-known pacifist ideals is that the British, being well aware of the *Nautilus*, had made him a secret offer; some French officials were certain that he had been suborned by their enemies, and the rejection of Fulton's plans may have been caused by these fears.

Whatever the background to Fulton's change of allegiance, the Government of William Pitt showed as much interest in the *Nautilus* as Napoleon's had in 1801. A high-powered committee, including the gifted inventor of military rockets, Major Congreve, was appointed, and a target-brig was blown up off Walmer. But an invention which inspired revulsion in French naval officers was hardly likely to appeal to the world's largest navy, and Lord St Vincent pronounced sentence: "Pitt was the greatest fool that ever existed to encourage a mode of warfare, which those who command the seas did not want and which, if successful, would deprive them of it".

The British have been ridiculed for adopting this negative attitude, but it is hard to see what else they should have done. The *Nautilus* was ingenious, but she was conceived when there was no practical alternative to hand-propulsion and no reliable means of sinking ships from under water. A light steam engine was still some fifty years away, as was the fish torpedo, and until these became practical a submarine had as little chance of reaching a target in the open sea as she had of sinking it. Added to which, these very small submarines had such limited visibility that navigation was extremely difficult.

THE NEXT STEP

Bauer's *Plongeur Marin*
Wilhelm Bauer's *Plongeur Marin* of 1850 looked like an iron tank, but proved that she could submerge. The big wheel moved a weight to and fro to make her dive in a succession of dips. She was also noteworthy as the first submarine from which anyone escaped after an accident

The next step forward was in 1850, when a Bavarian NCO named Wilhelm Bauer produced a submarine called *Le Plongeur Marin*, the Sea Diver. The Danish fleet was blockading the German coast, and with the backing of several influential citizens of Kiel, a boat was laid down in a private shipyard. *Le Plongeur Marin* had some features in common with Fulton's design, but she was built of sheet iron, and resembled a large oblong tank. Water was admitted into a double bottom to ballast the boat down, but when awash a heavy weight was moved backwards and forwards to produce a series of dips.

Despite her limitations, the boat was successful in making the Danish ships keep a more respectful distance, but in February 1851 Bauer achieved unenviable fame when his submarine's hull plating buckled under pressure, and he found himself on the bottom of Kiel harbour. By sheer force of personality Bauer persuaded his two panic-stricken seamen to do the one thing which could save them: admit more water to the boat until the pressure was equalised. Eventually they listened to him, and when the pressure was right the two hatches burst open and all three men shot to the surface. Not until 1887 was the *Plongeur* rediscovered during dredging operations, and she was subsequently exhibited at the Naval School in Kiel.

Bauer's friends seem to have deserted him, and as he lacked sufficient funds to continue he was forced to offer his services to the Austrian Government. After getting involved in a political squabble which quickly obscured any of the merits of his invention, Bauer decided to try his luck in England, but despite getting the attention of Prince Albert he had little success. There is a story that the celebrated naval architect Scott Russell sacked Bauer, and then adapted his ideas and offered a submarine to the Admiralty during the Crimean War, but little evidence of this has survived.

However, Bauer was able to persuade the Russians to listen to him, and he was allowed to build *Le Diable Marin*. As the Russians were as secretive in 1856 as they

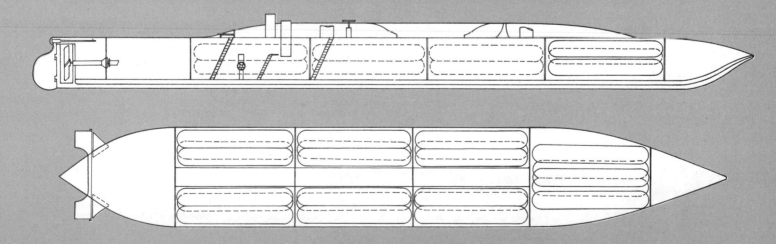

French *Plongeur*
The French *Plongeur* of 1863 was the first submarine to look anything like the modern ones. Although most of the hull was filled with reservoirs for compressed air she lacked sufficient pressure to blow her ballast tanks. The spar torpedo provided was a virtual suicide weapon, which was a further discouragement

are now, very little is known except that Bauer took his submarine below the surface of Kronstadt harbour with several musicians during the coronation of Tsar Alexander II, and during the royal salute the band struck up 'God Preserve the Tsar'. *Le Diable Marin* was later sunk, and thereafter Bauer drifted into obscurity, although he is now regarded as a man of great talent and perseverance who furthered the design of the submarine more than any of his predecessors.

The Anglo-French alliance during the Crimean War itself lasted only a short while, and one of the reasons for the tension between the two nations was the French discovery that they were enjoying a temporary lead over the British in ship-design. They had been able to offer the plans of their armoured batteries to the British, and when Dupuy de Lôme produced his plans for the ironclad frigate *Gloire* it seemed that France might be able to beat the British by sheer ingenuity.

It is against this background of revolution and innovation that a French officer, Captain Bourgois, suggested that a submarine propelled by compressed air would be a sound investment as a coast-defence weapon against ironclads. His ideas were put forward in 1858, the year in which the *Gloire* was ordered, and a year later the Minister of Marine called on various designers to produce detailed designs. The plans of M. Brun were accepted, and in 1863 the *Plongeur* was launched at Rochefort.

As a contemporary model has survived we are rather better informed about this boat than others. She was large, 140 ft long and 10 ft. in internal diameter from deck to keel, and had a spar torpedo. The boat's hull had an elliptical cross-section and the upper deck was flat, which gave her a marked resemblance to 20th century French submarines. Internally she had 23 reservoirs for compressed air at 180 lb/sq in, driving a four-cylinder engine sited right aft. Ballast tanks allowed the boat to be trimmed down, and regulating pistons gave a final adjustment of displacement, but the *Plongeur* differed radically from earlier boats in her ability to empty her ballast tanks by blowing the water out with compressed air. The low pressure in the reservoirs meant that this was a slow process, and as she proved difficult to handle with only a pair of hydroplanes aft, she was far too clumsy to be an effective weapon of war. With the suicidal properties of the spar torpedo to discourage them further, the French authorities discontinued their experiments, but they had made a big contribution to progress.

Seven years after Bauer's success in Russia, another naval blockade provided the stimulus for fresh progress. This time it was the American Civil War which was the focus for heroism and brilliant improvisation. As the Confederate forces were faced by a large fleet they saw themselves as giant-killers and the 'submersible torpedo-boats' produced by their designers were soon called 'Davids'.

The first type of 'David' was a totally new departure, for she was powered by a steam engine, and thus overcame one of the main limitations of earlier boats. She was not, however, a true submarine, for like Van Drebbel's boat she could only be trimmed down until she was awash. A small narrow superstructure containing the hatchway and the funnel remained above water, and as it was only ten feet long it could be mistaken for a baulk of timber at night. A suitable

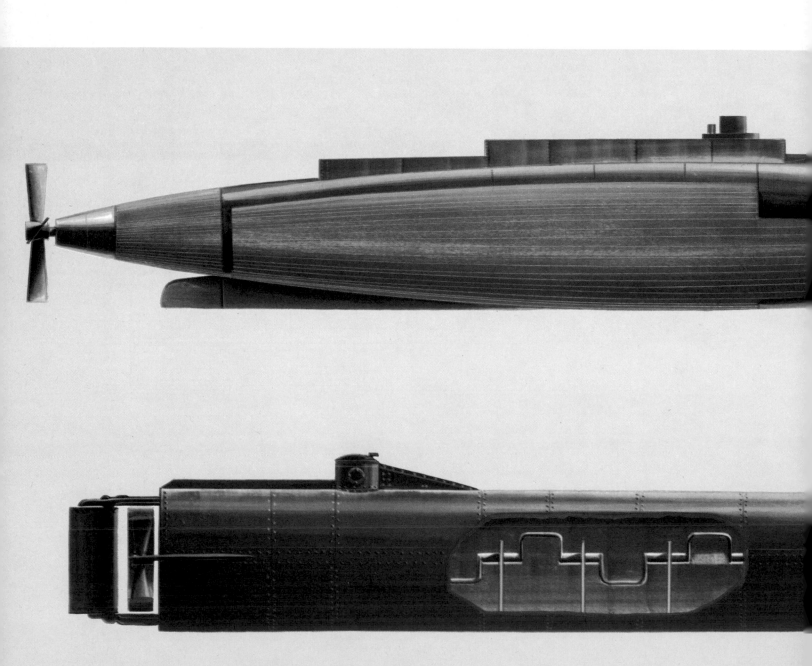

weapon was still lacking, however. All that a 'David' could bring to bear was a spar torpedo, a long pole tipped with a 134-lb canister of gunpowder fitted with a series of seven chemical impact fuses. Neither Bushnell nor Fulton would have thought much of such a kamikaze weapon, for nothing short of a miracle would prevent the 'David' from being swamped by the shock wave from the explosion of her 'torpedo', as she was never more than 20 ft away.

Nor was this the only danger – the very first 'David' was swamped during her trials by the wash of a passing steamer. But volunteers came forward to man her after she had been raised, and on 5 October 1863 she carried out an attack on Federal warships off Charleston, South Carolina. Under Lt Glassell the little craft headed towards the Federal ironclad *New Ironsides,* and when challenged by the watch she was close enough to disconcert her large adversary by firing a volley of rifle fire from her hatchway, killing an officer on board. Shortly afterwards came a powerful explosion which shook the *New Ironsides* and blew a hole in her side. Inevitably the little 'David' was swamped,

and only two crew members and Glassell were able to escape. Despite their efforts the Federal ironclad was only damaged, and this gave rise to a certain over-confidence among Federal officers. Just over four months later their complacency was shaken when an improved 'David', known from its inventor as the *Hunley,* attacked the new Federal steam sloop *Housatonic* off Charleston.

Although given the generic term 'David', this latest example was radically different to the steam-driven submersibles which had been used the year before. She was actually the third boat in a series built by a group headed by Horace L Hunley, the first two having been unsuccessful prototypes. The third boat was built at Mobile, Alabama, and sent by rail to Charleston, where she sank during trials on 15 October 1863, killing Hunley.

A new crew was assembled and trained to man the submarine when she was salvaged, and as a compliment to her late designer and commander she was named CSS *H L Hunley.* She was propelled by hand, but in order to provide sufficient power, an eight-man team

worked a pump handle arrangement to drive a single screw, while the commander conned the boat from forward. She was closed down, and had a pair of hydroplanes forward to keep her below the surface; the air supply was considered sufficient to last for two or three hours. On 17 February 1864, *H L Hunley* successfully sank the *Housatonic,* but nothing further was seen of her or Lt George E Dixon (actually a volunteer from the 21st Alabama Infantry Regiment) and his men. Some years later, divers examining the wreck of the *Housatonic* found a cylindrical hull alongside the sunken sloop, with nine skeletons aboard.

Another type of 'David' was used to attack the *Minnesota* off Newport News in April 1864. This was a picket-boat fitted with ballast tanks, and having a bullet-proof turtle-back deck fitted to make her silhouette as insignificant as possible. She was unusual in that she carried out a successful attack and escaped to tell the tale. The only other recorded attack was made in the North Edisto River at about the same time, but the target's propeller broke the spar torpedo, and the 'David' escaped.

American 'David'
The 'Davids' of the American Civil War were the first submarines to be used in war. This is the first type of steam-propelled David, which could trim down to leave only the funnel and hatchway above water. The spar torpedo was still the only weapon available for sinking ships, and this was her main weakness

American *H L Hunley*
Another type of Confederate submersible, the *H L Hunley* was hand-propelled. This drawing shows the cranks which had to be operated by eight men, and although slower than the steam-driven type, this David was able to submerge properly. She was the first submarine to sink an enemy ship

TORPEDOES:

The next noteworthy submarine design came from a Liverpool clergyman, the Rev. George Garrett, and it led in turn to the first commercially-built submarines. Technology was at last coming to the aid of designers, particularly with the perfection of the electric motor and the lead-acid storage battery, but a whole swarm of contrivances were investigated by 19th century inventors in an effort to store power under water. In 1878 Garrett built a small submarine out of steel plates, which submerged by the proven method of admitting water to alter the displacement of the boat. Like so many before it, this little egg-shaped boat was propelled by a hand-screw, and seems to have been sufficiently successful for Garrett to embark on a more ambitious project a year later.

The *Resurgam*

This was based on the original design in that the five-foot diameter was retained, but the hull was increased from 15 to 45 ft, and the ends were pointed. The second boat, christened the *Resurgam*, was steam-powered on the surface, and while running on the surface a full head of steam was raised to provide latent heat for heating water stored in special tanks. This system was already in use in Lamm's fireless locomotive to avoid making smoke on London's underground railways, and was good enough to drive the *Resurgam* at 2–3 knots for ten miles. Unfortunately Garrett's limited resources meant that he had to restrict the boat's size, and the boiler and pressurised tank took up so much room that the three-man crew had to crawl through 12- or 14-in spaces.

American *Intelligent Whale*

The *Intelligent Whale* was the Yankee North's answer to the Confederate Davids. She was hand-propelled like the *Hunley*, but proved hard to manoeuvre and lacked a suitable weapon. Furthermore, the end of the Civil War robbed her of targets, so she was never used

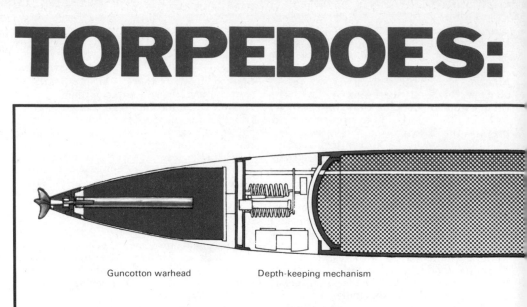

Guncotton warhead   Depth-keeping mechanism

Garrett had no qualms about using his ten-year-old son as a deckhand, presumably because the boy could squeeze through such spaces more easily, and the lad recorded years later that he had to lie on his back and pull himself along.

The experiment faced failure when the *Resurgam* was wrecked while carrying out sea trials off the Welsh coast, but Garrett was fortunate enough to attract the attention of the famous Swedish industrialist and inventor Thorsten Nordenfelt. As a supplier of arms to the world Nordenfelt could see the advantages of a workable submarine, and he willingly provided capital for a prototype to be built under Garrett's supervision at Stockholm in 1882.

By this time the Whitehead 'fish' or locomotive torpedo had come into service in many navies, and so another major obstacle to submarine progress had been eliminated. But the problem of propulsion remained, and Garrett's method of using latent heat from hot water tanks was

Whitehead Torpedo

The Whitehead torpedo, which was perfected in 1868, was the armament which the submarine needed before its potential as an effective and deadly weapon of war could be realised. It allowed the submarine to attack targets from a safe distance, and its speed made evasion difficult

retained. Vertical propellers were provided to take the boat below the surface, once she had been trimmed down to run awash, and a pair of bow hydroplanes assisted in depth-keeping. She was cigar-shaped, but without the conning tower of Garrett's *Resurgam*, and was the first submarine to have a surface armament, a 1-in Nordenfelt machine-gun. The Whitehead torpedo was fired from a bow tube placed in an external casing over the bow.

Trials took place at Landskrona in September 1885, and although moderately successful they proved that the submarine was not yet reliable enough. Although the steam engine gave a theoretical range of 15 miles underwater at four knots, the

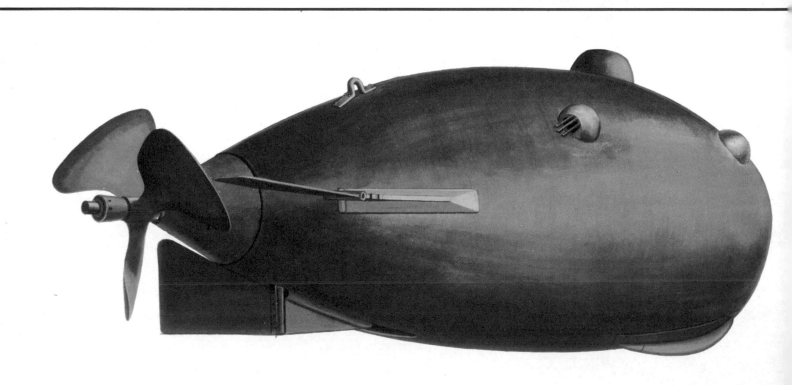

THE IDEAL WEAPON

Air reservoir | Compressed air motor | Rudders and propellers

boat (known as *Nordenfelt No.1*) proved unable to stay dived for more than three minutes and had great difficulty in keeping a constant depth-line. She proved quite successful while running awash on the surface, though, and this would have been of considerable value for an attack against the defences of the period. The air-supply was sufficient for six hours, but the slightest leakage from the furnaces or smoke-boxes produced carbon-monoxide poisoning. A contemporary account records the sinister fact that some men became drowsy, and cheerfully adds that any crew member badly affected needed to rest for 'several days'. Garrett himself was poisoned and made unfit for duty for three weeks.

Despite these problems, *Nordenfelt No.1* was sold to Greece for £9,000 in 1886, and the firm started work a year later on two improved submarines for the Turkish Government. These were built in England, near Chertsey, and were to be known as the *Abdul Mejid* and *Abdul Hamid*. Despite

the relative failure of the prototype, the Turks were anxious to keep abreast of submarine development, both on account of their dislike of the Greeks and on account of their fear of Russian ideas. In 1879 the Russians had ordered fifty small pedal-operated boats of the type designed by Drzewiecki, and although they proved to be quite useless their existence made the Turks apprehensive.

No volunteers

The two boats were shipped out to Turkey in sections, and re-erected at the government yard at the Golden Horn. Garrett received a commission as an Ottoman officer and, as no Turkish volunteers could be found, an English crew was provided. As with the prototype the biggest problem was securing a steady depth-line; the vertical screws proved to have little effect, and the large ballast tanks did nothing to help, since the water tended to surge backwards and forwards. On the only recorded occasion on which a

torpedo was fired, the bow leapt up violently and the boat plunged backwards to the bottom. The motion must have been unpleasant at the best of times, for she was described as being hardly ever on an even keel for more than a few seconds at a time.

The Turks were unable to recruit even the six men required to man one submarine, and the second boat was never finished. This was never announced, however, and for years the world thought that Turkey had two operational submarines. In 1914 the Germans found their remains in a dockyard shed, and tried to recondition them, but by that time they were beyond repair.

British *Resurgam*
The *Resurgam* was designed by the Reverend George Garrett and built in Liverpool in 1879. She overcame the propulsion problem by using a steam engine, but had no weapons of any kind. She was bad at depth-keeping because of her large ballast tanks and the absence of any diving planes

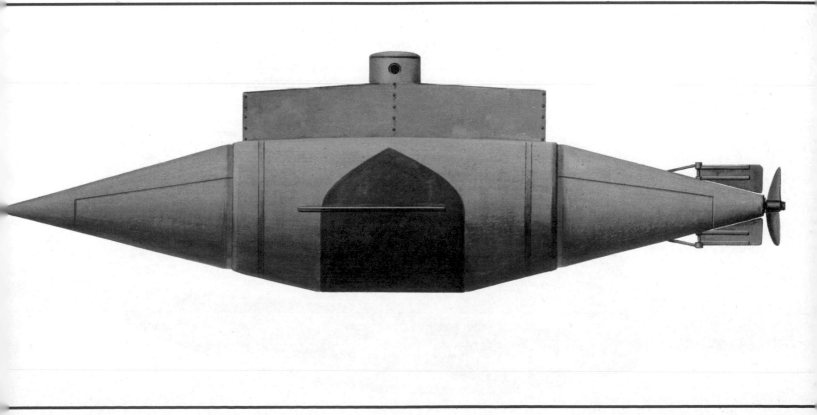

Like all arms-suppliers, Nordenfelt found himself supplying rival customers with counters to his own equipment, and it was not long before the Russians showed interest in the newest Nordenfelt submarine. This had begun as a speculative venture in 1887, and was considerably larger than the previous boats, being 125 ft long and 12 ft. in diameter. Her hull was made of 5/16-in plate, and the topside was 1 in thick as protection against light shells and machine-gun bullets. She differed in shape from the others in having a hull which was fuller throughout its length, with a blunt bow enclosing two torpedo-tubes, one above the other. The new shape was adopted to improve the underwater stability, and the vertical propellers were placed much further apart for the same reason. Two funnels were positioned close together amidships, and there were two small conning towers, one forward and one aft. She reached 14 knots on the surface, and was reported to be capable of 5 knots underwater, with a range of 20 miles.

As the first submarine to be seen publicly in England since the 17th century, she attracted a lot of attention,

and after trials she made her début at the 1887 Naval Review held to celebrate Queen Victoria's Golden Jubilee. Being painted a dull neutral grey she proved very hard to see. She seems to have been the first warship to adopt this serviceable colour-scheme. Despite the efforts of Garrett and Nordenfelt's designers the inherent problems were not solved, and the boat continued to be unreliable in depth-keeping. The ballast and hot water tanks were still too large, and surges exaggerated any movement. Neither of the inventors were able to design an adequate form of compensation for the change of weight caused by discharging a torpedo, and the heat in the engine room reached a staggering 150°F.

In spite of the submarine's inability to meet the claims of its designers the Russian Government offered to buy it, presumably to match the Turkish and Greek submarines, and having failed to find the answer in its own Drzewiecki boats. They did stipulate, however, that she should be capable of repeating her specified performance at Kronstadt in deep water, a wise precaution in view of what happened. *Nordenfelt No. 2* went out

to the Baltic in tow of Garrett's yacht, the *Lodestar*, but due to an error of navigation ran aground off the coast of Denmark. Although refloated two weeks later she was not accepted by the Russians, and she was written off as a total loss; the hull was subsequently scrapped by the salvage company. This brought an end to any collaboration between Garrett and Nordenfelt, and Garrett emigrated to the United States.

Nordenfelt persevered, and was able to sell his designs to the Germans in 1890. Two boats, called *W1* and *W2*, were built at Kiel and Danzig respectively, followed by an improved type built by Howaldt's yard at Kiel, but none of these proved successful in service. It is clear that Garrett-Nordenfelt designs were fundamentally unsound, in that they lacked a fixed centre of gravity, had only rudimentary depth-control, and were underpowered. Had the two inventors worked out the stability problems before rushing on to submarines four times as big as the prototype they might have contributed more. The ideal submarine weapon had arrived, but the propulsion problem still held up development.

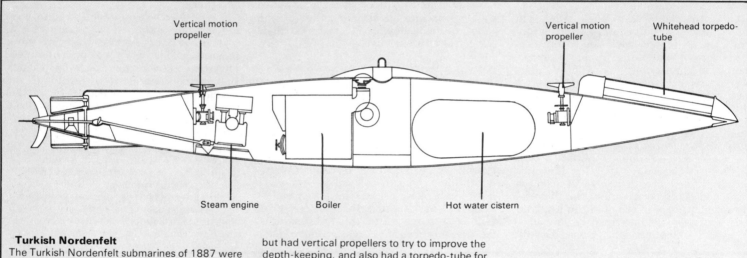

Vertical motion propeller   Vertical motion propeller   Whitehead torpedo-tube

Steam engine   Boiler   Hot water cistern

Turkish Nordenfelt
The Turkish Nordenfelt submarines of 1887 were the result of Garrett receiving financial backing from the famous Swedish armaments tycoon. They were similar in principle to the *Resurgam*, but had vertical propellers to try to improve the depth-keeping, and also had a torpedo-tube for firing a Whitehead torpedo. It proved so difficult to find Turkish volunteers to man them that the second submarine was never assembled

German Nordenfelt
Two German Nordenfelts were built in Germany in 1890, but they proved no more successful than their predecessors. Very little is known about these submarines, but the 'snout' appears to be the torpedo-tube

THE PROPULSION PROBLEM

Spanish Peral
Peral's electrically-driven submarine was built in
Spain in 1886, but was never accepted by the
Spanish Navy because of official obstruction.
The electric motor proved to be the answer to the
propulsion problem, and all subsequent
submarines owed something to this prototype

The propulsion problem was being tackled, for at the time that Garrett and Nordenfelt were pushing ahead with their designs, a young Spanish naval officer, Lieutenant Isaac Peral, was working on an electric submarine. It is a strange quirk of fortune that a small, under-developed country like Spain should have produced the first modern submarine, when the leading naval and shipbuilding power, Great Britain, was still unable to find a suitable method of propulsion. Peral was not the first Spaniard to build a submarine (an engineer called Montjuriol had built a copy of Bauer's boat called *El Ictineo* in 1860), but his boat was the first to use an underwater propulsion system totally independent of the atmosphere. She was powered by 420 electric accumulators (batteries) driving two 30 hp main motors, and three 5 hp auxiliary motors for pumping out ballast tanks. The vertical screws of the Nordenfelt boats were copied, and there was a single tube for firing a Schwarzkopf (German) torpedo.

Peral's ideas were generally sound, and had he been allowed to develop them it is probable that he would have cured the depth-keeping problems which inevitably plagued his submarine. But the Spanish naval authorities ordered a long-winded enquiry into the design, harping on its drawbacks and Peral's lack of experience. Peral was naturally indignant when he tried without success to get permission to build an improved submarine. The idea was finally killed off in 1890 in a long series of windy arguments and official verdicts, and it was not until the Spanish-American War of 1898 that the Spanish Government realised the value of submarines. The American Navy admitted that the existence of only two Peral submarines at Manila would have made their squadron far more cautious, and might have prevented it from destroying the Spanish cruisers with such impunity.

France in the lead
The accumulator battery and the electric motor were the keys to underwater navigation, for they offered a reasonable power-to-weight ratio and needed no oxygen. The country which had made most progress in the design of electric motors was France, and it is surprising that a Frenchman did not stumble on the idea of a battery-driven submarine before a Spaniard. The French civil engineer Claude Goubet produced a very small two-man boat in 1887, but as he failed to provide a means of keeping longitudinal stability it had little value. But the French Navy, influenced by the doctrines of the 'Jeune Ecole' which stressed the need for cheap forms of indirect attack, showed enough interest to make it worth Goubet's while to design a larger boat.

Goubet II was built at Cherbourg in 1886-1889, and had a 26-ft bronze hull. Her two operators could bring her to an awash condition by flooding the ballast tanks, and then they admitted more water to destroy her reserve of buoyancy. But the lack of any diving planes made this boat just as hard to control as her prototype, and she eventually finished up

French *Goubet II*
M. Goubet's submarine (1886) was operated by
two men sitting back-to-back, but without any
effective weapon she had no practical purpose,
and ended her life in an amusement park on
Lake Geneva

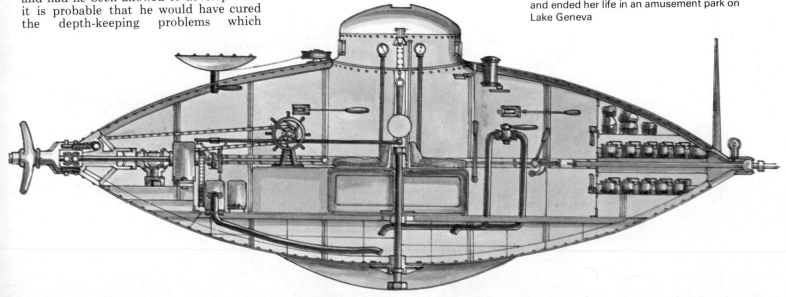

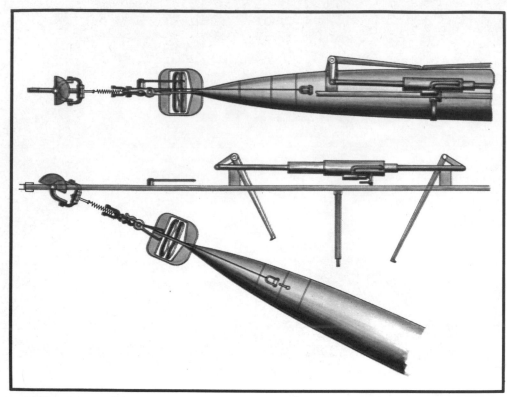

Drzewiecki's Drop-collar
The Drzewiecki drop-collar allowed for a crude angling of the torpedo. It was used in early French and Russian submarines in preference to internal torpedo-tubes, but it proved too delicate and temperamental, and was discarded during the First World War

as the property of an amusement park on Lake Geneva. Goubet, like so many others, spent the rest of his life trying to promote his ideas without success, and died a bitter man.

His frustration must have been inflamed when the great naval architect Dupuy de Lôme started work on his own design for a submersible. Although de Lôme died in 1885 his disciple, Gustave Zedé, carried on where he had left off, and the plans of the first modern submarine were sent to the Minister of Marine, Admiral Aube, in January 1886. Approval followed and an order was placed with the *Société des Forges et Chantiers de la Mediterranée* at Toulon on 22 November 1886.

A giant step

As the details of this giant step forward had not been fully worked out it was April 1887 before the hull could be laid down, and more than a year before it could be launched. The new boat was 60 ft long, built of sheet steel, with a circular cross-section and a cigar-shaped form. The diameter of the hull was approximately 5 ft 10 in and it had a displacement of 30 metric tons on the surface (31 tons submerged). Great attention was paid to hull strength, and the frames were only some 20 in apart. The original electric motors developed 55 ehp for an estimated surface speed of 6.5 knots, but this proved unrealistic in practice as the motor was too light. A more efficient type was later installed, giving only 33 ehp, but the accumulator batteries gave a lot of trouble. This was one drawback to electric propulsion, for the 564 accumulators needed to produce 33 ehp weighed over 2,000 lb, and the motor itself weighed twice as much.

The little boat was named *Gymnote* ('Eel') when launched, and she immediately began an intensive programme of trials in Toulon harbour in September 1888. Depth-keeping was bad, as she had been fitted with two of the vertical propellers which proved so useless in the Garrett-Nordenfelt designs, and also

because only one diving rudder was fitted. In 1892 two sets of hydroplanes were added, a pair forward and a pair amidships, and the conning tower was raised to improve safety while travelling on the surface.

At this time the *Gymnote* was armed with a single tube for firing a 14-in Whitehead torpedo fitted in her bow, but later opinion in French circles hardened against the hull-mounted torpedo-tube for submarines, and when the *Gymnote* was rebuilt in 1898 she was given a pair of 'drop-collars' for a 14-in torpedo on either side of the conning tower. This device was the invention of the Russian designer Drzewiecki, and comprised a sling which held the torpedo at any desired angle before launching. Its main advantage was that it reduced the problem of compensating for the loss of weight, the torpedo forming a big percentage of total displacement in the small submarines of the period, and its advocates also pointed out that the choice of angles made it easier to hit the target.

But in practice the drop-collars were

French *Gustave Zedé*
The *Gustave Zedé* was a bigger version of the *Gymnote*, and she carried three torpedoes. Without hydroplanes her depth-keeping was bad, and eventually three sets were added to cure this fault. She was an important step forward, but far from successful

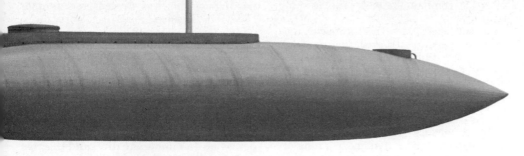

French *Gymnote*
The French *Gymnote* was the first successful modern submarine. When she appeared in 1888 she had virtually no superstructure, and this made surface-running very dangerous. She also proved bad at depth-keeping, but despite these problems she proved so promising that another submarine was built

French *Gymnote*
The *Gymnote* was rebuilt twice to improve her performance. She is seen here as she appeared after her second reconstruction in 1898, with a raised conning tower and external torpedoes carried in drop-collars. She also has an extended deck-casing to improve conditions for her crew on the surface

liable to damage from seaweed and flotsam, and the angling mechanism proved very uncertain in its operation. A contemporary account says, 'When the gear is in working order it appears very neat, and to see a torpedo move itself off when one is looking through a scuttle ten feet under water possesses great fascination for a torpedo man; the suspense as to whether it will release at the exact angle it is set for, adds zest to the experience.'

The *Gymnote*, although she was a credit to her designers, was too small and rudimentary to be more than an experi-

mental boat, and in October 1890 plans were finalised for a much larger boat to be called the *Sirène,* which would be able to develop the virtues of the prototype. Gustave Zedé was a sick man, and the design work was left to his deputy Romazotti; when Zedé died the Minister of Marine ordered the name of the new boat to be changed to *Gustave Zedé* to commemorate his achievement. She was launched at the Mourillon yard in Toulon in June 1893, but like the *Gymnote* she needed an enormous amount of patient trial and error before she could be described as a success.

Problems of size
Everything about the *Gustave Zedé* was bigger, probably the reason why she had so many snags. The hull was 159 ft in length and 10 ft 5 in. in diameter; the electric motors developed 208 ehp and no fewer than three 17.7-in torpedoes were carried, for firing from a similar bow-

mounted tube. As in the earlier boat, the electric propulsion was not satisfactory, and the lack of hydroplanes made it impossible for her to keep an even depthline. But Romazotti and his subordinates persevered, fitting a final total of three sets of planes — forward, amidships and astern, The importance of having a casing had not been realised, and it had to be added to reduce the chance of the boat being swamped by a stray wave, and to give the crew somewhere to stand. The final solution was to raise the conning tower and provide a light 'flying bridge' extension.

Romazotti was obviously dubious about the big jump in size, and he had prepared another set of plans for a smaller submarine. As soon as the *Gustave Zedé* finished her lengthy trials, six years after her launch, the third boat was begun and was named *Morse* at her launch. She resembled the *Gustave Zedé* in many ways, but she introduced the periscope as an aid to navigation, and had Drzewiecki drop-collars for two torpedoes in addition to her internal tube. The *Morse* proved to be a greater success than her predecessors, but another submarine was building at Cherbourg at the same time, and this one caused such a sensation that the *Morse* was rather put in the shade.

The new Minister of Marine, M. Lockroy, had in 1896 proposed an open competition for a 200-ton submarine with a range of 100 miles on the surface and 10 miles submerged. Twenty-nine designs were submitted from all over the world, but the winner was a Frenchman, Maxime Laubeuf, with a truly remarkable boat, the *Narval*. What made Laubeuf's design different was the provision of separate propulsion systems for surface and submerged operation, and a double hull to accommodate water ballast and fuel.

The surface system was a single-shaft triple-expansion reciprocating steam engine, developing 220 ihp; the speed realised was just under 10 knots, but this failure to meet the original specification was overlooked. An 80 ehp motor drove the boat at 5.3 knots below the surface, but the effectiveness of the *Narval* was increased because she could recharge the accumulators from a dynamo running off the steam engine. For this reason she was christened a 'submersible' to distinguish her from the all-electric 'sousmarins' like the *Morse*. This has caused considerable confusion because it is so inappropriate; today diesel-electric boats are called submersibles to distinguish them from nuclear submarines, in the sense that the 'conventional' boats can spend so much less time fully submerged.

The *Narval* resembled later submarines in having a flat deck-casing to give her better handling on the surface. The need to shut down the boiler meant that she took some 15 minutes to dive, and this was undoubtedly her chief drawback. She had no torpedo-tubes, being armed with four drop-collars, two forward of the conning tower and two aft, in recesses at the edge of the deck-casing. The problem of coal storage was overcome by using oil fuel, and this was stored in the double hull. Laubeuf emphasised strength of construction, with $\frac{1}{4}$-in plating on the outer hull, and $\frac{1}{2}$-in plating on the inner, and the *Narval* proved the value of this when she survived a collision with a naval tug — it was the tug that sank.

As with aviation, the French embraced the submarine concept with enthusiasm, and submarines multiplied. The *Narval* came into service in June 1900, and by the end of 1903 there were four more of very similar type, two improved versions of the *Morse*, and three of a new class designed at Rochefort by M. Maugas, all in service. A further 33 boats of various types were either building or on order, giving the French almost as many submarines as the rest of the world put together: the United States had 8, Great Britain 9, Germany 4, Russia 9, Italy 6 and Spain 1, for a total of 37.

French *Narval*
The French *Narval* of 1899 is the true parent of the modern submarine with her double hull and dual propulsion system. Note the funnel for her steam engine, the broad deck-casing for running on the surface, and the four Drzewiecki drop-collars

Basic Submarine Types
Below are shown the basic types of submarine hulls. *Left to right:* Single hull with saddle tanks; double hull with internal saddle tanks; modern double hull with deck-casing

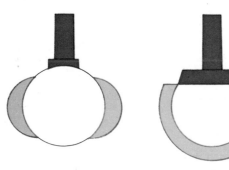

THE BUILD-UP TO WAR

The only country to show the same initial degree of interest in the submarine was the United States. As early as 1893 the Ordnance Bureau of the US Navy had appropriated $200,000 for building a submarine, with a view to stimulating private designers. With the exploits of Bushnell, Fulton, Hunley and others behind them, the Americans had always shown an interest in submarines, and three inventors produced material of sufficient credibility to arouse the interest of the Navy. Of these, Baker's boat soon dropped out, leaving John P Holland and Simon Lake as the contenders for the prize. Holland was an Irish-American who had been designing submarines in secret to destroy the British, from about the time of Garrett's experiments in England. His first effort was virtually a piloted

torpedo, reminiscent of German and Japanese ideas of the Second World War, and the design submitted in 1893 to the Bureau was his seventh. Lake, by comparison, only built his prototype *after* his design had been rejected by the Bureau.

Although Holland won the competition there was a long way to go. After several administrative delays a contract for construction was signed in March 1895, and the boat was launched as the *Plunger* in· 1897. There were so many changes in design during the building that Holland washed his hands of the whole venture, and the trials of the wretched *Plunger* were never completed. Holland and his company, the Holland Boat Company, decided to build *Holland No. 8* as a speculative venture to prove the soundness of the basic design. His faith was rewarded

Above: The French submarine *Espadon* under construction in 1900. The early years of the 20th century saw a tremendous upsurge in interest in the submarine, and many nations, particularly the French, began a spate of submarine building. By 1903, the French had almost as many submarines as the rest of the world put together

with the undisputed success of the second boat, and when he offered her to the United States Navy she was bought for $120,000, on 11 April 1900.

She had a fat cigar-shaped hull just under 54 ft long and 10 ft 3 in in diameter, and her electric motor could drive her at 5 knots for about four hours. Like the French *Narval* she had a separate surface propulsion system, but she used an Otto petroleum engine, which, with its good power/weight ratio and ease of stopping and starting, proved better suited for quick diving. She did not have the double hull of the *Narval*, and this excellent feature of Laubeuf's design was not accepted in British and American circles for another 15 years.

One reason for the great difference in size between French submarines and the American newcomer was the relative lightness of the Otto gasoline engine, which could deliver more power for less weight than the French boats' steam engine or all-electric drive. Below the surface all three prototypes could make speeds of 5–6 knots, but electric power on the surface demanded so much weight that submarines of any reasonable size would clearly have to have a dual propulsion system. The French ordered a large class of electric-powered submarines of the *Naïade* class in 1901, but during construction they were given a benzol motor to increase their radius of action.

Submarines with wheels

Holland's rival, Simon Lake, continued his studies after losing the US Navy contract. In 1894/5 he built a tiny 14-ft prototype of yellow pine, lined with felt and coated with tar. She was fitted with wheels driven by hand with a chain and sprocket, for Lake wanted his submersible boat to travel about on the seabed. He also provided a diving chamber to allow a diver to leave the hull, for he thought that the submarine's greatest value was for cutting underwater cables and destroying defensive minefields. Here lay the cause of Lake's failure, for although he modified his ideas subsequently he never seemed to grasp fully the submarine's potential as a ship-destroyer on the high seas. Even when he received enough backing to build the *Argonaut I* he still insisted on giving her wheels, as he did with the much larger *Protector* in 1901.

This boat was built to compete with *Holland No. 8*, and had many advantages to recommend her, such as a better hull-form for running on the surface, and three torpedo-tubes as against the single tube and two quite useless Zahlinski dynamite guns fitted in the Holland boat. Not only was the *Protector* very strongly built but her diving was smoother than the Holland's, yet those wheels seem to have annoyed the US Navy to the point where they turned her down. This was not the end of Lake's story, for he sold her to the Russians and subsequently received orders for four more. All five were sent to

French *Naïade*
In 1901 the French began a class of 20 small electric submersibles, the *Naïade* Class. When the Italian Navy wanted to build midget submarines for harbour defence in 1915 they asked the French for details of these 70-ton submarines

US Holland
The first Holland submarines built for the US Navy were the Plunger type, later renamed the 'A' Class. The first British submarines, called simply *Holland 1* to *5*, were almost identical. A feature of all early Holland designs was the 'fat cigar' shape, with a very small deck-casing and conning tower. Armament: one 18-in torpedo tube; Speed: 8 knots (surfaced) 7 knots (submerged)

Comparison of French and American designs			
	Gustave Zedé	*Narval*	*Holland No. 8*
Displacement (tonnes)* surface/submerged	261/270	117/202	64/74
Length overall (ft)	159	111.5	55.75
Diameter (ft)	10.4	12.5	10.3
Draught (surface) (ft)	10.6	6.1	8.5
Power (surface)	208 ehp	250 shp	45 ihp
Power (submerged)	208 ehp	80 ehp	50 ehp
Speed (knots) surface/submerged	9.22/6.5	9.88/5.3	8/5
*1 tonne = 0.9842064 long tons			

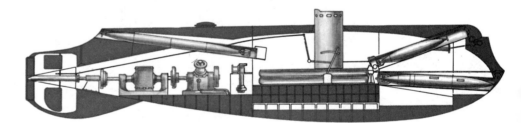

Holland's *Plunger*
The first Holland submarine, the *Plunger* was never finished because of disagreements between the designer and the US Navy. The inclined tubes are the barrels for the two Zahlinski dynamite guns which were to be fitted

Vladivostok in sections, and were assembled in time for the Russo-Japanese War. Neither side achieved much with their submarines in that conflict, though the existence of the Lake submarines is said to have made the Japanese defer an attack on Vladivostok.

Up to this point the British had maintained a position of masterly inactivity, as if they hoped that the rash of submarine building and designing would simply go away. Taking their cue from Lord St Vincent in 1801 they preferred to say that the submarine was only of use to a weaker navy, and as late as 1900 the official policy was to show no interest whatsoever. But it is now quite obvious that the Admiralty had been showing signs of life as far back as 1895, and the Director of Naval Construction had been instructed to draw up contingency plans for building submarines. However, with so little knowledge and so many claims being made by designers, the British decided to wait and see which designs showed most promise. The result was an announcement in 1901 that the Admiralty had ordered five submarine boats of the Holland type, with the intention of using them for experiments and training.

The boats which were ordered were very similar to the seven 'Improved Hollands' ordered by the US Navy in 1900, and were built by Vickers Sons & Maxim at Barrow from drawings bought from the Holland Company. This alone indicates how casually the USN took the submarine, for it is inconceivable that the French would have supplied drawings of the *Narval* to the British. The five British boats, named simply *Holland Nos. 1, 2, 3, 4* and *5,* were completed in 1901/2, and proved as successful as their American counterparts. An improved version was immediately put in hand by Vickers and became the 'A' class, the first British-designed submarine since Garrett's *Resurgam.*

Britain moves in

The British, having been so slow to move into the submarine field, now showed much more interest in their new toys than the Americans. After launching the seven *Plunger* Class or 'Improved Holland' type, the US Navy launched only two in 1906, two more in 1907 and six in 1909, during which time the British launched or completed 58 boats to their own designs. The French had not stopped at the *Narval* either, and had launched almost as many as the British. The Germans, however, had only built *U1* in 1906, and by the end of 1909 had added only three more boats.

With Bauer's efforts to inspire them, the Germans had not been as slow as they seemed. In 1890, as we have seen, two Nordenfelts had been built, one at Kiel and the other at Danzig, but they suffered from the faults inherent in the design. In 1902 an electrically-driven submersible of improved design was built by Howaldt's yard at Kiel, and although she was tried in Eckenfürth Bay she does not appear to have been a success either, and disappeared from the scene very quickly.

An indication of the growing suspicion of German intentions can be seen in the next development, which was an accusation by French newspapers that the Germans had stolen the plans of a new French submarine, the *Aigrette,* and had secretly constructed a submarine at Kiel. Like most rumours, this one had a grain of truth, in that a French inventor, M. d'Equevilley, after failing to interest the French Ministry of Marine, had sold his ideas to Krupps. The boat was never taken into German service, as she was bought by the Russians, along with two sisters, as part of the frantic efforts to make good the losses of the Russo-Japanese War. A fourth boat of similar design was launched in August 1906 at the Germania Yard at Kiel as *U1,* the Imperial German Navy's first submarine.

With a length of 101 ft 3 in, she was slightly smaller than the *Narval,* and nearly twice the size of the Holland prototypes. She had a double hull like the *Narval,* but instead of steam she used a Körting heavy oil engine, which gave her a surface speed of 10.8 knots. Like the French boat, she had a flat deck-casing and a hull-form which was more suited to surface running than the bluff bow and whaleback hull favoured by Holland. If we know a lot about *U1* it is because she survives as a museum exhibit in Munich. Her builders recovered her in 1919 after she had been laid up for scrapping. Although damaged by bombing during the Second World War, she was restored and is now in the Deutsches Museum.

Thus by 1906 the submarine had arrived, and was not only proving workable but reliable as well. It was clear now that a dual propulsion system was essential in

Lake's *Protector*

Lake's submarine *Protector*, showing the wheels stowed within the keel. These were to allow the submarine to move on the sea bed, because Lake intended his submarines to send out divers to cut submarine cables or demolish harbour defences. His designs were overshadowed by Holland's, but they proved successful in service

order to compensate for the limited endurance of accumulators, but opinion was divided as to the best method of propulsion on the surface. The French were still happy to use steam as late as 1905, in the 12 *Pluviôse* type, while the British clung to the gasoline engine until 1907. There were obvious disadvantages to steam operation, of which the worst were the time taken to dive and the heat generated inside the boat; the main drawback of using gasoline was the danger from gasoline vapour, which could easily explode from an electric spark. The solution lay in a new variant of the internal combustion engine which used a less volatile fuel. This was the Diesel engine, which soon displaced the gasoline engine in the world's submarines. The following list gives the launch dates of the first diesel-engined submarines in each major navy:

Aigrette (French) ....23 January 1904
Minoga (Russian) c.1906
D2 (British) ....25 May 1910
Skipjack (American) 27 May 1911
U19 (German) ....10 October 1912

Although Russia could claim that Peter II had ordered a submarine to be built as far back as 1729, their first serious efforts date from Bauer's *tour de force* during Alexander II's coronation in 1856. Thereafter they showed great interest in the Nordenfelt boats, as we have seen, and built 30 small pedal-driven boats to Drzewiecki's design as a counter to the imaginary threat from Turkey's submarines.

At the turn of the century the *Peter Kochka* was begun at the Baltic Works, St Petersburg. She was a small boat, displacing only 60 tons on the surface, and was armed with two Drzewiecki drop-collars. A similar boat, the *Forel,* was sent in sections to Vladivostok via the Trans-Siberian Railway to provide defence for the harbour, but she was apparently never fully assembled.

War with Japan

The first Russian submarine in service was the *Delfin,* begun in 1902 and completed in 1904. She was 77 ft long, and had a Panhard gasoline engine for surface running; her armament was the same as the earlier prototypes, two torpedoes in drop-collars. Meanwhile, the tension between Russia and Japan was clearly leading to war, and in a frantic effort to reinforce the fleet in the Far East the Russians bought the *Protector* from Simon Lake. Subsequently, four more were ordered, the *Sig, Kefal, Paltus* and *Buichok,* and six of the Holland type, *Som, Peskar, Sterljad, Beluga, Schuka, Lossos* and *Schudak.* Only one of the Hollands, the *Som,* appears to have been built in the

Russian *Forel*

The *Forel* was built for Russia in 1902, and was the first submarine built by Krupps. She displaced only 16 tons, and was not a success, but the experience proved invaluable when Krupps designed the next class of submarines for the Russians

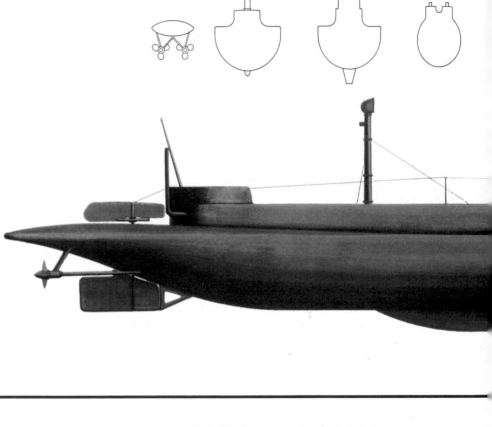

United States, as she appears in the records as ex-*Fulton*, but as the Russian records show the *Som* and the others as built at the Nevskii Works she was probably dismantled and shipped out to the Baltic like the Lake boats.

The next class was a Russian design by Professor Bubnov, and comprised six *Kasatka* class, armed with four torpedoes in drop-collars. In 1904 the Germans built a prototype for the Baltic fleet named *Forel*, and then three of the *Kambala* type to the d'Equevilley design, for the Black Sea Fleet, which were delivered in 1907. Four more boats were built to a Lake design, the *Alligator* class, which were 134 ft 5 in long, and displaced 409 tons on the surface. They had an extremely heavy torpedo armament, two torpedo-tubes in the hull, a twin rotating tube in the deck-casing, and two drop-collars, but the class proved unreliable in service, and needed constant repair. Despite this, the *Drakon* carried out more patrols than any other Russian submarine during the First World War.

The next two submarines mark a big step forward in Russian submarine design. The *Minoga* of 1905 was the first Russian submarine to be driven by a diesel engine, but she did not prove very successful. The *Akula*, on the other hand, was considered to be the most successful of the pre-war designs, and had a heavy armament of two bow torpedo-tubes, two stern tubes and four drop-collars. These two boats were built in the Baltic, but a third interesting boat, the *Krab*, was begun in 1908 at Nikolaiev in the Black Sea. She was intended as a submarine minelayer, the first in the world, but as she was not completed until 1915 her achievement was overshadowed by German and British developments.

Europe was moving inexorably towards war, as each nation sought to insure itself against the possibility of aggression from its neighbours. In the last few years of peace the rate of submarine building was stepped up. The chart on pp. 24-25 shows the classes in service with the navies of the world in 1914.

Russian *Minoga*

The *Minoga* (1906) was the first Russian submarine to have diesel propulsion. She carried two torpedoes in drop-collars and had a surface speed of 11 knots on a displacement of 122 tons. The diesels were not reliable, and in any case she was too small to be successful. The *Minoga's* diesel engine is shown, right

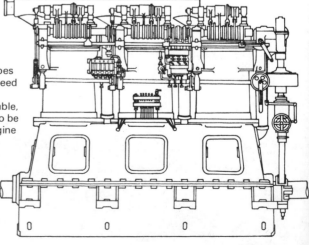

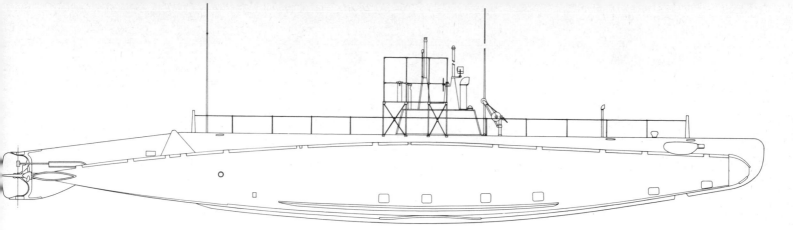

USS *Skipjack*

The *Skipjack*, launched in 1911, was the first US Navy submarine to be driven by diesel engines. She was 135 ft 3 in long, and was armed with four 18-in torpedoes. She and her sister entered service as *E1* and *E2* to conform with the USN policy of abolishing the old fish names

Russian Submarine Specifications 1908–1914

	Minoga	*Akula*	*Krab*
Displacement (tonnes) surface/submerged	123/152	370/468	560/740
Length (ft)	106	187	174
Beam (ft)	9	12	14
Draught (surface) (ft)	9	11	13
Machinery (surface)	2 × 120 bhp	3 × 300 bhp	4 × 300 bhp
Machinery (submerged)	70 ehp	300 ehp	2 × 330 ehp
Speed (knots) surface/submerged	11/5	10.65/6.39	11/7.5
Armament	2 bow TT	2 bow TT 2 stern TT 4 ext. TT	2 bow TT 2 ext. TT 60 mines

German *U1*

U1 was the first submarine built for the German Navy, and was based on three earlier submarines built by Krupps for the Russian Navy to a French design. She was completed in 1906 and was only a partial success. She spent most of her time on training and experimental duties and was re-acquired after the First World War by her builders as a museum exhibit. Although damaged during the Second World War, she has been restored and can be seen in the Deutsches Museum in Munich. Displacement: 237 tons (surfaced) 282 tons (submerged). Armament: 1 18-in torpedo-tube (bow); 3 torpedoes carried. Speed: 10.8 knots (surfaced) 8.7 knots (submerged)

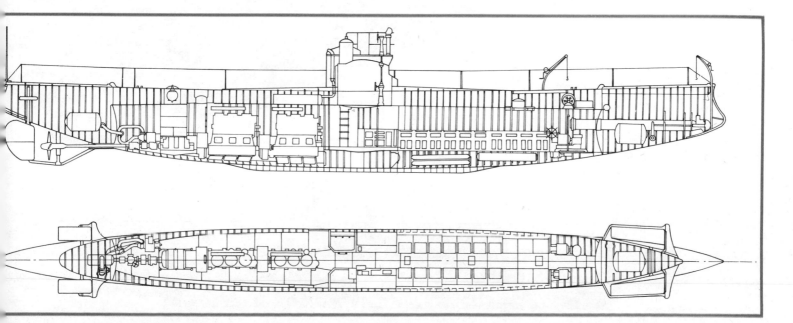

1914: THE LINE-UP

Austria – 6 boats + 1 building
U1–2 (1911)
U3–4 (1909)
U5–6 (1910)
U12 (1914)
Note: U7–11 were under construction in
Germany but taken over by Germany

France – 45 boats + 25 building
4 *Sirène* Class (1901/2)
2 *Aigrette* Class (1905–8)
Argonaute (1901)
6 *Emeraude* Class (1908–10)
Circe (1909)
12 *Pluviôse* Class (1908–11)
16 *Brumaire* Class
Archimède (1911)
Mariotte (1913)
Amiral Bougois (1914)
Charles Brun (1913)
Note: The *Gustave Zedé* (ii) was completing and a
further 24 boats built or planned

Germany – 29 boats
U1 (1906)
U2 (1908)
U3–4 (1909)
U5–8 (1910/11)
U9–12 (1910/11)
U13–15 (1912)
U16 (1911)
U17–18 (1912)
U19–22 (1913)
U23–26 (1913/14)
U27–29 (1914)

Great Britain – 77 boats
A2 and *A4–6* ⎫
A7–13 ⎬ (1905–8)
B1 and *B3–11* (1905/6)
C1–38 (1906–10)
D1–8 (1909–12)
E1–9 and *AE1–2* (1913/14)

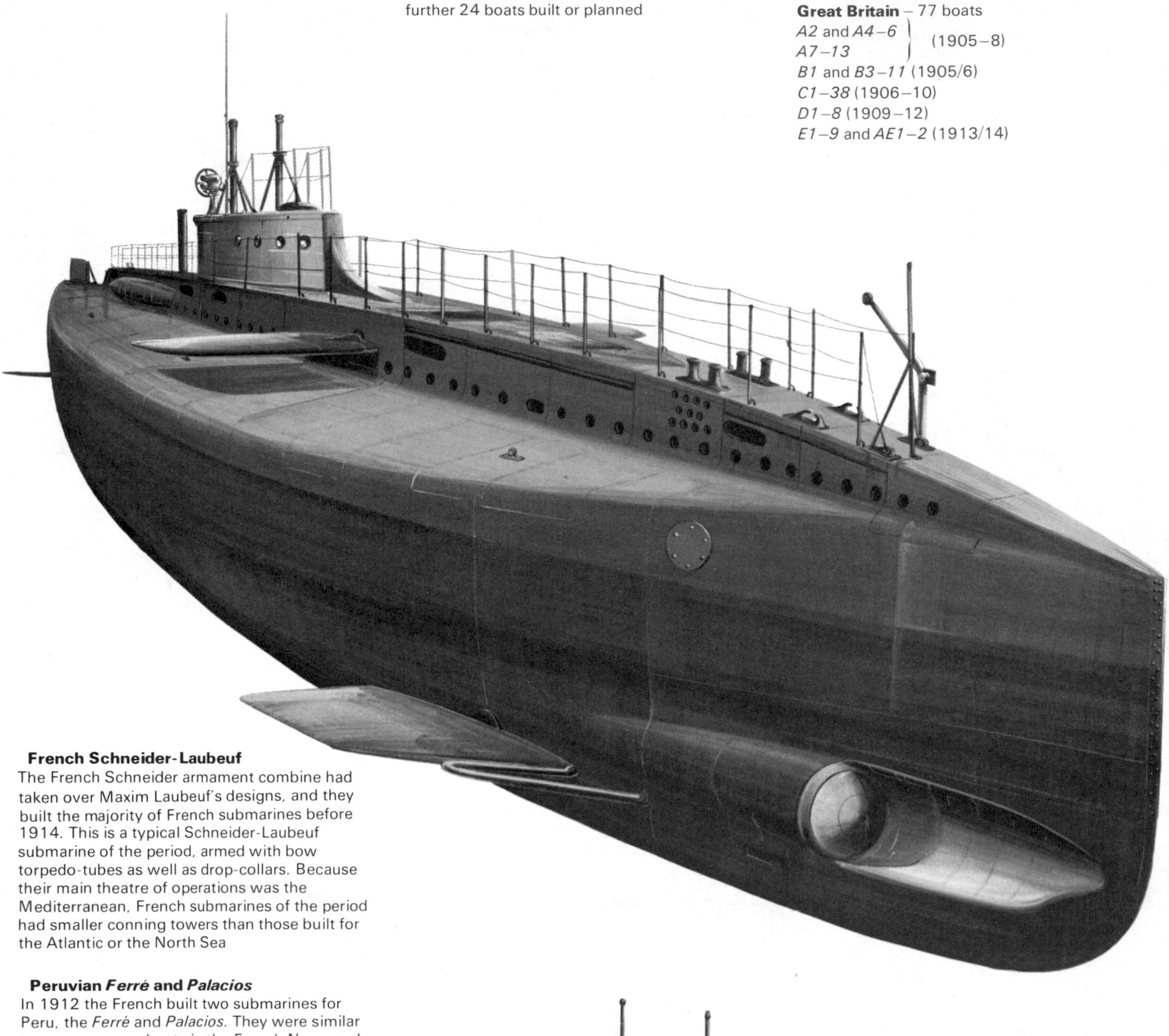

French Schneider-Laubeuf
The French Schneider armament combine had
taken over Maxim Laubeuf's designs, and they
built the majority of French submarines before
1914. This is a typical Schneider-Laubeuf
submarine of the period, armed with bow
torpedo-tubes as well as drop-collars. Because
their main theatre of operations was the
Mediterranean, French submarines of the period
had smaller conning towers than those built for
the Atlantic or the North Sea

Peruvian *Ferré* and *Palacios*
In 1912 the French built two submarines for
Peru, the *Ferré* and *Palacios*. They were similar
to contemporary boats in the French Navy, and
were armed with a bow torpedo-tube and four
drop-collars

Italy – 18 boats + 2 building
Delfino (1896)
5 *Glauco* Class (1905–09)
Foca (1909)
7 *Medusa* Class (1912/13)
Atropo (1913)
2 *Nautilus* Class (1913)
Giacinto Pullino (1913)
Note: Another of the *Pullino* Class was completing, in addition to the *Argonauta* and six large *Micca* Class just begun

Denmark – 7 boats + 2 building
Dykkeren
6 *Havfruen* Class
Note: Two more *Havfruen* Class under construction

Greece – 2 boats
2 *Delphin Class (1912/13)*

Netherlands – 7 boats + 4 building
O1
O2–5 and *K1*
Note: O6–7 and *K2–3* under construction

Japan – 13 boats + 2 building
Nos 1–5 (1905)
Nos 6–7 (1906)
Nos 8–9 (1909)
Nos 10–12 (1911)
No 13 (1912)
Note: Nos 14 and *15* were under construction in France

Norway – 4 boats
Kobben (1909)
A2–4 (1914)

Peru – 2 boats
2 *Ferré* Class (1912/13)

Portugal – 1 boat
Espadarte (1913)

Russia (Baltic) – 19 boats + 1 building
5 *Som* Class
3 *Ossetyr* Class
2 *Okun* Class
Minoga
Akula
4 *Kaïman* Class
N1–3

Russia (Arctic) – 1 boat
Delfin

Russia (Black Sea) – 8 boats + 1 building
4 *Okun* Class
2 *Karp* Class
2 *Som* Class
Note: Krab completing

Sweden – 5 boats
Kajen
Hvalen
Nos 2–4

United States – 35 boats + 6 building
A1–8 (1903)
B1–3 (1907)
C1–5 (1908–10)
D1–3 (1909/10)
E1–2 (1912)
F1–4 (1912/13)
G1–3 (1912/13)
G4 (1914)
H1–3 (1914)
K1–2 1914)
Note: 6 more 'K' Class completing

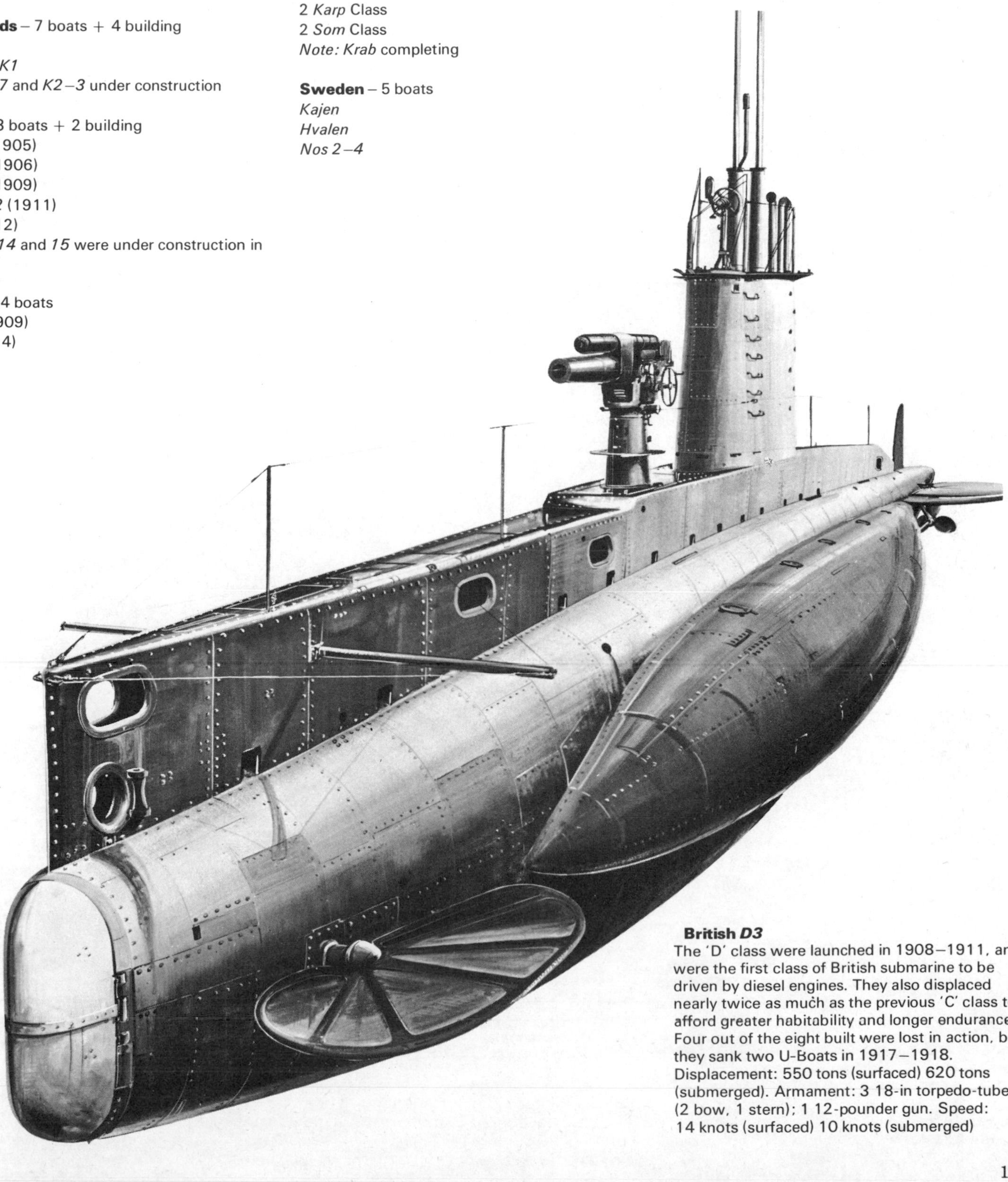

British *D3*
The 'D' class were launched in 1908–1911, and were the first class of British submarine to be driven by diesel engines. They also displaced nearly twice as much as the previous 'C' class to afford greater habitability and longer endurance. Four out of the eight built were lost in action, but they sank two U-Boats in 1917–1918. Displacement: 550 tons (surfaced) 620 tons (submerged). Armament: 3 18-in torpedo-tubes (2 bow, 1 stern); 1 12-pounder gun. Speed: 14 knots (surfaced) 10 knots (submerged)

SUBMARINES AT WAR
GETTING DOWN TO BUSINESS

After centuries of experiment, the submarine had arrived. With a workable method of propulsion and armed with a lethal weapon, her military potential was finally to be put to the test. And though still often frighteningly vulnerable, she was to have an impact which few could have foreseen

The first moves to be made by submarines when war broke out in August 1914 were timid in the extreme. Neither side was ready to do more than establish patrol lines, the Germans being obsessed with the need to guard against the expected onslaught by the British, and the British in turn only watching out for movements of surface ships. The British set up a patrol line in the Heligoland Bight immediately, and it was here that the U-Boats were stationed too. Information from the six British boats led to a spirited foray by surface forces later in the month, but due to a variety of circumstances the U-Boats took no part in the action. But the U-Boats had not been idle for, on 6 August, ten were sent on their first offensive patrol; they were to try to find out more about British dispositions, and to go as far north as the Norway—Orkneys line. This was a hazardous trip for submarines at this early stage, and particularly so for the U-Boats, which had never ventured so far afield, even in peacetime.

The U-Boats' pioneer cruise showed what the new weapon could achieve, but it also showed its limitations. *U9* broke down on the second day, but the others reached Fair Isle and even sighted British battleships at gunnery practice. At dawn the next day the British cruiser *Birmingham* suddenly caught sight of *U15*, apparently immobilised with engine trouble, and turned to ram. With hardly any damage to herself the cruiser sliced through the luckless submarine, which went down with all hands. When the rest of the U-Boats returned to Heligoland it was discovered that *U13* was also missing, and she is believed to have been mined on 12 August. The first attack on the British had not merely failed, but cost two U-Boats.

There were compensating factors however; on the one hand the British had cause to be uneasy, as their pre-war estimates of a U-Boat's radius of action had been too low, while on the other hand, the easy sinking of *U15* caused a marked degree of complacency about the risk to surface ships. This was to be rudely dispelled on 22 September, when *U9*, under the first of the U-Boat aces, Kapitän-Leutnant Otto Weddigen, sank three 12,000-ton armoured cruisers within the space of little over an hour. The three ships were, even by the standards of 1914, in an exposed position, and were known to their crews as the 'Live Bait Squadron',

but the joke rang hollow when it was realised that HMS *Aboukir, Cressy* and *Hogue* had taken over 1,100 men with them. On 15 October, Weddigen was again able to strike a numbing blow against the Royal Navy, when he sank the 23-year old cruiser *Hawke* off Aberdeen. Once more the loss of life was heavy, about 500 officers and men, for these older ships had only minimal protection against modern torpedoes, and carried large crews.

The only answer

The British by now had learned the hard way that the only answer to U-Boat attack was to screen all ships with destroyers, and soon units of the Grand Fleet moved at all times with a large force of escorting destroyers. Although the destroyer had no special weapons for dealing with submarines she was fast, highly manoeuvrable and so difficult a target that she could normally ignore the threat to her own safety. Apart from using her quick-firing guns she could ram a submarine in the same way as the *Birmingham* had sunk *U15*. This rapidly became the standard method, and new destroyers were fitted with a strengthened forefoot to their bows to act as a 'can-opener'.

Bundesarchiv

But there was no means as yet of detecting a submarine, and all countermeasures depended on a submarine giving her presence away, ie. waiting for the sight of a periscope or an accidental surfacing. Unfortunately such opportunities were rare, particularly with experienced submarine commanders, and in any case a periscope was hard to spot in rough weather.

The discomfiture of the British was completed when they realised that nothing prevented U-Boats from entering their main fleet's base at Scapa Flow. The result was a major upheaval, with the Grand Fleet moving to a series of temporary refuges while the necessary defences were installed at Scapa Flow, principally net barrages and blockships to seal the approach channels. Thus the submarine had achieved its first strategic victory over the surface warship, and had the German High Seas Fleet been in a position to take advantage of the U-Boats' achievement the Grand Fleet would have been caught in a difficult situation.

To make things worse, the British lacked a suitable mine, so even the defensive fields laid by minelayers proved useless. Indicator nets were the next step; these

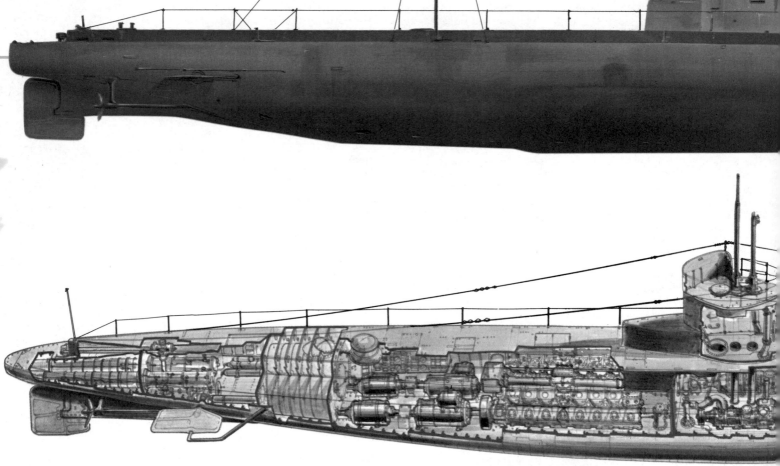

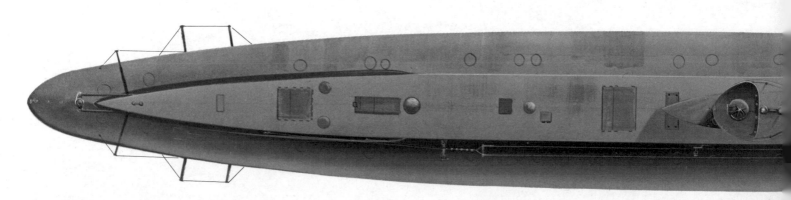

were nets of heavy wire mesh, kept afloat by indicator buoys and attended by armed drifters. Not only did a submarine run the risk of fouling her hydroplanes and propellers in trying to force a way through the net, but she gave her position away to the drifters above.

So, to give the drifters a weapon to attack a submarine which surfaced alongside, the lance bomb was developed. This was an explosive charge and detonator fixed to the end of an ash pole, and intended to be hurled downwards on to the deck of a submarine. Unlikely as it may sound, a lance bomb was once used, but it inflicted only minor damage to the submarine.

At the outbreak of war all belligerent and neutral countries regarded themselves as bound by International Law and the Hague Convention as far as the conduct of warfare at sea was concerned. With little precedent later than the

Napoleonic Wars to guide them, the maritime nations of the world assumed that a submarine (or any warship, for that matter) was not allowed to open fire on an enemy merchant ship 'on its lawful occasions' ie. not carrying offensive weapons and not acting in a hostile manner. On the contrary, the submarine would have to stop the merchantman, examine her papers, identify herself and then sink the victim or sail her home under a prize crew.

This idea was very favourable to the British as the major sea power and the world's largest mercantile shipowners, but it took little account of the peculiar nature of the submarine. Since it is impossible to stop and search a ship without being on the surface, a submarine would be almost completely ineffective as a weapon against commerce; moreover, she carried too small a crew to provide prize crews for her captures, or to accommodate prisoners.

German *U31*

U31 was a typical U-Boat of pre-1914 design, ordered in 1912 but not completed until late 1914. She was lost in the North Sea in January 1915 from unknown causes (probably a mine). She was armed with two torpedo-tubes in the bow and two in the stern, and carried a 10.5-cm deck gun. On the surface her two-shaft diesels gave her an endurance of 4,440 miles at 8 knots, but when submerged this fell to 80 miles at 5 knots. Length: 212 ft 6 in. Beam: 20 ft 9 in. Crew: 35 officers and men

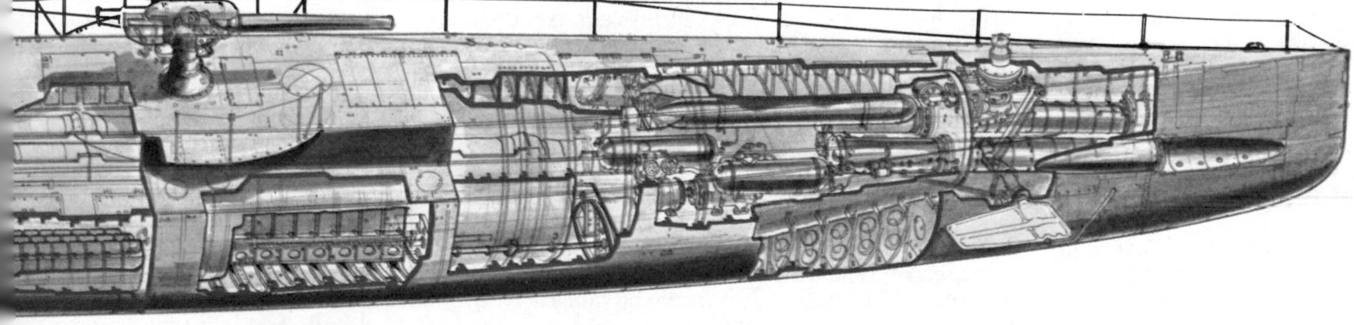

Every student of Mahan's books on naval strategy knew in 1914 that while Great Britain's seaborne commerce was her main strength, it was also a great source of weakness. At first the Germans had tried using their cruisers on the trade-routes to dislocate shipping, but by the beginning of January 1915, eight of the nine German cruisers operating outside the North Sea were either sunk or securely blockaded by Allied forces, and despite the vigour of their operations they had inflicted less than two per cent loss on British shipping.

On 20 October 1914, *U17* under K/L Feldkirchner stopped, searched and scuttled the steamer *Glitra* off Norway — the first time a submarine had tried to abide by the rules, and also one of the last. This insignificant little ship has gone down in history as the first victim of the submarine war on trade, but it was not long before other U-Boats began to attack shipping. As all British warships were now escorted by a screen of destroyers, there were fewer naval targets, and inevitably merchant ships made easier prey.

The problems faced by a submarine commander in identifying the type of target are demonstrated by *U24*'s torpedoing of the SS *Amiral Ganteaume* without warning off Cap Gris Nez on 26 October 1914: as the ship was loaded with Belgian refugees, the sinking was denounced as an atrocity, but in fact she was probably mistaken for a French troop transport.

No time for niceties

The view from a submarine's periscope is very limited, and was even more so with the crude instruments available in World War I; there was distortion of size and blurring of the image, so any careful examination of a ship from a submerged submarine (which would involve counting guns, number of people visible and type of uniform worn, etc.) was quite impossible. Furthermore, the vessel's slow speed under water gave the submarine commander little time for a leisurely assessment of possibilities, and the time available for making an attack could be limited to minutes or even seconds. In short, the very nature of the submarine, which made it such a lethal weapon against ships, also made a breach of international maritime law inevitable.

The *Glitra* sinking certainly inspired the idea of using U-Boats against British shipping, and the German Naval Staff were encouraged by Great Britain's ruthless interpretation of the law of contraband. Under the impression that all foodstuffs had been commandeered by the German government, the British had retaliated by treating cargoes of food as contraband, even when destined for a neutral port such as Copenhagen, providing that their ultimate destination could be proved to be Germany.

The problem was that both sides had drifted into total war, but everybody was still under the impression that life and business for civilians on both sides would carry on as usual while the dirty work was done by the armed forces. But as the land war in Flanders bogged down, and hopes of reaching Berlin or Paris by Christmas faded, it became clear to the leaders of both sides that the war would be a long one, and that it would also be a grim economic struggle. The Germans declared the waters around the British Isles a War Zone on 4 February 1915 and warned that British and French ships entering it would be sunk without warning, and that it would 'not always be possible' to prevent attacks on neutral shipping. In other words, the U-Boats were to be unleashed in an all-out offensive to cut off supplies to Great Britain and France.

The losses quickly mounted up; 32,000 tons of British shipping had been sunk in January 1915, and 15,900 tons of French and neutral shipping, but by March the figures had risen to 71,400 tons and 9,300 tons respectively. After a drop in April the figures jumped to 84,300 tons and 35,700 tons a month later, and by August they had climbed inexorably to the peak of 148,400 tons of British shipping and 37,400 tons of French and neutral shipping.

International opinion was soon up in arms, and no country's attitude was more crucial than that of the United States. The demands of the British war economy provided a growing boost to American industry, and manufacturers were only too happy to provide the sinews of war to both sides. As the British blockade prevented supplies from reaching Germany there was some friction between British and American interests, but on the other hand the needs of the British and the French were so enormous that the loss of the potential German market was hardly noticed. Furthermore, American public opinion had been prejudiced against Germany from the outbreak of war, first by her violation of Belgian neutrality and then by stories of brutality during the advance through Belgium and France.

Although there was a certain amount of latent anti-British sentiment to be exploited by German propaganda, this was more than balanced by a sentimental regard for France which went back to the War of Independence, and so State Department irritation at British high-handedness in operating the blockade was frequently eclipsed by far greater anger over the deaths of American citizens in neutral ships sunk without warning. The fiercest outburst came after the torpedoing of the British liner *Lusitania* by *U20* off Southern Ireland on 7 May, for she was running on the regular route from New York to Liverpool and was carrying 159 American passengers. The British were naturally quick to denounce the sinking, but the outcry in the United States was far stronger, and a diplomatic Note from Washington to Berlin demanded that German submarines should refrain from sinking ships carrying passengers.

Looking back on the *Lusitania* incident we should try to be as dispassionate as possible. Although some lurid claims have been made recently, there is no credible evidence to suggest that the *Lusitania* was armed, or that she was carrying a large cargo of high explosives. True, she was carrying 5,500 cases of small-arms ammunition and shell-fuses, totalling 37 tons, but this is hardly a lethal cargo, since rifle ammunition and nose-caps are not liable to be set off by a nearby torpedo explosion.

Much has been made of a mysterious second explosion reported by survivors, but this can easily be attributed to an implosion of the boilers, and if anyone doubts that a large ship would sink so quickly from a single hit, the very large boiler-rooms in a liner would fill rapidly and cause the ship to sink fast. Most of the accusations about hidden guns and vast cargoes of TNT prove on analysis to be either counter-claims made by Germany to evade charges of inhumanity, or confusion in the minds of laymen as to the differences between an armed merchant cruiser, an ammunition ship and a liner.

In any case, K/L Schwieger's own report shows that he had been warned to look out for troopships from Canada, but first mistook the liner for a '*number of destroyers in line*'; only when the ship came closer did she turn out to be a large four-funnelled ship, and Schwieger immediately fired a torpedo from a bow tube. There is no mention in his report of seeing guns, for it would have been impossible to pick out that sort of detail, and when he reported the second explosion he simply put forward boilers, coal or munitions as a likely cause, without further comment.

The British had gambled that the Germans would not dare to sink a liner carrying American nationals; when they did so, and then insisted on justifying their conduct, the British seized the opportunity to work up American sympathy. Although the sinking of the *Lusitania* was neither the first occasion on which American citizens were killed, nor the reason for America's entry into the War, it did mark a clear turning point in American public opinion, which finally decided that its sympathies lay more with the Allies.

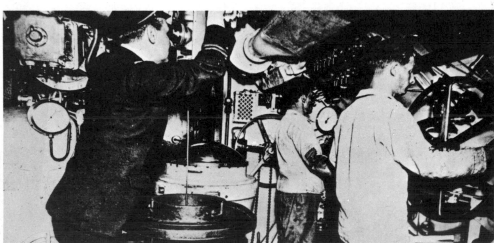

Left: Inside the control room of a submarine, showing the cramped conditions in which the crew had to work

Imperial War Museum

THE MEDITERRANEAN
IN SEARCH OF TARGETS

At first the war in the Mediterranean involved little or no submarine activity, despite the fact that most of the French submarines were stationed at Toulon and Bizerta. The lack of targets was partly responsible, for the overwhelming number of British and French ships in the Mediterranean had no difficulty in blockading Austrian and Turkish ships in their harbours. There were only seven Austrian submarines, all based at Cattaro (now Kotor in Yugoslavia) and they did not achieve anything approaching the Germans' exploits in the North Sea. But after an unsuccessful attack on the French armoured cruiser *Waldeck Rousseau* by the submarine *VI* (all Austrian submarines were originally known by a distinguishing Roman numeral; they did not adopt the U-prefix until late in 1915), the battleship *Jean Bart* was badly damaged by a torpedo from *XII*, and only reached Malta with difficulty.

This boat had a quaint history, for she had been ordered by the builders at Fiume for demonstration purposes; she was then taken over in August 1914, and became *XII*. Four months later, in April 1915, the armoured cruiser *Léon Gambetta* was sunk by two torpedoes in a skilful night attack by *V*, under Linienschiff-Leutnant von Trapp. Including Admiral Sénés, 650 officers and men were lost.

Meanwhile, the French submarines did not remain idle, and in December 1914 the *Curie* made a very bold attempt to enter Pola harbour, hoping to torpedo one of the Austrian warships based there. The barrage of nets proved too strong, and when she became hopelessly entangled her captain blew tanks and scuttled her before surrendering to the Austrians. Naturally the Austrians were interested in the *Curie*, which was a modern submarine completed in 1913, and they salvaged her. After repairs she was recommissioned in March 1915 as *XIV* (subsequently *U14*), and finally returned to French ownership after the Armistice.

In March 1915, much greater submarine activity was sparked off by the Anglo-French expedition to the Dardanelles. Suddenly Germany's new partner, Turkey, was under attack, and it was felt that a small reinforcement of submarines offered the only hope of interfering with the massive Allied naval effort. Accordingly, K/L Hersing was asked to attempt a passage of the Straits of Gibraltar in *U21*, and he left the Ems on 25 April 1915 via Spain and Cattaro. Although he was spotted by a patrolling torpedo-boat off Gibraltar, Hersing made a landfall at Cattaro without incident on 13 May, where he completed some urgent repairs before heading for Gallipoli. In the meantime the Germans had taken steps to reinforce the Austrians by sending ten new coastal U-Boats in sections down to Cattaro by rail. These were six of the 127-ton UB-type coastal submarines, *UB1*, *UB3*, *UBs7* and *8* and *UBs14* and *15*, and four of the 168-ton UC-type small mine-laying boats, *UCs12–15*.

After re-assembly they were commissioned under the German flag, and three of them were sent to Gallipoli in May 1915 in a brave attempt to distract the Allies. One of them, *UB3*, was lost without trace in the Aegean, but the other two passed through the Dardanelles and reached Constantinople safely. This was to be their only success for the moment, and it was left to *U21* to strike the first important blow. On 25 May, Hersing stalked the battleships *Swiftsure* and *Vengeance* without success, and then saw the *Triumph* off Gapa Tepe, firing her 10-in guns at the Turkish positions. The battleship was moving, with her anti-torpedo nets out, and Hersing had to wait for two hours for a good shot, but when it came, one torpedo hit her amidships and sent the old battleship over on her beam ends.

Hersing escaped by diving *under* the sinking *Triumph*, an appalling risk which was justified by his escape without detection. Two days later he saw the old battle-ship *Majestic* off Cape Helles, and moved into the attack. This time, the target was at anchor with nets out, and surrounded by colliers and patrols, but all to no avail. To a man like Hersing it was only a matter of time before a gap opened, and when it did he fired a single torpedo. Seven minutes later the one-time pride of the Channel Fleet heeled over and sank in 150 ft of water.

Although his targets were old and highly vulnerable ships with virtually no chance of surviving a torpedo hit in a vital spot, the Admiral commanding at the Dardanelles felt that he was about to see his entire supporting fleet of warships and transports picked off one by one, and so all bombarding ships larger than destroyers were sent away to Mudros. This alone put new heart into the hard-pressed Turkish infantry, and correspondingly dismayed their enemies. But the greatest enthusiasm was in Constantinople, where *U21* had a Roman triumph on 5 June.

'Tin tadpoles'

The entry of Italy into the War on the Allied side on 24 May gave the German and Austrian submarines new targets. On 9 June the light cruiser HMS *Dublin* was badly damaged by a torpedo from *IV*, and a day later the newly re-assembled *UB15* caught the Italian submarine *Medusa* on the surface off Venice, and sank her. These UB-craft were tiny and only barely adequate, and were known to their crews as 'tin tadpoles', but the same *UB15* was able to torpedo the armoured cruiser *Amalfi* in the Gulf of Venice. Yet another cruiser was sunk on 18 July, when *IV* sank the *Giuseppe Garibaldi* off Gravosa, near Ragusa, while *V* sank the submarine *Nereide* on 5 August near Pelagosa.

For a time the pretence was kept up that the German submarines were operated by the Austrian Navy, and *UB15* and *UB1* were formally transferred in June 1915 as *X* and *XI*. By October all the Austrian submarines bore U-prefixes with Arabic

Italian 'F' Class
The Italian Fiat-Laurenti designs were most successful, and were built under licence for several foreign navies. The 21 units of the 'F' Class were built during the First World War, and served until the 1930s. Armament: two 17.7-in torpedo-tubes; one 3-in AA gun. Speed: 12½ knots (surfaced) 8 knots (submerged)

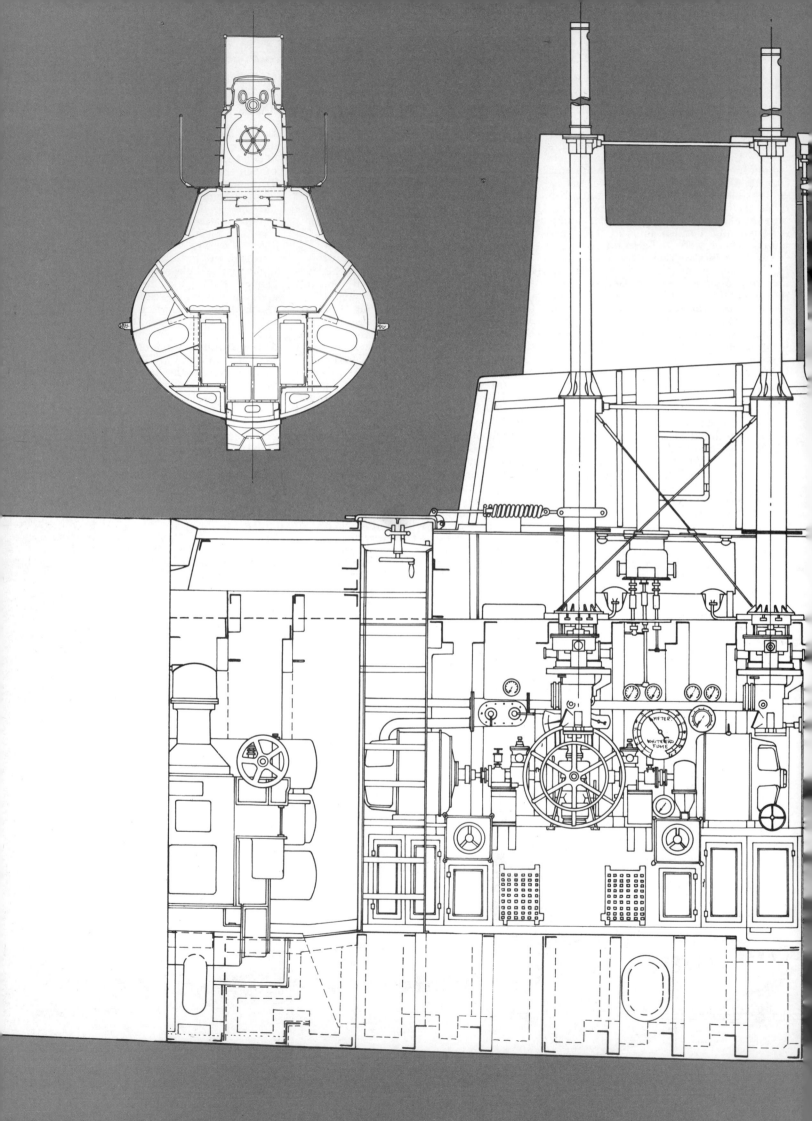

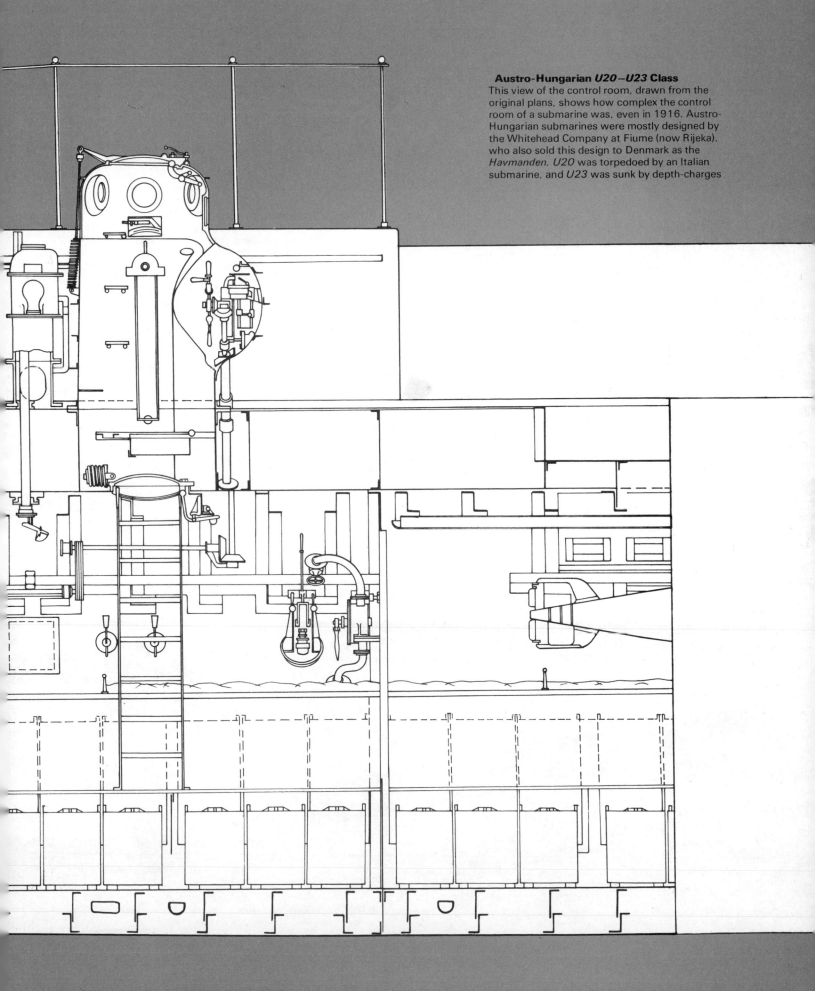

Austro-Hungarian *U20—U23* Class
This view of the control room, drawn from the original plans, shows how complex the control room of a submarine was, even in 1916. Austro-Hungarian submarines were mostly designed by the Whitehead Company at Fiume (now Rijeka), who also sold this design to Denmark as the *Havmanden. U20* was torpedoed by an Italian submarine, and *U23* was sunk by depth-charges

numerals, just like the German U-Boats, (and in many cases duplicating the German numbers). The five U-Boats at Constantinople, however, were not handed over to the Turks, but formed instead into a half-flotilla for operations in the Sea of Marmora and the Black Sea. Hersing in *U21* was the senior officer, and during the summer of 1915 he was reinforced by *UB14* and *UC13*. He and his captains pursued a vigorous campaign, but *UC13* was lost by stranding in the Black Sea, while his own boat developed defects which forced him to return to Cattaro for repairs lasting four months.

Forcing the Narrows

The British and French had not allocated any modern submarines to the Dardanelles forces at first, as they had

envisaged it as nothing more than a shore bombardment and landing of troops. At the end of 1914, however, three of the elderly 'B' class boats from Malta and the French boats *Brumaire* and *Circé* were sent to help maintain the blockade of the Dardanelles. This was principally to guard against a breakout by the German battle cruiser *Goeben* and her consort, the light cruiser *Breslau*, but it soon became clear to the naval staff that it might be possible to take a submarine up the 27 miles of the Narrows between the Gallipoli Peninsula and the mainland of Asia Minor, to attack any German or Turkish warships which could be found.

Only a submarine could get through the five rows of mines which guarded the Narrows; the biggest problem was whether these small, under-powered boats could

breast the 4–5-knot current which swept through the mile-wide gap between Chanak (Cannakale) and Kilid Bahir. The competition was fierce among the five boats, but finally the British *B11* was chosen on account of new batteries; her hydroplanes were fitted with special guards to prevent mine-cables from fouling them, and she was sent off on 1 December 1914.

After an exciting passage, the little submarine reached the smoother waters above the Narrows, and found to her delight that an elderly Turkish warship, the *Messudieh*, was lying at anchor. Lt Holbrook closed to 800 yards, fired one 18-in torpedo, and the target rolled over and sank. Hailed in the Allied newspapers as a battleship, the *Messudieh* was in reality a very old steam frigate recon-

British 'B' Class

The British 'B' Class were the second stage in the development of the original Holland design bought from the Americans in 1901. Their gasoline engines were their weak point, and they were too small for anything more than harbour defence. Yet in December 1914 *B11* managed to get through the Dardanelles minefields and torpedoed the Turkish ''battleship'' *Messudieh*

SURFACE TRIM

Submarine Diving Technique

When a submarine dives she admits water to flood her ballast tanks, and thus destroys her positive buoyancy. Once below the surface she manoeuvres by moving her hydroplanes

structed for coastal defence, but it was an audacious success to put against the recent achievements of the U-Boats.

More significantly, it showed the Allies how they could strike at the Turks, for if *B11* could penetrate the Narrows, a larger boat with more power and endurance could even reach the Sea of Marmora which lay between the Narrows and Constantinople. An immediate request for larger submarines was made by the officer commanding the British submarines at the Dardanelles, and as soon as the landing operations were sanctioned, orders were given for no fewer than seven of the 'E' Class to go out to the Dardanelles with the other naval reinforcements. The stage was set for one of the classic submarine campaigns of history.

The first attempt to force the Straits met with disaster, when *E15* ran aground off Kephez Point after being caught by the fierce current. As she was under the guns of Fort Dardanos it proved extremely difficult to prevent the Turks from salvaging an example of the very latest type of British submarine. After attempts to torpedo her, using both destroyers and submarines, two battleships tried to destroy her with gunfire; success was finally achieved by sending in a pair of picket boats armed with small torpedoes.

But the fiasco was only a minor interruption, and by 26 April 1915 the Australian submarine *AE2* was signalling from the Sea of Marmora; although she did not last long, being sunk by a Turkish torpedo-boat a day later, her sister *E14* had already arrived. Nor were the French submarines inactive, but unfortunately the *Saphir* ran

aground off Nagara Point in similar circumstances to *E15*, and the *Joule* was mined on 1 May, making the toll four out of five. But the Allied armies had sustained such tremendous casualties during their landings on 26 April that *E14*'s report of three ships sunk — and the alarm and confusion spread among the Turks — made it imperative to try to exert more pressure on the Turkish seaborne supply route. On 19 May, *E11* relieved *E14*, and began a career of destruction which earned Lt-Cdr Nasmith the Victoria Cross.

Building up strength

During the following months *E2, E7, E11, E12, E20, H1* and the French *Turquoise* were among the submarines which successfully forced the mine-barrier and the currents of the Narrows to get to the

AWASH

PERISCOPE DEPTH

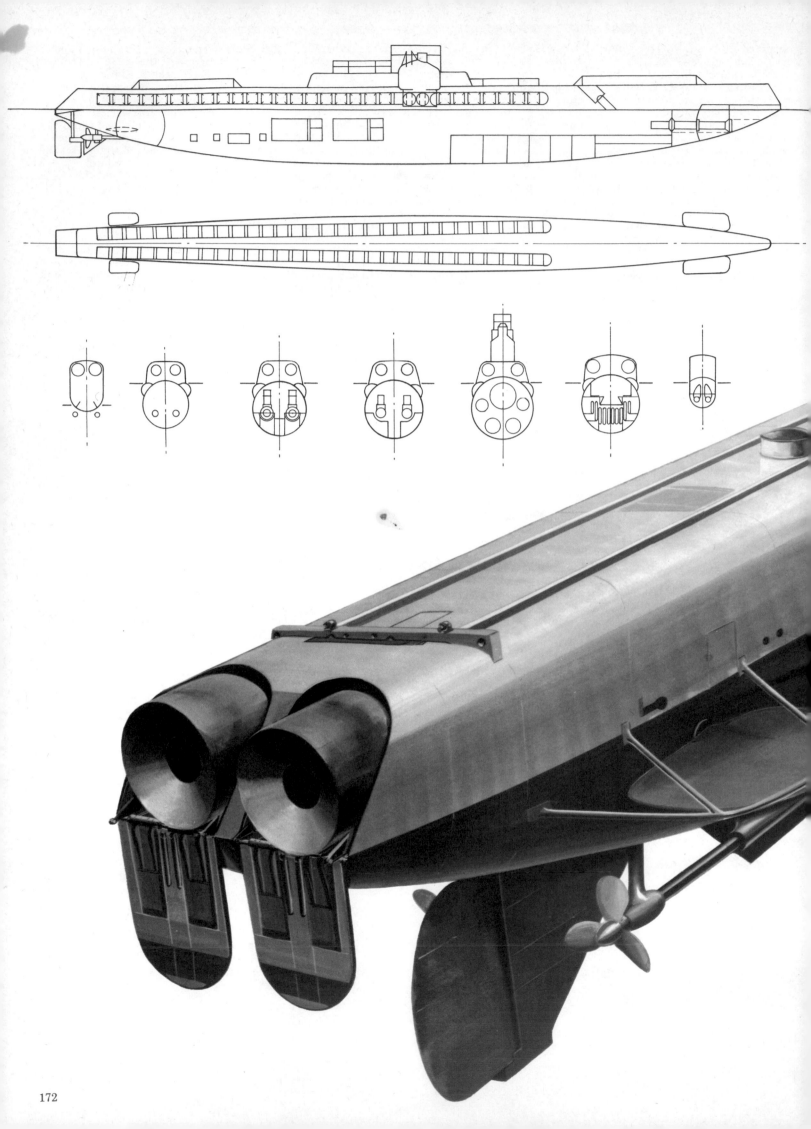

Sea of Marmora. Unfortunately the first German submarines had also penetrated the Straits, as we have seen, and on 30 October *UB15* was able to torpedo *E20*, as a result of information found that day aboard the grounded *Turquoise*.

After *E11*'s first patrol, when many targets such as dhows had been too small to warrant a torpedo, she was fitted with a 12-pounder (3-in) gun bolted on to the deck-casing, while *E14* had a 6-pounder (57-mm) gun. Both submarines found their deck-guns so useful that Malta Dockyard was forced to refit all the submarines in a similar fashion; *E12* was given a 4-in gun, and the ill-fated *E20* had a 6-in howitzer which was never tested in action. Not only could 'soft-skinned' targets such as boats and small steamers be stopped by the threat of gunfire, but also rail-traffic, for the main rail-link between Constantinople and Gallipoli ran close to the shore. It did not take the submarine commanders long to realise that they could shell troop-trains, and even lob shells into tunnels when ship targets were not available. From this point on, the gun became an indispensable feature of most submarines until the end of the Second World War.

Russian *Krab*

The Russian *Krab* was the world's first submarine minelayer, but as she was not completed until 1915 she was overtaken by the German UC-Boats. Although she had many teething problems she laid some successful fields in the Black Sea. She was scuttled by British forces in the spring of 1919, during the Anglo-French intervention against the Bolsheviks, but was raised in 1935 and scrapped

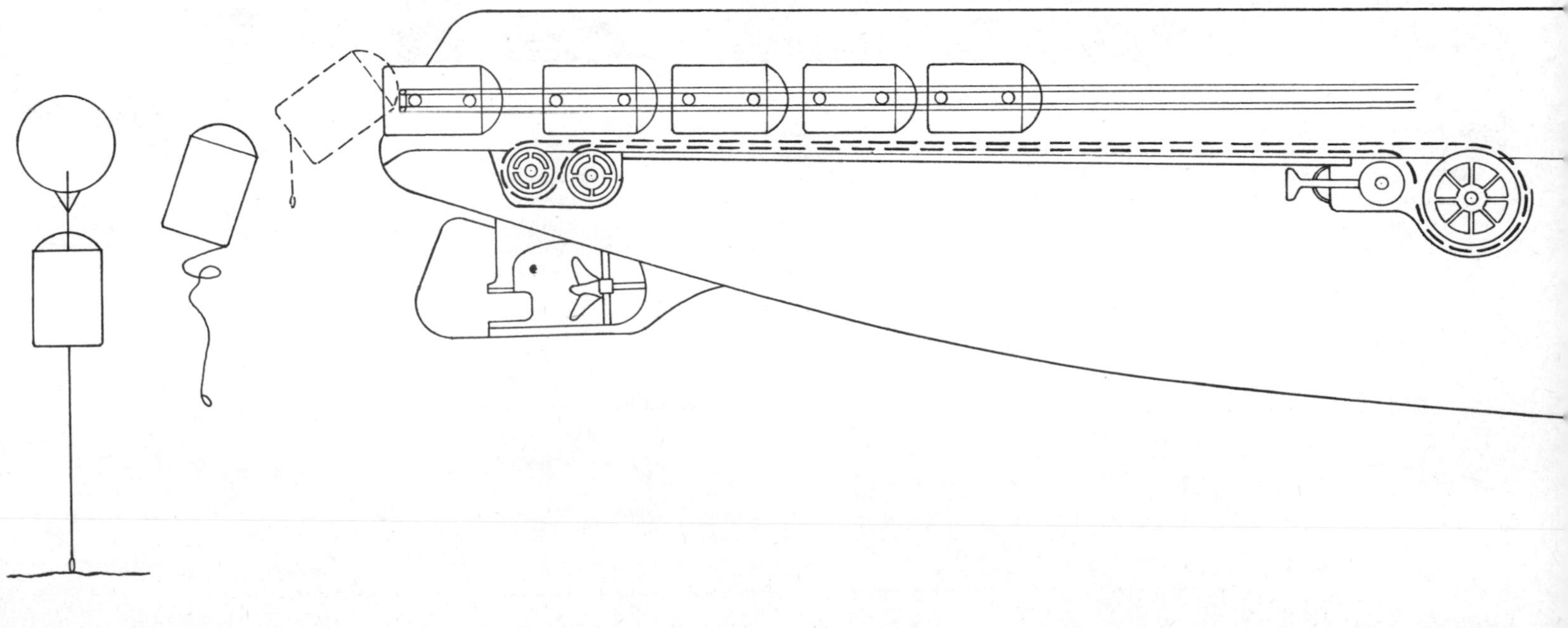

National Maritime Museum, London

A photograph of a captured German mine, taken during the First World War. When laid by a submarine, the frame and mine sank to the sea bed where a soluble plug released the mine on a length of cable and allowed it to float to the correct height; then it was anchored by the legs. This was an accurate system, but had the drawback that the plug was liable to dissolve too quickly, releasing the mine immediately under the submarine

German *UC1* (above)

The first German minelayer, *UC1* appeared in 1915. Apart from a machine-gun on deck she had no armament, but she carried twelve mines in six vertical chutes. The drawing shows how each mine was loaded in a frame; it was laid downwards through a hatch in the keel. This class had very limited endurance

German *UC26*

An inboard view of the German minelayer *UC26*, showing how much of the forward space was taken up with the mine-wells. The *blue* areas indicate torpedo-tube spaces; *red* indicates machinery; *mauve* indicates the control room and conning tower and *yellow* indicates the accommodation spaces

German UC71

The minelayer *UC71* had two external torpedo-tubes to leave more internal space for her mines. All the later minelayers were given a torpedo armament to allow them to sink ships on their homeward trip. This submarine did not commission until 1917, and survived the war only to be sunk by accident while crossing the North Sea to surrender

Although the failure of the Gallipoli Campaign and the final evacuation of the Peninsula in January 1916 meant the withdrawal of Allied submarines from the Sea of Marmora, there was still a lot of work left for them to do. Their skilled commanders were sent home for service in the North Sea, but the boats themselves remained. Six British submarines were sent to join the French boats watching the mine barrage in the Straits of Otranto, laid to prevent the Austro-Hungarian Fleet from breaking out of the Adriatic, and eight were dispersed on anti-U-Boat patrols. Only *E2* was left to keep a lonely vigil off the Dardanelles, guarding against a breakout by the *Goeben* and the *Breslau*; unfortunately, when the German ships did finally appear, on 19 January 1918, the *E2* was in dock with a fractured shaft. In a last desperate attempt to cripple the battle cruiser, *E14* was transferred from Corfu and, although she penetrated the Narrows with some difficulty, she failed to find her target, and was sunk by Turkish patrol vessels on 27 January.

The little 'B' Class boats, which had done so much better than expected in 1914/15, were by 1916 regarded as unsafe to dive, and six were converted by the Italians to surface patrol vessels in 1916/17. *B6–B11* became *S6–S11*, with raised wheelhouses and 12-pounder guns, but on 9 August 1916 *B10* was sunk by an enemy aircraft while under conversion at Venice.

Submarine Minelaying Techniques

There are two main systems of laying mines from submarines. *Above:* vertical chutes inside the pressure hull (or in the saddle tanks). *Below:* a horizontal deck or tubes. Both types needed precise compensating gear to adjust the trim while laying, to prevent the submarine from suddenly 'porpoising'

British 'M' Class

The British replied to the U-Cruisers with the 'M' Class, which mounted 12-in guns removed from battleships. The three 'M' Class were never tested in action, but they evolved a special method of using their guns. Known as the 'dip-chick' method, it involved a sudden rise to the surface, a round fired from the 12-in gun, and then a rapid dive again, all in 30 seconds

German *UB86* and *UB59*

Two examples of the UB type of small U-Boat, which were developed from small coastal submarines first ordered in November 1914. *UB59* (right) and *UB86* were both 500-tonners armed with four bow tubes, one stern tube and a deck gun. This type, the UBIII, grew steadily in size until it equalled the pre-war U-series, and it was chosen as the model for the Type VII U-Boats when Germany began to build U-Boats again under Hitler

US 'H' Class
The American 'H' Class were built to a successful design which was also used in Canada and Italy. *H4—9* were originally ordered by the Imperial Russian Navy as *AG17—20* (AG = American Holland) but after the Revolution in 1917 they were taken over by the US Navy. Armament: four 18-in torpedo-tubes. Speed: 14 knots (surfaced) 10 knots (submerged)

THE BALTIC
A DISTURBED PEACE

The other theatre in which British submarines distinguished themselves was the Baltic. As early as October 1914 two British submarines, *E1* and *E9*, set out from Gorleston, bound for Libau (now Liepaja), which was held by the Russians as a forward base. In some ways the passage of the Kattegat and the Baltic was as hazardous as the Dardanelles. The shallowness of the water and the number of German patrol craft, combined with a large number of minefields, made the Baltic a difficult area for submarines, but they did have the advantage of a friendly Russian base from which to operate.

When the first two boats arrived at Libau, however, they found the Russians busily engaged in demolishing the port in expectation of its capture by advancing German troops, and the British were forced to reshape their plans hurriedly. The Russians had set up a new base for the submarines at Lapvik in the Gulf of Finland, and here they were able to rest and effect repairs. The third boat, *E11* under Nasmith, had to turn back because of persistent attacks by patrol craft in the Kattegat, and was transferred to the Dardanelles—where, as we have already seen, there was no shortage of action.

The mere presence of two hostile submarines had a disturbing effect on German dispositions in the Western Baltic, for this was the secluded training area and private preserve of the High Seas Fleet. Outnumbering the Russian Fleet at Kronstadt, and facing a submarine force which lacked the leadership and the modern boats (many of the new Russian boats were without engines, as these had been ordered in Germany) which could have made it more dangerous, the Germans had good reason to think themselves secure in the western half of the Baltic.

The first intimation to the contrary came when *E1*, while on passage to Libau, fired a torpedo at the cruiser SMS *Viktoria Luise* which ran under the target, and when *E11*'s attempted passage was detected it was obvious that more than one submarine was involved. Max Horton, promoted to Commander on 1 January 1915, caused further unrest by taking *E9* out of Lapvik during the depth of the Russian winter, when ships were normally iced in. Entering Kiel Bay, he found the destroyer *S120*, but the torpedo hit the bottom under her and she was only severely shaken. The German Commander-in-Chief was convinced that the British had an entire flotilla, with a secret depot-ship hidden in a bay, and two squadrons of heavy ships were withdrawn to Swinemünde while the depot-ship was located.

Extraordinary exertions

But the main victims of *E1* and *E9* were the ships carrying iron ore from Sweden to Germany, and when the thaw came the two submarines ranged far and wide in pursuit of targets. The Russian *Drakon* was also able to drive off the cruiser SMS *Thetis* on 14 May, and this ship was again attacked unsuccessfully by the *Alligator* a month later. The *Okun* was similarly unable to hit a squadron of cruisers, and escaped from a ramming by a destroyer with slight damage. But reinforcements were on the way, for the British Government had been agreeably surprised by the extraordinary exertions of Horton and Laurence in *E9* and *E1*. Four more 'E' Class, *E8*, *E13*, *E18* and *E19* were to go out to join their sisters, while the old 'C' Class boats, *C26*, *C27*, *C32* and *C35*, were to be stripped down, sent by sea to Arkhangelsk, and then transported by rail and canal barge to Lapvik. *E8* arrived first, on 18 August, but the next one, *E13*, ran aground off the Danish island of Saltholm, and was destroyed by German torpedo boats. The other two arrived without mishap, making a total of five modern submarines at Lapvik, with four smaller 'Cs' available as soon as they could be re-assembled.

The results were soon evident. On 5 October one Russian and two British submarines sortied from Reval, and several merchant ships were sunk. Later that month four steamers and two cruisers were sunk by the British, while the Russian *Kaïman*, *Krokodil*, *Makrel*, *Som* and *Alligator* accounted for two between them. The year 1916 seemed to start well enough, and in May the British were again joined by the Russians, but the Germans' success on land swung the tide of battle slowly in their favour. Then came the so-called 'February Revolution' in March 1917, followed by a steady decline in the effectiveness of the submarine effort as Russian support for the British flotilla became less enthusiastic.

After the October Revolution came the Peace Treaty of Brest-Litovsk, in which the Germans stipulated to the new Communist masters of what was shortly to become the Red Fleet that the British submarines must be surrendered. There was only one way out for the submariners, and on 8 April 1918 a still-friendly Russian icebreaker led the surviving seven submarines out of their final base at Helsingfors (Helsinki) to be scuttled in deep water. The Baltic was no longer 'Horton's Sea'.

Russian *Akula*

The *Akula* was considered by the Russians to be their most successful design before 1914. She was much bigger than the *Minoga*, and was armed with eight torpedoes in drop-collars. After an active career in the Baltic she was lost in a German minefield near the Gulf of Riga in November 1915

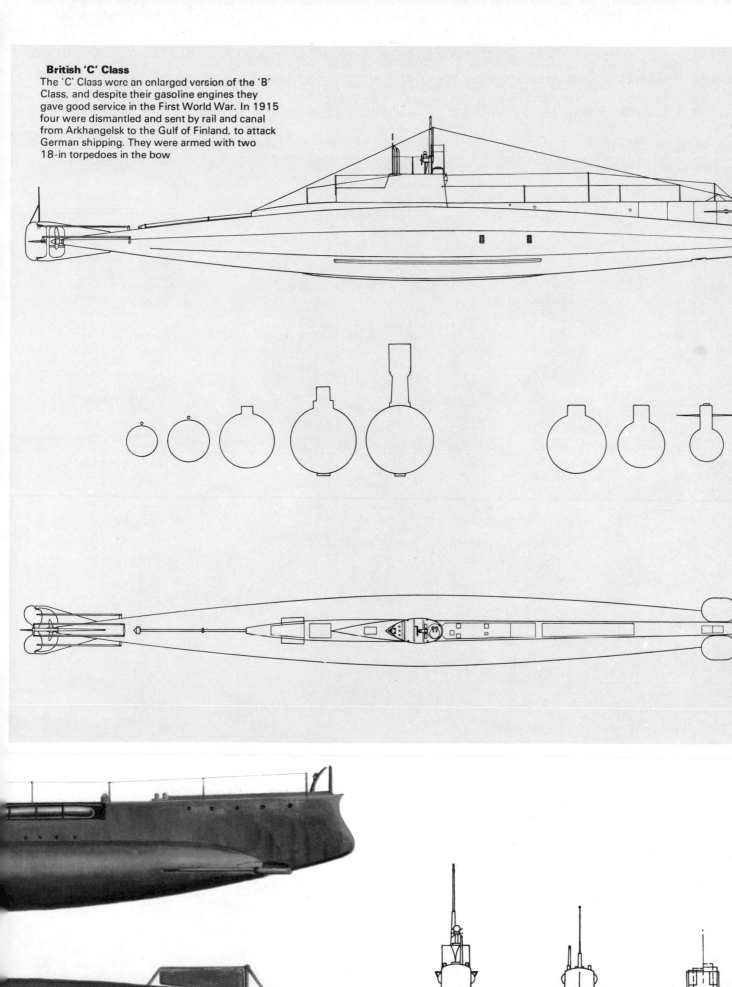

British 'C' Class

The 'C' Class were an enlarged version of the 'B' Class, and despite their gasoline engines they gave good service in the First World War. In 1915 four were dismantled and sent by rail and canal from Arkhangelsk to the Gulf of Finland, to attack German shipping. They were armed with two 18-in torpedoes in the bow

THE NORTH SEA
THE BRINK OF DEFEAT

Robert Hunt Library

In the main theatre of operations, the North Sea, both the British and the Germans introduced many new submarines, both repetitions of existing classes and novel types. The Germans had *U31–U41* and *U43–U50* under construction in August 1914 (*U42* was building in Italy, but she was seized in June 1915 as the *Balilla*), and they promptly ordered *U51–U56*. These were very similar to the preceding class – 720-tonners armed with two bow and two stern tubes firing 20-in torpedoes. They were driven by two 1,100 bhp diesel engines on the surface, and two 550 ehp electric motors submerged.

Like their British counterparts in the Sea of Marmora, German U-Boat commanders realised that some small targets could be sunk just as easily with a gun as with an expensive, irreplaceable torpedo, and the ocean-going submarines soon mounted heavier guns than the small 37-mm on a disappearing mounting which had been standard up to *U18*. A variety of 3.4-in (88-mm) and 4.1-in (105-mm) were carried in 1915–18 by all but the smaller boats, most of which were equipped with a small 4-pounder (50-mm) gun.

The next batch of boats ordered was the *U57* class of six units, followed by orders up to *U70*, placed by early 1915. These were the workhorses of the U-Boat fleet, known as the 'Mittel-U' type, fitted with two to four bow torpedo-tubes, and one or two stern tubes. They displaced 750 tons on the surface and approximately 830 tons submerged, but these figures changed as wartime improvements were made. Speeds varied, but they ranged between 15.5 and 17.5 knots on the surface from twin diesels, and 8 to 9 knots from the twin electric motors while submerged.

In November 1914, when the German High Command realised that there would be no early victory on land, orders were placed for two new types of U-Boat to allow the Navy to prosecute the war more effectively. These were the little 'UB' coastal submarines and the 'UC' minelayers, which were comparable in size to the early British 'A' and 'B' classes. However, both types were developed until they were bigger and more successful than the earlier Mittel-U types.

The first minelayers, *UC1* to *UC15*, were unique in that they had no torpedo armament, and they carried only 12 mines, stowed in six vertically inclined tubes. Also, they reverted to using the Körting heavy oil engine which had been such an undesirable feature of the early U-Boats. Their low endurance and lack of sea-keeping meant that they could only lay mines in the Channel and off the South East coast of England, but they nevertheless added a new and sinister dimension to the submarine war.

For some time the British were only dimly aware of the danger, when mysterious fields were discovered off the East Coast in June 1915, but on 3 July, after a steamer reported colliding with a submerged object, British divers found the wreck of the newly completed *UC2*. The Italians salvaged the wreck of *UC12* in March 1916 after she had blown herself up on her own mines in Taranto harbour, and the British recovered *UC5* almost intact when she ran aground on Shipwash Sand in April. More news came to light when the French found charts of minefields aboard *UB26*, after she had been caught in nets outside Le Havre.

The British reacted in a similar fashion to the Germans and ordered a further 38 of the 'E' Class in November 1914; unlike the Germans they had put a number of experimental submarines in hand in 1913, in order to evaluate foreign ideas. Three of the 'S' Class were built to the Italian Laurenti design, using Fiat diesels, and the four 'Ws' were built to French plans purchased from Schneider-Laubeuf. Vickers had also been allowed to build four 'V' Class to their own designs, while there were two more very unusual types, a large ocean-going boat and one driven by steam. Although the French had given up the idea of steam-propulsion as long ago as 1908, the Admiralty was looking for a surface speed which was beyond the capacity of existing diesel engines.

Too novel for war

Had the war not started when it did this interesting spawning of types might have had more effect, but as it turned out the 'S' and 'W' Classes proved too novel for wartime use, and all seven were transferred to Italy between October 1915 and August 1916, on the grounds that the Italian Navy might know how to work them. The big ocean-going boat was called *Nautilus*, the first British submarine to have a name instead of a number. Although she was a dismal failure and never became

German 'UB' and 'UC' type specifications

	UB1–17	UB18–46	UB48–136	UC1–15	UC16–79	UC90–120
Length (ft)	92	118.5	181.5	111.5	170	184
Breadth (ft)	10.25	14.25	191.3	10.3	17.1	18.2
Draught (ft)	10	12.15	12	10	12	12.35
Displacement (tons) surface/submerged	128/143	275/304	521/657	170/185	417/509	496/575
Surface hp	1 × 60	2 × 282	2 × 1100	1 × 90	2 × 500 or 2 × 600	2 × 600 or 2 × 650
Submerged hp	1 × 120	2 × 280	2 × 760	1 × 138	2 × 460	2 × 600
Oil fuel (tons)	3.5	22	34	2.5	46.6	63.6
Endurance at 5–8 knots (miles)	1,600	6,500	8,500	800	8,700	8,000
Speed (knots) surface/submerged	6.5/5.5	9/5.8	13.5/7.5	6.5/5	11–12/7	11–12/6.5
Torpedo tubes (in)	2 × 17.7 Bow	2 × 19.7 Bow	4 Bow; 1 Stern	None	2 Bow; 1 Stern	1 Stern; 2 ext.
Guns	1 MG	1 × 50mm or 1 × 88mm	1 × 105mm	1 MG	1 × 88mm	1 × 105mm
Complement	14	23	34	16	28	32

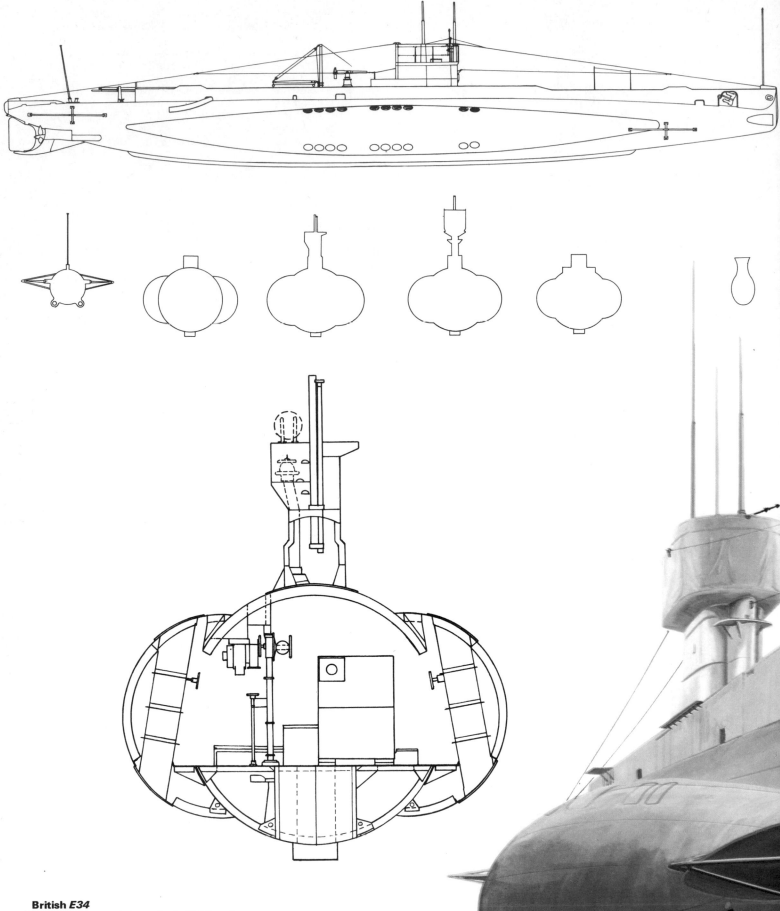

British E34

The 'E' Class came into service in 1914 and were the standard wartime design. In all, 56 were built, but in 1915, after the capture of *UC2*, six were altered to minelayers. Unlike the German boats, the *E34* and her sisters had vertical mine tubes in their saddle tanks. Sixteen tubes carried two mines each, making a total of 32 mines

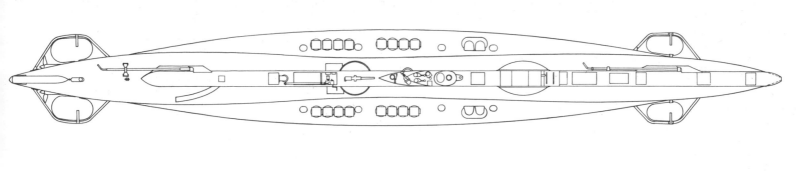

operational, the steam-driven *Swordfish* did carry out trials and proved that steam turbines could be used in submarines. Beyond that point she could not be made to go, and in July 1917 she was recommissioned as a surface patrol vessel, with built-up superstructure and guns like those of the little 'B' Class in the Mediterranean.

Being able to tap the enormous resources of America gave the British a great advantage. As part of a deal arranged with the head of Bethlehem Steel, Charles M Schwab, Vickers' Canadian subsidiary company in Montreal was given a contract to build ten submarines based on the contemporary 'H' Class building for the US Navy and for the Russians as the 'AG' Class, while the Fore River Plant at Quincy, Massachusetts, was to build a further ten. The American-built group, numbered H11 to H20, were to be delivered unarmed to Canadian Vickers, who would

then arm them, but this stretching of the neutrality laws finally goaded the State Department into action, and they were held up until the United States entered the war in 1917.

As it turned out, the British had by then more submarines than they could man, and six of the 'Hs' were ceded to Chile as compensation for warships seized in 1914, while the Canadians were given two. Out of the first group, H1 and H4 were sent to the Dardanelles in 1915; H3 was lost in a minefield off Cattaro in 1916, but H6 went aground off the coast of Holland and, after being interned, was purchased by the Dutch Navy. A further eight 'Hs' were built in Canada for the Italian Navy, and the Royal Navy liked theirs so much that in 1917 they ordered a further 34 to a modified design — which must constitute a record: one basic design was built in three countries, and the class served in seven navies. Incidentally,

H5's crossing of the Atlantic established a record for the longest voyage by a submarine to date.

The Admiralty panics
One notable feature of the naval war was the way in which the Admiralty was apt to be panicked by rumours. In 1915 a report was received in England to the effect that new German U-Boats would be capable of much higher surface speeds, and to meet this threat it was thought necessary to build 20-knot submarines. A further requirement was for long endurance and a more powerful wireless set, for the 'D' and 'E' Class boats patrolling in the Heligoland Bight could only transmit over a range of 50 miles. The resulting 'J' Class were over 100 feet longer than the 'E' Class, and had the remarkable speed of 19 knots on the surface, making them the fastest submarines in the world.

Unfortunately this led to the dangerous

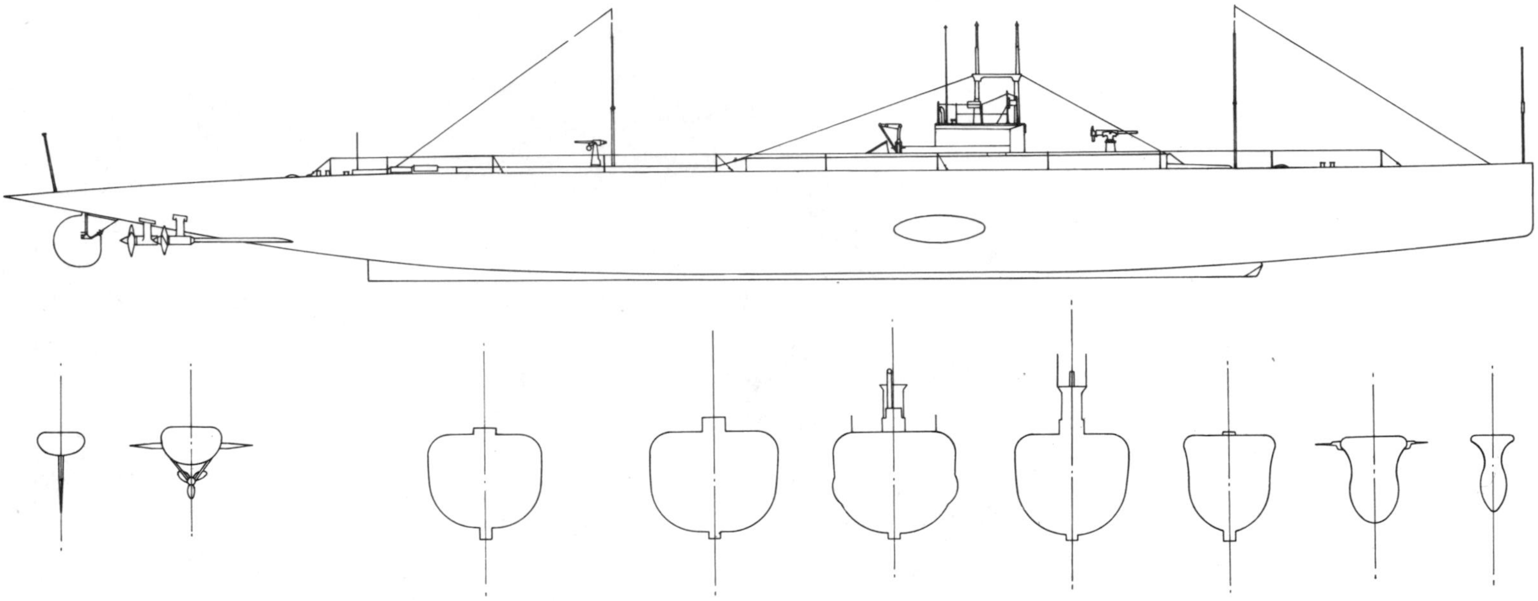

British J2
The British 'J' Class were designed for greater endurance than previous classes, and had long-range wireless to enable them to reconnoitre in enemy waters. They also had triple-shaft diesels to drive them at 19 knots, in an attempt to provide a submarine capable of operating with surface ships. After the war the survivors were transferred to the Royal Australian Navy

illusion that it would be a great advantage to have submarines capable of operating with the main battle fleet, the object being to lure the enemy's ships into a submarine trap. Up to this point the submarine's development had been rapid but logical, and under the stress of war enormous improvements in efficiency were being made, but now the designers were faced by an insoluble problem; the diesel could not be up-rated or developed any further, and even in the 'J' Class engine-power had only been achieved by linking three Vickers 1,200 bhp 12-cylinder engines. As a result, when Vickers were planning early in 1915 a so-called 'Fleet Submarine' there was no question of giving her the speed of a battleship (21 knots) with diesel engines, and so their designers fell back on the steam turbine unit which was being installed in the experimental *Swordfish*.

The ill-starred 'K' Class were the most bizarre submarines yet seen, for their 10,000 shaft hp turbines could drive them at 24 knots, with an auxiliary diesel for charging the batteries in addition to the electric motors giving them a total of three propulsion systems. In anticipation of their role in a surface action they were at first armed with twin revolving 18-in torpedo-tubes in the superstructure, as well as four bow and four beam tubes.

"Too many holes"

The 'K' boats merit a history of their own to do them full justice, but it will suffice to say here that their short-comings derived from two different causes: first, they were doing the wrong job, and second, their highly ingenious design was so complex that it was vulnerable to small defects. Submarines have never had any part to play in company with large war-ships; they have always been weapons of stealth and ambush. Furthermore, they are so dangerous that even friendly war-ships are likely to shoot first and ask questions later, and because of their low profile they are badly equipped for sur-face navigation at speed in close formation. The 'K' Class had two oil-fired boilers, each with a small funnel which had to fold down into a watertight well, and as these boilers required large air-intakes, these also needed watertight seals. In the succinct words of a contemporary sub-mariner, 'too many damned holes', and a minor obstruction like a paint canister or a wire rope was sufficient to jam a vent open just as the submarine was ready to dive.

A chapter of accidents befell the seven-teen boats of the 'K' Class, some of them the sort of mishaps that submarines are prone to suffer, but because of their role with the Fleet they were unduly exposed to the risk of collision. The worst event was the 'Battle of May Island' on the night of 31 January 1918, when two flotillas of 'K'

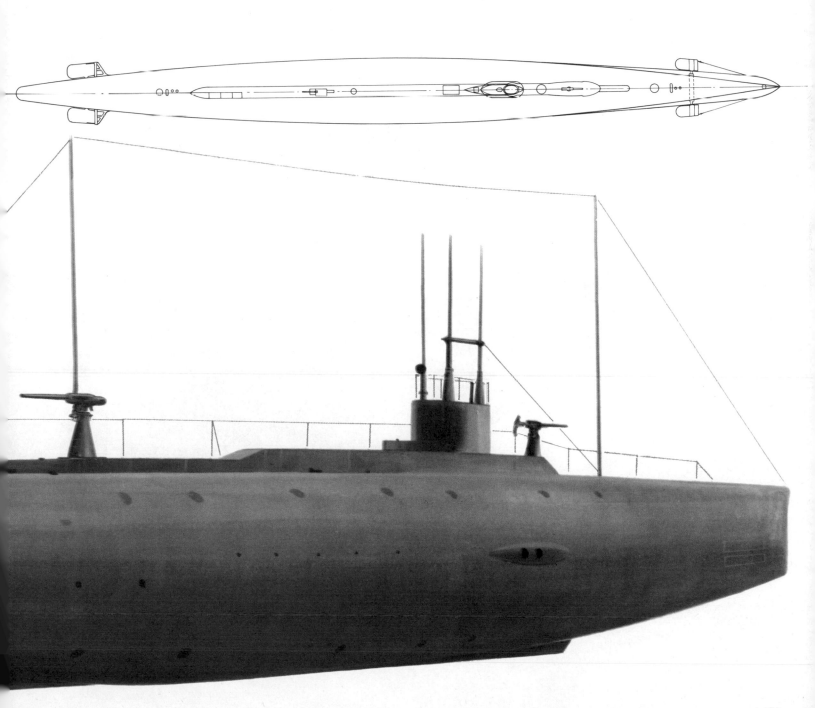

H21 returning to Harwich with a broom tied to her periscope. This is an old naval joke dating back to the 17th century, when the Dutch Admiral Tromp tied a whip to his mast, claiming he would whip the British. When Admiral Blake got the better of him in their next encounter, he tied a broom to his mast, to show he had swept the Dutch from the sea

British *K11*

K11 was one of the 'K' Class, the notorious Fleet submarines powered by steam turbines. They reached the phenomenal speed of 24 knots on the surface, but suffered a number of tragic accidents. She is shown as completed, with a low bow, and low conning tower, but the class later had a 'swan bow' and a raised conning tower. They had a heavy torpedo armament of four bow torpedo-tubes, four beam tubes and two more tubes in a training mount in the superstructure

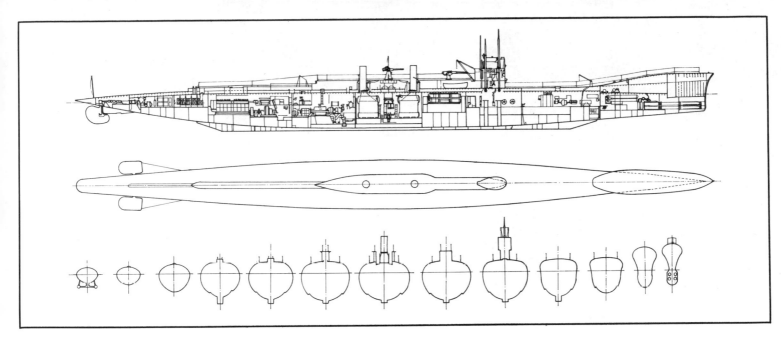

British *Swordfish* (top)
The *Swordfish* was the first British submarine to adopt steam propulsion, the only way to provide high surface speed. She was not a success, and was finally converted into a surface patrol vessel in 1917, but she paved the way for the 'K' Class

British 'K' Class
The 'K' Class had to be redesigned to eliminate various faults. The internal view above shows the arrangement of boilers and machinery, and shows how the bow was raised to accommodate a quick-blowing tank to help them surface faster. The funnels folded down into wells which were sealed with hatches

German *U151*

The *U151* Class were the first 'U-Cruisers', armed with two 15-cm (5.9-in) guns, but they were actually converted from mercantile submarines intended to carry cargoes to and from the United States. Being designed for cargo-carrying they were not very successful when armed, and carried a weak torpedo-armament for their size

boats operating with battle cruisers on a night exercise were involved in multiple collisions. *K4* was sunk by *K6*, and *K17* was sunk by a cruiser. To confirm the growing suspicion of a hoodoo on the class, an inquiry revealed that the disaster was caused by a jammed helm in *K22*, which was actually *K13* renamed after she had drowned most of her crew on her maiden voyage. With their long hulls they proved very difficult to handle, for at 338 ft overall and displacing 2,650 tons when submerged, they were larger than any contemporary submarine including the German 'U-Cruisers'.

Profiting by their capture of a UC-Boat, the British rapidly made provisions for submarine minelaying, and altered six 'E' Class during construction, but instead of putting the chutes inside the pressure hull as in the German boats, they put them in the side ballast tanks, ten chutes in all, with two mines in each. To compensate for the extra weight the two 18-in beam torpedo-tubes were omitted.

The next British development was also inspired by German ideas, for the news of U-Cruisers with 5.9-in guns prompted the Admiralty to order four submarines armed with a single 12-in gun each. These were the famous 'M' Class, of which the fourth was cancelled and only *M1* saw war service; they mark the ultimate in gun-armed submarines. It is generally thought that

they were intended to emulate the exploits of submarines in the Sea of Marmora, but recent evidence of trials against simulated submarine targets suggests that they were intended for use against U-Boats, although the reasoning behind this remains obscure.

The other notable British development was the anti-submarine submarine, or to give it a more modern name, the hunter-killer type. Twelve of these craft, the 'R' Class, were ordered in December 1917, and they were nearly 30 years ahead of their time in having a streamlined fish-shaped hull, single-shaft machinery and enlarged battery-capacity to give a higher speed underwater than on the surface. Not only were the 'R' Class ahead of their time, they actually worked quite well, and reached 14 knots submerged, which remained a record until the closing stages of World War II. Had they been equipped with a better detection device than the hydrophone they could have hastened the development of the modern submarine, but even so an 'R' boat is credited with torpedoing a U-Boat in October 1918 — and if the torpedo had not failed to explode, the class might have earned more respect; instead they were seen as freaks.

German developments

Returning to the Germans, production of the 'Mittel-U', 'UB' and 'UC' types continued throughout the war, but there were a number of other interesting designs as well. In January 1915 orders were placed for ten 'UE' Class ocean-going minelayers, *U71* to *80*, and they differed in many ways from the UC type. Apart from being bigger, they were fitted with horizontal

mine-tubes aft, in place of vertical wells; the mines were stowed in a large mine-room and then passed into the open ends of the tubes at the beginning of the lay. To provide the fuel capacity for an endurance of 7,800 miles at 7 knots in a hull which was no longer than the 'Mittel-U', the hull was given more diameter (16.4 ft) to accommodate the main ballast tanks internally; the saddle tanks could then be used to stow extra fuel. The disposition of the ballast tanks was ingenious, since one large one extended under the mine room and up the sides of the motor room and a smaller one was under the engine room and on either side of it. There were no internal torpedo-tubes, just two in the superstructure.

A further ten, *U117–126*, were ordered in May 1916, but they differed in many ways. By increasing the size considerably the designers were able to increase range, mine capacity and armament, and thus made very formidable craft out of these 'UE II' boats. Not only was the mine-room extended to enable 42 mines to be stowed, but 24 torpedoes could be carried, 12 externally in watertight cylinders and 12 internally, to be fired from four bow tubes. In addition, the gun armament was heavy, comprising a 5.9-in or two 4.1-in guns, and one can see in the 'UE II' Class the forerunner of successful Second World War designs like the Type IXA.

A development which attracted much more interest and caused great alarm at the time was the 'UK' or 'U-Cruiser' type of large boat with 5.9-in guns. This was a result of experience in 1915/16 very similar to that of British submarines, when it was shown that gunfire would sink a small target more effectively than a torpedo. The first class was the *U135–138* group ordered in May 1916, and they were followed three months later by *U139–141*; orders for an even larger type, *U142–150*, were never completed.

The importance of the gun-calibre was grossly over-estimated in the minds of both the British and the Germans. In practice a U-Cruiser could do nothing that a smaller U-Boat could not do with a gun of 88-mm or 105-mm calibre, and the time taken to build these large and clumsy submarines would have been better spent

German U155

U155 was the former mercantile submarine *Deutschland*, and she carried the heavy armament of two 15-cm and two 8.8-cm guns. To compensate for her weak torpedo armament of only two bow tubes she was later fitted with four external tubes, shown by dotted lines. In 1916 she made two famous trips to the United States, but was converted after America's entry into the war. The photographs below show *top*: U155 at sea; *centre* and *bottom*: postcards printed after the war of, respectively, the torpedo room, and the control room, looking forward

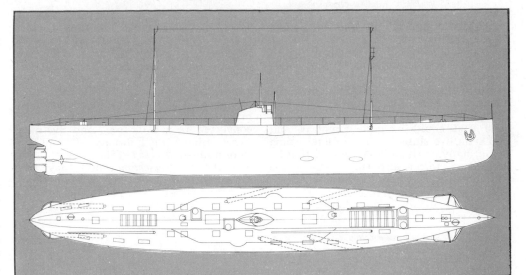

in building more of the standard types. On the British side there was wild talk of re-arming merchant ships with 6-in or 7.5-in guns, with no thought of the limitations of a submarine in a straight artillery duel. It is one thing for a submarine to shell a target from close range and quite another for her to face a ship armed with a 4.7-in or 6-in gun, for the submarine is so low in the water and so devoid of any fire-control equipment that her shooting is bound to be poor. U-Boats very rarely got the better of duels with decoy-vessels (Q-ships), and were either sunk outright or escaped with damage.

The effect of the British blockade was almost complete from the beginning of the war, for those German merchant ships which were not captured or sunk by Allied warships very quickly made for neutral ports and were interned. In 1915 it was decided to build two mercantile submarines which could run the blockade with ease, not so much for the cargoes they could carry but for the tremendous effect it would have on American opinion. Not only would the British be shown to have no defence against the U-Boat, but the Americans would be given a gentle warning about the dangers they would face if they chose to side with the enemies of Germany.

Intimidation fails

At one time it was hoped that the Kaiser would sanction a declaration of unrestricted submarine warfare to coincide with the arrival of the first submarines in American waters. It was thought that this double blow to the hopes of the pro-Allied politicians in the United States would paralyse any effective moves to put pressure on Germany, but one can doubt today whether this would have happened, any more than it did at the time of Pearl Harbour, 25 years later. In the event the Germans overplayed their hand.

The first cargo-carrier, *Deutschland*, left Kiel on 23 June 1916 under Captain König, carrying dyes, mail and precious stones; she made a landfall at Baltimore, Maryland on 9 July and, as she was clearly not armed, the US authorities had to treat her as a merchantman. After loading copper, nickel, silver and zinc, and having created world-wide interest, she sailed for Bremen on 2 August. Her sister *Bremen* was ordered to make a similar voyage to Norfolk, Virginia but this time *U53* was ordered to 'blow a path' through the waiting warships and to make an unannounced visit to Newport, Rhode Island. Although the *Bremen* disappeared without trace somewhere off the Orkneys (she was probably mined), the *U53* under Hans Rose reached Newport on 7 October.

The appearance of a belligerent warship caught the US Navy completely off balance; after an amusing conversation

with an American admiral who was frantically spinning out the talk while waiting for instructions from Washington, Rose took his submarine out of US territorial waters as quietly as he had come. Then, in accordance with his orders, he began to sink shipping within sight of the Nantucket lightship. Despite American annoyance at this effrontery there was little that could be done about it, and *U53* sank five ships in all before returning to Germany, with Rose convinced that he had struck terror into the hearts of the United States Navy and Government.

But fear does not always breed subservience, and the Americans became more worried than ever about Germany's long-term intentions. The mission was already pointless as the *Bremen* had failed to arrive, and the Kaiser could not bring himself to sanction an all-out U-Boat offensive. The surviving mercantile submarine *Deutschland* was ordered to be converted to a U-Cruiser, and five more were ordered in February 1917. These were numbered *U151–157*, of which *U155* was the ex-*Deutschland*, and they were armed with two 5.9-in guns and two 88-mm

guns staggered forward and aft of the conning tower. The large cargo hold abaft the conning tower was converted to a magazine for shells and charges, and the refrigerating plant provided for cooling the hold was removed. One unusual feature was the fact that the surface power was exactly the same as the submerged power.

The only other development of interest was the 'UF' type, a small submarine intended for operations off the Flanders coast. Between December 1917 and July 1918, 92 were ordered but none was completed before the Armistice. They approxi-

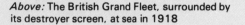

Above: The British Grand Fleet, surrounded by its destroyer screen, at sea in 1918

British *R12*

The British 'R' Class are outstanding as the first attempt to produce an anti-submarine submarine, or 'hunter-killer' as they are known today. They were also a quarter of a century before their time in having a streamlined hull designed for higher speed under water than on the surface. The bulbous bow contained listening gear, and the armament of six 18-in torpedoes was designed for maximum effect against submarines. Speed: 9 knots (surfaced) 14 knots (submerged)

'UK' (U-cruiser) type specifications			
	U135	U139	U142
Length (ft)	275.5	302.5	320
Beam (ft)	25	29.5	31.5
Draught	14.5	15.1	17.5
Displacement (tons) surface/submerged	1190/1560	1950/2500	2160/2760
Machinery (hp) surface/submerged	3500/1940	3500/1760	6000/2600
Fuel (tons)	66	102	
Torpedo tubes (19.7 in)	4 Bow; 2 Stern	4 Bow; 2 Stern	4 Bow; 2 Stern
Guns	1 × 5.9-in	2 × 5.9-in	2 × 5.9-in
Crew	46	62	83

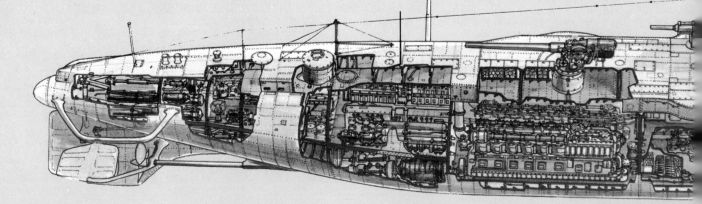

mated to the *UB18* class in size, but had more power and higher speed. Only two other types call for comment, the *UA* which was originally ordered as the Norwegian *A5*, and the cancelled 'UD' Class, which were 4,000-ton underwater cruisers incorporating the same armament as the *U151* class. When the Armistice came in November 1918 the Imperial German Navy had ordered 811 submarines of all types, 768 of them after the outbreak of war. Out of this vast number over 400 were either cancelled or incomplete, and 178 were lost.

This means that over 47 per cent of the German Navy's U-Boat arm was lost, with 515 officers and 4,849 other ranks, or roughly 40 per cent of the total personnel. Against this fearful casualty rate they could boast over 11 million tons of shipping sunk and a further 7.5 million tons damaged. Great Britain alone lost over 2,000 merchant ships and 14,000 merchant seamen from the activities of submarines, and nearly lost the war through starvation.

During the appalling month of April 1917, when merchant ship losses rose to 881,000 tons, and one ship in four destined for the British Isles was sunk, the food reserves were calculated at only six weeks. Had these losses not been checked, the submarine would have won by itself a war in which enormous armies were still trying to achieve a victory after three years. Had the British Isles been starved out the sequence of events would have been inexorable: a negotiated peace between Great Britain and Germany followed by the collapse of France. Not even the resources of the United States could have reversed the verdict, for her troops and supplies would never have reached Europe.

Robert Hunt Library

British *L52*
The British *L52* represents the final evolution of the standard submarine in the Royal Navy. Basically an improved 'E' Class, they had a heavy torpedo- and gun-armament, and were highly successful in service. Three survived until the Second World War. They were armed with six 21-in torpedo-tubes and two 4-in guns

German U-boat losses				
	'U' Type	*'UB' Type*	*'UC' Type*	*Total*
1914	5	–	–	5
1915	14	2	3	19
1916	7	8	7	22
1917	19	12	32	63
1918	17	42	10	69
Total	62	64	52	178

German *U139*
The *U139* Class of 1917 were a more balanced design of U-Cruiser, with a heavy torpedo-armament to balance their gun-armament. They had a strong influence on post-war design, particularly in Japan and the United States

THE SURFACE SHIPS FIGHT BACK
WEAPONS AND TACTICS

In the spring of 1917, the German U-boat offensive came close to crippling Britain by cutting off her supplies. But the development of anti-submarine weapons, such as the depth-charge shown exploding here, and of defensive tactics, notably the convoy system, soon turned the tide of war against the submarine. It became the hunted rather than the hunter

Imperial War Museum

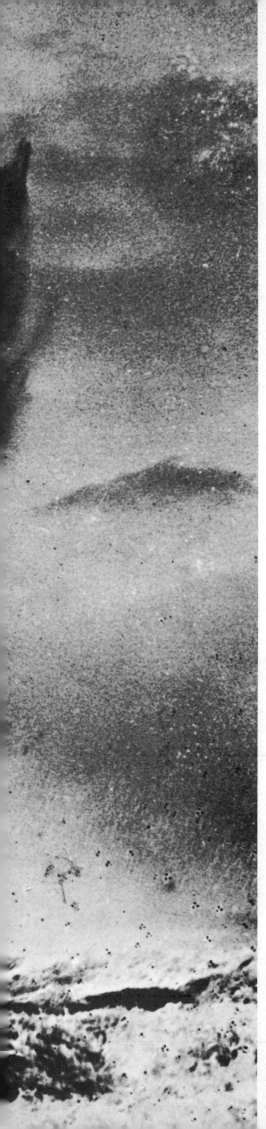

As we have already seen, the only weapons against the submarine in 1914 were the ram and the gun. However, both these methods depended on the submarine surfacing or giving away her position, and so opportunities for using them were limited. In all only 14 U-Boats were sunk by ramming, and it tended to damage the attacking ship. In 1918 the old destroyer *Fairy* sank after damage sustained from ramming *UC75*, but at the other end of the scale *U29* was sunk by the battleship HMS *Dreadnought* like a cobra crushed by an elephant.

However, there were two passive methods of defence, minefields and nets, and these were quickly put into effect by both sides. First came indicator nets and then mine nets, which had small charges attached to the netting to explode on contact. Although the British took some time to develop a properly effective mine, when they finally introduced the H2 pattern in 1916 it rapidly became the most effective weapon against U-Boats and sank 25 per cent of the total.

Underwater weapons

The depth-charge was introduced in 1916 to solve the problem of attacking a submerged submarine; it was basically a 300-lb bomb fitted with a hydrostatic device to detonate it at a pre-set depth. Then came the battle to devise a sensor to detect the submarine before it attacked, and out of this were developed various types of hydrophone. This was simply an underwater listening device which was made directional to trace the noise made by a submarine's electric motors. In July 1916 the motor boat *Salmon* brought off the first successful attack using both depth-charges and hydrophones, when she sank *UC7*. Late in 1918 scientists began to test more advanced methods of sonic location, and from the initials of the Anti-Submarine Devices Investigation Committee came the name Asdic, but that story belongs to the post-war period.

The simplest defence for a ship was to follow a zigzag course, for the U-Boat's commander had to estimate the target's course and speed by eye. Any error in estimation of the speed or inclination of the target could result in the torpedo missing, and so ships were also given false bow-waves to give a wrong impression of high speed. This in turn led to 'dazzle-painting', a form of camouflage which utilised extreme colour variations and linear patterns to obscure features such as the waterline, deckline or bridge structures which helped the U-Boat commander to estimate course and angle of inclination. Submarines also used camouflage to make themselves hard to pick out at a distance, and were even reported to have hoisted sails on occasions to imitate fishing vessels.

Although the depth-charge eventually proved to be the best weapon against a submerged U-Boat there were a number of intermediate steps. The first was the explosive sweep, which was developed from minesweeping gear and comprised a charge towed from a destroyer's stern, and kept below the surface by a special float. If the sweep fouled a submerged object this registered on an indicator, and the sweep could then be fired electrically. Another device was the explosive para-vane, two of which could be towed at high speed by a destroyer, in the hope that a submarine would draw the infernal machine on to herself. But both these gadgets proved very unpopular with ships' captains, who did not relish the idea of towing explosive charges with a penchant for wrapping themselves around propeller shafts.

The depth-charge thrower was only the culminating development in a series of projectors which could hurl an explosive charge some distance from the ship to the area in which the submarine had last been seen. There was the 7.5-in howitzer, which was simply a breech-loading recoilless weapon firing a spherical bomb; it was trained by means of a shoulder-piece, and as it weighed only 35 cwt it could be mounted in small ships like trawlers. The 10-in bomb-thrower was muzzle-loading, and could fire either a normal shell or a spherical stick-bomb weighing 200 lb; its main weakness was the tendency of the stick to rust to the barrel.

An even more fearsome weapon was the 11-in breech-loading howitzer, which fired a 350-lb shell some 3,000 yards; it could only be carried by cruisers, and as it fired a conventional shell it was mainly for use against diving or surfaced submarines.

By far the most spectacular weapon against submarines was the decoy vessel or 'Q-Ship', simply a merchant ship with concealed armament and designed to lure a U-Boat within gun-range and then open fire. The first Q-Ship victims were quite easily trapped, but inevitably some U-Boats escaped and reported the news, and so a deadly game of bluff developed. The impression given had to be one of an innocent steamer whose crew had taken to the boats, and so a 'panic party' had to leave the ship in the lifeboats, leaving the gun-crews still concealed behind cover. If the U-Boat commander was mildly suspicious he might then indulge in some leisurely gunnery practice, and in some cases three 'panic parties' left before the lethal game could be resolved.

As the U-Boat always had the option of simply torpedoing the Q-Ship some of them were filled with timber to increase their chances of staying afloat, in the hope that the U-Boat would then surface to finish her off with her deck-gun. In 1917 a specially constructed Q-Ship was completed, HMS *Hyderabad*; she had one 4-in gun, two 12-pounders, four bomb-throwers, and torpedo-tubes and depth-charges, all on a draft of only 6 ft 9 in so that torpedoes would pass under her. Many of the 'Flower' Class escort sloops were either modified or completed as 'Flower-Qs', resembling small coasters, and twenty of the so-called P-Boats were similarly converted to PC-Boats. The essential difference between these ships and the Q-Ships was that they functioned as normal warships, whereas the decoys were clandestine by nature and adopted false names so as to mislead spies.

The trawler trap

A variation of the decoy trick was tried in 1915, when U-Boats began to attack the British trawler-fleet off the north-east coast of Scotland. In each group of trawlers was one naval trawler (commissioned but unarmed), which was towing an old 'C' Class submarine, to which she was also connected by telephone. The

theory was that the trawler would give the essential data to the submarine via the telephone link, and the submarine would then slip the tow and work herself into a position for attacking the U-Boat. The first time it was tried, in June 1915, the cable refused to slip, but despite the fact that the submarine *C24* had 100 fathoms of tow rope and telephone cable dangling from her bows she managed to torpedo *U40*. Nearly a month later *C27* had another chance; this time the telephone link failed, but the submarine commander was able to work out what was happening on the surface and finally succeeded in torpedoing *U23*.

However, the problem still remained of how to find submarines, and in April 1917 the shipping losses showed clearly that all counter-measures had failed. The fundamental problem was — and still is — that the ocean was far too big for the escorts to cover. The answer was Convoy, or sailing merchant ships in groups defended by warships, the classic counter to harassment of seaborne commerce since the 14th century. But for a variety of reasons,

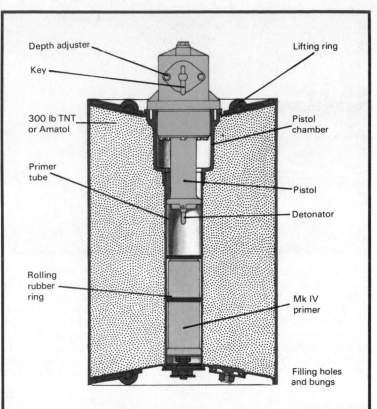

British Depth-charge

The 'D' Type depth-charge Mk III. This simple weapon proved to be the most successful method of sinking U-Boats, but it was not ready until 1916, and only available in quantity in 1917. The hydrostatic device was set to the estimated depth of the U-Boat by hand, and the depth-charge was then rolled off the stern of the escort. Known to the Germans as the 'Wasserbom' or 'Wabo' for short, it could destroy a U-Boat up to 25 ft away, and inflict damage as much as 50 ft away

Labels on diagram: Depth adjuster; Key; 300 lb TNT or Amatol; Primer tube; Rolling rubber ring; Lifting ring; Pistol chamber; Pistol; Detonator; Mk IV primer; Filling holes and bungs

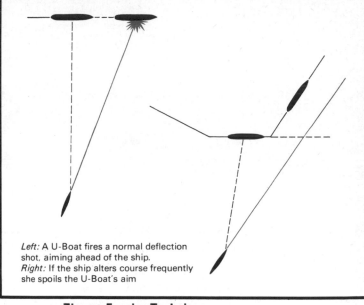

Left: A U-Boat fires a normal deflection shot, aiming ahead of the ship.
Right: If the ship alters course frequently she spoils the U-Boat's aim

Zig-zag Evasion Technique

Zig-zagging was an important defence for ships against U-Boats. One of the biggest problems was the co-ordination of zig-zagging in a convoy formation; to avoid collisions, it was done to a pre-arranged system

Explosive Sweep

The Explosive Sweep was an early device for towing behind destroyers. It was fitted with an electric indicator which registered an obstruction, and the explosive charge could then be fired from the destroyer

Dazzle-painted Anti-submarine escorts

These innocent-looking coasters were in fact commissioned warships. The sloops *Gardenia*, shown here in her official dazzle-painted scheme, and *Polyanthus* (opposite, top) were converted during construction from conventional escorts, while *PC69* (opposite, centre) was a converted P-Boat or patrol vessel. They were armed with a variety of 4-in and 3-in guns, depth-charges and bomb-throwers, and differed from the 'Q-Ship' decoys in that they were warships pure and simple. The armament was concealed behind shutters under the deck-houses amidships and at the stern

20th century naval tacticians could not accept that a method which had proved itself during the Napoleonic Wars could have any validity in the age of steam and armour. As late as January 1917 the Naval Staff stated that convoy could not be recommended as a defence against submarines, despite the fact that the Grand Fleet's immunity to submarine attack had

been, in essence, due to a form of convoying ever since the outbreak of war.

There was no 'inventor' of convoy in 1917, but much of the credit must go to influential advisers like the Secretary to the Cabinet, Hankey, who pressed it on Lloyd George, the British Prime Minister. The first change was in February 1917, when at French insistence the cross-

Channel collier traffic was convoyed; in April 1917 at the worst moment of the U-Boat war the collier losses were 0.19 per cent. With grave misgivings the first ocean convoy sailed at the end of April, and within one month the loss rate dropped from 25 to 0.24 per cent.

The system worked for the simple reason that convoys concentrated the

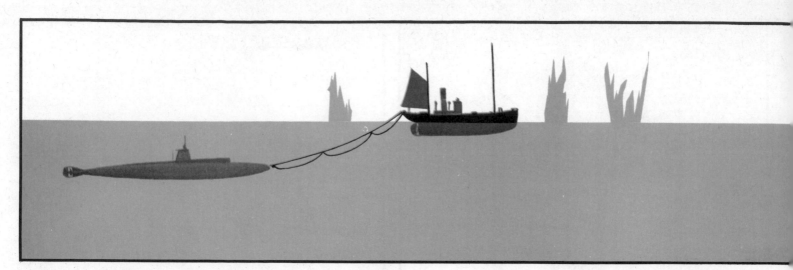

targets and so forced the U-Boats to come to the convoys, where they could be attacked. The memoirs of U-Boat commanders bear this out, for they had hitherto lain in wait at strategic points where merchantmen were bound to pass, whereas after the introduction of convoys the seas were suddenly emptied of shipping. And when shipping did appear it was surrounded by destroyers, sloops and patrol vessels of all sizes.

Once the appalling slaughter of merchant ships was halted, the U-Boats were put on the defensive. A new minelaying offensive was mounted against the U-Boat bases in the Heligoland Bight and on the Flanders coast. With the aid of crypt-analysis British minelayers laid both conventional and magnetic mines in the U-Boats' exit routes, and losses began to rise. Although the enormous Anglo-American Northern Barrage between Norway and the Orkneys was of little use in sinking submarines, the Dover Barrage was finally made submarine-proof in 1918. In the Mediterranean the Allies tried to seal German and Austrian sub-

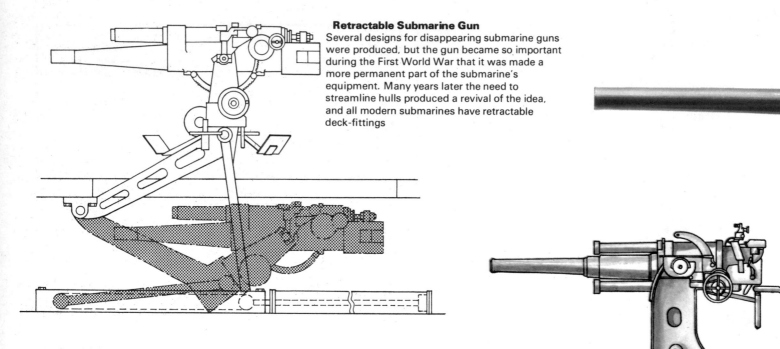

Retractable Submarine Gun
Several designs for disappearing submarine guns were produced, but the gun became so important during the First World War that it was made a more permanent part of the submarine's equipment. Many years later the need to streamline hulls produced a revival of the idea, and all modern submarines have retractable deck-fittings

German 8.8-cm Submarine Gun
The German 8.8-cm/L 30 on its disappearing mounting was a feature of the *U19* Class, but as more reliance came to be placed on gunfire the housing mechanism proved too cumbersome, and in later U-Boats it gave way to a permanent deck gun. The gun-crew had to get on deck as quickly as possible, and ammunition was passed up the hatch

Fielding Submarine Gun
A Mr Fielding patented this idea for a bow-mounted gun in a submarine

marines in the Adriatic with the Otranto Barrage, but with less success due to the depth of water.

In the final analysis it was the convoys that forced the U-Boats to take greater risks, both in entering mined waters and in broadcasting the endless stream of messages that gave the Allies the intelligence that they needed. Convoyed ships totalled 84,000, of which the U-Boats sank only 257, or 0.4 per cent; during the same period 2,616 ships were lost while sailing independently.

The other weapon to be developed during World War I as a potent anti-submarine measure was the aircraft. Technically the first submarine to be sunk by air attack was the British *B10*, in dock at Venice in August 1916, but the first true attack on a submarine at sea was made by two Austrian seaplanes against the French *Foucault* off Cattaro on 15 September 1916. The submarine was taken by surprise and was forced to the surface after being damaged. The British introduced 'Blimps', or non-rigid airships, for anti-submarine patrols, and they

'Trawler-submarine trap' (above left)
Early in 1915 two U-Boats were sunk by this method. The trawler towed a 'C' Class submarine instead of a trawl, and when a U-Boat attacked with her deck-gun, the trawler informed the towed submarine via a telephone cable attached to the tow. With information about the bearing of the U-Boat the 'C' Class submarine would then slip the tow and work herself into a position to torpedo the U-Boat

Explosive Paravanes (above)
A variant of the explosive sweep was a pair of explosive paravanes towed behind a destroyer at high speed. If either paravane fouled a U-Boat it exploded on contact, or they could be detonated from the destroyer. Neither device was popular with destroyer commanders, who never fancied the idea of steaming at high speed with a few hundred pounds of TNT trailing astern

6-Pounder Hotchkiss Gun
The 6-pounder Hotchkiss was fitted to many British submarines in 1915 as an emergency measure after the success of the campaign in the Sea of Marmora. This model had a range of 4,500 yards at $9\frac{1}{2}°$ elevation, and its 2.268-in shell travelled at 1,818 feet per second. Later, guns of this type were handed over to the Army for use in the first tanks

German 15-cm Submarine Gun
The German 15-cm/L 45 was mounted in the U-Cruisers of the *U151* and *U139* Classes

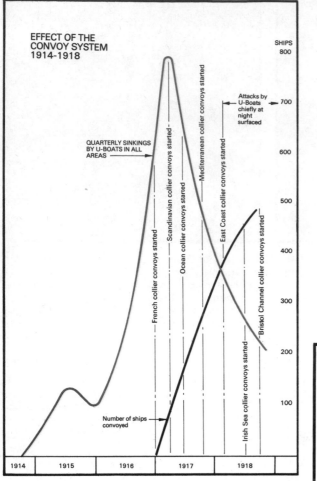

EFFECT OF THE
CONVOY SYSTEM
1914-1918

SHIPS
800

700

600

500

400

300

200

100

QUARTERLY SINKINGS
BY U-BOATS IN ALL
AREAS

Attacks by
U-Boats
chiefly at
night
surfaced

French collier convoys started

Scandinavian collier convoys started

Ocean collier convoys started

Mediterranean collier convoys started

East Coast collier convoys started

Irish Sea collier convoys started

Bristol Channel collier convoys started

Number of ships
convoyed

1914 | 1915 | 1916 | 1917 | 1918

These graphs illustrate the effects of the convoy system on the U-boats' anti-trade war. The number of merchant ships sunk by submarines fell dramatically *(above)* in direct relation to the number of ships convoyed, and in spite of the number of U-boats at sea *(below)*

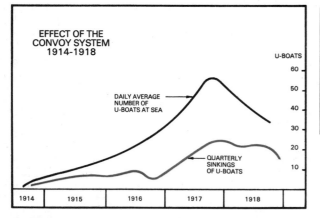

EFFECT OF THE
CONVOY SYSTEM
1914-1918

U-BOATS
60
50
40
30
20
10

DAILY AVERAGE
NUMBER OF
U-BOATS AT SEA

QUARTERLY
SINKINGS
OF U-BOATS

1914 | 1915 | 1916 | 1917 | 1918

7.5-in Bomb Thrower

This was only one of a series of interim weapons produced before the depth-charge thrower was introduced. It propelled its 100-lb stick-bomb to a range of 2,100 yards at its maximum elevation of 45°, but its usefulness was limited because the bomb had no hydrostatic fuse to allow it to explode at a fixed depth. It was meant primarily for disabling a submarine on the surface or just after she had submerged

Loading Torpedoes

Striking down a torpedo in a U-Boat. This remains essentially the same today in all submarines because of their narrow beam. The torpedo is lowered by a boom or derrick rigged temporarily on deck, through a loading hatch onto guide-rails, and then down into the torpedo room

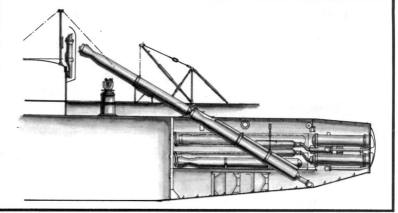

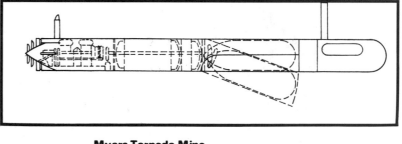

Myers Torpedo Mine

Among several ideas patented during the First World War was the 'torpedo mine' designed by a Mr Myers. It was a torpedo which dropped a mine at the end of its run

proved particularly valuable when convoys were introduced. The Davis Gun was specially introduced to provide a recoilless weapon for aircraft and airships to use against submarines, and of course bombs and machine-guns were available. It has been claimed that in all only two ships were sunk in convoys that were accompanied by aircraft.

What defence had the U-Boat against all these counter-measures? She faced armed merchant ships, Q-Ships and ordinary warships, as well as a growing horde of armed yachts and similar auxiliary patrol craft. The early war days showed that a sharp-eyed lookout was essential to give warning of the approach of a warship, but as long as the submarine was still functioning she could dive in time. Nets were countered by fitting net-

cutters on the bows, either a saw-backed frame as in U-Boats or a hardened edge to the bow as favoured in British submarines.

Periscope design also improved, from the early crude single instrument to the provision of separate search and attack periscopes. The search periscope had a wide-angle lens to allow the maximum field of vision, whereas the attack type had a narrow field; by the end of the war special air-search periscopes had been produced, with a high-angle head to allow a search for aircraft. Aircraft could also be met with gunfire, but the state of anti-aircraft gunnery was in an even cruder state than aerial bombing, and the outcome of aircraft/submarine duels was largely a matter of luck at this stage.

The biggest problem was the lack of

endurance while running submerged, and there was a steady growth in battery capacity as wartime construction progressed. Although the provision of deck-guns became standard as a means of conserving torpedoes, the Germans were forced to rely on the torpedo after the introduction of convoy in 1917, for there was little reward in engaging a large number of merchant ships and escorts on the surface.

As submarines had increased in size it became possible to provide extra torpedoes as reloads, and this reached its peak in the UEII Class, with an extra 12 torpedoes stowed outside the pressure hull. As early as 1915 the British *E14* went on patrol in the Sea of Marmora with spare torpedoes lashed on the casing, but this was an extreme measure that was not

German Air/Sea Search Periscope
The growing danger from aircraft is reflected in this German Goerz air/sea search periscope, which could tilt from the horizontal to 80° elevation. The growing complexity of submarine operations led to the provision of separate periscopes, a wide-angle one for search purposes, and a narrow-angle one for attack

Depth-charge Thrower (below right)
The English firm of Thornycroft designed a small mortar for throwing depth-charges about 75 yards clear of the ship. With one on each side of the stern and a rack for dropping depth-charges, it was then possible to drop a 'pattern' with more chance of destroying the U-Boat

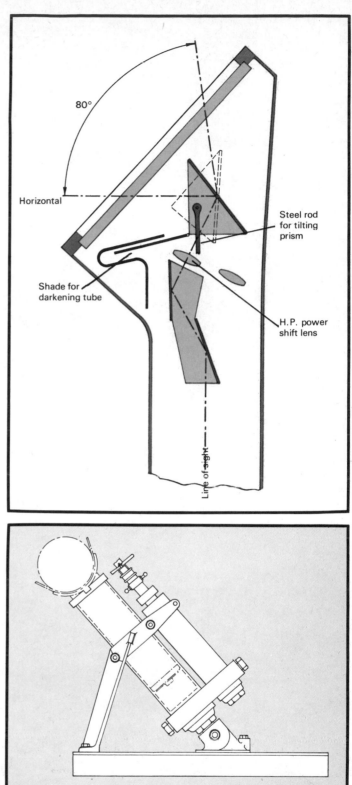

80°

Horizontal

Steel rod for tilting prism

Shade for darkening tube

H.P. power shift lens

Line of sight

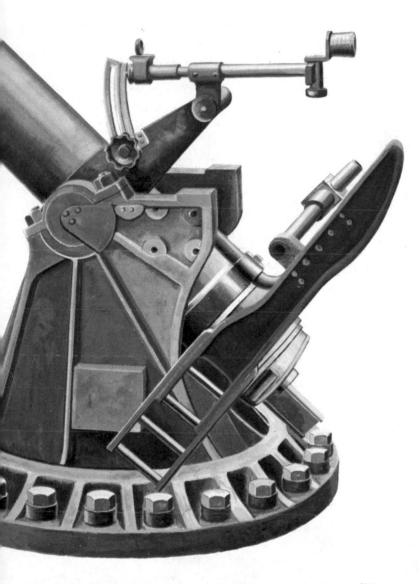

encouraged. On one occasion a British submarine commander swam out to an unexploded torpedo to screw down the safety device before reloading it into the tube.

The war showed that submarines could function in worse conditions than had ever been dreamed of in peacetime. Conning towers were modified to allow greater protection to personnel, but the submarines proved to be more robust than many surface ships. Spray interference and lack of visibility were the limiting factors because of a submarine's low silhouette, but as submariners knew, really rough weather could be dodged simply by submerging, as the effect of waves does not go very deep.

The worst problems of habitability were the cramped quarters and the ever-present condensation. One of the most grisly

reports on conditions was sent in from a British submarine in the Sea of Marmora, when the crew were stricken by dysentery, but that could be matched by stories of U-Boats operating in the North Atlantic in winter. Many of the problems could only be solved by increasing the size of submarines, and there was a clear link between the size of a boat and her efficiency on a long patrol. This was one of the main post-war improvements.

The submarine came of age during the First World War in more ways than one. First came the realisation at top level that she was a dangerous threat to all surface ships, and then as the war went on came the perfection of the weapon itself. This particularly involved the personnel, as submariners learned how to use their boats to the best of their ability, but it

was matched by increased reliability of the equipment. Machinery improved dramatically, and so did torpedoes, and by 1918 the submarine had gone through a revolution of design as rapid as the one undergone by the military aircraft in the same period.

When we look at those quaint examples and wonder how men could dare to put to sea in them we must remember that in 1918 a submariner might wonder how anyone had the courage to take a Holland or a Lake boat to sea. The answer must surely be that submariners have always had a special brand of nerve to enable them to master their strange element. That is the sad paradox of the submarine, that it called for the highest type of bravery and yet waged the most ruthless form of warfare.

Depth charges exploding after being dropped by a destroyer
over the spot indicated by its submarine detection apparatus

Admiralty Photograph

The engine room of a British submarine with the engines cut and the crew at action stations waiting for the signal to dive

SUBMARINES SINCE 1919
Antony Preston

In both the First and Second World Wars, the submarine came close to winning a decisive victory. Twice, it almost succeeded in cutting off Britain's supply routes and completely crippling the Allied war effort in Europe. Today, however, those achievements pale in comparison with the almost limitless power of the ICBM-armed nuclear submarine.

In this chapter we take up the story of the submarine at the end of the First World War, when it had uncontestably claimed a major place in the arsenal of any military-minded nation. We trace its development in the inter-war period, its vital role in all the major theatres of the Second World War and then follow the story up to the present day.

CONTENTS

A Russian nuclear submarine running on the surface

BETWEEN THE WARS

A WHOLESOME RESPECT

The experience of the First World War had left no doubt of the military value of the submarine. As victors and vanquished alike gradually began the inevitable re-armament, they could not afford to ignore the new weapon — and, for the Allies at least, the surrendered German U-Boats provided a good starting-point

When the exhausted world powers turned to negotiation in 1918, as an alternative to the four years of destruction which had been endured, it was with a wholesome respect for the submarine. Whether the war would have ended sooner without the submarine is arguable, but there can be no doubt that it would not have been so ruinously expensive. The British Empire, having started the war as the world's largest ship-owner and operator, lost over 9 million tons, as against 4 million tons lost by all other countries put together. This represented about 90 per cent of the steamships under British registration in 1914, and the loss of national wealth went far beyond the actual cost of the cargoes.

The submarine had proven its worth as a fighting weapon during the First World War, as the fearful slaughter of ships showed only too well. When the Armistice was signed on 11 November 1918 between Germany and the Allies, one of the key clauses stipulated that the U-Boats must be surrendered at a designated port. All boats fit for sea had to retain their armament, but those unfit for sea were to be disarmed and immobilised.

On the morning of 20 November a melancholy procession began, with batches of U-Boats going to the British east coast port of Harwich until the early months of 1919; others surrendered at Sevastopol or in neutral ports, and even more were put out of action in German ports. A total of 176 boats were surrendered, and immediately the victors seized the chance to study the sinister weapon which had cost them so much in blood and treasure. The U-Boats were parcelled out as follows:

Great Britain
105 boats, of which at least U126, U161 and one of the UC90 class wore the White Ensign for a time

France
46 boats of which 10 were incorporated into the French Navy and renamed:

U79/Victor Reveille	U162/Pierre Marrast
U105/Jean Autrice	U166/Jean Roulier
U108/Léon Mignot	UB98/Trinité Schillemans
U119/Réné Audry	UB99/Carissan
U139/Halbronn	UB155/Jean Corré

Japan
7 boats renamed:

U125 – O1	UC99 – O5
U46 – O2	UB125 – O6
U55 – O3	UB143 – O7
UC90 – O3	

Italy: 10 **USA:** 6 **Belgium:** 2 originally allocated to Great Britain

With the exception of the ten French boats listed, all these submarines were scrapped and disposed of by 1922/23 by agreement between the nations concerned (the French arrangement having been a special case) to compensate for wartime losses. But the lessons had been learned and would be incorporated in future construction.

Despite the fact that wartime experience had not justified the 'U-cruiser' type, with its large, clumsy hull and superfluous heavy guns, every navy plumped for cruiser-submarines. The two nations whose navies were expanding rapidly were Japan and the United States, and both took possession of the larger types of U-Boat as their share of surrendered tonnage. The United States took over U140, a 311-ft vessel armed with two 5·9-in guns, and incorporated many of her features into the so-called V-series, the *Barracuda* Class, and the *Narwhal* Class, both with high endurance and heavy torpedo-armament, and in the case of the two *Narwhals*, having two 6-in guns. The sixth in the V-series was the giant *Argonaut* which was also based on U140, but incorporated the minelaying system of the UEII type U117, which was also among the US Navy's booty.

The first Japanese cruiser-submarine was the *I52* laid down in 1922, and she was modelled on the *O1* (ex-*U125*), another

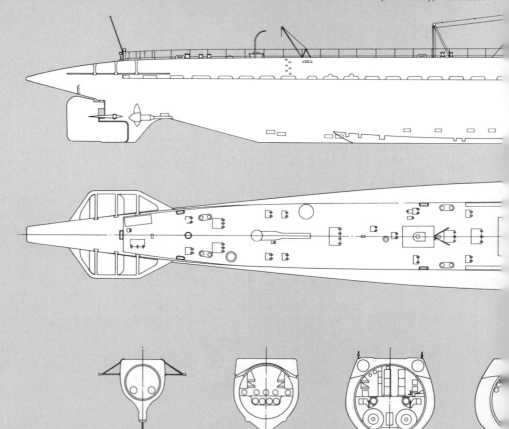

UEII type. A year later an even larger type, the 'Junsen Type 1' or Cruiser Submarine Type 1 was begun; the four vessels *I1–4* displaced 2,135 tons on the surface and 2,791 tons submerged, had an armament of two 5·5-in guns and carried 20 torpedoes. In 1926 *I1* showed her capabilities by cruising for 25,000 miles and diving to 260 ft, the deepest dive recorded by a Japanese submarine up to that date. No mines were carried, as the minelaying features of the UEII type were incorporated in a further class, the *I21–24*, which approximated more closely to the original design in size.

The British also rushed headlong into experiments with cruiser-submarines, and in 1923 they launched the giant *X1* under conditions of exaggerated secrecy. She was based on the uncompleted *U173* class of giant U-cruisers, and even used similar M.A.N. twin diesels for surface running. German diesel engines had enjoyed a high reputation for reliability, but in this case they proved to be the reason for many of *X1*'s problems; although extremely safe and capable of diving very deep, with a radius of 12,400 miles on the surface, she was plagued by mechanical troubles and

American *Nautilus*

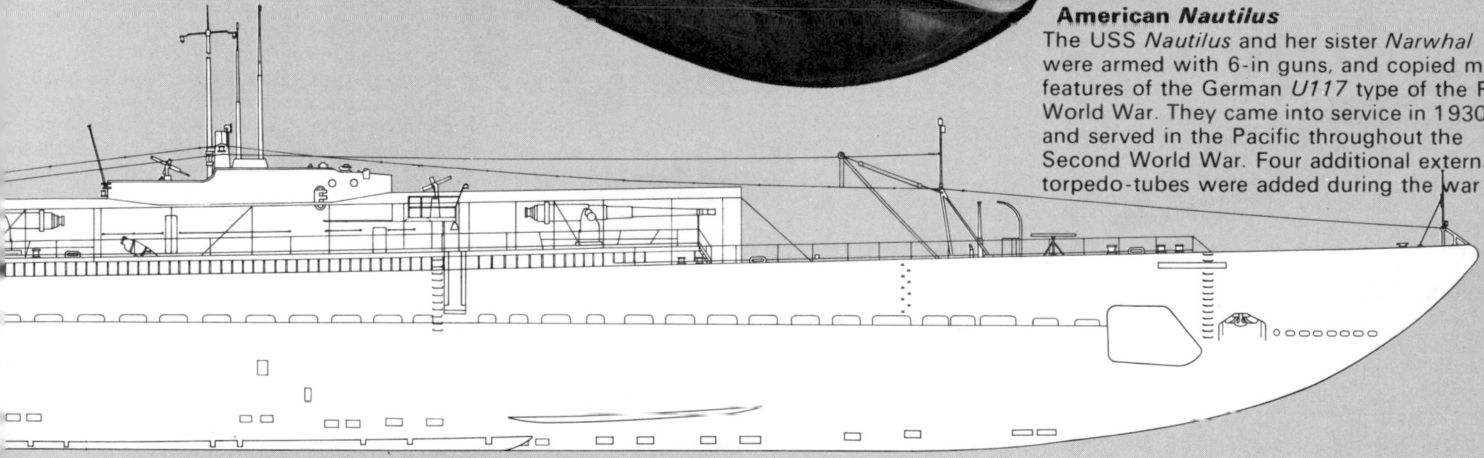

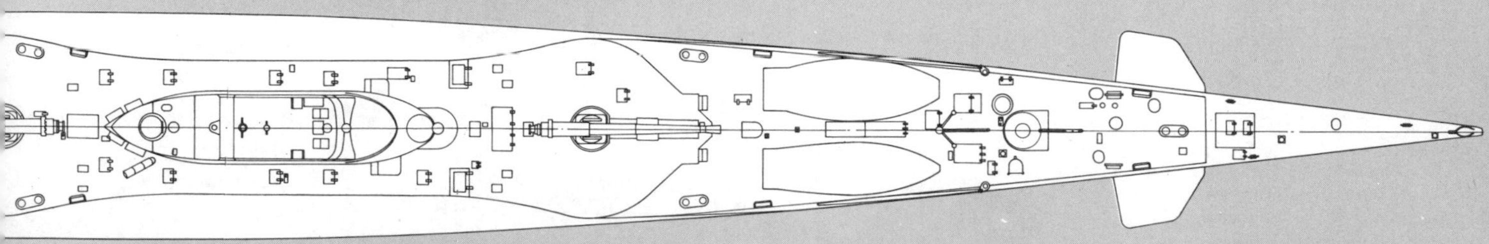

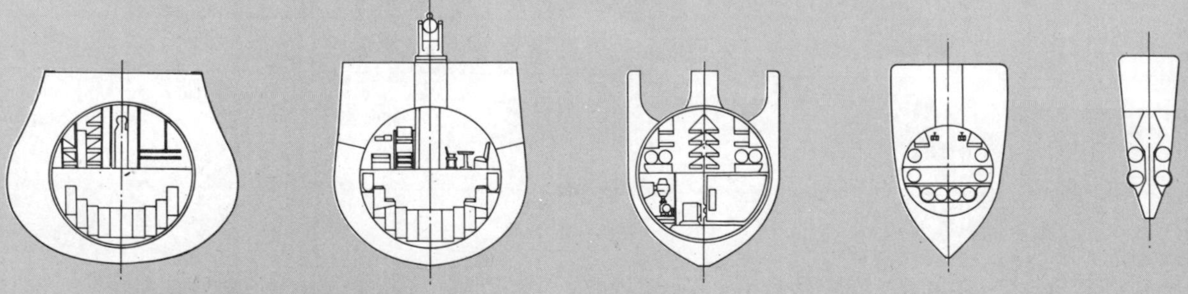

The USS *Nautilus* and her sister *Narwhal* were armed with 6-in guns, and copied many features of the German *U117* type of the First World War. They came into service in 1930/31 and served in the Pacific throughout the Second World War. Four additional external torpedo-tubes were added during the war

was finally scrapped after only five years' active service. Thereafter British interest in giant submarines lapsed, and only the French stayed in the game, with their *Surcouf*.

Nothing if not logical, the French took the terms of the Washington Treaty at face value, and as the Treaty stated that submarines might carry guns no bigger than 8 in, that was the calibre chosen. This unique submarine carried not only a seaplane but a twin 8-in turret and twelve torpedo tubes, with ten reloads. An interesting innovation was the provision of a quadruple mounting for firing small (15·7-in) torpedoes against merchant ships; although fast, these torpedoes had a range of only 1,500 yards.

Although the Italian Navy developed large submarines from their UEII type, *U120*, they avoided the extreme examples produced elsewhere. While the number of torpedo-tubes was increased, the gun-calibre was kept down to 3·9 in or 4·7 in, thus avoiding the chief pitfall of the big submarine.

British experience in the recent conflict had taught them one thing, the need for a heavy bow salvo of torpedoes to give greater accuracy at long ranges. This arose because, unlike U-Boats, British submarines had normally attacked well-defended warships. The knowledge that anti-submarine tactics had improved beyond all measure, and would continue to do so, led British submariners to accept the need to fire from a greater distance, and so from the *L52* class of 1917, British submarines had a standard armament of six 21-in bow torpedo tubes. By comparison, Japanese and American submarines still had only four bow tubes at the expense of two stern tubes, and German U-Boats had largely been armed with two bow and two stern tubes, although in the later boats an extra pair was fitted.

Aircraft from submarines

The other important development in the years after the Armistice was the operation of aircraft from submarines. War experience had shown the importance of reconnaissance to the submarine, especially for locating targets when operating in distant waters. In January 1915 *U12* had operated

German Arado 231 Seaplane
The single-seater Arado 231 was intended to be launched from U-Boats, although no U-Boat seems to have been designed to meet this requirement. Naturally the design was restricted by limitations on size, and the aircraft could only fly 310 miles at a maximum speed of 106 mph. The wing span of 33 ft 4½ in could be reduced to 6 ft 6½ in when folded (above), and the length was 25 ft 7½ in

Sopwith Baby
With its 25 ft 8 in wingspan and maximum speed of 100 mph, the Sopwith Baby was successfully flown off a British submarine in 1916. Performance and range were too limited to produce any positive results, however, as was the case with similar experiments with German U-Boats.

In 1916 the Norwegian Navy bought Farman floatplanes for trials, and when they broke down or ran out of fuel submarines were able to recover them by surfacing gently underneath. In this photograph a recovered seaplane is being lifted off the casing of submarine *A4*. Note the spare float lashed to the submarine's casing

Stored German Arado 231

a Friedrichshafen FF-29 off her foredeck, and in April 1916 the British *E22* flew off two Sopwith Baby seaplanes from a stern ramp. This latter experiment was an attempt to extend the range of seaplanes to shoot down Zeppelins rather than to extend the submarine's capability, but it did prove the feasibility of the idea. As early as October 1915 the Admiralty had considered the need for a watertight hangar, but this idea had to wait until after the war. The Germans built three small Hansa-Brandenburg W-20s in 1917, and the V-19 Putbus for operation from U-Boats, but these were never used at sea.

By 1919 the aircraft themselves had developed, and it was not long before experiments were put in hand. In 1923 the United States Navy submarine *S1* appeared with a tubular hangar abaft her conning tower. This housed a folding seaplane, which could be run out to the stern after assembly, but as no catapult was provided the seaplane had to taxi before takeoff. The experiment proved quite satisfactory, and a specially designed aircraft was built, the Martin Kitten, but the idea was killed off by lack of funds.

In 1925 the British decided to remove the

Martin Kitten
The Martin Kitten was the first aircraft specially designed for operating from submarines. 4 were ordered in 1922 but only one prototype survives. It is unusual in having wingtip ailerons and also in having wheels instead of floats. This meant that the aircraft had to do a crash-landing after completing its mission, but the cockpit is so cramped that the pilot would have extreme difficulty in baling out. In fact, pilots would probably have been chosen for their lack of stature and expendability if it had gone into service.

Norwegian Navy

British *M2* Hangar
In 1925 the two surviving 12-in gunned submarines *M2* and *M3* had their guns removed. To test the concept of using aircraft to seek targets for submarines, *M2* was equipped with a hangar forward of the conning tower, and a catapult. She could operate a single Parnall Peto

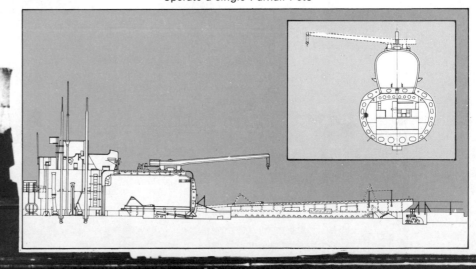

12-in guns from their two surviving 'M' Class submarines, and *M2* was converted to carry a seaplane. A large hangar was built forward of the conning tower, with a large crane on its roof; a light inclined catapult was built on the forward casing, and a specially designed Parnall Peto seaplane was carried. The biggest problem of handling an aircraft on board a submarine was the lack of space, and this dictated very small machines, which in turn lacked the capacity for fuel which would have made them more useful.

Then, in 1932, the Japanese launched their prototype *I5*. They stowed the fuselage and floats in one hangar and the wings in another, sited to port and starboard under the conning tower. The time taken to assemble the seaplane was so long that the submarine would almost certainly have been sunk in the middle of the operation. The *I6* had the same problem, but she did at least have a catapult like the *M2*. Thereafter a seaplane and catapult became a feature of the larger types of Japanese submarines, and special tactics were devised to exploit the combination.

The sister of *M2* was converted to a minelayer at the same time, as a development of the *U71* type. *M3* had a free-flooding casing (i.e. outside the pressure hull) containing twin mine-tracks, which ran from well forward past the conning tower. She was a great success, although ungainly in appearance, and she was followed by a class of six more. The main innovation in the *M3* was the provision of powered chain conveyor gear, which allowed the use of a normal mine and sinker, rather than the special type of mine which had to be used in all First World War minelayers.

The Washington Disarmament Conference of 1921/22 and the Treaty which resulted were the outcome of the rivalry which had grown up between the United States and Japan during the First World War. Although the Treaty is best known for its limitations on large, surface warships, it also dealt with submarines. The British delegation was not unnaturally content to see the submarine banned, but this was a futile quest so soon after the great submarine campaign of 1915–18. The Italians and French were particularly anxious to

retain a large fleet of submarines as a cheap alternative to new battleships and aircraft carriers, and the Japanese made little secret of their intentions to build up a big fleet to threaten American superiority in the Pacific. Lord St Vincent's words of 1801 had come true, and neither of the two largest navies really wanted to see any progress made with the weapon most likely to destroy their own superiority.

The best that could be done was to limit the gun-calibre to 8 in, as in heavy cruisers, but the French were particularly obdurate in rejecting limitations on numbers of submarines and in blocking attempts to outlaw unrestricted warfare. The world's

British *X1*
X1 was the largest British submarine ever built until the advent of nuclear propulsion, and was in many ways superior to other cruiser-submarines. Her radius of action was 12,400 miles on the surface, and she could remain submerged for over two days, thanks to her large battery capacity. In addition, her two twin gun-mountings were carried high above the waterline to free them from spray interference, but despite all these advantages her unreliable machinery prevented her from being a success

French *Surcouf*
Not only the largest submarine in the world, the *Surcouf* was also the only one to have the maximum calibre of guns allowed under the Washington Disarmament Treaty. Her 8-in guns were carried in a twin power-operated turret, and could each fire three 260-lb shells per minute to a range of 30,000 yards. In addition, she carried a seaplane in a cylindrical hangar abaft the conning tower. She operated under the Free French flag in the Second World War, but was accidentally rammed by an American freighter in 1942

Cruiser-submarine comparative specifications					
Type	Tonnage (surf/sub)	Length/ Beam (ft)	Speed (kts) (surf/sub)	Guns	Torpedoes
U117 (Germ.)	1164/1512	276·5/24·5	14·7/7	1×5·9 in	4×20 in (20 reloads)
U139 (Germ.)	1930/2483	311/29·75	15·8/7·6	2×5·9 in	6×20 in
U151 (Germ.)	1512/1875	213·25/29·25	12·4/5·2	2×5·9 in; 2×3·4 in	2×20 in
U173 (Germ.)	2115/2790	320/29·75	17·5/8·5	2×5·9 in; 2×3·4 in	6×20 in
Barracuda (US)	2000/2620	341/27·25	18/11	1×5 in	6×21 in
Argonaut (US)	2710/4080	381/34	15/8	2×6 in	4×21 in
Narwhal (US)	2730/4050	371/33·25	17/8	2×6 in	6×21 in
X1 (UK)	2425/3585	363·5/29·75	19·5/9	4×5·2 in	6×21 in (6 reloads)
Surcouf (Fr.)	2880/4304	361/29·5	18·5/10	2×8 in	8×21·7 in (10 reloads) 4×15·7 in
I52 (Jap.)	1500/2500	330·75/25	22/10	1×4·7 in; 1×3 in	8×21 in (9 reloads)
I1 (Jap.)	2135/2791	320/30·25	18/8	2×5·5 in	6×21 in (14 reloads)
Ettore Fieramosca (Ital.)	1556/2128	275·6/27·25	19/14	1×4·7 in	8×21 in (6 reloads)

major navies, denied the opportunity of building unlimited numbers of surface warships as much by economics as by international agreement, plunged into an orgy of submarine building.

The smaller navies were also conscious of the value of submarines, and the Netherlands and the Scandinavian countries had developed their own designs with some success. The Royal Swedish Navy had been building submarines since 1908, but the first fully indigenous design, the *Sjölejonet* Class, was not ordered until 1934. They displaced 580 tons on the surface, were 210 ft in length, and had a submerged speed of 9 knots. The disposition of torpedo tubes was unusual – three 53-cm (21-in) bow tubes, two rotating deck tubes similar to those on French boats, and a single stern tube; two single 40-mm deck guns were carried in retractable mountings, an idea derived from Dutch submarines. Three were completed in 1938/9, and a further six were ordered when the international situation worsened.

Denmark lacked the resources of Sweden, but she too produced original designs like the 'H' Class, whereas Norway was more

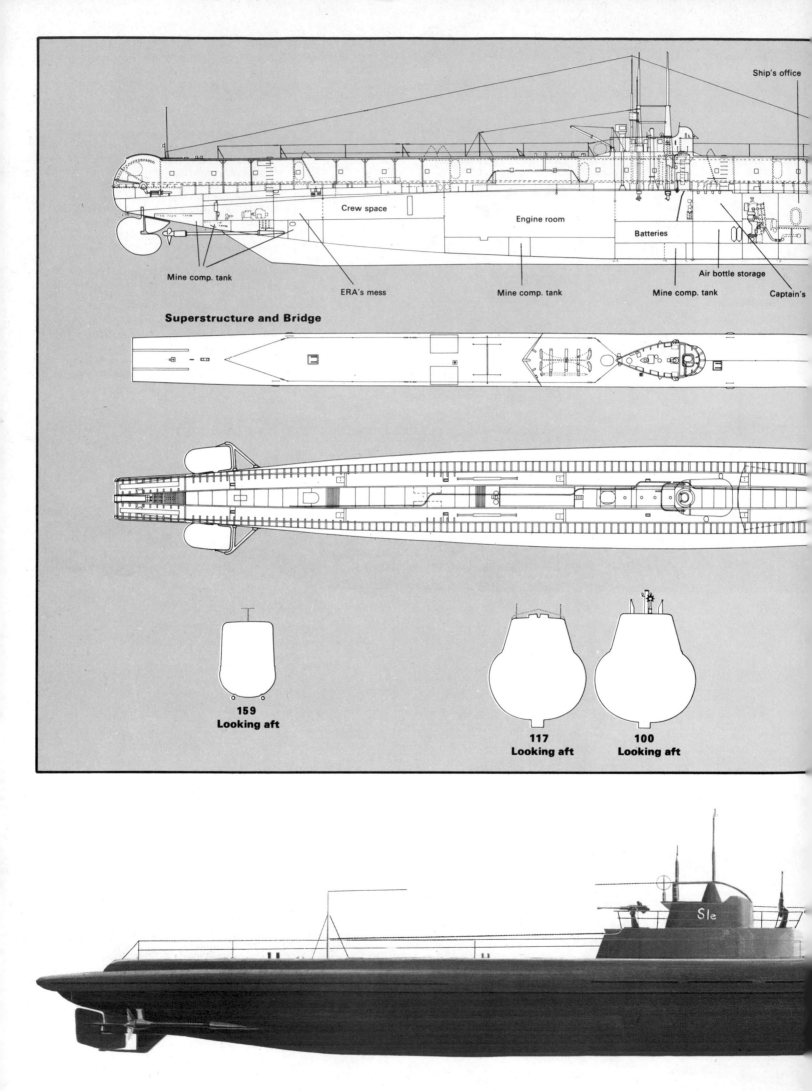

Mine comp. tank

Crew space

Engine room

Batteries

Ship's office

ERA's mess

Mine comp. tank

Air bottle storage

Mine comp. tank

Captain's

Superstructure and Bridge

159
Looking aft

117
Looking aft

100
Looking aft

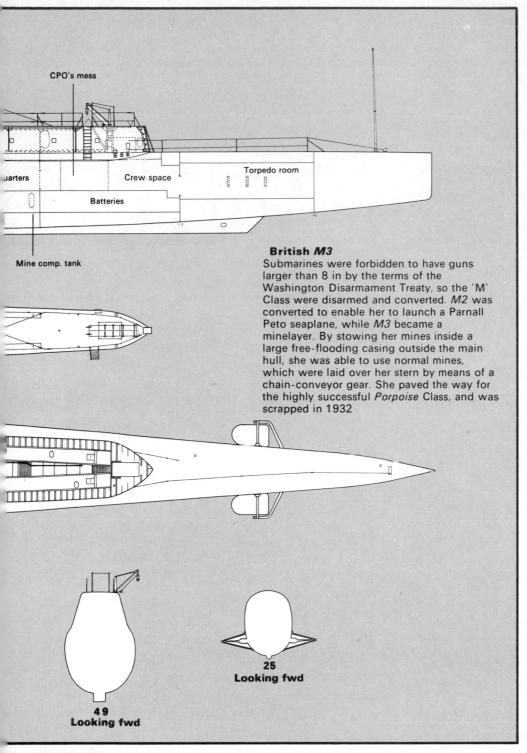

Submarine Building 1921–1936						
Programme	Britain	USA	France	Italy	Japan	Russia
1921	1				3	
1922			9		4	
1923	3	1	10		9	
1924			2	4		
1925		2	9	8		
1926	6		11	3		
1927	6		9	6	1	3
1928	6*		7	4		
1929	6*	1	11	7		25†
1930	3		11	12		4
1931	3	2		5	9	6
1932	3			4		12
1933	3	4				5
1934	3	6	2	10	4	20
1935	3	6		20		25†
1936	8	6	2	11		26

*3 cancelled from each programme. †These programmes were subsequently spread over later years.

British M3

Submarines were forbidden to have guns larger than 8 in by the terms of the Washington Disarmament Treaty, so the 'M' Class were disarmed and converted. *M2* was converted to enable her to launch a Parnall Peto seaplane, while *M3* became a minelayer. By stowing her mines inside a large free-flooding casing outside the main hull, she was able to use normal mines, which were laid over her stern by means of a chain-conveyor gear. She paved the way for the highly successful *Porpoise* Class, and was scrapped in 1932

CPO's mess
uarters
Crew space
Torpedo room
Batteries
Mine comp. tank

49 Looking fwd

25 Looking fwd

Swedish *Sjölejonet*

The *Sjölejonet* Class were ordered in 1934, and were the first fully Swedish design of submarine. They had an unusual arrangement of torpedo-tubes, with three in the bow (two over, one under), and one internal tube and an external pair of revolving tubes aft. They also mounted two short-barrelled 40-mm Bofors guns on disappearing mountings, as a defence against aircraft. *Displacement*: 650 tons (surfaced) 760 tons (submerged) *Speed*: 16 knots (surfaced) 9 knots (submerged)

content to rely on foreign designs. The 'B' Class were completed in the early 1920s to an American Electric Boat Company design of 1914 vintage, but *B1* nevertheless served in the Second World War. Poland had a small force of five boats, comprising the Dutch-built *Sep* and *Orzel* and a trio of French-built 980-tonners, the *Rys*, *Wilk* and *Zbik*, of which the *Orzel* and *Wilk* managed to escape to Britain in September 1939 in a desperate dash for freedom.

The Dutch had originally built two types of submarine, those with 'K' numbers for the East Indies, and those with 'O' numbers for home waters, but in 1937 the two series were combined under 'O' for 'Onterzeeboot'. The *O21* class of five boats were laid down in 1937/38 for general service at home and in the Far East. They were conventional in all ways but one: they were the first to incorporate an 'air mast' for charging batteries while running at periscope depth, a vital step in extending the submerged endurance of submarines.

Alas, like other prophets the Dutch were without honour in their own country, and with their Allies for that matter; when *O21–24* arrived in England in May 1940 the first thing the Royal Navy did was remove the air masts, and only in 1943 did the Germans realise the worth of the gadget they had found in a Dutch shipyard. Looking around in desperation for an antidote to the danger of recharging batteries on the surface at night, when aircraft and escorts were using radar, they re-examined the air mast and perfected it as the 'schnorchel'.

After their spectacular experiment with the *Surcouf* the French Navy reverted to more conventional submarines. In March 1920 the Chairman of the Naval Estimates Committee in Parliament had suggested quite seriously that a fleet of 250 to 300 submarines would answer all needs hitherto met by cruisers and battleships. Fortunately this extreme argument was met by a reasoned rebuttal, for it was clear to naval officers that, despite its potency, the submarine had only recently suffered a catastrophic defeat. Furthermore it was correctly argued that on a ton-for-ton basis the complexity of a submarine made it just as expensive as a surface ship to build and maintain, and also reduced its effective life. Although submarines were to be built in large numbers, they were nonetheless part of a balanced fleet. Two types were built after 1922, 1st Class boats of some 1,000 tons, and 2nd Class boats of 600 tons, the larger being intended for overseas patrol duties and the smaller ones for defensive patrol duties in home waters.

An interesting feature of French submarines of this period was their external torpedo-tubes, fitted in training mounts in the casing and capable of being trained over a wide arc. The purpose of this fitting was to assist the submarine in sinking merchant ships, and the idea was extended by the provision of 15·7-in (400-mm) light short-range torpedoes for use against 'soft-skinned' targets. Unfortunately this torpedo proved a total failure, and even the 24V 21·7-in (550-mm) proved unreliable on gyro-angling runs, although good on a straight run.

Two notable French classes of submarine were built between the wars. The six *Saphir* Class minelayers were of moderate dimensions, and had their mines in vertical wells in the saddle tanks. Although this was officially known as the Normand-Fenaux system it was actually a later version of the British system introduced in the 'E' Class in 1915. The *Rubis* operated with great success under the Free French flag during the Second World War, and notched up a high score of victims. Thirty-one large ocean-going boats of the so-called '1500-tonne' type were laid down in batches each year under the 1924–30 programmes, and proved successful; two travelled over 14,000 miles from Toulon to Saigon in 1935 without mishap.

The most famous of the class was the *Casabianca*, which was the only vessel to escape the holocaust which ensued when the Germans tried to capture Toulon by treachery in 1942. She joined the Allies in North Africa and sank three enemy ships during the invasion of Corsica a year later. The next class of large submarines had only just been started when their hulls were scuttled to prevent them from falling into German hands in June 1940, and a similar fate befell their 2nd Class contemporaries.

Russia rebuilds

The Russian Navy, or the Red Fleet as it became after the Revolution, took some years to recuperate from the aftermath of the Civil War and the anti-Bolshevik intervention by Great Britain and the rest of the erstwhile allies of the First World War. Many of the submarines which survived the vicissitudes of 1917–19 were unserviceable, and unfortunately the majority of the new construction had been scuttled. Only ten boats remained in the Baltic by 1922, one in the Arctic and five in the Black Sea. It was to be another nine years before the first new submarines joined the Fleet, which explains why the British submarine *L55* was salvaged and incorporated into the Red Fleet; she had been sunk in 1919 during the Intervention, but was raised in 1928 and recommissioned in 1931.

The first of the new programme was the *Dekabrist* or 'D' Class of six units, which came into service in 1931/32. Based on an Italian design, they displaced 989 tons on the surface, and were armed with a 4-in deck gun, a smaller 45-mm gun and eight 21-in torpedo tubes. The *Leninets* or 'L' Class which followed were of similar size and characteristics, but based on *L55*, and took longer to build; it took from 1933 to 1942 to commission 24 units, and one was never completed. At the same time a smaller

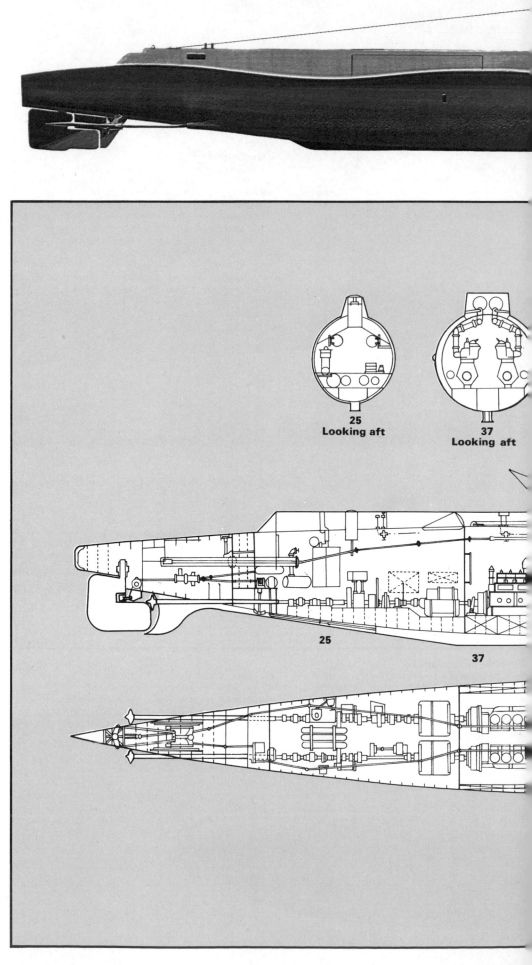

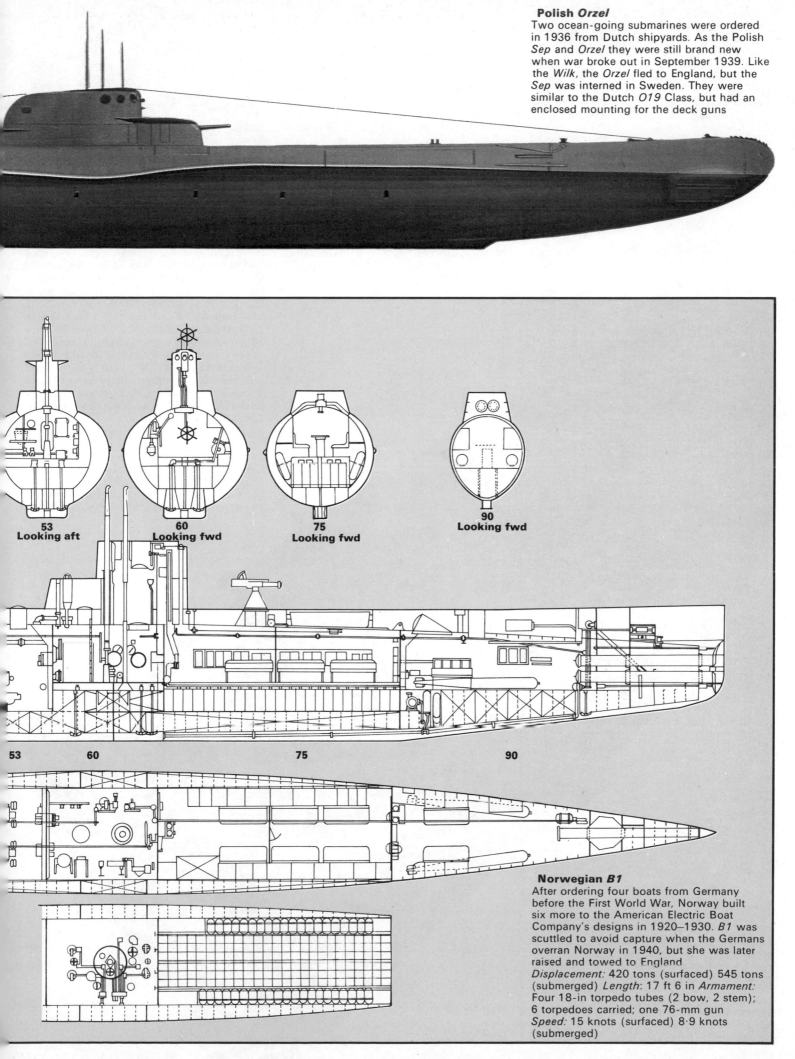

Polish *Orzel*
Two ocean-going submarines were ordered in 1936 from Dutch shipyards. As the Polish *Sep* and *Orzel* they were still brand new when war broke out in September 1939. Like the *Wilk*, the *Orzel* fled to England, but the *Sep* was interned in Sweden. They were similar to the Dutch *O19* Class, but had an enclosed mounting for the deck guns

53
Looking aft

60
Looking fwd

75
Looking fwd

90
Looking fwd

53   60   75   90

Norwegian *B1*
After ordering four boats from Germany before the First World War, Norway built six more to the American Electric Boat Company's designs in 1920–1930. *B1* was scuttled to avoid capture when the Germans overran Norway in 1940, but she was later raised and towed to England
Displacement: 420 tons (surfaced) 545 tons (submerged) *Length:* 17 ft 6 in *Armament:* Four 18-in torpedo tubes (2 bow, 2 stem); 6 torpedoes carried; one 76-mm gun
Speed: 15 knots (surfaced) 8·9 knots (submerged)

type was designed, known as the *Shchuka* (Pike) or 'Shch' Class; 90 were commissioned in 1933–42, and three were scrapped incomplete. They displaced 580 tons on the surface, and had six 21-in torpedo-tubes and a 45-mm deck gun. A further intermediate type, the *Stalinets* Class (33 units) and a general patrol type known as the *Pravda* Class (3 units) came into service from 1936 onwards.

The *Pravdas* did not prove very successful, but the *Stalinets* Class were very satisfactory in service, because they were able, by a roundabout route, to make use of German expertise. This came about because the Russian dictator, Marshal Stalin, was anxious to help Germany to evade the restrictions of the Versailles Treaty, which prevented Germany from building U-Boats. German design firms were set up outside Germany, in Spain, Holland and Russia to keep the nucleus of a design team together, and although the orders which resulted went to shipbuilders in the countries concerned, the know-how was German. As a price for their help the Russians obtained plans of the Type IA which was built in Spain for Turkey as the *Gür*, and this design became the basis of the *Stalinets* or 'S' Class.

All these submarines were generally simi-

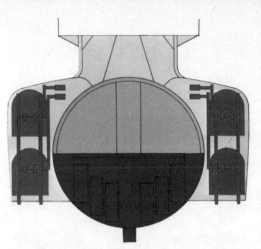

lar in dimensions to the submarines being built outside the USSR, but there were two more types which represented the upper and lower extremes. The 'Malyutka' (small) Class displaced only 161 tons in surface trim, and had two 21-in torpedo-tubes; they bore some resemblance to the little 'tin tadpoles' of the German UBI Class in 1915. Between 1933 and 1937 over 50 were added to the Russian strength, and two improved types were commissioned between 1938 and 1944. The 'M' types were built in sections, the original Malyutka VI and VIbis series having four sections, the Malyutka XII series six sections, and the final Malyutka XV series seven sections, all small enough to allow shipment by rail and canal for assembly wherever needed.

The other Russian submarine type was the 'Kreiser' or 'Katyusha' type, a big cruiser submarine of 1,390 tons on the surface, armed with two 3·9-in (100-mm) guns, two 45-mm and ten 21-in torpedo-tubes.

French *Rubis*

The French Navy ordered ten minelaying submarines between 1925 and 1939. The *Rubis* was operating under British control at the fall of France in 1940, and under the Free French flag she carried out over twenty successful minelaying trips between 1940 and 1945. Her sister *Perle* survived to be sunk in error by an Allied aircraft in 1944, but the rest were either scuttled incomplete or captured in a wrecked condition in 1942 by the Germans

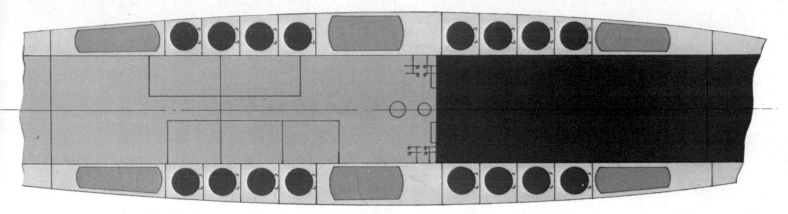

The surface speed was 18 knots to allow them to operate with surface units, and 13 numbered units were commissioned between 1940 and 1942. As the numbers ran as high as *K51* it must be assumed that a large number were not completed during the War. They could dive in 50 seconds, a good time for a large boat.

When Hitler gave the order to attack Russia in 1941, this was the approximate strength of the Red Fleet:

Baltic
7 'K' Class (*K24, K51–56*) – some building
3 'P' Class (*P1–3*)
13 'S' Class (*S1–13*)
4 'L' Class (*L1–3, L21*)
1 'D' Class (*D2*)
1 *L55*
5 'B' Class (*B2, B4–6, B8*)
22 'Shch' Class (*Shch 301–11, 317–320, 322–324, 405–408*)
22 'Malyutka' Class

Far East
4 'S' Class (*S52–53, S57–58*)
12 'L' Class (*L7–14, L16–19*)
41 'Shch' Class (*Shch 101–141*)
30 'Malyutka' Class

Normand-Fenaux Minelaying System
The *Saphir* Class used a system derived from the British method first used in the 'E' Class in 1915. Eight wells on each side, in the saddle tanks, held two mines stowed vertically. The mines were armed and set mechanically from within the pressure hull, and the loss of weight was automatically compensated for. The supply of French Sauter-Harlé mines soon gave out, but by a stroke of good luck Vickers were producing a mine of almost identical pattern for Rumania in 1939, and this was easily adapted

the ex-Estonian *Kalev* and *Lembit* were commissioned as Red Fleet units. They were British-built, and rather similar to the British 'P' Class. In 1944 the British Government transferred four submarines under Lend-Lease for use in the Arctic; these were the *V1* (ex-HMS *Sunfish*) and *V2–4* (ex-*Unbroken*, *Unison* and *Ursula*). In one respect the Russian submarine service was unique in that it assigned numbers according to the Fleet in which the submarines were serving. The two large numbered classes, the 'Shch' and 'Malyutka' types seem to have changed numbers when transferred from, say, the Baltic to the Arctic. Thus Shch *101–141* served in the

endurance, and a reload was provided for each tube in order to extend the operating time. One unfortunate feature was introduced as a result of economy: because the dimensions were restricted, some of the fuel tanks had to be carried in the upper half of the saddle tanks. As it was virtually impossible in a riveted hull to have an oil-tight seam these external tanks tended to give away the submarine's position by leaving a tell-tale oil slick on the surface.

The 'P' and 'R' Classes were generally similar to the 'O' Class but slightly larger. In 1929 a new design for a 'fleet' submarine was produced, the 'River' type with the unusually high surface speed of 22 knots. To accommodate a pair of 10-cylinder diesels the stern torpedo-tubes had to be omitted, and although the design proved successful in service it was soon realised that the concept was wrong. The speed of surface warships had risen since 1915, when the fleet submarine requirement had been put forward, and the only use for 22 knots' speed was in a campaign against commerce in the Pacific or the Indian Ocean.

As the result of the success of the *M3*, six submarine minelayers were built between 1930 and 1938, the famous *Porpoise* Class.

Arctic
6 'K' Class (*K21–23, K1–3*)
12 'S' Class (*S14–16, S19, S51, S54–56, S101–104*)
3 'L' Class (*L15, L20, L22*)
2 'D' Class (*D1, D3*)
8 'Shch' Class (*Shch 401–404, 421–424*)
17 'Malyutka' Class

Black Sea
8 'S' Class (*S31–38*)
6 'L' Class (*L4–6, L23–25*)
3 'D' Class (*D4–6*)
5 'A' Class (*A1–5*)
16 'Shch' Class (*Shch 201–216*)
28 'Malyutka' Class

In addition to these submarines, of which some were still under construction, the Russians took over four boats as a result of their 'liberation' of the independent Baltic republics in 1940, but of these only

Russian 'Shch' Class
This class took its name from the initial letters of the prototype *Shchuka* ('Pike'), and was a medium-sized patrol type begun in 1932. By 1941 nearly a hundred had been built, and they continued in production until 1942. From what can be pieced together it seems that some thirty were sunk during the Second World War

Far East, but Shch *201–216* served in the Black Sea, and when a permanent transfer was made the number seems to have changed as well.

After their attempts to ban the submarine at the Washington Conference, the British settled down to serious submarine construction in 1923. The *L52* Class of 1917 was chosen as the model, and the 'O' Class which resulted was longer and beamier but carried the same heavy bow salvo of six 21-in tubes and two stern tubes. A drop in surface speed of two knots to 15½ knots was more than compensated for by a much increased

These 270-ft boats displaced 1,520 tons on the surface and had a capacity of 50 standard Mk XVI mines in a full-length deck outside the pressure hull. The need for specialised submarine minelayers lapsed when the Royal Navy produced a mine which could be laid from a 21-in torpedo-tube, but the minelayers proved even more successful when used as supply submarines to run precious cargoes to Malta in 1941/42. Their capacious mine-decks were filled with such assorted items as machine-gun ammunition, glycol coolant for Spitfires, and food.

Under the 1929 Estimates a new type of medium patrol submarine was introduced, the 640-ton 'S' Class. They were a breakaway from the large 'O', 'P' and 'R' type, and were meant for work in European and Mediterranean waters which were too confined for large submarines. The result was a great success, and the 'S' Class eventually ran to some 60 units, the largest single class built

Comparison of Russian Type 1A and 'S' Class designs

	1A	Gür	Stalinets
Tonnage (surf/sub)	862/983	750/960	780/1050
Length (ft)	237·5	237·5	256
Beam (ft)	20·25	20·3	21
Draught (ft)	14	13·5	13
Machinery	2800 bhp 1000 chp	2800 bhp 1000 chp	4200 bhp 2200 chp
Speed (surf/ sub) (knots)	17¾/8¼	20/9	20/8½
Torpedo-tubes	6×21-in 4b 2s	6×21-in 4b 2s	6×21-in 4b 2s
Guns	1×4·1-in 1×20-mm	1×4-in	1×3-in 1×45-mm

French *Casabianca*

Thirty-one '1500-tonne' 1st Class submarines were built between 1924 and 1939 for overseas work. Most were scuttled, either at Brest in 1940 or at Toulon in 1942, but the *Casabianca* was able to make her escape from Toulon to join the Allies in North Africa. Later she distinguished herself in the liberation of Corsica by sinking a sub-chaser and damaging another.
Displacement: 1,570 tons (surfaced) 2,084 tons (submerged) *Length:* 302 ft 9 in *Beam:* 27 ft *Armament:* Nine 21·7-in torpedo-tubes (4 forward, 3 and 2 aft); two 15·7-in torpedo-tubes (external aft); one 3·9-in gun; two 13·2-mm AA guns
Speed: 19 knots (surfaced) 10 knots (submerged)

British *Olympus*

The success of the prototype *Oberon* led to the introduction of six 'O' Class submarines in 1926 for service in the Far East. They were the first of a series of similar boats which incorporated the lessons of the recent war, and although quite successful they suffered from having external fuel tanks which leaked oil. This, combined with their size, led to four of the six being lost in the Mediterranean in 1940–42 for the Royal Navy. By positioning all fuel tanks inside the pressure hull they cured the worst fault of their predecessors, and had a good diving time. They were too small for overseas work, however, and had to be complemented by the equally famous 'T' Class, which were 70 ft longer, and displaced just over 1,000 tons. Whereas the 'S' Class had six bow tubes only, the 'Ts' had eight bow tubes, including two in a bulbous bow casing, and an extra pair of tubes in the casing amidships, giving them the phenomenal bow salvo of *ten* tubes.

Nothing has been said so far of German developments, for of course Germany was not allowed to have U-Boats under the Treaty of Versailles. As we have seen, the German Navy made sure that it kept abreast of submarine developments by financing design work in other countries. Thus when Hitler and his National Socialist government repudiated the Versailles Treaty and began rebuilding the armed forces in 1934, there was a great deal of expertise available.

particularly in having a much increased number of reload torpedoes.

Among the many experimental ideas was one for a submarine carrying two small motor torpedo-boats on deck in cylindrical hangars. Like the operation of aircraft this was an idea which looked better on the drawing board than it did to an anxious U-Boat commander worrying about the length of time taken to get things in and out of hangars, and it was quietly dropped. Likewise the 2,500-ton minelayers of the Type XA and a trio of aircraft-carrying 3,000-ton U-cruisers were abandoned, no doubt with a sigh of relief from the submariners.

The standard sea-going U-Boat which evolved from this series of prototypes was the Type VII. The first group, known as VIIAs, were developed from a German design built in Finland but in turn the Finnish

The Type VIIC U-Boat had a waterline length of 220 ft, a beam of just over 20 ft, and displaced about 770 tons on the surface. She was of fairly conventional design, with saddle tanks, four bow tubes and two stern tubes; her diesels drove her at 17 knots on the surface and the electric motors could produce 7½ knots for a limited time under water.

Although not an ideal type for the Second World War as it turned out, the Type VII series was simple to build and very handy. Its principal drawback was its endurance, 6,500 miles at 12 knots, which proved insufficient for extended operations, while its lack of internal space imposed extra burdens on personnel. British submariners would have been surprised to learn that their German counterparts regarded Royal Navy submarine accommodation as palatial. Despite these inherent problems the U-Boat Arm waged a most determined and ferocious campaign from the Arctic to the Indian Ocean in conditions ranging from merely spartan to utterly vile.

Five basic types were considered; sea-going types of 500–750 tons, ocean going boats of 1,000 tons, U-cruisers of 1,500 tons, and coastal submarines and minelayers of 250–500 tons. The sea-going type was based on the Turkish *Gür* which had been built in Spain to a pre-1934 German design, but the first coastal type was based on the UBII Type of the First World War. The ocean-going boats of Type IXA were based on the *U117* or UEII Type of the First World War,

Russian 'K' Class

This class was also known as the *Katyusha* Class, and they were large ocean-going submarines with a heavy armament.
Displacement: 1,390 tons (surfaced)
Armament: Ten or twelve 21-in torpedo-tubes; two 3·9-in guns; two 45-mm AA guns

boat owed a lot to the old UBIII Type of the First World War. *U27* was the first to be launched in 1936, and by the outbreak of the Second World War the improved Type VIIB was in service. The Type VIIC which followed had many improvements over the original A type, such as more powerful diesel engines and greater fuel capacity, and became the standard wartime type. By 1941 the first had been launched, and as the 600-odd which were built came very close to winning the war for Hitler and Nazi Germany, a closer look is indicated.

At this point it is opportune to revert to progress in anti-submarine warfare, for this had kept pace with the frightening increase in the submarine's efficiency between 1919 and 1939. First, the British Admiralty had learned the lessons of 1917, and convoy was to be their standard defence for merchant ships. Meanwhile, in 1918 a secret committee of scientists had been set up to investigate methods of detecting submarines, and their researches had resulted in the brilliant discovery that a sonic beam could be bounced off a submarine's hull and be measured to give a bearing and range. Known from the initials of its parental committee, the Anti-Submarine Devices Investigation Committee, ASDIC, worked on the simple principle of passing an electric current through a quartz plate. Although the Germans suspected its existence, they did not uncover the secret until details were captured in France in 1940.

By 1939 the Admiralty had ensured that some 200 escort vessels were fitted with Asdic, and all anti-submarine tactics had been developed to make use of its remarkable properties. It led, however, to a dangerous under-estimation of the threat from submarines, and there were people in the Admiralty who talked of the submarine being a weapon of the past. Not only were there too few escort vessels for the amount of shipping to be protected, but the Asdic had its blind spots; it could not be used against a surfaced submarine, and at that stage in its development it could not hold the target when the searching ship passed overhead. Thus an attack with depth-charges always had to be carried out 'blind'.

The aircraft had shown itself to be a dangerous enemy to submarines during the First World War, and the increased range of aircraft in 1939 made them far more dangerous. It was not foreseen that the ordinary aircraft bomb would be ineffective against submarines, and the lack of sufficient numbers would also prevent aircraft

British *Sealion*

In 1929 the first orders were placed for medium-sized patrol submarines, as the Royal Navy became aware of the need for smaller boats to work in Northern European waters. The problem of leaking fuel tanks was solved by putting them inside the pressure hull, and as speed and submerged endurance were not sacrificed the 'S' Class was most successful. An improved version was put into mass production during the Second World War, making this class the largest single group of submarines built for the Royal Navy: more than sixty units were built over a period of fifteen years.
Displacement: 735 tons (full load, surfaced)
Armament: Six 21-in torpedo-tubes (forward); one 3-in gun *Speed:* 13½ knots (surfaced) 10 knots (submerged)

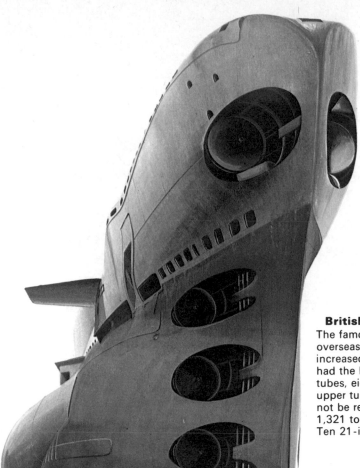

from making a full contribution at first, but ultimately they proved the submarine's worst enemy. Another less-publicised weapon which was available was the mine. In 1917/18 mines had accounted for 49 U-Boats, over a quarter of the total sunk, but for some reason the value of offensive mining against submarines was still disputed in 1939. Nevertheless, the Royal Navy had developed the magnetic mine which it had used in 1918, and had large stocks of an anti-submarine pattern in hand.

When war broke out between Britain, France and Germany on 3 September 1939, the German Navy had 56 U-Boats in commission, with five more nearing completion. Some 40 of these were already at their war stations around the British Isles, and despite the fact that Hitler's instructions forbade 'unrestricted' warfare against merchant shipping, one of them sank the liner *Athenia* without warning on the first day of the war. Hitler's instructions were based on his reluctance to antagonise neutral

British *Thrasher*
The famous 'T' Class were designed for overseas operations, and so size had to be increased to approximately 1,100 tons. They had the heavy armament of ten torpedo-tubes, eight in the bow and two aft. The two upper tubes were externally fitted, and could not be reloaded at sea. *Displacement:* 1,321 tons (full load, surfaced) *Armament:* Ten 21-in torpedo-tubes; one 4-in gun

British *Thunderbolt*
This member of the 'T' Class was far better known as the *Thetis* after being lost in a tragic accident in Liverpool Bay in June 1939. To avoid any suggestion of a jinx on the boat the Admiralty put her into service under a new name, but this did not stop her from being sunk by an Italian corvette north of Sicily in 1943. Despite the *Thetis* disaster, the 'T' Class had a high reputation for reliability, and fifty-five were built between 1937 and 1945

opinion, but as early as 1937 the Admiralty had assumed that these restrictions would not be obeyed.

The *Athenia* sinking was a genuine mistake, as the commander of *U30* mistook her for a troop transport; other U-Boats behaved in a humane manner towards their victims in this early period of the war. It was known to the journalists as the 'Phoney War', and some people talked of a sinister plot between the Allies and Hitler, but there was nothing phoney about the 199 merchant ships sunk by the end of March 1940. Nor had the U-Boats escaped lightly, as 18 had been sunk in the same period.

The U-Boats had also scored some notable

successes against warships. Two weeks after the outbreak of war the aircraft carrier *Ark Royal* was attacked by *U39*, but the carrier's escorting destroyers pounced and sank her. Three days later, however, another carrier, HMS *Courageous*, was sunk by *U29*, and on 14 October *U47* brought off a brilliant coup by sinking the battleship *Royal Oak* in her supposedly secure base at

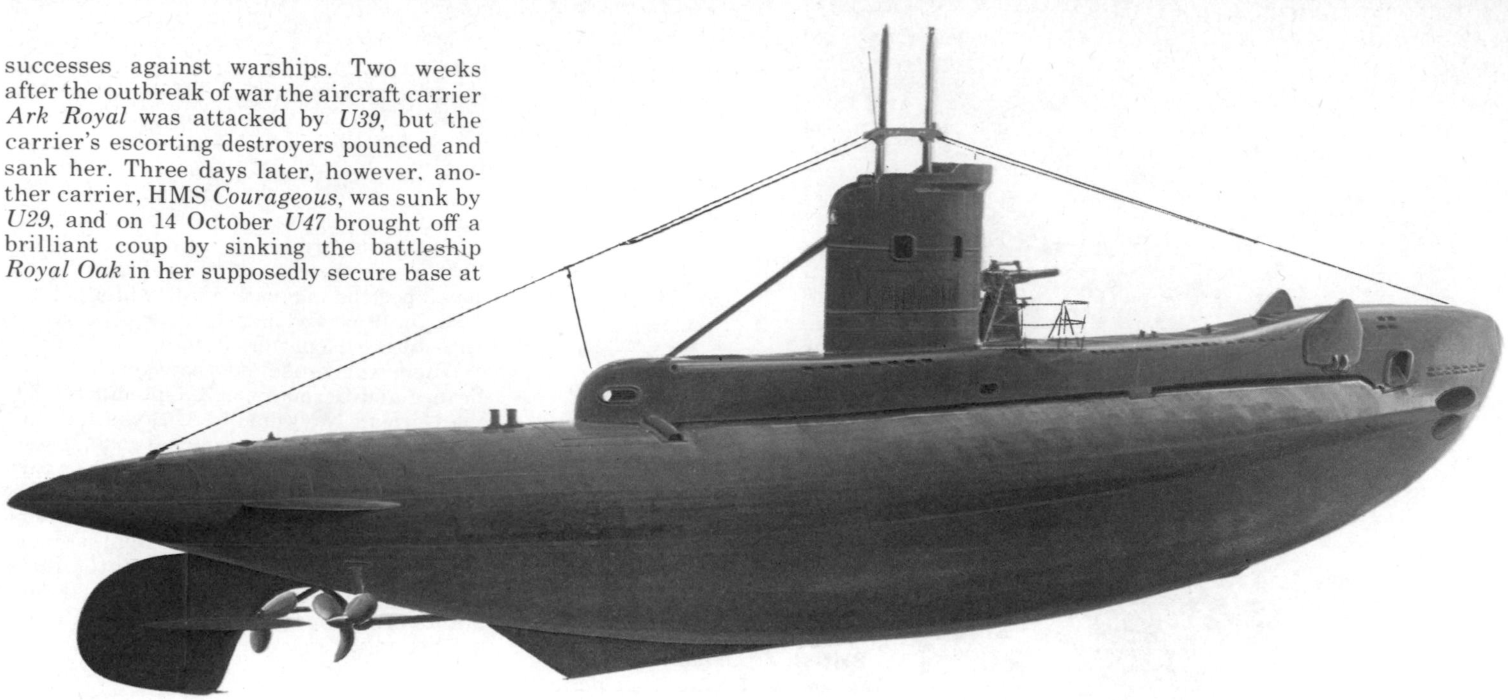

Scapa Flow. Kapitän-Leutnant Prien took his U-Boat in through the tortuous channels past the rusting blockships which had lain there since 1914, and finally found the battleship at anchor. After one salvo of torpedoes missed, Prien reloaded and fired a spread of three which detonated under the *Royal Oak*'s keel; she capsized and sank with 833 of her crew.

The *Royal Oak* was an elderly second-line unit whose loss could hardly rank with that of the carrier *Courageous* in military value, but *U47*'s exploit had far more impact. The realisation that Scapa Flow could be penetrated by a submarine forced the British to remove their entire Home Fleet to a series of temporary anchorages, just as the Grand Fleet had gone a-wandering in 1914 after a submarine scare. At a crucial moment the whole British strategy for penning the German Navy's surface warships in the North Sea had been drastically changed, all by one submariner and his crew's determination and courage.

Only 38 British submarines were available in September 1939, and although the British blockade of the North Sea denied them any big opportunities for attacking German shipping, they had an important role to play. They were immediately deployed to extend air patrol lines, in order to give warning of enemy naval movements, and to harass U-Boats and surface warships in their home waters. What was not realised for some time, however, was that a policy of sending submarines to lie off enemy bases would expose the submarines to a high loss rate. This is because a base acts like a convoy – in fact a convoy with a reduced perimeter – and thus the advantage swings to the enemy's anti-submarine forces.

In April and May 1940 there was a sudden lull in U-Boat activity, and only 20 ships were sunk; this was because Admiral Dönitz had recalled most of his boats to regroup for the invasion of Norway. The British also had plans for Norway, as they wanted to lay minefields to interrupt the iron-ore traffic from Narvik to Germany. After the end of the campaign only submarine minelayers could be used, and to strengthen the effort the Admiralty persuaded the French Government to lend them the *Rubis*. This famous submarine laid her

British Upholder (left)

The first three 'U' Class were ordered in 1936 to serve as unarmed targets for anti-submarine vessels, but they were completed with torpedo-tubes to allow them to carry out normal submarine training as well. In 1940 it was realised that their small size suited them for the North Sea and Mediterranean, and so they were put into quantity production. HMS *Upholder* was commanded by Lt Cdr Wanklyn VC, and she sank over 90,000 tons of German and Italian shipping in the Mediterranean before she was herself sunk in April 1942.

Displacement: 648 tons (full load, surfaced)
Armament: Four 21-in torpedo-tubes; one 3-in AA gun *Speed:* 11¾ knots (surfaced) 9 knots (submerged)

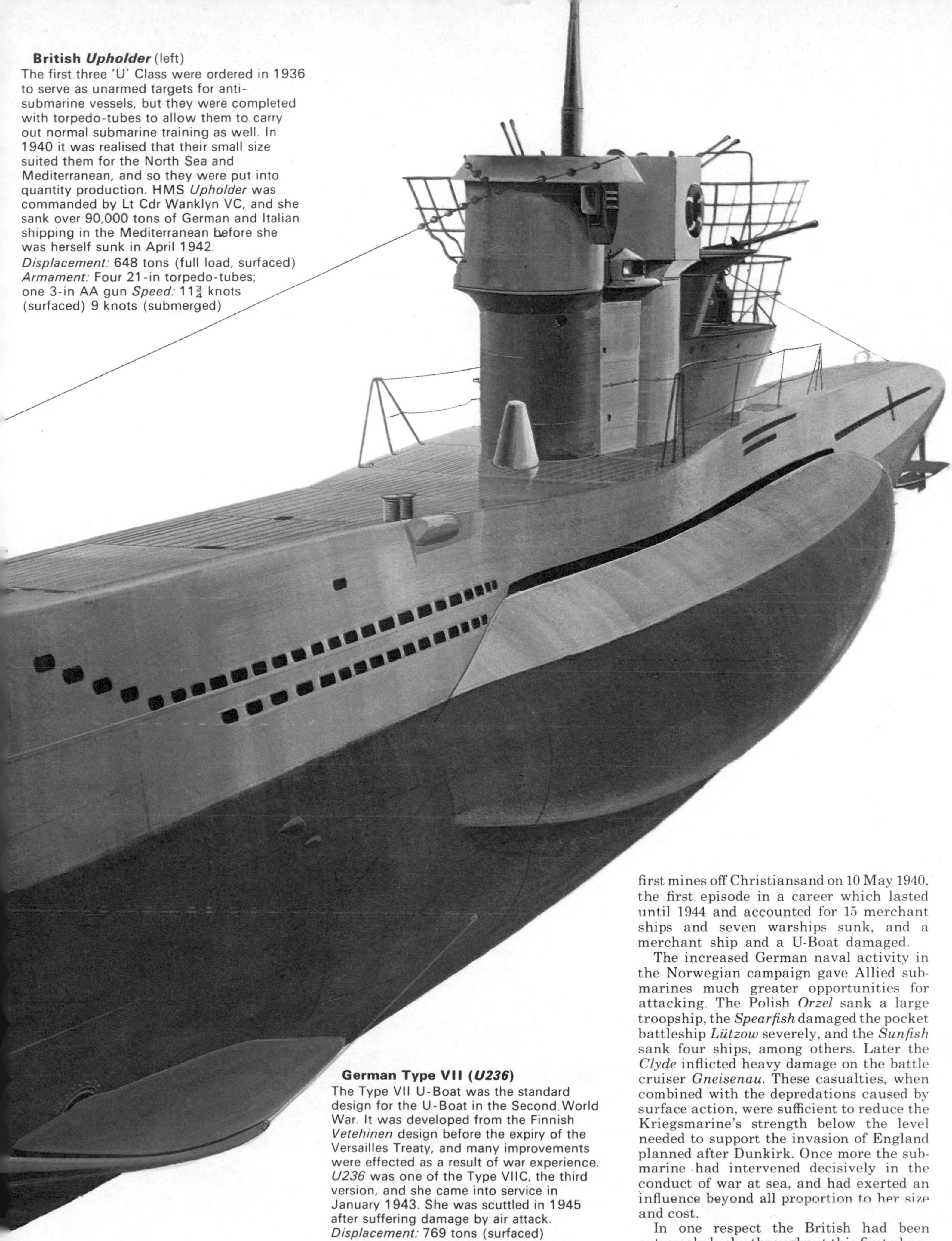

German Type VII (U236)

The Type VII U-Boat was the standard design for the U-Boat in the Second World War. It was developed from the Finnish *Vetehinen* design before the expiry of the Versailles Treaty, and many improvements were effected as a result of war experience. *U236* was one of the Type VIIC, the third version, and she came into service in January 1943. She was scuttled in 1945 after suffering damage by air attack.

Displacement: 769 tons (surfaced)
Armament: Five 21-in torpedo-tubes; 14 torpedoes carried; plus a variety of light AA guns *Speed:* 17 knots (surfaced) 7½ knots (submerged)

first mines off Christiansand on 10 May 1940, the first episode in a career which lasted until 1944 and accounted for 15 merchant ships and seven warships sunk, and a merchant ship and a U-Boat damaged.

The increased German naval activity in the Norwegian campaign gave Allied submarines much greater opportunities for attacking. The Polish *Orzel* sank a large troopship, the *Spearfish* damaged the pocket battleship *Lützow* severely, and the *Sunfish* sank four ships, among others. Later the *Clyde* inflicted heavy damage on the battle cruiser *Gneisenau*. These casualties, when combined with the depredations caused by surface action, were sufficient to reduce the Kriegsmarine's strength below the level needed to support the invasion of England planned after Dunkirk. Once more the submarine had intervened decisively in the conduct of war at sea, and had exerted an influence beyond all proportion to her size and cost.

In one respect the British had been extremely lucky throughout this first phase of submarine warfare; whereas their own torpedoes were reliable the Germans' magnetic pistols had proved to be uncertain.

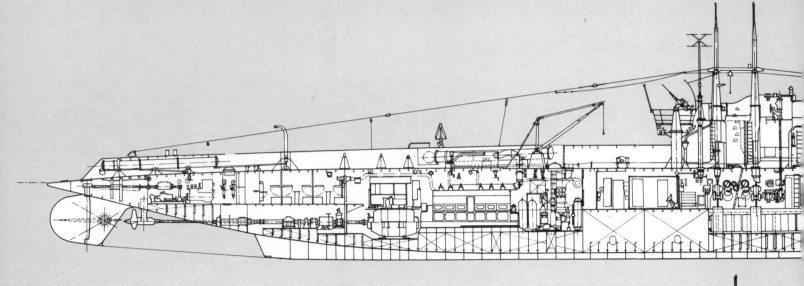

151   147   110

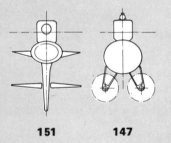

151   147

110   80

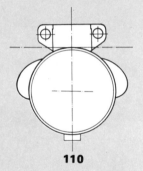

British *Telemachus*
Like the German Type VII the British 'T' Class
went through many wartime modifications.
This example shows how many changes had
been made in the original design: a changed
bow shape, external tubes now facing aft,
and a platform on the conning tower for a
20-mm AA gun. She was completed in 1943
and scrapped in 1961

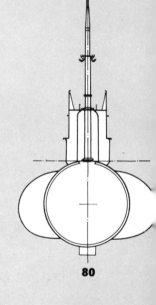

German Type IXB
These ocean-going boats were developed
from the UEII Type of the First World War,
and had more endurance than the Type VII
series. They proved less suitable for the
Western Approaches and were used in
distant waters, but their average of tonnage
sunk was as high as any other group of
U-Boats. Their main drawback was that they
took too long to build, and only 14 were
built. *Displacement:* 1,051 tons (surfaced)
Armament: Six 21-in torpedo-tubes; 22
torpedoes carried; one 105-mm gun; one
37-mm gun; one 20-mm gun *Speed:*
$18\frac{1}{4}$ knots (surfaced) $7\frac{1}{4}$ knots (submerged)

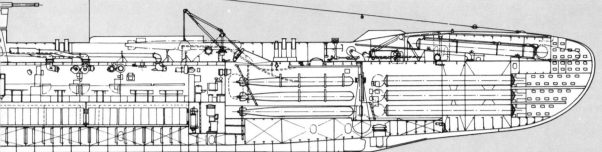

An estimated 30 attacks by U-Boats against British ships during the Spring of 1940 yielded only the submarine *Thistle* to *U4* off Skudesnes. Both the British and the Germans had been experimenting with magnetic pistols for torpedo warheads before 1939, the advantage being that a torpedo exploding beneath the keel of a

67   **23**   **12**

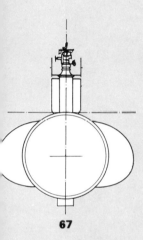

67   **23**   **12**

large warship would do far more damage than it could by exploding against its side.

New weapons often create their own antidote, and so it happened in this case that a process called 'degaussing' was immediately introduced to reduce a ship's magnetism. This could be met by increasing the sensitivity of the magnetic pistol, but the pistol was then liable to interference from the Earth's magnetic field, with the result that a deep-running torpedo might explode either prematurely or not at all.

Conforming to the well-known tendency for military and naval tactics to move in circles, the Royal Air Force matched the failure of German torpedoes by dropping bombs which did not sink U-Boats. Pre-war practice had made airmen over-optimistic about the accuracy of bombing runs against submarines, and also about the value of the conventional bomb. A bomb needs a direct hit, which is hard to achieve against the small, slender target presented by a submarine, whereas a near miss from a depth-charge can inflict vital damage to the hull. The answer to the problem was simple; the Mark VII naval pattern depth-charge was modified to make it more suitable for dropping from aircraft and came into service before the end of 1940. Later, however, properly designed airborne depth-charges were produced.

The collapse of France brought about a tremendous change in the naval situation, quite apart from the threat posed by German hopes of invading the British Isles. For a start, the loss or immobilisation of

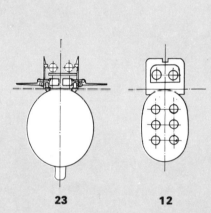

almost the entire French Fleet threw the whole burden of protecting shipping on the Royal Navy. Then the entry of Italy into the war as a partner of Germany meant that British ship-movements in the Mediterranean would be menaced by over 100 Italian submarines, in addition to whatever number of U-Boats could be spared from the Atlantic. A third factor was the greatly increased number of U-Boat bases available.

THE HUNTER OR THE HUNTED?

Imperial War Museum

Once more, Germany was attempting to strangle Britain's supply lines with an all-out submarine campaign. But while the outcome was never certain, time was against the U-Boats. Experienced commanders could not be replaced, and the manpower and materials shortage affected the U-Boats as much as any other branch of Germany's armed forces. For the second time they would come within sight of victory, and for the second time they would be denied it

By the end of 1940 many U-Boats had been moved to the French Atlantic ports, with 12 flotillas based on Brest, La Rochelle, La Pallice, St Nazaire, Lorient and Bordeaux. Being so much nearer to the Western Approaches and the North Atlantic gave them greater operating time, and so made them far more effective than before. For the same reason, when the Italian Navy offered some of its submarines to the Germans for use in the Atlantic it was decided to base them on Bordeaux rather than make them travel all the way from the Mediterranean.

The first Italian submarines to make a passage of the Straits of Gibraltar were the *Giuseppe Finzi* and *Pietro Calvi* in June 1940. After further attempts had shown how difficult it could be, owing to the currents in the Straits, the Italian Naval Staff decided to embark on the expense of setting up a permanent base at Bordeaux, and this was begun in August 1940. It came to be known as BETASOM, from *Beta* (= 'B' for Bordeaux), and *Som* (= Sommergibili), and by January 1941 the base was able to cater

for 27 submarines. This massive effort would have been very helpful to the Germans, but for the fact that the design of the Italian submarines proved so poor. They had prodigiously large conning towers, some of which were equipped with a galley and a lavatory for the comfort of watchkeepers, but had only modest surface speed.

BETASOM did its best to remedy the defects, and many desirable features of the German U-Boats were incorporated when possible. The main patrol area was off the Azores, and in the 2½ years in which Italian submarines operated they sank almost 1 million tons of Allied shipping, or an average of some 31,000 tons sunk by the 32 boats involved. When the Italians tried to make a separate peace in 1943, two of the surviving boats at Bordeaux were seized by the Germans and taken into the Kriegsmarine as *UIT21* and *22* (UIT stood for U-Italian).

As soon as the German base facilities were ready Admiral Dönitz switched to the attack once more. In August 1940 Hitler

Above: A Mosquito bomber armed with rockets attacks a diving submarine

declared a total blockade of the British Isles, thus freeing the U-Boats from the restrictions that had been in force since the beginning of the war. Success did not come easily, for the growing skill of British escorts made coastal waters too dangerous for the U-Boats, and so they had to move out westwards. Here they found the going easier, and between June and November 1940 losses of shipping rose to nearly 1,600,000 tons. Fortunately the United States replaced its 'Cash and Carry' legislation with an agreement to 'lend' war equipment, particularly 50 old but useful destroyers, in exchange for a 99-year lease on various bases throughout the British Empire.

The 'bases for equipment' exchange had little immediate effect on the U-Boat war as the destroyers took some time to be refitted as anti-submarine vessels, but it put heart into the British when they most needed it. It also depressed the Germans, who felt that America was once more trying to rob Germany of her rightful victory, and many senior Nazis urged Hitler to declare war on the United States before she could re-arm and rescue the British. But the Germans had their own problems, particularly in maintaining an adequate number of U-Boats at sea. Surprisingly little equipment from the navies of Europe had fallen into German hands, despite the swift collapse of resistance in May and June; dockyards were wrecked and although some captured submarine hulls were salvageable it would take months before they could be put back into service. The building programme had been stepped up, but like other branches of the armed services, the U-Boat Arm had been equipped for a short war, and pre-war planning for expansion had been unrealistic.

Only four U-Boats were launched between the outbreak of war and the end of 1939, and a further 60 followed in 1940. But in the same period British air and surface forces had sunk 32, and accidents had increased the total to 34. This was a much heavier loss rate than the U-Boats had sustained in the early years of the First World War, and proved that the British convoy escorts were skilled opponents. The withdrawal of destroyers from escort duties to meet the threat of German invasion after Dunkirk had denuded the convoys to a dangerous extent, and although the U-Boats scored more kills than ever before, there were only about thirty at sea at any moment, too few to exploit their enemy's weakness. This was the period of the great U-Boat aces, like Prien and Kretschmer, and some of them sank the staggering total of 200,000 tons of shipping apiece, an achievement which earned them the award of the Knight's Cross with Oak Leaves.

Birth of the 'wolf-packs'
The aces soon found that a night attack on the surface made a U-Boat almost invulnerable. The British escorts' Asdic could not detect a surfaced submarine, and it took an exceptionally sharp lookout to spot the conning tower of a U-Boat. Kretschmer went a step further, and took his U-Boat inside the columns of the convoy, the last place an escort commander would think of looking, and from this 'sanctuary' he could sink ships with impunity while his torpedoes lasted. The answer to this tactic was surface-warning Radar, but in 1940 no escorts were fitted with it, so merchant ships were fitted with illuminant rockets known as Snowflakes; when these were launched at the orders of the escort commander any U-Boat near the convoy would find itself suddenly exposed to view.

It was at this time that Admiral Dönitz began to intervene more directly in the conduct of U-Boat operations. Realising that the exploits of the aces could not be emulated by the newer submarine commanders and crews, he was anxious to use the large numbers of new boats in 'wolf packs'. The essence of the wolf pack tactics was the swamping of a convoy and its escorts by a co-ordinated attack from a group of U-Boats. To achieve this a U-Boat which made contact with a convoy was given strict orders not to attack but to signal its course and position to U-Boat Headquarters, which would then make contact with other U-Boats in the area and direct them to the original U-Boat's position. When the pack was assembled it was launched against the luckless convoy in a series of night attacks, night after night if necessary.

The chief danger from wolf pack tactics was that a U-Boat was both fast and hard to detect on the surface. Running at 17 knots on her diesels, a U-Boat could outpace the trawlers, corvettes and sloops which made up the bulk of convoy escorts in 1940 and 1941. Destroyers were faster, but too few, and in any case the lack of a radar set in all but a few ships made it difficult for any escort to sight a U-Boat. The new tactics were introduced between October 1940 and March 1941, and they proved deadly.

Another factor contributing to their success was the aerial reconnaissance provided by Focke-Wulf Condor aircraft operating from French airfields. These four-engined aircraft were able to locate convoys and shadow them for the benefit of the U-Boats, and until air-cover could be provided for convoys there was virtually no defence against them.

As stated before, the small size of the Type VII U-Boats prevented them from ranging too far in pursuit of targets, and to offset this a 'U-tanker' was introduced. The Type XIV was known to the Germans and the British as the 'Milch Cow', and each one could carry 432 tons of spare fuel and four torpedoes for transfer on the surface. Only ten were completed in 1941/42, and as Allied anti-submarine forces were told to give them top priority all were sunk. A further ten were cancelled because the growing threat from aircraft made refuelling on the surface too dangerous. For the

same reason a series of much larger supply boats, the Types XV and XVI were also cancelled.

The British adopted several counter-measures to meet the new threat. In May 1941 the first Type 271 surface search radar set went to sea in a corvette, and as it could detect a conning tower at $2\frac{1}{2}$ miles or more it put paid to surface attacks at night. Another device was High-Frequency Direction-Finding, known for short as Huff-Duff or H/F–D/F. Its principle was well known, but the British had been able to produce a set of great sensitivity which was small enough to be installed in an escort, and this meant that the vital signals sent by a shadowing U-Boat could be traced to within a quarter of a mile. The result was that the U-Boat could at least be forced to dive, and thus silenced; an immediate alteration of the convoy's course then gave the U-Boats the lengthy task of relocating the convoy and re-assembling the wolf pack.

March 1941 was a bad month for the U-Boats. Five U-Boats were sunk in the North Atlantic, including the three aces Prien (U47), Kretschmer (U99) and Schepke (U100). A month later U110 fell into British hands for long enough to allow boarders to recover her code-books. The result of this exploit was good enough for the Admiralty to keep its secret until well after the end of the Second World War. Even today it is not known exactly how much knowledge of German cyphers was gained, but it can be assumed that some of the successes against U-Boats in 1941 were attributable to the capture of U110.

There was no quick answer to the Focke-Wulf Condor, but an interim remedy was to fit some merchant ships with a catapult for launching a single Hurricane fighter aircraft. Although there was no way of recovering the fighter, it was a fair exchange for the degree of immunity conferred on the convoy if the shadower was shot down. Ideally each convoy needed its own aircraft carrier, but in 1941 this was quite beyond the Royal Navy, even if there had been sufficient aircraft to equip the carriers.

The other area in which improvements were made was weaponry. The difficulty in holding a submarine contact with Asdic as the contact came closer to the searching ship has already been mentioned; the answer was to provide a weapon which could project bombs or depth-charges ahead of the ship, while she still held the U-Boat in the Asdic beam. Development of such weapons took time, and in the meantime it was only possible to increase the number of depth-

Italian *Brin*
The 1,000-ton *Brin* Class of four boats were completed in 1938, but a year later another two were added to replace an earlier pair transferred to General Franco during the Spanish Civil War. *Armament:* Eight 21-in torpedo-tubes (forward); one 3·9-in gun; four 13·2-mm machine-guns *Speed:* 17·4 knots (surfaced) 8·7 knots (submerged)

charges which could be dropped. Before the war two depth-charge throwers and a short rack of charges was considered enough, but by 1941 most escort destroyers had surrendered a gun on the quarter-deck for a heavy outfit of four throwers and two extended racks of depth-charges. Better reloading gear was provided so that an escort could keep up a continuous attack, and the pattern of dropping charges was revised to give the maximum chance of destruction.

The standard Mark VII depth-charge had already been modified for use in aircraft, but it was also made heavier to make it sink faster. This was an attempt to reduce that gap between the time the Asdic beam lost contact with the U-Boat, and the explosion of the first charge; obviously the shorter the time interval the more precise was the attack. Another more deadly weapon was the Mark X depth-charge, a 15-ft long canister packed with Minol, one of the new explosives developed during the war. This 1-ton monster could only be fired from a torpedo-tube, and when it exploded at great depth its concussive effect produced damage over a greater radius. It had its drawbacks however: being the equivalent of a full pattern of ten ordinary depth-charges it could blow the ship's stern off if set too shallow or if the ship was moving too slowly.

In 1941 the first 'Hedgehog' appeared. This was a spigot mortar for firing 24 small bombs well ahead of the ship in an elliptical pattern. Each bomb had a 32-lb charge of Torpex (another new explosive) and a hit from one could sink a U-Boat. It allowed the firing ship to hold the target in the Asdic beam, but unlike the ordinary depth-charge a near miss did no harm at all to the U-Boat. In 1943 the British produced a fearsome weapon called 'Squid', which fired three full-sized depth-charges ahead of the ship, and thus combined the advantages of both the earlier weapons.

To be on the receiving end of these weapons was a harrowing experience. For a start there was the audible 'pinging' of the Asdic, and then if a searching escort gained contact would come the repeated concussion of patterns of depth-charges, each one containing 300 lb of high explosive. Light bulbs were shattered and small leaks could be started in the pressure hull. These were particularly dangerous as the mixture of seawater with the sulphuric acid in the batteries generated chlorine gas, which attacks the mucous membranes of the breathing passages.

A prolonged attack could keep the U-Boat down until her air-supply was exhausted even if she had not suffered structural damage. Evasive action was difficult because the noise of the electric motors could be detected by the enemy. If a submarine was trapped by a number of escorts and kept down until her air-supply ran out the choice of options was not inviting: to stay down and die of asphyxiation or blow tanks and try to fight it out on the surface.

Other ideas were germinating. At the end of 1941 the British converted a small merchant ship, the ex-German banana boat *Empire Audacity* into the first 'escort carrier', HMS *Audacity*. She carried only six Martlet fighter aircraft, which had to be parked aft on her small wooden flight deck as there had been no time to provide a lift or hangar. The purpose of this conversion was to provide a defence against the Focke-Wulf Condors which were causing a great deal of trouble to the convoys running from the British Isles to Gibraltar, but it proved that small utility aircraft carriers were a possibility. *Audacity* served for only a month before she was torpedoed off Portugal during a fierce convoy battle, but her aircraft had made so much difference that more conversions were ordered.

The entry of the United States into the war in the same month changed the whole situation, for she alone could provide the numbers of aircraft and the building resources to convert more escort carriers. As a result of strenuous British entreaties six mercantile hulls were converted in April and May 1942, and five of them were immediately transferred to the Royal Navy. However, the Americans were badly equipped for anti-submarine warfare, despite their decisive intervention in 1917, and the first result of their entry into the war was merely an inflation of the losses of merchant shipping. The U-Boats moved over to the Caribbean and the East Coast of the United States, where they found so many juicy targets that they christened the early months of 1942 the 'Happy Times'. It took only 21 U-Boats to sink 500 ships in six months.

The Americans' unpreparedness cannot be blamed on surprise, for the US Navy had been escorting ships bound for the British Isles to a 'Mid-Ocean Meeting Point', called MOMP for short, since September 1941. One destroyer had been sunk and another severely damaged by U-Boat torpedoes during this quasi-war, and the British had freely handed over information about their anti-submarine measures. Furthermore, the Admiralty had ordered 50 American-designed escorts early in 1941.

How was it, then, that the US Navy appeared to have no way of protecting shipping in its own coastal waters? The answer is that senior officers still doubted the wisdom of convoys, even after all experience had shown how vulnerable unescorted ships were to submarine attack. The Americans, having a large number of elderly destroyers, and no specialised escorts like the British sloops and corvettes, pinned their hopes on 'hunting groups', or high-speed patrols by destroyers to seek out the U-Boats before they could attack. It was seriously held by some officers that convoy was too defensive a measure to appeal to the aggressive American spirit – it might suit the more dogged, patient British but it was too old-fashioned an idea to be used by dynamic Americans.

Of course this argument had been the one used by the British from 1914 to 1917 to justify their own 'aggressive' tactics, and it ignored the inescapable fact that it was impossible to cover the ocean with patrol vessels. The submarine by virtue of its invisibility need only hide until the patrolling group had passed, and this is just what happened. During the 'Happy Times' U-Boat commanders reported that they could almost set their watches by the American patrols, which signalled their approach by plumes of smoke and impressive bow waves as a squadron of destroyers tore past at 30 knots. Once past, the length of their patrol line ensured that they would not be back for some time, and the U-Boat could rely on a free hand in running down solitary merchantmen once more. Furthermore security was bad, the American coastline was ablaze with lights, and the merchantmen chattered to one another in plain language, giving their positions regularly. Under these circumstances it is hardly surprising that 505 ships (nearly a third of the total for the whole year) were sunk in American waters before June 1942, when the US Navy finally organised all shipping into convoys.

Galling though these losses were, the

German 'Milch Cow' Type XIV
To extend the range of the Type VII U-Boats, the German Navy built ten submarine tankers in 1941. With a fatter and shorter hull than the Type IX boats, and less power, they could carry sufficient fuel to keep four or five U-Boats at sea for twice as long as usual, and they also carried four spare torpedoes in external stowage. They were made top priority targets for Allied ships and all ten were sunk. *Displacement:* 1,688 tons (surfaced) *Armament:* Two 37-mm AA guns; one 20-mm AA gun; no torpedo-tubes

British and Americans were able to co-ordinate their counter-measures very well. The programme of 50 British destroyer escorts (BDEs) was hurriedly expanded to 250, and further designs were put into mass-production, so that eventually over 1,000 hulls were on order by 1943. As an emergency measure, Lend-Lease was put into reverse to allow 25 'Flower' Class corvettes to be transferred to the USN, and the new British escort design, the 'River' Class frigate was put into production in American yards. But convoy proved to be the essential measure once again, and when introduced brought the shipping losses back under control.

Not that the position of the Allies was anything but alarming. In 1941 Great Britain had lost a total of 4,328,558 tons of shipping, representing 1,299 ships in all; U-Boats had sunk over 2 million tons (432 ships) while surface raiders, aircraft and mines accounted for the rest. But in 1942 the U-Boats alone sank over 6 million tons, while the total losses from all causes amounted to 7,790,697 tons (1,664 ships). It was April 1917 all over again, except that this time all possible counter-measures had been put into effect and yet the U-Boats were winning. In January 1942 the Germans had 91 U-Boats operational, and although 87 were lost during the year, new construction meant that 212 were operational by December.

The scent of victory

Dönitz and his submarines could smell the scent of victory in the air, and he exhorted them to greater efforts. It was essential for the U-Boats to prevent the Americans from bringing their enormous resources to bear on Europe, and Dönitz calculated that it would take a monthly loss rate of 800,000 tons of Allied shipping to starve out the British and prevent the Americans from implementing their strategic plans to liberate the Mediterranean and the Continent of Europe.

The average monthly losses of shipping in 1942 were running at 650,000 tons, which was far beyond the rate of replacement, so the first priority for the United States was to build more merchant ships. With boundless ingenuity and energy American shipyards devised methods of mass-producing ships, and soon 'Liberty' and 'Victory' standard hulls began to appear in numbers. The British were beginning to see the results of their large warship-building programmes of 1940/41, and in 1942 the first 'River' Class frigates appeared, 1,400-ton twin-screw ships with enough endurance to cross the Atlantic and more speed than a surfaced U-Boat. With more radar sets and H/F-D/F sets available for escort vessels the existing convoy escorts were also better equipped to fight off wolf pack attacks, and this was reflected in the large number of sinkings in 1942.

The U-Boats were helped at this time by the so-called 'black gaps' in mid-Atlantic, five areas which were out of range of shore-based aircraft. In these areas U-Boats could stalk convoys without the fear of being forced to dive by an aircraft, and they sank many ships with little loss to themselves. The introduction of more escort carriers in the late summer of 1942 and the provision of a handful of VLR (Very Long Range) Liberator bombers helped to close the air gap, but the numbers of both would remain small until 1943.

A useful interim measure was the MAC-ship or Merchant Aircraft Carrier, which

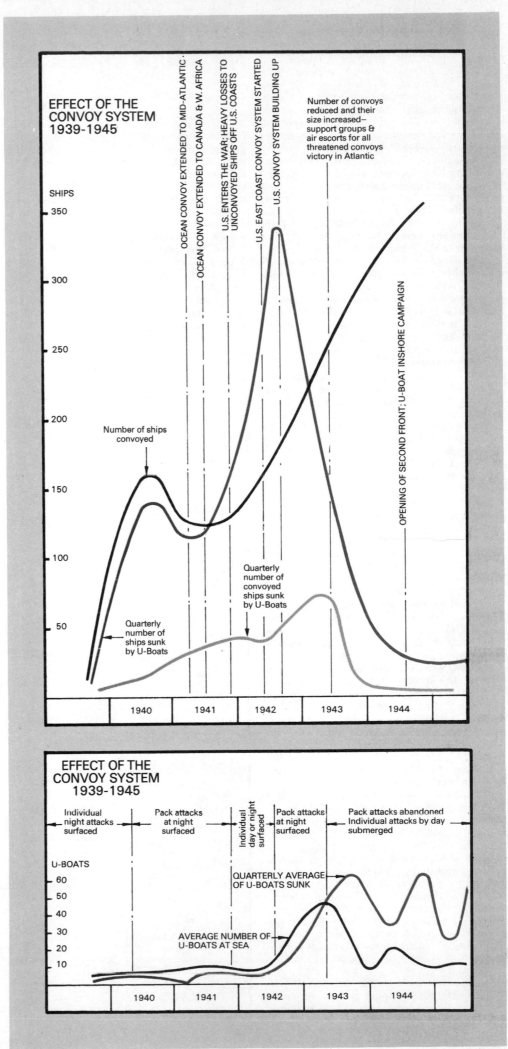

was an oil-tanker or grain-carrier equipped with a plywood flight deck to allow her to operate four aircraft. The virtue of this compromise was that it did not prevent the ship from continuing to carry her valuable cargoes, whereas an escort carrier was completely gutted and converted to a warship. On the other hand an escort carrier operated from 15 to 24 aircraft, and had the necessary communications equipment for controlling aircraft over a convoy.

The U-Boats continued their grim war of extermination, for their goal of 800,000 tons of enemy shipping sunk per month seemed within reach. Indeed Admiral Dönitz believed that they had reached the magic figure, but as in the First World War, U-Boat commanders tended to over-estimate the tonnage of their victims. As we have seen, the losses did not exceed 650,000 tons, which meant that the collapse of the Allies was further away than Dönitz thought. New torpedoes and devices were coming forward, and it was hoped that these would tip the scale. The most important were the homing torpedo and a radar impulse detector, the torpedo to increase the rate of hits and the detector to reduce the chances of being surprised by ship or aircraft on the surface.

The first homing torpedo was issued in January 1943, and was known as the T4 or 'Falke', but after only thirty had been used it was replaced by the better-known T5 'Zaunkönig'. This was the weapon known to the British as the 'Gnat' (for German Naval Acoustic Torpedo), and it travelled at the relatively low speed of 25 knots to reduce interference from its own noise.

Two factors combined to frustrate the Allies' efforts to beat the U-Boat offensive in 1942. The first was the Americans' virtual withdrawal of their escort forces from the Atlantic in June 1942, because these were needed for the Pacific against the Japanese. The second factor was the need to earmark escorts for the large convoys which would be needed for the invasion of North Africa, 'Operation Torch'. Although they were still responsible for coastal escort work, the American ships retained in the Atlantic now formed 2 per cent of the escort forces available, with the British and Canadians sharing the burden in a 50:48 ratio. This dilution of effort was unavoidable, but it gave the U-Boats a chance to inflict even heavier losses than they might have done, when the escorts were at full stretch.

To counterbalance this problem the large number of escort vessels coming into service did allow the British to organise the first experimental support group in September 1942. This was a group of escorts which operated independently in search of U-Boats, but kept itself at readiness to go to the aid of a hard-pressed convoy. It should not be confused with the old-style hunting groups, because it was based on the convoy system rather than being a replacement for it. The basic idea was to leave the convoy's escort to look after the close-range defence, while the support group could pursue and harry U-Boats to destruction. All too frequently a convoy escort had to leave a promising contact because she had to return to the convoy, and the support group idea promised to increase the number of sinkings. This is exactly what happened, particularly because support groups were able to operate in the areas where U-Boats were concentrated.

At the start of 1943 both sides were in a strong position. The U-Boats were well led and their achievements in 1942 meant that officers and men were experienced. Against them were ranged a growing force of aircraft and ships equally determined and skilled. Behind both antagonists were the designers and scientists, whose influence would prove decisive.

The first round went to the U-Boats in March. Acting on intelligence gathered after German cryptanalysts broke into the British convoy cypher, Admiral Dönitz arranged a heavy concentration of U-Boats against two eastbound convoys. This led to a successful interception, by a total of 39 U-Boats, of the slow convoy 5C-122, totalling 52 ships, and the faster HX-229, with only 25 ships. Finding the fast convoy first, the U-Boats were able to sink eight ships in a space of less than eight hours. The slow convoy fared rather better when another group of U-Boats attacked, but one U-Boat, *U338*, was able to sink four merchant ships with five torpedoes. During the next three days the convoys were joined to give their escorts a chance to fight back, but even this did not prevent the U-Boats from sinking another nine ships. In all 140,000 tons of shipping had been sunk, for the loss of only three U-Boats.

This great convoy battle marks the high point of the U-Boat offensive. Dönitz almost achieved his dream of making the convoy system unworkable, for the immediate reaction at the Admiralty was to consider the reintroduction of independent sailings until fresh counter-measures could be devised. At no time did Hitler come closer to victory, for if his U-Boats had cut communications

THE CRISIS

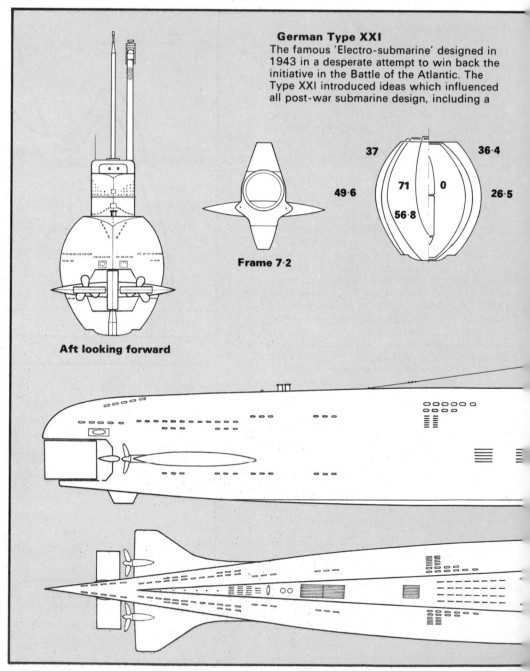

German Type XXI
The famous 'Electro-submarine' designed in 1943 in a desperate attempt to win back the initiative in the Battle of the Atlantic. The Type XXI introduced ideas which influenced all post-war submarine design, including a

Frame 7·2

Aft looking forward

between Britain and North America, not only would the British have been starved into impotence, but he would have been free to turn his whole might against Russia. Fortunately March 1943 was the turning point, and the U-Boats were shortly to receive their most devastating setback.

The first gleam of hope for the Allies was the intervention of escort carriers and support groups, which had been held back to cover 'Operation Torch'. With that landing successfully achieved, all the vital ships and aircraft which had been taken away from the Atlantic were now thrown back into the battle. Then President Roosevelt intervened to make 61 VLR Liberators available to the RAF, a welcome reversal of policy. But the scientists made the biggest contribution, for they had perfected a short-wave radar set for use in aircraft, the ASV (Air to Surface Vessel) set. ASV transmissions could not be picked up by the U-Boats' existing radar receivers, and losses to aircraft attack rose alarmingly. In May another great convoy battle was fought, but this time aircraft and two support groups intervened, with the result that eight out of twelve U-Boats were lost. It was in a frantic effort to find an answer to this unexpected

reversal of fortune that the U-Boat Command committed two fundamental blunders.

Basing his calculations on the premise that the Metox receiver would give ample warning of any radar-assisted attack, Dönitz decided that submarines could meet aircraft on equal terms provided that each U-Boat had its anti-aircraft armament increased. Conning tower platforms were extended, and a variety of weapons was added forward and aft. The common weapon was the 2-cm Flak 'vierling', a deadly four-barrelled automatic weapon, but single 2-cm and 37-mm weapons were also added, and twin 2-cm. As the main opponents were Sunderland flying boats and Liberator bombers, neither of them very fast or manoeuvrable aircraft, such an array of guns made a surfaced U-Boat an ugly customer, particularly when air crew were not expecting her to stay on the surface to fight it out.

This was the first of the blunders made by Dönitz and his advisers, for skilled air crew did not take long to devise tactics which neutralised the so-called 'aircraft trap' They simply flew around the U-Boat out of range, while calling up the nearest warship to come and sink her; if at any time the

U-Boat started to dive, the aircraft then rapidly switched to the attack. This led to the 'Battle of Seconds', the U-Boat crews' term for the vital 30-40 seconds needed to clear decks before diving, and many inexperienced U-Boat personnel died simply because they could not get below fast enough.

The second error made by the Germans was a more technical one. Faced with disturbing reports from U-Boat commanders about attacks from aircraft at night when the Metox receiver had given no indication of a radar search, the German scientists refused to consider the possibility of centimetric wave-bands on the grounds that they had already tried this idea without success. A similar reluctance to accept the existence of H/F-D/F in 1942 had caused casualties, but in the spring of 1943 such a mistake was deadly.

The problem was not helped when a captured British bomb-aimer casually revealed that aircraft could track the emissions from a Metox set. When the Germans found that the Metox set did produce emissions which could be tracked, they jumped to the wrong conclusion, and blamed the Metox for all their problems.

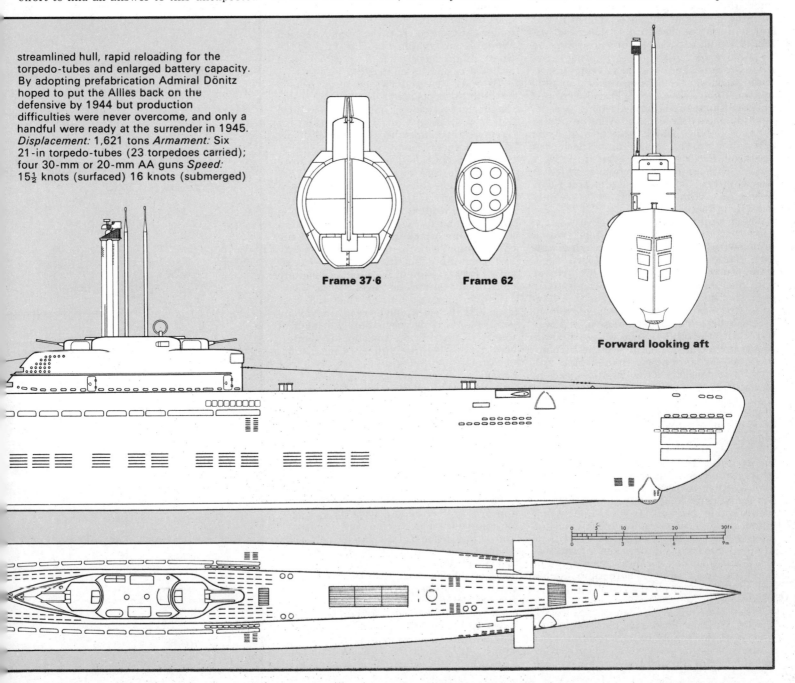

streamlined hull, rapid reloading for the torpedo-tubes and enlarged battery capacity. By adopting prefabrication Admiral Dönitz hoped to put the Allies back on the defensive by 1944 but production difficulties were never overcome, and only a handful were ready at the surrender in 1945. *Displacement:* 1,621 tons *Armament:* Six 21-in torpedo-tubes (23 torpedoes carried); four 30-mm or 20-mm AA guns *Speed:* 15½ knots (surfaced) 16 knots (submerged)

Frame 37·6

Frame 62

Forward looking aft

However, a new receiver which cured the fault did nothing to halt the sinkings, and only when it was too late to affect the outcome did the Germans discover that however many signals were emitted by the Metox, the centimetric wave-band of the ASV set gave far more accurate bearings, and it was this which was causing the losses.

The collapse of the U-Boat campaign was dramatic. In May a pair of convoys like SC-122 and HX-229 reached Britain without loss, having sunk six U-Boats on the way. In the same month escorts achieved a record, with more U-Boats than merchant ships sunk, and the figures show how savagely the escorts were mauling the U-Boats in revenge:

Month	Shipping sunk	U-Boats sunk
April	245,000 tons	15
May	165,000 tons	40
June	18,000 tons	17
July	123,000 tons	37

Dönitz had no choice but to withdraw his U-Boats from the battle and concede a temporary defeat, while his technicians and scientists worked on the new weapons which were under development.

The new acoustic torpedoes have been mentioned, but there was also the 'Schnorchel', that half-forgotten Dutch device for running diesels at periscope depth. It was hurriedly introduced into service, and was made a standard fitting for new construction as a move to reduce the crippling losses from aircraft. There were passive devices as well, such as the 'Pillenwerfer' or Submarine Bubble Target (SBT), which was a chemical compound released from a torpedo-tube; it acted like a giant Alka-Seltzer to produce bubbles which gave a false Asdic echo, but rarely fooled an experienced operator. Periscopes and even hulls were coated with rubber compounds which it was hoped would absorb Asdic and radar pulses, but again these measures were only partially effective.

The ace up the Germans' sleeve was the new Walther propulsion system, which promised to revolutionise submarine warfare. This was basically a closed cycle steam turbine, which burned an oxidant with oil fuel to dispense with atmospheric oxygen. The Walther system used a concentrated form of hydrogen peroxide known as Perhydrol which decomposed and was burnt with the oil fuel to produce a mixture of gas and steam which drove the turbine. It offered far more power than electric propulsion, and promised underwater speeds in excess of 25 knots.

The first Walther turbine had been tested in an experimental submarine as far back as 1940, but the first production U-Boat to receive it was *U791*. She was not commissioned, but experience with her was incorporated into the Type XVIIA U-Boats, which were coastal submarines powered by two Walther turbines coupled to a single shaft, and capable of about 25 knots. Under considerable pressure from U-Boat Command, the designers produced drawings for improved types, the XVIIB and XVIIG, but to speed construction only one of the turbines was installed. Despite this a speed of 20 knots was attained, more than double that of the conventional Type VII and Type IX U-Boats in service.

There were many drawbacks, however, and the Walther submarine must rank with some of Hitler's more bizarre tank projects as an interesting idea which absorbed far too much material and time at the expense

of less ambitious projects which were suffering setbacks.

The chief difficulty was in the manufacture and storage of the fuel, known as 'Ingolin'. This was highly unstable, and any impurity in the storage tanks led to decomposition and spontaneous combustion; only clinical sterility would do, and eventually synthetic rubber was discovered to be the least dangerous material for lining the tanks. Ingolin was also very expensive to make, costing about eight times as much as oil, and was consumed at a prodigious rate, so that a Type XVIIA boat could only travel 80 miles at top speed – which put the clock back to about 1900 as far as operational radius was concerned.

These problems were realised by Dönitz, and at a conference with Hitler in July 1943 he mentioned the existence of a new interim design known as the 'Electro' submarine, which was to bridge the gap between the ordinary schnorchel-equipped U-Boats and the first Type XVII boats. This was the famous Type XXI, actually a conventionally-propelled submarine, but redesigned to make use of every possible advance to offset the recent Allied successes. The improvements can be summarised as basically a streamlined hull to reduce underwater drag, and enlarged battery-capacity to give higher underwater speed. Had the Type XXI been available in greater numbers in 1944 U-Boats might have made a comeback and inflicted casualties at the 1942 level.

To boost the underwater speed from 9 knots to $15\frac{1}{2}$ knots it was necessary to treble the battery capacity, but they were also fitted with silent auxiliary motors for 'creeping' at 5 knots. To allow attacks from safer distances the torpedo salvo was increased to six tubes, and 17 reloads were carried. Wartime experience showed that a torpedo-tube took at least 10 minutes to reload by hand, so the Type XXIs were given mechanical loading to reduce the strain on the crew and to give them the chance to follow up an attack quickly. Although the conventional conning tower had given way to a streamlined 'fin', the menace of aircraft called for two pairs of AA guns in remotely controlled positions on top of the fin.

Dönitz promised Hitler that the first Type XXI U-Boat would be ready in November 1944, but Hitler immediately demanded that the Konstruktion-Amt should do better, even if it meant three-shift working. Reichsminister Albert Speer was given the job of organising the mass-production of Type XXIs, and he hoped to produce 20 per month. But in that strange mixture of efficiency and muddle which characterised the war effort of the Third Reich, the obsolescent Type VIIC was allowed to continue in production, while the Type XXI was entrusted to 'diluted' labour, i.e. a small proportion of skilled workmen padded out with old men, women and even children.

The territorial ambitions of the Germans now proved their undoing. The Army's need for manpower and the aircraft industry's over-riding demands for strategic materials meant that even if the U-Boat programme had been completed it was unlikely that the boats could have been manned. Dönitz told Hitler that in the second half of 1943 production would be running at 27 U-Boats per month, and it was hoped to increase this to 30 per month by 1945. But the existing programme was using 6,000 tons of steel each month, 4,500 tons for U-Boat hulls and 1,500 tons for torpedoes. He also pointed out

that if production rose to 40 U-Boats per month extra personnel would have to be found. The Kriegsmarine's allowance was 102,984 men, and the estimated manpower requirement was already 334,838 men short.

The Army had taken the largest amount of manpower since April 1942, when Hitler had been preparing for his ill-conceived

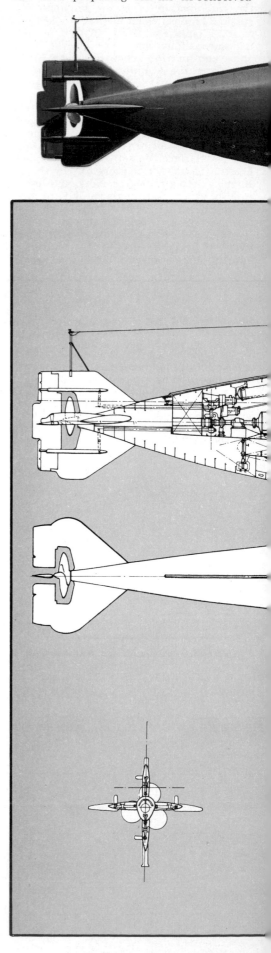

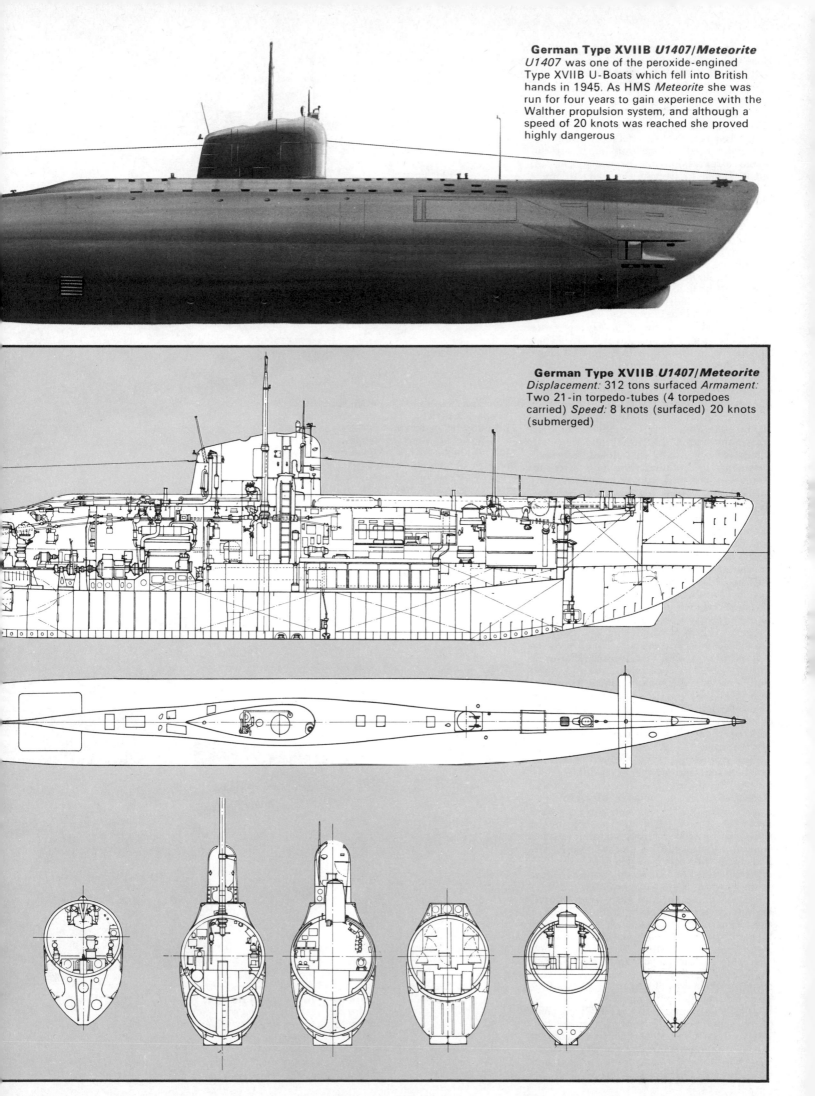

German Type XVIIB *U1407/Meteorite*
U1407 was one of the peroxide-engined
Type XVIIB U-Boats which fell into British
hands in 1945. As HMS *Meteorite* she was
run for four years to gain experience with the
Walther propulsion system, and although a
speed of 20 knots was reached she proved
highly dangerous

German Type XVIIB *U1407/Meteorite*
Displacement: 312 tons surfaced *Armament:*
Two 21-in torpedo-tubes (4 torpedoes
carried) *Speed:* 8 knots (surfaced) 20 knots
(submerged)

invasion of Russia. At the 1943 rate of U-Boat production (25–30 boats per month) this left the Navy short of 200,000 men. The officer candidates who had entered in the autumn of 1939 had all become commanders by the summer of 1943, and it would be necessary to transfer some officers from the Army and Air Force to make up numbers. This was finally done, and many of the 'expatriate' submariners proved successful, but it is easy to see why the sledgehammer blows of the Allies in the spring of 1943 were able to bring about the collapse of morale in the U-Boat Arm. All had given of their best, and continued to do so, but there was no way of wringing greater effort out of them.

Although the U-Boats continued to be dangerous, throughout the rest of 1943 and 1944 they lacked the ferocious determination that had characterised their earlier efforts. The schnorchel was partly to blame, for its value was negative rather than positive; while using it a U-Boat was relatively safe, but she did not have that freedom of movement which she had once enjoyed on the surface. Even her dangerous acoustic torpedoes were rendered harmless by noise-makers towed astern of escorts, known as 'Foxers', and the schnorchel could be detected by radar in smooth conditions. The invasion of Normandy in 1944 meant the end of the Biscay and Brittany bases, and the loss of Italy closed the Mediterranean to U-Boats. The only area in which U-Boats still enjoyed any measure of success was in Northern Norway and the Arctic, against Allied convoys to Russia.

The emphasis switched to midget submarines and special assault craft known generically as 'K-craft', to hold up invasion fleets. Many different types were built, but they scored very few successes, even against the vast D-Day Invasion fleet of 5,000 ships. The best-known were the 'Molch' (Salamander), 'Hecht' (Pike), 'Seehund' (Seal), 'Biber' (Beaver), 'Marder' (Marten) and 'Neger' (Negro) of which the Seehund type proved the most successful. Like all midgets they were only effective in fairly sheltered waters, and Allied counter-measures were sufficient to avoid serious losses. However they did prove one interesting point: they were so light that the blast from a depth-charge merely swept them aside without sinking them. The effect on the crew is not recorded.

Finally the first Type XXI U-Boats were finished, and four were commissioned early in 1945. But it is not possible to put a revolutionary type of submarine straight into service, and *U2511* did not leave for her first operational patrol until a week before the German surrender. A smaller, cruder coastal version, known as the Type XXIII, had come into service a little earlier, and although the handful completed had a few successes they were also too late.

The end came on 7 May 1945, when Dönitz, by now Hitler's successor and also head of the German Navy, broadcast instructions to all U-Boats to cease hostilities and to comply with the Allies' conditions. They were told to surface, and to fly a black flag while making their way to the nearest warship to make a formal surrender. In this way hundreds of U-Boats made their way to Lisahally in Northern Ireland. There they lay in their melancholy lines, just as they had at Harwich in 1919. Twice in a generation U-Boats had taken on the world, twice they had nearly won a great victory, and now they had failed once again.

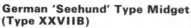

German 'Seehund' Type Midget (Type XXVIIB)
This two-man midget was developed from the XXVIIA 'Hecht', and was the most successful of the German midgets. Like the others, it was armed with underslung torpedoes. Some 450 were completed by 1945 and a further 650 were cancelled. *Displacement:* 15 tons (surfaced) *Armament:* Two 21-in torpedoes *Speed* 7¾ knots (surfaced) 6 knots (submerged)

German 'Molch' Type Midget
A third one-man type, from a different builder. Molch was similar to Biber, and nearly 400 were completed

German 'Marder' Type Midget
A one-man torpedo, with a G7E torpedo slung underneath the main body. About 300 Marders were completed

German 'Biber' Type Midget
Another one-man type, but armed with two torpedoes. Over 300 were completed. Like Marder, Biber was intended for use against invasion fleets, and could be moved by road or rail to their area of operations

BRITISH MIDGET SUBMARINES

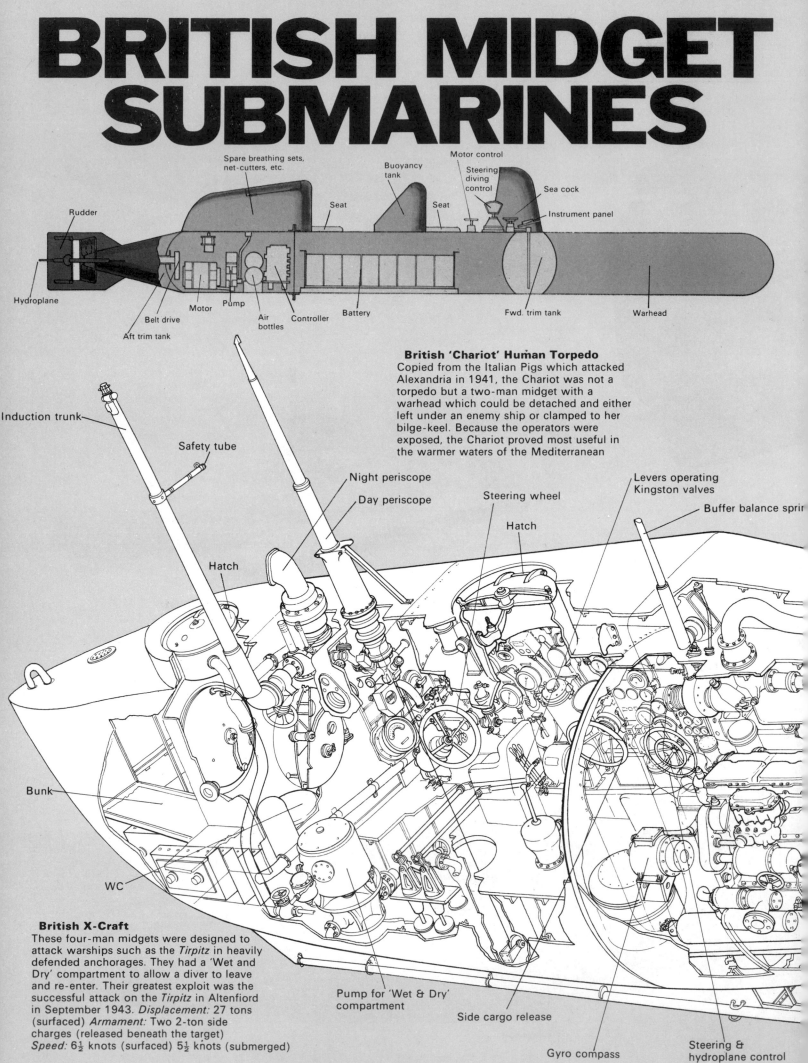

Spare breathing sets, net-cutters, etc.

Buoyancy tank

Motor control

Steering diving control

Seat

Seat

Sea cock

Instrument panel

Rudder

Hydroplane

Belt drive

Aft trim tank

Motor

Pump

Air bottles

Controller

Battery

Fwd. trim tank

Warhead

British 'Chariot' Human Torpedo
Copied from the Italian Pigs which attacked Alexandria in 1941, the Chariot was not a torpedo but a two-man midget with a warhead which could be detached and either left under an enemy ship or clamped to her bilge-keel. Because the operators were exposed, the Chariot proved most useful in the warmer waters of the Mediterranean

Induction trunk

Safety tube

Night periscope

Day periscope

Steering wheel

Hatch

Levers operating Kingston valves

Buffer balance sprin

Hatch

Bunk

WC

British X-Craft
These four-man midgets were designed to attack warships such as the *Tirpitz* in heavily defended anchorages. They had a 'Wet and Dry' compartment to allow a diver to leave and re-enter. Their greatest exploit was the successful attack on the *Tirpitz* in Altenfiord in September 1943. *Displacement:* 27 tons (surfaced) *Armament:* Two 2-ton side charges (released beneath the target) *Speed:* 6½ knots (surfaced) 5½ knots (submerged)

Pump for 'Wet & Dry' compartment

Side cargo release

Gyro compass

Steering & hydroplane control

Although the last in the field, the British made the most impressive use of midget submarines. They copied the Italian 'pigs', calling them 'Chariots', and then designed a range of battery-driven midgets to penetrate the Norwegian anchorages which were sheltering German heavy units. In 1941/42 ships like the *Bismarck* and *Tirpitz* were beyond the range of heavy bombers, and there was no other way to penetrate a Norwegian fiord.

One of the leading advocates of midget submarines was Commander Varley, who had served in submarines in the First World War. His firm built the prototype *X3*, while Portsmouth Dockyard built *X4*. Six production models were begun in December 1942, and by September 1943 they and their hand-picked crews were ready to attack the battleship *Tirpitz* in Altenfiord. Unlike the Italian and Japanese midgets, these 'X-craft' did not have torpedoes, but carried side-charges, containing a half ton of explosive each, which were dropped underneath the target. Although fitted with a diesel engine as well as an electric motor, they were too small to undertake long passages and were always towed to their target area by full-sized submarines.

The attack on the *Tirpitz* on 22 September 1943 was a great success, for although the charges did not sink her, they inflicted such damage on her that she was eventually moved south for repairs. Here she was at last within range of bombers, and she was finally eliminated little more than a year later. All six of the X-craft were lost, including one which broke down on the way out, and the surviving one, *X10*, which was scuttled afterwards. A slightly enlarged version, the XE-craft, was built for the Far East. They had more stowage space and had the blessing of air-conditioning to reduce the strain on the four- or five-man crew. There was also an air-lock to allow a diver to leave the midget and place limpet mines on the target's hull, and spring-loaded legs to make it easier for the midget to rest on the bottom.

Before the Normandy invasion in June 1944 midgets were used to reconnoitre landing beaches, and to provide information on tides and obstructions. On D-Day itself several acted as navigation beacons well inshore to guide the first assault wave. In the Far East they revived Simon Lake's ideas of fifty years earlier by sending out divers to cut submarine cables. Chariots were used in Norway, but the water proved far too cold for the crews, and they proved better suited to the Mediterranean where they sank the Italian cruisers *Gorizia*, *Bolzano* and *Ulpio Traiano*.

British 'Welman' Type Midget
A one-man craft capable of fixing a 560-lb charge to its target by magnetic clips. It is not known how many Welmans were produced, but they proved unreliable

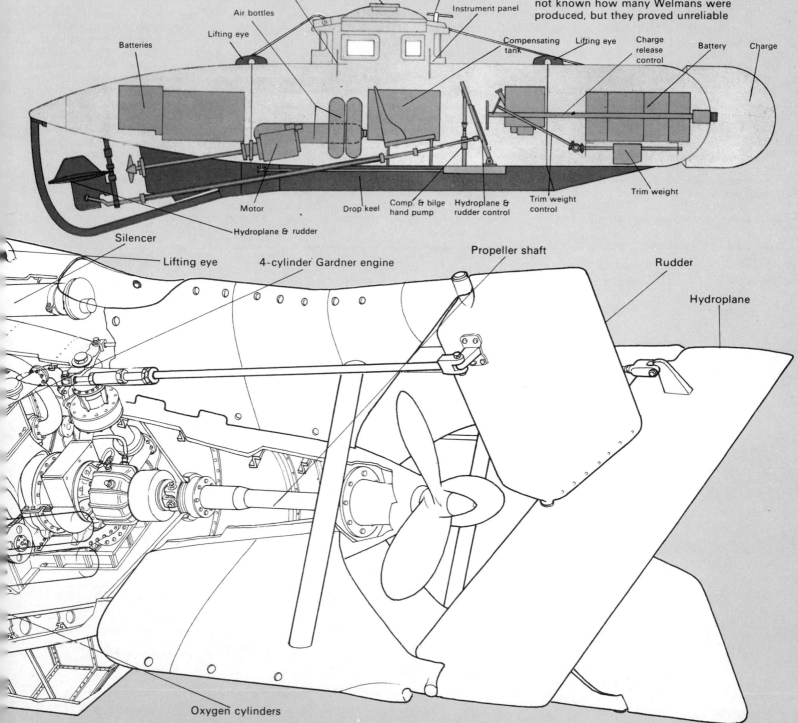

SUBMARINES IN THE MEDITERRANEAN

The submarine **war** that the British had feared in the Mediterranean when Italy entered the war in June 1940 did not take the form expected. This was partly due to the inertia of the Italian Navy, whose few energetic submariners were shortly to be sent to Bordeaux, but particularly because Admiral Dönitz was so reluctant to weaken the U-Boat offensive in the Atlantic by sending boats to the Mediterranean. For the British submarines, however, there were tempting targets in the form of Italian shipping taking supplies to the Italian and German troops fighting in North Africa. On the other hand the Mediterranean was dangerous for submarines: land-based aircraft were within a short flying distance at any time, and they could spot a submarine at a depth of up to 50 feet in calm weather, as against the North Sea, where a submarine is virtually invisible at periscope depth, or the Atlantic, where visibility extends only 30 feet down in ideal conditions.

Reverses to British fortunes, both on land and at sea, made it very hard to exploit the weakness of the Italians. The Luftwaffe had reinforced the Regia Aeronautica, which gave the Axis Powers air superiority over large areas of the Mediterranean and thus made the British submarines' job very difficult. Losses were heavy among the large submarines of the 'O', 'P' and 'R' Classes, not least because of their leaky external fuel tanks.

Nevertheless, in the early months of 1941 there were many successes. It is odd to note that British submarines were still forbidden to sink merchant ships without warning, and it was not until February 1941 that the Cabinet removed the restriction, on the assumption that all shipping found south of 35 46' N was hostile. By May over 100,000 tons of German and Italian shipping had been sunk by submarines operating out of Malta, Gibraltar and Alexandria.

In mid-1941 British submarine activity reached a new peak, when the three flotillas sank a further 150,000 tons of shipping. It was a repetition of the Sea of Marmora campaign of 1915, with the gun being used as much as the torpedo, and coastal targets such as bridges and railway lines coming under attack. Quite apart from the loss of supplies to the Italians and the German Africa Korps, which was described by the Germans as 'unendurable', these widespread activities strained a naval organisation which had never been very strong. Had this situation continued the British were heading for an impressive victory over their enemies at relatively small cost, but just when they seemed unstoppable, disaster struck.

U-Boats in the Mediterranean

Once again, the submarine had taken a hand. At last the losses and demoralisation of Axis naval forces in the Mediterranean forced the Germans to allow some of their precious U-Boats to be transferred to the Mediterranean. When they arrived they found that the British anti-submarine tactics had grown rusty because of the poor performance of the Italians. The sequence of events was a grim lesson for the British, who had grown used to their freedom. The first important victim was the aircraft carrier *Ark Royal*, torpedoed in the Western Mediterranean by *U81* and *U205* on 13 November 1941. Next to go was the battleship *Barham*, torpedoed in the Eastern

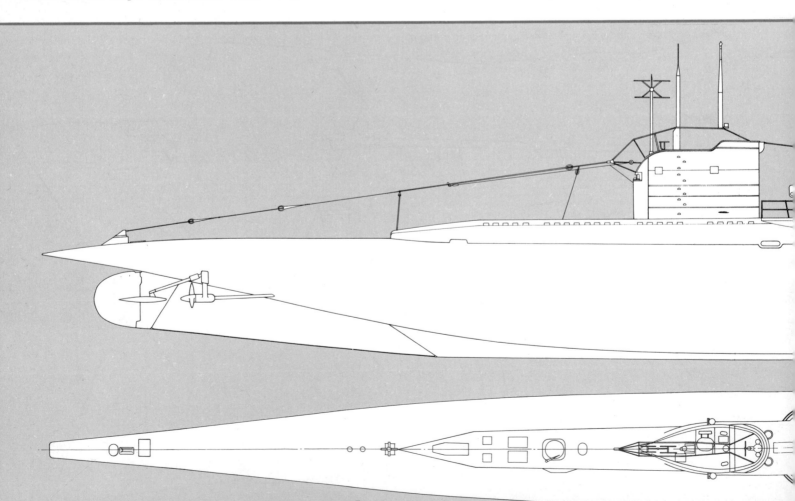

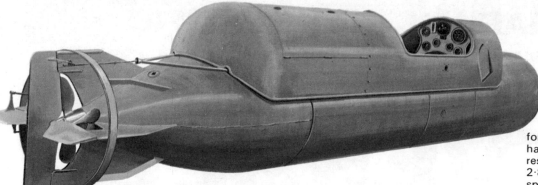

Mediterranean by *U331* on 25 November, and the light cruiser *Galatea*, sunk by *U557* on 15 December.

The exploits of Italian submarines were hardly notable for their vigour, but in one area the Italian Navy showed not only ingenuity but great personal courage. During the First World War they had pioneered midget submarines as well as special assault craft for penetrating defended harbours. Profiting by this experience they developed the 'Maiali' or 'Pig', a torpedo-shaped small submersible craft which was controlled by two men wearing self-contained underwater breathing apparatus (SCUBA gear). The operators rode the body of the craft, hence its nick-name of 'human torpedo', but it differed from a torpedo in that it was simply a slow-moving underwater vehicle to allow two frogmen to move about an anchorage. The 'warhead' was detached from the nose of the 'pig' and then attached to any convenient projection on the bottom of the target vessel, such as a bilge keel, by clamps.

The 'pigs' could not travel far, so the submarines *Scire* and *Gondar* were converted to carry three each in watertight containers on deck. After an abortive attempt against ships in Gibraltar in September 1941 the *Scire* was sent to Alexandria two months later. On the night of 18 December she put her three crews over the side; as luck would have it, a British cruiser was entering the harbour and so the three 'pigs' were able to slip through the net defences without any difficulty. They found their targets, the battleships *Queen Elizabeth* and *Valiant* and an oiler, and duly placed their charges. Early the next morning the charges went off, causing heavy damage to the two battleships. Coming so soon after the other losses, it meant that the Royal Navy's heavy units in the Mediterranean had been wiped out, and that the initiative had passed to the Germans and Italians.

Other events in the Far East were to add to the Royal Navy's problems. For on 7 December the Japanese had launched their crippling attack on the American Pacific Fleet at Pearl Harbour, and had followed this by sinking the British capital ships *Prince of Wales* and *Repulse*. Aircraft, warships and shipping had to be switched to the Far East, stripping the Mediterranean to the bone. The only naval forces left to harass the Axis supply lines were submarines, but now they had to operate in the face of enemy air superiority. Their base at Malta was under constant air attack, and it became necessary to submerge and lie on the bottom of the harbour by day, surfacing to recharge batteries at night.

As early as May 1941 Malta's position had been precarious, and so the minelaying submarine HMS *Rorqual* was sent on an experimental supply run. She took three weeks to convert at Alexandria, and finally sailed on 5 June with over 100 tons of urgently-needed stores, including high-octane fuel, kerosene and medical supplies. A second trip on 25 June showed that with careful attention to stowage even more fuel could be carried, and later in the year the fleet submarine *Clyde* took 1,200 tons of supplies, at a time when hardly any surface ships could get through. More runs were made by the *Osiris*, *Porpoise* and *Urge*, and by the middle of 1942 submarines had taken 65,000 tons into Grand Harbour, a staggering feat which was only matched by the efforts of the Japanese in the Pacific.

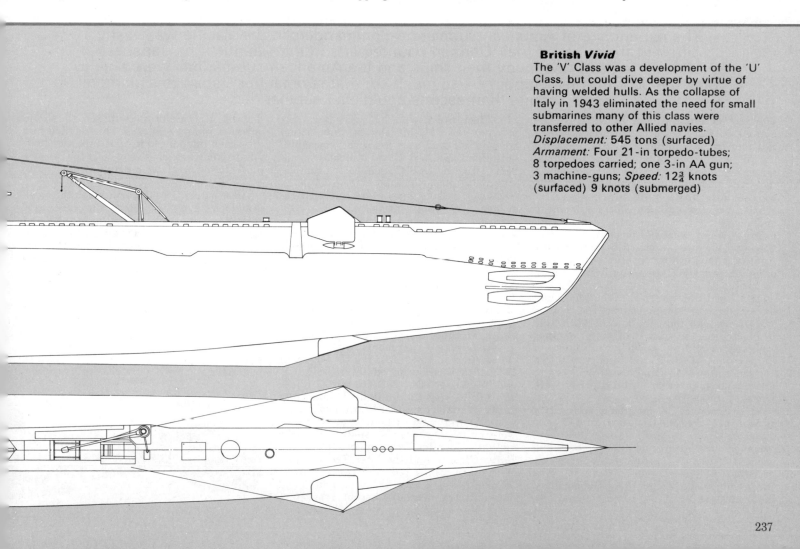

British *Vivid*
The 'V' Class was a development of the 'U' Class, but could dive deeper by virtue of having welded hulls. As the collapse of Italy in 1943 eliminated the need for small submarines many of this class were transferred to other Allied navies.
Displacement: 545 tons (surfaced)
Armament: Four 21-in torpedo-tubes; 8 torpedoes carried; one 3-in AA gun; 3 machine-guns; *Speed:* 12¾ knots (surfaced) 9 knots (submerged)

THE ROLES REVERSED

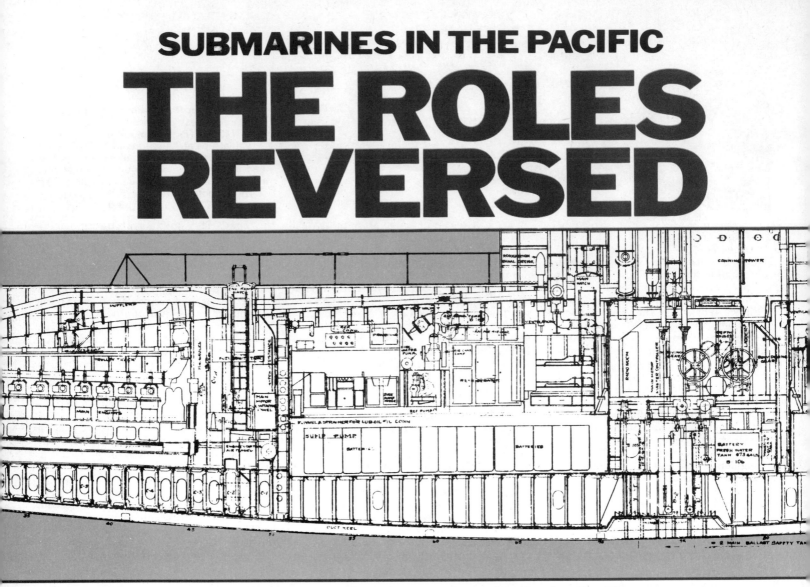

The experience of American submarine-commanders in the Pacific was vastly different from that of their German counterparts in the Atlantic. The Japanese stubbornly refused to convoy their ships and the American submarines were able to play havoc with their shipping — so much so, that submarines began to sink more escorts than escorts could sink submarines

The destruction and immobilisation of the United States Navy's battleships at Pearl Harbour left it with only two ways of carrying the war to the Japanese: carrier-borne aircraft and submarines. By December 1941 the USN had 113 submarines, of which 64 were elderly boats built during the First World War and suitable only for training and coastal work, nine large cruiser-submarines which were not mechanically reliable, and 40 newer submarines. Fortunately Congress had authorised a further 73 boats, of which some 30 were actually under construction.

Although the number of builders had dwindled to three as a result of the Depression, American industry had little trouble in expanding the output of diesel engines and electric motors, so when the Bureau of Ships asked for three additional yards, two commercial builders and one Navy Yard to undertake submarine building, they were able to provide them.

At this point it is opportune to insert a note about the classification of US submarines. From 1911 all submarines were assigned class letters and hull numbers, and the old fish and reptile names were discarded. The 'V' series were distinguished by the numbers *V1–V9* as Fleet Submarines, but in 1920 the designations SS (Submarine),

SF (Fleet Submarine), SC (Cruiser Submarine) and SM (Minelaying Submarine) were introduced as a temporary measure, with their own A, B, C and D pendant numbers. Thus the USS *Cachalot*, for example, was simultaneously known for a while as *SS170*, *C1* and *V8*, but in 1940 this multiple system was swept away, and only SS-numbers were retained. The fish names were reintroduced in 1931 with the *Barracuda* (*SS163*) and continued until the first Polaris submarine was launched in 1959.

American standardisation

The Pacific was seen clearly as the area of any future conflict, so American designs emphasised high surface endurance, habitability and good torpedo capacity. After the unsatisfactory experiments with cruiser-submarines in the 1920s, the 'P' Group of 1933–1938 was developed through the 'S' and 'T' classes into the 1,500-ton 'G' Class of 1940. In view of the limited number of yards available, standardisation of design was essential, and although three classes were built, they were so similar as to be virtually identical, the famous *Gato* and *Balao* Classes, and the later *Tench* Class. With an overall length of 311 ft 9 in and a beam of 27 ft 3 in, they had welded hulls and diesel-electric drive, i.e. diesel generators

driving electric motors coupled to the shafts through reduction gears. This method had also been introduced in contemporary British submarines, and replaced the former dual diesel or electric drive in older submarines.

All wartime US submarines had the same double hull divided into eight watertight compartments, with six ballast tanks and four fuel tanks, though stronger hulls were introduced in the *Balao* and *Tench* Classes. The armament was heavy, six torpedo-tubes forward and four aft, with stowage for 14 reload torpedoes, and a deck gun. During the war the gun changed from one 3-in/50 cal to 4-in or 5-in and a heavy battery of 40-mm or 20-mm AA guns, and the configuration of conning towers changed to accommodate them. But for all their heavy armament and generally excellent design, US submarines began the war with a serious disadvantage:

like the German U-Boats they suffered from defective torpedoes. The magnetic pistol was to blame as well, and for the first two years many attacks on Japanese targets were useless. It is strange that two countries with a high reputation for their engineering standards should have introduced a new weapon without spotting its weakness until long after it had entered service.

The Japanese, on the other hand, did not approach the submarine problem as systematically as the Americans. By 1940 there was a noticeable lack of medium-sized boats to supplement the large cruiser-types which

Type, a long-range cruising submarine intended to act as the headquarters for hunting groups of smaller submarines. The surface displacement was nearly 3,000 tons, and aircraft were carried, but most of the additional displacement was used to increase endurance – to as much as 22,000 miles in the *I12*.

These submarines were meant to play their part in a grandiose plan to seek out and ambush American surface forces across the wide expanse of the Pacific, and they were supplemented by midgets to attack the enemy if he should refuse to leave his

early in 1945. A much better-known development was the *Kaiten*, basically a piloted version of the famous 24-in Type 93 'Long Lance' torpedo. The three later models of *Kaiten* used a high-speed hydrogen-peroxide engine, but suffered so many production problems that the Model 4 was fitted with a conventional torpedo motor and carried a much heavier warhead in compensation.

The main problem for the Japanese at the beginning of the war was not one of design, but the question of how they intended to use their submarines. From the start the long-

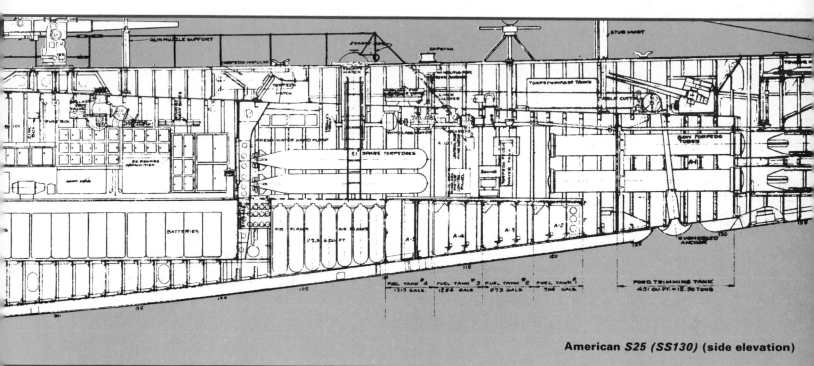

American S25 (SS130) (side elevation)

seemed to fascinate their admirals unduly. The 1940 Additional Programme tried to rectify this with an order for more than 80 of the K6 Type, 1,100-tonners armed with four torpedo-tubes. Although rather small they had a theoretical range of 11,000 miles at 12 knots, about equal to an early *Gato*, and were considered to be a very successful design. Production problems resulted in only 18 being completed, *RO35–RO50* and *RO55* and *RO56*, and all but one were sunk.

The same programme saw the commencement of 9 'medium' 600-tonners of the KS Type, a strange decision in view of the distances involved in the Pacific, but under the 1941 Emergency War Programme there was an immediate return to giant aircraft-carrying submarines with the *I40* and *I46* Classes. The *I12* was a repeat of the 1937 A1

defended harbours. The aerial attack on Pearl Harbour was intended to be supported by a torpedo attack from some Type A midgets, and one of the minor mysteries of that debâcle is how the Americans sighted and sank one of them at the entrance to Pearl Harbour *before* the main attack without alerting the defences. The attack was not a success, nor was a similar attack on Sydney Harbour in 1942, but in the same year the British battleship *Ramillies* was badly damaged by a midget launched from a parent submarine off Madagascar.

The nation that introduced the Kamikaze concept had little difficulty in applying it to naval warfare, and in 1943 the first of a range of suicide craft was developed, the *Kairyu*; it was a development of the Type A midget, but production did not start until

cherished aim of a general fleet action was paramount in the Imperial Japanese Navy's plans, and all submarine tactics had to be subordinated to that idea. Too much attention was paid to the need to maintain an offensive and aggressive outlook, which led to the grave error of assuming that warships were the only important targets for submarines. It also led to the equally serious error of neglecting the defence of merchant ships on the grounds that convoying was merely a defensive measure.

The lessons were painfully learned by the Japanese as American submarines proceeded to cut their lines of communication.

'American S25 (SS130)
The 'S' Class was the last design produced for the USN in the First World War, and in 1941 a few units were stationed in the Far East. They proved to have too little endurance for the Pacific, and so they were withdrawn. *S25* was lent to the Royal Navy for training, and then became the Polish *Jastrzab*. She was sunk in error by friendly ships in 1942

American _Gato_

The _USS Gato_ was the lead ship of a class authorised in 1941, before the United States entered the war. Over 200 of this very good design were ordered by 1945, and they were the backbone of the US Navy's submarine onslaught on Japan. _Displacement:_ 1,526 tons (surfaced) _Armament:_ Ten 21-in torpedo-tubes (6 forward, 4 aft); 14 reloads; one 3-in gun _Speed:_ $20\frac{1}{4}$ knots (surfaced) $8\frac{3}{4}$ knots (submerged)

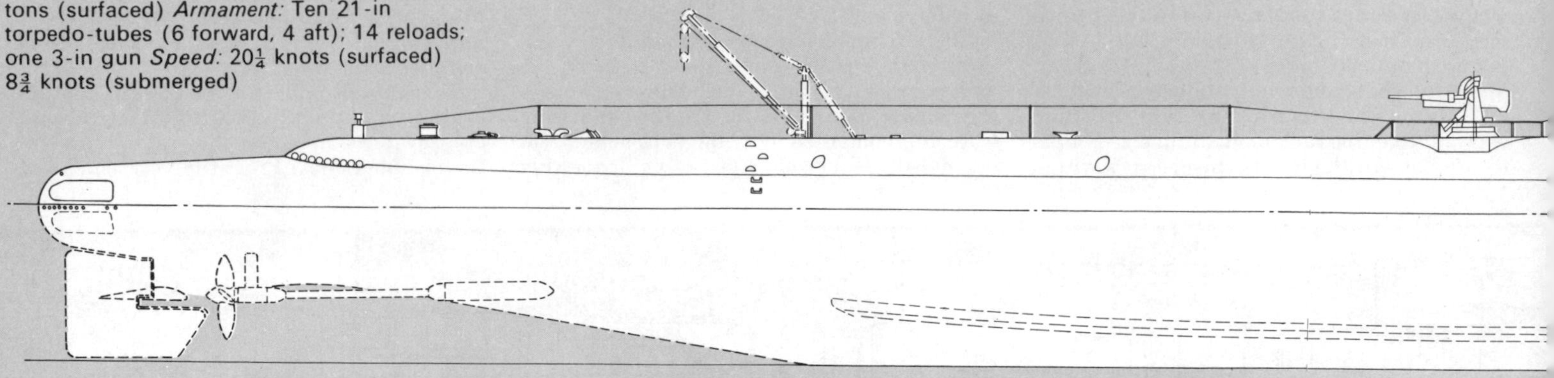

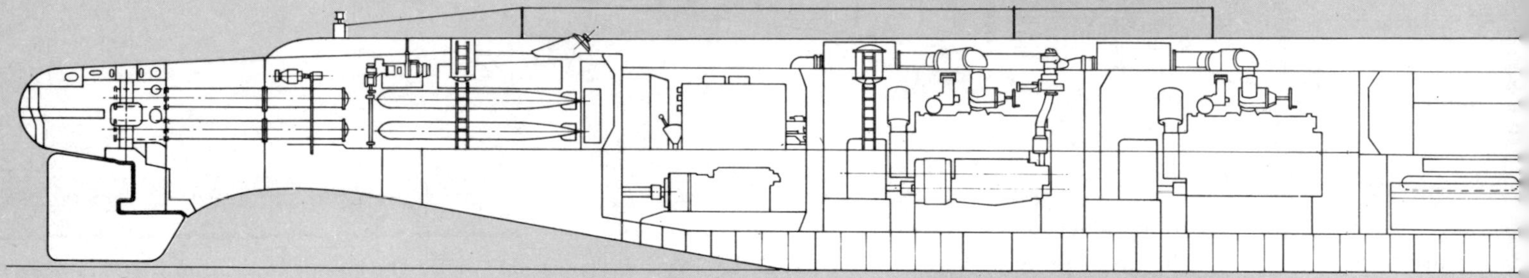

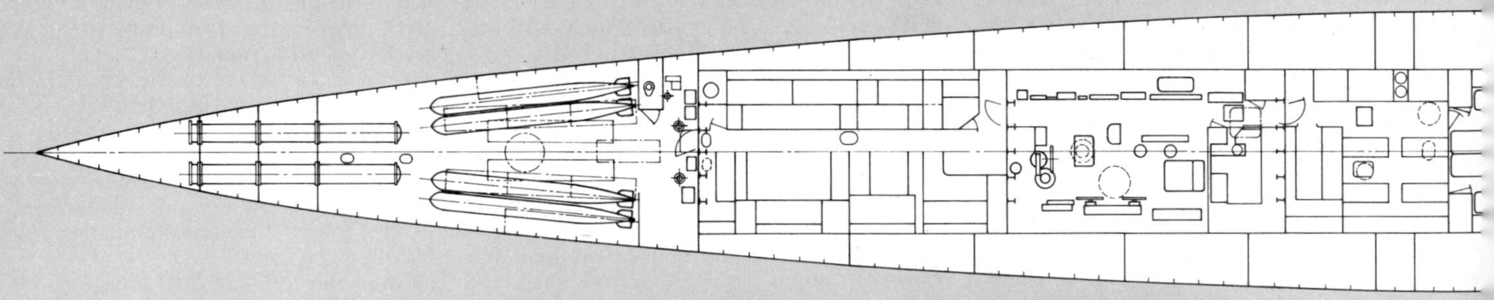

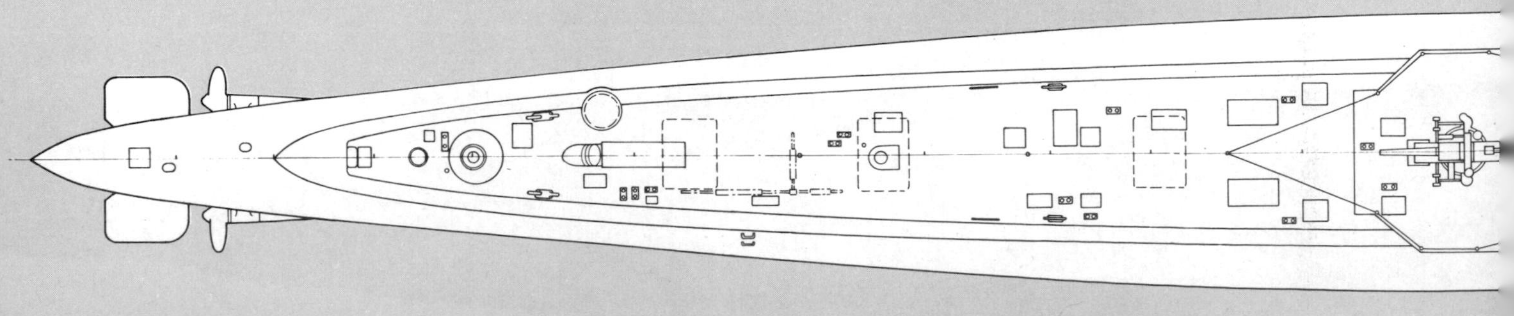

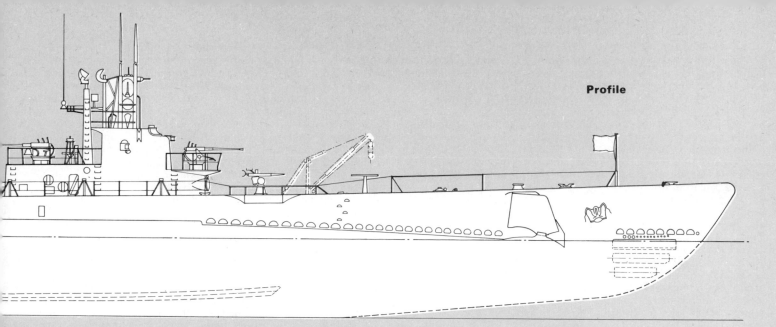

Profile

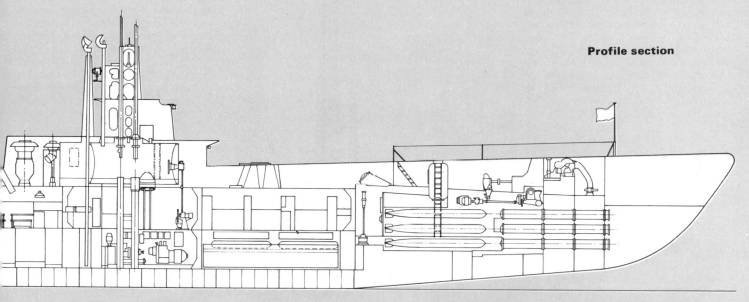

Profile section

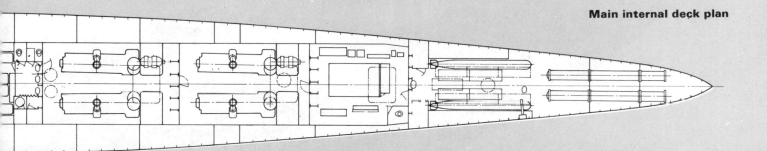

Main internal deck plan

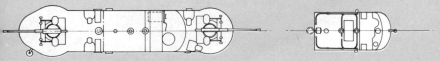

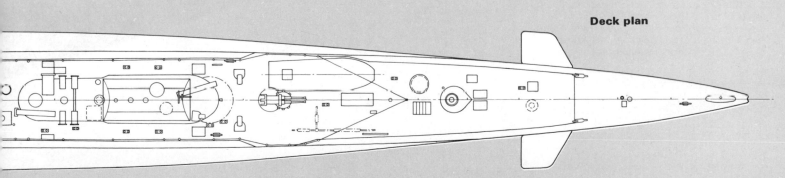

Deck plan

Losses of vital tonnage went up, so that it became harder and harder to reinforce the perimeter of island bases, which were essential to the Japanese maritime strategy. Worse, the homeland depended on imports for 20 per cent of the food consumed, 24 per cent of its coal, 88 per cent of all iron ore, and 90 per cent of its oil.

In the light of these statistics it is hard to understand why the Imperial Navy did not complete any escort vessels until 1940. Apart from a handful of old destroyers converted, the only further effort made by 1941 was the construction of another 22 escorts, and even they were given a low priority. The Japanese High Command did not expect the American submarines would be able to penetrate the defensive perimeter, and it was not until late in 1943 that any sort of convoy system was introduced. Even then, it was a very reluctant gesture and it was hampered by the desperate shortage of escorts. Over 4 million tons of shipping was sunk by American submarines, and by mines laid by submarines and aircraft, and when the war ended in August 1945 the Japanese mercantile marine comprised only 231 ships – in 1939 *Lloyd's Register* listed 2,337 ships!

The American submarines in the Pacific were supported by a small number of British and Dutch submarines, and after the col-lapse of Italy in 1943 the British were able to transfer reinforcements from the Mediterranean. By early 1944 there were three flotillas in the Far East, two at Trincomalee and a third at Fremantle in Australia, operating under American command. Because of their smaller size the British and Dutch boats were principally employed about the 10-fathom line west of Singapore where the big US submarines found it difficult to operate.

By comparison with the staggering losses inflicted by the American submarines, the tonnages sunk by the British and Dutch were modest, largely because the Japanese had withdrawn many of their units. But many small coasters and junks were destroyed by gunfire. HMS *Tally Ho* sank the cruiser *Kuma* off Penang, however, while *Taurus* sank the submarine *I34* in the same locality. When the patrol was extended the losses went up, and HMS *Trenchant*'s CO was awarded the US Legion of Merit for sinking the cruiser *Ashigara*. The midget submarines *XE1* and *XE3* disabled the cruiser *Takao* in Singapore, and two 'Chariots' from HMS *Trenchant* attacked merchant shipping at Phuket in Thailand. Excluding minor vessels under 500 tons, British and Dutch submarines sank a total of 87,000 tons of shipping.

Japanese counter-measures were poor, and only 60 US submarines were sunk, with a much lower loss ratio than that suffered by the German U-Boats. When the war ended the Japanese authorities told the Americans that their anti-submarine forces had sunk 486 boats! American submarines were also able to sink eight aircraft carriers and 12 cruisers, the classic examples being the torpedoing of the 62,000-ton *Shinano* by the *Archerfish*, and an ambush by the *Dace* and *Darter* which sank two heavy cruisers and damaged a third. Such was the ascendancy of American submarines over the Japanese that they were able to tackle escorts with

American *Drum* (SS228)
The *Gato* Class was the standard wartime design for the USN, and proved a superb weapon for the Pacific. As the war progressed the AA armament was increased, because American submarines operated on the surface for much of the time. The *Drum* is preserved at Mobile, Alabama. *Displacement:* 1,526 tons (surfaced) *Armament:* Ten 21-in torpedo tubes (6 forward, 4 aft); 24 torpedoes carried; one 3-in gun; two ·5 and two ·3 machine-guns *Speed:* 20¼ knots (surfaced) 8¾ knots (submerged)

impunity. Their outstanding tactic was the 'down the throat shot', a full salvo fired at short range at an escort bearing down on the submarine. It required very fine judgment and an iron nerve, but it meant that US submarines sometimes sank escorts faster than they could sink submarines.

The German wolf pack system was introduced in the Pacific in 1943, but the Americans used groups of only three boats, with such exotic nicknames as 'Laughlin's Loopers', 'Ed's Eradicators' and 'Ben's Busters'. With the advantage of radar, which the Japanese escorts lacked, they were able to track their targets with ease and avoid any counter-attacks. Like the Germans, the Americans found that attacking on the surface at night was very profitable, but unlike the British the Japanese escorts could not stop submarines from racing ahead to a new attacking position, because of their lack of radar.

Triumph at Midway

By comparison the US Navy suffered relatively little from Japanese submarine attacks. The battleship *North Carolina* was torpedoed by *I15* in 1942 but survived, as did the carrier *Saratoga* when hit by *I26*. The greatest Japanese triumphs took place at Midway when *I168* put four torpedoes into the crippled carrier *Yorktown*, and the sinking of the carrier *Wasp* by *I19* south of the Solomons. The main reason for this was the high degree of skill shown by American anti-submarine forces, as underlined when the destroyer escort *England* sank six submarines in twelve days in May 1944. But the concentration on warship targets by the Japanese freed the Americans from having to organise a massive convoy system in the Pacific, and released escorts for more urgent duties with the front-line forces.

Japanese submarines were well aware of the need to attack American shipping, but failed to get a hearing from their superiors. When things began to go badly in 1942 the response was to hurl submarines into useless attacks on landing forces, or to use them to transport supplies to isolated Army garrisons. Not satisfied with this, the Army began to build transport submarines of its

Japanese *I368*

The Type D1 was designed to carry supplies to isolated Japanese garrisons in the Pacific, and had a radius of action of 15,000 miles on the surface. The bow torpedo-tubes were removed after trials, and they relied solely on their guns for defence. One or two Daihatsu landing craft could be carried in wells on the deck casing

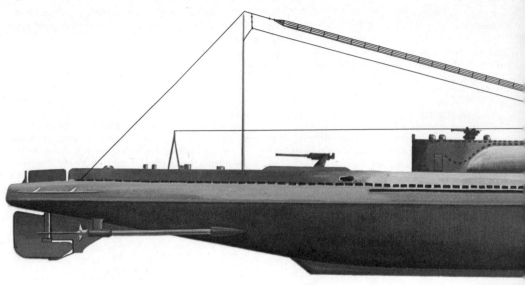

own, surely the most monumental dispersion of effort in the history of naval warfare; about 28 were built, and they were manned by Army personnel. When permission was given to attack communications it was too late, and in any case reliance was placed on the *Kaiten*, which were hardly suitable for extended operations. Like the Italian 'pigs' the *Kaiten* were transported on the decks of submarines, and were launched when close to the operational area.

The last flowering of Japanese submarine design was typically ambitious. In 1942 they ordered 17 of the Type STo, the largest submarines ever seen up to that time. These were the famous *I400* Class, an amalgamation of the Type A, B and C submarines, to produce an aircraft-carrying boat which could attack the Panama Canal. For this purpose they were meant to carry two seaplane bombers, but were altered to carry three in the hangar. In layout they followed the previous big submarines, but to keep the draught down as much as possible a peculiar double cylindrical hull was tried, with the cylinders side-by-side. The armament was heavy, eight 21-in bow torpedo-tubes with 20 reloads, and four torpedoes and 15 bombs carried for the seaplanes.

Only three of these giants were completed by August 1945, when Japan capitulated. When American technical experts examined them they found a lot of evidence of technical assistance from the Germans. Many German U-Boats had made trips out to the Far East to collect cargoes of rubber, tin and wolfram, and the Japanese had been very anxious to copy the features which made these boats so superior to their own. The *I400* Class had a schnorchel, and even had the same rubber coating on the hull which was being tried out in Germany as a means of absorbing Asdic pulses.

Costly failure

It would not be correct to suggest that the Japanese submarine effort was only directed towards large submarines, because in one way they anticipated the Germans in developing a boat with high underwater speed. In 1937/38 they built *No.71* in conditions of utmost secrecy, even to the point of launching her behind a smokescreen. She was small, only 140 ft long and displacing 213 tons on the surface, but she reached 21 knots under water. Although she never entered service, being nothing more than an experimental boat, she revived the ideas which had been tested and forgotten with the British 'R' Class twenty years earlier. During the war two operational classes were built to develop her ideas, the small *Ha201* Class and the larger *I201*s.

Despite these interesting developments the Japanese submarine effort during the

American 5-in Submarine Gun
The 5-in/25 cal. Mk XIII gun shown was mounted on board USS *Tigrone* (*SS419*), one of the few *Tench* Class to be completed before the end of the war. Many weapons were carried by US submarines, but this pattern was the most popular. *Weight:* 2·7 tons *Range:* 14,500 yards at 40° elevation *Weight of shell:* 53 lb

Japanese *I70*
The lack of numerical sequence makes Japanese submarine classes hard to follow; *I70*'s sisters were renumbered *I168–169* and *I171–172*. They were big ocean-going submarines with a range of 14,000 miles on the surface. *I70* was sunk by carrier aircraft only three days after the attack on Pearl Harbor. *Displacement:* 1,785 tons (surfaced) *Armament:* Six 21-in torpedo-tubes; 14 torpedoes carried; one 3·9-in AA gun; one 13-mm machine-gun *Speed:* 23 knots (surfaced) $8\frac{1}{4}$ knots (submerged)

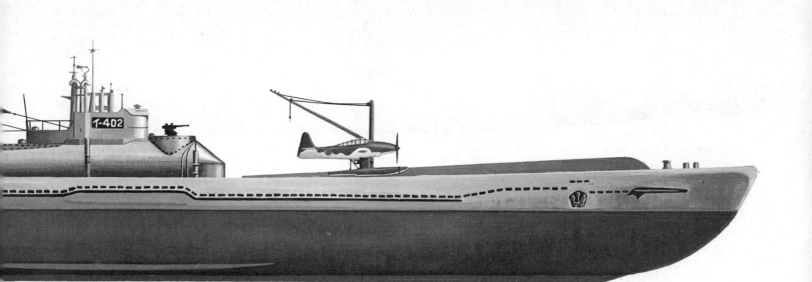

Japanese *I402*

The *I400* Class were ordered under the modified 1942 programme and were the largest submarines built up to that time. The intention was to provide them with three seaplane bombers in order to attack the Panama Canal, but the aircraft never reached production. Only three boats were completed by August 1945, and they were surrendered to the American occupying forces. *Displacement:* 5,223 tons (surfaced) *Armament:* Eight 21-in torpedo-tubes; 20 torpedoes carried; one 5·5-in gun; ten 25-mm AA guns

Japanese 'Kaiten' Midget

This was the naval equivalent of the Kamikaze, being a piloted version of the Type 93 Long Lance torpedo. It could travel 25,000 yards at 30 knots, and was launched from full-sized submarines or from surface warships

Second World War was a costly failure. Losses were extremely heavy; out of 245 submarines which served in the war (excluding ex-German and Italian boats taken over and midgets) 149 were sunk, a loss ratio of 60 per cent. There were few successes to match the exploits of the Germans, largely because the peacetime policy and training had proved totally wrong. The only successes of the aircraft-submarine tactics which the Japanese had developed so diligently came in 1942; a scout plane reconnoitred Diego Suarez harbour before a midget was sent in to torpedo a British battleship and another tried to set the Oregon pine forests alight with incendiary bombs. Otherwise this costly programme was entirely wasted.

By the end of 1942 the first Japanese submarines had been converted to run supplies to beleaguered Army garrisons on outlying islands, and this was to be the fate of the majority of the larger boats. Armament was reduced and the casing was modified to carry a 'Daihatsu' landing craft or such items as amphibious tanks. Although the Imperial Japanese Navy prided itself on its aggressive attitude to sea power, it allowed the Army to dictate requirements to the extent that its powerful submarine force was reduced to a supply service. Had those same submarines been put to better use they might have had far more effect on the war to the benefit of both Army and Navy, but as it was they suffered heavy losses in running food and ammunition to garrisons who were already doomed. When the surviving submarines were converted back into *Kaiten* carriers it did at least bring them back to a fighting role, but by then it was too late.

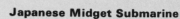

Japanese Midget Submarine

The Japanese began experiments with midgets in the mid-1930s and the Type A were used unsuccessfully at Pearl Harbor and against Sydney harbour in Australia. Their most notable success was the torpedoing of the battleship *Ramillies* in Madagascar in 1942. *Displacement:* 46 tons (submerged) *Armament:* Two 18-in torpedoes *Speed:* 23 knots (surfaced) 19 knots (submerged)

Ironically, the last success of Japanese submarines was the most spectacular, and it occurred when all was lost. On 30 July 1945 the heavy cruiser USS *Indianapolis*, after shipping the first atomic bomb out to the Pacific, was steaming between Guam and Leyte. So accustomed had the US Navy become to the lack of enterprise shown by Japanese submarines that this valuable warship was unescorted, but her course took her across the patrol line of *I58*. Lieutenant Commander Hashimoto fired a full salvo of six torpedoes, and two hit, causing the cruiser to sink in twelve minutes. To punish the Americans further for their complacency it was three days before anybody noticed that the *Indianapolis* had not arrived at her destination, and so 883 of her crew died in the US Navy's worst disaster at sea.

Japanese 'Kairyu' Suicide Midget

The Type A midget was developed into a suicide boat, but production difficulties made it impossible to find engines or torpedoes for many of them. Over 200 were built.
Displacement: 19½ tons (submerged)
Armament: Two 18-in torpedoes or a nose-charge of 600 Kg TNT *Speed:* 17½ knots (surfaced) 10 knots (submerged)

THE SPOILS OF VICTORY

Associated Press

At the end of the Second World War, as at the end of the First, the victors were quick to examine and learn from the German and Japanese submarines they had captured. But it would not be long before even more remarkable advances would affect the submarine: the day of nuclear-propelled submarines, armed with missiles rather than torpedoes, was fast approaching

As soon as Germany had surrendered to the victorious Allies, teams of intelligence officers and submarine experts moved into German shipyards and naval bases to seize as much as they could. Naturally there had been widespread sabotage and destruction of material by bombing, but the British, Americans and Russians were able to locate examples of the Type XXI, and even the few Walther boats which had been completed. In addition the British and Americans had the pick of all the U-Boats which had been interned at Lisahally in accordance with the surrender terms. Similarly when Japan capitulated in August 1945 large numbers of Japanese submarines fell into Allied hands.

Naturally, everybody was most interested in the Type XXI, as it proved to be a sound design. The Walther boats were treated with more reserve, mainly because it was

going to take some time to find out how to work them. The Russians obtained some Walther hulls, and even went to the length of loading the incomplete aircraft carrier *Graf Zeppelin* with U-Boat hull sections in her hangar; their enthusiasm over-reached itself, and the towed hulk sank after hitting a mine in the Gulf of Finland.

All navies knew how close the Allies had come to defeat at the hands of the U-Boats, and so the years immediately after 1945 were marked by prolonged experiments in submarine design, and also in anti-submarine warfare. The Type XXI features, the streamlined hull and large battery capacity, were immediately incorporated into new designs. The deck gun began to disappear, for it caused too much drag, and the former bulky conning tower with its platforms and periscope standards was streamlined into a fin, known in the USN as a 'sail'. The schnorchel

The Blöhm und Voss shipyard at Hamburg after its capture by the British in 1945. Submarines are in various stages of construction.

became a standard fitting, known in American submarines as a 'snorkel' and to the British as a 'snort'.

Propulsion remained the tried and proven diesel-electric drive for the moment, but the Walther turbine promised the dream of a 'true submarine', independent of outside oxygen. The three major submarine powers, Great Britain, the United States and Soviet Russia all experimented with the idea, although the Americans soon decided to drop it because of its complexities. The Russian experiments remain shrouded in secrecy to this day, although it is known that Walther-engined boats were tested. The British ran the salvaged *U1407* as HMS *Meteorite* from 1946 to 1950. She was regarded as about 75 per cent safe, and her crew were doubtless thankful to see the last of her. But she spawned two improved versions, the 225-ft *Explorer* and *Excalibur*, which entered service in 1956–58.

These two submarines were not unnaturally known as the 'blonde' submarines because of their peroxide fuel. They served a useful purpose in as much as they gave the Royal Navy's anti-submarine forces some valuable practice against fast targets. Their main use, however, was to prove finally that the Walther system was only a stopgap. There was more than one contemporary report of explosions in the two submarines, and at least one instance when the entire crew was forced to stand on the casing to avoid the noxious fumes which had suddenly filled the boat.

The reason the Americans had been so lukewarm towards the Walther system was that they had practical experience of nuclear energy. When the war ended the only use made of nuclear power had been in the form of bombs, but it was clear that a controlled reaction would be feasible. Nuclear energy provides a limitless source of heat, and makes no demands on oxygen for combustion. The disadvantage was merely that of weight and size, for a reactor needs thick lead shielding to prevent radiation, quite apart from its bulk. Therefore American nuclear physicists bent their research towards producing a reactor small enough to power a submarine.

While the designers were groping towards

Russian 'W' Class

This class, like so many others, clearly owed much to the German Type XXI, and was probably begun as soon as Soviet designers had absorbed all the knowledge gained after the German surrender. The first units appeared in 1950 and about 200 were built by 1958. Many of these are now serving with satellite navies, and the class is obsolescent. *Displacement:* 1,030 tons (surfaced) *Armament:* Six 21-in torpedo-tubes (four forward, two aft) eighteen torpedoes carried *Speed:* 17 knots (surfaced) 15 knots (submerged)

nuclear propulsion, the immediate problem for the US Navy was to modernise their submarine fleet to incorporate all the lessons of the war. A number of the *Tench* Class were completing to a slightly improved *Balao* design, and they were altered. The new design was known as the 'Guppy' type, standing for Greater Underwater Propulsive Power, and incorporated a lengthened and streamlined hull with larger batteries, as well as a modified sail and snorkel.

Many of the older *Gato* and *Balao* classes were converted in similar fashion, but even more were allocated to experimental duties.

British *Amphion*

For the Pacific, the Royal Navy needed a larger submarine with more endurance, and the 'A' Class resulted. They were not as large as the American boats, but they had air-conditioning and a radius of action of 10,000 miles. The early boats like *Amphion* had a low bow, but after trials this was raised

British Tireless
The early 'T' Class had riveted hulls, and therefore they could not be fully modernised. The later ones, like *Tireless*, were given a form of 'guppy' conversion in 1951–56, being lengthened and streamlined to give greater speed and endurance. *Displacement* 1,280 tons (surfaced) *Armament:* Six 21-in torpedo-tubes (guns and after tubes removed) *Speed:* 15 knots (surfaced) 15 knots (submerged)

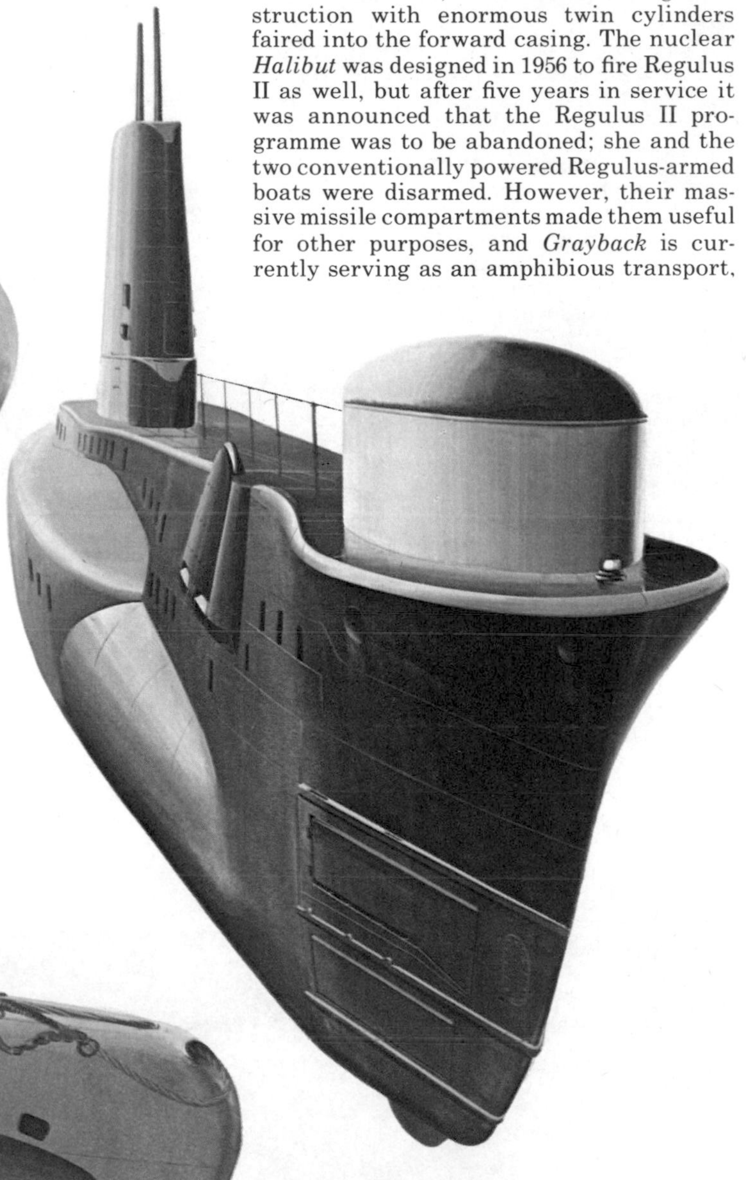

British Alaric
The 'A' Class were given a modernisation on the same lines as the 'T' Class, involving a complete rebuilding of the forward and after sections of the hull, lengthening and streamlining. The two external tubes forward and the two aft were removed, leaving them a total of six tubes, and no gun armament

Every wartime idea was tried and developed, including oilers and supply submarines. In 1948/49 the *Carbonero* and *Cusk* were fitted to operate the 'Loon' guided weapon system, an improved version of the German V1 'doodlebug', launched from a catapult abaft the conning tower. From these experiments came the Regulus I missile, an air-breathing anti-ship missile with a 500-mile range, and the *Tunny* and *Barbero* were fitted with cylindrical hangars to house two missiles.

The Regulus II missile which followed was 57 ft long, compared with only 32 ft for Regulus I, so it demanded a much bigger submarine. The *Grayback* and *Growler*, built in 1952–58, were fitted during construction with enormous twin cylinders faired into the forward casing. The nuclear *Halibut* was designed in 1956 to fire Regulus II as well, but after five years in service it was announced that the Regulus II programme was to be abandoned; she and the two conventionally powered Regulus-armed boats were disarmed. However, their massive missile compartments made them useful for other purposes, and *Grayback* is currently serving as an amphibious transport, while *Halibut* is acting as a 'mother ship' for the Deep Submergence Research Vehicle programme.

During the Cold War period the United States was preoccupied with the threat of Russian air attack with nuclear weapons, and put great faith in a seaward early-warning radar 'picket line'. Most of the pickets were surface warships fitted with elaborate radar and communications, but several submarines were fitted out as radar

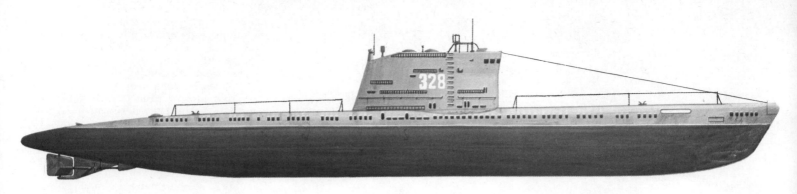

Russian Z-V Type

Between 1958 and 1961 seven of the conventional 'Z' Class were rebuilt to fire two ballistic missiles. This was part of a crash programme to counter the US Navy's sudden breakthrough in perfecting the Polaris system, but unlike the American boats these Russian conversions had to launch their missiles on the surface. None are now operational

Russian 'G' Class

This was an improved version of the Z-V Class, with three ballistic missiles. The 22 boats of this class now have the 650-mile range Serb (SS-N-5) missile in place of the older Sark, and an additional unit of the class was built in China

British *Oberon* Class

The thirteen *Oberons* are the Royal Navy's latest conventional submersibles, and also its most successful export design, as a number have been built for other navies. They embody many features of the German Type XXI, and have the reputation of being the most silent submarines in service.
Displacement: 1,610 tons (surfaced)
Armament: Eight 21-in torpedo-tubes (6 forward, 2 aft); 30 torpedoes carried *Speed:* 12 knots (surfaced) 17 knots (submerged)

pickets to provide more flexibility. This led to the construction of an enormous nuclear radar picket submarine, the *Triton*. She was the largest submarine ever built at the time (1959) and had two nuclear reactors; this power enabled her to circumnavigate the world submerged in 1960, a 41,500-mile voyage at an average speed of 18 knots.

All this time Russia's submarine force remained an enigma. Armed with as much information about German developments as her technicians could get, she worked hard

to modernise her fleet. By the early 1950s the first of the new 'W' Class were seen; although claimed to have been started in 1944 it is clear that they owed a lot to the Type XXI. They became the standard post-war type, and many were transferred to other navies. In 1961 work began on converting twelve to missile-firing submarines on the lines of the American *Tunny* and *Barbero*. One boat carried a single Shaddock surface-to-surface missile in a cylinder which elevated 20–25° for firing, but others

carried twin cylinders, and the third variant carried four Shaddock cylinders faired into a streamlined fin. There was also a radar picket version.

The next Russian submarine type to appear was the 'Z' Class, whose existence was doubted until 1952, when the first blurred photographs appeared in Western magazines. This was the class which was reputed to have tried the Walther propulsion system in the first few units, but the remainder quickly reverted to diesel-electric

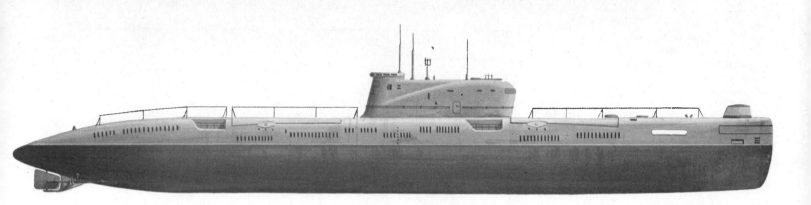

Russian 'J' Class
This class of conventional submersibles carry four Shaddock surface-to-surface cruise missiles in launchers housed in the deck casing. Sixteen were completed by 1967

Russian 'Y' Class
This is the Russian version of the Polaris submarines, with sixteen vertical tubes for launching the 1,350-mile range SS-N-6 missile. The first were reported in 1968 and 32 have been built

French *Daphne* Class
Like the British *Oberons*, the *Daphne* Class has proved a successful export to foreign navies, despite the fact that three have been lost in accidents. The eleven boats came into service between 1964 and 1970.
Displacement: 869 tons (surfaced)
Armament: Twelve 21·7-in (550-mm) torpedo-tubes (8 forward, 4 aft); at least 16 torpedoes carried *Speed:* 12½ knots (surfaced) 16 knots (submerged)

propulsion. They were more closely related to the Type XXI than the previous class, and at least 25 were built. A further ten were converted to fire two ballistic missiles from vertical tubes in the fin, and a slightly enlarged version called the 'G' Class was built at the same time to fire three missiles.

Great importance was attached in Western newspapers throughout the 1950s to the size of the Russian submarine fleet, but at the time its numbers were swollen by the large number of obsolescent 'M', 'S' and 'Shch' Class and othe boats which had survived the Second World War. When the new construction came into service it was possible to pay off these old submarines, and by the end of the decade it is doubtful if any were still used for anything but training.

The best submersibles

The Royal Navy contented itself with modernising its 'T' and 'A' Class boats during the 1950s, along the lines of the American 'Guppy' programme. Unfortunately the earlier 'Ts' and the 'S' Class had riveted hulls, which made them unsuitable for modernisation, but several were modified for experimental work. At the same time a new class of submarines was built to incorporate the latest ideas. These were known as the *Porpoise* Class, and they were followed by the very similar *Oberon* Class, which acquired an enviable reputation for reliability and quietness. Since 1962 a total of 14 have been sold to foreign buyers, and they are regarded as the best conventional submersibles available.

The French had to rebuild their submarine force from scratch after the war. Apart from a handful of worn-out pre-war submarines, and some borrowed from the British, they had only five incomplete hulls which were worth rebuilding. Taking advantage of a British offer of four 'S' Class for training, they set to work to redesign the five *Creole* Class hulls which had survived the war. These came into service between 1946 and 1953, and lessons were incorporated in the six *Narval* Class built in 1951–5. Two more classes were designed in the 1950s, of which the later *Daphne* Class of 1957–67 proved as commercially successful as the British *Oberons*.

Holland found herself in a similar situation in 1945, with her fleet comprising worn-out or borrowed submarines. In 1954 the *Dolfijn*, first of a unique class, was laid down. She had a triple hull, with three separate cylinders disposed in a triangle. This novel idea had the advantage of making better use of the internal space available, and also gave great strength, but it has not been repeated in any other navy.

The Swedish Navy had not suffered any loss, being neutral in the Second World War, but to maintain that neutrality it was necessary to keep abreast of developments. The *Sjölojenet* Class was streamlined and modernised, and four new classes were built. Of these the *Sjöormen* Class is the latest. The other Scandinavian navies also continued the tradition of building submarines in their own yards. The exception was Finland, which had to pay a heavy price for being on the wrong side in the war, and was forbidden to possess submarines.

The other Baltic navy to get back into the submarine business was, inevitably, Germany. In 1956 two sunken Type XXIII boats were salvaged and reconditioned for training duties as the *Hai* and *Hecht*. A third boat, the former Type XXI *U2540*, was in 1960

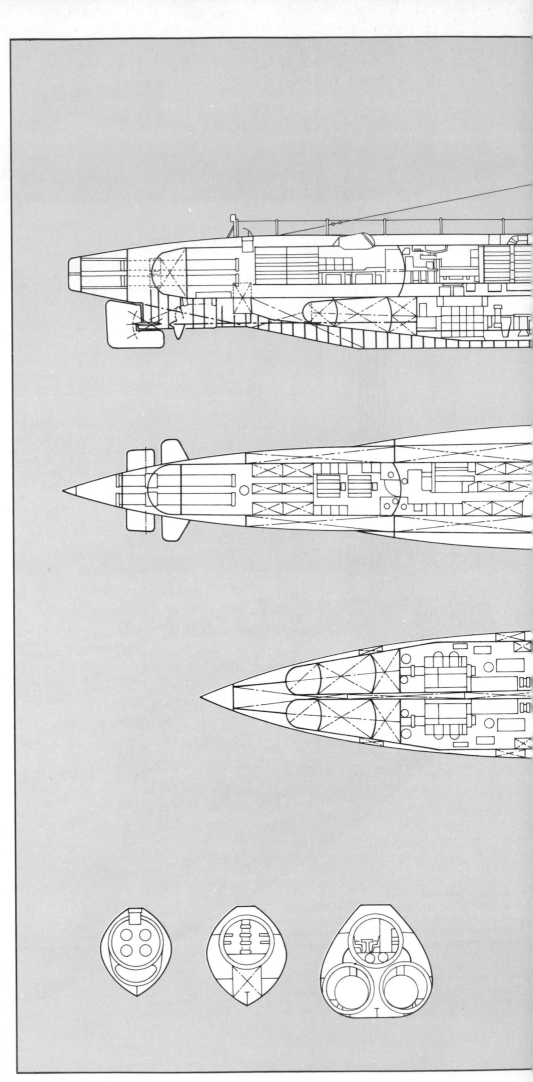

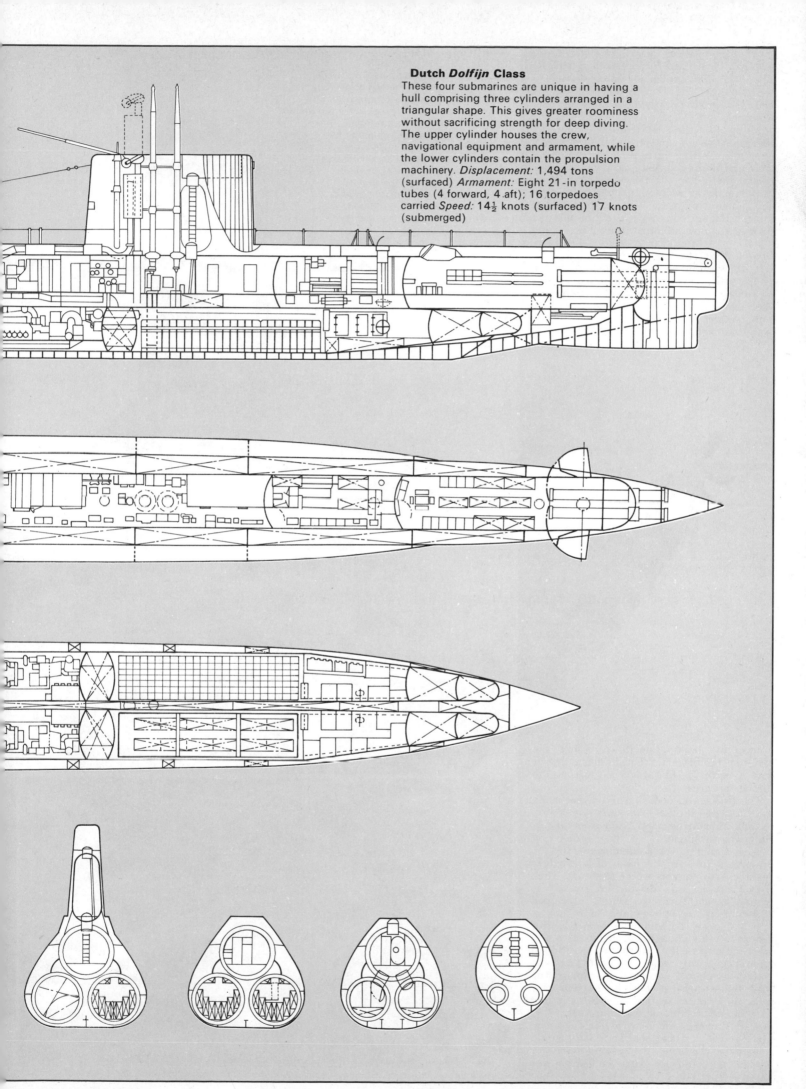

Dutch *Dolfijn* Class
These four submarines are unique in having a hull comprising three cylinders arranged in a triangular shape. This gives greater roominess without sacrificing strength for deep diving. The upper cylinder houses the crew, navigational equipment and armament, while the lower cylinders contain the propulsion machinery. *Displacement:* 1,494 tons (surfaced) *Armament:* Eight 21-in torpedo tubes (4 forward, 4 aft); 16 torpedoes carried *Speed:* 14½ knots (surfaced) 17 knots (submerged)

recommissioned as the *Wilhelm Bauer*, and has been used for research purposes. The first indigenous design appeared in 1961, when *U1* was launched at Kiel but *U1* and *U2* had to be rebuilt to remedy structural weakness.

Meanwhile the Americans had been developing the concept of the 'hunter-killer' submarine, using ultra-sensitive listening gear and improved Asdic, known as Sonar in the USN. The submarine makes a good anti-submarine weapon, primarily because she is operating in the same medium as her quarry, but perfection of the techniques had to wait for new silent-running motors and efficient tracking gear. A serious disadvantage is that she has to operate virtually 'blind', without the rapid communication and readily accessible visual data available to surface ships. But the real weakness is that despite all the improvements in propulsion and streamlining, a 'fast' underwater submarine is only fast for a matter of

hours, and must slow down before she exhausts her batteries. Until nuclear power was a reality, this was the obstacle to further progress.

The first water-cooled reactor was ready in 1952, when the USS *Nautilus* was begun. It took submarine propulsion back nearly 50 years to the days of the French and British steam-powered submarines, for the only way to use the heat of a nuclear reactor is to convert water to steam. Thus the *Nautilus* was driven by twin-shaft geared steam turbines, which developed 13,400 shaft horsepower and drove her at approximately 20 knots underwater. Her size inevitably made her clumsier than any wartime submarine, but it had its hidden advantages; only a large hull could provide the crew comfort necessary to support the high endurance provided by nuclear propulsion. In other words, the designers had come up against an old truism in submarine design: that crew efficiency is related to size, and even if a much smaller reactor could have been produced, the crew of a smaller submarine could not cruise submerged for extended periods.

American *George Washington (SSBN598)*

This was the West's first submarine to be armed with ballistic missiles, and was a result of President Kennedy's acceleration of the Polaris development programme. She fired two of her sixteen missiles for the first time in July 1960. To bring Polaris into service as quickly as possible, the five modified *Skipjack* type hulls were lengthened by 130 ft to accommodate the launching tubes. *Displacement:* 5,900 tons (surfaced) *Armament:* Sixteen Polaris intermediate range ballistic missiles; six 21-in torpedo-tubes *Speed:* 20 knots (surfaced) 25–30 knots (submerged)

Official US Navy Photograph

A rare picture of an American nuclear submarine in dry dock – the *Barbel (SS580)*

The size of the *Nautilus*, about 3,500 tons on the surface, and a three-decked hull over 300 ft long, allowed her 100 crew members a standard of accommodation which was better in some ways than surface ships of the same size. And they needed it, for in 1955, when *Nautilus* was completed, she made a run from New London to Puerto Rico fully submerged. This feat was eclipsed by her submerged crossing of the North Pole on 3 August 1958, when she proved to the world that a new era of submarine warfare had begun. Between 1955 and 1957 she steamed 62,562 miles on the original core of uranium, then logged 91,324 miles on her second core, and about 150,000 miles on the third.

In 1957 a second nuclear submarine was completed, the USS *Seawolf*. Slightly larger than the *Nautilus*, she was built to test another type of reactor using liquid sodium as a coolant in place of pressurised water. Although not as successful as the other prototype, she provided valuable experience for the first 'production models', the four *Skate* Class, which were completed in 1957–59. Their success convinced the US Navy that all future submarines should be nuclear-powered, and that decision marked a personal triumph for Admiral Hyman Rickover, who has been aptly named the 'Father of the Nuclear Submarine'.

Official US Navy photograph

The USS *Ray (SSN653)* shown here is an attack submarine of the *Sturgeon* Class, the largest group of nuclear submarines built to one design. They are intended to seek out and destroy other submarines and have their four torpedo-tubes amidships, to leave the bow position clear for a large sonar

In 1952 an experimental submarine had been ordered as a 'Hydro-dynamic test vehicle'. As the USS *Albacore* she entered service at the end of 1953. She revolutionised submarine design, because her 'teardrop' hull form gave more speed and manoeuvrability than any submarine had ever had. Her whale-shaped hull had no deck-casing, and the 'sail' was reduced to a thin dorsal fin. Since first commissioning, the *Albacore* has tested a variety of advanced equipment, but her main features have become the standard for later submarines; in particular the circular hull-sections and the single propeller shaft are a repetition of the British 'R' Class of 1918.

The next development of the nuclear submarine was a revival of a German project to launch a V2 ballistic missile from a pod towed by a submarine. Being a liquid-fuelled rocket, the V2 was ill-suited for use at sea, but postwar progress with solid fuels led to the Polaris missile system. This is a submarine-launched intermediate range ballistic missile (IRBM) capable of being fired from below the surface of the sea. It offers three main advantages over the big land-based inter-continental ballistic missiles (ICBM):

1 By moving the launching point out to sea the likelihood of a pre-emptive attack by enemy ICBMs is reduced.

2 Since the furthest point on land is only about 1,700 miles from the sea, the Polaris missile needs much less fuel than ICBMs, and can be smaller.

3 The difficulty of finding submarines in the oceans of the world means that in the foreseeable future there is no counter-measure.

Polaris works on a very simple principle of physics, the fact that water is incompressible; a missile is ejected from the submarine by gas or steam, its rocket motor ignites as it leaves the water, and the resulting downblast uses the 'hard' water underneath as a launching pad.

One major problem had to be solved before the Polaris system could be made to work, that of navigation. As a nuclear submarine dare not surface frequently to check her position by star-sights or radio-fixes, prolonged submarine voyages demand a much higher standard of navigation than ever before. The answer came in the SINS, the Ship's Inertial Navigation System, basically a computerised method of checking the vessel's actual movement from her point of departure by means of accelero-meters and gyroscopes. With SINS to track all drift and movement a nuclear submarine can dispense with magnetic compasses and dead reckoning errors, which makes a journey under the North Polar ice cap feasible. Furthermore, since a Polaris missile needs to know the distance to its target, it can be updated constantly by a fire control computer adjusting the firing trajectory from data provided by SINS.

Another problem created by Polaris and nuclear propulsion was habitability. If maximum benefit was to be gained from a submarine with virtually unlimited endurance, the human element had to be catered for. Intensive research into ventilation systems showed that it might be pos-

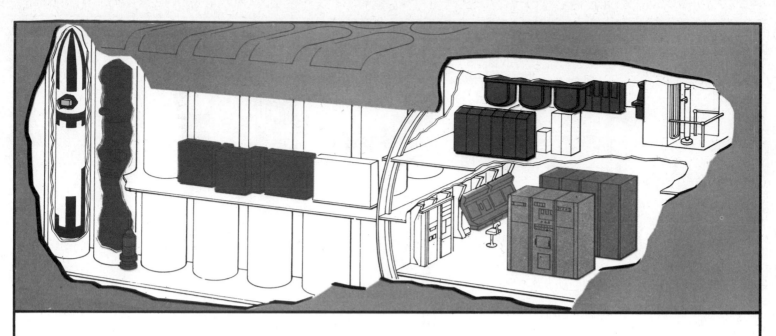

Official US Navy Diagram of Fleet Ballistic Missile System

Ship's Inertial Navigation System (SINS) maintains constant plot of ship's position for navigation and fire control

Fire Control computers receive information on ship's location and true north (from SINS), target locations and other information, and compute on a continuous basis trajectory information for rapid transmission to missile memory

Missile test and readiness equipment (MTRE) provides complete readiness checkout of all missiles and associated equipments

Launcher control prepares the 16 missile tubes for launch, including pressurization to insure that when the missile hatch is opened the tube remains free of water until missile is launched

Missile guidance 'memory' receives and stores trajectory data from the fire control system

Missile Control panel reflects status of all missiles. Sequence of missiles to be fired is selected here, and final launching circuit is closed here after captain has given permission to fire

Once all events have taken place to enable launch, closing firing key causes gas generator to ignite, whose exhaust forces missile out of tube

Only after it is safely out of the launch tube does missile ignite, to protect crew and ship. Once launched, the inertial guidance system in the missile directs the remainder of flight free of outside control

Polaris/Poseidon Installation (left)
This section through a US nuclear submarine shows the installation of an A-3 Polaris on the left, and its successor Poseidon on the right. They would never be installed together

American *Skipjack*
In 1959 the *Skipjack* introduced the revolutionary 'teardrop' hull which gave much greater speed and manoeuvrability than the older type of hull. The rounded casing is reminiscent of a whale, and makes for bad handling on the surface, but once submerged the submarine performs far better

Russian *Leninskii Komsomol*
In 1963 the Russians reported that this submarine had crossed under the North Polar ice cap. She is one of the 'N' Class, the first Soviet nuclear fleet submarines to enter service. The small conning tower set far forward is a feature of this class and of the improved 'V' Class. *Displacement:* 3,500 tons (surfaced) *Armament:* Six 21-in; four 16-in torpedo-tubes *Speed:* 20 knots (surfaced) 25 knots (submerged)

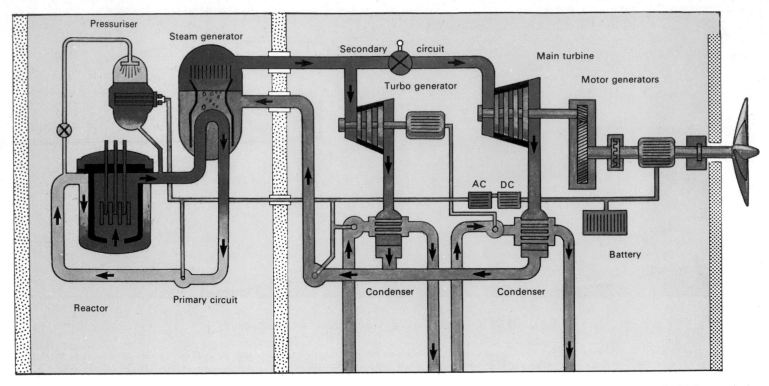

Pressuriser, Steam generator, Secondary circuit, Turbo generator, Main turbine, Motor generators, AC, DC, Battery, Condenser, Condenser, Reactor, Primary circuit

sible to extend a submarine's submerged endurance to three months or more by recycling the air – in other words, making the crew breathe their own air after it had been refreshed with oxygen and 'scrubbed' to remove toxic gases. Many interesting points came to light, particularly the need to have paints which did not give off toxic vapours, but now nuclear submarines are limited only by the endurance of their crews. This gives the submarine the same advantage that used to be enjoyed by the sailing ship – independence of bases as long as the food and water last.

The accumulation of waste causes severe problems as a hundred men will account for a large amount of potato peelings: the latest submarines are big, but they do not have unlimited space, and it is not always safe to jettison rubbish. For the same reason modern submarines have self-contained sewage systems which are pumped out when they return to base; this is also necessary because the pressure at great depths makes flushing the 'head' too difficult. Because of the extended cruise period, colours of furniture and furnishings have to be brighter and more harmonious than they were when always seen by artificial light.

Fortunately their great size allows nuclear submarines to have three decks, and so the accommodation can be made spacious. Crew comfort helps to reduce the strain of long patrols, but it is also necessary to provide films and gymnastic apparatus to combat boredom and the lack of exercise.

As soon as the United States Government knew that the A-1 Polaris missile was work able, permission was given to build the first of a fleet of 41 submarines, each capable of launching 16 Polaris missiles. As each missile's H-Bomb warhead was equal in power to all the high-explosive bombs dropped in the Second World War, the deterrent effect of such a system was obvious. Before the end of 1957 two newly ordered attack submarines had been redesignated Polaris submarines. A further three followed in 1958, and the five became the *George Washington* Class, the first Fleet Ballistic Missile (FBM) submarines

Nuclear Propulsion Power Plant
This diagram shows the basic components of the propulsion system of a nuclear submarine

in the world. To mark their importance, both in size and purpose, they were also the first USN submarines to be named after people rather than reptiles or fishes.

The next class, the five *Ethan Allen* Class, differed principally in being properly designed for their task, rather than hurriedly adapted from a smaller type. They and the 31 *Lafayette* Class which followed from 1960 onwards were better arranged internally than the original *George Washingtons*, and had improvements such as quieter machinery, but they retain the basic layout of two rows of eight missile tubes abaft the 'sail'.

The arms race begins
The news of the success of Polaris, after many pundits had said it would not be ready for another ten years, spurred the Soviet Navy on to develop a similar underwater deterrent. As we have seen, some of their conventional submersibles had been modified to fire two or three surface-to-surface missiles, but in 1958 work began on converting the first of ten 'Z' Class to fire IRBMs. The same system was used as before, two or three tubes housed in the fin, which opened like a clam shell to allow firing. Thirty 'G' Class were specially built for the job, and then came the nuclear powered 'H' Class, still using the same system. Not until 1968 did the first news leak out of a Russian version of the Polaris system, when the 'Y' Class appeared, with a very similar configuration to the American boats. Incidentally, all Russian class-designations are those assigned by NATO and bear no relation to what the Red Fleet may call them.

The first Russian nuclear hunter-killer submarines came into service between 1961 and 1963. Known in the West as the 'N' or 'November' Class, they numbered 15 units, and at least two were named. The *Leninskii Komsomol* emulated the *Nautilus* in the summer of 1962 by crossing the North Pole submerged, but in 1970 one of the class sank south-west of the British Isles. The 'V' or 'Victor' Class which followed were generally similar but greatly improved in detail, and

the 12 in service command a high reputation in Western intelligence circles.

The next country to build nuclear submarines was Great Britain, which had been experimenting with nuclear energy for some years. To save time a reactor was bought from the United States in 1958, to power HMS *Dreadnought*, the Royal Navy's first 'nuke', and the British reactor went into a second prototype, HMS *Valiant*, two years later. Since then a further two classes have been ordered, making a total of seven completed and four building. In 1963 it was announced that the Royal Navy would buy the A-3 Polaris weapon system from the United States and install it in their own hulls. These materialised in 1967–69 as the four *Resolution* Class, which replaced the

RAF's bomber force as Great Britain's strategic deterrent.

France was hardly likely to allow the British to have an 'independent' nuclear deterrent, but when the United States refused to supply Polaris missiles they went ahead with their own version, the MSBS M-1 (Mer-Sol-Balistique-Stratégique). A nuclear submarine had been laid down in 1958, but after being cancelled a year later she was redesigned as an experimental submarine to test the missiles and other equipment, and was appropriately named *Gymnote* after Gustave Zedé's prototype. She fired the first ballistic missiles, but the first operational FBM, *Le Redoutable*, did not come into service until 1971.

Apart from the People's Republic of China, whose intentions remain inscrutable, the only other country to contemplate the huge expense of nuclear propulsion was Holland. However, the two hulls planned in the early 1960s were replaced by conventional submarines, leaving only four navies with nuclear submarines. Red China certainly has the capability to build both nuclear submarines and Polaris-type missiles, but apart from a mysterious sighting of an *Albacore*-hulled submarine under construction in 1969, nothing is known.

The US Navy has improved the firepower of its later FBM submarines by arming them with the more powerful Poseidon missile. Very similar in appearance to the A-3 Polaris, Poseidon is two feet wider in diameter and three feet taller, but this modest increase in dimensions conceals many differences. Poseidon has twice the payload, which allows it to carry multiple warheads; this makes counter-measures even harder than before, since each missile can have three possible targets. The modifications include alterations to the missile tubes and replacement of the fire control system.

Despite the clear advantages of nuclear propulsion, conventional submersibles are still being designed and built. Nor are they confined to the smaller navies who cannot afford the cost of nuclear boats, for a new class of Russian diesel-electric submarines has been seen. One reason for this is that nuclear propulsion makes very heavy demands on skilled personnel, quite apart from its cost, and another is that the size of present-day nuclear submarines makes them unsuitable for coastal waters. There are areas in which small submersibles can function more effectively than the big fleet types, and so there are a number of French, British and German designs available for sale to foreign buyers.

Today the submarine represents the most potent naval weapon available. The nuclear submarine in particular represents a terrible threat to all surface warships, for her speed enables her to close in, attack with a variety of weapons such as guided torpedoes or even missiles, and then withdraw at high speed. The awesome destructive power of Polaris has already been described, but its value is enhanced because, unlike any other submarine weapon, it can be fired at a range of 2,000 miles or more. Even today the old convoy maxim holds good, that an attack submarine must sooner or later approach her target, and thus risk a counter-attack; a Polaris submarine, on the other hand, *avoids* all contact, and so she has the world's oceans in which to hide.

The future of the submarine could hardly be brighter. Advances in the design of nuclear reactors will probably reduce their size, and new weapons will increase their capabilities. But their great potential is also stimulating research on counter-measures. By the end of the 1970s we might well see a breakthrough similar in its effect to Asdic, such as a device to enable submarines to be tracked from satellites. Until then the submarine will continue to be the deadly weapon she has become in the last 30 years.

British *Resolution*

The *Resolution* was the first British Polaris or FBM (Fleet Ballistic Missile) submarine to be ordered in 1964. She was commissioned in 1967 as the most powerful warship ever to fly the White Ensign. She and her three sisters are armed with sixteen Polaris A-3 2,300-mile range missiles, with hydrogen bomb warheads. Although the missiles and their fire-control systems are American, the reactor and hull are British-designed, and they differ from the US Navy's submarines in having six bow torpedo-tubes. *Displacement:* 7,500 tons (surfaced)

SUBMARINE WEAPONS
&ANTI-SUBMARINE WEAPONS
THE ULTIMATE WARSHIP?

Admiralty Photograph

The submarine has come a long way from being armed simply with torpedoes and light AA guns — and effective counter-measures are even more difficult to find than during the desperate days of World War II

At the start of the Second World War the submarine had only one primary weapon, the thermal torpedo, which was kept on course only by gyroscopic stabilisation. She also carried a deck gun of 3-in to 6-in calibre for use against 'soft-skinned' targets such as merchant ships, but this was essentially an auxiliary weapon. Gyro-angling enabled the torpedo to change its angle during the run, and thus made it easier for a submarine to reach a good attacking position. Magnetic influence pistols were being introduced to make a torpedo explode within lethal distance under a target, like a proximity fuse, but these proved unreliable when first used.

During the war all operational submarines tended to have their anti-aircraft armament increased. This normally meant adding light automatic AA guns of 20-mm to 40-mm calibre on platforms on the conning tower, the most notable examples of this trend being the German U-Boats, which had a 'winter garden' crammed with Flak

pieces. The need to reduce drag for high underwater speed put an end to this, and both AA guns and the original deck gun became redundant.

The greatest improvement in torpedo design was the provision of homing devices to enable the torpedo to 'seek' its own target. The German acoustic torpedoes showed the way, and by 1945 there were several patterns under development in both the US Navy and the Royal Navy. After the war all navies developed similar weapons, but the limitations of acoustic homing (mainly the danger of a torpedo homing on its own submarine's noise) led to the development of wire guided torpedoes.

Wire guidance is very much older than it sounds, for it was the method by which the first Whitehead torpedo was controlled. The Brennan and Nordenfelt torpedoes of the 1880s also relied on a trailing wire paid out from a spool, but today's torpedoes are considerably more complex. Basically, fine wire is paid out from a spool inside the

A torpedo being loaded aboard a British submarine

torpedo body, and instructions are sent from the fire control system by impulse down the wire. Even with older patterns of torpedo it has been possible to substitute an umbilical link for the hand-cranked spindles which were formerly used to set the torpedoes before firing.

American submarines have for some time been fitted with Subroc, an advanced weapon system which has no equivalent elsewhere. Briefly, Subroc is fired from a 21-in torpedo tube, and then a rocket motor is fired underwater to lift it clear of the surface and send it on a ballistic course; at the end of its trajectory it re-enters the water and acts as a depth-charge. The essential fire control data is provided by the Passive Underwater Firecontrol Feasibility System (PUFFS), which takes bearings from propeller noises.

Aircraft, particularly the helicopter with

its ability to hover overhead, remain the submarine's worst enemy. At first the only defence was the passive one of providing a sensor at the masthead to detect the noise of a helicopter's engine, but now Vickers Ltd have produced the Submarine Launched Airflight Missile (SLAM) to allow a submarine some means of retaliation. SLAM is an adaptation of the land-based Blowpipe missile, a light close-range ground-to-air weapon which can be fired from the shoulder. It comprises a compact launcher with six missiles, stowed in the fin but raised to fire,

American Twin 20-mm Gun
Many wartime submarines in the Pacific used this twin hand-operated version of the 20-mm Oerlikon light AA gun. It was mounted on a platform on the conning tower or on deck, and was also used against small surface targets

and controlled by television guidance from the submarine's control room. In recent trials in the old British submarine *Aeneas*, the system proved successful, and it could seriously reduce the effectiveness of anti-submarine helicopters.

The Polaris system for firing ballistic missiles has already been described, but the Russians are now the only submarine power to employ cruise missiles. The Americans dropped their Regulus I and Regulus II systems because they both involved operation on the surface, which has become too risky for submarines. One wonders, therefore, about the value of the Russian Shaddock and Sark missiles in the early missile submarines.

The ultimate in submarine firepower is the American Trident project, formerly known as the Underwater Long-Range Missile System (ULMS). The project calls for ten submarines of about 15,000 tons displacement (submerged), each one armed with 24 Trident missiles capable of travelling 6,000 miles. The size of missile would permit even more multiple warheads than the Poseidon, as well as decoys and jamming devices to enable its warheads to beat the most advanced defences. The cost is estimated to be $1,000 million per submarine, but the *détente* between Russia and the West

will hopefully allow such a terrifying idea to be cancelled.

The depth-charge remained the principal weapon against the submarine throughout the Second World War, although it was supplemented by the aircraft bomb, and by specialised weapons such as Hedgehog. After 1945 a variety of launchers replaced the old-style depth-charge throwers and racks, to eliminate the need for an escort to pass over the submarine before dropping her charges.

Quick-reaction defence
The British favoured a three-barrelled mortar firing full-sized depth-charges. The first pattern was the Squid, but it was replaced by the Limbo, which had more range and could be trained over a wider arc. Limbo also had the advantage of being able to pre-set depth-charges with data supplied direct from the Sonar plot, and it remains in service today as a useful quick-reaction defence against a submarine which gets within a mile.

The US Navy and others favoured a rocket projectile to carry the explosive charge to the submarine. There are several versions of this type of weapon such as the now obsolete American Weapon Alfa, the Bofors quadruple launcher and the Norwegian Terne, but they all suffer from the basic weakness of carrying a small explosive charge, which reduces their chances of damaging a submarine.

The homing torpedo has been turned against the submarine, and it makes a

potent weapon, especially when dropped by a helicopter. One way of destroying submarines by homing torpedoes is to programme the torpedo in a descending spiral; another is to use wire guidance. Significantly the three most advanced anti-submarine missile systems in existence today are merely delivery systems for homing torpedoes.

The American Asroc system works like Subroc, but in reverse. It fires a missile on a ballistic trajectory to the target area, and then parachutes a torpedo into the sea. The French Lamafon is a 21-in torpedo with

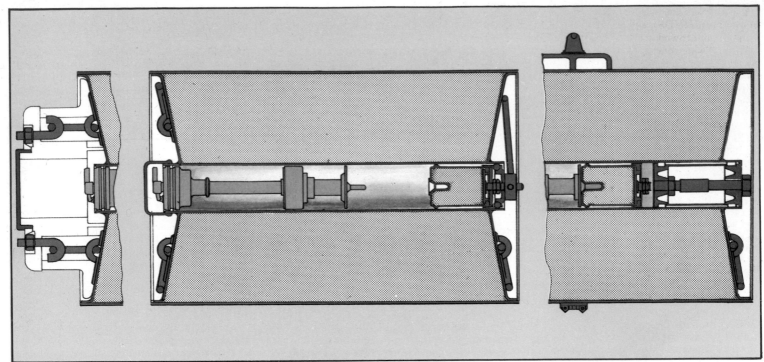

wings and tail, which is launched by rocket and then glides to its target area. The Anglo-Australian Ikara system differs from the earlier two in that the missile is actually a small delta-winged aircraft carrying a torpedo; its virtue is that it can be flown on a revised course to counteract evasive manoeuvres by the submarine, and when it reaches the area the carrier breaks up and releases the homing torpedo.

The original Asdic and hydrophones which were the only detection devices of the Second World War have been much improved and developed. These devices are now known as active and passive Sonar respectively, and the way in which they can be used has changed. Some U-Boats found that they could hide under 'thermal layers' of seawater of a different temperature, which made the Asdic beams bounce

British Depth-charges (above)
Left: The Mk VII (Heavy) was simply a charge with an added weight to make it sink rapidly. *Right:* The Mk VII (Aircraft Pattern) was the first airborne depth-charge. *Centre:* the Mk VII was the standard British depth-charge and differed little from the 'D' Type of the First World War

American Aircraft Depth-charge (below)
During the war considerable time was spent on re-designing the old 'ash-can' shape of the depth-charge to improve its flight-path and its rate of sinking. This was the US Navy's airborne depth-charge

Hedgehog Attack Pattern
The Hedgehog mortar could be fired while the U-Boat was still held in the Asdic beam. The elliptical spread of the bombs was intended to give the best chance of hitting a submarine, and a detonation meant a certain 'kill' except in very shallow water

American Depth-charge Projector (right)
A later development of the British wartime depth-charge thrower. Basically a spigot mortar, two or three would be mounted on each side of a ship, and set to project a pattern of charges

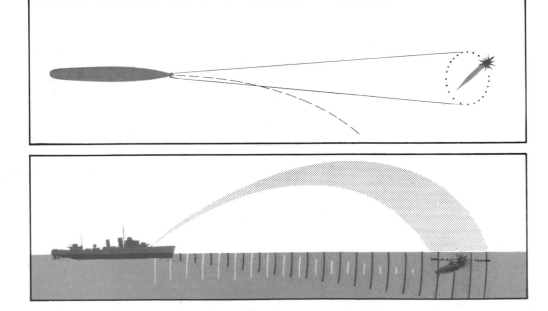

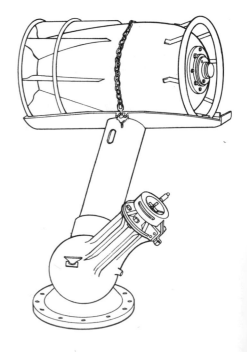

off. This has been countered by the Variable Depth Sonar (VDS), which is simply a Sonar transducer towed behind an escort and lowered to search beneath a thermal layer. The US Navy has developed very powerful Sonar sets, and they are frequently mounted under the bow, where the hull turbulence is at a minimum. Helicopters can use their dipping Sonars for the same purpose, and formidable machines like the Sikorsky Sea King have space for homing torpedoes as well.

However, the most potent anti-submarine weapon which has emerged is the submarine herself. She has many advantages, and they are multiplied by nuclear propulsion. Because she operates below the surface a nuclear hunter-killer suffers no reduction of speed from bad weather, and she can either use a thermal layer for her own protection or simply pass through it. She is her own sonar platform, with performance as good as her opponent's, and if she goes deep the pressure of water will reduce the noise of cavitation from her propeller. Her main problem is that she is operating in a semi-blind situation, and does not have the easy communication enjoyed by surface warships, but this is a small problem to set against her undoubted abilities as a submarine-killer. Here again, we should not be surprised to see a radical improvement within the next few years.

At this point we leave the submarine. She is at the height of her powers, having developed from a crude submersible torpedo-boat to a giant warship capable of cruising at will beneath the surface of the sea. History shows that every weapon is eventually displaced by a new one, but for the moment the submarine has no challenger.

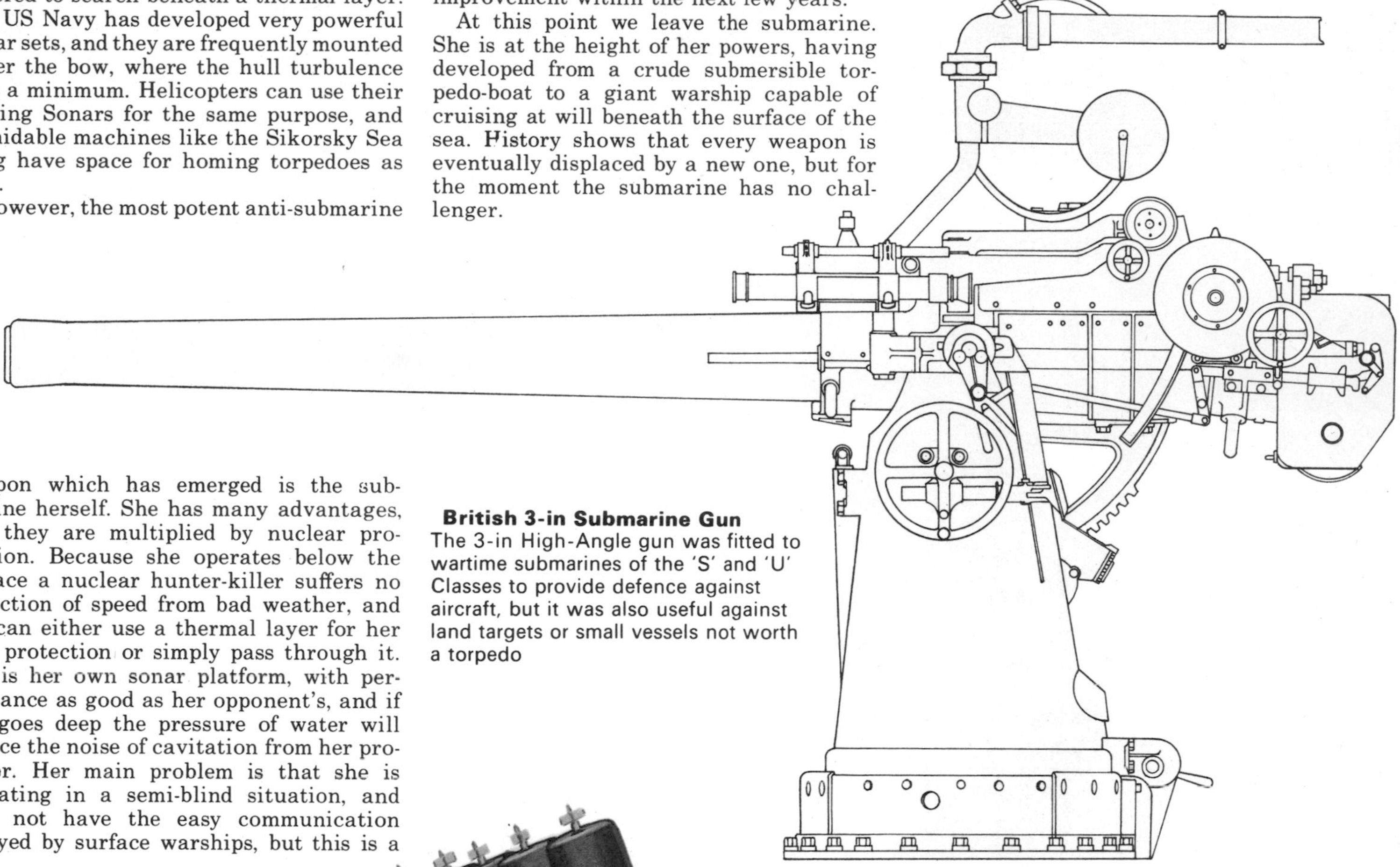

British 3-in Submarine Gun
The 3-in High-Angle gun was fitted to wartime submarines of the 'S' and 'U' Classes to provide defence against aircraft, but it was also useful against land targets or small vessels not worth a torpedo

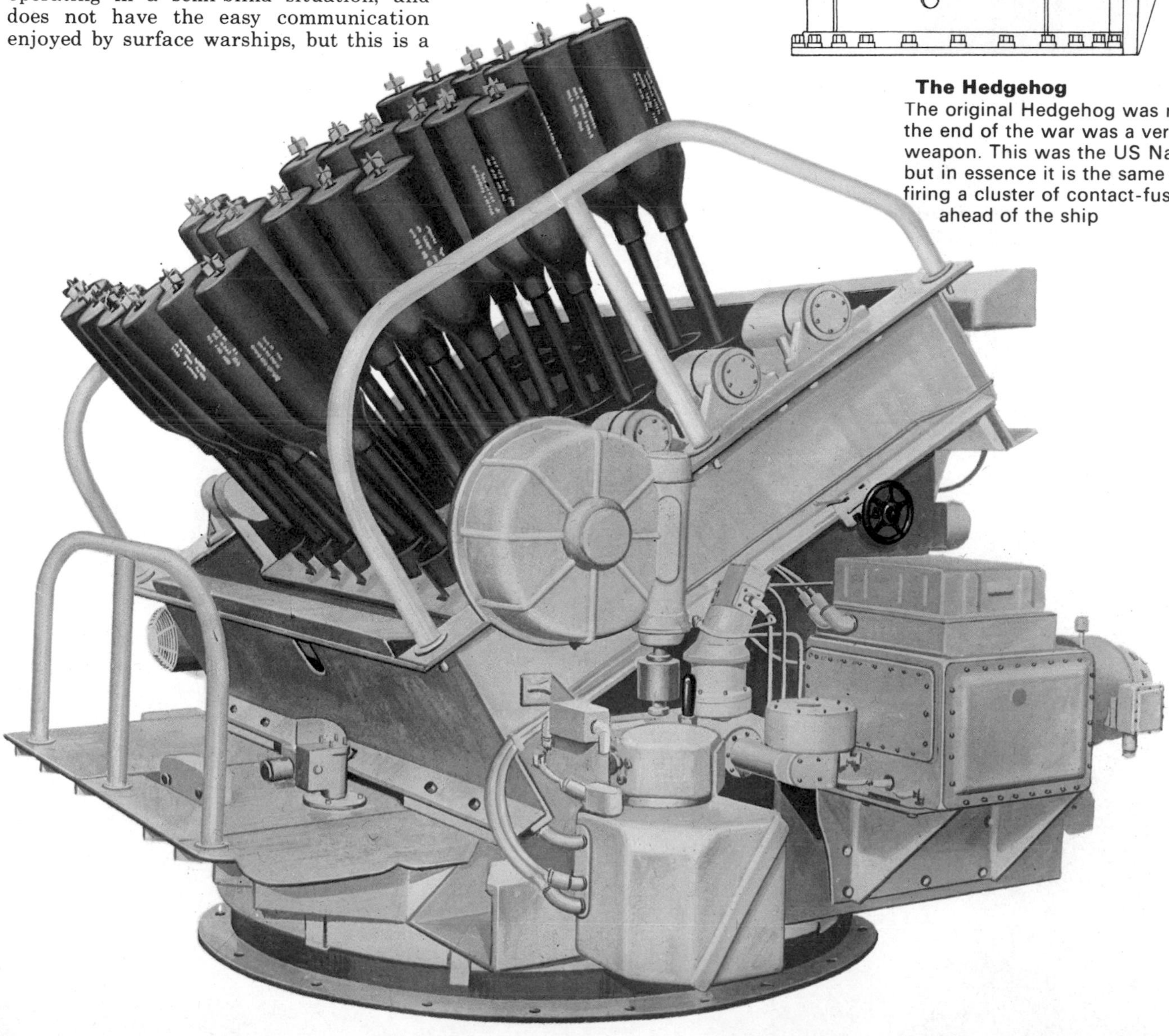

The Hedgehog
The original Hedgehog was refined, and by the end of the war was a very elaborate weapon. This was the US Navy's version, but in essence it is the same spigot mortar firing a cluster of contact-fused bombs ahead of the ship

Curtiss BF2C fighter-bombers in flight. It was the
last Curtiss biplane to serve with the US Navy

US Navy

EARLY NAVAL AIRCRAFT
Louis S. Casey

In 1914 the ultimate expression of naval power was the battleship. Already however, eight years after the Wright brothers' first flight, courageous and daring pioneers in America and Great Britain had made the first landings on warships at sea. Naval warfare had been expanded into a third dimension and naval flying took off with the outbreak of war.

Shipborne fighters and Zeppelins duelled over the North Sea. Torpedo-bombers went into action, like the submarine, threatening the supremacy of the big-gun ship. By 1918 true aircraft carriers were in service and special classes of aircraft were being designed to equip them.

This is the story of naval aircraft from the beginning to the outbreak of the Second World War – from Eugene Ely's first flight from the *USS Birmingham* in 1910 to the dive-bombers of 1939 designed to crack open a battleship.

CONTENTS

HMS Furious *as a seaplane carrier in 1917. Her
first conversion has added a flying-off deck forward,
but the 18-in gun aft remains as a reminder of her
origins as a battlecruiser*

THE BEGINNING OF CARRIER AVIATION

The first aeroplane flight from a ship took place on November 14, 1910, when Eugene Ely flew a Curtiss Model D from an 83-ft ramp on the bows of the light cruiser Birmingham *off Norfolk, Virginia. The Curtiss' wheels, floats and propeller hit the water, but Ely retained control and landed ashore*

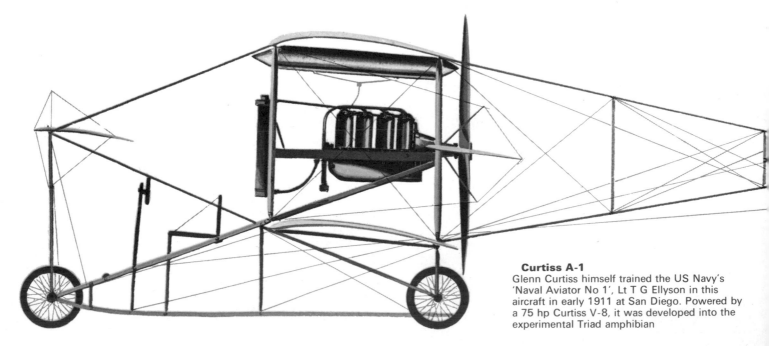

Curtiss A-1
Glenn Curtiss himself trained the US Navy's 'Naval Aviator No 1', Lt T G Ellyson in this aircraft in early 1911 at San Diego. Powered by a 75 hp Curtiss V-8, it was developed into the experimental Triad amphibian

When the Wright brothers made the first powered flight at Kitty Hawk in 1903, a new dimension was added to war. The potential of aircraft at sea was also made obvious to a courageous group of naval pioneers. The carrier aircraft was born.

Naval aviation had its beginnings less than seven years after the Wright brothers' first flight. A ramp was built over the bows of the light cruiser USS *Birmingham* at the instigation of Capt Chambers of the US Navy, who had learned of the interest in ship-to-shore mail flights by the Hamburg-American Steamship Line. The shipping line's pilot could not make the first attempt at a take-off from this platform, so a Curtiss demonstration pilot named Eugene Ely was recruited for the experiment.

The aircraft was a Curtiss Model D biplane, the Albany Flier, which Glenn Curtiss himself had used on his spectacular flight from Albany to New York in May 1910. It was hoisted aboard the *Birmingham* at Norfolk, Virginia, and positioned at the top of the ramp, which was a mere 83 ft long by 24 ft wide. The Albany Flyer's front wheel was just 57 ft from the forward edge of the platform.

The date of the attempt was set for November 13, 1910, but strong winds forced a postponement until the following day. After further delays Ely gave the go-ahead and at 1516, before the ship's anchor was even out of the water, he accelerated down the 5° ramp. Curtiss had developed a number of safety features for his overwater flight to New York, and these were also installed for Ely's historic mission. Canister floats were attached beneath the wings and a bag of corks was fitted to the keel. As the Albany

Ely wore a football helmet and a bicycle inner tube for safety during his landing on the Pennsylvania. *Swimmers and life-boats also stood by*

Flyer dropped the 37 ft off the ship's bows the canisters, along with the wheels, frame and propeller tips, hit the sea surface. The damaged propeller set the whole aircraft vibrating, and Ely prudently decided to make for the nearest land. This was Willoughby Spit, two and a half miles away, where he made a successful landing.

Undaunted by this experience, Ely agreed to attempt a unique double by making the first landing aboard a ship. A wooden deck, 120 ft long by 32 ft wide, was built over the after deck and rear turrets of the cruiser USS *Pennsylvania*. Every effort was made to reduce the dangers of this hazardous experiment. The deck sloped up at its far end and canvas was lashed to the front and sides,

screening the superstructure and acting as a safety net. Ely himself wrapped a pair of inner tubes around his body to keep himself afloat if he should come down in the water, and as an additional precaution life-boats and teams of swimmers stood by.

The aircraft, a Curtiss D IV Military fitted with canister floats under the lower wings but with no bag of corks, was to be brought to a halt by an arrester system consisting of 22 transverse ropes stretched between 50-lb sandbags. Timbers held the ropes slightly above the deck so that they could be engaged by three pairs of small grapnel hooks attached between the wheels.

January 18, 1911, was the chosen date, and despite adverse weather conditions Ely elected to press on. He took off from San Francisco's Presidio Field and headed for the *Pennsylvania* at anchor out in the bay. A 10 mph wind was blowing from the stern, and as Ely ran in for his downwind landing

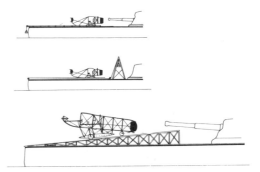
Early proposals for shipboard catapults included using weights to accelerate the aircraft under the force of gravity, but Eugene Ely relied on a simple ramp for his historic flight

On January 18, 1911, Ely carried out the second half of his mission by landing aboard the cruiser Pennsylvania *in San Francisco Bay. He landed on a 120-ft wooden platform built over the ship's stern and after turret, using an arrester system of ropes stretched between 100 lb sandbags*

the breeze swung round slightly to one side. As the aircraft crossed the ship's stern at about 40 mph the pilot eased the nose up to lose speed and caught the twelfth and successive ropes, bringing the machine to a halt about 50 ft from the superstructure looming up ahead.

Three-quarters of an hour later the aircraft had been turned round into what was now a headwind, and Ely made an uneventful flight back to land. The foundation had been laid for aircraft operations from ships, and the elegantly simple arrester system was to prove superior to other more complicated arrangements tried out in the following years. At the last moment it had been decided to make the first landing with the *Pennsylvania* stationary rather than under way, and it was left to the Royal Navy – which was to prove more enthusiastic than the USN about naval aviation in its infancy – to pioneer operations from moving ships.

On May 4, 1912, Cdr C R Samson piloted a Short Hydroplane from a ramp built over the forward gun turret of the battleship HMS *Hibernia* as she steamed into wind at about 12 knots. Lt Malone repeated Samson's pioneering flight, and the dawn of practical military aviation at sea was at hand.

Cdr C R Samson's Short Hydroplane about to be launched from HMS Hibernia, *May 1912*

Imperial War Museum

The first takeoff and landing aboard a navy ship by Eugene Ely and the first takeoff from HMS *Hibernia* while she was under way, demonstrated the basic techniques for aircraft launch and retrieval, as we know them today.

To the credit of the Royal Navy, they began experiments which eventually led to the development of shipborne aircraft and the techniques and ships to handle these planes. One wonders, when looking back over the development of naval aviation, why the navies of the world, particularly the British, United States, and Japanese, the major sea powers of that day, failed to grasp and perfect the techniques as demonstrated by Ely. Failure to utilize these techniques can probably be attributed to the battleship fixation of the senior naval

personnel of these nations. The thought of having their ships' decks encumbered or obstructed by the gear necessary to handle aircraft was out of the question.

Development of ships' facilities for the handling of aircraft was accelerated due to the demand for some kind of ship with sufficient speed to accompany the fleet and to act as a carrier for the numerous aircraft required. The aircraft were desired for reconnaissance, offensive action and fire control for the heavy guns of the capital ships of the fleet. From these experimental installations, it became obvious that the aeroplane did indeed have a definite place in naval warfare.

It was also determined that something more reliable and efficient than seaplane tenders was required, for with seaplanes, frail as they were at this time, it was often impossible to launch and retrieve them under certain sea conditions. Often the

NAVAL AIRCRAFT: THE FIRST WAR

US Experimental Steam Catapault, 1912

Avro 504

Remembered mostly as a trainer, the Avro 504 also saw service as a bomber and reconnaissance aircraft. On 21 November 1914, three aircraft of the Royal Naval Air Service bombed the Zeppelin sheds at Friedrichshafen in one of the most daring raids of the war. The Avro 504 was also used to attack Zeppelins in flight

Span: 36 ft *Length:* 29 ft 5 in *Engine:* Gnôme, 80 hp *Max speed:* 82 mph *Range:* 250 miles *Armament:* Lewis mg (some) *Bombload:* 4 × 20-lb

Imperial War Museum

Sopwith Tabloid, the only landplane embarked aboard HMS Ark Royal

Caudron GIII
One of the earliest types used by the RNAS
Span: 43 ft 11 in *Length:* 21 ft *Engine:*
Gnôme, 80 hp *Max speed:* 69 mph *Ceiling:*
10,000 ft *Armament:* 1 mg *Bombload:* 20 lb

Officer cadets of the fledgling RNAS learn the basics of aircraft structure—1914. On the blackboard is a Farman FM7

Imperial War Museum

Sopwith Pup (Type 9901a)

When Pups were first supplied to the early aircraft carriers, there was very little knowledge of the problems of deck flying. Experiments proved that a simple skid undercarriage could withstand the shock of landing better than wheels. The skid-equipped Type 9901a was built in some numbers for service throughout the fleet

Span: 26 ft 6 in *Length:* 19 ft 3·75 in *Engine:* Gnôme, 80 hp *Max speed:* 105 mph at 5000 ft *Ceiling:* 17,500 ft *Armament:* Vickers mg

most desirable situations coincided with the worst sea and weather conditions. To remedy this, the Cunard liner *Campania* was fitted with a deck almost 230 ft long and seaplanes were launched under conditions which would have made operations impossible under the old system of hoisting aircraft over the side of the ship for a water takeoff.

Launching from the *Campania* was accomplished by use of the Gregory-Riley wheel gear. This interesting and successful gear consisted of a cross-axle which was fixed to the bottom of the floats. Outboard of the floats, an ordinary aircraft wheel was mounted. Incorporated in the device were springs which tended to force the wheels off but were prevented from doing so by a pair of safety pins, inserted into the axle, to which wires were attached leading to the cockpit. As soon as the aircraft lifted off the deck, the pilot pulled the pins clear and the wheels shot outward and off the plane.

The Gregory-Riley gear was also useful in making takeoffs from aerodromes, where they experienced no more difficulty than ordinary wheeled craft. An improved version of this system had a deck built over the

aircraft close to the ship and rescue the pilot.

After Dunning's fatal accident, a deck was built aft of the bridge and wires were strung fore and aft with ropes athwartship, similar to Ely's arresting system. As this system developed, hooks were attached to the axle which engaged the longitudinal wires to prevent a recurrence of Dunning's fate. It was, potentially, very wasteful of aircraft, however, and resulted in a short lifetime of only three landings using this system. This was the system developed on the Isle of Grain referred to elsewhere in the text.

A parallel development of short duration was barge flying. Commander C R Samson, RN, who, on 10 January 1912, made the takeoff from HMS *Africa*, produced an idea and developed it to a working system. He had a flat-bottomed barge towed behind a fast, powerful destroyer. Mounted on the barge was a Sopwith Camel which was equipped with a quick-release mooring. With the combined sea breeze and the top speed of the destroyer, the flying speed of the Camel was reached enabling the plane to lift off from the barge. This was another

appears to be a slightly modified Sopwith Baby) with a wing span 2 ft greater than the 25 ft 8 in of the Sopwith version. The Hamble Baby was powered by the 110-hp Clerget, the Sopwith by the 130-hp Clerget. The Fairey Campania seaplane was a two-place floatplane of 61 ft 8 in of span (upper wing) and powered by a 275-hp Rolls-Royce engine.

Fairey Aviation produced the Type 3B powered by the 260-hp Sunbeam Maori engine. This, too, had biplane wings of unequal span, the upper span being 61 ft 0 in. Very similar was the Short 320, which was larger, 74 ft 6 in, and powered by the more powerful 320-hp Sunbeam Cossack engine. Last, but by no means least, was the Short Type 184, which proved to be one of the most durable of the lot. It was powered by a

forward hangar on HMS *Furious*. The deck was, in fact, the roof of the hangar and sloped downward towards the bow. Though this was something of an improvement, it left much to be desired, for the run available was only 200 ft.

It was on this deck that Squadron Commander Dunning made his ill-fated landing. His first landing on 2 August 1917, was successful. On this landing a deck crew assisted with the final touch-down of his Sopwith Pup. On the second landing, a tyre burst on touchdown, causing the Pup to swerve over the side of the ship and Dunning was drowned. Prior to this experimental landing, the usual procedure was to land the

short-lived experiment, but one that produced results, for shortly after Samson's experimental 'fly-offs', another pilot made a similar takeoff and shot down a far-ranging Zeppelin over the North Sea.

Aircraft involved in all these experiments were of wood and fabric structure and some, as in the case of the Camel and the Pup, were First World War fighters and well-known to anyone familiar with aircraft of that period. In addition, such aircraft as the Sopwith 1½ Strutter, P V N Griffin, Parnall Panther, Fairey Type 3A, Beardmore SB3D and the Hamble Baby were all used as ship's aircraft.

The Hamble Baby was a seaplane, (which

variety of engines, starting with the 225-hp Sunbeam engine.

Over 650 of these planes were produced during 1914-18 as torpedo reconnaissance aircraft and one is credited with the first successful aerial torpedo launching in the Sea of Marmara. It was also one of the early aircraft types sold to the Japanese navy in 1916 to begin their aviation training programme. Along with these, the Japanese acquired Sopwith Tabloid fighters and Deperdussin training seaplanes and the venerable Avro 504s.

Opposite is a comparison list of aircraft classified as ship's aircraft during this period of adapting aircraft to naval use.

From a barge towed behind a destroyer a Sopwith Camel takes off into a North Sea headwind

Sq Cdr E H Dunning makes the first successful deck landing on HMS Furious in a Sopwith Pup, August 2, 1917. He had to fly around the bridge and funnel to land on the downward sloping deck

Imperial War Museum

Sopwith 1½-Strutter

Deliveries to the RNAS began in the early spring of 1916, the aircraft being used as a bomber in its own right as well as an escort. The 1½-Strutter was the first British aircraft fitted with synchronizing gear to allow the guns to fire through the propeller, and its inherent stability compensated for a lack of manoeuvrability. A single-seat version was developed to carry out long-range bombing raids
   Span: 33 ft 6 in *Length:* 25 ft 3 in *Engine:* Clerget or Le Rhône, 80—135 hp *Max speed:* 106 mph *Ceiling:* 16,000 ft *Endurance:* up to 4 hr *Armament (single-seat bomber):* forward-firing Vickers mg *Bombload:* 225 lb

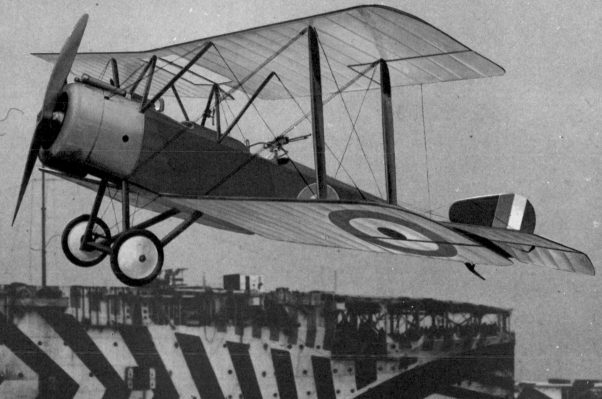

The world's first true aircraft carrier, HMS Argus. She was completed in September 1918, could make 21 knots, had a displacement of 15,775 tons and could accommodate up to 20 aircraft in her hangars

	Span	Length	Height
Wight Seaplane	65 ft 6 in	44 ft 8 in	15 ft 10 in
Sopwith 2F1 Camel	28 ft 0 in	18 ft 9 in	8 ft 6 in
Sopwith Torpedo Plane	45 ft 9 in	28 ft 6 in	11 ft 0 in
Beardmore SB 3D	25 ft 1 in	19 ft 4 in	8 ft 8 in
Fairey Type 3A	61 ft 0 in	35 ft 6 in	13 ft 0 in
Parnall Panther	29 ft 6 in	24 ft 11 in	10 ft 9 in
PVN Griffin	41 ft 6 in	27 ft 3 in	10 ft 11 in
Sopwith 1½ Strutter	33 ft 6 in	25 ft 3 in	10 ft 3 in
Sopwith Baby	25 ft 8 in	23 ft 0 in	10 ft 10 in
Fairey Campania	61 ft 8 in	43 ft 3 in	15 ft 1 in
Fairey Type 3B	61 ft 0 in	35 ft 6 in	13 ft 0 in
Short 184	63 ft 5 in	40 ft 8 in	13 ft 2 in
Short No 320	74 ft 6 in	45 ft 9 in	17 ft 4 in

Sopwith Camel F1

RNAS squadrons on the Western Front began exchanging their much-loved Triplanes for Camels in the summer of 1917. Naval Camels also operated in Italy and the Aegean. A few F1 Camels were used as ships' aircraft and launched from towed lighters but the smaller span Camel 2F1 was specifically developed as a fleet fighter and for anti-Zeppelin operations in the North Sea. Camel flights embarked aboard HMS *Furious* in 1918 and made a successful raid against airship sheds at Tondern. Naval 2F1s from *Vindictive* were operating against the Bolsheviks in the Baltic in 1919. The Camel was the First World War's most successful fighter, with 1294 aircraft downed to its credit. **1** Upper wing cutout for visibility **2** Ring sight **3** Vickers gun **4** Ammunition tank **5** Wooden propeller **6** Aluminium cowling **7** Rotary engine **8** Oil tank **9** Wing rib **10** Aileron control wire **11** Compression rib **12** and **13** Wing bracing wires **14** Main spars **15** Aileron operating horn **16** Aileron connecting wire **17** Bungee-sprung wheel **18** Rudder bar **19** Wicker seat **20** Fuel tank **21** Control column **22** Wire-braced wooden fuselage **23** Tailplane structure **24** Iron-shod skid **25** Fin and rudder **26** Bungee skid spring **27** Throttle and mixture controls **28** Instrument panel **29** Flying wire **30** Landing wire **31** Incidence bracing wires

Span: 28 ft *Length:* 18 ft 8 in *Engine:* Clerget (130 hp), Le Rhône (110 hp) or Bentley (150 hp) rotaries *Max speed:* 130 mph at sea level *Ceiling:* 24,000 ft *Endurance:* 2½ hrs *Armament:* 2 Vickers mg (Performance figures are for Le Rhône engine)

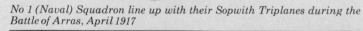

No 1 (Naval) Squadron line up with their Sopwith Triplanes during the Battle of Arras, April 1917

Youthful RNAS Flight-Lieutenants lament the crash of a Sopwith 1½-Strutter on a Western Front airfield

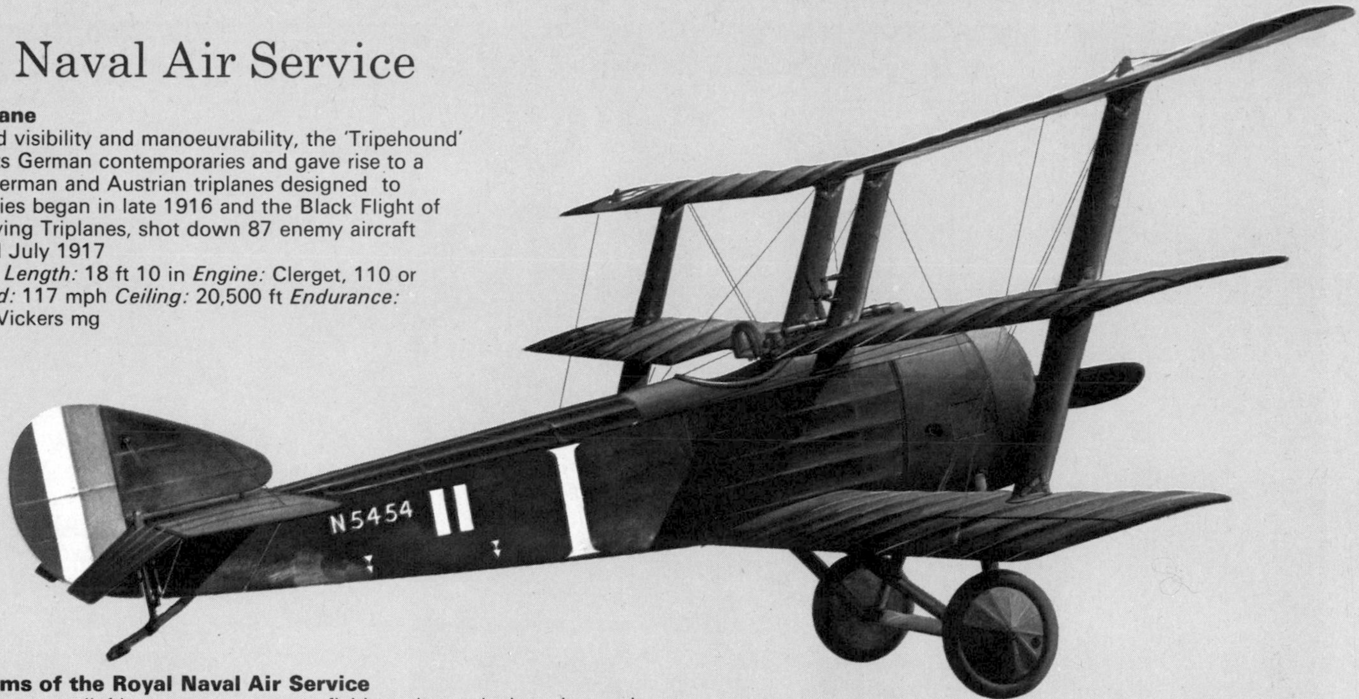

Sopwith Triplane

Designed for good visibility and manoeuvrability, the 'Tripehound' could out-climb its German contemporaries and gave rise to a whole family of German and Austrian triplanes designed to counter it. Deliveries began in late 1916 and the Black Flight of five Canadians, flying Triplanes, shot down 87 enemy aircraft between May and July 1917

Span: 26 ft 6 in *Length:* 18 ft 10 in *Engine:* Clerget, 110 or 130 hp *Max speed:* 117 mph *Ceiling:* 20,500 ft *Endurance:* 2¾ hr *Armament:* Vickers mg

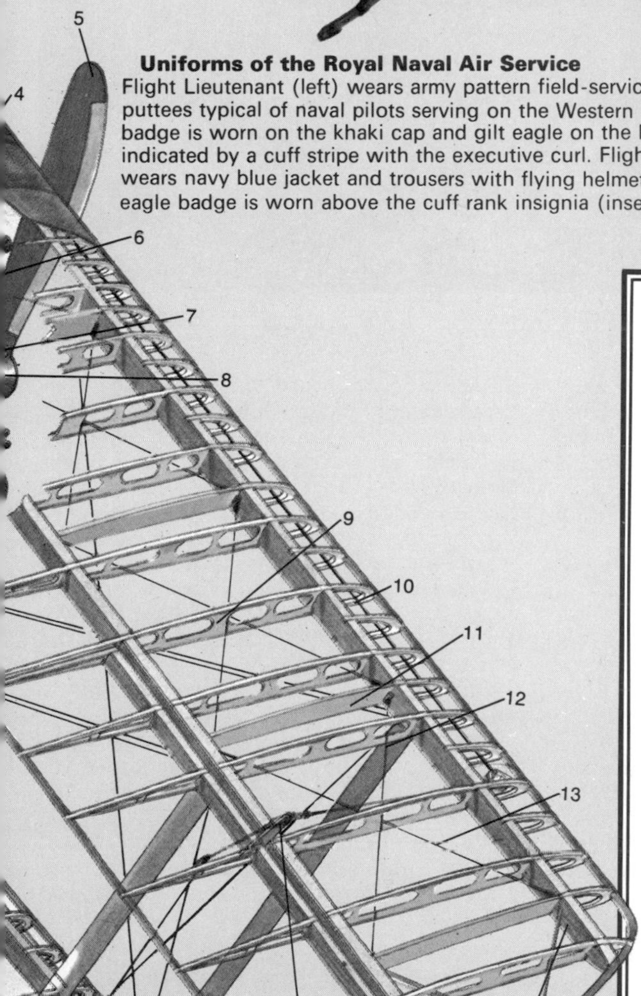

Uniforms of the Royal Naval Air Service

Flight Lieutenant (left) wears army pattern field-service tunic, breeches and puttees typical of naval pilots serving on the Western Front. The RNAS cap badge is worn on the khaki cap and gilt eagle on the left breast. Rank is indicated by a cuff stripe with the executive curl. Flight Commander (right) wears navy blue jacket and trousers with flying helmet and coat. The gilt eagle badge is worn above the cuff rank insignia (inset) RNAS cap badge

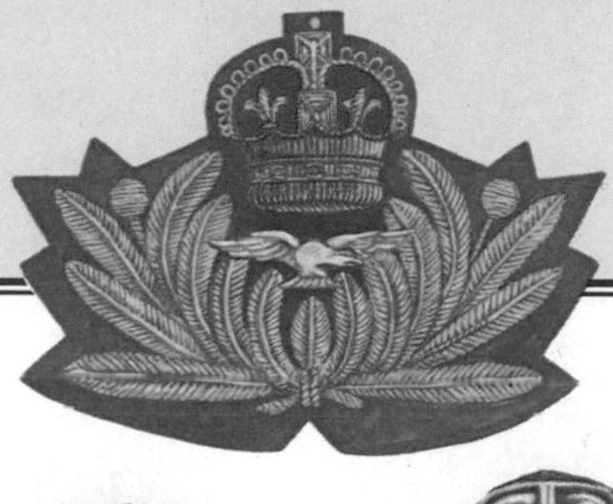

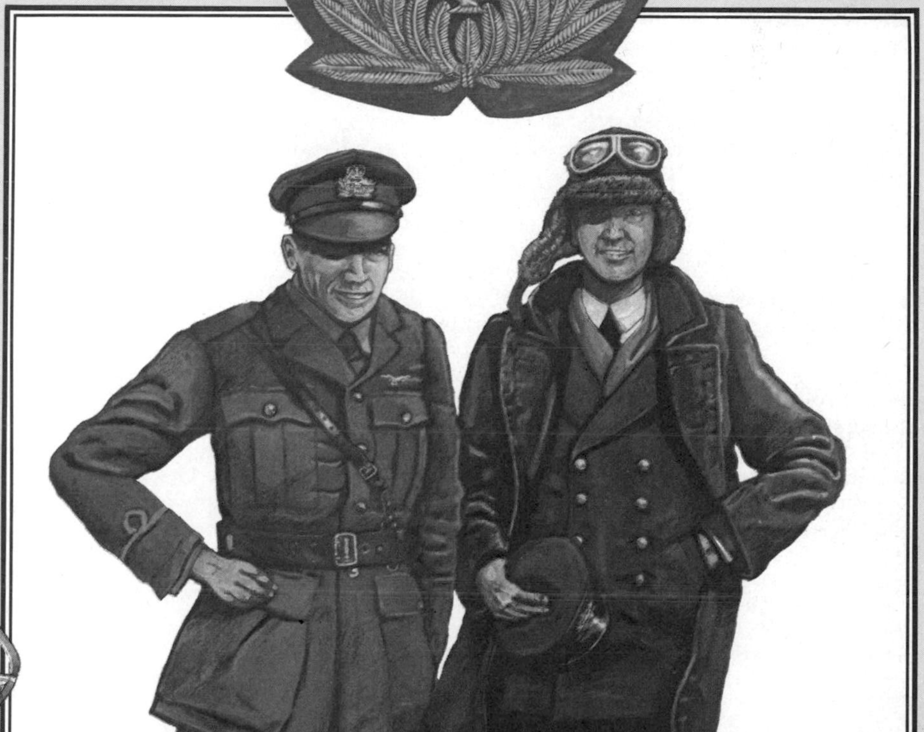

Christy Campbell

When the Handley Page 0/100 heavy bomber, seen here outside the manufacturer's factory at Cricklewood, entered service in November 1916 it allowed the RNAS to step up its daylight bombing. The 0/100 could carry three times the load of the Short Bomber and six times that of the DH4

The Sopwith 1½ Strutter, and Sopwith Pup, in particular, and others on occasion, were fitted with skids which were mated with parallel U-shaped tracks which guided them down the sloping decks for their take-off 'run' and which, on landing, caused the aircraft to come to a halt after a very short run. In addition, they protected the propeller as the plane nosed down from this friction with the landing deck. These skids were also used on aircraft intended for takeoff from the turrets of battleships and cruisers during the early experimental stage of naval aviation both in Britain and the United States. The Japanese, who were at this time only beginning to adapt aircraft to naval use, apparently bypassed this stage on the advice of their British Technical Training Mission.

With the demonstration of the deck landing technique, the loss of aircraft with each flight was nearly at an end. Each flight had previously ended in a 'ditched' landing. Of course, with the use of flotation bags much of the plane could be salvaged but, depending on the circumstances and sea condition, the probability of re-using the airframe more than once or twice was very slim, especially since the prevailing construction was of fabric-covered wood.

With this important milestone achieved, aircraft carrier development centred on landing decks which were built on the after-decks of the *Argus*, *Hermes* and *Vindictive* (originally the *Cavendish*). The latter was nearing completion and orders were given to include a landing deck aft, in addition to the flying-off deck forward.

These ships were a step along the way toward what we now know as aircraft carriers. The forward and aft flight decks were ponderous in the extreme. Aircraft would land on the aft deck and were then man-handled around the control bridge and other superstructure on a trolley type arrangement to avoid damaging the wing or other flight components. After struggling with the aircraft past the bridge, it was positioned on the forward deck for takeoff. It was not long before the unpracticality of this arrangement became evident and the *Argus* was modified once again.

The cruiser *Hermes* had been fitted with a flying-off deck in 1913, but when war broke out, she was fitted with trackways over the foredeck. Unfortunately, little use was obtained from *Hermes*, for she was sunk by a German submarine in October 1914.

In 1913, a merchant ship, then under construction, was purchased and modified for the operation of seaplanes. Named the *Ark Royal*, she was fitted with a flying-off deck, 103 ft long, and stowage space for 10 seaplanes, plus shops for maintaining the planes. *Ark Royal* was launched in 1915 but

A Caproni Ca 5 fitted with torpedo shackles in place of its normal bomb racks. More than 250 of the type were built in 1918

Short Bomber

Developed from the Short 184 seaplane, the Bomber—which was never assigned an official name—was designed as a long-range heavy bomber and was used to attack targets such as Ostend and Zeebrugge. It was not a great success operationally, however

Span: 85 ft *Length:* 45 ft *Engine:* Rolls-Royce Eagle, 250 hp *Max speed:* 77 mph *Ceiling:* 9500 ft *Endurance:* 6 hr *Armament:* Lewis mg *Bombload:* 920 lb

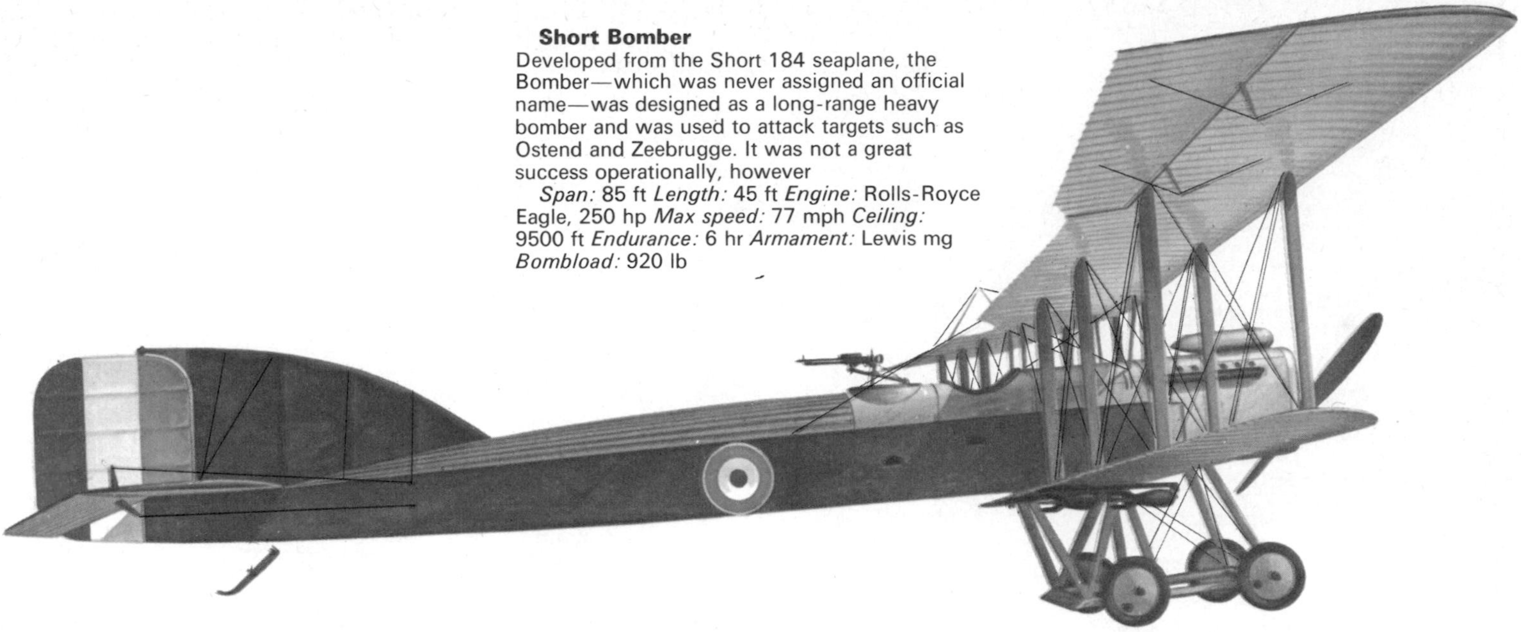

Caproni Ca 5

Caproni returned to the biplane layout for the Ca 5, having adopted a triplane configuration for the Ca 4s. The Ca 5s were beginning to replace the earlier Ca 3s as the war ended, and the type was regarded as Italy's best heavy bomber of the period. Capronis were used throughout the First World War to attack Austro-Hungarian targets such as the naval base at Pola and the seaport of Trieste

Span: 77 ft *Length:* 41 ft 4 in *Engines:* three Fiat A 12 bis, 330 hp each *Max speed:* 100 mph *Range:* 400 miles *Armament:* 2 Revelli mg *Bombload:* 2000 lb

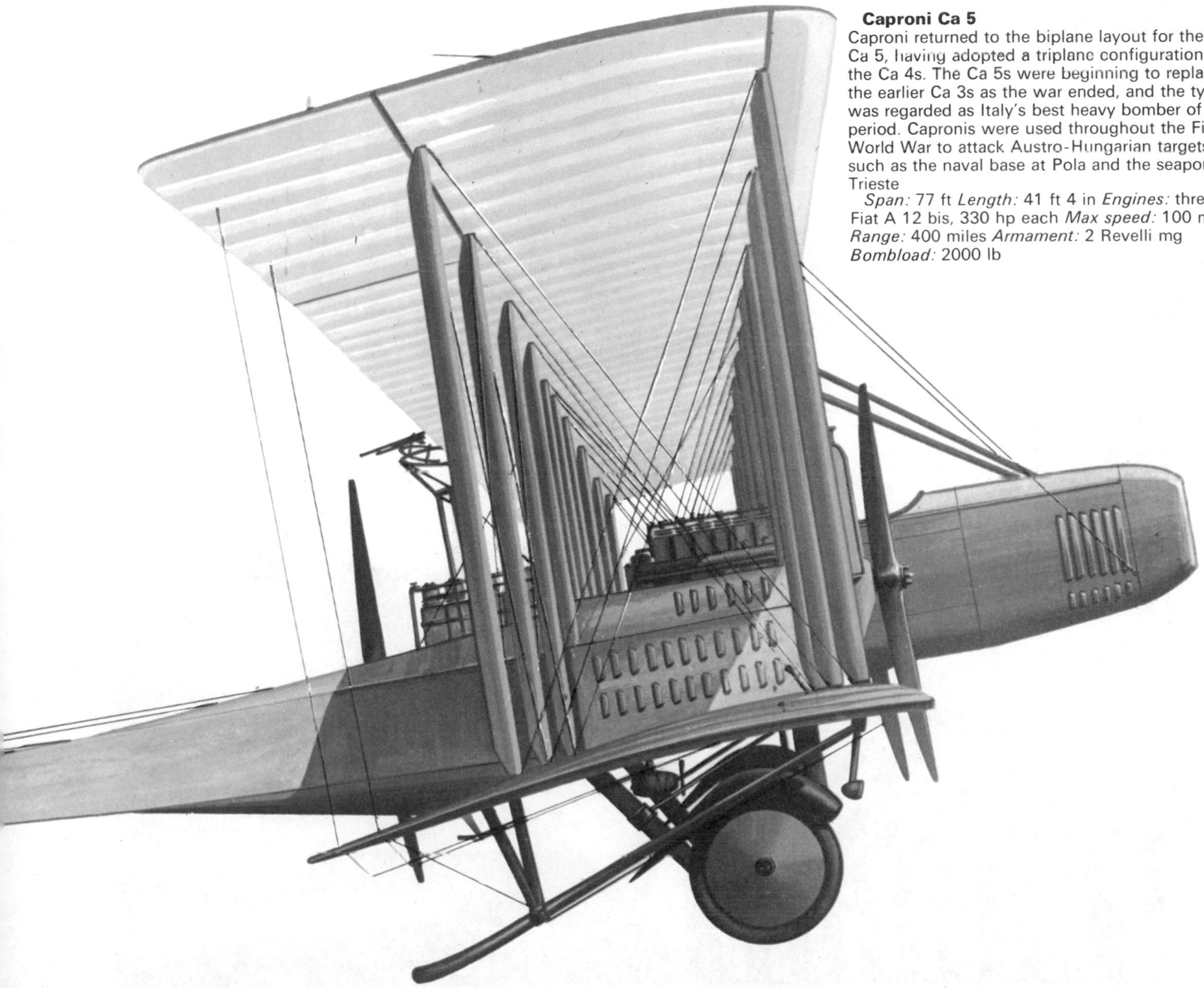

Below: HMS Furious

When *Furious* joined the fleet in July 1917 it was as a hybrid vessel, aircraft carrier forward and cruiser aft. A hangar was built in place of the forward 18-in gun, the roof forming a flying-off deck. A landing deck was later added behind the funnel, but operations proved too dangerous and flying was confined to launching. Up to 12 Sopwith Pups and eight Short seaplanes could be accommodated in the two hangars
Displacement: 22,000 tons *Length:* 786 ft overall *Max speed:* 32·5 knots *Armament (1918–1925):* 11×5·5-in guns, 18×21-in torpedo tubes, up to 33 aircraft

Below left: HMS Riviera

Converted into a seaplane carrier from a ferry. The aircraft were housed in a hangar at the stern, being hoisted out for launching and back in again after alighting
Displacement: 1675 tons *Length:* 311 ft *Max speed:* 23 knots *Armament:* 2×4-in and one 6-pounder guns

HMS Campania *was fitted with a 120-ft flying-off deck forward, but this was never used in action. Seaplanes were hoisted overboard to take off from the open sea instead*

Imperial War Museum

HMS Argus

Converted from the unfinished Italian liner *Conte Rosso,* the *Argus* was fitted with a clear flight deck 550 ft long by 68 ft wide. The chart house was mounted on a lift, and exhaust gases were ducted to ports in the stern. A squadron of Sopwith Cuckoos was embarked in late 1918, marking the first deployment of carrier-based torpedo bombers, but the war ended before the vessel could see action
Displacement: 15,775 tons *Length:* 565 ft *Max speed:* 20·75 knots *Armament:* 6×4-in AA guns, up to 20 aircraft

her speed of 11 knots made her unusable with the fleet. She saw service in the Mediterranean as a base and maintenance ship.

At the beginning of the First World War, *Empress*, *Engadine* and *Riviera*, three cross-channel steamers, were fitted out to operate the ship planes and later the *Vindex*, in 1915, and *Manxman*, in 1916, were added to the list of ships converted to handle aircraft.

Prior to the commissioning of HMS *Eagle* in 1920, all the existing carriers had a level, squared-off flight deck at the stern. This resulted in a number of mishaps, usually the result of pilots approaching too high to assure their clearing the flight deck and the down-draught usually associated with it when the ship was operating at speed. To reduce or eliminate this problem, the *Eagle's* deck was constructed with a round-down to catch and correct for a low approach. Prior to this, a low approach often resulted in a sheared-off landing gear or worse. The round-down prevented further mishaps attributable to this.

The end of the First World War brought with it an economic retrenchment characteristic of post-war years when all the belligerents are physically and financially exhausted. This situation had its effect on carrier development which was reduced to experimental status which, in fact, it was.

The pressure to develop the equipment and operating techniques was no longer present. Great Britain had the *Argus* and the *Furious* operating in their earliest configurations. The United States was converting the collier *Jupiter* which became the first US carrier, *Langley*, and the Japanese were building their first carrier, from the keel up, to be christened *Hosho*.

Though the combinations varied from nation to nation and by date, the service functions for carrier aircraft were: fighters, torpedo-attack, bombers, reconnaissance, utility and trainers.

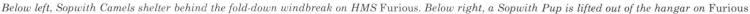

Below left, Sopwith Camels shelter behind the fold-down windbreak on HMS Furious. *Below right, a Sopwith Pup is lifted out of the hangar on* Furious

Imperial War Museum

Imperial War Museum

NEW POWER AT SEA

The development of carrier aviation has progressed in cycles of approximately six years, starting from 1910 when Ely made the first flight off the USS *Birmingham*.

The experimental period examined in the first chapter lasted up to 1915, when adapted landplanes were the dominant aircraft and flight decks were being installed fore and aft on battleships and cruiser hulls. Daring and courageous pilots were feeling their way with techniques that were eventually to bring the combination of aircraft and warship to its ultimate development and use during the Second World War.

For lack of better terminology, we will categorize the descriptions of further stages of development by 'generations' within the operational type groupings. The first generation, the period from 1915 to 1921, still relied on aircraft types developed in, and in many cases left over from, the First World War. They were still star performers, not because of their excellence, but because of their availability during a period of limited resources. The aircraft to dominate this period were the Sopwith Camel, Pup, and 1½ Strutter; added to these were the relative newcomers, the Sopwith Cuckoo and Parnall Panther.

The second generation, 1922-1927, included US types, for with the conversion of the collier *Jupiter* into the carrier *Langley*, the United States began the long road to the mastery of carrier operations. Prior to this period, US Naval aviation had been concentrated on the flying boat and lighter-than-air craft to combat the submarine.

The third generation appeared in the years 1928-1933/4, the Depression years, but in aviation these were the golden years of the great air races and the smashing of one record after another. Great strides were made in the development of powerplants, airframes and overall designs. Fuels and lubricants were rapidly developed, largely in response to the racing activities where men, machines and motors (engines) were pushed to new limits.

The fourth generation, from 1934-1939, could be called the build-up years or the years of trial, when planes and aircrews were being tempered and tested as the world moved steadily toward conflict. The men that were destined to command the naval armadas of the Second World War were in training and developing the tactical and technical skills that were to be used in the war years. The transition to monoplanes was begun and the biplane, with the notable exceptions of the Fairey Swordfish and Albacore, disappeared from the decks of the carriers. With varying degrees of urgency, monoplane aircraft became the dominant first-line aircraft, just in time for the beginning of the Second World War and the fifth generation, the test of all that had gone before.

Whether by fate or pre-ordained destiny, all the lessons learned came to a focus during this period. The carrier task force replaced the dreadnought as the decisive weapon of naval warfare. One by one, the battleships slipped away, many the victims of carrier aircraft.

A Blackburn Dart torpedo bomber overflies HMS Hermes, *the first vessel to be designed from the outset as an aircraft carrier*

: FIGHTERS 1918-39

The first generation of carrier fighters were the tired, war-weary Sopwith 1½ Strutters and the Sopwith Pups, both of which had seen their day by 1918. However, rather than lose what little momentum had already been gained, these aircraft, along with the Nieuport Nightjar/Sparrowhawk, were used to carry on the many experiments that lay ahead before carrier aviation would be an accomplished fact. These aircraft were party to experiments in the handling of aircraft aboard the flat-deck carriers: such manoeuvres as launching, landing, stowing, flotation, and maintaining aircraft at sea all needed development.

The Sopwith aircraft – the 1½ Strutter and the Pup – were of conventional construction for First World War service. They were of wood and fabric structure, suitably braced by wires internally as well as externally. Both were powered by rotary engines. Their wing area was sufficient to give them a low wing loading and consequently low landing speeds. Coupled with these low landing speeds was good manoeuvrability which made them good, if not ideal, for deck flying. The low speeds made them appear to float from and particularly onto, the decks of the carriers, especially when the ship was underway producing a wind over the deck that approached in velocity the normal landing speeds of the aircraft.

Versatile 1½ Strutter

The development of flotation bags and early versions of the arrester gear were developed with the 1½ Strutter as was the technique of flying off a short forward deck.

It became one of the earliest multipurpose aircraft. At various times, sometimes interchangeably, 1½ Strutters were called upon to serve as fighters, reconnaissance aircraft, as well as single and two-seat bombers.

Performance was not spectacular. Speeds of nearly 100 miles per hour were all that could reasonably be expected. Armament, when it was carried, was limited to single rifle-calibre guns mounted on the cowling and on a flexible mounting in the rear cockpit.

The Pup, in addition to its wartime success, found use aboard ships. It was the first type used to take off from the turrets of battleships and return to short after-decks. These feats were performed on skids before wheel brakes and arrester hooks were standard naval aircraft equipment. The

Nieuport Nightjar

When the Gloster company took over the Nieuport designs in 1920, they produced the Nightjar as the naval counterpart to the RAF's Nighthawk—the major difference being the Nightjar's Bentley engine and the provision of arrester gear. This fighter flew patrols during the Chanak crisis of 1922

Span: 28 ft *Length:* 19 ft 2 in *Engine:* Bentley BR 2, 230 hp *Max speed:* 152 mph at sea level *Ceiling:* 23,000 ft *Endurance:* 2 hrs *Armament:* 2 Vickers mg

Nakajima A1N1
The A1N1, a licence-built Gloster Gambet and closely resembling the Gamecock, was designated Type 3 by the Japanese Navy. It made extensive use of duralumin to combine light weight with high structural strength
Span: 31 ft 10 in *Length:* 21 ft 4 in *Engine:* Bristol Jupiter VI *Max speed:* 136 mph *Endurance:* 3¼ hr *Ceiling:* 23,000 ft *Armament:* 2 Vickers 7·7-mm mg *Bombload:* 4×20-lb

Pup was the aircraft type used by Lt S D Culley when he took off from a planing barge (lighter) in the North Sea to destroy the Zeppelin L53 at the end of July 1918.

The Nieuport Nightjar was another of the transition aircraft that used the rotary engine. It came into service in 1922 as a follow-on to the Sopwiths. Whether it used a rotary Bentley BR.2 engine because of familiarity with the type of engine in naval service, or because of shortage of funds dictating the rotary's continued use, is not known. The RAF used virtually the same airframe and installed either the Armstrong-Siddeley Jaguar or Bristol Jupiter radial engines, re-christening it the Nighthawk.

The name change was in itself worthwhile. The Nightjars were part of the first group of aircraft purchased by the developing Japanese naval aviation units. In spite of lack of arrester system or brakes, and in addition to the well-known torque from rotary engines, the Japanese mastered handling these Nightjars in their training programme. It is reported that 50 Nightjars and Sparrowhawks were consigned to Japan; however, it is unknown whether the Japanese Nieuports were the same as, or in addition to, those used by the Royal Navy. In any event, they served for a relatively short period until 1924.

The 'Unbreakables'
The second generation group of carrier fighter aircraft, while still predominantly of British design and manufacture, included in addition the Naval Aircraft Factory (US) TS-1 aircraft. The Fairey Flycatcher and Parnall Plover were readied to replace the Nighthawk in British carrier service.

The Flycatchers served long and well and were often called the 'Unbreakables', as they survived all that the Fleet Air Arm pilots and conditions could offer. They went on board HMS *Argus* for deck-handling trials in early 1923 and served until the early 1930s.

They were of conventional construction for their time, primarily wood with metal fittings and fabric covering. Though on close examination the fuselage profile was conventional, the addition of a rather odd shaped fin and rudder reminds one of a hobby-horse.

All pilot reports for the Flycatchers were very favourable. They were able to execute and survive virtually everything they were called on to perform. For their day, they were the ultimate carrier fighter. They were compact, with a span of 29 ft and length of 23 ft. They fitted the carrier aircraft lift with room to spare. In addition, they had built-in fixtures for float attachment and were often used in this configuration, particularly during Mediterranean cruises. They were very responsive to the controls, and visibility, particularly for deck landings, was excellent, in spite of the air-cooled radial Armstrong-Siddeley Jaguar engine. A robust, if ungainly-looking landing gear assured a reasonable landing. In conjunction with this, their specially patented camber-changing wings served as flaps during the landings. These, or equivalent systems, in varying combinations with other high-lift devices, are now being adapted to a wide range of military and civil types of aircraft, particularly the category now known as V/STOL aircraft.

Unlike the Nightjar/Sparrowhawk, the Flycatcher did not get a second innings in another naval service. They were used only by the Fleet Air Arm until they were declared obsolete in 1935.

One of the many guises allowed the Flycatcher was that of an amphibian. In this form, the floats, which were rather ordinary fitments to these aircraft, were suitably sprung with shock absorbers and wheels were installed in pockets within the floats just forward of the step. This installation permitted very little ground clearance when the Flycatcher was taxiing about the airfield or the deck, but did make them amphibious by definition.

Practically, however, they experienced considerable difficulty in getting 'unstuck'. This phenomenon was experienced previously in 1913 when Glenn H Curtiss, at the insistence of Captain W I Chambers, constructed the OWL (for Over Water and Land). The results were the same, water

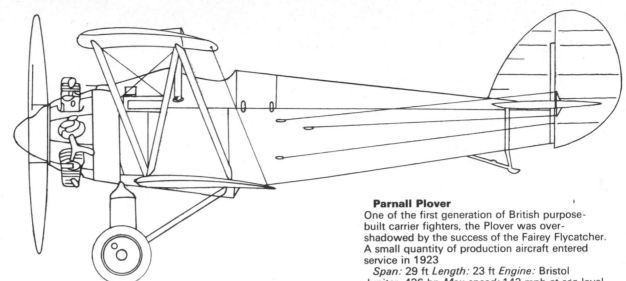

Parnall Plover
One of the first generation of British purpose-built carrier fighters, the Plover was over-shadowed by the success of the Fairey Flycatcher. A small quantity of production aircraft entered service in 1923
Span: 29 ft *Length:* 23 ft *Engine:* Bristol Jupiter, 436 hp *Max speed:* 142 mph at sea level *Ceiling:* 23,000 ft *Armament:* 2 Vickers mg

cavitating in the wheel pockets did little to help the cause of getting airborne.

Built to the same specifications as the Flycatcher (6/22), the Parnall Plover did not enjoy the same degree of affection as did the Flycatcher, partially due, no doubt, to word getting around about a weakness of the centre section. In any event, their service life was limited, as was the production run. Unlike the Flycatcher, the Plover did not have the patented drooping ailerons though it did have full-span ailerons on both upper and lower wings.

On the other side of the Atlantic, the US Navy was completing the *Langley* and with it the Naval Aircraft Factory was designing a single-place fighter not unlike its British counterparts. The resulting carrier fighter was designated the TS-1. It was designed by NAF and 34 were built by the Curtiss Aeroplane and Motor Company. Five planes were built by NAF as a financial check on the contract-built planes.

The TS went through a number of modifications, all part of the experimentation so necessary to this early phase of development. The first models had the fuselage suspended slightly above the lower wing.

The centre section of the lower wing served as the fuel tank.

About this same time, A V 'Fred' Verville had returned from an inspection tour of European aviation manufacturers with General 'Billy' Mitchell. One of the items reported on was an aerofoil-shaped fuel tank suspended on the landing gear axle of a Fokker aircraft. The idea seemed good from a safety point of view, since a crash would surely sever the tank from the fuselage and reduce the risk of fire. The principal short-coming was that the steady shocks of taxiing and landing continually ruptured

Fairey Flycatcher I
The first post-war quantity production naval fighter, the Flycatcher, was a superbly rugged, compact and manoeuvrable machine ideal for carrier operations and was the mainstay of FAA fighter squadrons in the 1920s and early '30s
Span: 29 ft *Length:* 23 ft *Engine:* Armstrong Siddeley Jaguar IV, 425 hp *Max speed:* 133·5 mph at 5000 ft *Ceiling:* 20,100 ft *Armament:* 2 Vickers mg

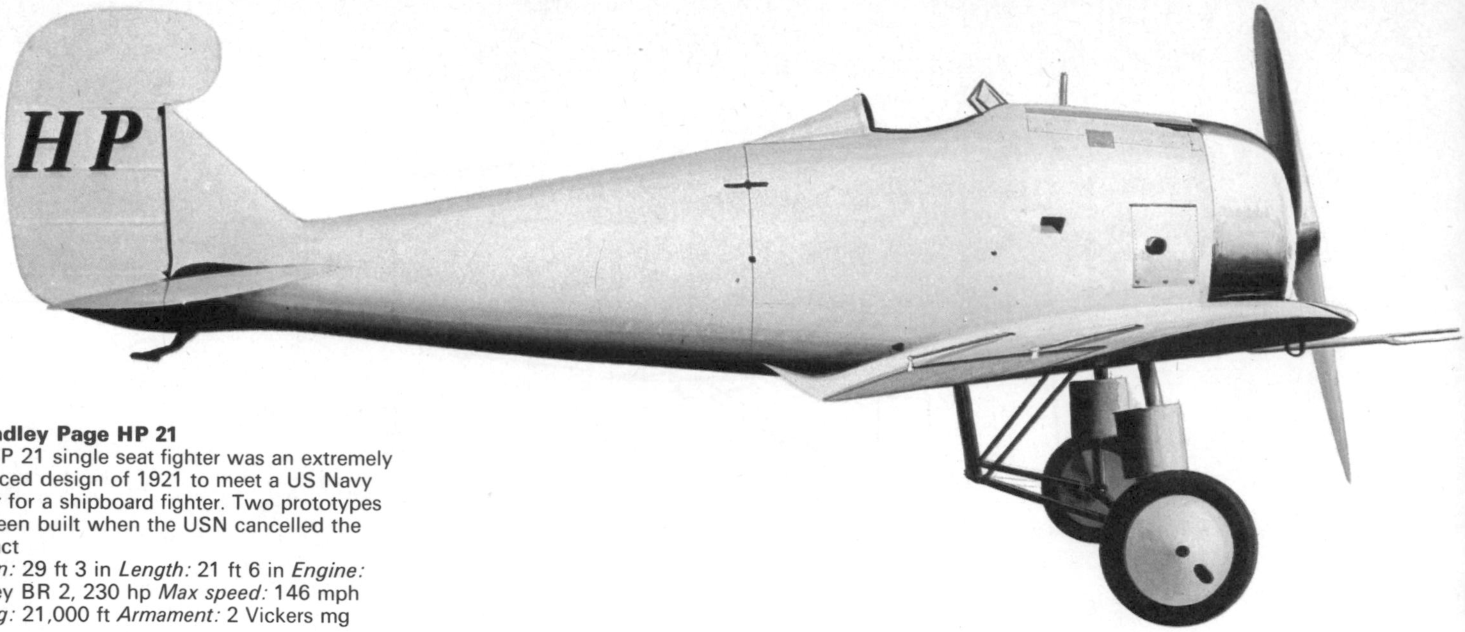

Handley Page HP 21
The HP 21 single seat fighter was an extremely advanced design of 1921 to meet a US Navy tender for a shipboard fighter. Two prototypes had been built when the USN cancelled the contract
Span: 29 ft 3 in *Length:* 21 ft 6 in *Engine:* Bentley BR 2, 230 hp *Max speed:* 146 mph *Ceiling:* 21,000 ft *Armament:* 2 Vickers mg

the soldered joints of the fuel tank, resulting in a high maintenance commitment. On the TS-1 the addition of arrester hooks would have also taken their toll on the tank. As a result, the tank, incorporated in the centre section of the lower wing, was a compromise – not on the axle, but still not in the fuselage.

The TS-1 was an extremely rugged machine which featured a wide gear tread and could also be fitted with floats. The structure was still wood and fabric, though a contract was negotiated with Curtiss to produce an all-metal version which was designated the F4C and built by Charles W Hall as part of continuing experimen-tation with carrier-type aircraft. The results of this latter experiment, constructing the design out of metal, produced a weight reduction of 300 pounds but, by itself, was not sufficient grounds for further orders. Time had run out for the TS-1/F4C and European designs were surpassing it in performance.

US Naval Fighters
Like its British contemporaries, the TS-1 was fitted for float gear in addition to its wheel landing gear. Also it served as a test bed for the 240-hp water-cooled Aeromarine engine (TS-2) and 180-hp Wright-built His-pano Model E (TS-3). As if these changes were not enough chopping and changing, the TS-3 was further modified by stream-lining the fuselage, lowering the upper wing flush with the top of the fuselage, and changing the aerofoil – no small chore – all in the interest of making a trainer for the US 1923 Schneider Trophy team.

The third generation of carrier aircraft were among those to benefit from the in-creased development impetus of the golden years of aviation between 1928 and 1933/4. Certainly these were the fun years and yet they were also the years of learning, and carrier aviation development advanced con-siderably during this period.

Both Boeing and Curtiss had succeeded in capturing contracts with the Army Air

Curtiss F6C-2
Two examples of this shipboard fighter were ordered by the United States Navy in March 1925, in addition to seven F6C-1s. A variant of the Army's Hawk fighter, the F6C could be fitted with either wheels or floats. The USN later ordered 35 of the F6C-3 model, with arrester gear added, and 31 F6C-4s with Pratt & Whitney engines
Span: 31 ft 6 in *Length:* 22 ft 8 in *Engine:* Curtiss D-12, 400 hp *Max speed:* 159 mph *Range:* 330 miles *Ceiling:* 22,700 ft *Armament:* 2×0·30-in mg

A Nieuport 17 flies off the French sloop Bapaume. *Catching up with US and British experiments, the French began a series of flying-off tests in 1920. As a result the French Admiralty decided to complete a battleship hull as the Béarn—France's only carrier*

Corps for the production of sleek fighters based on the proven Curtiss D-12 liquid-cooled in-line engine. Boeing produced the PW-9 for the Air Corps, and not to be outdone, the Navy ordered 16 planes, which for practical purposes were the same, designated FB-1s. The first ten went to Marine squadrons without deck landing gear installed. After that, the deck landing equipment, including axle hooks and strengthened fuselage, were incorporated in the FB-2.

A succession of model modifications ensued, changing from D-12 water-cooled engines to radial air-cooled engines and back to the Packard water-cooled engines. Like the TS, time and design improvements overtook the FBs, but fortunately a successor was ready – the F2B – to start a new performance escalation in company with the rival Curtiss F6C series.

The FBs left their mark though, with a good production record for their day of 43 planes. Fortunately, one still survives, an FB-5 which one day will inspire current and future generations. They also marked the early stage of optional armament installation, permitting the substitution of a ·50 calibre machine-gun in place of one of the two ·30 calibre guns.

The Curtiss F6Cs, dubbed Hawks by their manufacturer, began this series and were powered by the Curtiss D-12 liquid-cooled engine. With the completion of the F6C-3s the change was begun to air-cooled engines, and the -4s, powered by the Pratt & Whitney R-1340, finished the series. Here again the technology of the times was passing them by, in spite of their aesthetically attractive lines.

Learning the Lessons

A specially modified and redesigned F6C-3 was fitted for racing purposes and was piloted by Captain Arthur H Page, USMC. A high-wing monoplane, redesignated as XF6C-6, it featured racy lines which were accentuated by elongated, streamlined wheel pants, which made this plane the talk of the US National Air Races in September, 1930. Page was off to an early lead in the race and continued to gain until the 17th lap of a 20-lap race. He then crashed, a victim of carbon monoxide poisoning. This was one of many such lessons learned during this period, too often at the cost of the life of a courageous pilot.

Though greater in span than the 29 ft of the Flycatcher, the Boeing at 30 ft and the Curtiss at 37 ft 6 in were still small and readily accommodated on the aircraft carrier lifts. The time was not right for folding wings, at least not for the fighters.

As evidence of increasing interest in naval aviation, appropriations were forthcoming to purchase no less than 75 of the Curtiss F6C series in addition to 76 aircraft combining the earlier FBs and F2Bs, really a breakthrough in the mid-1920s. The carriers *Langley*, *Lexington*, and *Saratoga*

The Americans too began with fighters on big ships, a Nieuport 28 up on the flying-off platform of the battleship USS Oklahoma, *1920*

US Navy

Boeing F3B-1

A carrier-based fighter-bomber, the F3B-1 was developed from the F2B-1 and originally had the same wings as its predecessor. Larger wings were incorporated before the type entered production, however, to improve the high-altitude performance. The US Navy bought 73 F3B-1s

Span: 33 ft *Length:* 24ft 10 in *Engine:* Pratt & Whitney Wasp A, 425 hp *Max speed:* 156 mph *Ceiling:* 20,900 ft *Range:* 350 miles *Armament:* 2 mg *Bombload:* 125 lb

were by now in commission and we were seeing the last of the tube-and-fabric aircraft and the end of the convertibility requirements (convertible to floats or wheels as the need arose, but always provided for in the design specifications).

Boeing, still adhering to the 30 ft span, produced an improved aircraft, the F3B-1, in 1928. An order for 74 insured that the fighter groups aboard the carriers would receive the improved models though the service life was to be shortened by the development of the Boeing F4B, probably the

most famous and appealing US carrier fighter of all time.

The F4Bs, in their developmental sequence, topped the list for orders of a single type and its variants. A compact, handsome biplane, the F4B was built with semi-monocoque fuselage and corrugated metal control surfaces in contrast to the bolted square-section aluminium frame as used in the F3Bs. Like the Fleet Air Arm's Fly-catcher, these F4Bs caught the fancy of the pilots who flew them, and most of those who didn't as well. Performance-wise, they were good for their day. Powered by a Pratt & Whitney R-1340-16, the F4B-4 had a top speed of over 185 mph. As a series, F4B-1 to F4B-4, they remained operational over a seven-year period until 1937, when they were replaced by the Grumman fighters.

About this time (1928), decisions were

Boeing F4B-2

Boeing built 586 aircraft in the F4B/P-12 series for the US Navy and Army respectively between 1928 and 1933, establishing a production record which stood until 1940. The Navy ordered 46 F4B-2s, with Frise ailerons, ring cowl and split-axle undercarriage, following an earlier purchase of the basic F4B-1

Span: 30 ft *Length:* 20 ft 1 in *Engine:* Pratt & Whitney R-1340-17, 525 hp *Max speed:* 186 mph *Ceiling:* 26,900 ft *Range:* 400 miles *Armament:* 2×0·30-in or 1×0·30-in and 1×0·50-in mg

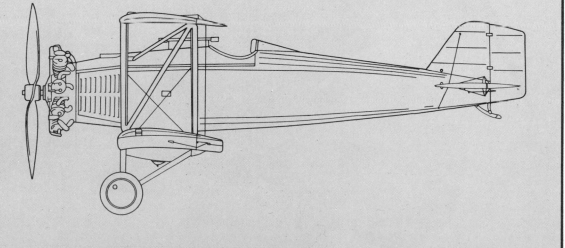

Boeing F4B-4

The second in the series to have an all-metal fuselage, the F4B-4 introduced the broad-chord tail and an enlarged head-rest for the pilot. The US Navy bought 74 of these single-seat fighters, and a further 14 were exported to Brazil

Span: 30 ft *Length:* 20 ft 5 in *Engine:* Pratt & Whitney R-1340-16, 550 hp *Max speed:* 187 mph *Ceiling:* 27,500 ft *Range:* 400 miles *Armament:* 2×0·30-in or 1×0·50-in and 1×0·30-in mg

Curtiss TS-1

The first fighter designed specially for the United States Navy, the TS-1 was delivered from December 1922 for operations aboard the USS *Langley*. In an unusual arrangement, the fuel tank was mounted under the fuselage so that it could be jettisoned in an emergency. Curtiss built 34 of the aircraft, which was later redesignated FC-1, and the Naval Aircraft Factory assembled a further five

Span: 25 ft *Length:* 22 ft 1 in *Engine:* Wright J-1, 200 hp *Max speed:* 125 mph *Ceiling:* 16,250 ft *Range:* 480 miles *Armament:* 0·30-in mg

Curtiss F9C Sparrowhawk

Designed as a shipboard fighter, the Sparrowhawk was instead used to defend the early-warning and reconnaissance airships USS *Akron* and *Macon*. The F9C's small size and light weight made it ideal for this role as a parasite fighter: the aircraft were launched from a hangar inside the airship and recovered by means of a power-operated trapeze. The Sparrowhawk's operational career ended when the *Macon* crashed in 1935, the *Akron* having been lost two years earlier

Span: 25 ft 6 in *Length:* 20 ft 1 in *Engine:* Wright R-975, 420 hp *Max speed:* 176 mph *Ceiling:* 19,200 ft *Range:* 366 miles *Armament:* 2×0·30-in mg

Curtiss F11C-3

A retractable-undercarriage development of the F11C-2, with a higher top speed. In March 1934 the designation was changed to BF2C-1. The type was the US Navy's last Curtiss biplane
 Span: 31 ft 6 in *Length:* 23 ft *Engine:* Wright SR-1820-78 Cyclone *Max speed:* 225 mph *Ceiling:* 27,000 ft *Range:* 800 miles *Armament:* 2×0·30-in mg *Bombload:* 4×116-lb and 1×474-lb

Curtiss F11C-2 Goshawk

Developed from the F6C and the Army's P-6E Hawk, the Goshawk first flew in March 1932 and, following evaluation by the United States Navy, was ordered in October of that year. Twenty-seven F11C-2s were delivered during the following spring, and the last of the batch of 28 was converted to F11C-3 standard with retractable undercarriage. In March 1934 the F11C-2s were redesignated BFC-2s to emphasize their bombing role
 Span: 31 ft 6 in *Length:* 25 ft *Engine:* Wright SR-1820-78 Cyclone, 750 hp *Max speed:* 205 mph *Ceiling:* 24,300 ft *Range:* 560 miles *Armament:* 2×0·30-in mg *Bombload:* 920 lb

Curtiss F7C-1

Developed as a private venture and first flown in February 1927, the F7C-1 was ordered by the United States Navy in June of that year and delivered from December 1928. Only the first prototype was fitted with arrestor gear, and the aircraft was also tested as a floatplane. It was not a success, and the 17 production examples were transferred to the US Marine Corps
 Span: 32 ft 8 in *Length:* 22 ft 2 in *Engine:* Pratt & Whitney R-1340-B Wasp, 450 hp *Max speed:* 151 mph *Ceiling:* 23,350 ft *Range:* 330 miles *Armament:* 2 mg

made to include two-place fighters in the inventory of carrier aircraft. In theory, the purpose was to increase the range of these fighting aircraft and to do so would require an additional crew member to relieve the pilot, to navigate, and to communicate. The US Navy chose to adapt the airframe of the well-tested Curtiss Falcon then in service with the Army Air Service. The major change for naval use was the installation of the well-tried, almost standardized Pratt & Whitney R-1340 Wasp engine. The distinctive swept-back upper wing gave the Falcons a rakish look that seemed to inspire diving. The resulting F8C-1s were delivered to the Marines in 1928 and assigned to Nicaragua and China. During this assignment they were called upon to serve in a variety of missions in an all-purpose role of fighter, dive bomber, air evacuation and observation.

During their tour of Nicaragua, the first dive bombing experiments were carried out. To take full advantage of the dive bombing ability later versions were modified in many details to improve this capability, including provisions for carrying a 500-lb bomb under the fuselage or two 116-lb bombs under each wing. These F8C-4s were given the name Helldiver, a name that was to remain in use far beyond the F8Cs. It was still appropriate and used with the SB2Cs of the Second World War.

French Carrier

With the completion of the *Béarn* in 1926, the French modified existing aircraft types for carrier duty. Modification consisted of

built carrier fighters to be accepted. In appearance, it bore a strong resemblance to the Gloster Grebe which had been a 1924-25 fighter in the Royal Air Force. This was replaced in the mid-thirties by the Nakajima Type 90s which bore more than a passing resemblance to the Curtiss Hawk series. 100 of these were built.

Japan was moving ahead with its programme of catching up with the other major powers in the field of aircraft design and construction. It was approaching independence in both aircraft and engine design, though the engines that powered these two aircraft were derived from foreign designs. In the Nakajima Kotobuki engine, design features were to be found which were directly traceable to the British Bristol Jupiter air-cooled radial.

Following the Wibault 74/75 in service aboard the *Béarn* in 1933 were a token number of three Morane-Saulnier 226s and a Morane-Saulnier 226 *bis*, equipped with folding wings. The interesting thing about these fighters selected for service aboard the French carrier was that they were all high-wing parasol monoplanes in contrast to the biplane fighters in service with the British, American and Japanese services. The introduction of a monoplane fighter as early as 1927 was revolutionary, and the fact that it was a parasol configuration showed that there were several design options to achieve the highly desirable line of vision forward and downward for deck landing operations.

The third fighter-type selected by the French Navy, to replace the ancient Wibault

Morane-Saulnier MS 225

Twelve MS 225 parasol monoplanes were delivered to the French Navy in 1933, flying from the shore station at Hyères. The success of the landplane inspired the MS 226, the 225 with tailwheel and arrester gear for duties aboard the *Béarn*. The 226 *bis* was an experimental version with folding wings
Span: 34 ft 7·75 in *Length:* 23 ft 9·25 in *Engine:* Gnôme-Rhône 9Kbrs, 500 hp *Max speed:* 207 mph at 13,125 ft *Ceiling:* 34,500 ft *Range:* 590 miles

Wibault 74

The exceptionally strong series of Wibault 7 fighters, the prototype of which first flew in 1924, carried the comparatively heavy armament for their day of four machine-guns. The Wibault 74 and 75 were the naval versions with arrester gear and served aboard the *Béarn* until 1934
Span: 36 ft 0·75 in *Length:* 24 ft 11·25 in *Engine:* Gnôme-Rhône Jupiter 9 Ady, 480 hp *Max speed:* 137 mph *Ceiling:* 26,900 ft *Range:* 373 miles

adding a tail hook and strengthening the airframe and landing gear to absorb the stress associated with deck landings. The first fighter to see service aboard the *Béarn* was the Wibault 74/75, based on the Wibault 72 design. With virtually all dimensions identical, except for an increase of 60 hp

from the same series GR 9 Jupiter engine, the naval version suffered performance-wise, a good example of the penalty borne by naval aircraft.

Model 72
3350 lb   156 mph   27,900 ft   420 hp
(GR9 Ac Jupiter)

Model 74/75
3416 lb   137 mph   26,900 ft   480 hp
(GR9 Ady Jupiter)

In 1930, Japan emerged with the first of its home-designed fighters, though they were based on the designs of British and US manufacturers. In 1927, a single-seat Nakajima biplane was one of the first Japanese-

74/75s, was the Dewoitine D 373. Forty of these carrier versions of the D 371 were ordered. Again, a high-wing parasol was selected for the conversion process. In this case the landing hook and flaps were fitted. As in the previous case, a second version was included in the conversion and was designated D 376. In this version the engineering was carried one step further to include provision for folding the wing for stowage aboard ship. In this case the performance penalty was one of additional weight which reduced the service ceiling by 3300 ft and the range slightly. The D 373s served until after the outbreak of war, but were withdrawn from service due to a high incidence of engine failure involving the crankshaft.

Loire-Gordou-Leseurre 32
An advanced design when the prototype first
flew in 1925, the LGL 32 was in the front line of
the French fighter force in the early 1930s. A
batch were specially modified for service aboard
the *Béarn*
 Span: 40 ft 0·25 in *Length:* 29 ft 9·25 in
Engine: Jupiter, 420 hp *Max speed:* 155 mph
Ceiling: 31,800 ft *Range:* 310 miles

Grumman FF-1

The FF-1 was the first US Navy fighter with a retractable undercarriage and, though itself a two-seater, was faster than any of its single-seat contemporaries. The US Navy bought 27, a number of which were fitted with dual controls for training. These were designated FF-2. The type was also built in Canada, and operated by the Royal Canadian Air Force as the Goblin I

Span: 34 ft 6 in *Length:* 24 ft 6 in *Engine:* Wright R-1820-78, 775 hp *Max speed:* 207 mph *Ceiling:* 21,100 ft *Range:* 920 miles *Armament:* 2 mg

In 1932, the Hawker Nimrod replaced the much-loved Fairey Flycatchers after a decade of faithful service. The Nimrod was the naval version of the Hawker Fury which was highly regarded by the RAF. This was the era of steel and duraluminium construction with fabric cover still in vogue. Wood and glue fastening were rapidly disappearing from aircraft construction and anodizing of aluminium structures was becoming the standard practice for the preservation of airframes.

The Nimrod and the similar Osprey were favourites on the British carriers. They had low wing-loading, a good power-to-weight ratio, good aerobatic handling and formation flying with them was a pleasure. One might reflect on the many formation photographs taken during the mid-1930s and recall how many were photos of the Nimrod or the Osprey in naval service or their counterparts, the Fury or the Hart, in RAF service. It was a pleasure to fly them in formation, for it was effortless.

During this era, cruises about the Mediterranean, down the Red Sea, and to the Far East were made aboard the *Eagle* or *Hermes*, the two carriers that alternated duty in the Far East.

Ospreys Accompany Nimrods

The Hawker Osprey was the two-place carrier fighter in the Royal Navy, very similar to the Curtiss F8Cs in the US Navy. The Ospreys, while designated as fighters, were in fact built to accompany each flight of Nimrods to provide a navigator for extended overwater flights. In practical fact they were not fast enough to keep up with the Nimrods and therefore saw limited service in this capacity. They were all equipped with float fittings and often operated with floats installed for patrolling rivers and bays of the Far East which were then under the protection of the Royal Navy.

The Nimrod was powered by the Rolls-Royce Kestrel II developing 590 hp and the Osprey by the 640-hp Rolls-Royce Kestrel V. Even with this power difference, the Osprey was so badly outclassed by the Nimrod that the pairing of these two types for navigation or other purposes was not considered

Hawker Osprey

A naval variation of the long-lived Hawker Hart day bomber, the Osprey fleet reconnaissance-fighter served with the FAA from November 1932 until the outbreak of war

Span: 37 ft 3 in *Length:* 29 ft 1 in *Engine:* Rolls-Royce Kestrel V, 640 hp *Max speed:* 176 mph at 14,000 ft *Ceiling:* 24,500 ft *Endurance:* 3·3 hrs *Armament:* Vickers Mk IIIN mg, Lewis mg

prudent. Like the Flycatcher, the Nimrod and Ospreys enjoyed a long, happy service life with the Fleet Air Arm. They were replaced by the Blackburn Skua in 1939. Some were retained until 1941, as target tugs.

Curtiss F11C series. Though these planes were some of the most attractive types used by the US Navy, they did not enjoy a long service life. In fact these had an experimental 'air' about them for they went through a number of modifications and designation changes with bewildering speed. Deliveries of the F11C-2s began in February 1933. By March 1934, they had been redesignated BFC-2s to indicate that they had become fighter-bombers. By changes in engines and finally a redesign of the landing gear to a retractable type, and a partial enclosure of the cockpit, the plane was designated an F11C-3 and subsequently a BF2C-1. It is interesting to note that the cleaning-up aerodynamically, particularly the landing gear, resulted in an increase in speed from 205 mph (BFC-2) to 225 mph (BF2C-1).

Hawker Nimrod

A strengthened version of the Hawker Fury interceptor, the Nimrod carried more fuel and had an increased wing area. It was supplied in both float and wheel versions to the FAA as a replacement for the Flycatcher

Span: 33 ft 6·5 in *Length:* 26 ft 11·75 in *Engine:* Rolls-Royce Kestrel IIS, 590 hp *Max speed:* 205 mph at 13,000 ft *Ceiling:* 26,900 ft *Range:* 305 miles *Armament:* 2 Vickers Mk III mg

Nakajima A2N

Also known as the Type 90, this highly manoeuvrable single-seat carrier-based fighter was popular with pilots and ground crew alike. It entered production in 1931 to replace the A1N and was regarded as a better dogfighter than its eventual successor, the A4N. One hundred were built
Span: 30 ft 10 in *Length:* 21 ft 7 in *Engine:* Nakajima-built Bristol Jupiter VI, 450 hp *Max speed:* 200 mph *Ceiling:* 32,000 ft *Range:* 400 miles *Armament:* 2 mg

About this same period (1931), Grumman Aircraft Engineering Corporation was stepping into the aircraft building field. Prior to this it had been building floats for conversion of landplanes to seaplanes. Its first design was in answer to a proposal for the construction of a two-place fighter. One of the features of this first effort, to be designated the FF-1, was the wheel retraction system.

This retraction system, which was similar to that used on the Curtiss BF2C-2 with beneficial results, was an adaptation of the retraction system used on the Loening amphibians. While the down position placed the wheels fairly close to the sides of the fuselage, requiring some care on the part of the pilots when landing and during ground operation, the wheels, when retracted, fitted snugly into pockets in the sides of the for-ward fuselage. The fuselage, of course, had been bellied down to permit this geometry and stowing. The result was a portly but attractive barrel-shaped fuselage which became a Grumman design feature for years.

The Grumman FF-1 proved itself to be a remarkable aircraft, for it was a two-place biplane fighter capable of out-flying its single-place contemporaries. Though it did accomplish this unusual feat it did not lead to large orders, for this period was the aftermath of the Depression in the US and large orders were out of the question.

Japanese Progress

The 27 FF-1s that were ordered did give naval pilots a taste of what was to come. They were modified to dual controls and served as training and 'check-out' planes for the single-place Grumman F2Fs and F3Fs. As a matter of interest, a single example of the FF-1 survives, completely restored in the US Naval Aviation Museum.

In 1934, Japan was rapidly closing the gap between its native-designed aircraft and those of the other naval powers, principally the US and Britain. The Japanese were still observing the products of the two other nations and, on occasion, making purchases of aircraft as a means of checking on their own progress and also with a view to checking for new design features. While this activity was progressing, they proceeded to build a replacement for the Type 90 carrier fighter. This new plane, the Nakajima A4N1 Type 95, filled the equipment progression gap.

The Type 95 displayed excellent manoeuvrability and was ordered in large quantities, 300 being built. It was to be the last of the biplane fighters in the Japanese Navy and, because of its very excellent manoeuvring ability, provided the comparison against which the next generation of monoplane fighters was judged. The Japanese placed great store on the ability

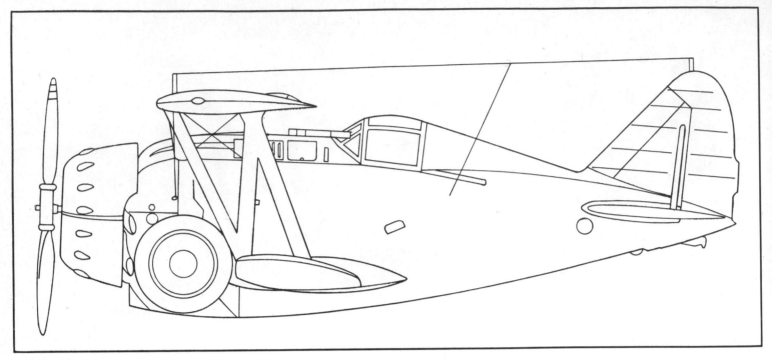

Grumman F2F-1

A single-seat fighter based on the FF-1 and its SF-1 derivative, the F2F retained the same general layout as its predecessors. The US Navy ordered 55, which were delivered from 1935 to equip the carriers *Lexington* and *Ranger*. They served until 1941, ending their life as gunnery trainers. The F2F-1 was developed into the F3F-1, with increased wingspan and a longer fuselage

Span: 28 ft 6 in *Length:* 21 ft 5 in *Engine:* Pratt & Whitney R-1535-72, 700 hp *Max speed:* 231 mph *Ceiling:* 27,100 ft *Range:* 985 miles *Armament:* 2×0·30-in mg *Bombload:* 225 lb

Grumman F3F-1

Developed from the F2F-1, with fuselage and wings lengthened to improve manoeuvrability, the prototype F3F-1 was ordered in October 1934. This aircraft crashed, but a second prototype was successful and 54 production models were delivered in 1936. This single-seat fighter, along with the F3F-2 and F3F-3 developed from it, remained in front-line service until the spring of 1941

Span: 32 ft *Length:* 23 ft 3 in *Engine:* Pratt & Whitney R-1535-84, 700 hp *Max speed:* 231 mph *Ceiling:* 28,500 ft *Range:* 880 miles *Armament:* 0·50-in Browning, 0·30-in Browning mg

of their fighters to execute manoeuvres with great agility. To a degree, it was their undoing, for they sacrificed other important factors, such as armour and airframe strength, to achieve this manoeuvrability.

The fourth generation of carrier fighter aircraft included the last of the biplane fighters and the first of the low-wing monoplane fighters. The Gloster Sea Gladiator was to be the last of the British biplane fighters and was a direct conversion of the RAF Gladiator. It provided a badly needed replacement for the Hawker Nimrod until the Blackburn Skua monoplane was ready for service. They were handsome, agile machines, but no match for the Messer-schmitt Bf 109s which they were to encounter off Norway. Where they did not encounter such opposition, they were able to provide fighter cover for spotting aircraft in the Mediterranean and at least provide a morale booster for Malta during the crisis days of 1941.

The final naval biplane fighters were the Grumman F2F and F3F aircraft. These rotund, pugnacious little planes were of all-metal structure with fabric-covered wings and control surfaces. The semi-monocoque metal fuselage snuggled in behind the big 700-hp Pratt & Whitney R-1535 Wasp (F2F) or the even larger 950-hp Wright Cyclone R-1820 engines (F3F-2).

Though the total numbers produced of each type was substantial (F2F – 56 built, F3F – 164 built), their first-line life was short.

The most advanced aircraft design of this generation was the Mitsubishi A5M Claude. The Japanese had caught up, in fact had passed, their rivals in the development of carrier-based fighters. They began flight tests on the A5M in February 1935 and eventually built 1000 aircraft of this type. As if in anticipation of the events to come, these A5M Claude fighters saw service in the Sino-Japanese war in 1937-41. Design-wise, it was a large step forward, bridging the gap between the fabric-covered biplanes and the Mitsubishi A6M Zero.

THREAT FROM ABOVE

The Vought SB2U Vindicator scout bomber, deliveries of which began at the end of 1937

While a form of dive-bombing or glide-bombing is reported to have been used during the First World War, the beginning of serious development of the technique is generally credited to a section of US Marine Corps pilots flying Curtiss OC-1s in Nicaragua in 1928. When a small group of Marines were isolated and surrounded by a bandit group, the main body of Marines, by signal panels, directed the Marine aviators operating with the expeditionary force to bomb the insurgents. Close proximity of the two opposing forces made precision attacks necessary. Because of this the bombing took the form of near-vertical dives to place the bombs on the enemy strong points without endangering the Marine company.

At that date the OC (for Observation Curtiss) was called a Curtiss Falcon, for they were Navy modifications of the Army's Falcon. The main change was from a water-cooled engine to the air-cooled Pratt & Whitney R-1340 Wasp. These first OC-1s were not equipped for carrier operation. They were purchased as F8C-1 two-place fighters but were almost immediately re-designated OC-1s. With the introduction of the second version, the F8C-4 (O2C-1), the name Helldiver came into use, as the type was built to make dive-bombing its principal function. The resulting F8C-4 was capable of carrying a single 500-lb bomb under the fuselage or four 116-lb bombs in racks under the wings.

Indicating an early appreciation of the potential of dive-bombing as a method of ordnance delivery, the Japanese produced a two-place biplane dive-bomber for carrier use. The Nakajima N-35 Tokubaku powered by a 650-hp Lorraine engine was comparable in speed and general structural details to the state of the art in the US aircraft

Typeface used on all US Navy aircraft 1920-41. It appeared on all machines somewhere. Dimensions to USN specifications

Martin BM-1
Originally designated the XT5M-1, the production BM-1 was the first aircraft to be allocated the US Navy's new 'B' prefix to indicate a bomber. Designed as a dive-bomber, the two-crew BM-1 entered service on the USS *Lexington* in July 1932. The 12 BM-1s were followed by 21 BM-2s
Span: 41 ft *Length:* 28 ft 9 in *Engine:* Pratt & Whitney R-1690-22, 525 hp *Max speed:* 145 mph *Ceiling:* 16,400 ft *Range:* 400 miles *Armament:* 2×0·30-in mg *Bombload:* 1000 lb

Curtiss F8C-4

The F8C series were designed as two-seat fighters which could also operate as light bombers and be used for observation. The F8C-4, powered by an uprated engine, made its appearance in May 1930. Twenty-seven were built, but they were transferred to reserve units after a short period of service with the Navy and Marine Corps

Span: 31 ft 1 in *Length:* 25 ft 11 in *Engine:* Pratt & Whitney R-1340-88, 450 hp *Max speed:* 137 mph *Ceiling:* 17,300 ft *Range:* 380 miles
Armament: 4×0·30-in mg *Bombload:* 500 lb

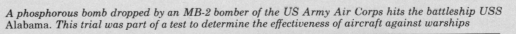

A phosphorous bomb dropped by an MB-2 bomber of the US Army Air Corps hits the battleship USS Alabama. *This trial was part of a test to determine the effectiveness of aircraft against warships*

US Navy

US Navy

The Curtiss BF2C-1, formerly designated F11C-3, featured a retractable undercarriage and was fitted with a new engine, raising its speed by 20 mph over the earlier BFC-2 fighter

industry. It was a 7-Shi development (1931) and was equivalent to the Curtiss F8C (O2C) Helldiver.

The same year, 1931, the US Navy was ordering a dive-bomber/torpedo-bomber, the Martin XT5M, and the Naval Aircraft Factory XT2N-1 two-place, dual purpose aircraft. The principal requirement for these aircraft was that they could pull out of a terminal-velocity dive with a 1000-lb bomb or torpedo attached. Bomb shackle hang-ups were not unheard of in those days. Deliveries of the first 12, designated BM-1s, began in September, 1931. Though the BM-1s and subsequently 16 BM-2s were designed primarily as dive-bombers, they were assigned initially to torpedo duties with VT-1S aboard the *Lexington*, and later when VT-1S was redesignated VB-1B in 1934 a second unit, VB-3B, used the Martins aboard the USS *Langley*. They were withdrawn from carrier duty in 1937, but continued to serve on utility duties until 1940.

Towards the end of the third generation of carrier aircraft, or the beginning of the fourth, depending on how you choose to break the periods, dive-bombing aircraft became popular in both the US and Japan. In fact, several feature films were produced with the dive-bomber as the main theme of the story. However, while they were a good public relations medium for the US Navy,

the films also resulted in a number of misconceptions about the technique, spectacular as it appeared in the films.

At the beginning of 1933 a new and attractive type of carrier fighter-bomber was delivered to the Navy—the Curtiss F11C-2. It was a single-place biplane with very attractive lines. Initially it had a neatly faired, single strut, fixed landing gear, but as the type progressed the landing gear became retractable with the wheels folding flush into the lower sides of the fuselage which had been bellied downward, guppy fashion, to accommodate the retraction mechanism and the fairings for the wheels when retracted.

Bombing Technique

Shortly after delivery in 1933, the 28 F11C-2s were redesignated BFC-2s. They were flown by the US Navy's famed High Hot Squadron VF-1B aboard the *Saratoga*. They remained in service until early 1938. Within the Navy Hawk series they were known as Goshawks and among the export models, basically the same aircraft, there were Turkey Hawks, etc. A pair of these Hawks was purchased by Ernst Udet in 1934 to demonstrate the technique of dive-bombing in Germany. The results of those demonstrations are well-known to the people of Europe who survived the opening days of

Vought SBU-1

Designed as a two-seat fighter as a replacement for the Curtiss Helldiver, the SBU-1 was re-designated before service in the new 'Scout-Bomber' category. Deliveries began in late 1935, and the SBUs were still in service in 1940

Span: 33 ft 3 in *Length:* 27 ft 9 in *Engine:* Pratt & Whitney R-1535-80, 700 hp *Max speed:* 205 mph at 8900 ft *Ceiling:* 24,400 ft *Range:* 548 miles *Armament:* 2 mg *Bombload:* 500 lb

Great Lakes BG-1

A dive-bomber incorporating elements of the TG-2, which was developed from the Martin T4M-1 torpedo bomber when that company was absorbed by Great Lakes in October 1928, the BG-1 was a two-seater able to carry a 1000-lb bomb under its fuselage. Deliveries to the US Navy began in October 1934, and nearly half the production run of 60 aircraft was supplied to the Marine Corps. The Great Lakes Aircraft Corporation went out of business in 1936, before it could produce any other original designs

Span: 36 ft *Length:* 28 ft 9 in *Engine:* Pratt & Whitney R-1535 Wasp, 750 hp *Max speed:* 188 mph *Ceiling:* 20,100 ft *Range:* 550 miles *Armament:* 2×0·30-in mg *Bombload:* 1000 lb

Northrop BT-1

The BT-1 first flew in 1935 incorporating Northrop's experience in attack bombers for the US Army. When Northrop in turn was taken over by Douglas the technology of this carrier-based scout/dive-bomber was incorporated in the SBD Dauntless

Span: 41 ft 6 in *Length:* 31 ft 8 in *Engine:* Pratt & Whitney R-1535, 825 hp *Max speed:* 222 mph *Ceiling:* 25,300 ft *Range:* 1150 miles

the Second World War and the attacks of the Luftwaffe. They were probably the first aircraft to be specifically designated as fighter-bombers and capable of carrying a bomb or bombs of sufficient size to have more than nuisance value in a tactical situation.

A contemporary of the Curtiss fighter-bombers was another two-place dive-bomber, the Great Lakes BG-1. It was an attractive plane, as large biplanes go, with a good profile and tapered wing planform. In ability, it was a substantial advance over the F8C

(O2C) Helldiver which it replaced at the beginning of 1934. The BG-1s were powered by the 750-hp Pratt & Whitney R-1535-82 engine which made it possible for them to carry a 1000-lb bomb, twice the load capacity of the F8Cs, for a range of nearly 550 miles. They were to remain in active service until 1938 at which time they were relegated to utility and training duties. Of the 60 BG-1s produced about half were assigned to a single carrier squadron, VB-3B/VB-4, for duty aboard the USS *Ranger* and the USS

Saratoga. They were the first of the two-place dive-bombers to incorporate enclosed cockpits for the crew.

Very similar to, though slightly smaller than the BG-1, was the Vought SBU-1 which was slightly faster than the BG-1 but carried only a 500-lb bomb similar to the earlier Helldivers. Range was equal to the BG-1 but the service ceiling was better than the Great Lakes. In comparison, the Great Lakes plane was a better performer with its 1000-lb load. It remained in service until the early 1940s.

Also in the 1933-34 period there was the Japanese Aichi D1A1, Type 94 dive-bomber. This was derived from the Heinkel He 50 single-seat biplane. The successor to this plane, the Type 96 or D1A2 Susie, built in 1936 was quite successful and was built in very large numbers of 428, at a time when

Loire-Nieuport 40/41

The LN 41 dive-bomber, developed from the LN 40 prototype, entered service in 1940 and was immediately thrown into action against invading German forces. Heavy losses were sustained, because the crews had not had sufficient time for training, but earlier trials had shown the aircraft to have a performance similar to that of the Ju 87

Span: 45 ft 11 in *Length:* 32 ft *Engine:* Hispano 12 Xcrs, 690 hp *Max speed:* 162 mph *Ceiling:* 31,200 ft *Range:* 745 miles

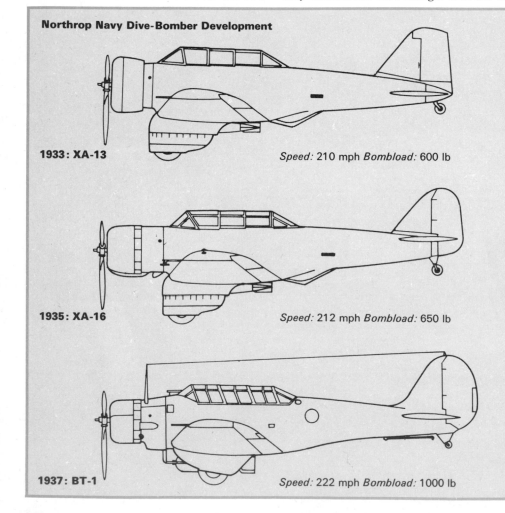

Northrop Navy Dive-Bomber Development

1933: XA-13   *Speed:* 210 mph *Bombload:* 600 lb

1935: XA-16   *Speed:* 212 mph *Bombload:* 650 lb

1937: BT-1   *Speed:* 222 mph *Bombload:* 1000 lb

the US was only ordering groups of 25 to 40 planes at a time. This gives some indication of the serious interest the Japanese Navy was taking in the dive-bombing tactic.

In 1937 two totally different aircraft, the biplane Curtiss SBC Helldiver and the monoplane Vought SB2U Vindicator, were received by the US Navy. The SBC clung to the biplane configuration, even though it

was to be the last biplane combat aircraft produced in the US. The SBC began as a parasol monoplane, the XF12C. Possibly inspired by the Morane-Saulnier 226 the XF12C-1 had many things in common with the Morane including the folding wing of the 226 *bis*. They were contemporaries and both probably were exploring the parasol monoplane configuration to improve the pilot visibility for carrier operations. Looking back, we can see some of the ungainly fuselage configurations—the result of trying to improve or at least maintain the proper degree of visibility over the nose or alongside the nose of the radial engine.

Biplane Comeback
Unlike the Morane, the XF12C-1 was a two-place fighter and the end of the two-place fighter was already in sight. During the testing programme it crashed. It was rebuilt as a scout aircraft, the XS4C-1, at the end of 1933. A second crash spelled the end of the parasol-wing configuration and when the plane was replaced, it was a totally new design, company model 77, US Naval designation XSBC-2. This time they reverted to the proven biplane configuration and completely redesigned the fuselage as well as incorporating a turtle deck of metal rather than the projecting greenhouse canopy of the XF12C-1. In 1936 the original Wright R-1510 was replaced by the Pratt & Whitney R-1535 Twin Wasp and the designation changed to SBC-3. The final configuration was the SBC-4, a few of which were delivered to the *Lexington* and about 15 to the US Marine Corps, but the majority were relegated to reserve squadrons.

Because of a desperate need for aircraft for the *Béarn*, the French were permitted to order 90 SBC-4s but only 44 were aboard when the *Béarn* sailed in June, 1940. Enroute across the Atlantic, the *Béarn* stopped

Vought SB2U Vindicators were the first low-wing monoplane dive-bombers to see service with the US Navy

at Martinique where it remained for the duration. The last photos of these SBC-4s indicated that they were last seen with tattered fabric rotting in a field in Martinique. The British took over the other French aircraft purchase contracts and in doing so, acquired five of the Helldivers which were rechristened Clevelands. Fortunately they never saw combat for they were no match for the fighters frequenting the skies of Europe at this time.

In April 1936, a single prototype Brewster SBA powered by a Wright R-1820-4 engine was produced. Eventually the Naval Aircraft Factory built 30 of these under the designation SBN-1s. Like the Brewster F2A fighters their landing gear did not stand up well to carrier landings and they were used as trainers aboard the USS *Hornet*. They were the first dive-bombers to carry their ordnance, a 500-lb bomb, internally. The successor to the SBA/SBN was the Brewster

Bermuda, known in the US Navy as the SB2A. In July 1940, the British Purchasing Commission ordered 750 of these aircraft and the Dutch Army ordered an additional 162 for the Royal Netherlands East Indies. In 1943 the US Navy purchased 80 SB2A-2s, and in 1944 the US Navy accepted 60 of the SB2A-3 variation—the only one to be equipped with arrester hooks and folding wings for use aboard carriers. With the fall of the Dutch East Indies, their 162 aircraft were acquired by the US Marine Corps to be used as trainers. The only distinctive feature about the SB2As was their ability to carry a bomb load of 1000 lb internally, twice that of their predecessor. They never were used in combat.

At the end of 1937 the US Navy began accepting the Vought SB2U-1s, a low-wing two-place dive-bomber and the first of the low-wing monoplane dive-bombers to actually see combat service. While the transition to monoplane configuration had been made with this aircraft, it was still of composite construction with substantial areas covered with fabric. It also had the distinction of being the first carrier based aircraft to have hydraulically operated wingfolding for stowage aboard ship. At the beginning of the Second World War, SB2Us were serving aboard the USS *Lexington*, USS *Saratoga*,

USS *Ranger*, and USS *Wasp*. They did see combat service in the early stages of the Second World War—flown by Marine pilots in 1942 and at the Battle of Midway.

Torpedo Bombers

STRIKE FROM THE SURFACE

Sopwith Cuckoo
The first landplane to be designed from the outset as a shipborne torpedo strike aircraft. Admiral Beatty put forward ambitious plans early in 1918 for a mass attack by 200 Cuckoos on German bases and ships in harbour. However, the first squadron only embarked on HMS *Argus* in October 1918 and were too late to be used operationally
1 Sunbeam Arab engine, 200 hp **2** Wicker pilot's seat **3** Fabric-covered wooden framework **4** Wire cross-bracing **5** External control runs **6** Long tail-skid to allow clearance for torpedo **7** Equal-span rearward-folding wings **8** Divided undercarriage to straddle torpedo **9** 18-in Mk IX torpedo, 1000 lb
   Span: 46 ft 9 in *Length:* 28 ft 6 in *Engine:* Sunbeam Arab, 200 hp *Max speed:* 98 mph at 10,000 ft *Ceiling:* 12,100 ft *Endurance:* 4 hrs *Armament:* 18-in Mk IX 1000-lb torpedo

The function of torpedo-bombers was three-fold: torpedo dropping, bombing and scouting. For naval aircraft the requirement for flexibility of loading is paramount. In almost all cases provision must be made for substituting fuel for ordnance load to alter the function of the aircraft from attack to scouting.

The Sopwith/Blackburn Cuckoo was the pioneer torpedo-bomber finally introduced in mid-1918. When Admiral Beatty heard of this type of plane, he asked for 200 to be produced as soon as possible. Until this time the Grand Fleet had not shown much interest in torpedo planes. However, the Germans were known to have seaplane torpedo planes ready at North Sea bases and the British fleet did not want to be short-handed with weapons in case the German High Seas Fleet decided to make a break for open water beyond the North Sea.

Though 350 were ordered, less than 100 were delivered by the time of the Armistice. Their first use was at the Torpedo Aeroplane School at East Fortune where, in-

cidentally, a pair of Cuckoo wings have recently been found (by the Royal Scottish Museum) supporting the roof of a building! Cuckoos served afloat and as shore-based aircraft until early 1923. By this time they had been embarked on the carriers in commission during this period, *Argus*, *Eagle* and *Furious*. As in the case of their contemporaries, they were of wooden structure and fabric covered. Their powerplants were either the 200-hp Sunbeam Arab or, in the case of the Cuckoo Mk II, the Wolseley Viper engine. Their speed was in keeping with their times, slightly over 100 mph.

The 18-in torpedo for which the Cuckoo was designed as a carrier was found to be inadequate for the job and an earlier Mk with greater explosive charge was proposed as a replacement. To carry this heavier torpedo, contracts were negotiated for the purchase of a Cuckoo replacement. As a result the Blackburn Blackburd was designed. It was not an attractive aircraft by any standards, but it was the first of a long line of Blackburn aircraft d signed as

torpedo aircraft and adopted as standard by the RAF. Being a contemporary or follow-on to the Cuckoo, it suffered from many of the disadvantages of the times, not the least of which were a clear-cut idea of what was wanted and how to design an aircraft for a carrier whose design was still experimental, especially the arrester system.

The Blackburd was ungainly, an ugly box with wings and a landing gear that could drop free after takeoff. The wheels, mounted on a solid axle, had to be dropped to permit launching a torpedo. After dropping the

Imperial War Museum

Short seaplane drops its torpedo. The type made history in 1915 when a Short Type 184 from HMS Ben-my-Chree *became the first aircraft in the world to sink an enemy ship—a Turkish steamer— by means of a torpedo*

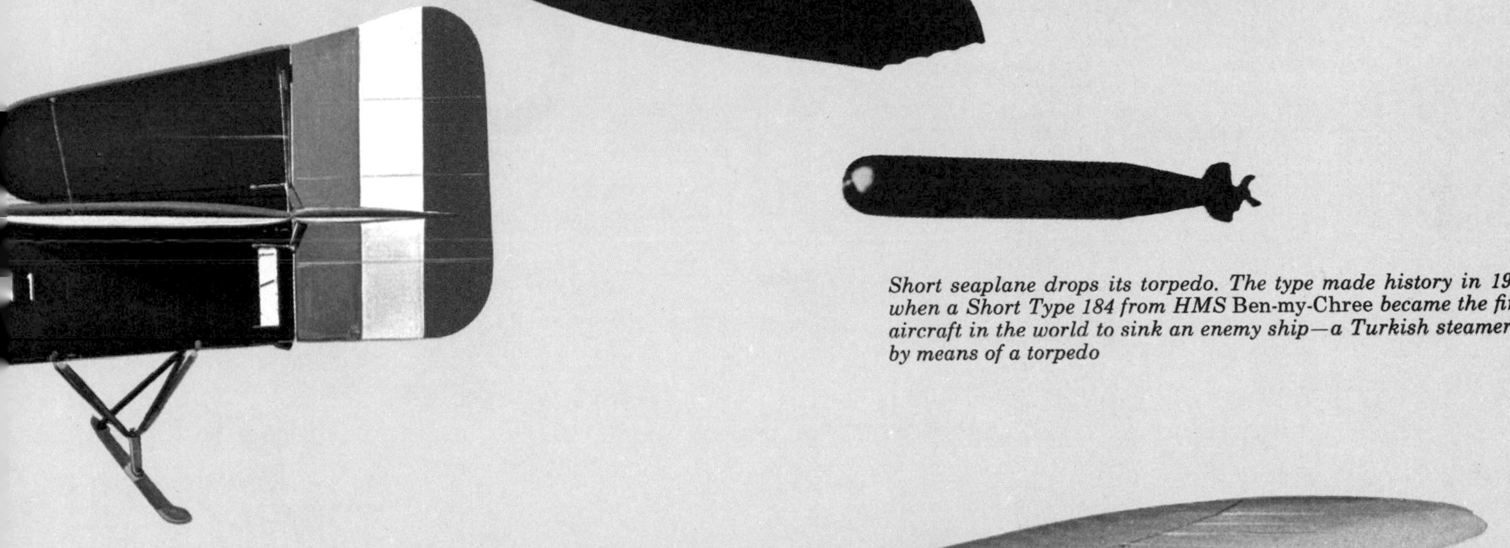

gear and launching its torpedo, the aircraft was landed aboard the carrier on a pair of skids which were very similar to those used on the contemporary Sopwith Pups and 1½ Strutters but adapted to the greater weight of the Blackburd.

The Germans had no carrier at this time and relied on float seaplanes for torpedo dropping, as did the US Navy. The Curtiss R-6Ls which were Liberty-powered float planes were modified to carry torpedoes after the war. The R-4 and R-6 series were generally referred to as scaled up JN-4 Jennies all of which had been designed as

Blackburn Blackburd

The first Blackburn aircraft designed specifically for torpedo-carrying, the Blackburd was intended for rapid and easy production. The wheels used for take-off had to be jettisoned before the torpedo could be released, leaving skids available for landing

Span: 52 ft 6 in *Length:* 36 ft 3 in *Engine:* Rolls-Royce Eagle VIII, 350 hp *Max speed:* 95 mph *Ceiling:* 12,000 ft *Endurance:* 3 hrs (with torpedo) *Bombload:* 1×1400 lb Mk VIII torpedo

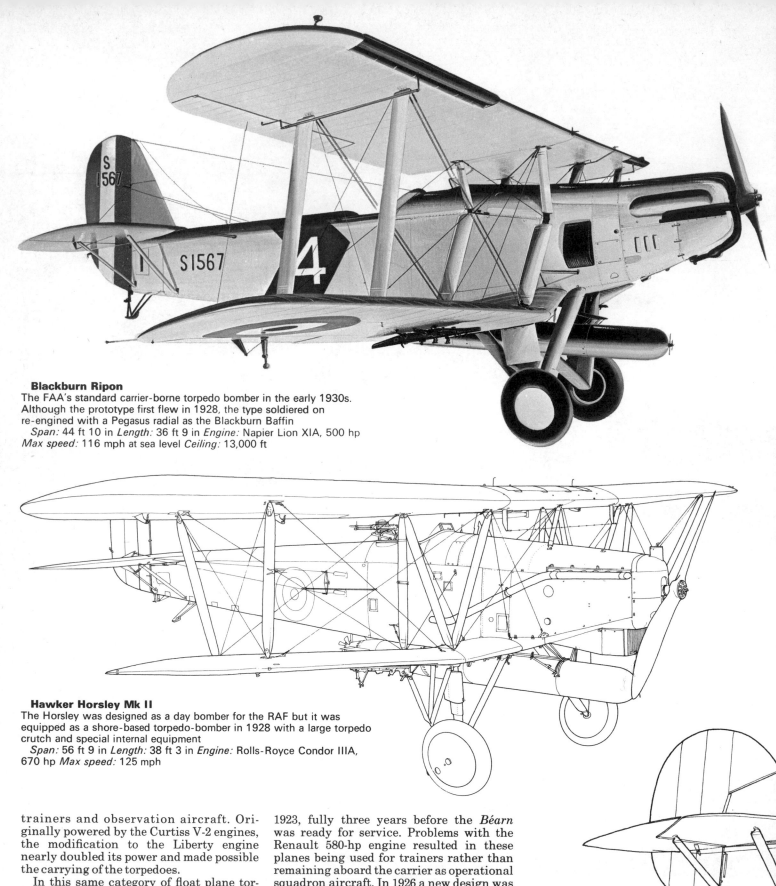

Blackburn Ripon
The FAA's standard carrier-borne torpedo bomber in the early 1930s. Although the prototype first flew in 1928, the type soldiered on re-engined with a Pegasus radial as the Blackburn Baffin
Span: 44 ft 10 in *Length:* 36 ft 9 in *Engine:* Napier Lion XIA, 500 hp
Max speed: 116 mph at sea level *Ceiling:* 13,000 ft

Hawker Horsley Mk II
The Horsley was designed as a day bomber for the RAF but it was equipped as a shore-based torpedo-bomber in 1928 with a large torpedo crutch and special internal equipment
Span: 56 ft 9 in *Length:* 38 ft 3 in *Engine:* Rolls-Royce Condor IIIA, 670 hp *Max speed:* 125 mph

trainers and observation aircraft. Originally powered by the Curtiss V-2 engines, the modification to the Liberty engine nearly doubled its power and made possible the carrying of the torpedoes.

In this same category of float plane torpedo-carriers was the Short 320 which was the largest float plane to enter service during the First World War. Though 110 aircraft of this type had been received by the end of the war, they were dropped in favour of the carrier-borne Cuckoos. Their performance was less than impressive though their 75-ft wingspan would not fail to catch one's eye for they were the same size as the Curtiss H-4 Small America flying boats undergoing trials at Felixstowe.

Second generation torpedo bombers included the Levasseur PL2A2 which was readied for the French carrier *Béarn*. The aircraft was flying in a squadron unit in 1923, fully three years before the *Béarn* was ready for service. Problems with the Renault 580-hp engine resulted in these planes being used for trainers rather than remaining aboard the carrier as operational squadron aircraft. In 1926 a new design was begun to replace the PL2s. The new model, the PL7, made its first flight in 1928, but details of the production model were not finalized until 1931. After experiencing structural failure in 1931, they were grounded until 1932. They were finally reinstated, serving until the beginning of the Second World War in 1939, as no replacement had been ordered.

In 1921 an improvement was made in the form of the torpedo plane. The fabric-covered box frame was still the basic form but a number of improvements were made, the most obvious being the landing gear. Instead of the droppable wheel and axle of the Blackburd, the landing gear of the Blackburn Dart was split to enable the torpedo to be loaded and dropped without first dropping the wheels. Though it was an improvement, the landing gear of the Dart was still an ungainly bridge-like structure with wheels attached to the outboard ends. The upper cowling between the pilot and the 450-hp Napier Lion engine sloped

The Levasseur PL7 was the last French carrier-based torpedo bomber. After being withdrawn from service because of structural failures the type was redeployed and remained operational until 1939

ECP Armées

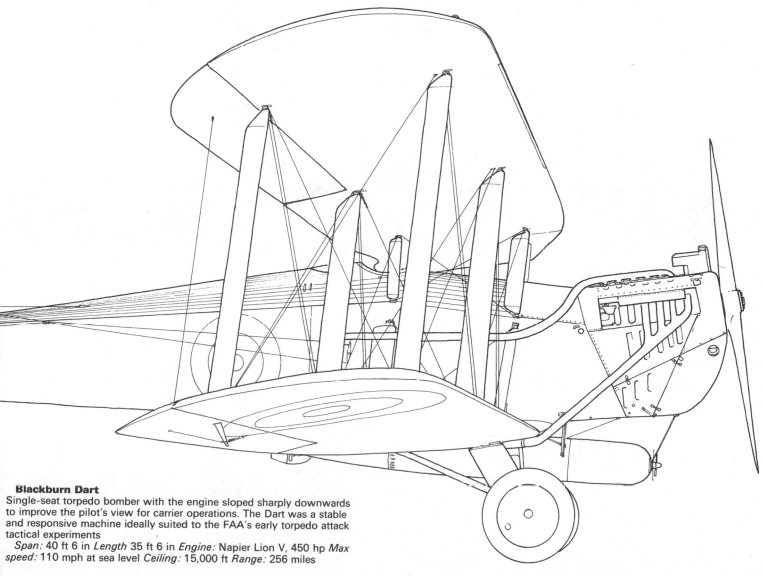

Blackburn Dart
Single-seat torpedo bomber with the engine sloped sharply downwards to improve the pilot's view for carrier operations. The Dart was a stable and responsive machine ideally suited to the FAA's early torpedo attack tactical experiments

Span: 40 ft 6 in *Length* 35 ft 6 in *Engine:* Napier Lion V, 450 hp *Max speed:* 110 mph at sea level *Ceiling:* 15,000 ft *Range:* 256 miles

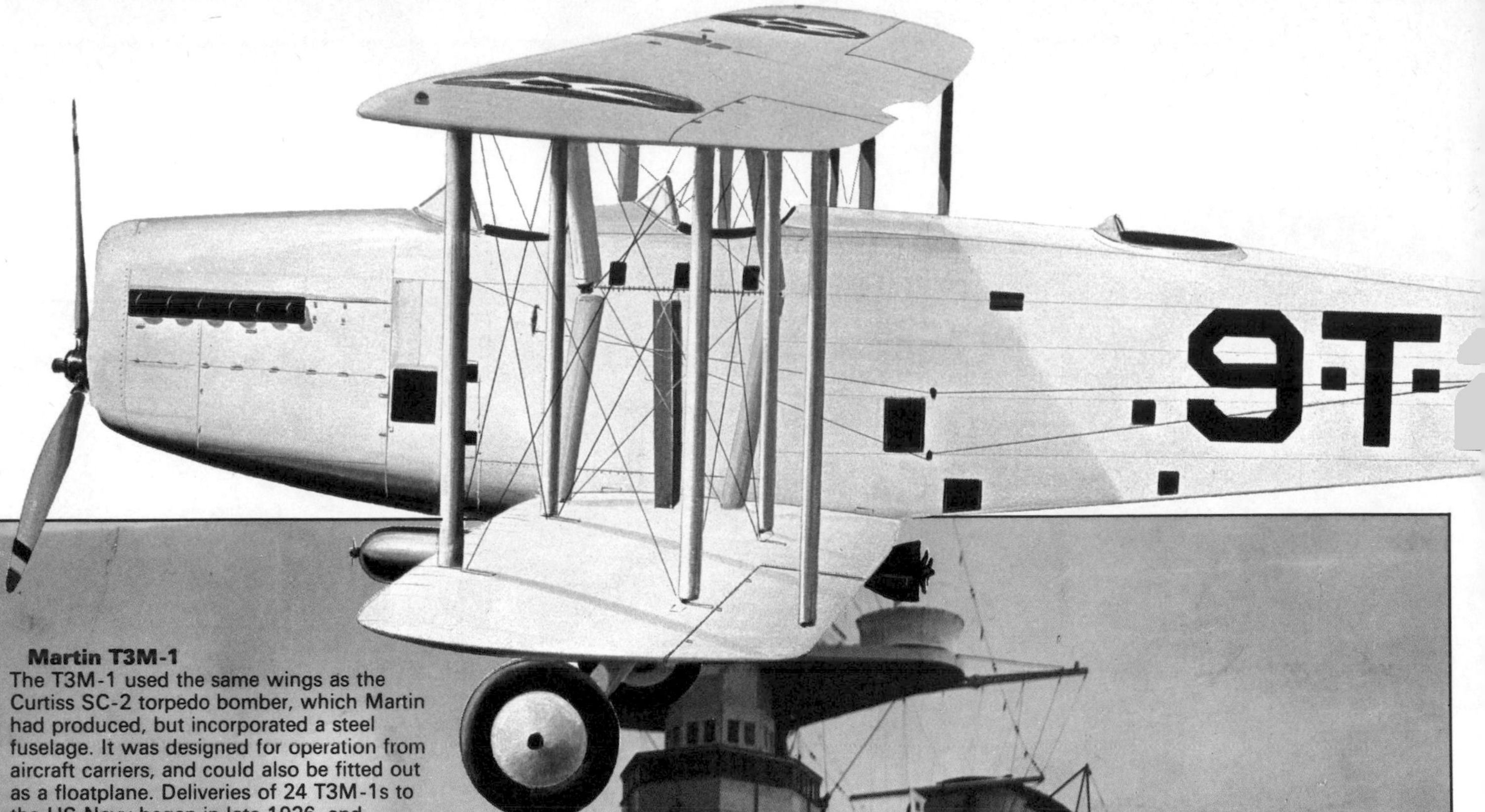

Martin T3M-1

The T3M-1 used the same wings as the Curtiss SC-2 torpedo bomber, which Martin had produced, but incorporated a steel fuselage. It was designed for operation from aircraft carriers, and could also be fitted out as a floatplane. Deliveries of 24 T3M-1s to the US Navy began in late 1926, and variants with uprated engines were later supplied

Span: 56 ft 7 in *Length:* 41 ft 9 in *Engine:* Wright T3B, 575 hp *Max speed:* 109 mph *Ceiling:* 5700 ft *Range:* 525 miles

In 1928 the Martin T4M torpedo bomber, seen here about to take off from the USS Saratoga, replaced the T3M-2. The T4M was powered by an air-cooled 525-hp Pratt & Whitney Hornet, many parts of which were interchangeable with the Wasp

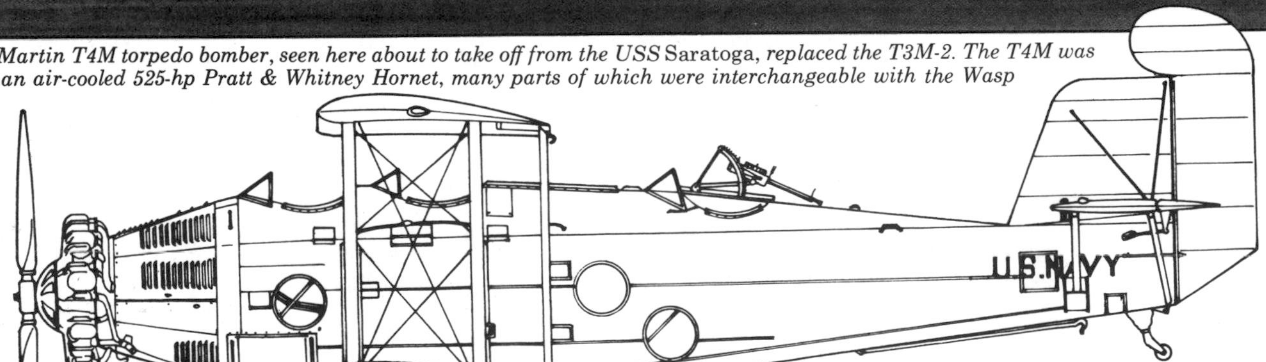

US Navy

Martin T4M-1

Developed from the T3M, which itself resulted from Martin's experience in building Curtiss torpedo bombers, the T4M-1 was fitted with a different engine as well as having a revised rudder shape and shorter wings. The US Navy bought 102 production T4M-1s, plus developments produced by the Great Lakes company. The aircraft were eventually replaced by monoplane torpedo bombers

Span: 53 ft *Length:* 35 ft 7 in *Engine:* Pratt & Whitney Hornet, 525 hp *Max speed:* 114 mph *Ceiling:* 10,150 ft *Range:* 365 miles

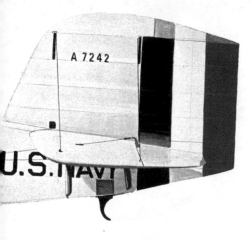

abruptly downward and to the sides to preserve the possible view forward for the approach and landing of this massive box-like structure with wings. For its time, it was produced in large numbers (117) and entered service in 1923. What it lacked in performance, it made up in ease of handling. It did its job well and was used in the many exercises that were necessary to mate the aircraft and ship. A tribute to its ease of handling is the fact that the Dart was the first plane to make a night landing aboard a carrier.

As originally produced it was a single-place aircraft but a twin float version was created and fitted with a second cockpit, for there was ample room for at *least* one additional crew member in the cavernous fuselage. Further testimony to the accept-ability of the Dart was the fact that pro-duction did not cease until 1927, four years

The Blackburn Shark torpedo bomber and recon-naissance aircraft combined experience gained with the Dart, Ripon and Baffin. It entered service in 1935 and was eventually replaced by the Sword-fish

John Batchelor

Blackburn Shark

Designed to operate both from land and as a seaplane, the Shark was a two/three-seat torpedo bomber and reconnaissance aircraft which entered service with the Fleet Air Arm in 1935. The 16 Mk Is were followed by 126 Mk IIs and 95 Mk IIIs, the type eventually being replaced as a front-line aircraft by the Swordfish in 1938
Span: 46 ft *Length:* 35 ft 2 in *Engine:* Armstrong Siddeley Tiger VIc, 700 hp *Max speed:* 152 mph *Ceiling:* 16,400 ft *Range:* 625 miles *Armament:* 1 Vickers mg, 1 Vickers-Berthier mg *Bombload:* torpedo or 1500 lb

after entering service, and reserve units continued to operate them as late as 1935. They were of wood and fabric construction with large two-bay constant chord biplane wings. Ailerons were fitted to both upper and lower wings and automatic slots were fitted to the upper wings in line with the ailerons. These features undoubtedly con-tributed to their controllability and long active service.

The Dart, when it was phased out, was followed by another Blackburn torpedo plane, the Ripon, which became the standard torpedo plane of the Fleet Air Arm late in 1929. There was a strong family resemblance though the fuselage took on more attractive lines and the landing gear improved visibly from that of the Blackburd and Dart. The angle of the cowling was retained for operational reasons and the power was increased by the installation of the 570-hp Napier Lion XIA. It was intended

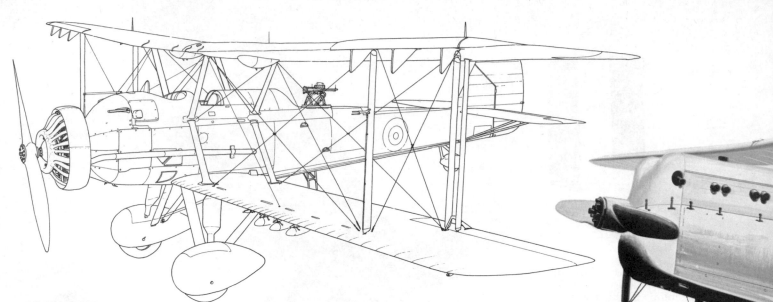

Vickers Vildebeest

Designed to succeed the Hawker Horsley as the RAF's torpedo bomber, the Vildebeest entered service in 1932 and was still operational with two Coastal Command squadrons in the Far East at the outbreak of the Second World War. The most numerous version was the three-crew Mk III, of which 111 were built. All variants could be operated as floatplanes or with a normal undercarriage

Span: 49 ft *Length:* 37 ft 8 in *Engine:* Bristol Perseus VIII, 825 hp *Max speed:* 156 mph *Ceiling:* 19,000 ft *Range:* 1625 miles *Armament:* 2 × 0.303-in mg *Bombload:* 18-in torpedo or 1100 lb of bombs

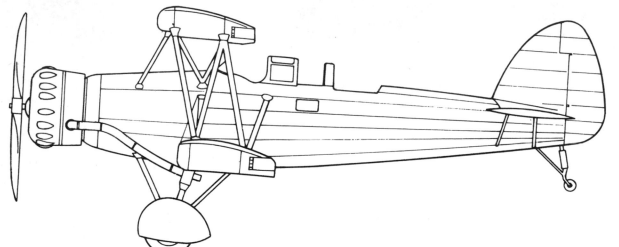

Yokosuka B4Y1

The B4Y1, a biplane torpedo bomber, was designed by Nakajima but built by the Yokosuka Naval Air Arsenal because the former company was engaged in other projects of greater priority. Great emphasis was placed on the use of aluminium alloy to reduce weight while retaining good structural strength, and 200 were supplied under the designation Type 96. Those still in service at the outbreak of the Second World War were given the code name 'Jean'

Span: 49 ft 2 in *Length:* 33 ft 3 in *Engine:* Nakajima Hikari, 710-840 hp *Max speed:* 173 mph *Range:* 980 miles *Armament:* 7.7-mm mg *Bombload:* torpedo

Mitsubishi B1M

The B1M was the first Japanese aircraft designed for torpedo operations, bombing and reconnaissance, and also the first to see combat. It was adopted by the Japanese Navy Air Force in 1924 and continued in service until 1938, being used in action during the war with China. Nearly 450 were built over a period of nine years

Span: 48 ft 6 in *Length:* 32 ft 1 in *Engine:* Napier Lion or Mitsubishi-built Hispano-Suiza, 450 hp *Max speed:* 130 mph *Endurance:* 2½ hr *Armament:* 2 or 4×7.7-mm mg *Bombload:* 1070 lb or torpedo

to be used, from the outset, as a dual purpose aircraft for torpedo work and long-range reconnaissance. For reconnaissance work it had a range of over 1000 miles (14 hours) and in the torpedo configuration its range was 815 miles, almost double that of its predecessor. To cope with the navigation, it was designed to carry a crew of two.

The Ripons merged with the Baffins that succeeded them. The Baffins were, in fact, originally called Ripon Vs in their prototype stage and as the Baffins came into service 68 surviving Ripons were converted to Baffin configuration. This change from Ripon to Baffin consisted mainly of changing engines from the water-cooled Napier Lion to the air-cooled Bristol Pegasus, cleaning up the landing gear details and increasing the length by about 2 ft—all very trivial. The results were interesting though, for with a slight reduction in available power and the substitution of the air-cooled engine, the airspeed actually increased by 10 mph.

In America, Martin T3M-1 and T3M-2s were produced in substantial numbers in 1926 and 1927, powered by the Wright and Packard engines. They carried equipment that gradual experience indicated was necessary. In September 1928, the first torpedo planes to go aboard a US carrier were the Martin T3M-2s, employed aboard the USS *Lexington*. These aircraft also had the distinction of being the last of the water-cooled engine torpedo planes in the US Navy. They were replaced in 1928 by the Martin T4M-1 powered by the Pratt & Whitney Hornet air-cooled engine which produced 525 hp. One of the most important features of this new engine was that many

parts were interchangeable with the Pratt & Whitney Wasp engines, already in extensive service use. This unique feature reduced the spare parts stocked aboard ship, a very important feature where space and weight, not to forget cost, are important. Almost identical to the T4M-1s were the Great Lakes TG-1s and TG-2s. These designations resulted when the Detroit Aircraft Company purchased the Cleveland plant of the Martin Company when Martin moved to Baltimore.

The fourth generation of torpedo bombers consisted of the Blackburn Shark, the Fairey Swordfish and the Douglas SBD.

Continuing its hold on the torpedo-plane market, Blackburn had in-hand a replacement for its own Baffin. During 1934-35 tests were underway on the Blackburn Shark. It still retained that all-important high position for the pilot for good visibility, but aside from that and the basic geometry of the machine, it was a rather drastic technological change from its predecessors.

Aside from this one peculiarity, the Shark had a well constructed, robust appearance which included a cowled air-cooled Armstrong-Siddeley Tiger VI engine of 760 hp. In addition to being a torpedo plane, it became a spotter-reconnaissance plane with provision for a third crew member. However, refinement in structure and powerplant performance of the Shark over its predecessors was not sufficient to give it more than passing notice in the progression of torpedo planes, for its successor was the Fairey Swordfish. The Swordfish's long career in the Second World War puts the biplane torpedo-bomber with the Avengers and Barracudas covered in that section.

Mitsubishi B2M

Built for the Japanese Navy as a replacement for the B1M, the B2M was a disappointment in service and never really replaced the earlier machine. It was in service from 1932 to 1937 and saw limited service during the Sino-Japanese war

Span: 49 ft 11 in *Length:* 33 ft 8 in *Engine:* Mitsubishi-built Hispano-Suiza, 600 hp *Max speed:* 132 mph *Ceiling:* 14,300 ft *Range:* 1100 miles *Armament:* 2×7.7-mm mg *Bombload:* 1764 lb torpedo

Observation/Utility/Trainers
SERVICING THE FLEET

Imperial War Museum

Sqn Cdr Bigsworth and the Avro 504B he used to attack Zeppelin LZ39 over Ostend on May 17, 1915. The Avro 504 was the Royal Navy's best combat aircraft in 1914 serving as bomber, fighter and reconnaissance aircraft but was soon relegated to secondary roles becoming an outstanding basic trainer

Westland Walrus
Designed as a shipboard utility aircraft the Walrus used surplus D.H.9 wings and was characterised by humps and bulges for its special equipment. The undercarriage was equipped with complex arresting gear and flotation bags
Span: 46 ft 2 in *Length:* 30 ft *Engine:* Napier Lion II, 450 hp *Max speed:* 110 mph

Aeromarine 39B
The USN's first shipboard trainer, first flown in 1917. In October 1922 Cdr G deC Chevalier USN made the first landing on the USS *Langley* in an Aeromarine 39B
Span: 47 ft *Length:* 30 ft 4.25 in *Engine:* Curtiss OXX6, 100 hp *Max speed:* 73 mph at sea level *Ceiling:* 5000 ft *Range:* 273 miles

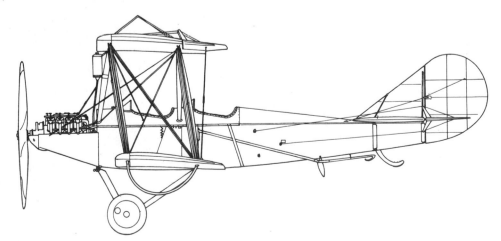

Though few in numbers, the variety of aircraft that came within this category covers the entire span of carrier aviation operations. From the very beginning, the aircraft that were first experimentally operated from carriers were trainers or multi-purpose aircraft. Probably best known of these is the Avro 504, which because of its docile flying characteristics and its period of operation, was used in almost every category including bombing and as an anti-Zeppelin fighter.

Though not operated from a carrier at that time, 504s were used in the historic RNAS raid of November 21, 1914, on the Zeppelin sheds at Friedrichshafen on Lake Constance. Three 504s, each armed with four 20-lb bombs, attacked from an altitude of 700 ft and succeeded in exploding a gas works with spectacular results and also severely damaged one Zeppelin. Later, on May 16-17, two RNAS Avros intercepted two Zeppelins in the vicinity of Ostend. Though the Zeppelins were damaged by the Avros' 20-lb bombs they escaped complete destruction.

The Avros were included in the aircraft types making the carrier landings and take-offs in the 1915-1917 period, and one of the first aircraft to be launched by catapult was an Avro 504H, piloted by Flight Commander R E Penny in 1917.

The 504s' extensive use as trainers is well known and, in this configuration were the first aircraft to be selected by the Japanese Navy when they began their carrier operations. Their simple wood and fabric airframe and generous wing area encouraged the use of these Avros whenever a new development was attempted. Their rotary engines made them the logical transition trainers for pilots training to fly the Parnall Panther, which was to be one of the first British aircraft to be designed from the outset for carrier operation.

Hump-Backed

The Panther was a two-place spotter/reconnaissance machine, but was not fitted with dual controls. It has a hump-backed fuselage, appearing to have the crew cockpits mounted on top of a Nieuport fuselage. The pilot was afforded a good view for car-rier landings by being perched on top of and slightly to the rear of the 230-hp Bentley BR2 rotary engine. The Panther was equipped with all the accoutrements of the early carrier aircraft including flotation bags, hydrofoil fitted to the landing gear and axle hooks to engage the landing wires then in use aboard the *Argus* and *Hermes*.

Additionally, the Panther was unique in that it could be folded for stowage aboard ship. The unusual aspect of this folding was that the fuselage was folded rather than the wings, as became standardized at a later date. The fold point was immediately behind the observer's cockpit and required an indentation in the curved starboard side of the fuselage at the hinge line, a concession to reducing the complexity of folding the fuselage. The wing span was 29 ft 6 in, keeping it marginally under the 30-ft limit of the aircraft lift aboard the carriers. Since Panthers were not intended for combat, their only armament was a single ·303 Lewis gun mounted for defence purposes in the rear observer's cockpit. Their airframe was constructed of wood with fabric covering.

Loening M-8-0
In 1918 the Loening company was asked to develop a two-seat fighter for the US Navy able to outperform the British Bristol Fighter. The result was the monoplane M-8-0 but the 46 production models delivered saw shipboard service as observation aircraft
Span: 32 ft 9 in *Length:* 24 ft *Engine:* Hispano-Suiza, 300 hp *Max speed:* 145 mph *Ceiling:* 22,000 ft *Armament:* 2 Lewis mg

Blackburn Blackburn
Built around a capacious cabin for the observer equipped with four portholes as befitted a carrier-borne observation aircraft, the ungainly Blackburn's pilot sat just below the top wing's leading edge for the best view on landing
Span: 45 ft 6 in *Length:* 36 ft 2 in *Engine.* Napier Lion IIB, 450 hp *Max speed:* 122 mph *Ceiling:* 15,500 ft *Endurance:* 4·25 hrs

Despite this construction and the idiosyncrasies of their rotary engines, they remained in service until 1926. In 1919, 12 Panthers were sold to the Japanese Navy as trainers for reconnaissance pilots.

The first aircraft actually designed for spotter/reconnaissance duties after the Armistice was the Westland Walrus. Its service life was overlapped by the Panther just described. The Walrus was the result of an economy drive that usually follows a major military effort. The de Havilland D.H.9As were redesigned into a configuration suitable for carrier deck operation. The resulting aircraft was surely one of the most unattractive of all times. There really was no redeeming feature to this aircraft other than the modest out-of-pocket initial cost. To make this conversion the D.H.9A was the point of departure, to which was added space for a third crew member, flotation gear, detachable wings and special landing gear fixtures to grasp the longitudinal deck cables in a manner similar to cable car grippers. These served as brakes for landing, since wheel brakes were not in use at this date. With a humped turtle deck aft of the rear cockpit, a pannier bulge beneath the fuselage for the observer, flotation bags extending from under the lower wings forward to the front of the engine and a radiator suspended beneath, the Walrus can only be described as a flying apparition. In 1925 the 36 Walruses were phased out of service to be replaced by Blackburn Blackburds and Avro Bisons, both designed for the same duty, spotter/reconnaissance.

As for the Avro Bison, there was some merit in this choice of name for, in profile and general overall ugliness, it could be compared with its namesake, the bison, a massive beast, native to the Plains states of

North America. The Bison was a slab-sided, hump-backed monstrosity whose one good feature appears to have been a very substantial 'picture window' for the observer on both sides of the fuselage just forward of the rear cockpit. Its wing span of 46 ft made it necessary to find a means for folding it. As it developed, the wing panels, completely rigged, were folded backward to rest between the wing stub and the horizontal stabilizer. Performance was less than spectacular. Since it was intended for spotting and reconnaissance this was no great failing though its range of 360 miles would not qualify it for any accolades.

Designed for Comfort
The Bison's successor, the Blackburn Blackburn, was slightly improved in performance with a range of about 440 miles. Along with the Bison and the Walrus, the Blackburn was designed with the comfort of the navigator/observer in mind and with little regard for aesthetics or aerodynamic streamlining. The pilot was 'mounted' directly above the rear of the Napier Lion engine, in what appears to be an appendage to the forward fuselage which extended to a notched break in the fuselage at the trailing edge of the lower wing. To the rear of this notch, a gunner's cockpit was installed with a Scarff ring mount. To the rear of the engine, directly under the pilot, and back to the trailing edge of the wing was the compartment for the navigator/observer. From the dimensions of the fuselage, in the area described, this crew member had an accommodation not unlike an 'efficiency apartment' complete with two porthole windows on each side to maintain the nautical flavour. These were the ugly sisters of the Blackburn Dart torpedo-bomber

which is to say they were really unattractive, for the Dart was not a thing of beauty. The total Mk I and Mk II Blackburns amounted to 62 aircraft constructed and operated from 1922 until they were declared obsolete in 1935.

A side-by-side seat trainer variant of the Blackburn known as the Blackburn Bull carried the design to absurd lengths. The drag was so high as to make its operation from existing land bases extremely risky, without adding the danger, if not the impossibility, of operating from a carrier. Only two aircraft of this type were built.

The second generation carrier aircraft had the benefit of technical improvements in a number of details but the aircraft in carrier service were still left-overs from First World War designs. As such, they were still of the wood and fabric structure characteristic of the period of their design but modified by the addition of a tail hook and the axle hooks that were then in favour.

The two aircraft trainer/utility types that figured prominently in early US carrier operation were the Aeromarine 39B and the Vought VE-7. The VE-7SF, piloted by Lt VC Griffin, made the first takeoff from the carrier USS *Langley* on October 17, 1922, and on October 26, 1922, Lt Cdr Godfrey de Chevalier landed an Aeromarine 39B aboard the USS *Langley* while underway.

The Fairey IIID was of later design but still of the wood and fabric construction as were the Aeromarine and Voughts. The IIIDs entered service in 1924 and continued service until 1930. They were developed from the IIIC which was well-proven, having been produced before the Armistice and used during the period following the war. The IIIDs were used extensively as carrier based landplanes from HMS *Argus* and also

The 450 hp Napier engine had great difficulty pulling this float-equipped Blackburn Blackburn through the air so great was the 'built in headwind' from wires, struts and the ungainly fuselage

as floatplanes with HMS *Vindictive*. This dual capability was a standard feature of most naval aircraft of this period, including the Aeromarine 39 and Vought VE-7, mentioned previously.

The third generation was characterized by a shift to metal fuselage structures with wood wing structure still the standard. Notable among these aircraft was the Fairey IIIF, a further refinement of the IIID, but really a complete redesign. The fuselage, of tubular steel construction, was refined aerodynamically as well. Possibly the best-known aircraft type between the wars, the IIIF served aboard every operating British carrier. During their operating life, from 1927 to 1940, over 350 of this aircraft were produced. During this extremely lengthy period numerous structural changes took place, the most significant of which was the transition to all-metal primary structure. Also during their tenure, another technical detail was resolved.

During the early days of carrier operation, the deck wires were stretched longitudinally to the detriment of aircraft landing gears. Then, because of excessive damage to landing gears, landing wires were eliminated altogether, but as aircraft weight and speeds increased interest in arrester systems were renewed. A Fairey IIIF was used to experiment with the tail hooks used, with the transverse arrester wires similar to those still in use aboard carriers today. The IIIF could be mounted on twin floats to be used aboard battleships and were fitted to carry a light load of bombs, up to 500 lb, under the wings. In keeping with their limited combat capability, they carried only one forward firing Vickers machine-gun and one free-swivelling Lewis gun in the rear cockpit.

The Fairey Seal followed the IIIF and was

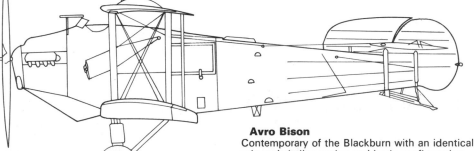

Avro Bison
Contemporary of the Blackburn with an identical role and similar engine and basic configuration
Span: 46 ft *Length:* 36 ft *Engine:* Napier Lion II, 480 hp *Max speed:* 110 mph *Ceiling:* 14,000 ft *Range:* 340 miles

Blackburn Shark comes in to land on HMS Courageous, *the handling crews already running to grab the plane as soon as it settles*

US Navy

Vought UO-1

The UO-1 two seat observation and gun spotter was fitted for catapulting from battleships and scout cruisers. It served aboard the *Langley*, and as shown here was rigged with an overwing hook for operation from airships
Span: 34 ft 1 in *Length:* 24 ft 2 in *Engine:* Wright J-1, 220 hp *Max speed:* 122 mph *Ceiling:* 18,200 ft

Specially modified N2Y-4 trainer makes a test drop from the US Navy's airship Akron *above Lakehurst, New Jersey, 1931*

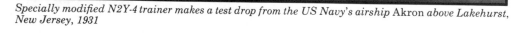

Fairey IIIF

More than 340 Fairey IIIFs were operated by the FAA as three-seat spotter/reconnaissance aircraft, making it the most widely used type of the inter-war years. It entered service in 1928 and operated from every Royal Navy aircraft carrier. The IIIF was the last FAA type designed specifically for reconnaissance, and it remained in service until 1940
Span: 45 ft 9 in *Length:* 34 ft 4 in *Engine:* (Mk IIIB) Napier Lion XIA, 570 hp *Max speed:* 120 mph *Ceiling:* 20,000 ft *Endurance:* 4 hrs *Armament:* 1 fixed Vickers mg, 1 Lewis gun *Bombload:* 500 lb

Vought O2U Corsair
Conceived as two seat fighter quickly convertible as a landplane or floatplane, the Corsair saw most service as an observation machine
Span: 34 ft 6 in *Length:* 24 ft 8 in *Engine:* Pratt & Whitney Wasp, 425 hp *Max speed:* 151 mph *Ceiling:* 22,100 ft *Range:* 580 miles *Armament:* 2 Browning mg, 2 Lewis mg

An early experiment with parasite fighters involved the airship R23 and Sopwith Camels in the summer of 1918. The aircraft was attached to a horizontal surface under the airship's keel. The war ended before the proposal could proceed beyond the experimental stage

Imperial War Museum

Imperial War Museum

North American SNJ-1
SNJ-1 was the naval designation for the
famous AT-6 advanced trainer, the prototype
for which first flew in 1938. Over 10,000 were
produced during the war
 Span: 42 ft 0.25 in *Length:* 29 ft *Engine:*
Pratt & Whitney R-1340-AN-1, 550 hp *Max
speed:* 212 mph *Ceiling:* 24,000 ft *Range:*
870 miles

essentially a IIIF converted to air-cooled
engine. The IIIF used the 570-hp Napier
Lion engine and the Seal was powered by
the 525-hp Armstrong-Siddeley Panther engine. In spite of the reduction of horsepower, the maximum speed actually increased from 120 mph for the IIIF to 138
mph for the Seal.

The concept of spotter/reconnaissance
aircraft was running out of favour with their
duties being added to new design requirements of other aircraft. As a result, some
squadrons were re-equipped with Fairey
Swordfish by 1938, the other squadrons
converting to the Blackburn Sharks (torpedo planes) as early as 1935, the year that
production of the Seals ended. As a part of
their training programme, both construc-
tion-wise and operationally, a number of
Seals were purchased by the Japanese Navy
but these were about the last of the aircraft
imports of any size, for they were about to

purchase their aircraft from Japanese manufacturers as a means of developing their
own design and production capabilities.

The Vought O2U Corsair was the US contemporary of the Fairey IIIF and, like the
IIIF, it was capable of operating from catapults or from carrier decks. A notable
difference in operating philosophy between
the British on one hand, and the American
and Japanese on the other hand, concerned
the floats. The British favoured two parallel
and equal displacement floats while the US
and the Japanese favoured a single main
float with smaller outrigger wing-tip floats
to maintain balance when at rest. The US
technique dates back to the first naval aircraft and the decision by Glenn H Curtiss to
use the single float. The single float prevented an imbalance should the float develop
a leak for any reason. A single float might
fill a compartment if damaged and prevent
takeoff, but the landing or takeoff, if poss-

ible, would be in a balanced condition. Also,
when taxiing at high speed, the single float
offers less resistance, the wing floats are
well clear of the water at planning speed,
and balance is achieved somewhat like
riding a bicycle. Additionally, waves striking twin floats unequally have a tendency
to twist the floats and their fittings. The
twin floats, however, generally speaking,
are easier to train on and make for easier
entry to and egress from the aircraft. Twin
floats find their greatest use in civil aircraft.

The O2Us entered operational service in
1927 with 130 O2U-1s, plus two prototypes.
They followed the pattern of their contemporaries: tandem two-place biplanes
with a single .30 cal machine-gun firing

forward. A pair of .30s were mounted on a Scarff ring in the rear cockpit. The O2Us were powered by a radial air-cooled Pratt & Whitney R1340-88, producing 450 hp. Speeds were improving and the Corsair showed its mettle by establishing a number of records for speed and weight carrying. As in the case of the Fairey IIIFs the landing gear still had a fixed solid axle. An innovation of the Vought planes was the 'cheek' fuel tanks which were mounted on the fuselage sides from the firewall back to the seat of the forward pilot's cockpit. They were faired to the contours of the fuselage.

The Japanese copied the Vought in almost every detail. In 1930, the Nakajima E4N2 and the E4N2-C (for carrier operation) reached operational status, the same year that the improved O3U-1 began to replace the O2Us. Other than rudder configuration there was little external difference between the Nakajima and the O3U-1. The E4N2 was followed by the E8N in 1933, which was an improved version and was an even closer match for the O3U series, even to engine power. The E8N1 and its variations were produced in quantity, totalling over 750 planes, and in a number of variations. Like its Vought counterpart, it was stressed for catapult launching and could be used on carriers as well. It was the standard Japanese reconnaissance aircraft until the introduction of the Nakajima C6N1 Myrt.

Among the more interesting carrier observation aircraft was the Loening OL-8A amphibian, 20 of which were built. A number of OL-8s were built but were not equipped for carrier operation. The first of this unique series of aircraft was built to match the performance of the de Havilland DH-4s which were still the standard Army aircraft at the time of their introduction. Grover C Loening anticipated difficulty in selling these to the military and, with this in mind, positioned the pilot and observer exactly as they were in the old DHs, figuring that if the crew felt at home with all their accustomed reference points, the chance for sale would be improved. As it turned out he was correct but the real breakthrough came when General Billy Mitchell had a forced landing in the Mississippi River while flying a DH on an inspection tour. After getting ashore, his first action was a phone call to the purchasing department which resulted in the purchase of five Loening amphibians. Additional small orders followed and the Navy purchased a number which were used by the McMillan Arctic expedition with Commander Richard

E Byrd as the detachment commander.

The Army used them for surveys and several famous flights, the most notable being the first South American Goodwill Flight in 1927. The importance of the flight was lost in the publicity resulting from the trans-atlantic attempts and their return to the US coincided with Lindberg's famous solo transatlantic flight in May 1927.

Various engine installations were used in the Loenings. The most interesting to Loening was the first inverted Liberty installation. Other than the Loenings, the only other widely used amphibians were the Supermarine Walrus and the Grumman JF-1 which, in general, resembled the Loening design formula.

The Walrus was of a flying boat configuration and was stressed for catapult launching which made it one of the most versatile spotter/reconnaissance aircraft to see naval service. Its versatility resulted in a very large production run of over 740 aircraft and a useful service from 1933 to 1944. This was a long period of service for an ungainly looking biplane in an era when transition to monoplanes was in progress. Like its equally improbable contemporary, the Fairey Swordfish, the Walrus was highly regarded by FAA crews.

Utility Amphibians

About the time the Walrus was entering service, on the other side of the Atlantic, Grumman Aircraft Engineering Company was testing a replacement for the Loening amphibians. The design concept for this aircraft followed that of the Loenings; a single central float joined to a fuselage that seated its crew in tandem, and had floats mounted at the outboard tips of its biplane wing. Their duties were utility and general communications, providing a link between ship and shore. The Grumman J2F Duck was built in small numbers until the expansion programme preceding the Second World War. At the end of 1940, Grumman received its last and largest order for 144 Ducks. As in the case of the TBFs, war was declared, and production was shifted to the Columbia Aircraft Corp. from where 330 were ordered. Grumman production facilities were fully committed to the production of the F6F Hellcats.

The last of the Curtiss biplanes in naval service was the SOC Seagull which, like so many Scout/Observation/Reconnaissance/ Spotter aircraft, was a jack of all trades. It was required to operate as a float plane from battleships and cruisers and be convertible to land operation and aboard carriers.

It is a fine point of distinction, but observation planes were attached to battleships and scouting planes were normally operated from cruisers. With the SOCs, the duties were combined. After 135 SOCs were delivered, the next 40 were land based with a single strut and fixed streamlined landing gear similar to that used on the F11Cs and the Army's P6E. On these latter two aircraft, the landing gear was an attractive appendage but on the SOC it resulted in an odd bird-legged appearance. Aircraft that were equipped for carrier operation were designated SOC-2A and SOC-3A. Though scheduled to be retired with the introduction of the SO3C Seagull, the SOCs were retained and used until the end of the Second World War when the SO3Cs failed to meet operational expectations and were retired.

ARMAMENT

While the original intended use of aircraft in warfare was to observe enemy actions, it was only a very short time before air-to-air combat developed. It is recorded that the first evidence of armament in conjunction with aircraft was the use of service pistols carried by observers or pilots. Quickly realizing the inadequacy of pistols, the next stage was carbines, which were only slightly better, but still ineffective in the developing combat techniques of 1914. When it was realized that machine-guns offered the only hope for shooting down an enemy aircraft, development of this weapon for use by aircraft crews proceeded rapidly.

During the First World War, the dominant armament was the .30 cal machine-gun, though at least in one case, a 37-mm cannon was mounted in the V of a Hispano-Suiza engine mounted in a Spad XIII. To a limited degree also, an 11-mm cartridge was used in

Vickers Mk II
Replaced the Mk I*, using a smaller, perforated casing than its predecessor. The Mk II had no fused spring box and was lighter than the earlier model *Weight:* 22 lb *Rate of fire:* 450-550 rpm *Muzzle velocity:* 2440 fps

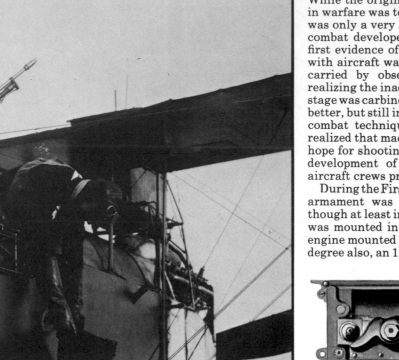

Imperial War Museum

The simplest form of air-craft armament in the First World War—apart from freely aimed rifles or pistols—was a machine gun used by the observer in reconnaissance aircraft such as this Short seaplane. The Lewis gun is attached to a Scarff ring mounting

Lewis Mounting
The Scarff mount (left), devised by Warrant Officer Scarff, RNAS, was adopted as standard by the RAF and remained in use until the start of the Second World War. Its main drawback was that if one gun jammed, it became almost impossible to fire the other. The earlier Foster mount (below on PV8) enabled the gun to be fired from the upper wing, over the propeller arc, by means of a cable

The PV8 lightweight fighter had a Lewis gun mounted above the upper wing

Imperial War Museum

aviation guns. Following the war, development of various aviation machine-guns and light cannon continued but, because of weight considerations, the cal 30 guns dominated the field. In many instances, new plane specifications stipulated the ability to mount one cal 30 (7·9 mm) and one cal 50 (12-13 mm) or two cal 30 guns.

Though development continued between the wars, it was not until stimulated by the preparation for war in the latter part of the 1930s that dedicated efforts were made to develop a suitable 20-mm aircraft cannon. During the evolutionary period of carrier aircraft, the 1920s and 1930s, the cal 30 guns were the mainstay of shipboard aircraft.

As the weight of the aircraft increased, with the addition of armour plate to protect the crew and vital parts of the aircraft, and with increased weight of projectiles, an increased rate of firing became necessary. The dual problems of slow rate of fire and magazines of limited capacity (as few as 60 rounds per gun) considerably dampened official and designers' enthusiasm for air-

Crashed Sopwith Pup reveals its Gnôme rotary engine and the Vickers .303 Mk 1* with ammunition panniers

An RNAS armourer works on the twin Lewis guns in the front cockpit of a Handley Page O/100 operated by No 14 (RNAS) squadron at Dunkirk on June 1, 1918. The bomber carried up to five Lewis guns

Imperial War Museum

Vickers .303 Mk 1*
The first Allied gun able to be synchronised to fire through propeller blades, this was a Mk 1 Vickers modified for air cooling with louvres cut in the barrel casing and belt containers for the ammunition *Weight:* 38 lb *Rate of fire:* 450-550 rpm *Muzzle velocity:* 2440 fps

craft cannon. As a result, the compromise solution was the development of the ·5-in cal 50 (12·5 – 13 mm) size gun for use by most military services.

While not capable of the same range as the cannon, nor easily adaptable to the use of explosive type projectiles, they were a decided improvement over the cal 30 (·303 – 7·9 mm) guns whose rate of fire had been their greatest asset. As the rate of fire of the ·5-in machine-gun was increased, a cyclical rate acceptably close to that of the cal 30 guns resulted.

Representative Machine-Guns for Naval Aircraft

Name	Country of origin	Ammunition	Cooling	Rate of fire (rpm)	Muzzle velocity (fps)
Lewis Air Mk II	Britain	0.303-in	Air	500–600	2440
Vickers Mk I*	Britain	0.303-in	Air	450–550	2440
Vickers Mk II	Britain	0.303-in	Air	450–550	2440
Madsen 23-mm	Denmark	23-mm	Air	500	2920
Darne Model 29 Aircraft	France	7.5-mm rimless	Air	1200	2700
Lubbe Air	Germany	20-mm	Air	360	2650
Semag	Switzerland	20-mm	Air	350	
American Armament Corp Type M	US	37-mm	Air	125	1250
Browning aircraft mg M1919	US	0.30-in	Air	1100	2750
Marlin aircraft mg M1917	US	0.30-in	Air	850–1000	2750

The next plateau was the cannon in the 20–30-mm range, dictated by steadily increasing weight of aircraft and speed. Development of this armament category was slow and did not reach quantity use until the Second World War when the Japanese used the 20-mm cannon in their nimble Mitsubishi A6M Zeke naval fighters. Unfortunately, the muzzle velocity of these Japanese cannon left much room for development as their rate of fire was not in the spectacular class. As the war progressed, aircraft of the US and British navies standardized on the 20-mm cannon as the next advance in armament.

Enemy Target

At about the same time that the 20-mm cannon began to find favour as a weapon for attack-type aircraft, rockets were added to the stores to be carried by naval aircraft. Air-to-air and air-to-ground missiles began to take over the roles of the aircraft gun. Like the cannon, the rocket could be adapted to a multitude of warheads and fuses, including proximity fuses which explode the missile even without the necessity of a direct hit on the enemy target.

Lubbe 20-mm
This German aircraft gun, which was developed about 1929, never entered service, although some were purchased by the United States. It is shown here with its spring-loaded magazine

Semag (Above)
Used both as an aircraft and anti-aircraft weapon, the Semag employed blowback operation and was fed from a 20-round magazine *Weight:* 95 lb *Rate of fire:* 350 rpm

American Armament Corp Type M (Left)
A fully automatic cannon designed specifically for aircraft use, this weapon was produced with barrels of various lengths depending on the aircraft on which it was to be mounted. The mechanism was standard but weight and muzzle velocity varied *Weight:* 330 lb *Rate of fire:* 125 rpm *Muzzle velocity:* 1250 fps

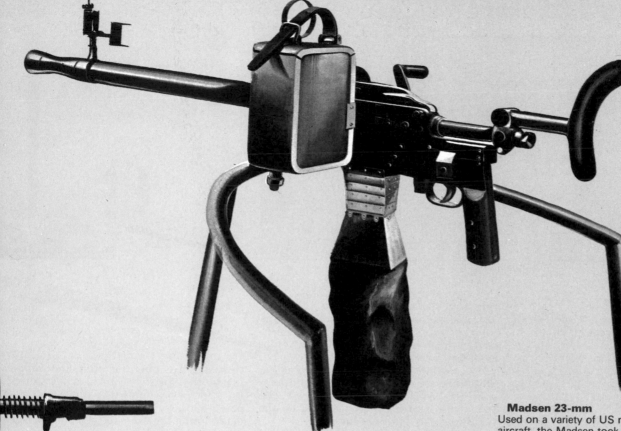

Madsen 23-mm
Used on a variety of US naval and military aircraft, the Madsen took advantage of the short range (500-600 yards) expected of aircraft cannon to increase the explosive content by reducing the amount of propellant compared with that necessary in naval guns *Weight:* 118 lb *Rate of fire:* 500 rpm *Muzzle velocity:* 2920 fps

SIGHTS

One of the least discussed equipment items for naval aircraft, and one of the most important, is its armament (gun) sight.

During the First World War, through the 1920s and, in many instances, into the Second World War period, a simple ring and post system was used. This consisted of a single post, sometimes with a small knob on top, and a second unit consisting of multiple concentric rings. In use, the pilot or gunner would manoeuvre his aircraft or flexible machine-gun, to bring the post, ring and target into alignment. The multiple rings

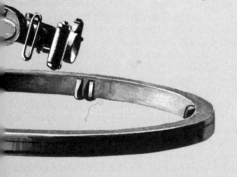

gave the pilot an opportunity to establish a rough estimate of lead or deflection.

A successor sight consisted of a telescope mounted on the cowling and through the windshield where it was adjusted for close proximity to the pilot's eye. Unfortunately, theoretical improvement was not matched by practical use. It was unusually restric-

tive, requiring the pilot to concentrate his vision only on the eyepiece of the sight. In addition, the optics of the sight had a bad characteristic of fogging up, thus rendering it inoperable.

It became quite apparent that a sight was required which allowed greater eye freedom and retained the degree of accuracy made possible by the telescope. The answer was the reflector sight introduced at the beginning of the Second World War. This sight consisted of an angled piece of glass, mounted on the glare shield above the pilot's instruments. Beneath this angled glass was a projector which projected a reticle pattern onto this glass for the pilot to see. It was like a ring and post sight suspended in air and when it was superimposed on an enemy plane it ensured that the plane and guns were boresighted on the target.

Computing Gunsights
By joint efforts the British and US scientific teams co-operated to produce the Illuminated Sight Mark 8 which was used extensively throughout the Second World War for fixed guns. By a succession of modifications, the Mark 8 was steadily improved during this period. Paralleling the development of this sight was the Illuminated Sight Mark 9 for use with free guns as used in turrets.

Computing gunsights were considered as early as 1937, but it was not until the closing days of the Second World War that the British produced a sight which was further developed for production by the Bureau of Ordnance of the US Navy.

With the introduction of the Mark 18 sight for turrets, the expenditure of ammunition dropped substantially and hits increased. The success of this Mark 18 sight resulted in an intensive redesign of this sight for fixed installation in fighter aircraft. When completed, it was designated the Gun Sight Mark 21. This Navy-developed sight, based on a basic British design, became the standard for all Allied air services.

No less important than gun sights were bomb sights, though as it turned out, the Army was the principal beneficiary of a gyro stabilized sight which began its development by the US Navy shortly after the end of the First World War. This sight became the most talked about 'secret weapon' of the Second World War.

The first model Mark II was accepted in 1929 and a later development, the Mark 15, began tests in 1931. As it turned out the Mark 15 was unsuitable for low level bombing, which was more typically a navy tactic. To meet this requirement, a 'field modification' was made using an Illuminated Sight Mark 9 as the basis. For dive bombing, 'straight down', or nearly so, the normal gunsight served well with the pilot applying aiming factors based on his own experience. A gratifying number of hits were scored in this manner.

While torpedo sights were available at the beginning of the Second World War, their shortcomings caused the pilots of these torpedo-bombers to favour the use of the gunsight and personal experience to place the torpedo in the most advantageous position in relation to its target.

FLOTATION GEAR

Ditched Sopwith Pup with its flotation bags inflated gets a tow back to a North Sea shore station

The first case of a landing aboard a carrier as we know it today, was in 1917 aboard the British carrier HMS *Furious*. At the time, only the forward part of the ship was used as a 200-ft flight deck. On this rudimentary deck, Squadron Commander Dunning made the first landing. With the ship steaming into the wind, Dunning threaded his way round the bridge until he was over the landing area forward, at which time he throttled back his Sopwith Pup and settled toward the deck where a landing crew caught the plane as it was about to make contact and guided it safely down.

With this successful landing, Dunning was confident of an equally successful, unassisted touchdown and directed that, on the second landing, the crew not assist until he was completely landed. Unfortunately, as he touched down for a second time, a tyre burst, causing his plane to swerve to one side and to plunge over the side of the

ship into the water, where Dunning was drowned before help could reach him. This freakish, tragic accident gave added incentive to the development of flotation equipment for aircraft and crew.

To save the aircraft after a ditching at sea, 'flotation gear' in the form of large air bags was installed in carrier-based aircraft. The size of the flotation bags depended on the type (size) of the aircraft involved.

The flotation bags themselves were constructed of multiple layers of rubberized fabric and were provided with fabric flaps for attaching them to the aircraft structure. The bags were stowed in containers built into the structure of the aircraft where they were faired in to prevent air drag. Installation was usually in the upper wing or in the sides of the forward fuselage, the location of the greatest concentration of weight.

Usually two bags were installed, but when the aircraft was unusually heavy, a

Squadron Commander Dunning's fatal accident as his Pup goes over the side of HMS Furious *with a burst tyre. Flotation equipment could have saved his life and the tragedy spurred on development work*

third bag was often installed and inflated inside the fuselage of the tail section. Location of bracing wires and the balance point of the aircraft were considered in determining the exact location of the bags. A release 'T' handle for simultaneous release of all bags was usually installed in the upper right side of the instrument panel or in the centre section of the upper wing, offset to the right side. A hand-operated air pump was also provided to top-off the flotation bags after inflation or to replace air lost as a result of a possible slow leak. The bags were capable of supporting a plane for about 10 hours in a relatively calm sea, but in a rough sea, rubbing against the fuselage or other structure could cause them to chafe and to lose pressure and, therefore, buoyancy.

With the beginning of the Second World War, all flotation gear was removed from US aircraft to increase payload and to sink the aircraft to avoid detection.

Inflatable Doughnut
Along with flotation bags for the aircraft, it was considered necessary to include personal flotation gear for the pilot and other crew members. This flotation gear consisted of an inflatable life raft and life preserver. The life raft consisted of an oval-shaped doughnut tube made of rubberized fabric and inflated by a CO_2 cartridge. These varied in size according to the crew complement for the plane. Later models of life rafts were made as a complete circle to reduce the risk of overturning. Life rafts were packaged in fabric carrying cases to prevent chafing or ripping. In addition, they were usually packed with survival gear and rations and installed in or near the cockpit.

Life rafts and life preservers were standard equipment during the Second World War, and were responsible for saving the lives of many air-crewmen during the Second World War. With the development of miniaturization, dehydration and special packing materials and techniques, it became possible to pack parachute seat cushions with relatively complete survival kits tailored for the geographic area of the earth over which the air operations were

Parnall Panther
Designed as a fleet reconnaissance aircraft specifically for use from carriers, the Panther's humpback cockpit gave the pilot an excellent view for deck landing. A hydrovane was fitted to prevent overturning in the event of a ditching and flotation bags were fitted to the top of the undercarriage.
Span: 26 ft 6 in *Length:* 24 ft 11 in *Engine:* Bentley BR 2, 230 hp
Max speed: 108 mph at 6500 ft *Ceiling:* 14,500 ft *Endurance:* 4.5 hrs
Armament: Lewis mg

taking place. In the case of carrier operations, these seat packs also included one-man life rafts, signal devices, dehydrated nourishing foods and first-aid materials.

The life preservers were initially kapok or cork filled; however, because of the bulk, these gave way to air-filled jacket-type 'Mae West' preservers that were worn at all times by carrier-based pilots.

The earliest form of inflatable life preserver dates back to November 14, 1910, when Eugene Ely made the first takeoff from aboard the USS *Birmingham*. As an added insurance Ely inflated two motor-cycle inner tubes and wrapped them around his neck and across his chest to form the earliest version of the Mae West.

During the final stages of the Second World War light-weight belt style preservers came into use. However, the standard aircraft life preserver has continued to be the horsecollar style.

POWERPLANTS

When the pilots of single-engine aircraft venture out over water beyond gliding distance back to a land mass, the psychological effect is equivalent to their engine switching to the 'automatic rough' operating condition. Whether this is literally correct or not, the response is normal for those pilots not accustomed to over-water flying.

Carrier-based pilots, whose daily operations are almost exclusively over water, understandably have a great interest in their engines and treat them with care and respect. In addition, powerplants that are adapted for naval use are designed, tested and maintained with maximum care. Reliability, durability and performance are the prime considerations in the selection of engines for carrier-based aircraft.

With these requirements in mind, it is interesting to note that the dominant engine type, during the years prior to the introduction of the turbine engine, has been the radial air-cooled engine. By type or numerical count, the liquid-cooled engine is in the minority. Though the liquid-cooled engine has undeniable qualities which merited its development, its use in carrier-based aircraft was not as extensive as its air-cooled counterpart. Plumbing, including the radiators, did not stand up well to the pounding which is normal in carrier operations.

The main reasons given for preference of the air-cooled engine in naval service were:
1. Generally, the air-cooled engine was lighter than the liquid-cooled engine of equivalent power. Radiators, plumbing and coolant liquids could add up to a 500-lb weight penalty per aircraft, a substantial amount when added to the weight of equipment such as tail hooks, beefed-up landing gear, etc.
2. The air-cooled engine was simple and easy to start with large tolerances between mov-

ing parts until operating temperatures were reached. Additionally, maintenance, installation and engine changing were simplified.
3. The air-cooled engine was less vulnerable in combat where the radiator and attendant plumbing were subject to battle damage and high stresses resulting from deck landing and handling.
4. There is limited space on a carrier. The more compactly-shaped radial engine and its lack of liquid-cooled system and attendant parts saved valuable space.

Performance Primary Requirement
In operation, carrier aircraft were brought in high above the fantail of the ship to insure that they clear it should the stern rise on the swell as the plane prepared to touch down. The plane was then dropped 15 to 20 ft in a semi-stalled condition to engage the tail hook with the arresting cable (pendant).

During the First World War and shortly thereafter, the primary requirement for aircraft engines was performance but, as carrier aviation developed, it became obvious that these jarring landings aboard carriers would soon put an end to the liquid-cooled engine as a naval powerplant.

A notable exception to this was the number of aircraft produced in the late 1930s and during the Second World War with liquid-cooled engines. It should be noted that a number were expediencies dictated by war-time production and modification of existing land-based planes to naval use. Examples included Hurricanes, Spitfires and even Mosquitoes in British service, and the planned use of the Bf 109 and Ju 87 for the German carrier *Graf Zeppelin*.

Following the First World War, the early days of carrier development, most aircraft were powered by the engines which were

war surplus or those which were under development during the closing stages of the war. This resulted in a number of powerplants which were unsuited for naval service. In the early 1920s, there were engines under development which held promise for naval use. The French were using the water-cooled Hispano-Suiza engines but soon made arrangements to build the British 400-hp Bristol Jupiter.

The British Air Ministry policy was definitely toward air-cooled engines to the extent, in some cases, of replacing water-cooled Rolls-Royce engines with air-cooled engines in existing airframes. The appearance of the aircraft suffered by the change, but the overall performance improved. The Japanese followed the practice of the British, generally, starting with the Nieuport Nighthawks powered by the Bentley 220 BR rotary engine. They became quite expert in handling this combination and landed aboard carriers with ease. These Nighthawks were re-engined with the 400-hp Bristol Jupiter.

In the US, a number of manufacturers attempted to meet naval requirements using liquid-cooled engines. Only Boeing and Curtiss enjoyed any real success, with aircraft powered by the Curtiss D-12 liquid-cooled engine. The Navy tested the TS, a single-seat shipboard fighter, in a number of configurations starting with the Wright-built, water-cooled Hispano-Suiza engine. Eventually, the TS (Curtiss F4C-1) was totally redesigned. The wings were redesigned using a new section and the Wright-Lawrence J-1 radial air-cooled engine was installed to bring it up to performance parity with contemporary British and Japanese naval fighters of 1923. The TS was overtaken by technical progress and was relegated to advance trainer status. In

British service, the Rolls-Royce Kestrel, Merlin and Griffon and the Napier Lion were the dominant liquid-cooled engines.

During the period 1923-25, the US Navy pinned its hopes on the air-cooled Wright P-1, followed by the R-1340 Wasp which was produced by the newly founded Pratt & Whitney company. The Wasp quickly dominated the field. During the 1930s, air-cooled engines powered the majority of carrier-based aircraft. The Bristol Pegasus, Perseus, Taurus, Hercules and Centaurus engines, the Armstrong-Siddeley Tiger, Jaguar and Puma engines in British naval service, and the Wright Cyclone, and Pratt & Whitney

Wasp and Hornet series engines in the US were produced in the greatest numbers.

The Japanese initially relied on licence-built engines, primarily of French and British design, but by the mid-1930s were developing their own designs of air-cooled engines for naval use, which were comparable to any in service with the other naval (carrier) powers. Liquid-cooled engines were used in several early carrier aircraft designs and even as late as the Second World War, the very clean, high-performance Yokosuka D4Y *Suisei* dive-bomber was designed to be powered by the licence-built Daimler-Benz DB601 liquid-

cooled Atsuta engine. Here again, maintenance problems plagued the engine from the beginning, though it was a well-proven engine in wide use in land-based planes. The aircraft was redesigned to install the Mitsubishi Kinsei 62 air-cooled radial engine. With few exceptions, Japanese carrier aircraft also used air-cooled engines.

Of passing interest was the design change in the British Bristol engines, beginning with the Taurus, to sleeve-valve rather than poppet-valve configuration.

As the Second World War approached, the engine production lines geared for all-out effort. Along with quantity production, a requirement for greater power was evident. To meet these requirements, twin-row air-cooled radial engines were developed and produced. Power output in the 3000-hp range became the designers' goal. In the case of the Wright R-3350 and the Pratt & Whitney R-4360 (four row, air-cooled) the maximum output reached 3000 hp.

The Gnôme Monosoupape rotary, 80 hp model
Advantages: Good power-to-weight and size-to-power ratios and relative mechanical simplicity.
Disadvantages: Fine tolerances required in maintenance, tendency to shed cylinders and no proper throttle (the only way of controlling the engine was by cutting the ignition to a number of cylinders). Unlike more conventional engines, the rotary had a stationary crankshaft, around which rotated the cylinders and crankcase, with the propeller bolted to their front. The crankshaft itself (**1**) is bolted to the aeroplane's structure. Into the crankshaft are led three inlets (only two are visible) (**2**) for air, fuel and lubricant

(castor oil, which does not mix with petrol). All three are taken to the crankcase (**3**), where the fuel and air are mixed and vaporised. The mixture is admitted to the cylinder through apertures in the sides of the piston and the base of the cylinder (**4** and **5**), which can only happen when the piston (**6**) is at the very bottom of its stroke. The mixture is compressed as the piston rises again and is detonated by the spark plug, which is fired by the magneto (**7**) when the cylinder is in the right place. This forces the engine round, and as it does, the chamber is cleared through the outlet valve (**8**) opened by a pushrod (**9**) operated from a cam (**10**) on the longitudinal axis of the engine

WING FOLDING

Beardmore WB III, an extensively redesigned Sopwith Pup with folding wings and retracting undercarriage. Modest production was undertaken and 18 were embarked aboard Furious.

Carrier-based aircraft necessarily have two options on wing design. They have wings of short span that fit within the limits imposed by the aircraft elevators of the carrier, or they have folding wings to permit stowage in the hangar decks, on the flight deck and again, most importantly, on the aircraft elevators that move the planes between these two decks.

Whatever the configuration, it should be remembered that folding wings and tail hooks are two of the several penalties and costs that a naval aircraft must bear over its land-based counterpart. The folding joint or joints must be designed so they will not exact any performance penalty on the operating crew. When in the flying position, the hinge must be at least as strong as an equivalent solid wing spar. To insure this strength, the spars must be reinforced and all control lines, fluid lines and electrical lines must pass through this fold point without, in any way, compromising the strength or reliability of the structure or function of the components.

Simplest Solution

Of the many variations of the folding wing principle, the overhead folding configuration, as used on the Vought F4U Corsair, Supermarine Seafire III, Hawker Sea Fury, Curtiss SB2C Helldiver, the Nakajima B5N1 Kate, B6N Jill, and the Aichi B7A2 Grace, offers the simplest solution geometrically speaking. One variant of the famed Mitsubishi A6M, the Model 21 Zeke, had, by all odds, the simplest folding wing. This consisted of manually folding the outboard one half meter of each wing tip upwards. Conversely, the low clearance aboard British carriers required a double fold in the wing of the Seafire III, with the main outboard wing panels folding upward and the tips, outboard of the aileron, folding downward.

The earliest form of wing folding, and one of the most difficult, was the rearward folding of the entire outboard bays of biplane wings. The geometry of this manoeuvre was a real design problem which involved rotating a completely rigged bay of a biplane, complete with flying wires, landing wires and drift wires and upper and lower wing panels, about a single vertical axis and stowing them in this assembled condition along each side of the fuselage, with trailing edges of the wing facing inward. Often the wing bays would rest on the horizontal stabilizer or special brackets which suspended the panels in that position, or with one panel above and one panel below the stabilizer.

The problems of handling these planes on the flight decks in even modest winds must have been quite impressive. Aircraft of this configuration were commonplace between 1920 and 1930, and the Fairey Swordfish and Albacores brought the type right up to the end of the Second World War, though by that time as types of aircraft they were long past their prime.

A third folding configuration involved a twist and a turn. From the flying position, the wing was twisted about its lateral axis and then, with the leading edge at the bottom point, in the case of the Grumman aircraft, the whole panel was rotated about a vertical axis toward the tail to lie parallel to the fuselage. The Fairey monoplane aircraft used a similar arrangement except that the trailing edge of the wing was rotated to the bottom position before the wing panel was rotated to the tail to lie parallel to the fuselage. The preference of the service for accessibility of armament while the wings were in the stowed position was a determining factor on which way the wing was to be stowed. The primary examples of each were the Grumman F4F Wildcat, F6F Hellcat, TBF Avenger, rotating the leading edge down and the Fairey Firefly, rotating the trailing edge downward.

Operating mechanisms varied with the manufacturer and model. Accumulated experience dictated operating systems all the way from full hydraulic operation, as used on the Vought SB2U Vindicator, to totally manual operation, as on such aircraft as the Mitsubishi A6M Model 21 previously mentioned. There were combinations of manual folding and hydraulic or mechanical safetying as well as hydraulic folding and manual or hydraulic safetying.

In all cases, deck crews were an essential part of the operation. In most cases, the price in weight and complexity dictated that human power was the primary operating medium, since crews were required during the action cycle at all times.

One monoplane folding system which was a design resurrection from the biplane era was the Fairey Barracuda torpedo-bomber which rotated the wing straight back, folding the wing of the plane about a vertical axis without any twist about the lateral axis.

Mitsubishi A6M Zero Wing Folding
Tip of each wing folds upwards manually to lose a metre from the total span to meet handling requirements on Japanese carriers

THE CARRIER GROWS UP

The first vessel to be completed as an aircraft carrier was HMS *Ark Royal* in 1914. A converted merchantman, she was fitted with a flying-off deck forward which was in fact never used in action. Instead she was operated as a seaplane carrier, deploying aircraft on fleet reconnaissance missions.

The next step towards the true aircraft carrier was HMS *Furious*, commissioned in 1917. She had started out as a light battle-cruiser before having a flying-off deck added over her forecastle and a hangar built underneath. The vessel was intended to operate Sopwith Pups and 1½-Strutters, which would be ditched after their mission. Trials were carried out in 1917 to see whether it was possible to land aircraft back on the flying-off deck, and Squadron Commander Dunning made a successful landing in a Sopwith Pup while the ship was steaming in Scapa Flow. On his second attempt, however, his aircraft ran off the side of the carrier and he was drowned. A landing deck was later added behind the superstructure, but air currents made operations too difficult and the futility of a hybrid vessel was eventually realized.

The United States Navy's first carrier was the converted collier USS *Langley*, which was commissioned in 1922. A continuous wooded flight deck was built above the hull, leaving space for aircraft storage —rather than a hangar—underneath. *Langley* was later converted to an aircraft tender, the forward 200 ft of deck being removed, and she was finally sunk in 1942.

HMS Ark Royal, *the first ship fully converted to an aircraft carrier, was completed in 1914 and began operations in the Dardanelles in February 1915. Her holds were converted into hangars and cranes were installed to handle her eight seaplanes. After only five months' service she was withdrawn from these duties*

The first true aircraft carrier was HMS Furious, *converted from a light battle cruiser by building a slanted flight deck over the forecastle. The space underneath formed a hangar, and later a landing deck which proved to be unusable—was added aft of the superstructure*

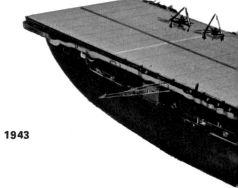

1943

The US Navy's first aircraft carrier was the USS Langley, *converted from a collier, which entered full-scale service in 1925 after three years of trials. She could carry up to 34 aircraft and was converted to a seaplane tender in 1937. The* Langley *was sunk in 1942*

HMS *Courageous* was the first carrier in which a really effective arrester gear was fitted. Wires connected to hydraulic cylinders were paid out gradually when engaged by a hook on the aircraft, giving smooth deceleration. This method of safely recovering aircraft, first installed in 1933, had endured to the present. *Courageous* was fitted with a 60-ft-long flying-off deck below the main flight deck, but this proved of little use in action because the vessel was sunk within a month of the outbreak of the Second World War when its Swordfishes failed to deter an attack by a German U-boat.

The US Navy's next two carriers were the more ambitious *Lexington* and *Saratoga*, converted from incomplete battle-cruisers. The massive funnel on the starboard side was a distinguishing feature.

The first US vessel designed from the outset as an aircraft carrier was the *Ranger*, commissioned in 1934. Although displacing only 14,500 tons, the *Ranger* could carry 75 aircraft because power, protection and

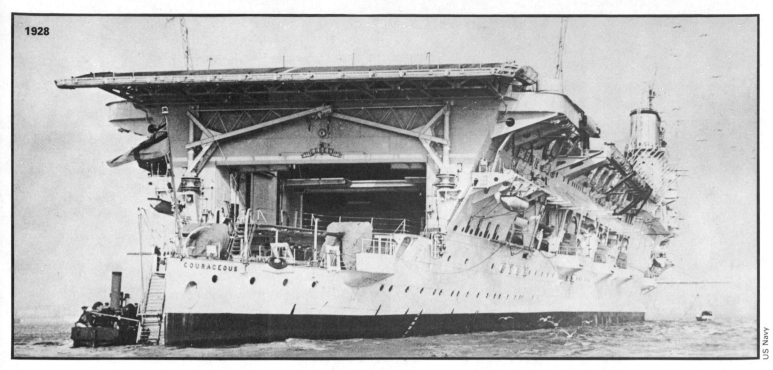

1928

HMS Courageous *was fitted with a 60-ft flying-off deck in addition to the normal flight deck, allowing light fighters such as the Fairey Flycatcher to take off independently of other operations. The* Courageous *and her sister ships* Furious *and* Glorious *were all converted from cruisers*

1933

The first United States Navy vessel designed from the outset as an aircraft carrier, USS Ranger *had a small island superstructure and three funnels which folded down during flying operations. The vessel, commissioned in June 1934, was too slow and under-armoured for Pacific operations but served in the Atlantic before being scrapped in 1947*

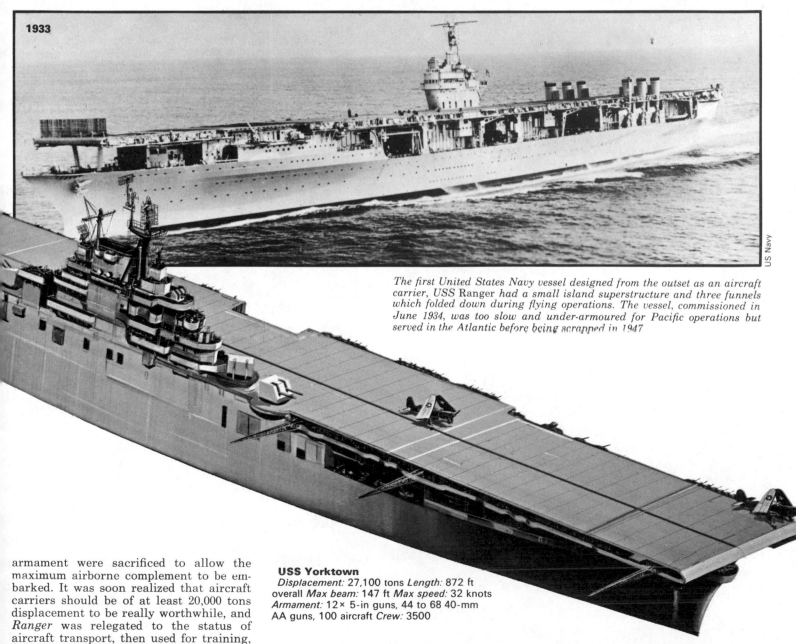

armament were sacrificed to allow the maximum airborne complement to be embarked. It was soon realized that aircraft carriers should be of at least 20,000 tons displacement to be really worthwhile, and *Ranger* was relegated to the status of aircraft transport, then used for training, before being scrapped in 1947.

USS Yorktown
Displacement: 27,100 tons *Length:* 872 ft overall *Max beam:* 147 ft *Max speed:* 32 knots *Armament:* 12× 5-in guns, 44 to 68 40-mm AA guns, 100 aircraft *Crew:* 3500

Helldiver dive-bombers massed on the flight deck of a newly commissioned US aircraft carrier 1941

John Batchelor

NAVAL AIRCRAFT OF THE SECOND WORLD WAR

Louis S. Casey

Carrier-borne aircraft revolutionised naval warfare during the Second World War. In the Atlantic and Mediterranean their work ranged from convoy protection to such dramatic actions as Taranto and the *Bismarck* and *Tirpitz* strikes; but it was in the vast reaches of the Pacific they came into their own.

With the Battle of the Coral Sea in 1942 a new era dawned: for the first time a naval engagement was fought by aircraft alone, without the surface ships of either side coming within sight of each other. Moreover, as the sinking of the *Repulse* and *Prince of Wales* in 1941, and of the *Yamato*, prize of the Japanese Navy, in 1945 demonstrated, the age of the battleship as king-pin of the fleet was over.

In this chapter we cover the naval aircraft of the United States, Britain and Japan during the Second World War, as well as the carriers from which they operated.

CONTENTS

Imperial War Museum

A Swordfish torpedo bomber takes off from HMS Furious on a reconnaissance patrol

WHEN AN AIRCRAFT LANDS AT SEA

With the Battle of the Coral Sea in May 1942, aircraft carriers came of age. The carrier was and still is the long arm of the navy and the aircraft of these carriers are the mailed fist to strike again and again at an enemy force whether it be on land or sea.

Until the Battle of the Coral Sea, the role of the carrier was that of a supporting force for the big ships of the navy – battleships, cruisers and heavy cruisers. When land armies move forward they take airstrips or create airstrips to bring their supporting air-power forward, shortening the round-trip time needed to rain blows on the enemy and to refuel, rearm and repair the aircraft involved. When a naval force moves forward, or in any direction in unison with the fleet or task force, the airstrip moves with it. Among the many advantages of this mobile airstrip is the complete continuity of action on the home base as well as complete familiarity of the pilots with this base, thus avoiding distracting elements which might take their minds off the job at hand. The parallel between the

airstrip and the carrier is fairly exact for the carrier provides the fuel and servicing for the aircraft as well as the combat direction and billeting for the crews.

Aircraft in warfare are often considered to be long-range artillery. In tactical situations this has validity, but with the added advantage that the firepower can be delivered from virtually any quarter, not just from along a relatively known static front-line of the battle area. This is particularly effective in naval engagements where dive-bombing and torpedo attacks can originate from every point of the compass or any vertical angle or altitude. From the carriers, they can strike swiftly and repeatedly, carrying out an old but certain prescription for military success of 'getting there firstest with the mostest'.

Originally, aircraft were accepted by the navies to be used for scouting/observation duties and to spot for the heavy guns of the fleet. Gradually, the aircraft evolved as the attack force itself. Single or small groups of aircraft operating from battleships or cruisers could harass opposing forces but rarely could they press home an attack of sufficient size and intensity to do significant damage to an enemy ship or fleet. To do so requires a large number of aircraft delivering repeated blows to keep the enemy force on the alert and unable to make the necessary repairs to remain in action. The destruction is cumulative, with the second, third and fourth attacks doing more damage than the first – if the attacks are in rapid succession and by sufficient numbers of aircraft. It is for this purpose that the carrier is designed – to keep the refuelling, repair and ordnance facilities close at hand. It is also important that carriers operate in groups to provide mutual support so that should one carrier deck be damaged, the remaining ships in the group are able to

service the aircraft of the damaged carrier.

While all the navies of the world had their own views and functional designations for their aircraft, the types generally desired were: Spotting Reconnaissance, Bombers, Fighters and Torpedo Bombers. In most cases the mission capability overlapped, such as in the case of fighter-bomber, scout-bombers and scout-observation. These multi-purpose aircraft resulted from the desire, if not the necessity, to keep the number of types as small as possible and to reduce the aircraft maintenance and supply problems to a minimum.

Generally speaking, carrier aircraft are designed to operate from a platform rather than from the water surface itself. The first instance of such a flight occurred on 14 November 1910 when Eugene Ely flew a Curtiss Model D biplane from a platform specifically constructed on the foredeck of the US light cruiser, USS *Birmingham*. Over-water safety features had been developed for the spectacular Albany-New York flight made by Glenn H Curtiss on 29 May 1910. These consisted of a pair of canister-type floats mounted under the wings and a long bag of corks attached to the centre keel of the plane.

When Capt Washington I Chambers of the US Navy learned of the interest in ship-to-shore mail flights by the Hamburg-American Steamship Line, he obtained permission to fit a platform on the USS *Birmingham*. This platform, 83 ft long and 24 ft wide, sloped down toward the bow at a 5° angle, placing the leading edge of the platform 37 ft above the water at the bow. However, circumstances prevented J A D McCurdy, the pilot for the steamship line (formerly of the Aerial Experiment Assn, and later Governor General of Canada), from completing the mail flight.

Take off from the 'Birmingham'

The same Albany Flyer that Curtiss had used for the Albany-New York flight was at that time participating in an air meet at Halethorp, Maryland, and Eugene Ely, a Curtiss exhibition pilot who was also taking part in the meet, volunteered to fly the plane. The plane was hoisted aboard the *Birmingham* with the front wheel positioned just 57 ft back from the front edge of the platform. Weather reports indicated the approach of strong winds for the following day, so the decision was made to attempt the flight on 14 November. After much delay due to low clouds, poor visibility and heavy rain showers, Ely climbed into the pilot seat of the Albany Flyer at about 1500. The *Birmingham* got under way and, while they still had 20 fathoms of anchor chain out, Ely gave the signal to the deck crew to let go. He cleared the deck at 1516 without benefit of much forward speed of the ship. Nosing down to gain the required flying speed, he struck the water with the wheels, frame, canisters and propeller tips.

The vibration resulting from the damaged propeller quickly convinced Ely that the prudent course would be toward the nearest land. In this instance it was a point of land, Willoughby Spit, two and a half miles distant, where he set the Albany Flyer down for a safe landing.

Unfortunately, like a good many other historic events it was much later before the importance of that flight was recognised. Ely's payment for the flight was a letter of thanks from the Secretary of the Navy, George von Lengerke Meyer. The aeroplane was not destined to revolutionise naval tactics – not at this date, anyway.

The second significant event involved the same pilot but a different ship, a different location and a different plane. The location was San Francisco Bay, the ship was the cruiser USS *Pennsylvania,* and the plane was a Curtiss D IV Military, the first of its kind, designed for the variable conditions of military aeronautics. In order to carry a second person for observation purposes, the wing area of the D IV was increased by the insertion of a 30-in panel in each wing cellule. So successful was this modification that varying sized panels up to a full extra panel or bay could be and often were added to increase the lifting capability of the otherwise standard Model D III Curtiss.

For this second experiment, a deck 120 ft long and 32 ft wide was constructed to

The Landing Signals Officer aboard the escort carrier Ravager *signals instructions to a Grumman F6F Hellcat. Once on his landing run, the pilot was subject to the commands of the LSO, who also decided the rate at which aircraft could land*

National Maritime Museum

cover the afterdeck equipment and turrets. This deck sloped upward at the forward end near the superstructure and after mast. As a further precaution canvas was laced to the front and sides of the deck, the forward panel extending upward to screen the superstructure and the side panels extending downward to serve as a final barrier net should the plane veer out of control. In addition to these precautions, the first aircraft arrester system was developed and used. At least three claims for its design are known: however, the fact that it was ingenious and simple in construction made it a success, so much so that the modern-day systems bear a strong resemblance to this original. It consisted of 22 ropes stretched across the beam of the flight deck, supported by timbers which held the lines slightly above the deck and with each rope tied to two 50-lb sand bags, one at each end. The plane was equipped with three pairs of small grapnel hooks attached laterally to the landing gear between the main wheels. As in the case of the Albany Flyer, two canister-type floats were attached under the wings outboard of the main landing wheels, but this time the cork bag used for the Albany flight was missing. To complete the safety precautions, Ely used a pair of crossed, inflated motorcycle inner tubes around his neck and under his arms.

The day before the experiment a decision was made not to get the ship under way for the test flight. On 18 January 1911 Ely took off from San Francisco's Presidio Field and headed for the smallest field ever encountered to this date. Conditions were at their worst with the ship headed into an ebb tide and a light 10 mph wind blowing from the stern, necessitating a down-wind landing. The wind changed slightly as he approached the deck, producing a slight cross-wind. However, when less than 100 ft from the deck, the plane steadied. As he cleared the lip of the afterdeck Ely pulled the plane up slightly to lose some of the speed, estimated to be a staggering 39-40 mph. He skimmed over the first eleven athwartship lines, hooked the twelfth and added successive lines as the speed dissipated until it came to rest after contacting the 22nd line and 50 ft short of the forward end of the deck. The dawn of the aircraft carrier was at hand.

The take-off 45 minutes later was uneventful. The tailwind was now a headwind as the plane was turned around for departure off the stern of the ship.

With two successful demonstrations, one would think that this new technique would have gained instant acclaim or at least a foothold – and be developed by the US Navy. Such was not the case, for the next step was taken by the British in making the first take-off from a ship under way. On 4 May 1912 Cdr C R Samson RN, and Lt Malone made two flights from HMS *Hibernia* while she was under way at a speed estimated to be 12 knots.

It was not until HMS *Argus* was launched in 1918 that a clear-deck aircraft carrier, as we know it today, was available. The outbreak of the First World War brought to a halt construction on the Italian Lloyd Sabaudo Company's liner, *Conte Rosso*, which was on the ways of Messrs Beardmore Ltd on the River Clyde. The half-completed hull was purchased by the British Admiralty and finished as the carrier HMS *Argus* complete with hangar deck, elevator and flight deck.

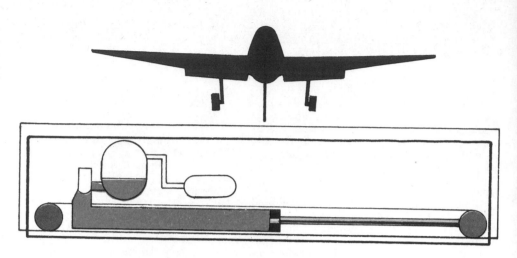

Approach
With the deck pendants raised, the arresting engines at battery, barrier cables raised and the landing area clear the aircraft carrier is ready to receive aircraft. The approaching plane has its wheels down, flaps down and arresting hook down preparatory to landing

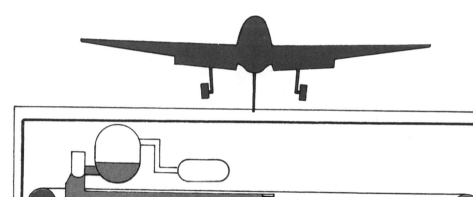

Engagement
The aircraft hook engages the cross-deck pendant pulling it forward, while the purchase cable is being pulled out from the deck edge sheaves

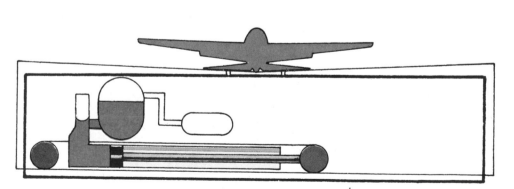

Arrestation
As the plane travels down the deck, purchase cable is pulled out causing the engine ram to be forced into the engine cylinder displacing hydraulic fluid under pressure through the control valve into the accumulator. This fluid metering process through the control valve restrains the pulling out of the purchase cable, and consequently the pendant cable

ARRESTED LANDING SYSTEMS

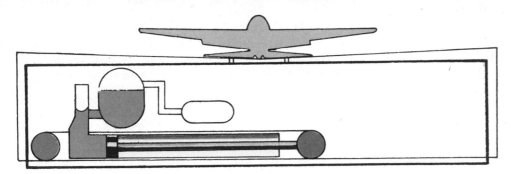

Arrestation Complete
The restraining action stops the motion of the plane, whereupon the control valve automatically closes, preventing it from being pulled back along the deck by the deck pendant, an action known as 'walkback'. 'Hookmen' run onto the flight deck and unhook the deck pendant from the plane. Barriers are lowered, plane moves forward and the pilot starts to fold his wings

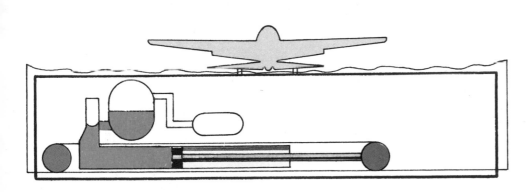

Taxiing from Arrester Gear and Retrieving
With the barrier down the plane moves over them and is 'spotted' ahead of the barriers or taken down the elevator to the hangar deck. Simultaneously the deck pendant is retrieved to its ready position by allowing the fluid from the accumulator to flow back into the cylinder and force the ram to battery position

Landing Signals Officer's Flag Signals

Everything OK

Landing hook not down

You're too slow— speed up

Too fast— slow down

You're low— climb a little

Cut engine and land

No good— go round again

Over this way a little

The first form of arrester was the rope and sandbag system used by Ely during his landing aboard the USS *Pennsylvania* on 18 January 1911 and described previously. During the early period of carrier development a number of other systems were tried, among them the very unsatisfactory and potentially dangerous practice of 'ditching' alongside an escort destroyer. If the pilot was fortunate enough to make a good landing or ditching, inflatable flotation bags were provided to keep the plane afloat until the pilot could be rescued. This system also had the disadvantage of sacrificing the plane and engine.

A second system was tried at the Marine Experimental Aircraft Depot on the Isle of Grain, Kent, UK, in late 1915. It consisted of an inclined wire ropeway fitted over the stern of the ship. While one BE fitted with a special gear did succeed in landing on this equipment, the idea was dropped in favour of a return to the earlier sandbag system.

Another system tried consisted of fore-and-aft wires supported on blocks about six inches above the deck. The aircraft was fitted with a number of hooks mounted on the axle which engaged one or more of the wires. To complete this system, the pilot lowered a tail hook to engage a set of transverse wires which were attached to the now standardised sand bags. These transverse wires were spaced at 30-ft intervals. The axle-mounted hooks ensured a straight run down the deck.

Landing without brakes

All these tests, it should be remembered, were before the fitting of internal wheel brakes. The high probability of a lateral gust of wind causing the aircraft to slew around was ever present. This resulted in a great number of damaged aircraft landing gears, propellers and wing tips as well as severe twisting strain on the airframe itself. The same system or a slightly modified version was used on the USS *Langley*, the first aircraft carrier commissioned in the US Navy. This ship began its service as the collier *Jupiter* and was later modified to the configuration of an aircraft carrier and recommissioned as USS *Langley*.

Another variation of the longitudinal 'grid' cable system was installed on HMS *Argus* in 1919. At first no transverse arrester cables were used: instead an ingenious system allowed the longitudinal wires to serve as brakes as well as guides. The aircraft had the hooks suspended from the axle as before. The cables were laid on the deck fore-and-aft and flush with the deck. The clearance necessary to bring the cables into contact with the hooks was provided by lowering the aircraft elevator, which was located near the centre of the flight deck, about nine inches. When the plane, on its landing rollout, dropped onto the lowered elevator, the hooks engaged the wires. At the forward part of the elevator an 'artificial hill' ramp brought the plane back to deck level and at the same time created sufficient tension on the cables for friction to bring the plane to a halt.

At the same time the aircraft required unusually high, stilt-like landing gear to ensure that the propeller would clear the wires. This required extra weight to provide the strength to withstand the twisting strains when the aircraft swerved from side to side. As might be expected, a number of aircraft sustained varying degrees of damage which had to be repaired before they could be flown from the deck again. The number of accidents caused by this system and equipment resulted in its abandonment seven years after its introduction. In 1924 the landing system reverted to that of the 1917 era, the rope and sand bag.

The sandbag system was improved by the addition of towers constructed on each side of the ship to support weights which looked like elevator weights. Via cables and sheaves from the deck, the weights were lifted in succession as the aircraft engaged the wires, much as sand bags had engaged in the older system. In the 1920s the 'Norden Gear' was installed in US Navy carriers. This machine consisted of a drum approximately three feet in diameter which had spiral grooves machined in its surface to accommodate the cable used. To make the cable wind on the drum in level layers the drum was designed to slide along an axle shaft, rather than incorporating a moving guide for the cable. Each drum – one for each cable end – was equipped with a brake drum to slow it down and an electric motor to retrieve the cable after it was unhooked from the landed aircraft.

Because of the tendency for one drum to run out of cable before its mate, as a result of off-centre contact by the tail hook, it was decided to bring both ends of each deck line (or pendant) together and attach them to a single arresting engine. These hydraulic arresting machines consisted of a cylinder in which hydraulic fluid was compressed and forced through an orifice – whose size could be controlled – to an air-filled accumulator. As the cable was paid out the fluid was compressed into the accumulator where the air was also compressed to provide the power for quick retrieval. The rate at which this hydraulic fluid was transferred was controlled by a valve which could be adjusted to allow for different aircraft weights and landing speeds.

To reduce the number of arrester gear units, the deck cables or pendants were attached in such a way that two pendants could be connected and both of them controlled by a single arrester.

A difficult act to follow

In the process of landing aircraft aboard a carrier during the Second World War, one individual stood out above all others – even the ship's commander. This was the LSO or Landing Signals Officer. His judgment determined the condition and rate of acceptance of landing aircraft. Once on the final leg of an approach to the carrier, the pilot set his speed and power at pre-tested levels and lined up at a predetermined altitude astern of the flight deck. From this point onward, he was subject to the commands of the LSO who communicated these instructions to the pilot by hand signals. Since hand signals are not readily visible, the LSO would use paddles similar to ping-pong paddles or other high visibility hardware which would ensure the visual communication of directions to the pilot.

Standing on a small platform at deck level near the aft end of the port side of the flight deck, the LSO would go through his signal routine for each aircraft. Part of his routine was standardised but most was based on experience of the incoming pilot, for the LSO quickly learned to know and anticipate any characteristics of the pilots and planes of his squadrons. He was in a very real sense a one-man act, and it was, as they say, 'a very difficult act to follow'.

Catapults used for aircraft launching are modern-day versions of those used by the Greeks and Romans as long ago as 340 BC to hurl missiles of stone against and into fortifications. In aviation history, assisted take-offs go back at least as far as the Wright Brothers and Dr Samuel P Langley, who was Secretary of the Smithsonian Institution in Washington, DC. It should be emphasised, however, that this does *not* include the first Wright plane of 1903, the first piloted heavier-than-air craft to fly under control in powered flight. The Wrights' catapult came later in 1904/5 and consisted of a tower on which was suspended a weight. Through a system of block and tackle, the weight was released and accelerated the plane up to flying speed.

The catapult of today dates back almost to the first association of aircraft with naval aviation. One of the first problems encountered in the marriage of the aeroplane with the ships of the fleet was the means of launching and retrieval of the aircraft without impairing the normal functioning of the ship. Realising this problem from the very beginning, Lt T G Ellyson, Naval Aviator 1, USN, and the head of the US Navy's Aviation Department, Capt W I Chambers, devoted time to producing at least two possible solutions to the problem.

The first, attributed to Glenn H Curtiss and Ellyson, was constructed and tried in 1911 at Hammondsport, NY, the home of Curtiss and the Curtiss Aeroplane & Motor Company. This device consisted of a cable 'slide' with the central cable fixed to a submerged post and the other end sloping upward from the shoreline to a platform. On each side of the main cable were two additional wires of comparatively smaller diameter which served as guides to keep the wings level until the aircraft attained control speed for the ailerons. Visualising a similar rig aboard ship, Ellyson made at least one successful flight from this slide. In doing so, he discovered that few problems were encountered with the control of the ailerons and the whole experimental take-off was over in a matter of seconds.

The second system, developed almost concurrently by Capt Chambers assisted by Naval Constructor H C Richardson and Lt Ellyson, was a true catapult though primitive in construction and operation. Again, it was Lt Ellyson who made the first launch from this type of catapult, which was powered by compressed air. The date was 12 November 1912; the location was the Washington Navy Yard. The device consisted of a track mounted on a barge along which a wheeled dolly was propelled by compressed air. The aircraft, a Curtiss Model E (the Navy's A-3) with Ellyson piloting, was launched successfully. For all its simplicity, this catapult contained all the ingredients of the system which, with refinement, was still in use in 1922.

This first catapult was designed for installation on the turret of a battleship. In the end this proved impractical, but for years battleships and cruisers carried and launched aircraft from catapults which

were deck mounted and independent of the turrets. The first major change from the compressed air type came in 1922 when a new catapult, designed to use gunpowder as the propellant, was designed by Lt Elmer Stone of the US Coast Guard and Mr C F Jeansen of the Bureau of Ordnance.

The development of catapults for use aboard carriers took place mostly during the Thirties when France, Germany and particularly England and the United States were carrying on secret developments. Japan, another of the nations involved in the development of aircraft carriers, did not carry out parallel programmes in catapult design. As far as is known, the Japanese did not have any satisfactory mechanical launching system for their carrier-borne aircraft until late in the war.

With the exception of the US, the other developments of carrier catapults relied on the obsolete and time-consuming use of a launching cradle which necessitated 'loading' each aircraft on the cradle prior to launching, and deck mounted tracks which obstructed movement of aircraft about the deck. The US, on the other hand, developed the expendable 'bridle' for flush deck operation. Using this very simple device it was possible to launch aircraft in rapid succession and with none of the complications inherent in stopping a heavy cradle at the end of each run. As a result, higher launching speeds and frequencies were possible and there were no tracks to restrict aircraft movement above the decks. The serious development of the flush-deck catapult began in 1934 at the Naval Aircraft Factory, Philadelphia, Pa. Carriers then under construction had these catapults installed but they were looked upon as a luxury rather than an everyday operational launching device. Remember, however, that aircraft weights and speeds were not great during that period. Under all but extreme sea or wind conditions the carrier deck was ample for take-offs and landings. Even during the early part of the Second World War its use was less than might be expected.

Cargo ships into carriers

The real requirement for catapults developed when the CVE 'Jeep' carriers (also known as MAC – Merchant Aircraft Carrier – ships) were developed by converting cargo ships into carriers in 1942 to provide the necessary escorts for convoys in the Atlantic. It became apparent that if these little, slow converted merchant ships were to be of any value they would have to use catapults to launch anything other than lightweight aircraft. The restricted deck area, the top-heavy character of the ship and its high degree of movement at sea required the mechanical boost available from the catapult. When at sea in anything but the calmest weather, the roll and pitch of the CVE Jeep carrier made unassisted take-offs hazardous to both the plane and the ship. On the other hand, the catapult made a straight-line take-off a certainty and the aircraft was accelerated to a reasonable speed even when loaded to full military gross weight.

CATAPULTS

A Sea Hurricane about to be launched from a CAM ship. Each mission for one of these planes meant the loss of the plane as well as a ducking for the pilot

The same Jeep-type carrier made use of its full capability on numerous occasions including the delivery of Army Curtiss P-40 fighters to cover landing operations in North Africa in November 1942. At the invasion of Guadalcanal in August 1942, Marine fighter reinforcements were launched from the USS *Long Island*. In fact, a number of Army-type aircraft were equipped with quick-attach fittings for carrier launch should the need arise.

The advantages of using catapults are many, but the principal ones are:

1. The ability to carry a larger number of aircraft (up to 40% more) which can be larger and heavier and therefore more effective since the only limit is on the number that can be landed aboard. Greater numbers of aircraft can be spotted on deck for launching, since less deck area is used for take-off.

2. Night operations without the use of lights to see the deck can be carried out routinely. The catapult maintains the aircraft in a straight line and accelerates the plane to a safe flying speed. On clearing the deck, the pilot continues normal climb procedures on instruments.

3. Rough weather operations can be carried out almost as routinely as the night operations. Again, the catapult assures a straight take-off in spite of the deck position. Furthermore, launch can be timed to the roll or pitch of the ship to place the plane in the most favourable position and speed.

4. Finally, the aircraft can be launched in crosswind conditions – in fact it was common practice to launch right out of the hangar deck! In pre-catapult times, it was necessary to head the carrier into the prevailing wind to assure the flow of air down the centre line of the deck. While this seems reasonable, it was not always the most practical since the rest of the task force might, for tactical reasons, be headed in a different direction, as much as 180° to the prevailing wind. Under the old unassisted system this could force the carrier to steam away from the protective screen of the fleet force and then have to turn and catch up. The alternative might mean depriving the fleet of a tactical

advantage in order to protect the carrier. Neither of these was necessary with the availability of the catapult.

The catapults used during the Second World War were essentially the same as those developed earlier, but with two important differences. Compressed air was still the propelling medium but an accumulator was used with the air over oil rather than direct application from an air compressor to the aircraft launching shuttle (hook). In these oil-pneumatic catapults the oil became the energy-transmitting medium, thereby reducing the amount of air lost on each shot. Only the amount of air necessary for the shot was expended and recompression was accomplished by oil pumps rather than air compressors.

The other important feature was the absence of any cradle. The aircraft was supported and operated on its own landing gear, thereby reducing the mass and moving parts that would necessarily accompany the use of a cradle in the form of accelerating and decelerating shock-absorbing buffers. With this new system increased rate and speed of launching were made possible since there was no cradle to be retrieved.

TORPEDO BOMBERS

AIMING A PUNCH WHERE IT HURTS

There is no denying the fact that the fighters and the dive-bombers are the glamour aircraft of carrier operations. However, the torpedo bomber certainly was one of the first types of carrier-borne aircraft, dating back to the First World War. The adaptation of the already developed torpedo to the new naval weapon, the aeroplane, was a natural evolutionary step. The torpedo was proving to be a potent alternative to the 16-in guns of the capital ships. It had been adapted to the submarine, the destroyer, the cruiser and the light, fast motor torpedo boat, giving each of these lesser fleet units the potential punch of the battleship. The problem, as always, was the delivery method.

Cruisers and destroyers usually did carry torpedoes as part of their ordnance complement but they were themselves sizeable targets for the big guns of an enemy fleet. The submarine, because of its stealth and difficulty of detection, had been the ideal and traditional delivery mechanism for the torpedo launching. But as the anti-submarine programme developed along with the submarine, the submarine as well as the motor torpedo boats (MTBs), became more vulnerable to attack from the air. Like the MTB, the aeroplane had the speed and the

manoeuvrability to take evasive action for its own protection while, at the same time continuing to press home an attack from any quarter, and it could be launched into an engagement from a floating or land base many miles from the scene of the battle. Each plane carried the same destructive punch as one of the large guns of the capital ships. Little wonder then that the torpedo was one of the first weapons to be adapted to the aeroplane.

The first attack
The concept of launching torpedoes from aircraft dates back to 1909 when T O M Sopwith built an aircraft known as the Cuckoo to a requirement suggested by Lt Murray Sueter, RN. The plane was not completed but served as an inspiration to Robert Blackburn who, having formed his own company, developed an improved version produced as the Blackburn Cuckoo. The earliest known success of aircraft torpedo attacks occurred in the First World War when two Short float seaplane aircraft from the seaplane carrier *Ben-my-Chree* each torpedoed a ship in the Sea of Marmara off Turkey.

Experience soon showed that launching seaplanes was at best a nuisance and at

worst a definite hazard since the carrier must necessarily slow to a near halt to launch and/or retrieve the aircraft. With the introduction of full-length flight decks on carriers, aircraft with wheeled undercarriages became the standard and made possible simplification of all operations. The torpedo carrier reconnaissance aircraft benefited in other ways too, since the weight and air resistance of floats had reduced performance to a degree which made the carriage of a torpedo only marginally possible. In one case, the Curtiss CT, in other respects quite an advanced aircraft, was a failure because the weight and drag imposed by the floats and struts did not permit the use of 1600-lb torpedoes. Otherwise, the CT was a very interesting aircraft. It was a twin-engine, low-wing monoplane developed at a time – 1920 – when biplanes were the standard.

A second major deterrent to the rapid development of the torpedo bomber was the torpedo itself. Directly adapted from the ship/submarine torpedo, the early airborne versions developed a number of problems when airlifted to their targets. Aerodynamic considerations and launching difficulties required very precise low level flying at the time of drop, imposing conditions on the

crew which made this branch of naval aviation little short of heroic. At the low altitude necessitated by the drop requirements, the torpedo plane was subject during its run not only to the hazard of direct hits: even a near miss could throw up a geyser which could be just as effective in deflecting the plane from its course.

Added to this ever-present barrage from a target or its supporting ships was the presence of defending fighters. These considered the heavily laden torpedo planes sitting ducks, particularly when they lined up for their run, for if the drop was to have any chance for success the bomber must hold its course – a very predictable course at low altitude, during which time fighters picked them off with discouraging regularity. Because of this, naval strategists did not consider the torpedo bomber a very practical weapon. The delicate structure and guidance mechanism of the Whitehead torpedo, which was designed for underwater or slightly above the water launching, made the low level aircraft delivery necessary. Consequently, anti-aircraft gunners of the fleets assumed that the torpedo craft would be like fish in a rain barrel. Records show these views to be unduly pessimistic, as the torpedo aircraft, particularly the Fairey Swordfish, gave a good account of themselves.

In spite of these normally hazardous conditions under which torpedo crews operated, this class of naval aircraft was considered to be very unspectacular until 11 November 1940 – when British Fleet Air Arm Fairey Swordfish (affectionately known as 'Stringbags') launched from the carrier HMS *Illustrious*, created havoc and sank or damaged a substantial number of ships of the Italian Battle Fleet in a daring strike on the Italian naval base at Taranto. This bold attack cost the British two Swordfish lost and two damaged – quite remarkable when one considers the volume

A Japanese Kate attempts to torpedo the USS South Dakota *during the Battle of Santa Cruz. Inset: A US Navy Avenger releases its torpedo in practice*

of anti-aircraft fire directed at the attackers.

During the Battle of Cape Matapan, Fairey Albacores and Swordfish, though insufficient in numbers, managed to divert a far superior Italian force from cutting off an outnumbered and outgunned British cruiser group. The torpedo planes succeeded in jamming the steering gear and flooding the Italian battleship *Vittorio Veneto* with about 4000 tons of water. This action slowed the ship sufficiently to allow the British Fleet to catch the battleship and its escorting cruisers and destroyers and blow them out of the water.

Relentless pounding

This was a long awaited test, for until this time torpedo bombers had not been tried in an open sea engagement. It was the beginning of a series of airborne torpedo attacks. During these battles the Italian fleet was repeatedly harassed by the Swordfish and the planes reduced the comfortable 100-mile lead of the Italian battleship to 30 or 40 miles in a matter of eight hours with repeated, relentless pounding. The cumulative damage principle took its toll. In the attempt to save the battleship, the Italians lost four cruisers and a number of destroyers which were sent to aid the badly mauled *Vittorio Veneto*. In spite of very heavy anti-aircraft fire and the almost pedestrian pace of the Swordfish, the British lost only one aircraft.

Again and again the torpedo bomber was to show its mettle by crippling some of the biggest and best-defended ships, as well as extracting a heavy toll of lesser fighting ships and supporting supply ships. In spite of the handicap of their torpedoes, which made them slow and lacking in manoeuvrability the torpedo planes of the

Royal Navy's Fleet Air Arm and the RAF managed to keep the waters around the European continent within their control.

The most dramatic service rendered by the Swordfish was the encounter with the *Bismarck*, the most powerful battleship then afloat. This super-ship, along with its escort, the battle-cruiser *Prinz Eugen*, broke out of the Baltic Sea into the North Atlantic on 23 May 1941 to attempt to destroy or at least harass the Atlantic 'bridge' of ships that was Great Britain's lifeline to North America. Virtually the whole of the British Home Fleet was concentrated on the efforts to destroy this threat to Britain's survival. Events that followed proved once again the importance of having an air arm in any fleet. The carrier HMS *Victorious*, only recently commissioned and carrying a large cargo of crated Hawker Hurricanes destined for Gibraltar, was pressed into service, though her complement of operational aircraft consisted of less than a dozen Swordfish and only half a dozen Fairey Fulmar fighters.

In a running fight with HMS *Hood* and *Prince of Wales,* the *Bismarck* emerged the victor with relatively minor damage but in need of dry docking before carrying out her intended mission. One of her fuel tanks had been damaged, reducing her cruising range measurably. During the night, *Victorious* proceeded to within striking range of her aircraft to deliver a night torpedo attack. The Swordfish, with the valuable assistance of the newly developed radar, succeeded in scoring a hit which did no significant damage, but the high speed manoeuvring necessary to avoid the torpedoes in the heavy weather increased the damage which had resulted from the running fight with the British battleships. The boiler-room of the *Bismarck* was flooded causing a further reduction in her speed. In the prevailing heavy weather, the *Bismarck* shook off her pursuers only to be rediscovered by an

RAF Catalina patrolling the area in mid morning on 26 May at a position only 11 hours away from Brest, the destination port, and only a few hours beyond the protective range of German land-based aircraft.

Once again, the Swordfish went into action, this time from HMS *Ark Royal* which had been despatched from Gibraltar. The second wave of 15 Swordfish, flying converging courses in low clouds and heavy weather, succeeded in severely damaging the *Bismarck's* propellers and steering gear and jamming the rudders. During the night, she circled helplessly while the British fleet gathered for the dawn attack. With the first light of dawn, *Rodney* and *King George V* pounded the *Bismarck* to ruins. The torpedo attack that followed from the cruiser *Dorsetshire* sent the pride of the German navy to the bottom of the ocean.

It is well to examine at this stage the conditions which prevailed during these engagements. One fact that stands out is the relatively small numbers of aircraft involved. As experience was gained, the aircraft were employed in progressively greater numbers and, instead of in-line attacks, the planes attacked simultaneously along converging courses. Poor weather and/or darkness also limited the fighter defensive cover, and out of it all came the Swordfish, the ungainly dinosaur of the aircraft world, certain game for defensive

fighters – though its manoeuvrability and slow speed succeeded on occasion in evading even the sleek monoplane fighters.

An inexpensive machine of the tube-and-fabric era, the Swordfish was easy to maintain. It could and usually did operate in the most deplorable weather conditions in spite of heaving decks that kept all other aircraft grounded.

Technically, the Swordfish was of a conventional design of composite construction, mainly steel tube and fabric with limited use of sheet metal sheathing adjacent to the engine, back to the diagonal line aft of the front cockpit and the cockpit enclosure from the upper longerons and back to the rear of the after cockpit. Its single nine-cylinder air-cooled Bristol Pegasus 30 radial engine was rated at 750 hp.

The Fairey Albacore, successor to the Swordfish, was from the same mould and the same manufacturer. The configuration was the same, that of a single-engine biplane with fixed landing gear. It was a 'cleaned up', modernised version of the Swordfish, designed to replace it, but in fact, the Swordfish outlived its successor. Reaching carrier operation status in late 1940, the Albacore took part in a number of actions, the most notable of which was the battle of Cape Matapan in March 1941.

Operated from shore bases as often as from carriers, Albacores provided protective cover for convoys and flew anti-submarine

patrols. They were prominent in minelaying and in flare dropping as well. Their service in North Africa during the Western Desert campaign was one of the highlights of their service career; there they dropped flares to illuminate Rommel's positions and concentrations of armour for RAF night bombers. During this operation, it is estimated that they released approximately 12,000 flares in addition to taking part in the bombing themselves.

While this action was taking place, a monoplane replacement was being developed. The Fairey Barracuda, developed under an Air Ministry R & D Specification S24/37, issued in January 1938, never enjoyed the confidence of its crews.

Following the first flight of the prototype on 7 December 1940, a long development period ensued resulting in a great number of structural, aerodynamic and powerplant 'fixes' that delayed its entry into operational service until September 1943. Coupled with the structural problems was that of retrain-

Final inspection of a torpedo loaded on a Swordfish on board HMS Battler, *July 1943*

Central Press

ing crews from the slow, forgiving and highly manoeuvrable Swordfish and Albacore. Spins resulting from heavy application of the rudder while in a turn and the ensuing loss of altitude were most distressing and tiring to the pilots whose full attention was required to perform the necessary evasive attack manoeuvres.

In addition to its basic role of a torpedo bomber, the Barracuda was to be fitted out with a plethora of equipment with which to carry out a wide variety of additional duties. During its operational life it was to carry radomes, rockets, bombs, mines, lifeboats and containers for the dropping and supply of agents behind the front lines in France.

The aircraft retained the manoeuvrability necessary for torpedo attack but, in addition, was stressed to carry out the dive-bombing role.

The greatest successes attributed to the Barracuda were the attacks on the German battleship, *Tirpitz*, which was blockaded in a Norwegian fjord. In the neutralising of this battleship and her escorting cruisers, the Barracuda accounted for 176 sorties, of which 174 got through to the target, although it was well protected by both natural and man-made defences. Only two aircraft were shot down by anti-aircraft fire. Previous to this, the Barracuda had been giving a good account of itself in anti-shipping operations along the coast of Europe, using its dual capability as a dive-bomber to account for an impressive total of shipping damaged or destroyed.

Torpedoes in the Pacific

The Pacific theatre also had its share of torpedo activity with less lopsided results than in the European/Mediterranean theatre. As a rule, conditions in the Pacific were not as favourable to the torpedo plane. The weather was better, for a start, and the presence of large numbers of fighters with each of the opposing sides made torpedo launching a decidedly hazardous occupation – not that any combat category is safe, even in the most favourable conditions.

Beginning with the Japanese surprise attack on Pearl Harbor on 7 December 1941, 40 Nakajima B5N 'Kate' torpedo bombers gave a good account of themselves in successfully dropping torpedoes in the shallow harbour, with 104 additional Kates operational in their alternate role of horizontal bombers from altitude. In conjunction with the Aichi D3A 'Vals', the Kate wrought destruction on a scale rarely seen before or since Pearl Harbor. The first wave of attackers consisted of 40 Kates armed with torpedoes, with 50 additional Kates armed as horizontal bombers. The second wave of attackers included 54 Kates. At the conclusion of the attack, over 2400 Americans had been killed, almost 1200 wounded, four battleships were sunk, another beached and three others badly damaged. All of this was accomplished at a relatively small cost. Of the 354 Japanese aircraft involved in the attack, 5 Kates, 9 Zeros and 15 Val dive-bombers had been lost. As earth-shaking and successful as this attack was, it was a preview of the carrier task force which became the standard of naval operations during the Pacific War.

The B5N Kate and the less numerous Mitsubishi B5M were similar in configuration and structure – both were low-wing monoplanes built to the same specifications. The B5M was a bit more conservative in design and retained the fixed landing gear which was the principal identification detail between these two very similar aircraft.

Both had folding wings to facilitate stowage on board carriers and both carried their ordnance, whether torpedo or bombs, externally. Both were developed to meet a specification issued in 1935: the Nakajima entry, being more advanced in engineering concept, was chosen for large-scale production and assignment to carrier duties.

Fairey Swordfish I
The antiquated 'Stringbag' had the superb handling essential for carrier flying, and delivered cripplingly accurate torpedo attacks in actions from Taranto to the sinking of the *Bismarck*
Span: 45 ft 6 in *Length:* 36 ft 4 in
Engine: Bristol Pegasus 30, 750 hp
Armament: 1 Vickers mg; 1 Lewis mg *Max Speed:* 139 mph at 4750 ft *Ceiling:* 10,700 ft
Range: 546 miles *Bombload:* 1 × 18-in torpedo or 1500 lb bombs or mines or 8 × 60-lb bombs

Fairey Albacore
Overshadowed by the Swordfish for which the Albacore was planned as a replacement, this rugged biplane fought at Matapan and in the Western Desert on flare-dropping missions and proved a useful anti-submarine aircraft
Span: 50 ft *Length:* 39 ft 9½ in *Engine:* Bristol Taurus II, 1065 hp *Armament:* 1 Vickers mg; 2 Vickers 'K' mg *Max Speed:* 161 mph at 4000 ft *Ceiling:* 20,700 ft *Range:* 930 miles
Bombload: 1 × 18-in torpedo or 2000 lb bombs

With the outbreak of hostilities in the Pacific in 1941, a major part of the US fleet of capital ships was sunk or put out of action. Fortunately, the carriers *Lexington*, *Saratoga* and *Enterprise*, still at sea, escaped the fate of the battleships and cruisers at Pearl Harbor. Forming part of the aircraft complement of the three carriers were the venerable Douglas TBD Devastators, by this time five years old and suffering from old age in the form of intergranular corrosion of their structure and sheet metal skin.

As a result the TBDs served only six months at the beginning of the war.

During this time they took part in the first action against the Japanese. Flying from the *Enterprise,* Torpedo Squadron VT 6, armed with bombs in a dawn attack, caused heavy damage to ships anchored at Kwajalein and, after re-arming with torpedoes, succeeded in accounting for two transports, two cargo ships, one cruiser and two submarines – which can be considered a good day's work. Later the same day, VT 6 bombed Taroa, destroying a number of grounded aircraft and an ammunition dump. At the same time VT 5 was busy bombing a large shore installation on Jaluit.

With these modest successes, the planes of the two squadrons suffered only minor hits by the shore anti-aircraft batteries.

Shortly afterwards, on 24 February 1942, the TBDs of VT 6 attacked Wake Island, followed by a raid on Marcus Island on 4 March. TBDs from the *Yorktown* and *Lexington* were equally busy with raids on Lae and Salamaua where they reverted to torpedo dropping to destroy 10 ships. On 7 May the planes of VT 2 and VT 5 succeeded in sinking the Japanese light carrier *Shoho* in co-operation with other aircraft in the fleet in coordinated attacks during the Battle of the Coral Sea.

Showdown at Midway

The most famous battle in which the TBDs participated was the Battle of Midway which began on 4 June 1942, with a combined total of 41 TBDs available from all the US carriers in the massed fleet. Aside from a few veterans of the actions previously listed, the bulk of the squadron crews were new and inexperienced, hastily assembled at the outbreak of the war, and most of them had never taken off with live torpedoes prior to this battle.

At Midway, the torpedo bombers faced a major part of the Japanese Navy including capital ships and four aircraft carriers bent on the destruction of Midway as an outpost of the US Navy. With this array of strength, which included the very capable, and by now well-proven, Zero navy fighters among its bag of weapons, the Japanese fleet was a most impressive adversary. The TBDs faced a 'stacked deck'. With good weather, but low clouds at about 2000 ft, with many

Fairey Barracuda Mk II
The three-seat Barracuda served as the FAA's workhorse, carrying everything from bombs, torpedoes, mines and rockets to lifeboats. Forty-two Barracudas crippled the mighty *Tirpitz* in Kaafiord, Norway on 3 April 1944
Span: 49 ft 2 in *Length:* 39 ft 9 in
Engine: Rolls-Royce Merlin 32, 1640 hp
Armament: 2 Vickers K mg *Max Speed:* 228 mph at 1750 ft *Ceiling:* 16,600 ft *Range:* 1150 miles unloaded *Bombload:* 1 × 1620-lb torpedo or 4 × 450-lb bombs or 6 × 250-lb bombs

Nakajima B5N2 'Kate'
B5Ns were in the forefront of the attack on Pearl Harbor, and during the following year carrier-based Kates were to deliver fatal blows to the carriers *Lexington*, *Yorktown* and *Hornet*
Span: 50 ft 10 in *Length:* 33 ft 9 in
Engine: Nakajima Sakae II, 970 hp at 9845 ft
Max Speed: 235 mph at 11,810 ft
Ceiling: 27,100 ft *Range:* 1237 miles
Armament: 1 × 7·7-mm mg *Bombload:* 1764 lb bombs or torpedo

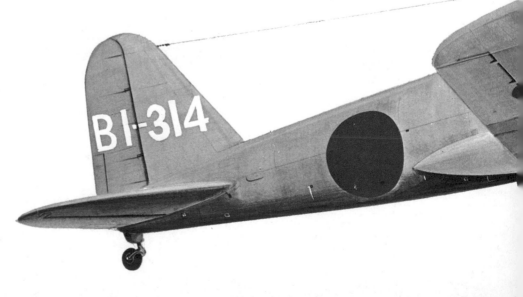

Associated Press

A US battleship blazes at Pearl Harbor. But the Japanese had failed to hit the vital carriers, which were fortunately still at sea when the attack occurred

Japanese ships to maintain an umbrella of anti-aircraft fire and the fighter squadrons of four Japanese carriers, the situation was at its worst for the TBDs. Added to this, the planes and their Mk 13 torpedoes were both outmoded and inadequate for the job, as events were to show.

The TBDs, with an approach speed of about 125 mph, were exposed to the murderous fire of the Japanese guns for about 15 minutes during their approach. The early models of the Mk 13 torpedoes could not be dropped at speeds above 100 mph or higher than 50 ft above the surface. Coupled with this was the necessity to aim for a quartering bow shot for these torpedoes with a maximum speed, under favourable conditions, of 30 knots could never catch a carrier or cruiser if launched from a rear quarter.

In the face of these odds, three squadrons of TBDs, the Torpedo Squadrons VT 8 from the *Hornet,* VT 6 from the *Enterprise* and VT 3 from the *Yorktown* pressed home the attack, only to lose the bulk of their planes and crew (the aircraft loss was 90%, the crew casualty rate was 85%). VT 8 lost all 15 planes with only one survivor, Ensign George Gray. VT 6 lost all but three aircraft and two aircraft of VT 3 survived, only to splash down just short of landing on board the *Yorktown.* Many concluded, incorrectly, that this was the end of the line for torpedo bombers.

The TBD was a conventional aircraft for its day, first entering service with the fleet in November 1937. It was of stressed skin construction and monoplane configuration. The low cantilever wing tapered in plan and profile from the root to the tips. About half-

343

way out, at the flap/aileron juncture, each wing could be folded hydraulically, making it the first type of aircraft to have this feature. The oval cross-section fuselage accommodated the crew of three – pilot, navigator/bombardier and radio-operator/gunner. A special window beneath the pilot permitted the bombardier, lying prone, to use a bombsight for launching an externally mounted torpedo or bombs.

Armament was minimal but typical of the times in which the TBD was designed. It consisted of one ·30 cal synchronised gun firing forward and one ·50 cal flexible-mounted gun in the rear cockpit. The Pratt & Whitney R-1830-64 engine developed 900 hp to give a weight to power ratio of over 11 lb per hp at 10,194 lb combat gross.

Replacement in the wings

At the Battle of Midway the heavy casualties suffered by the TBDs emphasised the need for an immediate replacement. Such a machine was in the wings, for Squadron VT 8 which had sustained such heavy losses at Midway was scheduled to be one of the first squadrons to be re-equipped with the Grumman TBF Avenger. In fact, six Midway-based Avengers of VT 8 attacked the Japanese fleet at Midway early on 4 June only to lose five aircraft in the ensuing battle. In this case it was not so much the quality of the aircraft involved as the numbers and the lack of coordinated fighter and dive-bomber attacks to keep the Japanese gunners' minds and guns off the torpedo planes as they began their attacks.

Two months later, on 7 August 1942, when the first amphibious assault began on Guadalcanal, the TBFs had replaced all the TBDs. From this date onward the TBFs were the standard torpedo bomber of the US Fleet and were used in very substantial numbers by the Royal Navy and other Allied navies. In the Pacific theatre alone, the TBFs took part in the Battles of the Eastern Solomons on 24-25 August 1942; Santa Cruz Islands (26-27 October 1942); Gilbert Islands (10 November to 10 December 1943); the Marshall Islands (29 January to 23 February 1944) and the Battle of the Philippine Sea, 19-24 June 1944.

A rugged aeroplane, the TBF was quite obviously a near relative to the F6F Hellcat fighter – so much so that at least one Japanese pilot, Saburo Sakai, one of the most famous fighter aces of all time, mistook a flight of Avengers for Hellcats. He proceeded to attack from below and to the rear only to find himself trapped in the concentrated crossfire from the ventral stinger guns in the TBF flight. This was the first torpedo plane to carry its load, whether the new 22-in, 2000-lb torpedo or the equivalent weight in 500-lb bombs, internally, thereby

Douglas TBD-1 Devastator

The backbone of the US Navy's carrier torpedo forces at the outbreak of the Pacific War, the Devastator was already obsolete. With its light armament and slow approach speed, it was easy prey for Zero pilots
Span: 50 ft *Length:* 32 ft 6 in *Engine:* Pratt & Whitney R-1830-64, 900 hp *Max Speed:* 225 mph *Range:* 985 miles *Armament:* 1 × ·30-in mg; 1 × ·50-in mg *Bombload:* 1000-lb bomb or 1 × 21-in torpedo

Nakajima B6N2 Tenzan (Heavenly Mountain) 'Jill'

The Japanese Navy had high hopes for this big carrier attack bomber, but in action its high landing speed restricted it to the larger carriers, while it proved an easy target for US Hellcats
Span: 48 ft 10 in *Length:* 35 ft 8 in *Engine:* Mitsubishi MK4T Kasei 25, 1680 hp at 6880 ft *Max speed:* 299 mph at 16,075 ft *Ceiling:* 29,660 ft *Range:* 1085 miles *Armament:* 2 × 7·7-mm mg *Bombload:* 1764-lb bombs or torpedo

cutting down on air resistance and increasing the maximum speed to around 250 mph, a good 80–100 mph faster than the old TBD.

Part of this increase was, of course, attributable to the nearly 1000 extra hp provided by the Wright R-2600 engine. This additional power also improved take-off performance, making it possible to get off the carrier decks in as little as 650 ft. In the case of the small CVE Jeep carriers, the additional boost required to launch the heavily laden TBFs led to accelerated development of the flush deck catapults for all-weather operations. The use of small merchant ships converted to CVEs was one of the most important steps in maintaining anti-submarine patrols with the Atlantic convoys, as well as providing close support for amphibious landings and anti-submarine patrols and resupplying the larger attack carriers after battle losses in the Pacific. The TBFs were an important and integral part of both of these operations.

Contrary to earlier concepts of torpedo plane design, the TBF was fat and business-like in appearance and in combat it grossed at nearly eight tons, an impressive load for a single-engine aircraft, and one which accounted for its relatively poor rate of climb. Testimony to the ruggedness of the TBF, usually referred to as the 'Turkey' by its crews, is the fact that even now, Avengers are still in demand and still in use as 'water bombers' in delivering fire-extinguishing chemicals for forest fire control.

The TBF and the F6F Hellcat were initially produced side-by-side, but increased demand for the F6F made it necessary to secure a second source of production for the TBF. A contract was negotiated with the Eastern Aircraft Division of General Motors at their Trenton, NJ plant and signed on 23 March 1942. In December 1943, Grumman, the parent plant, ended production of the TBFs after producing in excess of 2290 planes. Eastern Aircraft Division then became the primary constructor under the designation of TBMs, producing a total of 7546 planes.

A mid-wing monoplane of rather portly dimensions, the Avenger had accommoda-

tions for a three-man crew above the wing in a greenhouse canopy, the aft end of which was rounded off by a glazed ball turret. The wing, in plan form, had a straight centre section out to the folding point, at which juncture there was an almost equal taper of the leading and trailing edges of the outboard panels. The centre section housed the main fuel tanks and the retractable landing gear fittings and struts. Under the wing was a fairly spacious bomb-bay which could totally enclose the Mk 13 torpedo or alternatively four 500-lb bombs or an auxiliary fuel tank for long-range reconnaissance or ferrying. The wheels themselves were fully enclosed in the outer panels of the wings when the gear was retracted outward during flight. In spite of this outward retraction feature, the tread was quite generous, unlike the Messerschmitt Bf 109 and the Spitfire, both of which had a similar disposition of the undercarriage.

The big 18-cylinder Wright R-2600-8 was a powerful engine, developing 1700 hp initially, but was prone to overheat, requiring careful management by the pilot. Armament consisted initially of one ·50 cal machine-gun mounted on the starboard side of the cowling, synchronised to fire through the propeller (later models were fitted with two wing guns), and a single ·50 cal gun mounted in a Grumman-designed turret covering the upper rear field of fire. This single gun was mounted on the starboard side. Finally, in the bombardier's ventral position was a single ·30 cal machine-gun. Primary ordnance was the torpedo which increased in weight and improved in reliability as the war progressed. In addition, the TBF could carry bomb loads of up to 2000 lb, ranging from 100-lb bombs in salvo to single 2000-lb bombs, often supplemented by wing-mounted rocket launchers when engaged in supporting amphibious assaults.

Designed as a replacement for the Kate, the Nakajima B6N2 Tenzan (Heavenly Lightning) 'Jill' was the last Japanese aircraft designed as a carrier-based torpedo bomber to see action during the Second

GRUMMAN TBF AVENGER

Grumman TBF-1 Avenger
The Avenger had the defensive qualities and strike capability of a twin-engined aircraft, combined with the size and handling of a carrier aircraft. Carrying bombs, depth charges or torpedoes, the type was outstanding in US and Royal Navy service

Span: 54 ft 2 in *Length:* 40 ft *Engine:* Wright Cyclone GR-2600-8, 1850 hp
Armament: 2×·5-in mg in wings; 1×·3-in mg in ventral position; 1×·5-in mg in dorsal turret
Speed: 259 mph at 11,200 ft *Ceiling:* 23,000 ft
Range: 1000 miles loaded *Bombload:* 1×22-in torpedo or 2000 lb bombs

World War. It was initially powered by the 1800 hp Nakajima Mamoru engine which unfortunately experienced problems, delaying its development. Excessive vibration of the Mamoru engine led to the re-engining of the plane to make use of the Mitsubishi 'Kasei' Model 25 which was in series production by the time various other problems had been ironed out.

Delays caused by this programme of switching engines put back the entry of the plane to operational status until June 1944. Though the airframe was ready as early as March 1942 a US Technical Intelligence Report of the day stated that the Japanese

National Maritime Museum

FAA Avengers fly in box formation to exploit their defensive firepower

were not entirely satisfied with its performance (possibly a hint about the engine problems) and indicated that F4Fs could easily catch it at sea level and that the fuel tank protection was totally ineffective against ·50 cal incendiary ammunition. It was believed that Jill was the first Japanese plane to use water injection for 'flash performance' in evading fighters and during take-offs. Jill carried its one 1700-lb torpedo or two 550-lb bombs on external racks, offset to clear the propeller.

Jill was a substantial improvement over the Kate, with an increase of about 50 knots in speed and 50% in range, making it superior in performance to the Grumman TBF Avenger. Loss of the Japanese carriers and skilled pilots prevented this plane from being fully exploited in combat conditions. While it was used on board the remaining carriers, it was, for the most part, land based.

A distinctive recognition feature was the forward tilting vertical fin and rudder, a design feature which was dictated by the size of the elevators aboard Japanese carriers and the necessity of keeping within the overall length of 11 metres. A total of 1268 B6N2s were built.

A Japanese dive-bomber swoops on USS Hornet *while a torpedo plane circles, Battle of Santa Cruz*

Imperial War Museum

DIVE-BOMBERS

'WHEN WE SAY DIVE WE MEAN STRAIGHT DOWN'

Scout-bomber/strike-reconnaissance attack aircraft are better known as dive-bombers, dive-bombing being their most spectacular and devastating form of attack. Though tried in limited form by the Royal Flying Corps during 1918, the first true dive-bombing was carried out by the US Marines in 1919 in Haiti and later in Nicaragua in 1928, using Curtiss Helldivers, when the lives of their comrades on the ground would have been endangered by any less precise bombing method.

As early as 1927 the US Navy began to practise dive-bombing with all types of aircraft except the VPB patrol bombers and VTB torpedo bombers, using such machines as the Curtiss BFC and BF2C (redesignated Hawk III and Hawk IV). These were developments of the Hawk I and II export Hawks and the US Navy's F11 C-2 fighters. During his many visits to the US, Ernst Udet was intrigued by this form of bombing, which was then being demonstrated at air shows by Maj Al Williams, USMC Ret, and others. Using his Gulfhawk I, a Curtiss F6C owned by the Gulf Oil Company, Williams was a regular performer and crowd-pleaser as he roared straight down to deposit a bag of flour or a dummy bomb on a target in front of the grandstand with almost unerring accuracy.

Udet was sufficiently impressed to persuade his old First World War chum, Hermann Göring, to purchase two of the export Hawks for demonstration and testing back in Germany. These two aircraft, with manufacturer numbers 80 and 81, were delivered during the first two weeks of October 1933 and cost the then high price of $11,500 each. When Udet took delivery, he promptly christened them Iris and Ilse and set out to convince the budding Luftwaffe that this was the way of the future. Unfortunately one of the Hawks crashed in 1934 and the other was relegated to the Berlin Museum after having been flown extensively in demonstrations and outlived its usefulness. At the end of the Second World War this remaining Curtiss Hawk ended up in the Air Museum at Krakow, Poland.

The tactic of dive-bombing was continuously practised by the US Navy, to a lesser extent by the Fleet Air Arm and, presumably, by the Imperial Japanese Navy. The nature and size of ships make them very elusive targets, especially when they take evasive action, and there is little possible benefit from near misses by bombs dropped in salvo. Unless it is a very near miss, causing hull damage by concussion, conventional salvo bombing could waste a lot of bombs with little or no effect on the target. With a dodging and turning ship, the difficulty of getting a direct hit is increased many times.

'Battleship Row', Pearl Harbor, 7 December 1941 Bomb-aimer's view of stricken US Pacific Fleet

Single-engined aircraft normally used by the Navy do not carry many bombs, so it is necessary to use bombs of sufficient size to do meaningful damage and to place those bombs with great accuracy. Payloads rarely exceed 1½ tons, making it normal practice to use smaller bombs in quantity only against land or harbour targets. This does not mean that level bombing is not used in battle, for the sheer magnitude of bombs raining down on a fleet of ships or a landing zone from whatever source lends substantial assistance to the attacking force as a destructive and distractive element. There is also a strong possibility of a hit or near miss silencing a ship's anti-aircraft guns.

Dive-bombing, on the other hand, is a reasonably accurate delivery method in which the plane is lined up with the target so precisely that it is almost like sighting down the barrel of a gun. Evasive action is still possible, but the pilot can correct for this with small movements of the controls of his aircraft until the instant of release, which can be at a very low altitude, depending on the skill, daring and physical tolerance of the pilot.

Dive-bombers try to approach a target at high speed taking advantage of any cloud cover and, when possible, diving out of the sun in order to increase the problems for the defending anti-aircraft gunners. While speed is an asset in getting to the target, and away from it after the bomb is released, it is a disadvantage to build up too much speed in the dive. To do so increases the difficulty in aiming, as well as the stress on a plane

and crew during the pull-out. Aerodynamically clean, the dive-bomber would build up a tremendous speed if not retarded by some means. It is therefore necessary to fit these aircraft with speed-retarding dive brakes. These enable the pilot to adjust his dive speed to be fast enough to press home the attack and still slow enough to pick up the target and make a good recovery.

Confusing the Gunners

The ideal is a true vertical dive which enables the pilot to confuse the ship's gunners by giving him a choice of any angle for recovery. Simply by rolling the plane while in the vertical position, the pilot can avoid giving away his intended direction of recovery and thus confuse the gunners who would normally try to 'lead' him like a clay pigeon during his recovery trajectory, when the plane is most vulnerable. The pull-out rate and altitude is determined more by what the pilot can stand, physically, than by what the plane can take.

Dive-bomber pilots are quick to point out that 'when we say dive, we mean straight down'. However, it did not always work out that way in practice, for the pull-out often caused the pilot to black out due to blood being driven from the pilot's head by centrifugal force (referred to as 'Gs'). Medical scientists and technicians combined forces to develop anti-G suits to retard the flow of blood from the pilot's head by exerting pressure on arterial pressure points and the stomach area, reducing, or at least delaying, the normal tendency to black out.

Contrary to general belief, a pilot does not just line up a target, particularly a moving target, in his sights and hold this position. He continues to fly the plane, adjusting for wind, target movement and, most probably, bursts of flak. During the dive he must avoid skidding or the bomb will be deflected away from the aiming point. Finally, the pull-out point must be determined and this varies with the pilot's personal tolerance for the centrifugal force and the type of bomb, since he wants to be levelled out and well on his way before the bomb bursts.

Among the advantages of dive-bombing is the fact that anti-aircraft fire never has succeeded in stopping a dive-bombing attack, and it is far more accurate than other systems. Ideally, an attack should be a coordinated effort between the dive-bombers to disable the target ship and torpedo bombers to come in for the kill. As one wag put it, 'If you want to let in air, you use bombs, and if you want to let in water you use torpedoes'.

The spectacular aspect is well known but the second, and equally important, function of this type of aircraft is scouting for an enemy force. The strike-reconnaissance/scout-bomber must have the range to carry out this mission as well – and sometimes both missions must be combined. Such was the case when Lt-Cdr C Wade McClusky set out to find the large Japanese fleet which was headed for Midway Island.

The fleet had been reported by a US Army B-17 to be headed toward the island, but numbers and types of ships were missing from the brief radio transmission. McClusky led an air group of 33 Douglas SBDs of VB 6 and VS 6 off the *Enterprise* in search of the enemy force. Unknown to McClusky, the Japanese Fleet had turned and was steaming north-east instead of toward the island. Not finding them in the expected position, he continued to search until he made contact and began the attack that was to become the Battle of Midway. A few minutes later a second group, VS 3 and VS 5 from the *Yorktown*, led by Lt-Cdr Max Leslie, joined the battle. In the ensuing action, the Japanese lost four carriers, the *Kaga*, *Akagi*, *Hiryu* and *Soryu*. This decisive victory was accomplished at a cost of 32 casualties and the loss of all but six of the 41 torpedo bombers from VT 8 and VT 6.

At the outbreak of the Second World War the aircraft considered to be in this combat grouping were the British Blackburn Skua, the Japanese Aichi D3A Val and the US Douglas SBD Dauntless. As the war progressed, lessons learned in the various engagements were incorporated in the aircraft under development. Among the planes of this second grouping were the Nakajima B6N1/2 Jill and the Aichi B7A1 Grace, the Curtiss SB2C and the Fairey Barracuda (discussed under the heading of torpedo bomber/attack aircraft). The Barracuda, as noted, was designed or adapted to do virtually everything and ended up doing none of its tasks exceptionally well.

One of the least known aircraft of the war was the Blackburn Skua. This lack of recognition would be strange except that at the time the Skua was making its mark in history, censorship was the order of day. The Skua was not produced in any great quantities so it was not seen sitting around every airstrip as were Moths and Cubs. In fact records show that only 165 were manufactured. But among its accomplishments it is credited with the destruction of the first German plane by a British aircraft during the war. The event took place on 25 September 1939, when a Skua shot down one of three Dornier Do 18 flying boats which were shadowing British fleet units off the coast of Norway.

State of the art

The Skua, like the Aichi Val and the Douglas SBD, represented the state of the art of the late 1930s, each reaching fleet operation status in 1937–39 and all scheduled for replacement just prior to the outbreak of war. HMS *Ark Royal* received six Skuas in November 1938, just in time for the opening action of the war. Operationally, the Skua played a very active role in the early days of the war, not because of great faith in dive-bombing on the part of the Royal Navy who favoured the torpedo as a weapon, but because in many instances it was the only aircraft available.

Blackburn Skua
The Royal Navy's first operational monoplane was conceived as a dual purpose fighter and dive-bomber, and saw combat in Norway, over Dunkirk and Dakar
  Span: 46 ft 2 in *Length:* 35 ft 7 in
Engine: Bristol Perseus XII, 890 hp
Armament: 4 Browning mg; 1 Lewis mg *Max Speed:* 225 mph at 6500 ft *Ceiling:* 19,100 ft
Range: 760 miles *Bombload:* 1×500-lb bomb

Blackburn Roc
The tactical concept of the Roc – bringing its four-gun turret to bear in broadside attacks on enemy aircraft – proved a failure and the type saw little combat, ending its days as a target tug
  Span: 46 ft *Length:* 35 ft 7 in *Engine:* Bristol Perseus XII, 890 hp *Armament:* 4×·303 Browning mg *Max Speed:* 223 mph at 10,000 ft *Ceiling:* 18,000 ft *Range:* 810 miles

For example, in early April 1940 when the Germans launched their attack on Norway and Denmark, the cruisers *Köln* and *Königsberg* along with a gunnery training ship, *Bremse*, were to attack the port of Bergen. The shore-based batteries damaged the *Königsberg* sufficiently to cause her to tie up to a breakwater at Bergen. This news was transmitted to the Royal Navy who dispatched the only aircraft available, the Skua. Two squadrons, 803 and 800, totalling 16 Skuas, loaded with 500-lb bombs and enough fuel for a 600-mile round trip, managed to struggle off the airfield at Hatston in the Orkneys on 10 April 1940. Diving out of the sun, the traditional attack position for dive-bombers, the pilots of the Skuas managed to score at least three direct hits, plus numerous near misses which caused the *Königsberg* to disappear in a sheet of flames and debris. The cost to the Royal Navy was three damaged Skuas and one lost.

During the evacuation of Dunkirk in June 1940, all available aircraft were pressed into service to provide air cover. Skuas from 801 and 806 Squadrons took their place along with other aircraft types to provide much needed cover for the beleaguered British Expeditionary Force. After Dunkirk, the Skuas saw action in the Mediterranean, where 800 and 803 Squadrons, on board the *Ark Royal*, attacked units of the French Fleet, dive-bombing and putting out of action the new 35,000-ton battleship *Richelieu*.

There followed several engagements aiding convoys en route to the besieged island of Malta. Finally, in 1941, the Skuas were replaced by Fairey Fulmars for operational flying, but continued in service as trainers and for target towing. The rapid pace of aircraft development with the beginning of the war proved too fast for the sturdy Skua which had been designed in 1934 and first flown in 1937.

The Skua was an all-metal, single-engine monoplane. The fuselage, in compliance with specifications 0.27/34, was designed to be waterproof. It was divided into three watertight compartments to provide flotation should a ditching at sea be necessary. This was a valuable foresight as a number did ditch.

Production aircraft were fitted with the Bristol Perseus XII sleeve-valve engine – a unique engine, substituted for the Bristol Mercury which was required to outfit the Bristol Blenheim.

The Skua was the first all-metal monoplane to reach operational status with the Fleet Air Arm and was the first British aircraft designed specifically for dive-bombing. One surprising detail in view of its slow speed (225 mph max) was its alternative role of fighter and the location of the fuel tanks in the fuselage between the front and rear cockpits. A similar tank location in the De Havilland DH-4 of the First World War earned for it the unenviable name of 'Flying Coffin', but this was before self-sealing fuel tanks were developed.

The rugged but awkward angled landing

gear and tail hook, plus the folding wing panels, completed the Skua's fitting-out for carrier service. Range was 760 miles; endurance was 4.5 hours at cruising speed of 145–165 mph.

Its armament was modest. Typical of that found in aircraft at the beginning of the war, it consisted of four forward-firing ·303 cal Browning machine-guns mounted in the wings and a single ·303 cal Lewis gun in a flexible mount in the rear cockpit. Ordnance consisted of one 500-lb bomb carried externally on a fork mount to ensure clearance of the propeller and up to eight 30-lb bombs on external wing racks. The latter were used primarily for practice since the only bombs of any value in this weight class were anti-personnel fragmentation bombs.

The Aichi D3A 'Val', built in 1937, was by far the most important of the Japanese dive-bombers and was considered obsolete by the time it was used so effectively at Pearl Harbor. Although the Yokosuka D4Y1 Suisei (Comet), code named by the Allies 'Judy', was in the development stage, it was not to see service until February 1944 off Truk Island, so the Val really had the war to itself in the dive-bomber class. It was the first all-metal dive-bomber built by the Japanese and was based on engineering knowledge obtained from the Heinkel He 118 which had been purchased by the Japanese for study purposes.

Slow and vulnerable

The Val was not too popular because of its relatively slow top speed of 232 mph and was also quite vulnerable in spite of the agility characteristic of Japanese aircraft of that period. Like its contemporaries it carried a single 550-lb bomb externally. For shorter ranges this load was supplemented by two smaller bombs fitted to wing racks, each of about 130 lb.

The devastation of Pearl Harbor was largely due to the Val. Following that historic attack the Val's next appearance was in the Indian Ocean in April 1942 where, for the second time, the Japanese convinced an anxious world that sea power was at the mercy of air power, particularly if the ships did not have adequate defensive air power of their own. It was an expensive lesson in ships and men, for the British carrier *Hermes* and the cruisers *Cornwall* and *Dorsetshire* all were sunk.

Following the major battles of Midway and Coral Sea, where the Japanese lost the major part of their trained and experienced

The American battleship USS Arizona *reduced to a blazing hulk by Japanese dive and torpedo bombers*

US Navy

Imperial War Museum

'Vals' in formation. They were the first Japanese type to bomb US targets

aircrews, the accuracy of their bombing fell to 10% hits in contrast to the 80% and 82% hit ratio that prevailed when they attacked the British ships in the Indian Ocean. The Japanese never managed to replace the experienced pilots lost in these battles.

Failure of the Yokosuka D4Y Judy to meet the operational requirements resulted in a continuation of production of the Val in an improved model, the Aichi D3A2, fitted with a more powerful engine, the Kinsei 54, and additional fuel capacity to increase the operating range.

From China to Leyte Gulf

In addition to the Pearl Harbor attack and the fateful battles of the Coral Sea and Midway, the Val was present in the earlier operations in China, at Wake Island, Darwin, Eastern Solomons, Santa Cruz, Philippine Sea (known as the 'Marianas Turkey Shoot') and finally the Battle of Leyte Gulf. By this time, Japan no longer had a carrier force and all navy aircraft, regardless of their intended use, were forced to operate from land bases. From this point onward, attacks by the Japanese consisted mostly of Kamikaze attacks. For this, the remaining Vals were converted to single seat configuration.

The Val was a single engine, low-wing monoplane whose fixed landing gear had streamlined covering over the legs and pants over the wheels. The fixed landing gear was one of the most obvious indentification characteristics and contributed to lack of speed but was considered an asset when the plane was in its bombing dive. To facilitate stowage aboard carriers, the wing tips could be folded at a point six feet inboard from the tips. Like other aircraft of this period, its armament was not highly regarded. It carried two 7·7-mm guns firing

forward and a single 7·7-mm gun mounted in the rear cockpit for defensive purposes and for strafing the decks of enemy ships as the bomb run was completed.

A total of 1294 Vals were produced between 1937 and 1944, 478 of which were the earlier model 11s (D3A1), powered by the 1075 hp Mitsubishi Kinsei 43 radial air-cooled engine. The second variant, the Model 22, powered by the Mitsubishi Kinsei 54, a twin-row 14 cylinder engine, boosted the power to 1200 hp and increased the speed to 266 mph. A total of 816 of the Model 22s (D3A2s) were built between 1942 and 1944.

Aichi D3A2 'Val'

This rugged carrier-borne dive-bomber was in the forefront of the attacks on Pearl Harbor and on the Royal Navy in the Indian Ocean, and sank more Allied fighting ships than any other Axis aircraft type
Span: 47 ft 2 in *Length:* 33 ft 5 in *Engine:* Mitsubishi Kinsei 54, 1100 hp at 20,000 ft *Armament:* 3×7·7-mm mg *Max speed:* 267 mph at 9845 ft *Ceiling:* 34,450 ft *Range:* 840 miles *Bombload:* 1×550-lb plus 2×132-lb bombs

A flight of US Navy Dauntless dive-bombers heads for the Japanese base at Palau in the western Pacific

John Batchelor

DOUGLAS SBD DAUNTLESS

The SBD dive-bomber, approaching obsolescence by 1941, was one of the most important instruments in the American victories and still outperformed its successor, the Helldiver at Coral Sea, Midway, and the Philippine Sea
Span: 41 ft 6 in *Length:* 33 ft *Engine:* Wright Cyclone, 950 hp *Max speed:* 255 mph at 14,000 ft *Ceiling:* 25,200 ft *Range:* 773 miles *Armament:* 2 × ·5-in mg *Bombload:* 1 × 500-lb bomb

Designed in 1938 and accepted by the US Navy in February 1939, practically on the eve of war, the Douglas SBD Dauntless nevertheless represented pre-war technology. Fortunately, its design was quite adaptable, within limits, to changes dictated by combat experience. Above all it was a compact, rugged machine that could take a lot of punishment at the hands of both friend and foe. Friends were likely to expect too much from it in load carrying and handling and an enemy target or aircraft could be expected to throw everything at it.

The SBD had only barely passed its teething period when war broke out. The first planes were accepted in February 1939 and the first contract for 57 SBD-1s was negotiated during the first week of April 1939. Following the outbreak of hostilities, these orders were substantially increased with successive model changes indicating responses to lessons and tactics learned in the European war. These included increases in fuel, self-sealing fuel tanks and armour plate for the crew, as well as a more powerful engine, a Pratt & Whitney R 1820-52 delivering 1000 hp, to maintain the performance. Pearl Harbor added new urgency to production lines, and an additional 500 SBDs were ordered. By this time the armament had changed from two ·30 cal cowling-mounted guns to two ·50 cal machine-guns. A second ·30 cal gun was added to the rear cockpit. The SBDs produced under this expanding programme, plus the remaining SBD-2s, played a major role in the crucial battles of the Coral Sea and Midway.

The SBDs gave a good account of themselves in every enagagement of the Pacific theatre and, like the Aichi Vals, had a reprieve. This resulted from delays in getting the Curtiss SB2C, their intended successor, fully acceptable and modified for carrier operations. All told, they accounted for most of the damage sustained by the Japanese carriers and other enemy ships they encountered.

Like its counterpart in the Japanese Navy, the Val, the SBD almost had the war all to itself for its successor, the Curtiss SB2C did not satisfy operational requirements until late in 1943. In fact one eminent naval historian, Samuel Eliot Morison, in recording the Battle of the Philippine Sea, stated that 'the new Helldiver was outshone by the two remaining squadrons of Dauntless dive bombers . . . here the Dauntless fought her last battle'.

Aichi B7A Ryusei (Shooting Star) 'Grace'
Exceptionally large for a Japanese carrier
aircraft, the B7A was designed for a new class
of ships. The loss of the Imperial Navy's carriers
saw the big attack bomber operating only
fitfully from land bases

Span: 47 ft 3 in *Length:* 37 ft 8 in
Engine: Nakajima Homare 23, 1670 hp at 7875 ft
Armament: 2×20-mm cannon; 1×7·92-mm mg
Max speed: 352 mph at 21,490 ft *Ceiling:*
36,910 ft *Range:* 1151 miles *Bombload:* 1764-lb
torpedo or 1800 lb bombs

Armament of the SBD-5 (the most numerous variant of the type) consisted of two ·50 cal guns mounted in the top deck of the cowl and a brace of ·30 cal flexible-mounted guns in the rear cockpit for the radio-operator.

Ordnance could consist of a variety of loads including (published specifications to the contrary) a 1600-lb bomb on the centre rack plus two 100-lb bombs on wing mounts, all externally mounted. In a scouting configuration, drop-tanks could be attached to the wing mounts for greater endurance.

In the final version of the SBD-6, the engine was the 1350 hp Pratt & Whitney

Curtiss SB2C Helldiver
Designed to fit the standard US carrier deck-elevator, the Helldiver suffered constant stability problems but it won honours in the USN's last dive-bomber action at Leyte Gulf, and in the attacks on the Japanese super-battleships *Yamato* and *Musashi*
Span: 49 ft 9 in *Length:* 36 ft 8 in
Engine: Wright R-2600-8, 1700 hp *Max speed:* 294 mph *Ceiling:* 23,000 ft *Range:* 695 miles

R-1820-66 and the published weights were 6554 lb empty and 10,882 lb at gross take-off weight. Unlike most of its contemporaries, the SBDs did not have folding wings to improve their shipboard stowage ability. Instead they had the same basic wing construction as their parent, the Northrop XBT-2 (XSBD-1), the Northrop Gamma and the ubiquitous DC-3 Dakota. The similarities of design are more than incidental.

Designed to replace the Douglas SBD, the Curtiss SB2C Helldiver was long overdue in combat. A succession of problems and modification programmes delayed the first squadron delivery of SB2C-1s until December 1942, a full year after Pearl Harbor. The original contract for the XSB2C-1 had been negotiated and signed in May 1939. Between these two dates a seemingly endless series of problems conspired to delay production. Difficulty with stability and control tests, cooling problems and loss of test aircraft kept engineers and test pilots busy for many months trying to resolve the problems as they occurred. In addition to design problems there was the question of engineering the plane for production by the thousand. Parts that normally would have been handmade out of a number of small components now were redesigned for mass production, often resulting in single unit forgings to economise on both man-hours and weight.

Weight reduction was an ever-present

albatross around the necks of the SB2C engineers. The SB2C was designed to carry bombs 50% heavier than those carried by the SBD it was to replace, and this added weight was to be carried in an internal bomb-bay. This was difficult to accomplish for two reasons. Firstly, increasing loads were being hung on the SBD in response to combat necessity and bombs 50% heavier were also larger, making it difficult to carry them internally. Secondly, external racks, while increasing the frontal drag, also permitted a wider variety of sizes and configurations.

By the time the problem areas were determined and the appropriate corrections made by modifications, the war was well under way. Most of the really big and decisive battles were over by 11 November 1943 when Squadron VB 17 from the *Bunker Hill* equipped with SB2Cs attacked the harbour at Rabaul. From this date until the end of hostilities the Helldiver was the standard dive-bomber, USN, replacing the SBD in all remaining major actions of the war.

Only a small number of SB2Cs were ordered by Allied forces. The Royal Australian Air Force ordered 150 A-25As, a land-based Army version, but took delivery of only ten, since by this late date there was no longer a requirement for land-based dive-bombers. Twenty-six SBW-1Bs were delivered to the Royal Navy from Canadian Car & Foundry Production. Like the Helldiver, which carried on a traditional Curtiss name, the A-25As were also to carry a traditional name of 'Shrike'.

The 'Beast', as it was called by its crew, was not particularly well liked, although it established a good record before the end of the war. It could carry up to 2000 lb of bombs in the bomb-bay and was tested to carry a Mk 13 torpedo though this was never used during the service life of the aircraft. In a similar vein the SB2C-2 was tested with floats with the idea of using it for close support of expeditionary landings. This configuration was never to see combat use. Depending on the dash number, the SB2Cs were armed with either four ·50 cal machine-guns or two 20-mm cannons plus two ·30 cal machine-guns in a flexible mount for the rear seat gunner.

Cancellation recommended
Directional stability was to plague the design during all its operational life. The short fuselage required to fit two aircraft on to each of the 40 ft × 48 ft elevators contributed to this. To improve the directional stability, the engine was moved forward one foot and compensating area added to the fin and rudder. On shake-down carrier qualification tests aboard the *Yorktown*, the SB2Cs had many problems, including structural failure, collapsed tail wheels and missed hook contact. Based on this experience, the ship's commander, Capt J J Clark recommended cancellation of the entire contract. This was in June 1942, only six months after Pearl Harbor when all the emphasis was on planes to win the war. This was hardly the climate to start over again with a new design. As a result all parties pressed on, throwing good money after bad to make it work in spite of all its deficiencies. Under any other circumstances Captain Clark's recommendation would have spelled the end of this plane. The production lines turned out 600 SB2Cs before all the bugs were under control. The 601st plane was the first to be delivered

without a stop-over at one of the modification centres.

With the Pacific war nearly over and most of the Japanese carriers destroyed or damaged beyond repair there was really little left for the Helldivers to do. The one exception was the Battle of the Philippine Sea, where the SB2Cs gave a good account of themselves. They were to be the last dive-bombers of the Second World War.

After undergoing additional modifications to make them suitable for different tasks, the SB2Cs and their derivatives the A25s, were phased out of service and most of them scrapped.

Of limited importance during the Second World War, but built to requirements and from lessons learned in combat, the Aichi B7A1 *Ryusei* (Shooting Star) 'Grace' did

Yokosuka D4Y2 Suisei (Comet) 'Judy'
The fastest carrier-borne dive-bomber of the Second World War, the 'Judys' were very susceptible to battle damage and took a savage mauling in the 'Marianas Turkey Shoot'
Span: 37 ft 8 in *Length:* 33 ft 6 in
Engine: Aichi Atsuta AE1P, 1340 hp at 5580 ft
Armament: 2×7·7-mm mg; 1×13-mm mg
Max Speed: 360 mph at 17,225 ft
Ceiling: 35,105 ft *Range:* 909 miles
Bombload: 1234 lb

not establish any record of action from carriers although it was designed as a follow-on to the Nakajima B6N2 Jill and the D4Y Judy. Only 105 of these aircraft plus nine prototypes were completed before the end of hostilities and after the destruction of the Japanese carrier fleet.

The Grace was the first Japanese aircraft to be designed for internal stowage of a 1760-lb torpedo. In addition, it could carry a second torpedo externally. It was distinctive in design, having an inverted gull-shaped wing for the same reason as the Vought F4U Corsair, namely the need to shorten and therefore reduce weight of the retractable landing gear. It also featured coordinated droop ailerons (10°) which provided additional drag and lift when the flaps were lowered.

An 1825-hp Nakajima 'Homare' 12 engine made the Grace substantially faster than its predecessors with 356 mph being achieved during tests. Unfortunately, the engine was not fully developed, needed time-consuming maintenance and lacked reliability.

Among the dive-bomber category the Junkers Ju 87 is not generally known as a carrier-based type though as a dive-bomber it is probably better known than any other plane. The fact that it was considered and even stressed and fitted with catapult and arrester hook escapes any but the most intense researcher.

At the beginning of the war Germany had under construction an aircraft carrier, the *Graf Zeppelin*, which was abandoned early in the war. The principal dive-bomber, the Ju 87C or Stuka as it was best known, was to have been the dive-bomber assigned to this ship. The Ju 87C was a special modification of the Ju 87B-1 and was fitted with jettisonable landing gear in anticipation of the probability of a ditched landing. This

Towards the end of the war, many types of Japanese

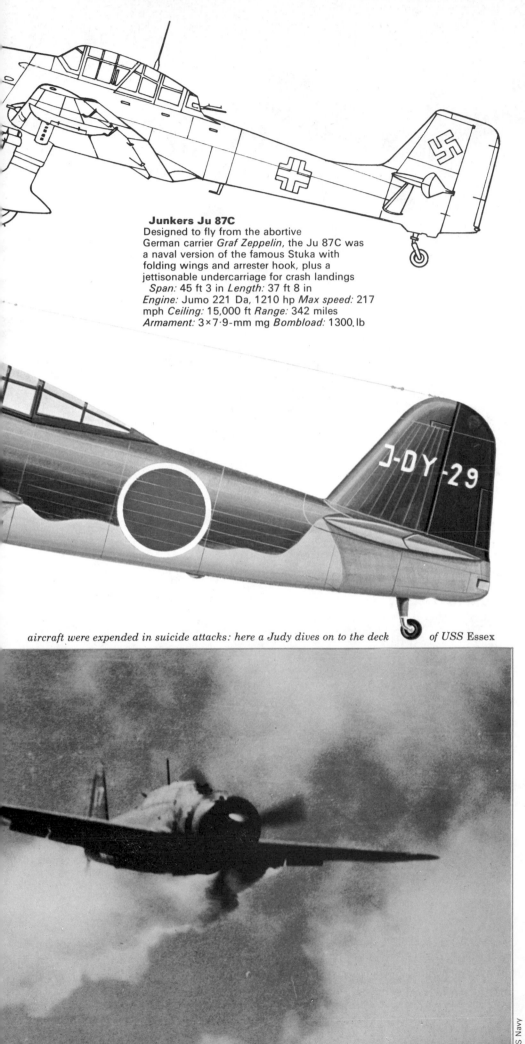

Junkers Ju 87C
Designed to fly from the abortive
German carrier *Graf Zeppelin*, the Ju 87C was
a naval version of the famous Stuka with
folding wings and arrester hook, plus a
jettisonable undercarriage for crash landings
Span: 45 ft 3 in *Length:* 37 ft 8 in
Engine: Jumo 221 Da, 1210 hp *Max speed:* 217
mph *Ceiling:* 15,000 ft *Range:* 342 miles
Armament: 3×7·9-mm mg *Bombload:* 1300 lb

aircraft were expended in suicide attacks: here a Judy dives on to the deck of USS *Essex*

US Navy

modification feature, to the best of our
knowledge, was not used by Germany's ally
Japan in the design of the Aichi D3A Val.

Only a few were produced and these were
converted back to the Ju 87B-1 configuration when the carrier plans were abandoned.

The last of the carrier-based attack bombers or dive-bombers built by the Japanese
was the Yokosuka D4Y1 *Suisei* (Comet),
Allied code name 'Judy', which first entered
service in its scout-reconnaissance role
during the Battle of Midway. It was produced in a variety of models and in surprisingly large numbers – 2038 – which exceeded
the production of Curtiss SB2Cs, even
though Japan was under direct attack
during the latter days of the war and disrup-
tion was certain to prevail during this time.

The Judy was interesting in a number of
respects, one of which was the use of the
liquid-cooled Aichi AE1A Atsuta 12 engine
which produced 1200 hp. Most carrier-based
aircraft, with the notable exception of the
D4Y1 and D4Y2 Judy and the British Fairey
Barracuda and Fulmar used air-cooled
engines. Even the later versions of the Judy,
D4Y3 and D4Y4, used air-cooled radial
engines, the Mitsubishi Kinsei Model 62.

In each of these exceptions to the existing
tradition, the resulting aircraft was very
attractive. The Aichi Atsuta 12 was a
version of the German Daimler-Benz engine
built under licence. Poor reliability prompted the Aichi engineers to suggest changing
the engine to the 1560-hp Mitsubishi Kinsei
62, an air-cooled radial. This modification
was designated D4Y3. Of the 2038 D4Ys
produced, at least 822 were powered by
radial air-cooled engines.

Reconnaissance only
Like all naval carrier aircraft, the Judy
was of a multi-purpose design, for dive-
bombing/attack, night-fighter and finally as
special attack (Kamikaze) aircraft. Until
March 1943 the Judy experienced wing
flutter when tested as a dive-bomber. As a
result they were restricted to their reconnaissance configuration when they made
their combat debut, flying from the aircraft
carrier *Soryu* during the Battle of Midway.
The D4Y2, powered by the 1400-hp Aichi
Atsuta 32, had the airframe strengthened,
making it serviceable in its intended principal role of dive-bomber. Unfortunately,
time was running out for the Japanese fleet,
much of which had slipped beneath the
Pacific waters. During the period when the
type was being strengthened, those produced were in action as reconnaissance
aircraft flying from all the carriers remaining in action.

The night-fighter conversion was an
interesting but relatively ineffective modification designed to attack B-29s which were
then making regular runs over Japan. In
this conversion a 20-mm cannon was fitted
in the fuselage to fire upward at a 30° angle.
Interesting as it was this was not an effective
weapon since the plane itself had very poor
performance. It had a 50 to 80 mph speed
advantage over its predecessor, the D3A
Val, and the contemporary SB2C. However,
the latter carried at least twice the load of
the D4Y and had almost twice the range.

Due to the pressure of the American
forces moving steadily toward the Japanese homeland, desperate measures were
adopted. The Kamikaze groups used specially designed aircraft, as well as modified
production aircraft. Like the remaining Vals,
the Judy was also used for this duty.

Grumman F4F Wildcat
Grumman's first monoplane fighter for the US Navy, this tubby, highly manoeuvrable fighter put up heroic resistance to the Japanese onslaught of 1941 and early 1942, and was rushed into British service as the 'Martlet I'
Span: 38 ft *Length:* 28 ft 9 in *Engine:* Pratt & Whitney R-1830-76 Twin Wasp, 1200 hp at take-off *Max speed:* 330 mph at 21,100 ft *Ceiling:* 37,500 ft *Range:* 845 miles at cruising speed *Armament:* 4×·5-in mg

FIGHTERS
BOMBER ESCORT OR CARRIER PROTECTOR?

Designed to maintain local mastery of the air, the fighter and the fighter pilot must both be a rather special combination. In the Second World War the lesson was learned once again that any air force must have a high proportion of fighters. This was soon apparent when aircraft carrier commanders found it necessary to hold in readiness a substantial number of their fighter complement to protect their own ships from enemy attacks. It was necessary to maintain a Combat Air Patrol (CAP) constantly ready to divert or destroy attacking enemy aircraft. The problem was how many to keep in orbit in the vicinity of the carrier or its task force when at the same time the torpedo planes and the dive-bombers needed air support during their attacks.

It was often necessary to keep the majority of the fighters close at hand to protect the carriers. When this happened, the small number that could accompany the torpedo planes and/or the dive-bombers were usually totally inadequate and often resulted in a high loss rate to the attack planes. Conversely, should the planes be assigned to accompany the dive-bombers and torpedo planes then the carrier with its critically important landing deck was left in a vulnerable situation. To accommodate both these requirements, the percentage of fighters in relation to other types of aircraft rose from roughly 18% to 60% of the aircraft complement of the carrier.

Another factor which made these aircraft ratios necessary was the increasing use of fighters in an attack role, loaded with ordnance almost beyond belief. In these cases, the fighters operated in the role of fighter-bombers delivering bombs, rockets and/or napalm on the first attack wave, and reverting to their fighter·role after

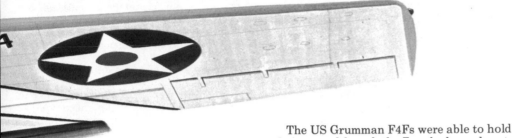

dropping their ordnance stores. It was partially because of the multitude of attack functions taken over by the fighters that scout-bombers became less and less necessary as the war progressed.

In fighter aircraft superior speed, while an important consideration, is not adequate in itself, nor is rate of climb the whole answer. Manoeuvrability by itself is also meaningless, but to combine the three in a machine superior to those of an opponent is the goal of the aircraft designer.

In the case of naval aircraft, additional requirements are imposed by their operation at sea and often far from friendly land bases. Among these requirements is adequate endurance and the strength to withstand launching and retrieval. Prior to the Second World War, two-seater fighters were purchased, and well into the early part of the war such planes as the Fairey Fulmar were operated – not because of any outstanding superiority but because of a lack of anything better. They were adequate when attacking slow bombers or reconnaissance aircraft but were at a grave disadvantage when opposed by single-seat fighters. The additional crew member and the accommodations for him penalised the plane's action. The most successful and most numerous naval fighters of the Second World War were single-seat planes.

Japan, among the major naval powers, had the best shipboard fighters when the war began. The French were woefully inadequate, as were the British, and the US was only slightly better off. The European nations had almost totally neglected sea-based airpower for a variety of reasons. The US was still suffering from short rations and shortsightedness, a hangover from the depression years.

The Mitsubishi A6M2 was the outstand-

ing fighter aircraft in the opening days of the Pacific war and came as a considerable surprise to most military authorities. The intensive security maintained by the Japanese largely accounted for this surprise. The A6M2, better known as the Zero or Zeke because of the designation of the aircraft as the Navy type '0' carrier fighter, was much maligned in the US as being a copy of one or more well known US aircraft. The Zero nevertheless gave a good account of itself and its pilots.

The US Grumman F4Fs were able to hold their own although the Zero had an advantage in most categories. By being able to absorb a lot of battle damage and still carry on, the F4F's four ·50 cal machine-guns were capable of tearing up the light structure and unprotected fuel tanks of the Zeros. High on the list of design criteria for the Japanese naval fighters was high manoeuvrability and high speed. To obtain these, it was necessary to compromise by using a light structure and by elimination of frills such as self-sealing fuel tanks and armour plate protection for the pilot and vital parts of the aircraft. They were, in fact, the correct choice for the war 'game-plan' of the Japanese commanders for a fast-moving war of short duration. Their misfortune was in not destroying the *Lexington* and *Enterprise* at Pearl Harbor.

New generation

The well-trained and heroic pilots of the US Navy, flying the rugged Wildcats and other carrier aircraft, held on and turned the tables when the new generation of planes was ready for combat operations. US planes like the Grumman F6F Hellcat were designed with the specific purpose of attaining air superiority over the Zero. The Japanese, on the other hand, did not have access to industrial resources to match those of the US, which was able to maintain production lines of F4Fs and SBDs while at the same time design and build the second generation aircraft.

The Japanese, in the meantime, were hard pressed to accomplish the same results although in retrospect one can only admire their determination, the variety of aircraft types and numbers produced during the war. The Zero, along with the Zeke and other

variations, was the principal Japanese carrier fighter from the beginning to the end of the war.

In the European theatre the British Navy paid a high price for peacetime lethargy or perhaps for the honest ignorance of fiscal and military officialdom. When the war clouds were growing in intensity, the Fleet Air Arm, which attained an independent status in May 1939, was still using the Gloster Sea Gladiator, a conversion of the RAF's last biplane fighter.

The success of the Hurricane and Spitfire prompted the Royal Navy to request a monoplane fighter. This resulted in the Fairey Fulmar, a two-seater which was to become the Navy's first all-metal monoplane fighter. The Blackburn Skua, previously mentioned, was to have been an all-purpose machine supposedly capable of operating as a fighter as well as a dive-bomber, but as a fighter it was badly outclassed.

With this situation Britain, hardpressed on many fronts, built Fairey Fireflys and adopted the Grumman Martlet I, basically the F4F with the single row Wright R-1820 instead of the more normal twin row Pratt & Whitney R-1830. These Martlets were originally ordered by the French and were diverted to the Fleet Air Arm after the French capitulation in June 1940. They were well tested and coming off production lines at a rate to satisfy US and British requirements.

Holding the line

The plane that held the line and kept the Imperial Japanese Navy busy during the early stages of the war was the Grumman F4F, a comparatively small single-engine, mid-wing monoplane. A pugnacious looking machine in the air, it was almost ugly on the deck, propped up on its narrow tread retractable landing gear. In the early models, the gear was manually retracted by thirty turns of a crank at the pilot's right hand. This feature was never particularly liked by pilots for more often than not it resulted in a porpoising flight path just after lift-off. In any event it was better than that of the Polikarpov I-15, the little Russian biplane fighter used by the Republicans in Spain. In the I-15, each landing gear leg had to be cranked up independently by hand, resulting in a roll, or partial roll, first one way and then another.

The F4Fs, christened 'Wildcats', were just coming into carrier service when war broke out. The fall of France in June 1940 resulted in increased orders for the Wildcat which, up to this point, was going through the normal peacetime development progression of service trials leading to full acceptance by the Navy. The original design competition was announced in 1935 to replace the Grumman F3F-1 biplane then in

USS Hornet, *the carrier that launched Doolittle's raid on Tokyo and was later sunk off Guadalcanal*

US Navy

service. The competition was won by the Brewster F2A Buffalo but the US Navy gave Grumman a contract for a new prototype, designated XF4F-3. This turned out to be a very fortunate occurrence because, in service, the Buffalo showed a distressing weakness of the landing gear.

However, the Buffalo could easily outmanoeuvre the Wildcat in simulated combat but, on returning to the carrier, the odds were in favour of an unserviceable plane – not because of combat damage but because of landing damage. The F4F on the other hand was rugged and reliable in all situations but was lacking in climb and manoeuvrability when compared with its antagonist, the Japanese Zero. It more than made up for these deficiencies in its firepower of four (and later six) wing-mounted ·50 cal machine-guns, self-sealing fuel tanks and armour for pilot protection. The merit of these features was clearly demonstrated by the nearly seven to one combat-kill ratio over its opponents, many of them Japanese Zeros.

One design feature which caused problems and resulted in one fatal crash was inflation, in the air, of the specified flotation air bags. Elimination of these and the mechanism for hydraulically folding the wings provided space in the wings and weight reduction which made it possible to add another pair of guns and ammunition to bring the armament up to six ·50 cal machine-guns. This battery of guns proved to be the answer to any other deficiencies the Wildcat might have had, for when the pilot got on a target there was little doubt about the outcome.

Having quickly learned of the manoeuvrability and climb characteristics of the Zero, the US Navy pilots concentrated on head-on or diving attacks. In the head-on attack the Wildcat had the advantage of the high velocity ·50 cal guns, while the Japanese 7·7-mm machine-guns barely scratched the Wildcat and their slow-firing, low-velocity 20-mm cannon were quite inaccurate. The diving attack used the strength of the Wildcat, while its ability to manoeuvre even at high speed was another plus factor since the Zero was found to have problems with aileron control at the higher speeds encountered in dives. The F4F was never redlined for terminal dive speeds which is testimony to its durability.

The Wildcat was considered to be a transitional fighter by the US Navy, intended to hold on until a second generation could be produced. Whatever the intent, it is recorded fact that the F4F was present and gave a good account of itself and its pilots in most of the major engagements in the Pacific and in the Atlantic as well.

The F4F was present at Pearl Harbor, where 11 Wildcats were caught on the ground and nine destroyed. As the war progressed the Japanese pushed on with their attacks on Wake Island. This was one of the most heroic defensive battles, and one which was to spur the American war production efforts, bringing the Wildcat to the attention of the American public. With seven of the newly arrived Wildcats destroyed during the first Japanese attack, the remaining aircraft, never more than three in the air at the same time, succeeded in destroying a twin-engine Japanese bomber and at least one Zero in air combat. In addition, Capt Henry T Elrod, USMC,

Fairey Fulmar I
The Royal Navy's first 8-gun fighter, the Fulmar kept the two-seater layout for a navigator/observer and was outmatched by its land-based contemporaries and their naval derivatives
Span: 46 ft 5 in *Length:* 40 ft 3 in
Engine: Rolls-Royce Merlin VIII, 1080 hp
Max speed: 280 mph *Ceiling:* 26,000 ft
Range: 800 miles *Armament:* 8 × ·303-in mg

Blackburn Firebrand TF 5
Conceived as early as 1939, the Firebrand torpedo-fighter was dogged by development difficulties, and became operational in 1945, too late to see action
Span: 51 ft 3½ in *Length:* 38 ft 9 in
Engine: Bristol Centaurus IX, 2520 hp
Armament: 4 × 20-mm cannon *Max speed:* 340 mph at 13,000 ft *Ceiling:* 28,500 ft *Range:* 740 miles *Bombload:* 1 × 1850-lb torpedo or 2 × 1000-lb bombs

bombed and sank a Japanese destroyer before the defenders were overrun.

One of the first American heroes of the war was Lt Edward H 'Butch' O'Hare. On 20 February 1942 he and his squadron were flying Wildcats from the *Lexington* when they encountered a large force of Mitsubishi G4M1 Bettys returning to their base after a raid. In the ensuing battle, O'Hare shot down five enemy aircraft and damaged a sixth. He became one of the first US aces of the war and received the Medal of Honor.

The first of the folding-wing variants was the F4F-4 the prototype of which had a hydraulic folding system which was abandoned. The geometry of the characteristic Grumman wing-folding system was such that the wings were rotated some 90° about a central axis and folded back flush alongside the fuselage. This made the folding comparatively easy and, at the same time, reduced the overall height and volume of the Wildcat for stowage aboard ship. The F4F-4 made its debut at the Battle of Midway.

The Wildcat in any of its variations was a rugged machine and could not be considered inspiringly handsome by even its most avid admirer, but it could and did do the job it was designed to do. It was a chunky little mid-wing monoplane with a narrow-tread retractable landing gear, the mechanics and geometry of which had been well tested in earlier Grumman designs and dated back in concept to such planes as the Loening amphibians of 1927.

Pre-war design

Like so many of its contemporaries, the F4F's design dated back to the mid 1930s, its successor, the Grumman F6F, being the first plane to be designed from lessons and techniques learned during the war. Skill and adaptability on the part of the pilots, many of whom became aces flying Wildcats, made up for the plane's deficiencies.

Modifications were made along the way to adapt to changing conditions. The original four guns were increased to six, the solid wing of the F4F-3 became folding wings in the F4F-4 and FM-1, propellers were changed along with power plants, and the single-stage Pratt and Whitney engine was improved with the addition of two-stage, two-speed superchargers. In the FM-2, produced by General Motors, the guns were again reduced in number to four and the plane reduced in weight to improve its operation from the Jeep Carriers.

Developed at a time when procurement of aircraft for British air services came within the jurisdiction of the RAF, the Fairey Fulmar was hurriedly designed to fill a gap, since none of the existing aircraft then in RAF service could readily be adapted to the requirements visualised for the new armoured carriers.

Some allowances should be made for the shortcomings of the Fulmar when compared with other fighters, for it was designed to a different set of conditions as reflected in the specifications. The RAF had reserved for itself and its aircraft the task of defending ships while they were in range of land-based enemy aircraft. With these segments accounted for, if not tested in practice, the Royal Navy's fighter requirements were reduced to that of accompanying torpedo and strike/dive-bomber aircraft and driving off any reconnaissance aircraft. To meet

these requirements, the Fulmar was designed to incorporate two seats, the rear one for an observer/navigator/telegrapher. Note that the term 'gunner' is conspicious by its absence, as the rear seat occupant was already burdened with three jobs. In any case a good number of observers would have willingly taken on the gunnery duty as well if the designers had only had the foresight to include one or more guns for the rear seat. Thus it was that the observer was 'along for the ride' when the combat situation was at its worst. The pilot could not count on enemy fighters to avoid a direct stern attack.

With its several shortcomings, including lack of armour protection for the pilot, the Fulmar did give a good account of itself during the opening days of the war in the European theatre, accounting for 112 enemy aircraft shot down and 80 more damaged, which was about one third of the total Royal Navy victories.

Liquid-cooled engine

The Admiralty's preference for an air-cooled engine was not incorporated in the design, making the Fulmar one of the few aircraft designed for carrier operation that used liquid-cooled engines. As designs for the Fairey Barracuda were firmed up, it was proposed and accepted to use the same engine, the Rolls-Royce Merlin 30 in both the Barracuda and the Fulmar II. This was intended to reduce the maintenance parts problem, although no great performance gains resulted from the change.

In armament the Fulmar was equal to the Hawker Hurricane, having eight wing-mounted ·303 cal machine-guns which were impressive in number, but not in range. With the development of radar, the spacious rear cockpit made the Fulmar a logical plane for the Fleet Air Arm to use as a night fighter where its lack of speed would be less detrimental. In addition, the range of the Fulmar would allow it to remain airborne for five hours or more when fitted with auxiliary fuel tanks.

In combat service, the 15 Fulmars of 806 Squadron did provide air superiority for the Fleet operating in the eastern Mediterranean until they were overcome by Luftwaffe aircraft in early January 1941. In most of

Mitsubishi A5M4 'Claude'
This single-seat carrier fighter had fought over China and given Japanese Navy fighter pilots combat experience. Although obsolescent by 1941, the last 'Claudes' (the Allied code-name) were expended as Kamikaze suicide aircraft
Span: 36 ft 1 in *Length:* 24 ft 10 in
Engine: Nakajima Kotobuti 41, 785 hp at 9485 ft *Armament:* 2×7·7-mm mg *Max speed:* 252 mph at 6890 ft *Ceiling:* 32,150 ft *Range:* 746 miles

**Mitsubishi A6M5 Reisen
(Zero Fighter) 'Zeke'**
Universally known as the 'Zero', the potency of the A6M fleet fighter gave the Allies a shock during the Japanese onslaught of 1941 and 1942, but the A6M5, the final production version, was outclassed by the new generation of US carrier fighters from 1943
Span: 36 ft 1 in *Length:* 29 ft 11 in
Engine: Nakajima Sakae NK1F, 1100 hp at 9350 ft *Armament:* 2×7·7-mm mg; 2×20-mm cannon *Max speed:* 351 mph at 19,685 ft *Ceiling:* 38,520 ft *Range:* 1194 miles

the actions in which the Fulmars participated they accounted for more enemy planes down than they lost themselves. Considering relative performance, these results are quite remarkable and a tribute to the crews. Only one specimen is known to survive: NI 854, in the Fleet Air Arm Museum, RNAS Yeovilton, Somerset.

Rude awakening

Until the surprise attack on Pearl Harbor, the Mitsubishi A6M2 'Zero' was comparatively unknown even to the organisation most likely to encounter it, the US Navy. Although it had been reported by Gen Claire Chennault in 1940 after his 'Flying Tigers' had encountered a number of them over China, little effort was made to determine the capability of this new fighter. Even if an attempt had been made to learn more, it is quite unlikely that any results would have been forthcoming, for the Japanese were the most security conscious of nations at that time.

As a result of the lack of knowledge of the Zero, the Allies of the Pacific theatre, particularly the US, suffered a rude awakening by the attack at Pearl Harbor and the seeming invincibility of the onrushing Japanese war machine as it pushed steadily down the Asian Coast and through the islands of the western Pacific. Following these surprises, intelligence teams and engineering and military analysts groped for an explanation of this successful design. It was reputed to be a copy of the best features of the Vought V-143, the Hughes Racer and, possibly, one or two other aircraft for good measure.

The fact was that this, like any other plane of that date, was 'a copy of all that preceded it' according to the designer, Jiro Horikoshi, who had been assigned to lead the Mitsubishi design team. It was in fact an example of the state of the art when the Zero was designed. It could not be attributed to any one or more designs as a copy. Like the bee, the design team sampled many designs, taking the best and blending them to achieve the results required.

With the outbreak of hostilities between Japan and China in July 1937, the performance requirements increased as a result of combat experience. Specifications had

Associated Press

The slightly damaged USS Maryland *against a backdrop of smoke after the Pearl Harbor attack*

increased to such a degree that a Nakajima design team elected to concentrate on other projects, pulling out of the competition and leaving the project and problems with the Mitsubishi team. They succeeded to a remarkable degree and produced a plane that will be remembered along with the First World War Spad and Fokker D VII.

It was a classic and exceptionally fine compromise, as all aircraft designs must be. The design started with a compromise choice of engine, the 875 hp Mitsubishi Suisei 13 engine, although the designer favoured the larger, more powerful but heavier Mitsubishi Kinsei 40 engine. It wasn't until much later – too late – in the war that the Kinsei was to be adopted. Contrary to general belief, the lack of protective armour for the pilot was not an oversight, or a result of disregard for the crew, but a hard compromise choice dictated by the performance characteristics considered to be essential. The gamble almost paid dividends, for the Japanese had things pretty much their way at first and for several months until the Zero's weaknesses were found and exploited by the US pilots.

The Zero's first flight
The first prototype, the A6M1, made its first flight on 1 April 1939. Storm clouds were gathering in Europe and the US Exclusion Act of 1924 was still a very sore point with the Japanese, not so much because of its results but because it implied that Japan was less than a major international power.

The aircraft was officially designated Navy type 0 carrier fighter on 31 July 1940, and shot down its first enemy aircraft on 13 September 1940 when 13 planes flying over China surprised and downed 27 Polikarpov I-15s and I-16s without suffering any losses themselves. At this time General Claire Chennault, who was then reorganising the Chinese Air Force, advised his colleagues in the US of this new fighter, but his warning was either ignored or forgotten.

The high point of the A6M2's service was the Pearl Harbor attack of 7 December 1941 and the invasion of Wake Island soon after. There followed a succession of victories as the Japanese pushed further south, eventually attacking Port Darwin, Australia, on 15 February 1942, destroying eight Australian aircraft in air combat and an additional 15 on the ground – again without losses to themselves. Following this, the Japanese fleet under Admiral Nagumo headed for the Indian Ocean where they sank the British fleet units consisting of HMS *Dorsetshire,* HMS *Cornwall* and the carrier HMS *Hermes.*

The Japanese were now riding high on wings of victory, but at the same time the

Mitsubishi A6M2 Zero
Jiro Horishoki's brilliant fighter design first saw action in September 1940 when A6M2s destroyed 99 Chinese aircraft for the loss of 2 Zeros. The A6M2 was the model in service during the 1941–42 period of runaway Japanese victories
  Span: 39 ft 4 in *Length:* 29 ft 9 in
Engine: Nakajima NK1F Sakae 12,950 hp at 13,780 ft *Max speed:* 331 mph at 16,000 ft
Ceiling: 32,810 ft *Range:* 1160 miles
Armament: 2 × 20-mm cannon; 2 × 7·7-mm mg

USS Yorktown *listing heavily after a savage battering during the Battle of Midway. But her Dauntlesses had smashed two Japanese carriers*

Japanese force consisting of less than 200 Zeros leapfrogged its way through the Philippines and down the coast of Asia, concentrating on the defeat of a hodgepodge of obsolescent aircraft such as Brewster F2A Buffaloes, Curtiss CW-21Bs, Hawk 75s, P-40s and Hawker Hurricanes.

The Zero was built in a number of variants and model improvements including the A6M2, Zero (Zeke), A6M2-N (float fighter 'Rufe'), A6M2-K (two-seat trainer), A6M3 'Hamp' (Models 22 & 23) and A6M5 Zeke 52 which itself had a number of variations.

By mid 1943, the Zero and the Hamp had been surpassed by most Allied fighters yet they were always potent adversaries when flown by an experienced pilot. The Grumman F6F in particular and the Vought F4U were to provide air superiority over the Zeros.

Inevitable end

In one last desperate role, the A6M2s were used as Kamikaze weapons. Equipped with one 500-lb bomb, the Zeke was used in the much described spectacular attacks on US ships. While the A6M2 Kamikaze accounted for a high percentage of the attacks and actual hits, the effort was not worth the price, for the US attacks had reached a crescendo of such proportions and determination that, at best, the Kamikaze could only hope to delay the inevitable.

The Vought F4U Corsair was unique in several respects, one of the war's most versatile aircraft, an excellent fighter and a dive-bomber/attack plane. It was capable of lugging and delivering external ordnance loads up to a total of 4000 lb. It was this dual capability that reduced the requirement for additional dive-bombers and other specialised aircraft such as the Curtiss SB2Cs.

The Corsair was the first fighter to be powered by a 2000 hp engine, and in later configurations such as the Goodyear-built F2G was powered by the 3500 hp Pratt & Whitney R-4360 engine. To use this high power at high altitudes it was necessary to install a large, slow-turning propeller. To provide ground clearance for this propeller and still keep the landing gear short and rugged for arrested landings was a problem which was solved by the unusual bent wing configuration. The resulting wing position made unnecessary the extensive filleting usually required to smooth out the air flow at the juncture of the wing and fuselage. The short landing gear also served as a dive brake, with the added advantage of retracting backward into the wing.

This configuration improved pilot visibility on the approach and final leg of landing and when landing, the stall occurred in the trough of the gull close to the fuselage.

US was marshalling its military strength and heading for the Battle of the Coral Sea on 7/8 May 1942, the first battle ever to be fought entirely by aircraft with the surface ships out of sight of each other. It was at this point of the war that the tide began to turn. The Grumman F4Fs held the line and each carrier force had one carrier seriously damaged, and the Japanese lost the light carrier *Shoho*.

Shortly afterwards, on 3/4 June 1942, the Battle of Midway was underway. Again, the Zero extracted a heavy price, but this time the victims were mostly the TBDs which, through an error in timing, were left unprotected during their run. In turn, the Japanese paid an extremely heavy price with the loss of most of their carrier force and their complement of aircraft and crew was sadly depleted as well. These carrier losses included the *Kaga*, *Akagi* and *Soryu*, and the *Hiryu* which was set afire, but not before her aircraft crippled the *Yorktown*.

In connection with this battle, a diversionary attack was made on the Aleutians during which one Zero was forced to land due to fuel loss. Though wrecked on landing in a bog and killing the pilot, this Zero was to play an important role. Salvaged and restored to flying condition, it was thoroughly tested at Anacostia and North Island Naval Air Stations, and its strong and weak points documented. With this final bit of technical intelligence, the US aircraft industry was able to finalise the design of aircraft then in production, notably the Grumman F6F Hellcat and the Vought F4U Corsair. The Hellcat was, in fact, the first fighter designed specifically to gain mastery over the Zero. Despite the fact that the Zero had been improved, it was no match for a plane built right from the start to conquer it.

With the Japanese carrier fleet no longer a threat, the remaining Zeros were forced to operate from land bases, where they distinguished themselves and their crews by having their endurance and that of their pilots developed to a degree that amazed everyone. During the first year of the war a

A Japanese Zero assembled from parts of five Zeros shot down in the battle for Buna airstrip. Information about the Zero's performance was vital to Allied pilots in their fight against it

US Air Force

Imperial War Museum

Chance-Vought F4U-7 Corsair
Earning a legendary reputation during the
Second World War, the ungainly Corsair was
still fighting over Indo-China in 1954 flown by
pilots of the French Navy Air Force
Span: 40 ft 11 in *Length:* 30 ft 8 in
Engine: Pratt & Whitney R-2800-18W Double
Wasp, 2000 hp at 1500 ft *Max speed:* 415 mph
at 19,500 ft *Ceiling:* 34,500 ft *Range:* 1562
miles *Armament:* 4×·5-in mg *Bombload:*
2×1000-lb bombs

The added advantage of this wing design was
that the folding point of the wing was also
located at the low point of the trough,
making it possible to maintain the low
clearance for the hydraulically actuated
folding system to be operated in the confined
spaces aboard carriers. Because of less
headroom aboard British carriers, the wing
tips of Corsairs assigned to the Royal Navy
were shortened by removal of eight inches
from each wing tip resulting in a squared
off wing tip and a slightly higher stalling
speed – but little else was changed.

The structure of the F4U was simplified by
using large single panels whenever possible
and fabricating these by arc welding whenever practical. One unusual feature was the
rather generous use of fabric in a plane of
this late date.

Veterans of the Second World War will
readily recall the distinctive sounds of
aircraft which caused instinctive reactions
among ground crews and particularly anti-
aircraft gunners and troops in the front
lines. The engine exhaust, propeller or
cooling system produced distinctive sounds
which inspired fear or exhilaration. In the
case of the Corsair, the whistling sound
generated by the wing root air intakes was
so pronounced that enemy troops referred
to it as 'Whistling Death', for it extracted
a high price in air combat and an even
greater one among the ground troops in its
role as an attack plane, bombing, launching
rockets and strafing.

Because of its rather unconventional
appearance it was also known by US and
Allied personnel as the 'Bent-wing Bird'.
With the exception of the Stuka and the
Grace, there was no other Second World
War aircraft with this unusual wing con-
figuration.

The Corsair had a prolonged adolescence.
While it was designed for carrier operation,
a variety of idiosyncrasies, including a
bounce when landing aboard carriers, kept
it from its intended role until 1944, although
the first 22 F4Us had been proclaimed
combat-ready as early as December 1942.
In spite of its early rejection from carrier
qualification it was operated by Marine
and Navy squadrons VMF 124 and VF 17
from land bases, establishing a victory/loss
ratio of better than 11 to 1.

The first action in which Corsairs took
part was to escort Consolidated PB4Y-1,
single-finned Navy Liberators, all the way

Fleet Air Arm Corsair II fighters in echelon formation. The type provided cover for the Tirpitz *raids*

National Maritime Museum

Side View of FG-1D Corsair
Goodyear-built FG-1D (the classification changed with a different maker) of 2nd Marine Air Division

Mitsubishi A7M2 Reppu (Hurricane) 'Sam'
Conceived as a replacement for the A6M Zero, with armour plate and self-sealing fuel tanks, the Reppu's production was strangled by earthquakes and B-29 raids and none saw action
Span: 45 ft 11 in *Length:* 36 ft 1 in
Engine: Mitsubishi MK9A, 1800 hp at 19,685 ft
Armament: 2×13·2-mm mg; 2×20-mm cannon
Max speed: 390 mph at 21,665 ft *Ceiling:* 35,760 ft *Range:* 2·5 hr cruising plus 30 min combat

to Bougainville, a task which had been impossible for the Grumman F4Fs. The new pilots got a thorough baptism of fire the next day when, together with an array of Liberators, P-40s and P-38s, they were attacked by 50 Zeros with a loss of two each of Liberators and P-40s and four P-38s. From this inauspicious beginning the tables turned, for the Corsairs completed their war service with the destruction of 2140 enemy aircraft in air combat against a loss of only 189.

In addition to daytime combat, the F4U was successfully adapted to night fighter duties by the use of a radar antenna pod mounted near the tip of the starboard wing. The night fighter group operated on a fire alarm basis, moving about the combat zone as the need arose.

In spite of its weight, the Corsair was more than a match for any aircraft that the Japanese had available and in simulated combat tests it proved superior to any other plane in the US service at that time. Of the 9418 Corsairs produced, Vought produced 4669 with the two subcontractors, Goodyear and Brewster, producing 4014 and 735 respectively. In service they were assigned to 19 Marine squadrons, a total of 6255 planes, and 19 squadrons of the Royal Navy (1977), many of which had the modified wing tips. In addition to the above

services, the Royal New Zealand Air Force acquired 425 during the war.

After the end of hostilities a number were allocated to various South American countries and to the air forces of a number of smaller nations, where they served well. Fortunately, a number of Corsairs of various modifications are still retained in museums around the world.

The Japanese name of Reppu (Violent Wind) was given to the Mitsubishi A7M1 in advance of its actual testing, which accounts for the misnomer. It was in fact a great disappointment in speed and climbing

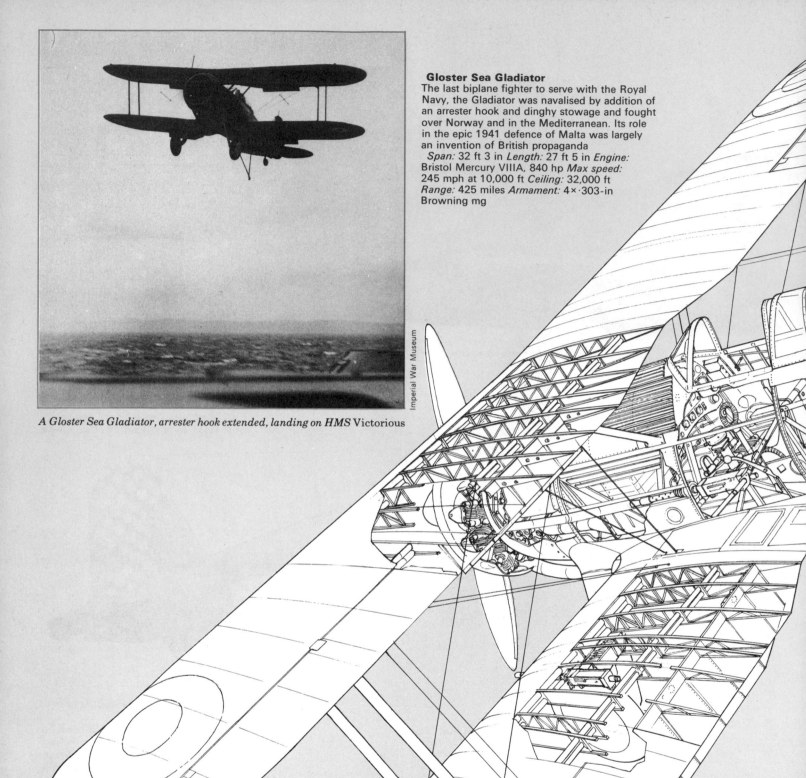

Imperial War Museum

A Gloster Sea Gladiator, arrester hook extended, landing on HMS Victorious

Gloster Sea Gladiator

The last biplane fighter to serve with the Royal Navy, the Gladiator was navalised by addition of an arrester hook and dinghy stowage and fought over Norway and in the Mediterranean. Its role in the epic 1941 defence of Malta was largely an invention of British propaganda
Span: 32 ft 3 in *Length:* 27 ft 5 in *Engine:* Bristol Mercury VIIIA, 840 hp *Max speed:* 245 mph at 10,000 ft *Ceiling:* 32,000 ft *Range:* 425 miles *Armament:* 4 × ·303-in Browning mg

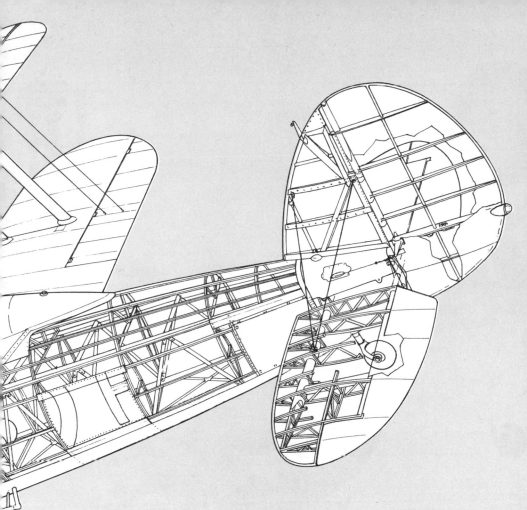

ability, both of which were intended to surpass the A6M Zero's capability. The main reason was the change in power plant from the Mitsubishi Mk 9A engine of 2100 hp to the more readily available Nakajima Homare of 1800 hp.

In addition the A7M1' was to have the qualities which the Zero lacked – greater firepower and armour – while retaining its desirable features, including carrier equipment. The resulting performance was so bad (347·5 mph max), that production was suspended in August 1944. A second model, A7M2, was completed in October, this time using the original engine. Maximum speed was 390 mph, 10 mph less than the specifications called for, but sufficient to result in a production order on an accelerated basis. In December 1944, the Nagoya industrial area where the A7M2s were under construction was hit by the double blow of an earthquake and intense B-29 raids, which disrupted production to the extent that only eight Reppus had been completed by the end of hostilities and none had reached operational status.

The last biplane fighter

The Gloster Sea Gladiator was a naval modification of the RAF's last biplane fighter. The outbreak of war in 1939 caught the Fleet Air Arm with these remnants of the biplane era. Though procurement thinking had changed to monoplanes, few if any were actually available. The Fairey Fulmars and Blackburn Skuas were rushed as an intermediate step into the monoplane era. The Sea Gladiator did not phase out in peacetime, however, for it did provide effective cover for the Fairey Swordfish during the Norwegian campaign. Fortunately, one of these may be retrieved from a Norwegian lake, which should have provided excellent preservation treatment in contrast to those forced down at sea.

By the latter part of 1940 all remaining Gladiators had been withdrawn in favour of the Skua. Its construction was aluminium, with surfaces and parts of the fuselage fabric covered.

Stubby and manoeuvrable in comparison with its contemporary Grumman F4F Wildcat/Martlet, the Brewster F2A Buffalo did see action in the defence of Crete and against the Japanese in the Dutch East Indies, as well as over Cairo, Rangoon, Burma and Singapore – and in the Battle of Midway where US Marine Squadron VMF 221 used 20 F2A Buffalos and 7 Grumman F4F-3s based on Midway itself. The loss of 13 Buffalos to the more manoeuvrable Zeros ended the career of the Buffalo.

Brewster F2A Buffalo
This diminutive, underpowered American fighter flew from British carriers as a stopgap measure during the defence of Crete in March 1941. Very few served with the US Navy
Span: 35 ft *Length:* 26 ft *Engine:* Wright Cyclone, 1200 hp *Max speed:* 313 mph at 13,500 ft *Ceiling:* 30,500 ft *Range:* 650 miles *Armament:* 2×·5-in mg

Fairey Firefly I
Combining the roles of fighter and long-range
reconnaissance aircraft, and fitted with folding
wings and full naval equipment, the Firefly was
one of the most complex fighters of its day
  Span: 44 ft 6 in *Length:* 37 ft 7 in
Engine: Rolls-Royce Griffon IIB, 1490 hp at
14,000 ft *Max speed:* 315 mph at 16,500 ft
Ceiling: 30,100 ft *Range:* 850 miles *Crew:* 2
Armament: 4×20-mm cannon *Bombload:* 2000 lb

Imperial War Museum

A formation of US Navy Grumman Hellcats, the type that replaced the Wildcat at war against the Zero

Grumman F6F Hellcat
Based on the Wildcat formula, but incorporating
the lessons of combat experience, the Hellcat's
speed and climb were excellent and it could
outmatch the Zero in a dogfight
  Span: 42 ft 10 in *Length:* 33 ft 6 in
Engine: Pratt & Whitney R-2800-10, 2000 hp at
1000 ft *Max speed:* 371 mph at 18,700 ft
Ceiling: 35,000 ft *Range:* 1495 miles
Armament: 6×·5-in mg plus 2×1000-lb bombs

The Buffalo had the unique distinction of winning the US Navy design competition against the Grumman F4F and still falling by the wayside. Production was not one of the Brewster Company's strong points, either with the Buffalo and Buccaneer/Bermuda of their own design or when they were called upon as a second source for the Vought F4U/F3A.

The US Navy found the Buffalo particularly susceptible to deck landing damage due to a weakness in the landing gear. As a result, the Grumman Wildcat superseded the Buffalo to become the standard carrier fighter of both the US Navy and the Fleet Air Arm until the Vought F4U and Grumman F6F replaced them.

In comparative tests with the Hurricane I, the Buffalo was slightly more manoeuvrable but slower to accelerate in a dive. Though designed for carrier operation, when sold to the British it was found to be one foot too large in wing span and could not be accommodated on carrier elevators. Instead it was used in the Near East over Cairo, where the fine silt was less harmful to the air-cooled radial engine than it had been to other planes' close tolerance liquid-cooled engines.

Other features which prevented it from assignment to serious combat were lack of firepower (the Buffalo had two ·50 cal and two ·30 cal machine-guns) and of armour plate, which was neither thick enough nor large enough. These were its major failings, its other deficiencies being sufficient to relegate it to training missions or desperation defence requirements.

A two-seat fighter/reconnaissance aircraft, the Fairey Firefly was built to a requirement dating back to the mid-1920s and as a replacement for the stop-gap Fairey Fulmar, which served well if not spectacularly during the early part of the war.

The war was well under way in Europe and the US was recovering from the shock of Pearl Harbor, the complete tally of the disaster not yet fully appreciated, when the Firefly prototype was first flown on 22 December 1941. While resembling the Fulmar in general plan and profile – making it hard to differentiate between them at a distance – the Firefly was, aerodynamically, an improvement, while the substitution of the 1730 hp R-R Griffon II B and later the 1990 hp Griffon XII did much to improve the performance with an immediate 40 mph increase in top speed.

Along with the increased performance, the armament was changed from the eight ·303 cal guns of the Fulmar to the four 20-mm cannon of the Firefly. The wing plan form adopted was quite similar to that of the graceful, elliptical wings of the Supermarine Spitfire. Were it not for the generous expanse of clear glass aft of the wing, the Firefly might easily have been mistaken for the Spitfire. The Firefly got a comparatively late start, but by the end of 1946 over 950 Mk 1s and night fighter modifications had been built, over 800 of them by the Fairey plants. The remainder were built by General Aircraft Company.

The Firefly distinguished itself in action in the Far East as an attack plane launching rockets against important targets such as the oil refineries in Sumatra in January 1945, effectively knocking out the major source of petroleum products for Japanese ships and aircraft. Earlier attempts by British Engineers to destroy refinery storage tanks during the retreat from the Malay Peninsula resulted in amusing and embarrassing results when the high octane fuel refused to burn. The intensity of fumes snuffed out attempts to ignite it with any of the normal – and some far from normal – forms of incendiary materials.

Night fighter Firefly

One of the principal variants of the Firefly Mk 1 was that of night fighter. As in the case of the Fulmar, the spacious rear cockpit was quite adequate for the radar equipment; however, the early forms of radome successfully cluttered up the otherwise clean aerodynamics, resulting in lower speeds, and the weight of the early radar equipment altered the centre of gravity, making it necessary to move the engine 18 inches forward to compensate. This combination of pilot and radar operator is practically standard for current combat aircraft including fighters. The radar/counter measures crew member in currently operational fighters is regarded as essential to the performance and safety of the aircraft. In the days of the Firefly, however, the second crew member was a definite obstacle to high performance in an aircraft when compared with the single-seat, single-engined contemporaries. Its top speed was 316 mph, only slightly greater than that of the Brewster Buffalo, whose every

performance was surpassed rather quickly and early in the war.

During the preliminaries to the sinking of the German battleship *Tirpitz*, the Firefly was used to attack auxiliary ships and silence anti-aircraft gun emplacements in preparation for the battleship's destruction by RAF Lancasters.

The Grumman F6F Hellcat, successor to the F4F Wildcat/Martlet, was built in the Grumman tradition of robust, rugged structure with good flight control characteristics and, in this case, performance adequate to gain air superiority over the Japanese Zero.

During the first 16 months of the Pacific War, the Wildcat was on its own and did a remarkable job considering that normal terms of measurement would have shown it to be inferior to its enemy, the Zero. The brutish Hellcat was designed to remedy the situation with speed and climb ability superior to the Zero's. It was the first plane built after Pearl Harbor and incorporated the features demanded by Navy pilots allowing them to initiate ·or break off combat at their choosing.

Grumman F8F Bearcat
The Bearcat appeared too late to see combat, but had brought the Grumman fighter design precepts to perfection. Lighter than the Hellcat by 3000 lb, its superior performance was gained at the expense of firepower
  Span: 35 ft 6 in *Length:* 28 ft *Engine:* Pratt & Whitney R-2800-22W Double Wasp, 2100 hp at take-off *Max speed:* 424 mph at 17,300 ft *Ceiling:* 33,700 ft *Range:* 955 miles *Armament:* 4 × ·5-in mg *Bombload:* 2000 lb or 4 × 5-in rockets

The results of tests on the Zero forced down in the Aleutians established the design parameters for the Hellcat which was then being designed. It was, in fact, designed to better the performance of the Zero as its primary mission. That reserves in structural strength were there also was important but almost of secondary importance at this time.

Like its sister-ship on the Grumman production lines, the TBF Avenger, the Hellcat was big and spacious inside and of simplified rugged structure to ensure ease of production and maintenance aboard carriers. Carrying this simplification further, the wings were folded manually with the locking pins operated hydraulically from the cockpit and made safe by manually controlled lock pins. For stowage aboard ship the wings were rotated about the front spar and then folded backward alongside the fuselage, leading-edge downward, like those of the Wildcat and the Avenger.

The landing gear rotated 90° as it retracted rearward, like that of the Curtiss P-40 and Vought F4U. Cover plates smoothed over the wheels and struts when fully retracted. When in the extended position, a cover plate at the upper end of the gear leg added to the drag produced by the gear. The six ·50 cal machine-guns were mounted in the panels just outboard of the line where the wings broke for folding.

The fuselage was a semimonocoque structure with rings and stringers, covered by stressed skin. Adequate armour plate was installed for pilot protection and a turn-over structure was incorporated as well.

Performance had been improved, with the speed 60 mph faster than the F4Fs. Range was increased and the ammunition carried was 400 rounds per gun – nearly doubling the capacity of the F4F. Most important, the Hellcat could be flown and flown well by the inexperienced pilots who were then coming into combat theatres fresh from the training centres.

The first flight of the XF6F-3 took place in July 1942 and the first full squadron of Hellcats was delivered by December of the same year. The F4F and the TBF production was farmed out to General Motors where the designation was changed to FM-1 and TBM, but little else changed as production continued unabated. Fourteen months from design to production was a record of which Grumman could be proud and one that instilled pride in the workers for the esprit de corps of Grumman employees was the envy of the other wartime manufacturers, especially their neighbour, Brewster.

The first combat flown in F6Fs was a VF 5 flight, in support of the strike aircraft from Task Force 15, consisting of *Essex*, light carrier *Independence* and the second *Yorktown* in their attack on the Marcus Islands on 31 August 1943. Numerous encounters further endeared the Hellcat to its pilots and improved their skills for the big battles just over the horizon. The Battle of the Philippine Sea, 19-20 June 1944 (known as the 'Marianas Turkey Shoot'), was one of the most decisive battles of the war. On 19 June aircraft of Task Force 58 destroyed 402 enemy aircraft, and by 10 August carrier aircraft had sunk 110,000 tons of enemy ships and destroyed 1223 enemy aircraft.

Staggering losses
The date, 20 June, was memorable for other reasons. In a dusk battle at extreme range, Task Force 58 lost 104 aircraft out of 216 launched. Of the Hellcats six were lost in the vicinity of the Japanese fleet of Admiral Ozawa, while 17 splashed down with dry tanks on the way home. The dive-bombers (SB2C – Helldiver) and torpedo bombers (TBF – Avenger) lost 60% or more of their planes over the target or en route back to Task Force 58. This battle and the Battle of Leyte Gulf, 23-26 October, resulted in 1046 enemy aircraft destroyed during the month of October and another 770 during November. The staggering losses in planes and aircraft carriers, as well as other surface ships, spelled the end of the once powerful Japanese carrier aviation.

In all these battles the Hellcat played an important role in protecting the strike force and defending the massed US carrier force against the determined and suicidal attacks of the Japanese carrier pilots.

The Hellcat also found favour with the Fleet Air Arm and was used extensively in Atlantic operation, notably from HMS *Emperor*, which carried out anti-shipping attacks along the Norwegian coast and provided fighter cover during eight attacks on the German battleship *Tirpitz* from April to August of 1944. Most of the Fleet Air Arm action took place in the Pacific where the F6F-5 (Hellcat II) was the standard. All told, the Royal Navy used over 1260 Hellcats. It was designed to do a job well and, by any standard, it succeeded.

The Hawker Sea Hurricane ('Hurricat' or 'Catafighter') was used as a stopgap measure when the German submarine and long-range Focke Wulf Fw 200 Condor became a menace in early 1941. The age of the Hurricane design made it unwise to expend design and fabrication effort to develop folding wings. Therefore, the plane was used as it was by catapulting it off CAM (Catapult Armed Merchantmen) ships. Each flight ended in a ducking for the pilot and loss of the aircraft, which probably accounts for the fact that only one Hurricane I is known to exist of all those that fought in or during the Battle of Britain. This one remaining Hurricane is on exhibition in the Science Museum in London.

The only situation where plane and pilot were recovered was during training, in port, or possibly when the convoy of which the CAM ship was a part was within range of land. Otherwise the normal method was for the pilot to take to his parachute and Mae West life preserver, hopefully to be picked up by ships of the convoy after the danger of attack was passed.

In addition to the CAM operation, a number of Hurricane IBs were adapted to operate from carriers by reinforcing the airframe to permit catapulting, and addition of an arrester hook. A number of variants were introduced with the addition of four 20-mm cannon mounted in the universal wing and, with a change in engine to the Merlin XX, these became Hurricane IICs.

Fleet Air Arm pilots originally flew the Hurricats off the CAMs but later were relieved by RAF pilots who well remember the shock of the catapult launching.

Of the carrier-based Sea Hurricanes, some were assigned to the CAM escort carrier HMS *Avenger* on the Russian Convoy PQ 18 to Murmansk, after the previous Convoy, PQ 17, which was without air cover, was pounded continuously en route by German aircraft based in Norway and Finland. On this convoy, the Sea Hurricanes accounted for five German aircraft destroyed and 17 more damaged with a loss of one pilot and four Hurricanes. They were to give a good account of themselves for some time, taking part in the defence of Malta and escorting convoys as late as August 1942 and during the North African Torch landings on 8–11 November 1942. By this time replacement aircraft, Seafires and Grumman F6F Hellcats, were being placed aboard the carriers. The remaining Sea Hurricanes were stripped of their sea-going gear and returned to land duties.

The Supermarine Seafire was a well-tried and proven design modified to naval operating standards. The rather unusual configuration of the Seafire III, when the wings were folded for storage aboard carriers, led to the nickname of 'Praying Mantis'. The tips were folded downwards at the wing tip joint at the outboard aileron gap; then the main panels, outboard of the coolant radiators, were folded upward to form an almost equilateral triangle. The main panels were unbolted by unscrewing locking bolts inside the wheel wells. The wings were supported in their folded position by tele-

scoping tubes which were normally stored in lateral slots in the upper wing surface. Folding was accomplished by a three or four man crew and reduced the original span to 13 ft 4 in, which was 23 ft less than the unfolded span of 36 ft 10 in.

Earlier Seafires made do with the non-folding standard Spitfire wing as most of them were conversions of existing standard models. Seafires were used extensively, taking over from the Sea Hurricanes in 1941 after it was shown that fast, single-engined, single-place fighters were needed aboard carriers and in naval operations.

On the offensive

The first operational use of the Seafire was from HMS *Furious*, *Formidable* and *Argus* flying in support of Operation Torch, the Allied landings in North Africa on 8–11 November 1942. Then, on 10 July 1943 the Seafires took to the offensive again, flying from HMS *Furious* and *Indomitable* in support of the Allied landings in Sicily. During this campaign, which lasted until 18 August, Allied airmen lost 274 planes and accounted for 1691 enemy aircraft.

Operation Avalanche, the invasion of the Italian mainland, began on 2 September. Fleet Air Arm squadrons operating from the escort carriers *Attacker*, *Battler*, *Hunter*, *Stalker* and *Unicorn* provided the total air cover for the beachhead during the early stages of this engagement. For the landing troops, the low wind velocity experienced was a pleasure since sea sickness was minimised but the Seafire pilots operating from

A Seafire Mk XV touches down aboard the Pretoria Castle. *Note the sting-type arrester hook*

the Jeep carriers soon realised that the maximum speed for the CVEs, about 17–18 mph, was not the best speed for the take-off and landing of the Seafire. During these hectic days amid low wind conditions a number of Seafires were damaged during deck operations, usually landings, when they came in too fast and tore the arrester hook from the aircraft.

The Seafires continued to serve well, flying top cover for the attacks on the *Tirpitz* and whenever their presence was needed, whether from shore or carrier base. The last action for the Seafires in the European theatre was in the Aegean Sea area during the latter part of 1944.

Meanwhile, in the Pacific theatre, the Seafires found themselves at a disadvantage, for ranges (or endurance) which had been quite acceptable in the European theatre were not adequate in the broad expanse of the Pacific. The normal two-hour endurance of the Seafire limited its usefulness as well as that of its carriers. The decision was made to retire the Seafires in favour of the F6F Hellcats and F4U Corsairs after nearly 1700 Seafires had been built or converted.

Although the Seafire was without a doubt the finest low-level fighter produced by the Allies, its range, firepower and ordnance capabilities did not match those of the later developed Hellcat and Corsair that had been designed from the outset for long endurance, heavy firepower and incredible ordnance capacity. These same features eventually made redundant such specially designed dive-bombers as the Curtiss SB2C.

A Hawker Hurricane 1A being catapulted from a Catapult Armed Merchantman (CAM ship). The Hurricane provided valuable cover for Atlantic and Arctic convoys. Each mission meant the loss of the plane, but the Hurricane was becoming obsolescent, and was unsuitable for conversion to a proper carrier plane. Mk 1B specifications: Span: 40 ft Length: 31 ft 5 in Engine: Rolls-Royce Merlin II, 1310 hp Max Speed: 298 mph at 16,400 ft Ceiling: 30,000 ft Armament: 8 × ·303 mg

Supermarine Seafire Mk III
A straightforward adaptation of the Spitfire, fitted with arrester hook and catapult spools, the Mk III had double-jointed folding wings (inset) to clear the low hangar ceilings typical of British aircraft carriers
Span: 36 ft 8 in *Length:* 30 ft *Engine:* Rolls-Royce Merlin 55, 1470 hp *Armament:* 4×·303-in mg; 4×20 mm cannon plus 1×500-lb or 2×250-lb bombs *Speed* 342 mph at 20,700 ft *Ceiling:* 37,500 ft *Range:* 508 miles

National Maritime Museum

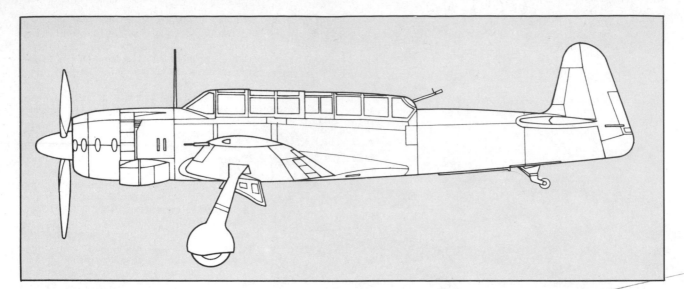

Nakajima C6N1 Sauiun (Painted Cloud) 'Myrt'
Conceived exclusively as a carrier reconnaissance aircraft, the C6N was a very effective fleet shadower, its range and speed (almost equal to those of the Hellcat) making it almost immune to interception
Span: 41 ft *Length:* 36 ft 1 in *Engine:* Nakajima NK9H Homare, 1600 hp at 6560 ft
Armament: 1×7·92-mm mg *Max speed:* 379 mph at 20,015 ft *Max range:* 3300 miles

Airspeed Fleet-Shadower Prototype
Built just before the Second World War but never put into production, the type was conceived as a means of extending a task force's range. With an 8-hour endurance and speed of only 45 knots, the type could pace an enemy fleet, but its extreme vulnerability, and the fact that aircraft already in service could do the job made it somewhat redundant

Curtiss SOC-2 Seagull
Built originally as a catapult floatplane, the
Seagull served aboard every carrier, battleship
and cruiser in the US Fleet during its career.
The SOC-2 was a landplane version and the
SOC-3 had interchangeable floats or wheel
undercarriage
 Span: 36 ft *Length:* 26 ft 6 in *Engine:* Pratt &
Whitney Wasp *Max speed:* 168 mph
Ceiling: 14,900 ft *Range:* 891 miles
Armament: 2×·30-in mg

MISCELLANEOUS TYPES
TRY HARDS AND TRAINERS

Among the aircraft intended for carrier use
and fitted with arrester hooks was the
Curtiss SO3C Seagull which was originally
designed as a catapult-launched observation aircraft. Fitting a fixed landing gear
of narrow tread to enable it to land aboard
carriers or on land did little to improve its
worth or acceptability. The instability of
wheel gear dissuaded pilots of both the US
Navy and British Fleet Air Arm (where it
was known as the Seamew) from using this
aircraft type. It is doubtful whether these
were ever carried or operated from carriers.
They were used to train radio operators and
gunners and as radio-controlled targets.
One unusual feature was the use of an air-
cooled 12 cylinder inverted V engine, the
Ranger SGV-770-6.

   Also intended for carrier use were the
aircraft designed to specifications as Fleet
Shadowers. These aircraft, Airspeed 39 and
General Aircraft Ltd 38, were designed to
meet Air Ministry specifications S23/27 for

carrier operation to shadow enemy fleets
during the night. Such activity was thought
to require slow speeds and long endurance.
As events developed, other aircraft normally carried by the carriers for scouting,
bombing and fighting could accomplish the
same mission, working in relays from
carriers or from shore bases. These were
preferred to the extremely vulnerable, slow
and underpowered Fleet Shadower.

Relegated to training
Finally, there were several aircraft that
mercifully did not get into serious combat
action, for the events which unfolded during
the early stages of the war would have made
their use suicidal. Two of these were the
Curtiss SBC-4 Helldiver biplanes, known as
Clevelands in France and Britain, which
were on their way to France during the first
days of the war and were unloaded in Martinique when France capitulated in June
1940; and the Vought SB2U-1 Vindicator,

Curtiss SBC-4 Helldiver
The last combat biplanes to be manufactured in
the USA, 186 SBCs were on strength with the
US Navy and Marine Air Corps at the time of
Pearl Harbor, although none saw action.
  Span: 34 ft *Length:* 27 ft 6 in *Engine:* Wright
R-1820-34 radial, 950 hp *Max speed:* 237 mph
at 15,200 ft *Ceiling:* 27,300 ft *Range:* 555 miles
Armament: 2×·30-in mg *Bombload:* 1000 lb

a monoplane dive-bomber known in the Fleet Air Arm as the Chesapeake. Those received by the Fleet Air Arm were aircraft taken over from the French purchase orders. Though they were issued to several naval squadrons they were quickly relegated to training duties since their unassisted take-off distance was too great for the escort-carriers. A number served with US Marine squadrons aboard the *Lexington*.

For reconnaissance purposes, the Japanese felt the need for a long-range/long-endurance aircraft similar to the British Fleet Shadower specifications. However, the Japanese knew that the answer would not be in the form of a 'low and slow' aircraft as was the concept of the Fleet Shadower. Instead, a design specification was laid down for a fast three-seat, low-wing monoplane, the Nakajima C6N1 'Myrt', which could do its scouting at longe range and, when the Hellcats and Corsairs swarmed out of the carrier hive, escape to fight again. Emphasis was placed on speed to such a degree that the Myrt could almost equal if not outrun a F6F.

While the Myrt was used during the Battle of the Marianas, the heavy loss of Japanese carriers during this battle forced these and other carrier types to use land bases.

As the war progressed, the necessity of throwing everything into combat became more pressing. As a result the Myrt was fitted to drop torpedoes and a number were converted to handle the jobs of night fighters when the frequency and intensity of B-29 raids increased over the home islands. The unconventional installation of a pair of 20-mm Type 99 cannon mounted obliquely in the fuselage eliminated one crew position from the normal three-man crew.

The first flight of the Myrt was in May 1943. During the remainder of the war, attempts were made to improve the altitude performance by fitting various engines with higher power ratings. Experimentation with these modifications was still underway when hostilities ceased. Like the Jill, the Myrt had a distinctive forward rake to the vertical fin and rudder to enable the plane to be accommodated on the elevators aboard the carrier. The only known survivor of the Myrt class is in the study collection of the National Air & Space Museum of the Smithsonian Institution.

Vought-Sikorsky SB2U-1 Vindicator
Known as 'Vibrators' by their Marine crews, the SB2 was one of the US Navy's first monoplane types. Some Vindicators were still in service during the Battle of Midway
Span: 42 ft *Length:* 33 ft 11 in *Engine:* Pratt & Whitney SB4-G, 750 hp *Max speed:* 257 mph at 11,000 ft *Ceiling:* 28,200 ft *Range:* 700 miles *Armament:* 5 mg *Bombload:* 1500 lb bombs

TORPEDOES
FOR LETTING IN WATER

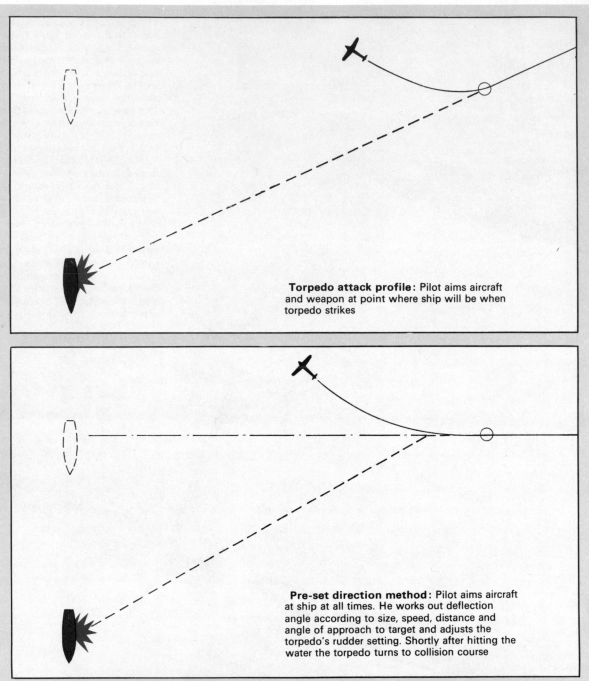

Torpedo attack profile: Pilot aims aircraft and weapon at point where ship will be when torpedo strikes

Pre-set direction method: Pilot aims aircraft at ship at all times. He works out deflection angle according to size, speed, distance and angle of approach to target and adjusts the torpedo's rudder setting. Shortly after hitting the water the torpedo turns to collision course

US Mk 13 Airborne Torpedo
A development of the original Whitehead torpedo, with vastly improved range and speed. Fully developed, the Mk 13 could deliver 600 lb of explosive at better than 40 knots over ranges of several miles. Thirteen feet long, with a 22·42-in diameter, the torpedo weighed about a ton. The steering mechanism and 700 hp steam engine were located in the rear of the torpedo, compressed air, fuel and water tanks in the middle, and the explosive in the nose

Imperial War Museum

The USS California *settles low in the water amid clouds of smoke after being torpedoed at Pearl Harbor*

Probably the most effective airborne anti-shipping weapon is the torpedo. The earliest known success with a torpedo dropped from a plane was in the Gallipoli campaign in the autumn of 1915, when two Short torpedo bombers carrying 14-in (diameter) torpedoes succeeded in sinking two ships, one a 5000-ton supply ship. The only basic differences between airborne torpedoes and the original torpedo designed by Robert Whitehead for the Austrian Navy in 1862 were a more precise directional gyro and improved propulsion systems.

Against the Whitehead torpedo's speed of 6 knots and range of several hundred yards, its Second World War counterpart had a speed of 30 knots and a range of over 4000 yards. In view of the experience gained in naval battles in the Pacific, notably the Battle of Midway, the all-round performance of the US Mk 13 torpedo was improved to the point where speeds exceeded 40 knots and combat ranges were increased to several miles. The latest development also included target-seeking capability and proximity fuse exploders. Moreover, the torpedoes could be dropped at up to 300 knots and from altitudes approaching 1000 ft.

The earlier US airborne torpedoes, such as the 18-in diameter Mk 7, required that the pilot fly a very precise attitude and altitude of about 50 feet at the instant of drop. To do otherwise could destroy the torpedo by breaking its back, or cause it to skip on impact with the surface of the water. Experience with the earlier torpedoes led to the development of a torpedo tailored to the aircraft's conditions and limitations.

The US Navy developed the Mk 13 as an aircraft torpedo and then adapted it for use on the PT torpedo boats as well, since its rugged construction was well suited to the severe conditions encountered by these high-speed boats. It was, in effect, a miniature submarine designed to carry a sizeable quantity (600 lb) of high explosive and detonate it against an enemy ship. If placed well, the torpedo could burst the plates of a battleship, but only if exploded below the protective armour belt which surrounded the hull at the waterline. To ensure maximum destructive capability, the depth settings ranged from 2–3 ft for shallow draught barge-type shipping to 10 ft for destroyers, cruisers or submarines on the surface and about 22 ft for battleships and aircraft carriers. When proximity fuses were used, the depth would be somewhat greater, causing the torpedo to explode under the ship to do the most damage.

The Mk 13 in its developed form weighed a little over one ton, and was powered by a very compact engine which developed about 700 hp to drive the torpedo at speeds in excess of 30 knots. The US favoured rotary engines, while European manufacturers preferred reciprocating engines with pistons displaced radially around the shaft. Though not used extensively, the Germans developed an electric motor which was claimed to be over 95% efficient and, more important, did not leave a trail of air bubbles to mark its course.

Limited usefulness

The 18-in US Mk 7 torpedoes were tried but attained only limited success as was the case with the 21-in Mk 14 and Mk 15 torpedoes. The Mk 14 was developed for use in submarines and the Mk 15 for use on destroyers. Both these types were 21 ft long and weighed about 1½ tons each, which limited their usefulness to larger patrol bombers such as the Catalina flying boats. The Mk 13 was much shorter, 13 ft long, slightly larger in diameter (22·42 in), and weighed about one ton. In addition, the Mk 13 required several attachments to make it operate successfully. To complete the torpedo for air drop, an air stabiliser, a plywood box-shaped fin, was fitted outside of the shroud ring which surrounded the counter-rotating propellers. The second accessory was a drag ring or blunt nose which was also made of wood and dubbed a 'pickle barrel'. This was fitted to the nose of the torpedo to take the initial shock of entry into the water and also to prevent skipping. Both of these fractured on impact with the water and dropped away. In the event that the torpedo was not housed inside the aircraft, as in the case of the TBDs, Barracudas and Swordfish, a streamlined cap was added forward of the pickle barrel drag rig. This cap pulled off at the time the torpedo was dropped.

In addition to the very precise driving mechanism, an extremely intricate guidance system was required to withstand the shock of launching and still keep it on course and at the required depth. The main charge was not easily exploded by impact. It was necessary therefore to add an exploder. Unfortunately, the mechanical impact exploder used on early models was a very temperamental device and caused a number of otherwise good hits to be wasted.

Early in the war these exploders were mechanically similar to bomb fuses and were not as reliable in operation as development and production costs would lead one to expect. Later versions set off a detonator of fulminate of mercury at the time of impact. The explosion of this detonator set off a booster charge which in turn ignited the main charge. In addition to the standard exploders, a magnetic proximity fuse was developed similar to those used for artillery and anti-aircraft shells. These were designated Mk 9 Exploders and made a near miss as effective as a direct hit.

The control mechanism was located in the rear third of the torpedo along with the powerful engine. The centre section housed an air flask with air pressures up to 2800 lb/sq in, and the fuel and water tanks for the steam engine. The nose section housed the explosive head.

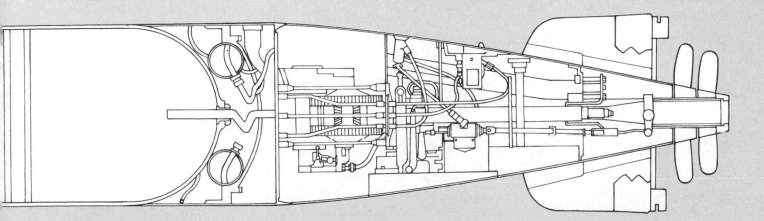

BOMBS
FOR LETTING IN AIR

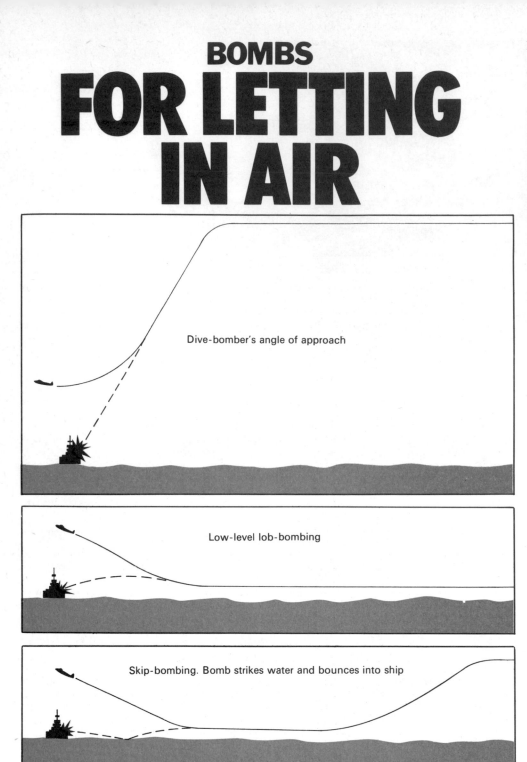

Dive-bomber's angle of approach

Low-level lob-bombing

Skip-bombing. Bomb strikes water and bounces into ship

Smoke and flames billow from the deck of USS Bunker Hill, *bombed during the attack on Pearl Harbor*

In addition to torpedoes, carried-based aircraft could normally be expected to deliver three other major classes of ordnance: bombs, mines and rockets.

Of these three, bombs probably would constitute the largest group from several points of view. They could be subdivided by weight, type and fusing. Weights, for combat, ranged from the relatively light fragmentation bombs in the 20/25-lb weight range, up to the 2000-lb bombs.

Bombs are classed according to use, such as general-purpose (GP), armour-piercing (AP), semi-armour-piercing, fragmentation and depth. In addition to these, there is a whole range of chemical bombs which are classified according to the filler used or incendiary, the latter being rated as an intensive or scatter incendiary.

The shapes vary, as do the proportions, but they generally follow a streamlined form with directional stabilising fins attached to the rear of the bomb. Later, after the war, bombs were stream-lined to become low-drag bombs. Not that it made much difference to the bombing aspect but it did make a difference to the plane carrying the bomb. The low-drag bomb could add several miles per hour to the speed of a supersonic plane when carried instead of the old standard bomb. In some cases low-profile bombs were required if the aircraft was to get airborne.

Packed with explosive

The General Purpose (GP) bomb is packed with explosive which amounts to some 50% of the bomb weight. It is suitable for attack on unarmoured ships, ground targets, personnel and other targets generally susceptible to blast effect and earth shock. The bomb casing is about half an inch thick, which gives it enough rigidity to penetrate through buildings or through several decks of unarmoured ships. GP bombs range in weight from 100 lb up to 2000 lb. They are normally double-fused, nose and tail, to ensure detonation in case of malfunction of the nose fuse as a result of impact with the plating or building structure. On occasion, the tail fuses are delayed action to further ensure the detonation. When operating from land bases, an additional fuse, a hydrostatic fuse, might be added in an athwartship fuse pocket of the bomb.

However, this is not a general practice when operating from carriers. In the event of the aircraft returning with a 'hang up', there is always the possibility of its breaking loose on the arrested landing and rolling down the deck. Should this occur, the probability of the bomb going overboard and exploding beneath the Home ship is quite high.

Armour-piercing (AP) bombs were developed for use in penetrating the heaviest deck armour or reinforced concrete. To accomplish this, the nose is machined to a smooth, long ogival shape. Because its main purpose is penetration, the nose and casing is very thick, resulting in the explosive being the smallest part of the bomb – approximately 15% of the total weight. Anticipating contact with a highly resistant surface, the nose fuse is not used on this bomb, for the impact would almost certainly crush the fuse, preventing its functioning. The most common fusing is a tail fuse, with a possible athwartship fusing to give a back-up capability. Unless this bomb is right on target in the case of a ship, no great damage can be expected.

Imperial War Museum

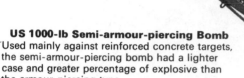

US 1000-lb Semi-armour-piercing Bomb
Used mainly against reinforced concrete targets,
the semi-armour-piercing bomb had a lighter
case and greater percentage of explosive than
the armour-piercing type
Total weight: 1000 lb *Length:* 70·4 in
Fin width: 20·72 in *Charge/weight ratio:* 31%

US 500-lb General Purpose Bomb
With a higher proportion of explosive than other
types of bomb, and a lighter case, the general
purpose bomb relied on blast and shock for its
effect, and was used against unarmoured
targets and personnel
Total weight: 500 lb *Length:* 59·16 in
Fin width: 18·94 in *Charge/weight ratio:* 51%

US 1000-lb Armour-piercing Bomb
Intended to break through armour before
exploding, the nose casing was pointed and
heavy, and the percentage of explosive small
Total weight: 1000 lb *Length:* 73 in
Fin width: 16·6 in *Charge/weight ratio:* 14·5%

A variation, the semi-armour-piercing
bomb, is intended primarily for reinforced
concrete and is lighter than the AP bomb,
making it possible to use a greater percentage of explosive.

Depth bombs were intended for submarines or other underwater targets. They
have comparatively thin shells since they
rely on the pressure wave against the hull
of a submarine or other ship. They are
armed for impact, air burst or hydrostatic
detonation. They have an explosive load of
up to 70% of the total weight.

One little-known use for these bombs was
to encourage enemy troops to come out of
lateral caves dug into the hills of Pacific
Islands. The fuses used in this instance
were nose contact or VT (proximity) fuses
to give an air burst on or slightly above the
ground, producing a blast effect rather than
a penetrating effect. The hydrostatic fuses
could be set to 25, 50, 75, 100 or 125 ft.

Fragmentation bombs might be mixed in
with other more destructive ordnance mostly to reduce the activity or effectiveness of
anti-aircraft gunners, with an additional
possibility of use on parked aircraft to
cause widespread damage if not destruction.
Fragments piercing an aircraft might render the plane unserviceable with multiple
shrapnel holes through cockpits, tyres and
possibly fuel and oil tanks.

Mines were to account for a large amount
of shipping sunk during the war, much of it
by those placed by aircraft. The term 'mine'
goes back to the first use of this system,
which involved miners tunnelling under a
defensive position to place a demolition
charge. Early mines were contact mines
with external horns which, when bumped
by a ship, would trigger an explosive charge.
In the Second World War modern versions
of these, and more advanced types such as
magnetic mines, were sown by aircraft in
harbours, along coastlines and in frequently used channels to reduce the amount
of shipping and resupply operations. Aircraft were perfect for this task, for they
could sow the original mine fields and, as
they were exploded or swept clear by the
defenders, it was a simple matter for one or
more planes to 'bolster' the mine field.

Some measure of the effectiveness of
aerial mine-laying can be gained by the
tonnage destroyed – 649,736 tons, with
1,377,780 tons damaged. British and German
aircraft were particularly active in this
regard in the European theatre as were the
US and the British in the Pacific. It was
estimated that 218,000 mines were sown
during the war, with aircraft dropping
about 85% of the total.

During the Second World War the
development of rockets, particularly air-to-
ground rockets, was accelerated. They were
highly favoured for aircraft launching as
they produced no strain on the launching
plane and their installation for carriage
was very simple and left little or no residual
fittings. Moreover, the battery of rockets
normally carried was equal in destructive
power to a destroyer's main battery.

Rockets for aircraft use ranged from the
2·75-in which was about 50 in long and
weighed about 20 lb, to the 5-in high velocity
aircraft rocket.

As in the case of gunnery, the pilot had to
adapt his flying to the rocket, for any
manoeuvre in progress at the moment of
firing would have an effect on the rocket's
direction. Time from launch to target
could be as short as three seconds.

Sea Hurricanes, an Albacore and a Swordfish preparing to take off from a British carrier en route to Malta

Imperial War Museum

US Navy

USS Essex, *her deck packed with Dauntlesses, Hellcats and Avengers with their wings folded*

CARRIERS
THE LONG ARM
OF THE NAVY

Though the subject of this work is carrier aircraft, it would not be complete without some reference to the floating air bases, the carriers themselves. Space does not permit a thorough history of the carrier. However, a brief resumé of its evolution is in order.

To the British must go the credit for the first flight deck carrier, the *Argus*, built in 1918, although, as described earlier, the concept of taking off and landing aboard a ship was first successfully accomplished by Eugene Ely aboard ships of the US Navy, the USS *Birmingham* and the USS *Pennsylvania*. The take-off from the *Birmingham* was on 14 November 1910 and the landing, followed by a take-off, was made on the USS *Pennsylvania* on 18 January 1911.

Experiments with float planes (hydroplanes) were carried out by the Royal Navy, but they and the ships which were modified to carry and service them left much to be desired. There was a transition period during which awkward compromises were constructed with the superstructure and boiler exhaust stacks protruding in the middle of two decks – one for take-off and an afterdeck for landing. The impracticality of this was quickly recognised and by 1918 the *Argus* was completed.

An interesting aside concerns the armament of these early carriers for most, if not all, still tried to maintain their ties with the 'battleship' navy by the inclusion of main gun batteries, ranging from 4-in up to 8-in guns. It is not too surprising, however, for some of the early carriers were, in fact, converted from cruisers whose below-deck accommodation was a compromise.

Treaty restrictions

The London Treaty restricted guns to 6·1-in and the Washington Treaty limited the displacement to 27,000 tons. The Washington Treaty further stated that all aircraft carriers in existence or under construction on 21 November 1921, were considered experimental and could be replaced within the overall national tonnage limitations, which were as follows:

Britain	135,000 total tons for carriers
United States	135,000 ,, ,, ,, ,,
Japan	81,000 ,, ,, ,, ,,
France	60,000 ,, ,, ,, ,,
Italy	60,000 ,, ,, ,, ,,

Carriers then in existence and considered experimental were the British *Argus*, *Hermes*, *Eagle* and *Furious*; the US *Langley*; and the Japanese *Hosho*. A few of the earlier carriers were designed from the keel up as aircraft carriers. The *Hermes*, the *Hosho*, the *Ryujo* and the *Ranger* were in this group. The *Lexington* and *Saratoga* were originally designed or intended to be battle cruisers.

With the outbreak of war in 1939, the practice of converting existing ships was adopted, particularly in the case of escort carriers to fill gaps in the defence of convoys and to support the larger carriers and amphibious landings.

Many details of carriers require special design. For example, the cavernous hangar deck was probably the most obvious difference from conventional warships, apart from the 'flat top'. These hangar decks, while appearing large when a carrier is in

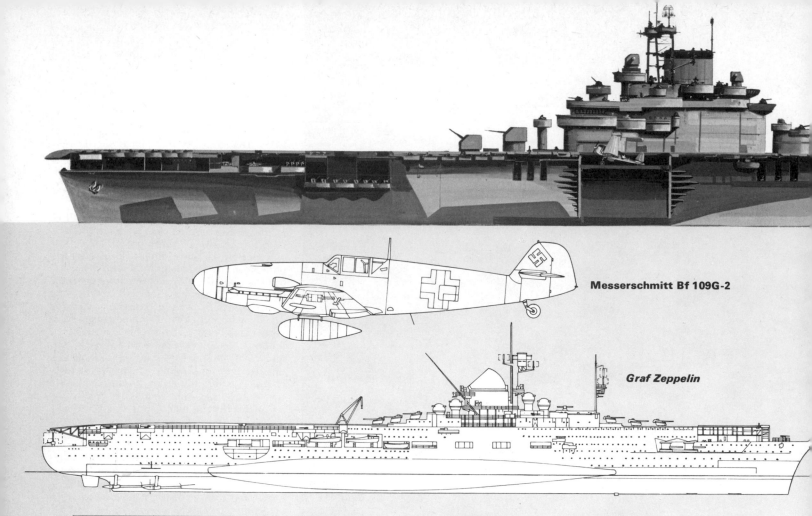

Messerschmitt Bf 109G-2

Graf Zeppelin

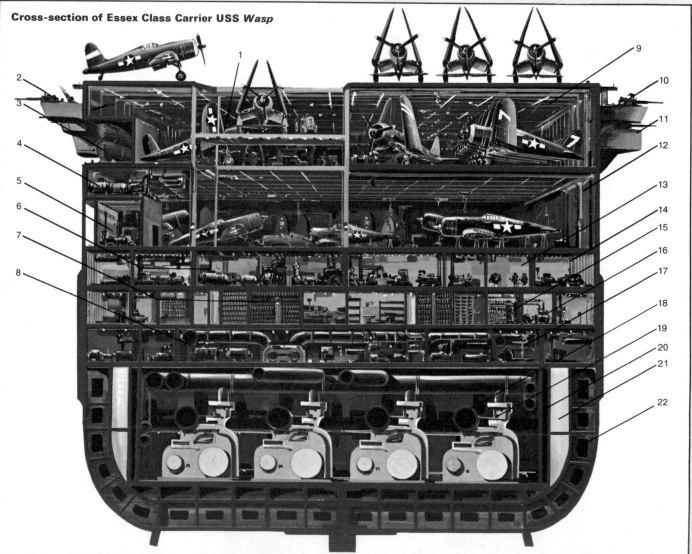

Cross-section of Essex Class Carrier USS *Wasp*

1

2

3

4

5

6

7

8

9

10

11

12

13

14

15

16

17

18

19

20

21

22

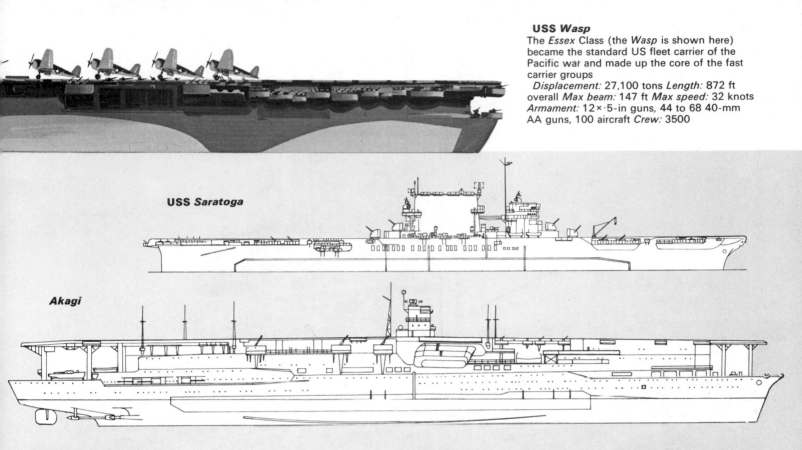

USS Wasp

The *Essex* Class (the *Wasp* is shown here) became the standard US fleet carrier of the Pacific war and made up the core of the fast carrier groups
  Displacement: 27,100 tons *Length:* 872 ft overall *Max beam:* 147 ft *Max speed:* 32 knots *Armament:* 12×·5-in guns, 44 to 68 40-mm AA guns, 100 aircraft *Crew:* 3500

USS *Saratoga*

Akagi

USS *Wasp* cross-section
1 Lift **2** 20- & 40-mm AA guns **3** Two lifeboats **4** Fan motors **5** Airframe workshop **6** Workshop deck & lift machinery **7** Ammo & aircraft stores **8** Air conditioning plant **9** Main hangar (aft) **10** AA guns **11** AA guns **12** Servicing hangar **13** Aero engine stores **14** Engine servicing shop **15** Port ammo stores **16** Emergency lighting plant **17** Engine-cooling motor **18** Steam pipes to turbines **19** Turbines **20** Fireproof coffer dam **21** Aviation spirit tank **22** Oil fuel tanks

Flugzeugtrager *Graf Zeppelin*
Germany's only aircraft carrier, the *Graf Zeppelin's* projected complement featured 12 Bf 109Gs and 28 Ju 87 dive-bombers (see page 31). Hitler's lack of interest in the surface fleet halted the project before completion
  Displacement. 23,200 tons
  Armament: 16×5·9-in; 12×4·1-in AA
  Complement: 1760 *Launched:* 8 December 1938

USS *Saratoga*
The *Saratoga* and her sister-ship the *Lexington* were the largest carriers in the world at the outbreak of the Second World War. Launched in 1925, the 'Old Sara' was to take a tremendous battering from Japanese submarines and Kamikazes yet survived the war.
  Displacement: 33,000 tons *Length:* 888 ft overall *Beam:* 105½ ft *Speed:* 34 knots *Armament:* 8×5-in guns; 125×20- & 40-mm AA guns, 90 aircraft *Crew:* 3300

Akagi
Launched in 1927, the *Akagi* was the Japanese Navy's first big fleet carrier. She had served as Admiral Nagumo's flagship at Pearl Harbor. At Midway the *Akagi* was found by dive-bombers from the *Enterprise* with her decks crammed with planes, and she was sunk along with the *Kaga, Soryu,* and *Hiryu*
  Displacement: 36,000 tons *Aircraft:* 91

port, are in fact marginally adequate in combat. Stowage of full-size aircraft, plus spares of almost every conceivable aircraft part, is in the areas overhead. Complete fuselages, propellers, wing panels as well as tail surfaces also find overhead stowage. Engines and other components find nooks and corners in which to be secured. Handling gear such as tractors, engine hoists, jacks and complete machine shop and engine overhaul facilities are all crowded into this hangar deck along with the work stands and maintenance personnel to service the planes.

High explosives are stowed much like shells in the average cruiser and get the same precautionary handling that shells might expect. However, aircraft require and get regular fuelling and oiling. The fuel, in particular, requires special handling to prevent static electricity from detonating the fumes. At sea there is the regular refuelling of the carrier with fuel for its own machinery in addition to the volatile 100 octane aviation gas.

Two distinct groups operate a carrier: the ship's crew mans the ship as it would any other naval vessel, while the second group is the air department. This consists of the air officer and assisting officers and crew whose responsibilities cover all the aviation activities. These include the operation, maintenance and storage of all aircraft, aircraft accessories, work shops and berthing and plane handling. Under the latter category are such jobs as handling crews to see that the planes are moved expeditiously and spotted either on the flight deck or hangar deck. In addition, there are plane directors, fuel squads, fire crews and ordnance men.

Under combat conditions a carrier is full to overflowing with men as well as machinery. During the long operational cruises,

space and facilities were at a premium. More often than not meals, showers and other personal necessities were taken in shifts. One consolation was the quality of food, which was usually above average, as was the cleanliness of the ship – kept that way by constant policing of crews of both the air department and ship's crew.

Structural details of the carrier are beyond the scope of this book. However, by illustration we are able to convey some of the detail and complexity of these ships, such as the machinery of the ship and its control. One of the principal features not covered previously is the aircraft elevator – or elevators – as they developed. While apparently taken for granted they are the all-important link between hangar deck and the flight deck and vice versa. Damage to the aircraft elevator could effectively silence the carrier. For this reason, modern carriers built as carriers include at least two or more elevators to preclude the possibility of restricting the expeditious handling of the aircraft.

Another fact worthy of mention is the influence that elevator size or weight limitations have on the design of the aircraft. For example, the Japanese aircraft Jill and Myrt had a distinctive forward rake to their fin and rudder and this was designed specifically to adapt to elevator size. In the case of the US Curtiss SB2C Helldiver, the designers never did completely solve the directional stability problems which were the result of designing the plane to fit the elevator rather than designing it to fly well.

The carriers were, and are, huge floating cities designed to place a potent force within combat range of anywhere in the world. They are the long arm of naval forces which enable the mailed fist, the aircraft, to strike repeated blows upon an enemy wherever he may be.

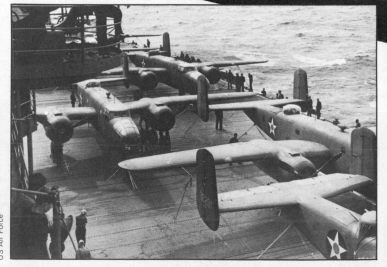

On 18 April 1942 Lt Col James H 'Jimmy' Doolittle led a raid on Tokyo flying Mitchells from the Hornet and carrying on to crash land in China. Above left he is receiving Japanese medals to be attached to the bombs – the first to fall on the home islands during the war. The flight deck of the Hornet (right) vividly illustrates the problems of flying the bulky B-25s from a carrier's deck, even with special preparations and stripped down planes

US Air Force

US Air Force

AND DOOLITTLE'S B25s

North American B-25B Mitchell
The Tokyo raid was carried out by specially
stripped versions of the USAAF's medium
bomber. With defensive armament removed, and
every available space crammed with fuel, the
B-25s were launched 823 miles from the
Japanese coast, and after dropping their bombs
the survivors went on to land in China.
Doolittle's version is shown here; original
specifications for the B-25 were:
Span: 67 ft 6 in *Length:* 52 ft 11 in
Engine: 2×Wright Double Cyclone, 1700 hp
Armament: 3×·50-in mg; 3×·30-in mg
Speed: 300 mph at 15,000 ft *Ceiling:* 23,500 ft
Range: 1300 miles *Bombload:* 4800 lb

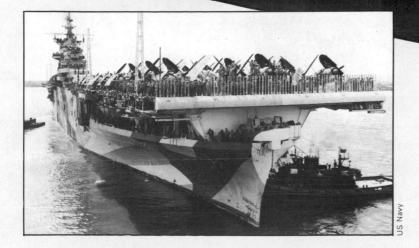

USS *Hornet*
Commissioned on 20 October 1941, the *Hornet*
had a displacement of 19,800 tons and a
complement of 2919 men. Doolittle's historic
B-25 raid was launched from her deck, and at
the Battle of Midway in June 1942 her
Avengers helped shatter two Japanese carriers,
the *Akagi* and the *Soryu*. However, she was
herself severely damaged, and was finally sunk
during the Battle of Santa Cruz after being hit by
two torpedoes, six bombs and two Kamikaze
aircraft, on 26 October 1942. A second *Hornet*,
CV 12 (the original was CV 8), was
commissioned in 1943 and is illustrated *opposite*

US Navy Classification System

The USN's formula for designating an aircraft type was generally divided into four units. The first unit of either one or two letters gave the function of the aircraft. The second was a number denoting the model. The third unit, of one letter indicated the maker and modifications were indicated by a further hyphenated number. Thus in the F6F-3 Hellcat formula, F is for fighter, 6F shows it is the sixth fighter type to be produced by Grumman, and -3 shows the third modification of the design. An X prefix denotes an experimental model. If an aircraft was sub-contracted to more than one firm, that firm's code letter would be used in the formula, hence the Vought F4U Corsair when built by Goodyear became the FG. (The second, model number unit is sometimes omitted when the number is 1.)

First Unit (Function)

A	Amphibian	P	Patrol
B	Bomber	PB	Patrol Bomber
F	Fighter	R	Transport (multi-engined)
G	Transport (1 engine)	S	Scout
H	Ambulance	SB	Scout-Bomber
J	Utility	SN	Scout-Trainer
JR	Utility-Transport	SO	Scout-Observation
N	Trainer	T	Torpedo
O	Observation	TB	Torpedo-Bomber
OS	Observation-Scout	X	Experimental

Third Unit (Maker)

A	Brewster	M	Martin/General Motors
B	Beechcraft/Boeing	N	Naval Aircraft Factory
C	Curtiss	O	Lockheed
D	Douglas	P	Spartan
E	Bellanca/Piper	Q	Stinson
F	Grumman	R	Ryan
G	Goodyear	S	Stearman
H	Howard	T	Timm
J	North American	U	Vought
K	Fairchild	V	Vultee
L	Bell	Y	Consolidated

A US Navy Avenger takes off straight out of the hangar deck of an aircraft carrier.

Smithsonian Institution